3rd Edition

Foundations of

Interpersonal Practice
in Social Work

3rd Edition

Foundations of Interpersonal Practice in Social Work

Promoting Competence in Generalist Practice

Brett A. Seabury
University of Michigan

Barbara H. Seabury
Private Practice

Charles D. Garvin
University of Michigan

Los Angeles | London | New Delhi
Singapore | Washington DC

For information:

SAGE Publications, Inc.
2455 Teller Road
Thousand Oaks,
    California 91320
E-mail: order@sagepub.com

SAGE Publications Ltd.
1 Oliver's Yard
55 City Road,
London EC1Y 1SP
United Kingdom

SAGE Publications India Pvt. Ltd.
B 1/I 1 Mohan Cooperative
    Industrial Area
Mathura Road, New Delhi 110 044
India

SAGE Publications Asia-Pacific
    Pte. Ltd.
33 Pekin Street #02-01
Far East Square
Singapore 048763

Printed in the United States of America

Library of Congress Cataloging-in-Publication Data

Seabury, Brett A., 1942-
Foundations of interpersonal practice in social work : promoting competence in generalist practice / Brett Seabury, Barbara Seabury, Charles D. Garvin. — 3rd ed.
    p. cm.
Prev. ed. entered under Garvin, Charles D. has title: Interpersonal practice in social work.
Includes bibliographical references and index.
ISBN 978-1-4129-6682-5 (cloth: acid-free paper) — ISBN 978-1-4129-6683-2 (pbk.: acid-free paper)
    1. Social service. 2. Interpersonal relations. 3. Social problems. 4. Public welfare. 5. Human services. I. Seabury, Barbara. II. Garvin, Charles D. III. Garvin, Charles D. Interpersonal practice in social work. IV. Title.
HV43.G33 2011
361.3′2—dc22   2010031275

This book is printed on acid-free paper.

10   11   12   13   14   10   9   8   7   6   5   4   3   2   1

Acquisitions Editor:	Kassie Graves
Associate Editor:	Leah Mori
Production Editor:	Brittany Bauhaus
Copy Editor:	Megan Markanich
Typesetter:	C&M Digitals (P) Ltd.
Proofreader:	Victoria Reed-Castro
Indexer:	Diggs Publication Services, Inc.
Cover Designer:	Candice Harman
Marketing Manager:	Stephanie Adams

BRIEF CONTENTS

CSWE Objectives   xv

Preface   xxi

Acknowledgments   xxiii

Chapter 1. Interpersonal Practice in Social Work:
    Nature and Scope   1

Chapter 2. Basic Assumptions and Concepts   17

Chapter 3. Values, Ideology, and Ethics of Professional
    Social Work   39

Chapter 4. Interpersonal Practice Beyond Diversity and
    Toward Social Justice: The Importance of
    Critical Consciousness   60

Chapter 5. Violence and Trauma   99

Chapter 6. Engagement and Relationship   124

Chapter 7. Becoming a Client   162

Chapter 8. Contracting   195

Chapter 9. Monitoring and Evaluating Change   216

Chapter 10. Assessing Individuals   245

Chapter 11. Individual Change   291

Chapter 12. Assessing Families   333

Chapter 13. Family Change   365

Chapter 14. Assessing Groups   401

Chapter 15. Group Change   438

Chapter 16. Assessing Organizations and Communities   475

Chapter 17. Change in Organizations and Communities   507

Chapter 18. Termination   541

Bibliography   564

Index   580

About the Authors   590

DETAILED CONTENTS

CSWE Objectives   xv

Preface   xxi

Acknowledgments   xxiii

Chapter 1. Interpersonal Practice in Social Work:
    Nature and Scope   1

  Definition of Social Work   9
  Interpersonal Practice   9
  Use of Ecological Concepts   10
  The Scope of Practice   11
    Fields of Service   11
    A Problem Focus   13
    Service Priorities   13
    How Agencies Affect Practice   14
    Agency Functions   15
  The Bases of Interpersonal Practice   15
    Social Work Action Repertoire   15
  Summary   16

Chapter 2. Basic Assumptions and Concepts   17

  Rationale   17
  Underlying Assumptions   20
  Metaphors   23
    Moral   24
    Disease   25
    Nature   27
    Mercenary   29
  Basic Concepts: Client, Worker, Target, and Action Systems 32
    The Client System   33
    The Worker System   33
    The Target System   35
    The Action System   35
  Summary   38

Chapter 3. Values, Ideology, and Ethics of Professional Social Work 39

The Ideology of the Social Work Profession 42
The Social Work Code of Ethics 43
    Informed Consent 45
    Social and Political Action 45
    Conflict of Interest 45
    Privacy and Confidentiality 46
    Sexual Relationships 46
    Gifts and Barter 47
    Cultural Competence and Sensitivity 47
    Discrimination 47
    Termination of Service 47
    Referral for Service 48
    Sexual Harassment 48
    Impairment of Colleagues 48
    Unethical Conduct of Colleagues 48
    Commitment to Employers 49
    Consequences, Sanctions, and Remedies for Code Violations 49
Value Conflicts in Practice 51
Practice Cases With Ethical Issues 54
Summary 58

**Chapter 4. Interpersonal Practice Beyond Diversity and Toward
Social Justice: The Importance of Critical Consciousness** 60

*Beth Glover Reed, Peter A. Newman, Zulema E. Suarez,
and Edith A. Lewis*

What Is Critical Consciousness? 65
Major Dimensions of Multiculturalism and Some Terminology 69
    Differences or Diversity Perspectives 70
    Definitions Related to "Difference" 74
    Perspectives That Incorporate Dominance 74
    Definitions Related to "Dominance" and Power 75
Key Social Group Categories and Related Terminology 77
How Do Multiple Identities Work? 80
    Positionality, Standpoint, and Critical Consciousness 81
    Positionality and Standpoint 81
Routes to Critical Consciousness and Multicultural Competence 84
    When One Has Experienced Discrimination and Oppression 87
    When One Has Been Privileged by One's Location 89
    Working Multiple Issues at Once 91
The Application of Critical Consciousness to Practice 91
Summary 97

Chapter 5. Violence and Trauma 99

Recognition of Violence and Trauma 100
Types of Trauma 102
Assessment of Trauma 103
Consequences of Trauma: Symptoms of Psychological
   and Emotional Injury 105
Treatment Options 107
Risk Screening Protocols 107
   Screening for Assault and Violence 108
   Issue of Safety in the Workplace 109
   Screening for Suicide 111
   Screening for Suspected Child Abuse 115
   Screening for Domestic Violence 118
   Screening for Substance Use 119
Summary 123

Chapter 6. Engagement and Relationship 124

Definition of the Social Work Relationship 126
Power Dimensions in Professional Relationships 129
Stages of the Professional Relationship 131
Transactional Nature of the Professional
   Relationship 135
Why Is Relationship So Important? 141
Conscious Use of Self 141
Importance of Hope 143
The Initiation of Relationships 144
   Accurate Communication 144
   Full Communication 149
   Feelings of Warmth and Caring 152
   Complementary Roles 153
   Trust 155
Relationships in Group Situations 156
Relationships in Family Situations 158
Summary 160

Chapter 7. Becoming a Client 162

Definition of a Client 164
Overview of the Clienthood Process 165
Pathways to Clienthood 169
   Voluntary Clients 169
   Nonvoluntary Clients 169
   Involuntary Clients 170

The Entry Process 170
    Feelings About Clienthood 171
    Perceptions of Agencies 172
    Events Leading to Clienthood 173
The Worker's Tasks With Applicants 175
Tasks With Nonclients 180
"Significant Others" in the Client's Life 180
Defining the Client in a Multiperson Client System 181
Agency Conditions and Definitions of Client 182
Continuance and Discontinuance 183
Orientation to the Client Role 188
    A Role Clarification Procedure 188
    Role Training 191
The Initiation of Problem Solving 191
    Specifying the Problem 191
    Problem Specification in Family and Group Systems 192
The Preliminary Contract 193
Summary 194

Chapter 8. Contracting **195**

Components of a Social Work Contract 195
Characteristics of a Social Work Contract 200
Value of the Contract Approach 206
Limits of Contracting 207
    The Hidden Agenda 208
    The Corrupt Contract 209
    Sabotage 210
Contracting With Families and Groups 211
Summary 215

Chapter 9. Monitoring and Evaluating Change **216**

Monitoring 218
    Process Recording 218
    Critical Incident Recording 219
    Electronic Recording 219
    Coded Recording Forms 222
    Other Monitoring Techniques 223
Evaluation 225
    The Design of the Evaluation 225
    The Measure of Change 228
    Rating Problem Solving Skills 233
    Rating Interpersonal Behaviors 234

Client Satisfaction Questionnaires 234
Evaluation of Family Change 235
Evaluation in Groups 236
Side Effects 237
Summary 243

Chapter 10. Assessing Individuals **245**

Purposes of Assessments 245
Issues in Use of Sources 247
Individual Assessment Framework 250
A Developmental Perspective 251
An Ecological Perspective 256
Stress Assessment 262
Crisis Assessment 267
Active Crisis 268
Vulnerable State 273
The Precipitating Factor 280
Assessment as a "Label" 282
PIE—The Person-in-Environment System 283
Summary 290

Chapter 11. Individual Change **291**

The Context of Interpersonal Change 292
The Treatment Plan 292
Formal and Informal Resources 294
The Alternative and Indigenous Healing System 296
Self-Help/Support Groups 297
Interventive Roles 301
Enabler 302
Trainer 304
Broker 312
Mediator 315
Resource Developer 322
Advocate 323
Overcoming Barriers 326
Crisis Intervention 327
Role Solutions 330
Summary 332

Chapter 12. Assessing Families **333**

What Is a Family? 334
Measurement of System Variables 335

Family Assessment 335

The Process of Family Assessment 336

Obtaining Family Assessment Data 338

    Initial Contact 338

    Tracking 339

    Enactments 340

    Tasks 341

    Collecting Data Directly From the Family 342

Categorizing Family Circumstances 344

Ways of Portraying Family Conditions 352

    Chronological Chart 353

    Family Resources 354

    Interaction With Other Systems 356

Summary 363

Chapter 13. Family Change **365**

Occasions for Family Interventions 366

Prior to the First Family Session 367

The Initial Sessions 369

The Family Change Stage 379

    Interventions Related to Family–Environment Transactions 380

    Family–Extended Family Transactions 384

    Transactions Within the Family 386

Phase of the Family Life Cycle 386

    Family Culture and Traditions 387

    Family Emotional Climate 390

    Family Communication Patterns 391

    Family Boundaries and Structure 392

Endings 399

Summary 400

Chapter 14. Assessing Groups **401**

Types of Groups 402

Therapeutic/Effectiveness Variables 404

    Instilling Hope 405

    Self-Sharing 405

    Feedback 405

    The Johari Window 406

    Universality 407

    Cohesiveness 408

    Receiving and Giving Advice 408

    Altruism 409

Learning Interpersonal Skills	409
Vicarious Learning	410
Catharsis	410
Humor	410
Socialization	411
Group Development	411
In-Session Phases Within a Closed Group	412
In-Session Phases in an Open-Ended Group	413
Stages of Group Development in Closed Groups	415
Composing the Group	416
Where, When, and How Many?	420
Agency Sanction and Approval	422
Assessing Group Dynamics	426
Norms	427
Communication	427
Sociometry	429
Roles	431
Geography	436
Summary	437

Chapter 15. Group Change | **438**

First Group Session	444
Second Group Session	447
The First Session of a Closed Group	450
Establishing Initial Relationships	451
Determining Purpose and Goals	452
Determining Group Norms and Ground Rules	454
Dealing With Feelings About the Group	454
Establishing the Preliminary Contract	455
Ending the First Session	456
Leadership Interventions	457
Leadership Moves and Structured Activities	459
Interpersonal Conflict in Groups	469
Conclusion	473
Summary	474

Chapter 16. Assessing Organizations and Communities | **475**

Organizational Assessment	477
Need for Understanding Organizations	477
How to Assess an Organization	479
Norms and Operating Rules	480

Decision Making Structure 483
Organizational Roles 488
Organizational Climate 492
Information Technology 494
Geography 495
Community Assessment 499
Need for Understanding Communities 499
Geographic Information Systems 503
Contemporary Issues in Community Assessment 504
Summary 504

Chapter 17. Change in Organizations and Communities 507

Ethics of Organizational and Community Change 508
Theories of Organizational Change 513
Problem Solving Framework 513
Problem Solving Steps 517
Community Change 534
Strategies, Tactics, and Interventions 535
Summary 539

Chapter 18. Termination 541

The Tasks of Termination 543
Warning and Initiation 543
Evaluation 544
Coping With Feelings 547
Maintaining Change 551
Utilizing Changes in a Variety of Circumstances 554
Engaging in New Services 556
Termination Issues in Group Work 557
Termination Issues With Families 558
Worker Termination 559
Problematic Terminations 561
Summary 563

Bibliography 564

Index 580

About the Authors 590

CSWE OBJECTIVES

All accredited social work schools and programs must cover mandated content in a variety of curricular areas. The Council on Social Work Education (CSWE) has developed objectives for the foundation area of the curriculum. In preparation for CSWE accreditation in 2008, the University of Michigan School of Social Work (UMSSW) developed 15 primary objectives and 44 sub-objectives that reflected CSWE's criteria. The framework presented below represents the key words of the 15 primary foundation objectives and indicates the specific chapters and pages in these chapters devoted to these objectives:

Key Words From the 15 Primary Foundation Objectives

- **Apply knowledge of critical and creative thinking**

    Ch 2. Basic Concepts and Assumptions, p. 5

    Ch 3. Values, Ideology, and Ethics of Professional Social Work, p. 23

    Ch 4. Interpersonal Practice Beyond Diversity and Toward Social Justice, p. 53

    Ch 5. Violence and Trauma, p. 15

    Ch 8. Contracting, p. 7

    Ch 10. Assessing Individuals, p. 60

    Ch 11. Individual Change, p. 8

    Ch 12. Assessing Families, p. 20

    Ch 14. Assessing Groups, p. 15

    Ch 16. Assessing Organizations and Communities, p. 5

- **Describe the value base, ethical standards, and principles of the social work profession**

  Ch 3. Values, Ideology, and Ethics of Professional Social Work, p. 23

  Ch 7. Becoming a Client, p. 4

  Ch 8. Contracting, p. 5

  Ch 9. Monitoring and Evaluating Change, p. 5

  Ch 15. Change in Groups, p. 7

  Ch 17. Change in Organizations and Communities, p. 4

- **Practice without discrimination**

  Ch 3. Values, Ideology, and Ethics of Professional Social Work, p. 5

  Ch 4. Interpersonal Practice Beyond Diversity and Toward Social Justice, p. 53

  Ch 7. Becoming a Client, p. 7

  Ch 10. Assessing Individuals, p. 6

  Ch 14. Assessing Groups, p. 3

  Ch 15. Change in Groups, p. 5

  Ch 16. Assessing Organizations and Communities, p. 3

  Ch 17. Termination, p. 2

- **Identify the major forms and mechanisms of oppression and discrimination**

  Ch 3. Values, Ideology, and Ethics of Professional Social Work, p. 23

  Ch 4. Interpersonal Practice Beyond Diversity and Toward Social Justice, p. 53

  Ch 5. Violence and Trauma, p. 30

  Ch 6. Engagement and Relationship, p. 3

  Ch 7. Becoming a Client, p. 22

  Ch 8. Contracting, p. 4

Ch 10. Assessing Individuals, p. 5

Ch 12. Assessing Families, p. 3

Ch 16. Assessing Organizations and Communities, p. 8

● **Identify the major milestones in the history of social welfare**

Ch 1. Interpersonal Practice in Social Work: Nature and Scope, p. 2.

● **Use a bio-psycho-social, strengths-based, multi-system perspective**

Ch 2. Basic Concepts and Assumptions, p. 15

Ch 5. Violence and Trauma, p. 30

Ch 7. Becoming a Client, p. 12

Ch 10. Assessing Individuals, p. 21

Ch 12. Assessing Families, p. 26

Ch 14. Assessing Groups, p. 4

Ch 18. Termination, p. 5

● **Use theoretical frameworks supported by empirical evidence**

Ch 2. Basic Concepts and Assumptions, p. 3

Ch 5. Violence and Trauma, p. 30

Ch 6. Engagement and Relationship, p. 22

Ch 7. Becoming a Client, p. 40

Ch 8. Contracting, p. 9

Ch 9. Monitoring and Evaluating Change, p. 39

Ch 11. Change in Individuals, p. 17

Ch 13. Change in Families, p. 32

Ch 14. Assessing Groups, p. 5

Ch 15. Change in Groups, p. 17

Ch 16. Assessing Organizations and Communities, p. 11

- **Analyze, formulate, and advocate for changes in social policies**

  Ch 11. Changes in Individuals, p. 3

  Ch 16. Assessing Organizations and Communities, p. 43

  Ch 17. Change in Organizations and Communities, p. 44

- **Apply research findings to practice and integrate evaluation measures into practice**

  Ch 9. Monitoring and Evaluating Change, p. 39

  Ch 11. Individual Change, p. 12

  Ch 13. Family Change, p. 10

  Ch 15. Group Change, p. 8

  Ch 17. Change in Organizations and Communities 3

  Ch 18. Termination, p. 10

- **Effectively communicate with and establish culturally appropriate collaborative relationships**

  Ch 1. Interpersonal Practice in Social Work: Nature and Scope, p. 10

  Ch 4. Interpersonal Practice Beyond Diversity and Toward Social Justice, p. 53

  Ch 6. Engagement and relationship, p. 50

  Ch 8. Contracting, p. 9

- **Use supervision and consultation appropriate to social work practice**

  Ch 3. Values, Ideology, and Ethics of Professional Social Work, p. 5

- **Assess the structure and processes of organizations and service delivery systems**

  Ch 7. Becoming a Client, p. 40

  Ch 16. Assessing Organizations and Communities, p. 30

- Assess the structure and process of neighborhoods and communities

  Ch 16. Assessing Organizations and Communities, p. 12

- Evaluate the structure and processes of social policies on service delivery

  Ch 7. Becoming a Client, p. 2

- Recognize when information is needed to inform professional decision making and how to access that information

  Ch 3. Values, Ideology, and Ethics of Professional Social Work, p. 5

  Ch 5. Violence and Trauma, p. 15

  Ch 16. Assessing Organizations and Communities, p. 3

PREFACE

The aim of this book is to teach the fundamental values, knowledge, and actions that constitute direct practice of social work. This book offers basic generalist practice methods that form the foundation and common elements in social work with individuals, families, and groups. The goal of the book is to teach social work students how to enhance clients' social functioning by helping them become more proficient in examining, understanding, and resolving clients' social problems.

Our approach stresses common elements in work with individuals, families, and groups. Our approach includes the value and ethical considerations that underlie interpersonal practice with an emphasis on enhancing individual–environmental transactions. Interpersonal practice is viewed as a problem solving, goal-oriented, contractually based set of procedures, which are designed to help people examine and resolve problems in living and improve their social functioning. In addition, we believe that a common pool of knowledge from the behavioral and social sciences as well as social work practice experience should form the basis of all interpersonal helping methods. Interpersonal practice should employ procedures that have been or can be tested for effectiveness, and interpersonal practice interventions should be continually monitored and evaluated by practitioners.

We hold several value positions that guide the way we present our view of interpersonal practice. We view social work throughout its history as having a strong commitment to working with people who are oppressed by social and environmental circumstances. Such people include but are not limited to African Americans, Native Americans, Asian Americans, Latinos and Latinas, gay men and lesbians, people suffering from disabilities, and people living in poverty. We also believe that women have been disadvantaged and harmed by the patriarchy that exists in our society. Consequently, we have sought throughout this book to emphasize social work methods that help these people to cope with oppressive circumstances and to work toward a socially just society.

The idea that practice should be committed to the pursuit of social justice means to us that this is a practice in which the worker recognizes that we live in a society in which many parts of the population are oppressed by their social status, ethnicity, gender, sexual orientation, age, or disability. This evolution of a critical consciousness is expected to lead practitioners and consumers to enhance their own and others' empowerment and to eradicate oppressive social circumstances. Although content about diversity issues is interwoven throughout the book, we have brought forward from the second edition the special chapter on economically and socially oppressed groups, which was written by known experts in the field.

We divided the book into three sections. The first section focuses on the foundation of the profession of social work (Chapters 1–5): ethics, values, assumptions, knowledge base, and contemporary societal problems. The second presents the basic generic knowledge and skills that interpersonal practitioners need in direct practice with individuals, families, and groups (Chapters 6–9)—that is, building relationships, engaging applicants in the helping process, contracting and planning service goals, and monitoring and evaluation measures that can be implemented in practice. The third section focuses on basic knowledge and skills in the assessment of individuals, families, and groups in their surrounding communities and organizations (Chapters 10, 12, 14, and 16). These assessment chapters are followed with intervention chapters for promoting individual, family, group, organizational, and community change (Chapters 11, 13, 15, and 17). The final chapter looks at the issues and tasks of termination with individuals, families, and groups (Chapter 18).

The third edition of the text has been thoroughly revised, and each chapter has undergone revision to make the content more "user-friendly" for students. We have used our partnership as a university social work professor and a social work practitioner to make the text both theoretical and practical by including many application exercises, practice case examples, and interactive simulations of practice. We have also included many links to Internet resources (in the Bibliography) that will enhance the learning opportunities for contemporary, Internet savvy students.

Two new chapters have been added that expand the earlier editions' discussions of social work practice issues: a chapter on values (Chapter 3) and a chapter on violence and trauma (Chapter 5). We have added practice case examples to the chapters in the text to engage students and help them apply concepts and skills to their field experience. The conceptual and theoretical discussions have been saturated with practice case examples, questions for critical thinking, and experiential exercises. The chapters on family and group change are organized around an interactive case of practice over several sessions. This structure encourages students to imagine that they are the interpersonal practitioner and to comment on the actions that are taking place in the case narrative.

Since social work practice often involves working with involuntary clients, we present difficult case situations in which an applicant is mandated or forced to see the practitioner. The authors believe that many of the barriers that exist with "unmotivated" clients can be successfully addressed, and clients can be empowered to make significant changes in their lives.

ACKNOWLEDGMENTS

We want to thank Charles Garvin for his senior authorship of the first two editions of this text and his presence in this third edition in the organization of the text and many of the conceptual discussions of practice interventions that have carried over from the earlier two editions. Charles has graciously bowed out of any authorship of this edition, and encouraged me (Brett A. Seabury, or BAS) to take over the authorship of this third edition at SAGE. He also encouraged me to find a successful practitioner, which I did (Barbara H. Seabury, or BHS), who could collaborate with me on this third edition. Because Charles has left his footprint on this edition, we have included his name in the title page of this text. However, any errors, omissions, and/or problems with this third edition are the responsibility of our authorship and revisions.

We also want to thank Kassie Graves, the acquisitions editor at SAGE, and her assistant Veronica Novak for their support, encouragement, and responsiveness while making revisions to this text. We also want to acknowledge the careful and comprehensive editing that Megan Markanich performed as a skilled copy editor. We also want to thank the feedback from outside reviewers who expressed their opinions about changes that should be incorporated into this edition:

Thomas E. Broffman, *Eastern Connecticut State University*

Marcia B. Cohen, *University of New England*

Lorri L. Glass, *Governors State University*

Elaine M. Maccio, *Louisiana State University*

We hope they will be able to see their suggestions in this third edition when it is published.

CHAPTER 1

INTERPERSONAL PRACTICE IN SOCIAL WORK

Nature and Scope

If you have built castles in the air, your work need not be lost, that is where they should be. Now put the foundations under them.

—Henry David Thoreau (1817–1862)

The purpose of this chapter is to introduce the student to interpersonal practice and to relate the content of this book to the purposes, domains, and definitions of social work practice. This analysis is necessary because social work now encompasses a vast array of activities in countless settings. The size alone of the social work enterprise creates many controversies as to what social workers should know and what they should seek to accomplish.

We begin this chapter with two different case examples—one from literature and one from interpersonal practice. These two case examples will be used to introduce the major themes that are played out in the following 17 chapters of this book. Hopefully this way of beginning the book will demonstrate our commitment to provide many living examples of how interpersonal practice works.

"The Bent Backs of Chang 'Dong"

. . . She had been in Chang 'Dong only two weeks when she asked an unanswerable question.

She was working in her kitchen with two of her Sarkanese neighbors, trying to make a small guava which grew in the jungle into jam . . . "Why is it that all the old people of Chang 'Dong are bent over?" "Every older person I have seen is bent over and walks as if his back is hurting." The two older neighbor women shrugged. "It is just that old people become bent," one of them answered. "That's the natural thing that happens to older people."

Three weeks after the monsoon ended, the older people in the village began to sweep out their homes, the paths leading from their houses to the road, and finally the road itself. This sweeping was inevitably done by older people. They used a broom made of palm fronds. It had a short handle, maybe two feet long, and naturally they bent over as they swept.

One day, as Emma was watching the wrinkled and stooped woman from the next house sweep the road, things fell into place. She went out to talk to the woman.

"Grandmother, I know why your back is twisted forward," she said. "It's because you do so much sweeping bent over that short broom. Sweeping in that position several hours a day gradually moulds you into a bent position. When people become old their muscles and bones are not as flexible as when they were young."

"Wife of the engineer, I do not think it is so," the old lady answered softly. "The old people of Southern Sarkhan have always had bent backs."

"Yes, and I'll bet that they all got them from sweeping several hours a day with a short- handled broom," Emma said. "Why don't you put a long handle on the broom and see how it works?" . . .

"Brooms are not meant to have long handles," the old lady said matter-of-factly. "It has never been that way. I have never seen a broom with a long handle, and even if the wood were available, I do not think we would waste it on long handles for brooms. Wood is a very scarce thing in Chang 'Dong." . . .

It would have been simple, of course, to have imported wooden poles, but long ago Homer had taught her that only things that people did for themselves would really change their behavior. . . . She was driving the jeep down a steep mountain road about forty mile from Chang 'Dong. Suddenly she jammed on the brakes. Lining one side of the road for perhaps twenty feet was a reed very similar to the short reed that grew in Chang 'Dong—except that this reed had a strong stalk that rose five feet into the air before it thinned out.

"Homer," she ordered her husband, "climb out and dig me up a half-dozen of those reeds. But don't disturb the roots."

When she got back to Chang 'Dong, she planted the reeds beside her house and tended them carefully. Then, one day, when several of her neighbors were in her house she casually cut a tall reed, bound the usual coconut fronds to it, and began to sweep. The women were aware that something was unusual, but for several minutes they could not figure out what was wrong. Then one of the women spoke. "She sweeps with her back straight," the woman said in surprise. "I have never seen such a thing."

Emma did not say a word. She continued to sweep right past them, out on the front porch, and then down the walk. The dust and debris flew in clouds; and everyone watching was aware of the greater efficiency of being able to sweep while standing up.

Emma, having finished her sweeping, returned to her house and began to prepare tea for her guests. She did not speak to them about the broom, but when they left, it was on the front porch, and all of her guests eyed it carefully as they departed.

The next day when Emma swept off her porch, there were three old grandmothers who watched from a distance. When she was finished Emma leaned her long-handled broom against the clump of reeds which she had brought down from the hills. The lesson was clear.

The next day, perhaps ten older people, including a number of men, watched Emma as she swept. This time when she was finished, an old man, his back bent so that he scurried with a crab-like motion, came over to Emma.

"Wife of the engineer, I would like to know where I might get a broom handle like the one you have," the man said. "I am not sure that our short-handled brooms have bent our backs like this but I am sure that your way of sweeping is a more powerful way."

Emma told him to help himself to one of the reeds growing beside the house. The old man hesitated. "I will take one and thank you; but if I take one, others may also ask, and soon your reeds will be gone."

"It is nothing to worry about, old man," Emma said. "There are many such reeds in the hills. I found these by the stream in Nangsha. Your people could walk up there and bring back as many as the village could use in a year on the back of a water buffalo." The old man did not cut one of Emma's reeds. Instead he turned and hurried back to the group of older people. They talked rapidly, and several hours later Emma saw them heading for the hills with a water buffalo in front of them.

... It was not until four years later, when Emma was back in Pittsburgh, that she learned the final results of her broom handle project. One day she got a letter in a large, handsome yellow-bamboo paper envelope. Inside, written in an exquisite script, was a letter from the headman of Chang 'Dong.

Wife of the engineer:

I am writing you to thank you for the thing that you did for the old people of Chang 'Dong. For many centuries, longer than any man can remembers, we have always had old people with bent backs in this village. And in every village that we know of the old people have always had bent backs.

We had always thought this was a part of growing old, and it was one of the reasons that we dreaded old age. But, wife of the engineer, you have changed all of that. By the lucky accident of your long-handled broom you showed us a new way to sweep. It is a small thing, but it has changed the lives of our old people. For four years, ever since you have left, we have been using the long reeds for broom handles. You will be happy to know that today there are few bent backs in the village of Chang 'Dong. Today the backs of our old people are straight and firm. No longer are their bodies painful during the months of the monsoon.

(Continued)

(Continued)

This is a small thing, I know, but for our people it is an important thing.

I know you are not of our religion, wife of the engineer, but perhaps you will be pleased to know that on the outskirts of the village we have constructed a small shrine in your memory. It is a simple affair; at the foot of the altar are these words: "In memory of the woman who unbent the backs of our people." And in front of the shrine there is a stack of the old short reeds which we used to use.

Again, wife of the engineer, we thank you and we think of you.

Source: Excerpt from William J. Lederer & Eugene Burdick. (1958). *The Ugly American.* Fawcett Publications, Greenwich, CT, pp. 196–201.

At this point in the chapter, we want the reader to think about the themes and patterns that appear in this case example. Here are some of the themes that we discern in this example, and you may have discovered others when you were reading this case example:

- Barriers may exist between people who come from very different life experiences, such as culture, religion, age, and economic class. This theme is played out in chapters on diversity, relationships, assessment of individuals, families, and groups.
- Even though people may not want to change, it may still be possible to help people make significant changes in their lives. This theme is presented in the chapters on clienthood; relationships; and the individual, family, and group change chapters.
- How do we engage vulnerable populations in ways that empower them to become active agents in the change process? The theme of empowerment of vulnerable clients is imbedded in the chapter on values, diversity, relationship, group change, and organizational and community change.
- How do we know that our efforts to help have been successful? The chapters on evaluation and monitoring, the group change chapter, and the termination chapter concern ways that interpersonal practitioners can understand the impact of their services.
- How much of helping depends on creativity, resourcefulness, and "working with what you have"? Though social work is in the age of evidence-based practice, there is a large measure of "art" in what interpersonal practitioners do to engage and help our clients to change. Examples of the "art" of practice can be found in the four change chapters (i.e., individual change, family change, group change, and organizational and community change).

- "Vicarious learning" (i.e., learning by watching others who are models) can be a powerful way that people can change. Vicarious learning is discussed in the chapter on group assessment.

The next case comes from author Barbara H. Seabury's (BHS) practice in a nonprofit agency in which she was employed as a social worker. Read the case example and look for themes and practice activities that you recognize in this case. This example is based on a real case situation, but it has been carefully disguised in order to protect the confidentiality of the clients.

The Mother's Group

Family and Children's Aid (FCA) is a nonprofit agency that is funded by United Way and, in part, by several contracts to provide services to clients of the state's Department of Human Services (DHS). One of the contracts that FCA accepted with DHS was to develop and lead a parenting group. The parents' children had been removed from their care and put in foster care homes because the parents had been found either abusive or neglectful. As a social worker from FCA, I (BHS) was asked to meet with a group of eight mothers who had been identified by DHS as lacking parenting skills. The goal to teach members parenting skills had been set by my agency and DHS. All of the mothers in the group were ordered by the Family Court to attend the group as one of the requirements they had to meet in order to regain custody of their children. The mothers could choose not to attend the group, but if they made that choice, they would seriously jeopardize their chances of regaining custody of their children. In effect, they had no choice. They had to comply and attend the group. I was required to report their attendance and participation to DHS.

All eight women came to the first group session. I began the group by introducing myself. I introduced myself as a social worker from FCA and explained that most of my practice was working with children and their families. I informed them that I had a graduate degree in social work and was a married mother with three children. What I didn't specifically tell them was that I lived in a nice house in a nice neighborhood and my children were all living with me and my husband, who was a supportive father. (Note: I recognized that I was older than most of the women and younger than two of them. I was different from these women in many ways, and I imagine they figured that out on their own.) I stated that raising children was a difficult and stressful job even under good circumstances. I expressed my understanding of the purpose of the group, which was to improve their parenting skills.

I asked the women to explain the circumstances that brought them into the group. Seven of the eight women shared the following information: (One of the women, who was the youngest member of the group, was silent, which was a pattern that she maintained in most of the sessions of the group.) The women shared that they had been sent to the group by a foster care

(Continued)

(Continued)

worker who had been assigned by DHS. The women had been through Family Court, where they had been told—not always in the nicest fashion—that they were neglectful or abusive parents. The judge had ordered them to get evaluated and treated by mental health professionals and to find better housing or clean up their existing living arrangement. They had been assigned court appointed attorneys. (Note: My experience with court appointed attorneys was that for the most part they took little interest in these clients.)

It was apparent to me that all of the women were poor. The highest level of education in the group was high school. All of the women had been getting financial aid from DHS before their children were removed. Now that the children were not in their care, their income was taken away, and they had very little money and were having to do whatever they could to maintain housing for themselves. Seven of the women were Caucasian and one was African American. All of the women were socially isolated single mothers. It also seemed to me that the women were angry, sad, and distrustful of authority and men. They described the men in their lives as unreliable, abusive, and transient. (I knew they probably didn't trust me either since I was part of that authority system.) They agreed to attend the group because they had to do that. The group was to meet weekly for 10 weeks. A meeting time for the group was arrived at for the next session.

As the group was leaving the room, one of the mothers stepped up to me and handed me a small rumpled piece of paper with several numbered items on it. I looked more carefully at the piece of paper. The writing reflected the mother's lack of education. But as I read what was written on the note I could tell that it was important to the author. I was impressed by her courage and strength. The small list represented a request for a different agenda for the group. The list included these requests: (1) for a lawyer to come to explain the legal process they all were required to go through in order to regain custody their children; (2) for a psychologist to come to talk about the psychological evaluations they had all been required to obtain; (3) for a legal expert to come and explain the mother's rights in the situation; and (4) for a foster care worker who was not one of theirs to talk about the responsibilities of a foster care worker in the court process. I told the woman that I would read over her list and talk about it next time with the entire group if that was OK with her.

All eight mothers came to the next session. I began the meeting by talking about the list that one member had presented to me at the end of the first session. The group was very interested in the list as I talked about it. They spoke more freely about not understanding what was happening to them in the court process. They didn't understand how the police could enter their house and remove their children without a search warrant or any warning. They didn't understand why they had been told by the authorities that they were neglectful or abusive. They missed their children and wanted them back. It was clear to me that as a group they were not ready for parenting techniques. They were trying to recover from the trauma and insult they felt as a result of the removal of their children. They really didn't understand what was happening to them or what they could do about any of it. My thought was that they needed to be understood and empowered. They needed to be given some of the advantages that a more middle-class, educated mother might have in the same situation. I agreed to work out a group agenda that was in line with their questions instead of the one I had originally presented in the first session. After the second meeting, I called DHS and told them what I thought was needed before parenting classes. DHS agreed on the new agenda but still wanted parenting classes later. DHS gave me latitude and called the group a support group. I had to report attendance but was not required to divulge what members said in the group.

The group continued to meet on a regular basis. I contacted professionals who agreed to come talk to the group. The first presenter was an attorney from the local law school who had worked in the child protection field in a different county. I felt she could give a neutral presentation on the law and the usual procedure that the parents would endure. The group had many questions for the attorney. Their expectations were often unrealistic. The rules in place in child abuse are different than in criminal cases. The group was able to discuss their experiences and help each other be more prepared with their attorneys and in court. The next presenter was a psychologist who was able to explain psychological testing in general terms. I felt one of the benefits for the women was that they could have the process demystified, made more concrete so that they were less afraid of what was happening to them. The presentations by outside professionals were combined with handouts that would help the women better deal with their situation. We talked about ways the mothers could be more assertive and practiced techniques.

The mothers got to know each other and began to be supportive of each other. I offered to facilitate a holiday party for them and their children if the group thought they would like that. They were excited about a party with their children. I contacted DHS to get approval for a party and an agreement to transport the children to and from the party. The parents had limited visitation with their children, so they were happy to have another special occasion. As a group, we planned a simple menu. I arranged to take a picture of each mother and her child(ren), so they had something they could take home with them.

The group continued and evolved. One of the more quiet mothers explained that she felt she could be honest in the group and say what she wanted. Others had expressed their concern that their foster care workers had lied to them about their rights and the threats that had been made about terminating parental rights. The mothers were more open and verbal. Some of the younger mothers began to bring concerns that they had about their children's behavior. The older mothers began to share stories how they had handled similar problems with their children. They were willing to continue the group for another 10 weeks. The new focus for the group would be parenting skills.

Again, we want the reader to think about the themes and issues that appear in this case example. Here are some of the themes that we discern in this example, and you may have discovered others when you were reading this case example:

- Like the first case example, there were many differences between the interpersonal practitioner and the members of the group. In spite of the social class differences and single parenthood, the interpersonal practitioner was able to bridge these differences by "starting where the client is," changing the initial group purpose in response to one member's suggestions, and encouraging group members to make decisions about what kind of group they would have. These kinds of issues are discussed in the diversity chapter, the relationship chapter, and in the group change chapter.

- The mothers were required by court mandate to attend the group as a condition of getting their children back. They were not happy with this coercive use of authority and the inherent power in the role of the interpersonal practitioner as an instrument of the court and DHS. The interpersonal practitioner was able to diffuse this resentment by demonstrating empathy for the mothers and empowering them to discover what their rights are when children are removed for neglect and abuse. These issues are discussed in the diversity, relationship, and clienthood chapters.

- The removal of children from parents is a traumatic experience for both parents and children. The interpersonal practitioner empathizes with the mothers and does not blame them for their predicament. By planning a party in which children and mothers can be reunited (even for a brief time) and photographing the mothers and their children, the interpersonal practitioner is responding to their needs and the pain of separation from their children. These issues can be found in the chapters on relationship, trauma, individual assessment, and individual change.

- The mothers are all struggling with the effects of social isolation. By providing them with a support group in which they can develop interpersonal relationships with other women facing the same problem, the interpersonal practitioner is intervening in a significant way to help them cope with their social isolation. These issues are discussed in the chapters on social work values, group assessment, and group change.

- The mothers are all struggling with powerful, fairly punitive, social institutions (i.e., police, protective services, and courts) that have descended on them for "deviant" behavior. By bringing in experts to teach them what their rights are and how these social institutions operate, the interpersonal practitioner is empowering them to understand the forces that are swirling uncontrollably around them. These issues are covered in the clienthood chapter and the individual assessment and change chapters.

Social work is affected by political processes, and the practice of social work has political consequences. The political system affects social work in several ways: First, social work has a commitment to serve populations that themselves are centers of controversy, such as persons who are in poverty; who experience racism, sexism, and homophobia; and who have been labeled deviant by society, such as the mentally ill, prison inmates, and perpetrators of physical and sexual violence. Second, the social welfare enterprise consumes a significant proportion of the resources of any country in the developed world. In the United States in fiscal year 1990, total welfare expenditures were estimated at 19% of the GDP, and in Canada and Western Europe, the expenditures for many welfare categories were larger than those in the United States (Bixby, 1995). More recent estimates in fiscal year 2005, which take into account both public and private expenditures, reflect an increase in total welfare expenditures driven by the rising costs in health care and health insurance (Hoefer, 2008).

DEFINITION OF SOCIAL WORK ●

How does social work define itself as a profession, and how does this definition relate to the functions of the profession? How do such definitions and functions manifest themselves in the various fields of social work practice, when these various agencies respond to different kinds of social problems? Because most social work practice takes place in social agencies, how does social agency sponsorship affect social work practice? These issues are the foci of the chapters on clienthood and organizational and community assessment and change.

A pervading theme of social work practice focuses on the interactions between individuals and their environments. The ultimate measure of the success of social work activity is the well-being of individuals within their environments. These environments range from the most immediate, such as friends and family; to larger entities, such as the workplace, neighborhoods, and the surrounding community; and finally to the largest systems, such as the state or the country.

In working to create optimal interactions between individuals and their environments, at times social workers will be helping individuals to change, at other times helping to make environmental change, and most often working to change the transactions between individuals and their environments. The decision to focus on individual change or environmental change or change involving both is based on the unique character of the case situation and is negotiated between the social worker and the individual concerned. Social work is "boundary" work (Hearn, 1993). Such a perspective requires social workers, however, to consider individuals and their environments as always in interaction and to apply measures consistent with this view.

INTERPERSONAL PRACTICE ●

Because this book is about interpersonal practice, it is important to locate this level of practice within all of social work practice. The primary focus of interpersonal practitioners involves work with individuals and their immediate environments, such as their families, social relationships, and peer groups. On occasion, interpersonal practitioners will help people to seek changes in larger entities, such as schools, welfare departments, hospitals, workplaces, and neighborhood groups that affect them. Specific chapters in this book deal with individual assessment and change, family assessment and change, group assessment and change, and organizational and community assessment and change.

Besides interpersonal practice, there are other social work roles that can be found in social work practice. When the unit of attention is communities, the profession refers to these workers as *community organizers* or *community practitioners*. When the focal activity is the effective and successful management of social welfare agencies, the profession refers to these workers as *administrators*. When the focal activity is the creation and establishment of programs and services, the profession refers to these workers as *social planners*. This last segment of practice includes departments of government as well as special interest groups. *Research-oriented workers* and *policy analysts* are also trained to provide new knowledge about services and how to evaluate them.

Despite what we have said about the differences between interpersonal practice and other levels of practice, such as community organization and administration, these distinctions are not as clear as one might think. This is especially true with reference to the topic of social justice. We believe that social justice is most likely to be attained and maintained in a society in which individuals see themselves as drawing from as well as contributing to their communities.

This concept of social justice and community conditions should be carefully considered by interpersonal practitioners. It suggests that individuals, as they develop a sense of themselves in their societies, will become increasingly committed to creating communities that promote the common good (Hartman, 2006). Social justice represents the community's concern for the welfare of everyone in the community. When individuals develop this attitude and understanding, they will be strengthened in their sense of importance and power. They will be on a path of individual growth and development.

Because of our convictions about the relationships between individual and community well-being, we focus to a great extent in this book on the interpersonal practitioners' understanding of and work with the community. Our discussions of work with families and groups stress the role of the worker in helping families and groups work on their relationships with their communities.

● USE OF ECOLOGICAL CONCEPTS

We discuss in more detail in later chapters the theories and knowledge that social workers utilize. It is important to note here that many social workers have come to believe that the historic mission of social work to enhance the transactions between individuals and their environments can best be fulfilled by using concepts from ecology. Ecology was originally a biological conception of the relationships between organisms and their environments and now has been broadened into one of humans and their social relations as well. Germain and Gitterman (1980), who have contributed to this development in social work, stated,

> The ecological perspective provides an adaptive, evolutionary view of human beings in constant interchange with all elements of their environment. Human beings change their physical and social environments and are changed by them through processes of continuous, reciprocal adaptation. When it goes well, reciprocal adaptation supports the growth and development of people and elaborates the life-supporting qualities of the environment. When reciprocal adaptation falters, however, physical and social environments may be polluted. (p. 5)

THE SCOPE OF PRACTICE ●

The major purpose of social work is to *prevent* or *resolve* problems in social functioning. Obviously, such problems result from how well people respond to their environment and how well the environment provides the resources and opportunities people require. When we define practice in this way, we require concepts and theories related to this definition. Role concepts, for example, are applied extensively in this book because they relate to how people act, as well as the expectations others hold for the role, the resources they provide for its enactment, the rewards, and punishments they offer the role performer (Biddle & Thomas, 1966).

Fields of Service

The emergence of fields of service is largely a result of how agency services developed in response to social needs or problems. Table 1.1 summarizes the major fields in which interpersonal practice in social work occurs.

In all these fields, the social work purpose is to improve social functioning—that is, to help people to interact in more functional ways with their situations and to change aspects of themselves and their situations that will enhance such interactions. For example, in a family agency, an interpersonal practitioner may help family members communicate their expectations of each other in order to improve their family role performance. In a criminal justice setting, an interpersonal practitioner may help a client develop behaviors that are more adaptive and also help the client transition from inmate to community roles after release from incarceration. In a VA hospital, an interpersonal practitioner may help a returning veteran transition from a military role to civilian roles. This transition back to civilian roles, such as spouse, parent, and breadwinner, may be complicated by physical and emotional disabilities in which the veteran will be required to learn new skills.

Table 1.1	Social Work Fields of Service

1. *Family Welfare.* The focus is on family roles, such as parent, stepparent, sibling, grandparent, etc. Relevant agencies are usually referred to as family agencies, although some focus only on roles such as youth and the aged. Other agencies also classified under this heading deal only with certain types of role problems, such as those that seek to prevent family violence. Some agencies deal only with people with similar issues, such as the elderly.

2. *Child Welfare.* The focus is on either strengthening family roles or helping the child reestablish roles in substitute families created under adoptive, foster care, or institutional arrangement. An important category of child welfare services is protective services, and these are brought into play when the dangers to the child are immediate and severe. Another specialized category of services, usually linked to the field of child welfare, is school social work. In that field, the emphasis is on how the student role may be affected by other roles, such as those within the family. Relevant agencies are usually referred to as child welfare, although these are increasingly combined with family agencies into family and children's agencies.

3. *Criminal Justice.* The focus is on helping people who have been in deviant roles to relinquish these in favor of socially acceptable ones. This often involves enhancing the client's performance as spouse, employee, and citizen. Relevant agencies include prisons, training schools, and courts.

4. *Physical Health Care.* The focus is on how people can best fulfill the requirements of their other roles, as well as the patient role, while entering or leaving the patient role. Relevant agencies include hospitals and rehabilitation programs.

5. *Mental Health Care.* The focus is on how people who require forms of mental health care, or who have entered the role of mental patient, can enhance their social functioning as spouse, parent, employee, or citizen. Relevant agencies include hospitals, community mental health programs, and clinics. We also classify agencies that help people with developmental disabilities here.

6. *Leisure Time and Youth Services.* The focus is on helping people fulfill all roles better through enhancing their creative potential and ability to work cooperatively with others. Youth services are often emphasized in community centers and "Y's," and these services focus on the developmental needs of people in that role. Relevant agencies include settlement houses and community centers.

7. *Income Maintenance, Job Training, and Employee Assistance in Industry.* Because relevant agencies focus on resource and provider and employment roles, we have grouped them together. The last-named category, industry, is one of the newest fields of practice for social workers. Agencies include welfare departments, personnel training and placement programs, and employee assistance departments in businesses and industries.

8. *Substance Abuse.* A number of agencies focus entirely on helping abusers of alcohol and drugs. Most of the fields of service already discussed also help many substance abusers, but these clients will also be referred to specialized agencies. Relevant agencies are alcohol and drug treatment programs.

9. *Private Practice.* Social workers in increasing numbers have entered private practice, often in addition to their agency practice. In most recent surveys of members of the National Association of Social Workers (NASW), about 23% of members are engaged in some form of private practice. Studies of private practitioners in social work over the past 2 decades show that this sector continues to grow (Mosley, Stoesz, Cnaan, Koney, & Lopez, 2008). Private practitioners operate independently or in partnership with other social workers. The people who seek help from such workers usually must be affluent enough to pay fees, although many are now covered by health insurance for this service. Most private practitioners offer psychotherapy, group therapy, and family and marital therapy.

10. *Faith-Based Programs.* Historically, social work has been connected to many religious institutions—e.g., Catholic Charities, The Salvation Army, Lutheran Social Services, and Jewish Child & Family Services. Presently a number of small, inner-city churches have developed community based programs to reach poor families in their neighborhoods. These services might include emergency food, clothing, housing, employment counseling, and recreational programs for youth.

A Problem Focus

Our model has in common with most social work models the idea that the purpose of social work practice is to enhance social functioning through the prevention or amelioration of *problems*. In interpersonal practice, we mean by problem some aspect of the transactions between a person and his or her environment that is unsatisfying or highly stressful for the person. Recently in interpersonal practice a solution-focused model has developed, which we view as relatively consistent with our problem focus (DeJong & Berg, 2002; O'Hanlon & Weiner-Davis, 1989; Walter & Peller, 1992). Because we believe that establishing goals is a central part of problem solving practice, we will discuss later in greater detail in this book how solution-focused practice is compatible with our model of interpersonal practice.

Service Priorities

An issue that has confronted social workers as long as there has been an awareness of the range of problems with which they can help is whether, with limited resources, some problems have a higher priority for service than others. We believe that the problems of certain groups in society are the priority ones for social work practice. These are the problems of people who are poor, oppressed, or have physical or emotional disabilities. We also included members of ethnic groups, such as African Americans, Latinos and Latinas, Native Americans, and Asian Americans, and sexual minority groups, such as lesbian, gay, bisexual, and transgender (LGBT) people because these groups have been the targets of racist, homophobic, and sexist practices.

We believe that social work has a historical commitment to these kinds of groups, as affluent persons or persons in powerful positions have access to many resources to resolve interpersonal difficulties and enhance personal development. This does not mean that we should withhold social work services from such groups but that they deserve a lower priority when scarce social work resources are an issue. This is consistent, for example, with the social work professional organization's (NASW) stance that recognizes the legitimacy of private practice but asserts the primacy of social services in welfare organizational settings.

How Agencies Affect Practice

The agency is not simply a physical setting for interpersonal practice, but it may strongly influence and determine what such practice will be. In the chapters on organizational assessment and change, we discuss how the worker, to serve clients better, can assess and change agency conditions. We believe that an understanding of the agency is essential for any comprehension of interpersonal practice today. The agency may determine who may "enter" the agency system through its recruitment policies and intake procedures. The agency can also determine which aspects of the client or the environment or both will become targets for change. For example, the policies of a department of social work in a school system were that clients must be students in the school, that they must be referred by their teachers, and that classroom behaviors are the targets to be changed. These policies then did not allow interpersonal practitioners in this school to see students on a walk-in basis, nor to work with student concerns about "bullying" in the lunchroom, nor to work with problems in the families of students. More about these issues are presented in the clienthood chapter.

Agency rules and procedures may indicate which persons in the agency are authorized to interact with the client, what social work approaches are approved by the agency, and what resources will be made available for the utilization of these approaches. In the example of a school social work department just cited, the policies of the department required all students who are referred to a social worker to also be interviewed by the school psychologist for possible psychological testing. The agency's descriptions of social work practice described the social worker's approaches as "individual problem solving," "referral," and "support." The interpersonal practitioner was not permitted to develop and run groups nor to communicate directly with parents. Any communication directed to the parents about their child had to go through the assistant principal's office, who was the school disciplinarian. Some agencies have policies that determine when a client may be terminated regardless of whether the client has achieved the goals of service. As a way of allocating scarce resources, some agencies limit services to a specified time period (e.g., 3 months) or number of social work sessions (e.g., 10 sessions), whether or not the goals of service have been reached.

Agency Functions

The functions of social welfare agencies that employ social workers are not identical to the functions of the social work profession. The ways in which professions evolve in society are seldom in full correspondence with the ways in which the institutions that employ their members evolve. There are a number of conflicts that emerge between the profession of social work and the agencies that employ social workers. These conflicts are discussed in some detail in the clienthood chapter and in the organizational and community assessment chapter.

THE BASES OF INTERPERSONAL PRACTICE ●

Social work professional practice consists of (1) a body of *knowledge*, (2) a set of *values*, and (3) a series of *actions* that are related to the knowledge and values. These actions are referred to as the interventive repertoire of the profession. Later in this book, we discuss values, knowledge, and actions that workers utilize in specific circumstances. Our purpose here is to provide a general introduction to interpersonal practice.

Social Work Action Repertoire

Social work practice consists of actions that are utilized in a manner consistent with social work values, a topic dealt with in detail in Chapter 2. The use of actions is also determined by reference to a body of knowledge. The rest of this book elaborates on this action repertoire; however, we introduce this topic here with a general discussion of actions employed by social workers. Because the word *intervention* is also commonly used to mean the actions of workers, we use these terms interchangeably.

One issue is whether social workers' professional actions are different from those employed by members of other human service professions. We cannot assert that social workers exclusively possess any techniques. The distinguishing features of social work are its focus on individual environmental transaction and the purposes that we have also described in regard to these, not how social workers carry out their purposes. This is not to deny that social workers have pioneered in the development of a number of procedures, such as those of family treatment, group work, individual problem solving, advocacy, and brokerage. (All of these will be discussed in detail later.)

A more generic approach in social work practice has led to several alternative ways of defining specialization in social work. One that has had considerable influence in social work education is the separation of training for practice with individuals, families, and groups (usually referred to as direct practice, clinical practice, interpersonal practice, or micro practice) from that with communities and organizations (usually referred to as indirect practice, macro practice, or social policy and administration).

The skills that are called for to implement change plans can also be categorized by whether they apply to individuals, to environmental systems affecting individuals, or to the interactions between the two. These skills can be clustered, and these clusters can constitute different worker roles. Thus, in facilitating changes in individuals, workers fulfill roles as *enablers* of change, as *teachers*, as *behavior modifiers*, or as *promoters* of insight and awareness of feelings. Workers who locate resources to meet the needs of clients function as *brokers*; workers who develop opportunities to meet the aspirations of clients function as *resource developers*; workers who argue the client's cause in relationship to organizational policies and procedures function as *advocates*; and workers who help clients negotiate with other individuals and systems so that the needs of both may be met function as *mediators*. These roles are elaborated in the individual change chapter.

● SUMMARY

In this chapter, we have sought to describe the current status of interpersonal practice in social work. To accomplish this, we have presented and discussed a definition of social work. This definition emphasizes the functions of the profession as preventing or resolving dysfunctional individual environmental transactions and as strengthening the potential of people to lead creative lives in their environments. We clarified the role of the interpersonal practitioner in social work as accomplishing this function through interactions with individuals, families, and groups.

We subsequently described the scope of interpersonal practice in terms of fields of practice and the types of agencies that employ such practitioners. We introduced our model of practice as one that employs the concept of social functioning, is problem focused, and gives priority to people who are oppressed in modern society.

Our model also recognizes that because most interpersonal practice occurs in agency settings the implications of this must be fully understood, and this topic was also elaborated upon. As we have stated, the purpose of this chapter was to introduce the reader to the range of roles and actions of social workers in interpersonal practice. These also constitute the subject matter of the rest of this book.

CHAPTER 2

BASIC ASSUMPTIONS AND CONCEPTS

The society which scorns excellence in plumbing as a humble activity and tolerates shoddiness in philosophy because it is an exalted activity will have neither good plumbing nor good philosophy: neither its pipes nor its theories will hold water.

—John W. Gardner, secretary of the Department of Health, Education and Welfare under President Lyndon Baines Johnson

In this chapter, we present the rationale, major assumptions, and basic theoretical concepts that underlie the model of practice that is presented in this book. This should help the reader understand the criteria that have been used for the selection of concepts and prescriptions. This discussion highlights our biases about practice, theoretical orientation, and, therefore, both the strengths and blind spots of our model.

RATIONALE

As discussed in Chapter 1, this book is designed to be generic in that it presents the common elements of social work practice with individuals, families, and small groups. However, to compose a book exclusively with generic concepts would leave out knowledge that a practitioner must have to work with individuals, families, and small groups. Therefore, we include specific knowledge we consider to be crucial to interpersonal practice. Our own experiences in practice and education have taught us that a beginning practitioner needs both types of knowledge to be effective with different-sized client systems.

Our theoretical approach to interpersonal practice is eclectic. We do not concentrate upon any one theory or ideology. Although the authors are strongly committed to eclectic practice, each brings different practical experiences, educational backgrounds, and theoretical interests to the book. This blend has created an expanded eclectic model, and we value the richness this creates.

Although this book is eclectic, we do not survey all theory used in practice either. Comparative theory books have been written, but we have no intention of including all practice theory in this book (Roberts & Nee, 1970; Roberts & Northen, 1976; Turner, 1996). We do draw from various practice theories (e.g., ecological, task centered, ego psychological, systems, and behavioral), and we seek to bring together knowledge from all behavioral and social sciences. In spite of the explosion of knowledge in the biological sciences—especially in genetics— we do not focus on emerging knowledge from this area because biological interventions are in the realm of medicine. Interpersonal practitioners do not diagnose disease, perform surgery, or prescribe medication.

The rationale behind our choice of concepts and prescriptions from various theories has been shaped by five general considerations: (1) *applicability*, (2) *practice potency*, (3) *empirically demonstrable efficacy*, (4) *generality*, and (5) *a diversity perspective*. Applicability means that concepts, prescriptions, and organizing variables should be readily operational in social work practice with individuals, families, and small groups. Our descriptions of concepts should clearly fit the world of practice and be understandable to beginning practitioners. High-level abstractions may be briefly discussed at points, but the focus of the book is on clear, operational conceptualizations. This revision of the book has included many more case examples and practice exercises designed to make the book user friendly to beginning social work students.

Practice potency means that principles and prescriptions should make a difference in practice and significantly shape and influence what an interpersonal practitioner can accomplish in work with individuals, families, and small groups. For example, a biochemical theory of human emotion may have empirical validity, yet a social worker cannot use this knowledge to intervene directly into the chemical structure of individuals to influence their emotions (although a psychiatrist may be able to); therefore, not all theories of human behavior can have practice potency for social workers. Successful practitioners also operate with many uncodified, untested principles that significantly shape their practice, and this "practice wisdom" is important to a model of interpersonal practice. For example, there are numerous structured activities that can be employed by interpersonal practitioners with groups that have not been systematically tested. However, these activities can have a powerful effect on the group process and on individual members of the group (Barlow, Blythe, & Edmonds, 1999; Carrell, 2000; Liebmann, 1986).

We would like to be able to write a book that is primarily based on our third criterion: empirically demonstrable efficacy. Social workers would be uniquely sought after as change agents if all of their interventions were empirically researched for effectiveness. Even though this past decade has created a push to develop evidence-based practice and empirically based interventions (Vaughn, Howard, & Thyer, 2008), we do not believe there is enough empirically validated, prescriptive knowledge in social work to create a comprehensive guide to interpersonal practice. Medicine has developed "standards of care" for many of its interventions, but we believe the social work profession has only begun to develop such standards. There are specific interventions that we will discuss in this book, such as mindfulness meditation, which is empirically based (Kabat-Zinn, 1990), but there are many other areas of interpersonal practice, such as advocacy interventions, that still need to be the focus of social work research.

Even modern, scientific medicine does not claim to have all of its procedures scientifically validated. The Office of Technology Assessment (OTA) of the U.S. Congress, assisted by an advisory board of medical faculty, has estimated that only about 10% to 20% of modern medical procedures have been scientifically validated in controlled studies (Carter, 1993). This estimate does not necessarily mean that practice procedures are ineffective, but that in this stage of knowledge development, many practice procedures need to be further refined and tested. Social work practice in the beginning of the 21st century is in a similar stage of development, with some procedures having scientific support and many others representing the art of practice wisdom.

With challenges to the standard, positivistic, scientific paradigm that are appearing in the social work research literature, it is likely that many other ways of knowing and codifying knowledge may emerge, and in the future more and more practice procedures can be refined and validated (Laird, 1993). With a shift in the research paradigm to more qualitative and subjective measures, it may be possible to explore important phenomena in our clients' lives and in the helping process that are difficult to reliably measure yet should not be ignored. For example, relationship issues are clearly central to the helping process yet are often relegated as nonspecific factors in outcome studies. And spirituality as a dimension is clearly significant in clients' lives yet is often ignored in research. The paradigm shift may bring more focus to these ephemeral variables and will in the long run help to clarify these dimensions of interpersonal practice.

Though our book attempts to blend the art of practice wisdom and empirically validated procedures, we strongly believe that it is interpersonal practitioners' responsibility to be constantly trying to validate the procedures they are employing in practice. "Muddling through" with a particular client may be necessary in the moment of the practice world, but in the long run, for professional development and knowledge development, the empirical base of interpersonal practice must be continuously and systematically expanded.

Our conceptualizations should have enough generality to fit a variety of practice settings and a wide range of clients with various social problems. Conceptualizations that are efficacious to a unique client, setting, or problem and are not generalizable to other practice situations are not emphasized. For example, the interventions of a medical social worker with a postoperative patient who has just undergone open heart surgery have been carefully detailed, yet the specific knowledge of such procedures may not be particularly useful to practitioners in other settings with clients facing other kinds of problems (Beagle, 1974).

Finally, our model must take into account the gender, racial, ethnic, sexual orientation, and class diversity perspective of our clients, colleagues, and other helping professions. Social work is a diverse profession composed of people from many racial, ethnic, and socioeconomic backgrounds. American society is pluralistic and becoming more so every day, and it is common that social workers interact on a daily basis with others who come from different backgrounds. Sometimes this diversity among worker, client, and colleague creates special problems when service is delivered. For example, look at the potential problems that may arise in an interaction between an urban, middle-class, middle-aged Baptist African American social worker and a rural, gay white male adolescent client who is living on the streets. It is our belief that interpersonal practitioners should be sensitive to how diversity may negatively impact practice when they interact with clients and colleagues from different racial, ethnic, gender, sexual orientation, and class backgrounds.

It is also important that interpersonal practitioners understand how their clients' diverse backgrounds have shaped the clients' values, attitudes, and experiences. Values, attitudes, and experiences will, in turn, shape how a client perceives what is important in life, what is problematic, and what are acceptable ways to get help or go about resolving particular problems. For example, in some subcultures in the United States, there would be strong taboos about going outside the family structure for emotional help, whereas in others, the family would never be consulted about such problems (Spiegal, 1964).

● UNDERLYING ASSUMPTIONS

Although we are trying to be broad and eclectic in our approach to interpersonal practice, there are ideological biases and assumptions that underlie our model of practice. As we discussed in Chapter 1, the general purpose of social work practice is to improve social functioning, and thus our general approach to practice is from a social problem perspective. Social problems are not viewed as special disease entities or syndromes that individuals succumb to but as inevitable social disruptions that all individuals experience and face at various stages of life. There is nothing abnormal or unique about social problems. They are the likely consequence of living in a rapidly changing, complex society, and no one can be assured of complete immunity. In our model, the primary task of the worker and client is to work together to resolve and cope with problems of living.

The framework for change in our model is goal oriented. Unlike some models of change that focus on historical antecedents to problems to uncover and neutralize them, our approach assumes that change is accomplished through a rationally planned, goal-oriented process.

Although we do not present rigid prescriptions regarding time limits for service, our model is clearly not open ended, extended, or long term. Studies of practice have consistently demonstrated that many clients who enter service voluntarily do not stay very long. Clients do not expect service to take a long time (Maluccio, 1979a). About half are gone by the sixth interview, and only about one third remain in service by the tenth interview (Garfield, 1980).

In the face of empirical evidence that clients do not stay around very long, a number of social work fields are developing time-limited service—even in areas in which service was traditionally considered to last several years. For example, child welfare services are being restructured into 3- or 6-month planning and intervention episodes in which children are expected to be returned home or an alternative, permanent plan (such as adoption) instituted (Stein, 1981). Community mental health services are also being reorganized along brief, time-limited service held to 10 or 20 sessions. With the advent of managed care and third-party payments, treatment episodes are being shortened in some cases to less than five sessions. Long-term, open-ended service may be a thing of the past or only for the very wealthy.

We conceptualize a service sequence as taking place within a 3-month—or shorter—time frame. We are not rigidly committed to a set time limit for service as are some models of practice—for example, one session (Talmon, 1990), one weekend (MacGregor, Ritchie, Serrano, & Schuster, 1964), or 12 prescribed visits (Mann, 1973), but we want to emphasize that most clients will remain briefly in service. Therefore in our world of managed care, service must be designed to be delivered in the shortest time possible. Interpersonal practitioners and clients have neither the luxury of exploring everything in detail yet they must move expeditiously to produce an optimal outcome.

This model has a contract orientation in which client participation and acceptance of service are important values. We believe there is enough research evidence to conclude that service is significantly facilitated when clients know what they are getting into and when they agree with it. What is more, we firmly believe that it is unethical to coerce or "trick" clients into service or into changing parts of their lives without their knowledge or consent.

Consistent with our contract orientation is our commitment to evaluation and accountability. We believe that a worker has a responsibility to develop and/or employ procedures to evaluate the overall effectiveness of service as well as the efficacy of particular actions and interventions. These evaluation procedures are important because the worker is accountable to client, agency, and profession—to the client to demonstrate the effect service has had on the target problems; to the agency to help determine how scarce resources are being utilized and with what effect; and to the profession to generate, validate, or challenge its knowledge base. Contracting and evaluation are such important concepts in our model that an entire chapter is devoted to each.

Another bias in our model is the importance of action as a primary dimension of interpersonal practice (Maluccio, 1975; Reid, 1978). The worker actively intervenes and actively facilitates the client's participation in the problem solving process. The worker is not only active but so is the client. "Doing" and "acting" are essential to the client's sense of mastery and competence (Maluccio, 1979b, 1981). Furthermore, in studies of discontinuance in the 1960s, poor and oppressed clients are turned off by service that primarily emphasizes "talking," "reflecting," and "understanding." Clients from lower socioeconomic groups expect, want, and seek action-oriented solutions to their problems, *not* an elaborate, detailed understanding of the cause and consequences of their present troubles (Aronson & Overall, 1966; Mayer & Timms, 1969; Overall & Aronson, 1963; Silverman, 1970). We are not against a worker being reflective or nondirective, at times, with clients, but our approach firmly emphasizes that the worker and client should actively engage in problem solving actions. We believe such an action-oriented approach is more likely to be empowering for the client and the worker and in the long run to be more efficacious for oppressed clients who have been regularly disenfranchised from societal opportunities and resources.

Such an action-oriented stand may be criticized by devotees of nondirective practice as "impulsive," "bullying," or "moving too fast." We are aware of the danger of acting prematurely and accept it as a potential problem of an action-oriented model. We are, however, much more concerned about the inaction and resultant frustration that many clients experience in reflective, nondirective practice. The needs and problems of oppressed clients are so great that a service model cannot afford to further frustrate these clients and thus contribute to their dropping out of service.

A final bias in our model is that interpersonal practice is a client-centered model. The client's values and view of their world are central to the decisions and actions that are taken in service. We recognize that some clients may be their own worst enemies and reluctant to make changes in their lives. We do not believe it is helpful to view clients as resistant because of their own stubbornness or limited way of viewing their life situation. Because of the ethnic, class, and diversity of experiences of our clients that clash with the various policies, procedures, and practices in our social agencies and the secular values of our profession, it is common that clients will be reluctant to respond to service and make changes in their lives.

We do not believe that we can reach out to clients when we "blame" them for being resistant or unmotivated. We tend to think that when clients are unable to use service, we need to work harder to understand the client and their situation and look for the things about our way of being helpful that turns off clients and limits our ability to reach them. We are not naive in believing that we can reach every applicant or client, and the client must be the final arbiter of the decision to receive service. Even when clients are mandated by court order to receive our service, in the end, it will be the client who decides whether changes will be accomplished. This perspective is not unique to us but can be found in the social work profession's attempts to work with perpetrators of domestic violence and child abuse and neglect, to serve severely mentally and emotionally disabled clients, and to work to eliminate society's most intransigent social problems— inequality and discrimination against special groups.

METAPHORS ●

The term *metaphor* is gaining popularity in clinical practice to describe the healing power that certain kinds of symbolic communications have in therapeutic practice (Barker, 1995; Burns, 2007; Haley, 1973; Kopp, 1971; Watzlawick, 1978). In this chapter, the term *metaphor* is used in a slightly different (though related) manner. The meaning employed here is philosophical and psycholinguistic (Black, 1962).

We shall use the term *metaphor* to describe the highly abstract, often implicit, organizing frameworks that practitioners use in attempting to understand and change their practice world. A metaphor is a general perspective or worldview that helps individuals organize the complexity of the world around them. Even though metaphors are highly abstract and far from the world of experience, they are important because they shape how a practitioner will experience the practice world. For example, metaphors may direct a practitioner to focus on some events and to exclude others. There are many metaphors that can be extrapolated from social work practice, but we have chosen to focus on four—*moral, disease, nature,* and *mercenary*—because these are evident in contemporary practice and often clash and conflict with each other.

Before we describe each metaphor and relate it to social work practice, we take note of several qualifiers. Unlike a theory that by definition is supposed to be testable or open to validation, a metaphor cannot be directly validated. The strength of a metaphor does not arise from its scientific correctness or empirical validity but instead from its utility and comprehensiveness. Metaphors are useful ways of broadly organizing the complexity of the world around us, and although individuals may believe strongly in one metaphor as compared with another, it is senseless to argue that one metaphor is better or more accurate than another. Each of the metaphors we describe has utility for social work practice, and each continues to help practitioners understand the human condition. Although our model of practice clearly reflects a bias toward the nature metaphor, the other three metaphors must be understood because of their impacts.

It is beyond the scope of this chapter to give a detailed explanation of the origins of each metaphor, but this discussion has been conducted before (Germain, 1970; Miller, 1980). The reason for discussing metaphors is to alert students to some of the inherent conflicts in practice that emerge when different practitioners or agencies approach a situation from divergent metaphorical bases. In some agencies, there is a mixture of metaphorical orientations that can be confusing and sometimes overwhelming to students who want to know the following: "What's the right way to do it?"

Moral

The moral metaphor is historically the oldest metaphor of the four. The central issue of the moral metaphor is good versus evil. The behaviors and conditions of people can be understood and categorized as bad, immoral, and evil or righteous, moral, and good. Many theories of human behavior are an extension of this metaphorical orientation. For example, in the Puritan work ethic, wealth and hard work are next to godliness and poverty and sloth are the work of the devil. The eugenics movement at the turn of the century suggested a rationale for sorting out superior races (good) from inferior races (bad). Nineteenth-century social work practice was influenced by this metaphor. Clients of that day were sorted into worthy and unworthy categories (Coll, 1969; Mencher, 1967). The forerunner to the modern-day practitioner was the morally superior "friendly visitor," whose job it was to visit the poor and lift their spirits through "moral suasion" (Lubove, 1969). Service delivery systems of the day were designed to limit or control "pauperism" through registration, restriction, and limited, in-kind aid (Coll, 1969).

The interventions that evolved from the moral metaphor were death, punishment, control, and isolation. Death and punishment were justifiable reactions to immorality and evil. Control and isolation were necessary to keep evil and immorality from spreading and influencing the rest of society. Witches were burned or drowned; thieves had their hands severed; debtors were imprisoned; infidels were banned or excommunicated from the community; and the poor, sick, and homeless were crowded into slums or workhouses to die of neglect or to be sold at public auction to the highest bidder.

The moral metaphor, however, is not something only of the past but continues to influence society and social workers today. The fundamentalist Christian condemnation of homosexuality and women's rights, the conservative backlash against legislation to legalize gay marriage, the growing support to reinstitute capital punishment, and the belief that AIDS is a plague (not a disease) sent by God to punish homosexuality are examples of the way in which the moral metaphor continues to exert influence on society today.

This metaphor also exerts influence on social workers. Alcoholism and drug addiction are viewed by some social workers as irresponsible behaviors (reflecting some weakness in the client's personality), and, therefore, remedial efforts must involve strong measures of control and "penance." Some workers are morally outraged at the behavior of parents who abuse their children and may be overly zealous in moving toward termination of parental rights as a solution to child abuse. Some support strong limits, controls, and even punishment for institutionalized juvenile offenders who are prone to violent behavior. And in contradiction to the profession's position on choice, some workers view abortion as murder.

The moral metaphor will always be with us because it is an inevitable consequence of any social system. The stability of social systems depends in part on normative structures, and whenever there are norms, there are bound to be norm breakers who must be addressed somehow by the social system. Many areas of social work practice can be conceptualized as focusing on norm breakers (corrections, protective services, etc.).

Disease

The disease metaphor has a shorter history than the moral metaphor and in many ways arose as a reaction to the latter. The early adherents to the disease metaphor were viewed as revolutionaries—Phillipe Pinel, Benjamin Rush, and Dorothea Dix all wanted to unchain the "mentally ill" and treat rather than punish them (White, 1956).

The central issue of the disease metaphor is health versus disease. From this orientation, various human conditions are seen as manifestations of disease entities or disease processes. As with the moral metaphor, these disease processes were undesirable and required eradication; however, unlike the moral metaphor, the victim or host was not responsible or culpable. The culprit was not the victim but some precipitating, noxious agent.

Understanding the human condition from a disease orientation required practitioners to search the host's past for the causes of the present disorder and to understand how the disease emerged and progressed (etiology). This led to categorizing the disease into a diagnosis that differentiated it from other disease entities and finally to prescribing some form of treatment to neutralize or eliminate the causes of the disorder. The development and scientific validation of germ theory strongly enhanced the power of the disease metaphor as did later developments such as the discovery of antibiotics and tranquilizers.

In addition to influencing biologically oriented practitioners (such as physicians), the disease metaphor also influenced psychology and sociology. The 19th century works of Emil Kraepelin, J. M. Charcot, and Pierre Janet enhanced the development of psychopathological categories as *a* way of understanding various "psychological diseases" (White, 1956). The metaphor even influenced sociology, and terms such as *social disease* or *social pathology* emerged. Even racism and poverty have been described as social diseases that can grow like cancers and destroy the entire body (society; Kerner Commission, 1968).

The primary intervention that flowed from the disease metaphor was treatment. Treatment or therapy was expected to eradicate or neutralize the noxious, causative agents and to promote the health of the host. Unfortunately, not all technologies developed from this metaphor have left the host so untouched, and some even seem to possess the punitive character of the moral metaphor. For example, in one application of the moral metaphor, exorcism was developed to eliminate the evil spirits that possessed a witch, but it also eliminated the host through burning at the stake, ritual drowning, or driving a stake through the heart. Many of the interventions of the disease metaphor were likewise brutal, such as bloodletting and lobotomies. Even with the development of modern technologies, the "cure" may have disastrous side effects for the host. For example, prolonged use of certain tranquilizers may lead to serious brain damage (i.e., tardive dyskinesia), and cancer patients face severe side effects from both radiation and chemotherapy.

Social work practice has been strongly influenced by the disease metaphor because of the profession's close association with medicine and psychiatry during the 20th century. Models of practice have been developed both in casework (the psychosocial study, diagnosis, treatment model of Hollis, 1964; Hollis & Woods, 1981) and group work (Glasser, Sarri, & Vinter, 1974) that relate this metaphor to practice. Today, social workers in a number of practice settings, in order to satisfy third-party vendors and insurance companies, must use diagnostic labels (American Psychiatric Association, 2000) to describe their clients and client conditions.

The problems with using labels as outlined in the *Diagnostic and Statistical Manual of Mental Disorders* (4th ed.) (*DSM–IV*) (American Psychiatric Association, 2000) is that such diagnostic systems attempt to categorize almost every conceivable form of human behavior into some "disease" category. Even though we recognize the thrust of *DSM–IV* to be multifaceted, is it reasonable to consider all forms of the human condition as potential diagnostic entities? For example, patients who choose not to follow their doctor's recommendation or advice are diagnosed as V15–81, or "Noncompliant with Medical Treatment." The *DSM–IV*, however, does not have a category for patients who follow their doctors' recommendations, and, therefore, one must assume that such patients are paradoxically "healthy"!

Another problem with the disease metaphor is the narrowing effect it has on the definition of problems. Troubles to be treated are seen as lying within individuals or parts of individuals (such as personality dynamics), and thus social causes, consequences, or related conditions tend to be ignored and not addressed. Social casework has been repeatedly criticized for ignoring the social environment (Grinnell, 1973), and many technologies that developed are open to criticism as conservative and even repressive because they do not address the social conditions of clients (Germain, 1968).

Nature

The nature metaphor has experienced increased interest over the past few decades, though it has been around as long as the disease metaphor. Today, allopathic, Western medicine is criticized by advocates of holistic and alternative medicine. Focusing on disease is no longer adequate in medical practice, and doctors must have knowledge of nutrition, physical activity, exercise, work and home environments, and *stress* to understand their patients' troubles.

The central issue of the nature metaphor is growth versus decay. From this metaphor, various aspects of the human condition can be understood as manifestations of growth, decay, or combinations of the two. Growth and decay are the inevitable consequences of two fundamental processes in the universe—one ontogenetic and the other ecological. The ontogenetic process is the inevitable journey that living organisms take from creation, development, maturation, to death. But this journey does not unfold in a vacuum, and the ontogenetic process is significantly influenced by environmental (ecological) factors. The processes of life that include growing, thriving, and finally dying are significantly shaped by the quality and quantity of environmental resources and opportunities. For example, poor nutrition, poor sanitation, or inadequate health care during pregnancy, infancy, and early childhood can dramatically influence physical size and intellectual capacity during adulthood, or even whether the individual will have an adulthood.

In contrast to the moral and disease metaphors, there is no implicitly desirable side to the contrasting aspects of the nature metaphor. Growth and decay are neither desirable nor undesirable but inevitable. Organisms and their ecosystems cannot escape either condition, and the optimal (desirable) state is a balance or match between organism and ecosystems. Although it may seem that decay is undesirable, it is absolutely essential to growth, both ontogenetically and ecologically. Our bodies continuously build, break down, and rebuild our cellular structures, and the fertilizers and nutrients of nature, so necessary to growth of organisms, are only made possible through the decay and breakdown of previous organisms. Decaying organisms and their by-products are the food for future generations.

The interventions that flow from the nature metaphor involve matching, balancing, fitting, and "tinkering." Intervention cannot create the ontogenetic and ecological forces, although ontogeny can be tinkered with through genetic engineering, and ecology can be disrupted through such changes as uncontrolled pollution or elimination of part of a food chain (such as draining wetlands). Interventions can attempt to improve the delicate balance between ontogeny and ecology. These can be directed at the interface between the ontogenetic state of the organism and the ecological factors that surround and shape it.

Although the life model (so named to contrast it to a disease model) of Germain and Gitterman (1980) is clearly an extension of the nature metaphor into social work practice, many other models of practice seem to fit this metaphor also. For example, crisis theory and crisis intervention conceive of a crisis as a normal, expectable event that happens to all systems that have the potential for growth as well as decline (Golan, 1978; Roberts, 2005). Opportunity theory presented delinquency not as some form of psychopathology or evil behavior but as a career to which youths were attracted when there were few opportunities for success in their social environment (Cloward & Ohlin, 1960). In fact, the social functioning perspective discussed in Chapter 1 is clearly consonant with the nature metaphor because social functioning involves *both* the individual and the social context.

The major value of the nature metaphor as an orientation for interpersonal practice is the breadth of possible interventions that flow from it. Interventions can be directed at individuals with regard to their ontogenetic development (a young, expectant parent may be helped to learn parenting skills), at significant parts of the environment (a worker may advocate against a school procedure that does not allow a pregnant student to continue in regular classes), at the transaction between individual and environment (a worker mediates to improve the relationship between the young, expectant parent and her own parents), or at all three at once or in various combinations. Unlike the moral and disease orientations, to improve the match or balance between individuals and their environments, a worker does not have to focus on individual change or adjustment. Balance can be achieved by changing environmental forces as well as by influencing basic transactions between individual and environment. In some cases, improvements may be achieved by moving individuals out of deleterious environmental situations into more growth-enhancing environments.

Although the nature metaphor is an attractive orientation for social workers, it is not without its limitations and deficiencies. The nature metaphor introduces tremendous complexity into the understanding of the human condition. Not *only* must a practitioner understand the basic developmental stages of organisms and social systems but the practitioner must also understand the ecological cycles and forces that impinge on the organism as well as the various transactions that occur between organism and environment. The sheer number of variables that account for optimal balance are staggering, and such an optimal state may be difficult to define empirically (in much the same way that "health" is an elusive condition of the disease metaphor). For example, many factors (both internal and environmental) produce stress on organisms as they develop. Some stresses are necessary to growth, but clearly others are debilitating. With too little stress, an organism may be understimulated, whereas with too much stress, an organism may be overwhelmed. The optimal balance is further complicated because each individual is at different ontogenetic stages and within his or her own individual range has different capacities to respond to and handle stress.

One way around the complexity issue is not to focus on optimal social functioning. This may be an ideal and cannot be empirically defined. Instead it may be more useful and empirically more demonstrable to focus on examples of social dysfunction—that is, situations in which there clearly is no optimal balance between individual and environment and to address these social problems of living to restore a better balance.

The nature metaphor is most congruent with our view of interpersonal practice and can be found in many of the concepts and procedures described in this book. However, at some points, the other metaphors may be reflected in our discussions of practice principles, too. No single metaphor is powerful or general enough to explain all of the human condition, and at times we rely on other metaphors as complementary ways of understanding.

Mercenary

The mercenary metaphor probably does not deserve full metaphor status as do the other three metaphors, but it has grown so pervasive and influential over the past few decades that it is presented here. Of all the metaphors that can be found operating in social work practice, this is probably the most recent. The rise of this metaphor is connected to political movements to privatize public services. Private, free market capitalism is revered, while tax support of public service programs is condemned and denounced (Hartmann, 2006). The basic issue of this metaphor is cost versus profit. In this view of the world, profit, the bottom line, and dollars are most important. What's desirable is holding down costs and increasing profits. If something can be done faster or with less inputs of raw material or labor, then it is more desirable than something that takes more time or uses up more resources and labor. This perspective ignores hidden costs and externalities, such as the devastation on communities when factories move overseas to take advantage of low wages and non-existing laws about pollution. Cost efficiency drives all practice consideration.

Devotees of this metaphor have worked diligently to convert all variables and processes of the universe into an economic unit (dollars, yen, rubles, etc.). Even the most complex of human processes can be converted into economic units, as was revealed in the famous Ford Pinto lawsuits that involved the exploding gas tank. In the civil and criminal trials against Ford, it was revealed that the Ford Motor Company had calculated the cost of recalling all Pintos and rearranging the gas tank versus the cost of settling the lawsuits that would result from rear end accidents in which car occupants would be maimed or burn to death. In their analysis of the probabilities of accidents and awarding of settlements in court, the corporation concluded that it would cost less to pay off the lawsuits of widows and maimed survivors than it would to change all gas tanks of Pintos still on the road (Dowie, 1977). In this example of how the mercenary metaphor operates, costs are the prime consideration—more so than any moral position about saving lives or maiming customers.

The results of the mercenary metaphor can be seen in the dramatic rise of the "privatization of public services." Hospitals, prisons, residential treatment centers, employee assistance programs, and even social service agencies are being reorganized to make a profit. The service ethic of providing a needed service to a population at risk is now being replaced by the need to make money. More than ever, modern agencies are engaged in socioeconomic creaming and are trying to reach those populations who have the ability to pay; and so, too, is the profession of social work, as the number of practitioners who engage in private practice has grown dramatically (Jayaratne, Davis-Sacks, & Chess, 1991).

The mercenary metaphor has its impact on clinical decision making. Clients who are accepted for service must have insurance or the ability to pay, must have a condition that is amenable to the limited services that are offered, and must not present a liability risk to the agency. Thus, suicidal clients may be avoided because of their liability risk, poor clients without insurance regardless of their problems will be referred or placed on long-term waiting lists, and the most difficult or intransigent client situations will be allowed to fall through the giant holes in the service delivery net. For workers, it is how many clients you have had contact with in a week that counts, not how many clients you have helped or finally reached that matters.

The mercenary metaphor has also influenced the kinds of intervention strategies that social workers are expected to engage in with clients. Group treatment is more desirable than individual treatment, short-term treatment is more desirable than long-term treatment, and declassification of positions is desirable so that less-trained personnel replace higher-trained personnel.

Unfortunately, the underlying rationale is not whether group treatment is effective with some clients, or whether a brief modality works with a particular client problem, or who in the agency might be best suited to deliver a particular kind of service; the overriding consideration is the cost savings of having clients seen briefly in large groups by low wage workers.

What value is it for practitioners to try to understand how metaphors shape social work practice? Many conflicts that arise in practice between practitioners are not just technological (a matter of what works best) but instead represent fundamental clashes in metaphorical orientation. It is not uncommon during a case conference for several professionals working with the same individual client to have conflicts about "what's wrong?" or "what's best for the client?" or "what's the best way to help?" These are the day-to-day practice decisions, but these decisions often create conflict among professionals. Because the moral, disease, nature, and mercenary metaphors presently exist in social work practice (as well as in most human services), all four of these orientations are represented in the perspectives or viewpoints of workers or professionals. For example, how can four professionals be expected to agree with each other when one sees the client's behavior as irresponsible, requiring sanctions and limits; the second sees the same client's behavior as psychopathological, requiring psychotherapy; the third sees the same client's behavior as a dysfunctional response to a stressful, non-need-meeting environment; and the fourth sees the same client's behavior as a poor candidate for service because of a long history of noncompliance and missed interviews that will appear on weekly census sheets as "no shows"?

Metaphors do not necessarily have to work against each other in the practice world. For example, medical social workers must sometimes juggle all four metaphors in a case to be effective. A medical social worker may be working with patients who are recovering from a particular disease. The onset, treatment, and recovery may be fairly predictable events, yet the worker may attempt to connect the patient with new resources (a nursing home) or mobilize support from the patient's intimate environment (encourage family involvement), so that recovery is facilitated and the patient reenters the social environment outside the hospital. The worker may have to take into account specific aspects of the disease and the prescribed medical regimen and attempt to balance these with elements of the posthospital situation, such as the patient's impoverished home environment, reliance on home remedies, dependence on an indigenous healer, and a dietary preference for certain ethnic foods, all of which may complicate recovery. Of course the worker will be expected to resolve all these issues within the prescribed time limits of managed care guidelines, for that particular medical diagnosis.

In summary, we remind the reader of several points. Metaphors are implicit and not easily recognized, although they fundamentally influence how social workers view clients and interventions. Practitioners rarely question their own metaphorical orientation, although they question that of others when it differs from their own. Metaphorical orientations may be very hard to change, so practice decisions that involve a conflict of metaphors may be difficult to resolve rationally. Instead, such conflicts in decision making are often resolved politically or institutionally—that is, by the most powerful individuals in a given situation. Therefore, the disease metaphor can be expected to prevail in medical and psychiatric settings, the moral metaphor in correctional or court-appointed services, the nature metaphor in organizations serving oppressed ethnic groups, and the mercenary metaphor seems to be emerging in all settings that will be able to survive public sector cutbacks (See Exercise 2.1).

Exercise 2.1

Influence of Metaphors

To see the influence of these metaphors, students are encouraged to attend a staffing or case conference in their agency. In a multidisciplinary case conference, it is likely that several or all of these metaphors will appear in the discussions of what is wrong with the client (or patient) and what needs to be done. Look for conflict between members of the team or conference, and you will probably find an underlying metaphor that is clashing in the arguments presented by different team members. Look to see which metaphor "wins"!

● BASIC CONCEPTS: CLIENT, WORKER, TARGET, AND ACTION SYSTEMS

Although we have suggested that the ideal unit of attention for interpersonal practitioners is the person-in-situation configuration, such a broad conception is useful for assessment but impractical for intervention. As the interpersonal practitioner attempts to understand a client and her problems, a systems perspective can uncover numerous variables. However, when it comes to intervention, the practitioner requires concepts to partialize, focus, and delimit the complexity of an individual's situation. Four systems concepts—*client system, worker system, target system,* and *action system*—are just such partializing concepts. Although there may be many variables and processes that are ongoing in a client's life, the concepts of client, worker, target, and action systems help to specify those people and interactions that are essential to change efforts.

The Client System

The client system is a term that derives from planned change literature (Lippitt, Watson, & Westley, 1958) and has also become common in social work literature as well (Pincus & Minahan, 1973). In this literature, the client system has been variously defined as the beneficiary of service or the individual or group asking for help. There are weaknesses with both these definitions. The client system may not be the only beneficiary of service, and in some cases, even unwilling targets may benefit from change efforts. Furthermore, just because you ask for help does not mean you will receive it. As we discuss in our clienthood chapter (Chapter 7), becoming a client is much more than just initiating or asking for help.

As we analyze in more detail later, clienthood does not occur until there is a contract or working agreement established between client and worker. The client system is defined by this contractual process. In some cases, the client system is the person or persons who request(s) help, whereas in other situations, a number of contacts with many different individuals may transpire before the identity of the client system emerges. For example, a wife may come to an initial interview and express concerns about her marriage. In the next session, the husband might be seen alone. Finally, in a third session, both husband and wife might agree to pursue marital counseling with the worker, and the couple becomes the client system.

In interpersonal practice, the most common client systems are individuals, couples (marital pairs, parent–child dyads), families (parents and children, several generations of a family), or some small groups. (In many cases, we consider the group members, the client system, and the group to be the action system.) Although "client system" is more bulky in usage than is "client," it does reflect the variable size of the unit that contracts with the worker, and we want to emphasize that interpersonal practice is much more than individual casework and involves work with many different-sized client systems.

The Worker System

The worker system consists of the interpersonal practitioner and the employing agency. The worker system is larger than the individual social worker who contracts with the client system. Individual workers are influenced by their employing agency's policies, procedures, and resources; by their fellow workers and supervisors; and by professional ethics and standards of practice. Figure 2.1 represents the components of this system.

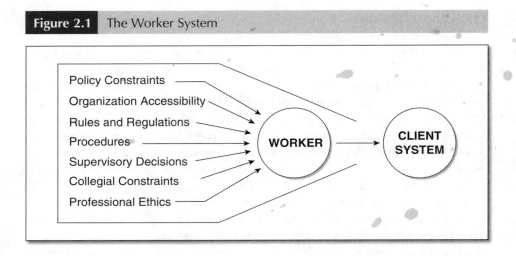

Figure 2.1 The Worker System

Policy Constraints
Organization Accessibility
Rules and Regulations
Procedures
Supervisory Decisions
Collegial Constraints
Professional Ethics

WORKER

CLIENT SYSTEM

Even in private practice, which is held up as a prime example of autonomous practice, the individual worker is not autonomous and is influenced by many forces. A private practitioner must meet licensing and registration requirements as well as those of insurance carriers or third-party vendors, must maintain a referral network, must collaborate with other professionals, and should secure case supervision or consultation. Even if autonomous practice were possible, we strongly believe it is undesirable because an interpersonal practitioner is an integral part of both an agency and a professional context that holds the individual practitioner accountable for practice decisions and behavior. Along with this comes the responsibility of individual workers to address and to change the dysfunctions in the worker system.

We have rejected the term *change agent system* from our model because it is both bulky and nonspecific. Social workers are a particular kind of change agent. A social worker cannot agree with helping clients to engage in violent actions (help a client "run over" his or her oppressive slumlord), nor can a social worker engage in sexual intercourse with clients, no matter how intense the clients' needs are to express their sexuality.

In some social work literature, the term *therapist* is used as a substitute for the term *worker*. This is an unfortunate trend because the term *therapist* is a much narrower conception than is the more generic and traditional term of *worker*. Interpersonal practitioners may engage in therapy or counseling with clients, but they also may be advocates, brokers, mediators, and evaluators. Our view of the worker system includes the notion that an interpersonal practitioner may engage in many roles when serving clients, and these roles are all given sanction and meaning by the organizational and professional context of social work practice.

The Target System

Target systems are those individuals or groups of individuals that the client and worker system seek to change or influence in order to achieve the client's goals. Although the term *target* has repugnant, militaristic connotations, the concept of target system has achieved common usage in social work literature. In some cases, the target system will be identical to the client system, as when a husband and wife contract with a worker to solve their marital problems. In other case situations, the target system is separate from the client system. In an advocacy situation, the target system may be a particular decision maker (DM) in an organization that withholds resources from a client system. In some cases, the target system may be a part of the worker system when client and worker attempt to change some aspect of the worker's agency that stands in the way of the client's goals.

When target and client systems do not overlap and do represent separate individuals, a question arises as to the ethics or responsibilities the worker has to the individual(s) who are identified as the target system. In some practice situations, the separate target system will be in agreement (issue consensus) with the goals the client and worker systems are pursuing; and the worker and client will have no problems contracting or interacting with it. However, target systems are not always in agreement with such goals. Sometimes they are apathetic about changes sought or more concerned about other issues. Sometimes the target system may be adamantly opposed to the change (Resnick & Patti, 1972). What are the worker's responsibilities to a target system that is in disagreement with the client system's goals or change objectives? Can a worker attempt to change someone against his or her will? Does a worker have to be open and relate honestly to the target? Can a worker and client secretly collude to make plans to change or manipulate a target system in ways it may not wish to change? These issues will be discussed more fully in the chapter on organizational change (Chapter 17).

The Action System

The action system involves the notion of social situation. The action system includes all the significant individuals involved in the change effort. It includes the client system, the worker system, the target system, and all other individuals the worker and client may enlist for particular actions, tasks, or objectives to be accomplished.

The action system conception is important to our model because it reinforces a view of social work as "boundary work" (Hearn, 1993). The action system in psychotherapy is usually the individual client and therapist interacting in a 50-minute office interview. The action systems in social work are much more complex—especially in working with oppressed clients. Besides the client and worker, the action system is likely to involve DMs from formal organizations (judges, employers, landlords, probation officers, and housing inspectors), other helping professionals (teachers, nurses, psychiatrists, psychologists, etc.), indigenous healers (spiritualists, curanderas, palmists, root doctors, and chiropractors), self-help groups (AA, Parents Anonymous, etc.), religious and community leaders (ministers, rabbis, priests, imams, and tribal councils), and relatives and family members of the client system.

Because action systems in social work practice can be so complex, an interpersonal practitioner must have skills not only in relating and contracting with clients but the worker must also have skills in coordinating, collaborating, monitoring, negotiating, and advocating with other individuals in the action system. An example is the responsibility of a worker in a mental health clinic (see Figure 2.2, The Action System). Consider the amount of effort in coordinating and collaborating with the various individuals involved in the life of this 15-year-old youth (client system) who is on parole and in a foster home. In this case example, there are 14 adults from seven different environmental systems in contact with this youth. The relationship between this youth and these adults varies greatly, the adults' perspective of this

Figure 2.2 The Action System

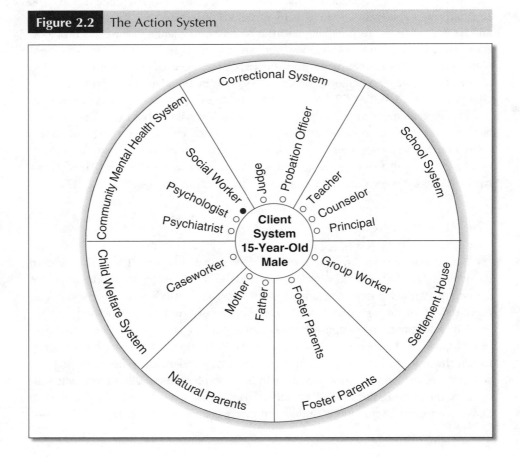

youth (underlying metaphor) is different depending on which system they are in, and a number of the adults are working at cross purposes with each other. In this particular case, the natural parents are in conflict with the child welfare agency and the foster parents, the school is in conflict with the mental health agency, and the settlement worker wants nothing to do with any of the other service providers in this case.

In concluding this discussion, we wish to emphasize that each system (client, worker, target, and action) must be carefully defined as service progresses. Such delineation is important because these systems constantly change as service unfolds. In the beginning of service, there is no a priori way to be certain what is the "best" or "right" client, target, or action system for a given case. The empirical referents for each of these systems will probably change (and usually do) as the case unfolds.

There is a tendency for practitioners to have a "favorite" unit of attention. Some prefer to work with individuals, some with couples, some with families, and some with community groups, etc., yet each way of conceptualizing a case has profound implications for what can be accomplished. In order to demonstrate how a given case may have many different client, target, and actions systems, we present a case that can be used to help students understand the various systems that interpersonal practitioners encounter in practice. Students may analyze the case and discover the various potential client, target, and action systems that exist in this case. What are the practice implications when different client systems are considered? (See Exercise 2.2.)

Exercise 2.2

Unit of Attention

It is your day to cover intake. You are placed in a satellite office of a family service agency that is located in an inner-city neighborhood. Because of the large immigrant population, you and all of your fellow workers are bilingual. A 10-year-old Guatemalan youth comes running into your agency in tears. He is crying that he will never see his mother again because the police have come and taken her away. You are able to get him to calm down enough to explain what happened. Earlier in the morning, during breakfast, the landlord and two men barged into the family's two room apartment and hauled their furniture onto the sidewalk. This was terrifying to the youth and his three younger sisters. His mother pleaded with the landlord not to evict them. She told him that she would stop withholding the rent, even though the landlord had not made the repairs that had been demanded by the housing inspector. The landlord shouted that he was fed up with "her kind," and when he reached to remove the crucifix from the wall, the youth's mother plunged a pair of scissors into his shoulder. The police were called, and his mother was taken off to jail. In this particular city, landlords have the right to evict tenants when they fall 2 months in arrears. This is the fourth family in the past 3 months to be evicted from this fourth floor walk-up.

● SUMMARY

This chapter has presented some of the major dimensions of our model of practice, dimensions that throughout this book we will utilize and expand on. These include the ideas that an understanding and sensitivity to diversity issues are essential to effective interpersonal practice. Modern interpersonal practice occurs in phases, is contractual, and is primarily short-term in nature. We indicated that the goals and the means to achieve goals are significantly influenced by four metaphors—moral, disease, nature, and mercenary. Although we lean toward the use of the nature metaphor, we recognize the necessity of incorporating other metaphors despite the paradoxes and contradictions that this may sometimes produce. We believe that an understanding of all four of these underlying metaphors will help students clarify some of the communication problems and conflicts that arise not only in conferences with members of other professions but also in interactions among social workers.

We presented the basic organizing principles—client, worker, target, and action systems—of our model. These concepts are the basis for understanding how an interpersonal practitioner assesses and intervenes in the practice situations of clients, and it is important that practitioners are clear about these boundaries in any practice situation. We do not consider this to be a "systems" book but rather an eclectic one that makes extensive but not exclusive use of systems concepts.

CHAPTER 3

VALUES, IDEOLOGY, AND ETHICS OF PROFESSIONAL SOCIAL WORK

Justice is inescapably judgmental. Whether we're arguing about financial bailouts or Purple hearts, surrogate motherhood or same-sex marriage, affirmative action or military service, CEO pay or the right to use a golf cart, questions of justice are bound up with competing notions of honor and virtue, pride and recognition. Justice is not only about the right way to distribute things. It is also about the right way to value things.

—Michael Sandell (2009, p. 261)

In this chapter, we explore the ideology, values, and ethics that underlie social work in the contemporary world. All social groupings develop norms for how they expect members of the group to behave. In large groups such as societies and nations, these norms are codified and written down as laws and regulations. Many of the laws in the United States have their roots in Judeo-Christian religious traditions. The Ten Commandments of the Old Testament may be viewed as either prescriptive or proscriptive. Prescriptive norms are those that suggest what are ideal and desirable, while proscriptive norms describe behaviors that are undesirable and taboo. For example, in the Ten Commandments, the commandment to honor thy father and mother is prescriptive and the commandment to not bear false witness against thy neighbor is proscriptive. The major difference between prescriptive and proscriptive norms is that proscriptive norms are more specific while prescriptive norms tend to reflect a wider range of possible behaviors. Most of the laws that exist in a given society reflect proscriptive norms, such as prohibitions against violence, murder, theft, drunk driving, etc.

The broadest group of norms that represent us all on planet earth can be seen in the United Nations' Universal Declaration of Human Rights (UDHR; United Nations, 2010). The UDHR specifies 30 rights that concern economic, political, and individual civil rights. Over many decades since 1948, this statement of human rights has generated a number of United Nation commissions and conventions designed to enforce these rights. For example, there are commissions on genocide, slavery, rights of women and children, etc. We do not have space in this chapter to get into all of the controversy that surrounds this document, but we do believe it is important that social workers become familiar with the various rights that are included.

Another broad set of norms for our planet is contained in The Earth Charter (TEC; www.earthcharterinaction.org). TEC expands the norms reflected in the UDHR to environmental sustainability and the ecological damage that is occurring on planet earth.

> The mission of the Earth Charter Initiative is to promote the transition to sustainable ways of living and a global society founded on a shared ethical framework that includes respect and care for the community of life, ecological integrity, universal human rights, respect for diversity, economic justice, democracy, and a culture of peace. (The Earth Charter Initiative, 2010)

TEC was created by a decade-long process that involved thousands of individuals and hundreds of organizations from all regions of the earth. TEC was created by experts and grassroot communities (See Exercise 3.1).

Exercise 3.1

Comparison of the Universal Declaration of Human Rights, The Earth Charter, and U.S. Constitution

Go to the websites for the UDHR (United Nations, 2010; www.un.org/en/documents/ udhr/), TEC, and the amendments to the U.S. Constitution (Mount, 2010; www.usconstitution .net/constquick.html), and peruse the principles in these three documents. Take the following quiz that highlights the similarities and differences between the UDHR, TEC, and the amendments to the U.S. Constitution.

	UDHR		TEC		U.S. Constitution	
A. Rights of women and girls	Y	N	Y	N	Y	N
B. Prohibitions against slavery	Y	N	Y	N	Y	N
C. Right to organize labor unions	Y	N	Y	N	Y	N
D. Rights of indigenous people	Y	N	Y	N	Y	N
E. Right of citizens to bear arms	Y	N	Y	N	Y	N
F. Prohibitions against genocide	Y	N	Y	N	Y	N
G. Prohibitions against torture	Y	N	Y	N	Y	N
H. Rights to education	Y	N	Y	N	Y	N
I. Prohibitions against nuclear, biological, and toxic weapons	Y	N	Y	N	Y	N
J. Right to equal protection	Y	N	Y	N	Y	N
K. Right to peaceful assembly	Y	N	Y	N	Y	N

We think the best way to "correct" this quiz is to share your answers with your classmates and see how they have answered this quiz. You may be surprised that the amendments to the U.S. Constitution do not have some of the rights outlined in the UDHR and TEC.

Along with the development of norms in a group, there also emerge a number of sanctions, penalties, and remedies for those in the group who violate particular norms. For example, the popular TV show *Law and Order* highlights in the first part of the show the laws that are being broken, and in the second part of the show the attempt by the court to prosecute the law breaker is highlighted. For some transgressions, the penalties may be severe, such as capital punishment or life in prison, and for others the penalties may be fines, community service, or probation.

We learn early in civic classes in school that justice is supposedly blind and the punishment fits the crime, but in the real world of social work, we know that our system of justice is not fair. Some norms breakers are more likely to be caught, prosecuted, convicted, and given more severe punishments than other members in our society. Poor people, ethnic and racial minorities, and undocumented immigrants are likely to have their rights violated through profiling, to be denied fair treatment in our judicial system, and more likely to receive severe penalties (Eitzen, Zinn, & Smith, 2009). Because social workers are likely to work with and represent clients from these vulnerable groups (Dover et al., 2008), the profession has strongly supported *social justice* as one of several values that inform the practice of the profession. In this book, many of the discussions about how we do interpersonal practice will center on social justice issues.

● THE IDEOLOGY OF THE SOCIAL WORK PROFESSION

Ideology is a body of beliefs and principles that characterizes the thinking of a particular group. It is an orientation, comprehensive vision, or way of thinking about issues. The profession of social work has explicitly articulated its ideology in its policy statements of 63 contemporary issues (National Association of Social Workers [NASW], 2009). Many of these issues are politically contentious, such as affirmative action; immigration; capital punishment; workplace discrimination; and rights of lesbian, gay, bisexual, and transgender people. The underlying theme of these policy statements could be characterized as "liberal" and "progressive."

George Will, a conservative columnist for the *Washington Post*, based on a study by the National Association of Scholars, has attacked social work education as mandating "an ideological orthodoxy to which students must subscribe concerning 'social justice' and 'oppression.'" His concern is why "are such schools of indoctrination permitted in institutions of higher education?" (Will, 2007). His perspective is correct that the ideological perspective of social work is progressive, but his criticism does not point to the "conservative" indoctrination in many departments of economics, public policy, business, and law at these same public institutions.

George Will's description of social work education is correct. The profession is committed to a socially just society and promotes social and political action to bring about change to society's most intransigence social problems. The profession's policy positions on women's rights and the gay rights can be especially difficult for entering students who come from conservative fundamentalist Christian backgrounds who view abortion and homosexual behavior as taboo. The profession has a long, antiwar tradition, which is reflected in its policy position on war, and students returning from military service in the wars in Iraq and Afghanistan find it hard to be in classes with younger students who have never experienced military service during wartime.

The profession also has a strong ideological commitment to inclusion and diversity and providing students with the skills to cope with the conflicts that emerge in a multicultural society. Returning vets and fundamentalist students may find themselves in the minority in their social work classes but so will many other students who are gay or transgender or from Chaldean, Native American, Latino backgrounds, etc. Conflicts arise because the profession has a strong commitment to celebrate this diversity and to teach students how to engage in conflict resolution skills through dialogue (Nagda, 2006; Nagda, Kim, & Truelove, 2004; Spencer, 2001; Spencer & Martineau, in press). For example, at the University of Michigan School of Social Work (UMSSW), we encourage students to form many different support groups (e.g., Christian social workers, Feminist Toolshed, men's discussion group, Latino social workers, social work veterans, Black social work students association, or Social Welfare Action Alliance), which we value as an important part of their educational process.

THE SOCIAL WORK CODE OF ETHICS ●

Most social workers belong to the National Association of Social Workers (NASW). Some are also members in other associations, such as the International Federation of Social Workers (IFSW) and the National Association of Black Social Workers (NABSW). All of these professional associations have codes of ethics, but we will focus in this chapter on the NASW *Code of Ethics* (National Association of Social Workers [NASW] Delegate Assembly, 2008). The code of ethics of the IFSW is much more condensed than NASW and focuses more directly on international issues: "Social workers should not allow their skills to be used for inhumane purposes, such as torture and terrorism" (International Federation of Social Workers [IFSW] & International Association of Schools of Social Work [IASSW], 2004). The *Code of Ethics* of the NABSW is also much more condensed than NASW and focuses more directly on the issues facing African American communities: "I adopt the concept of a Black extended family and embrace all Black people as my brothers and sisters, making no distinction between their destiny and my own" (National Association of Black Social Workers [NABSW], 2010).

The practice of social work is governed by guidelines and laws. Social workers make a commitment to ethical practice, but often they will be presented with ethical dilemmas that do not have easy answers. A good rule of practice is that if the social worker is unsure of what to do, he or she needs to seek out collaboration or supervision. If the social worker feels a need to make a special exception to an ethical guideline for a client, he or she needs to get consultation before acting. In the remainder of this chapter on values, we present NASW practice guidelines and a number of practice cases that involve ethical issues and dilemmas.

The NASW *Code of Ethics* (NASW Delegate Assembly, 2008) outlines the social worker's ethical responsibilities to clients, colleagues, practice settings, the social work profession, and the larger society. The code sets out standards of practice with the clients, colleagues, and practice settings. Every social worker should read and understand the entire code. This chapter will focus primarily on the social worker's ethical responsibilities to the client, with some attention to ethical responsibilities to colleagues and the profession. The Preamble to the NASW *Code of Ethics* sets out the basic ethical values for social workers:

> The primary mission of the social work profession is to enhance human well-being and help meet the basic human needs of all people, with particular attention to the needs and empowerment of people who are vulnerable, oppressed, and living in poverty. A historic and defining feature of social work is the profession's focus on individual wellbeing in a social context and the wellbeing of society. Fundamental to social work is attention to the environmental forces that create, contribute to, and address problems in living.

> Social workers promote social justice and social change with and on behalf of clients. "Clients" is used inclusively to refer to individuals, families, groups, organizations, and communities. Social workers are sensitive to cultural and ethnic diversity and strive to end discrimination, oppression, poverty, and other forms of social injustice. These activities may be in the form of direct practice, community organizing, supervision, consultation, administration, advocacy, social and political action, policy development and implementation, education, and research and evaluation. Social workers seek to enhance the capacity of people to address their own needs. Social workers also seek to promote the responsiveness of organizations, communities, and other social institutions to individuals' needs and social problems.

> The mission of the social work profession is rooted in a set of core values. These core values, embraced by social workers throughout the profession's history, are the foundation of social work's unique purpose and perspective:

> - service
> - social justice
> - dignity and worth of the person

- importance of human relationships
- integrity
- competence.

This constellation of core values reflects what is unique to the social work profession. Core values, and the principles that flow from them, must be balanced within the context and complexity of the human experience. (NASW Delegate Assembly, 2008)

The social worker's primary commitment is to the well-being of the client. The main goal of the social work relationship is to enhance the well-being of the client, not the social worker. The following discussion is not presented as a comprehensive review of the NASW *Code of Ethics*, but as a review of those issues that interpersonal practitioners are most likely to face in practice.

Informed Consent

Social workers should use clear and understandable language to inform clients of the purpose of the services, risks related to the services, limits to services because of the requirements of a third-party payer, relevant costs, reasonable alternatives, clients' right to refuse or withdraw consent, and the time frame covered by the consent. Social workers should provide clients with an opportunity to ask questions and should never pressure clients into engaging in any activity or intervention without a clear explanation of the activity and its purpose.

Social and Political Action

Unlike the expectations in the codes of conduct of many other professions, such as psychology, medicine, law, business, etc., social workers are expected to engage in social and political action that will improve the lives of clients. Social workers should act so that all people have equal access to the resources, employment, services, and opportunities to meet their basic human needs. Social workers should act to expand choice and opportunity for vulnerable, disadvantaged, oppressed, and exploited people and to promote conditions that encourage respect for cultural and social diversity.

Conflict of Interest

Social workers should not engage in dual or multiple relationships with clients or former clients when there is a risk of exploitation or potential harm to the client. A dual or multiple relationship occurs when social workers relate to clients in more than one role. For example, a social worker should not engage in psychotherapy and massage and financial counseling with a client. This ethic may be difficult to manage in rural social work when clients and workers may be members of the same place of worship or engage in business at a local farmers market when one or the other is selling organic produce. Conflicts will also arise in the military when military bearing (rank) may have an impact on the social work relationship.

Privacy and Confidentiality

Social workers need to protect their clients' privacy. Clients should be informed in clear language about the rules of confidentiality. The client should be informed of the possible limitations of privacy. For example, confidentiality may be compromised if the client is court-ordered to see the social worker. The client should understand that the social worker will be required to report to the court about the client's progress. The social worker needs to be aware that there are specific rules of confidentiality for clients concerning AIDS or substance abuse. The recent federal HIPPA regulations also define the requirement for confidentiality and suggest sanctions if the regulations are violated.

Social workers are required in many states to deliberately violate confidentiality when the client threatens to harm another person. In many states, social workers have a "duty to warn" or a "duty to inform" when threats are made. It may be necessary to warn the potential victim of the violence or to notify the police or some other authority about the threat of violence. This duty to warn is not universal in every state and is interpreted differently in many states, so that social workers must understand whether this duty exists in the state in which they practice and what is expected when this issue arises in practice. We suggest that interpersonal practitioners access NASW's website and learn the details of "duty to inform" (NASW, 2010).

Sexual Relationships

A most egregious ethical violation is a sexual boundary violation. There should be no sexual contact with the client. The use of any physical touch should be examined very carefully. There should be no sexualized language or harassment of the client. The social worker should not have a sexual relationship with family or close friends of a client. States have different rules about when a sexual relationship is permitted—if ever—with a former client. It is the responsibility of the social worker to maintain the boundary even though at times a client may want a sexual relationship.

Gifts and Barter

Whether or not a social worker should accept a gift from a client or give a gift to a client probably needs to be decided on a case by case basis. Clients are often grateful for the help they receive and want to give something in appreciation. A social worker should not accept a gift of great monetary value. To refuse a gift might also be seen as a rejection by the client. If the social worker works in an agency, the agency may have its own policies about gift receiving or giving.

Barter is the exchange of goods or services instead of money for payment. The use of barter is not considered ethical and should be avoided by social workers. In some communities, barter is a common means of conducting business. For example, in rural communities farmers may share equipment, and in poor communities, residents may exchange child care for transportation.

Cultural Competence and Sensitivity

Social workers work with clients with diverse cultural, religious, and ethnic backgrounds. Social workers need to educate themselves and be sensitive to their clients' multifaceted identities. It is important for interpersonal practitioners to understand and accept the ethnic and cultural differences of clients and not to impose their own values on their clients.

Discrimination

The code presents a daunting prescription for social workers in regard to discrimination. Social workers should not practice, condone, facilitate, or collaborate with any form of discrimination on the basis of race, ethnicity, national origin, color, sex, sexual orientation, gender identity or expression, age, marital status, political belief, religion, immigration status, or mental or physical disability.

Termination of Service

Social workers should terminate services to clients when such services no longer serve the clients' needs or interests. Social workers should take reasonable steps to avoid abandoning clients who are still in need of services. Social workers should rarely withdraw services precipitously and should assist in making appropriate arrangements for continuation of services when necessary.

Referral for Service

Social workers should refer clients to other professionals when the other professionals' specialized knowledge or expertise is needed to serve clients fully or when social workers believe that they are not being effective or making reasonable progress with clients and that additional service is required. Social workers are prohibited from giving or receiving payment for a referral when no professional service is provided by the referring social worker.

Sexual Harassment

Social workers should not sexually harass supervisees, students, trainees, or colleagues. Sexual harassment includes sexual advances, sexual solicitation, requests for sexual favors, and other verbal or physical conduct of a sexual nature.

Impairment of Colleagues

Social workers who have direct knowledge of a social work colleague's impairment, which is due to personal problems, psychosocial distress, substance abuse, or mental health difficulties and that interferes with practice effectiveness, should consult with that colleague when feasible and assist the colleague in taking remedial action. When a social worker believes that the colleague has not taken adequate steps to address the impairment, the social worker should take action through appropriate channels established by employers, agencies, NASW, licensing and regulatory bodies, and other professional organizations.

Unethical Conduct of Colleagues

Social workers should take adequate measures to discourage, prevent, expose, and correct the unethical conduct of colleagues. Social workers should be familiar with national, state, and local procedures for handling ethics complaints. Social workers who believe that a colleague has acted unethically should seek resolution by discussing their concerns with the colleague when feasible and when such discussion is likely to be productive. When necessary, social workers who believe that a colleague has acted unethically should take action through appropriate formal channels (such as contacting a state licensing board or regulatory body, an NASW committee on inquiry, or other professional ethics committees).

Commitment to Employers

Social workers should work to improve employing agencies' policies and procedures and the efficiency and effectiveness of their services. Social workers should act to prevent and eliminate discrimination in the employing organization's work assignments and in its employment policies and practices.

Consequences, Sanctions, and Remedies for Code Violations

If a social worker should commit an ethical violation, there are a variety of sanctions that may be levied. NASW has a complex adjudication procedure that will review ethics complaints from clients and other social workers, as well as recommend sanctions and remedial actions in ethics cases. The social worker's state professional licensing board can also sanction the social worker in a variety of ways with the ultimate sanction as the removal of the social worker's state license. When the social worker works in a social agency, the agency may have its own sanctions with the ultimate being the loss of employment. In some ethics cases, the client, the social worker, and/or the agency may end up in a civil or criminal proceeding.

Social work practice is also governed by the laws of society. It is against the law, for example, to commit insurance fraud. It is against the law in many states for a mental health professional to engage in sexual activity with a client. It is against the law to violate confidentiality as in the confidentiality of a child abuse report. It is required by law that social workers report suspected abuse to proper authorities. There can be criminal charges and civil lawsuits brought in order to sanction the professional for his or her behavior.

Though not all religious traditions believe in heaven and hell, we end this discussion of sanctions by a 14th century description of Dante Alighieri's *Inferno*. Dante describes a hell of many levels with each level corresponding to particular sins and evil. The farther down the circles go in his model, the more egregious the sin and the more devastating the punishment. In Figure 3.1, look down the levels until you come to "fraudulent counselors," which is just below "thieves" and just above "sowers of scandal and schism." This is the eighth level of hell, which is very near the bottom. This should be a reminder how important ethical behavior is in social work practice.

Figure 3.1 Dante's Inferno

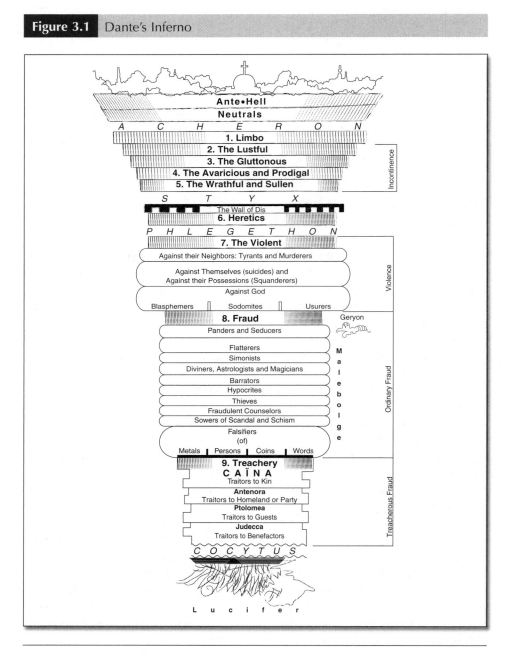

Source: Adapted from Mandelbaum, A. (Trans.). (1982). *The divine comedy of Dante Alighieri: Inferno.* New York: Bantam Classics.

VALUE CONFLICTS IN PRACTICE ●

Value conflicts in social work practice may emerge from four primary sources: (1) the personal values of the worker, (2) the personal values of the client, (3) the values of the social work profession, and (4) the laws and conventions of the community and state in which the social worker practices.

Social workers are human beings who have been shaped by their families, religion, and racial and ethnic identity. Because social workers come from different life experiences, the personal values of one social worker may be very different from the personal values of another social worker. A 25-year-old Jewish feminist lesbian social worker raised in New York City in an upper middle-class family will have different personal values from a 45-year-old Baptist heterosexual black male social worker raised in Birmingham, Alabama, in a working-class family. On race, age, gender, religion, sexual orientation, and geographical region, these two social workers have very little in common besides their membership in the NASW.

Though their personal values may be very different, both of these professional social workers may be engaged in ethical practice as outlined by the NASW *Code of Ethics*. And though their practice behaviors may reflect the ethical values of the profession, they may strongly disagree with some of the NASW policy positions on particular contemporary practice issues (NASW, 2009). For example, NASW has taken policy positions on a number of contemporary societal controversies, such as abortion, assisted suicide, and physical punishment of children. Individual social workers may disagree with NASW's position on a given issue and still be practicing social work. On these particular issues, NASW is pro-choice, against physical punishment, and clearly opposed to letting a worker do anything that assists a client in committing suicide except to encourage family involvement in the decision.

Another source of value conflict is the values that the clients bring into the practice situation. In the same way that individual workers may have radically different values, so may social workers and the clients they serve. A client may come from a different class, racial or ethnic group, religion, region of the country, and so on. A client may be racist, sexist, homophobic, anti-Semitic, and intolerant of others who are different. The 25-year-old Jewish feminist lesbian social worker previously mentioned would have to struggle with Rush Limbaugh as a client. Yet struggle she must because it is not the mission of a social worker to change the client's values, no matter how different their views may be from yours. Social workers are not missionaries trying to convert their clients. They may have missionary zeal for their work but not for changing their client's values.

In a multicultural society, it is very likely that interpersonal practitioners will encounter clients who have different values from their own personal values and different values from the profession of social work. This does not mean, however, that interpersonal practitioners screen out clients who have the "wrong" values. Instead, interpersonal practitioners must find a way to bridge value differences and conflicts. This is easier said than done, but practitioners have to do it all the time. One way of coping with these value conflicts is to try to understand how clients' experiences have shaped their values. When we understand the client as a product of his or her environment, it is easier to soften judgments about personal responsibility.

Another source of value conflicts may arise between the interpersonal practitioner and the community in which he or she practices. Sometimes local communities pass laws that directly conflict with the values of the profession and with the values of the individual social worker. For example, several states have passed legislation that removes gays and lesbians as protected groups under civil rights laws. Some towns have threatened to prosecute for murder doctors who perform abortions. Some communities have refused to comply with child abuse reporting requirements because they believed such reporting undermines parental authority and weakens the family.

Value conflicts are inevitable in the practice of social work, and some of the conflicts represent true dilemmas that have no solution. It is crucial that the social worker recognize value conflicts when they arise and at least work to clarify the nature of the conflict (Reamer, 1983, 2006). When we are in an interpersonal situation in which there are differences in values, there are a number of possible ways that we and others might react:

Celebrate ⟵→ Accept ⟵→ Tolerate ⟵→ Reject ⟵→ Persecute

Ideally, whenever value conflicts arise between individuals that are not life or limb threatening, it would be superb if individuals could resolve their differences by celebrating their diversity. This probably rarely happens in the real world, but in a multicultural society, it is a worthy goal. On the other end of the continuum, the worst outcome would be that one or another of the individuals would persecute the other for their value differences. Unfortunately, acts of persecution happen too often in our society in homophobic assaults, racist and anti-Semitic graffiti, and bullying in schools. At a bare minimum, the interpersonal practitioner must be able to tolerate the client's different values. From a professional perspective, it would be best if the worker could accept this diversity. As American society becomes more and more multicultural and pluralistic and more and more incidents of intolerance and persecution develop, it is critical for social work to realize the social responsibility to encourage society to be more accepting of differences. The Southern Poverty Law Center's Teaching Tolerance program (Southern Poverty Law Center, 2010) is a good example of how preventive and educational strategies may be used to improve relations between diverse groups of Americans.

The following practice scenario is offered as a simple quiz to help you think about value conflicts that arise in practice. Even though this exercise is constructed as a "quiz," some choices are not clear-cut. After you have taken this quiz, share your answers with your classmates or colleagues and see how they answered. In each question, V means "violation," NV means "no violation," and ? means "I have no idea." (See Exercise 3.2.)

Exercise 3.2

Ethics Quiz

Your field placement is at University Hospital in a medical social work position. You have been assigned a case of a 25-year-old married man who has tested HIV positive. Your responsibilities in this case are to provide him and his family with information about HIV/AIDS and to help them connect with resources. Which of the following actions might be considered violations of NASW Code of Ethics?

V   NV   ?   *You go to your supervisor and request that this case be assigned to another student because you are married and have a young child and do not want to risk contracting AIDS.*

V   NV   ?   *Your client refuses to tell his wife that he is HIV positive and refuses to change his present sexual practices, which do not include any form of disease prevention or condom use. Without his knowledge or permission, you contact his wife and warn her about her husband's HIV diagnosis.*

V   NV   ?   *You explain to your client that you will have to warn his wife about his HIV diagnosis whether he wants you to or not. You ask him to bring his wife to your next appointment so that all three of you can discuss this matter together.*

V   NV   ?   *Your client admits to you that he regularly engages in sexual intercourse with numerous partners outside his marriage. These are casual one night stands and he does not feel any responsibility to change his sexual practices with these liaisons. He adamantly refuses to use condoms or to warn these casual partners about his diagnosis. You explain to him that unless he does begin to use condoms, you will report him to the county health department, and they may require him to disclose all of his sexual contacts over the past 6 months.*

V   NV   ?   *You receive a phone call from Blue Cross Blue Shield (BCBS), and they request information on your client. They have recently developed a computer screening program that alerts them to potential AIDS carriers, and they want to know if your client has been diagnosed with AIDS. You inform BCBS that you are not authorized to release such information to anyone outside University Hospital.*

● PRACTICE CASES WITH ETHICAL ISSUES

The following case examples are based on real practice cases but have been carefully disguised to protect the identity of clients and agencies. These cases cover a wide range of practice situations and may be used to raise ethical issues in class discussions. We suggest that students read the entire NASW *Code of Ethics* before discussing these cases.

1. *You are a social worker in a family agency. You see a couple for marital counseling. They make good progress. Their marriage is so much better than when they started with you. They are very grateful to you for the progress, and they surprise you by bringing a beautiful, purebred golden retriever pup with them to their last session to thank you. They explain that they are registered breeders, and the pup is a runt from the last litter and would be difficult to sell. You are surprised. You love dogs and want to accept their gift.*

   What would you do?

   What are the consequences for the couple if you refuse the gift?

   What are the consequences for you if you accept the gift?

   Is it okay for you to buy the pup from them?

   Is there any acceptable solution?

2. *The client is a single mother with three children. Protective Services, a part of the Department of Human Services (DHS), is providing case management services to her in order to help her parent her children more effectively. She is eager for the help. Protective Services has referred her to an agency to provide in-home family therapy for her and her children. There has been no child abuse report. You are the mother's therapist. Your services are paid for by DHS. She complains to you that when the in-home therapists come they want to pray with her. You know that she has had very negative experiences with religion in her past. The client is not sure what she should do. She is afraid to refuse the services but also does not feel that she is getting help from the in-home service agency. She states that she feels worse after the in-home family therapists leave.*

   What would you do?

   What would you say to the client?

3. *You are a new social worker in a rehabilitation program for trau-matized clients. The client in question is a 40-year-old white woman who has experienced many sexual traumas throughout her life. She attends her sessions at the clinic in neatly pressed dresses, and it appears that it is important for her to look very nice. She has a 50-year-old white male social worker as her case manager. She seems to like his attentiveness and sometimes dresses in low-cut tight fitting dresses. You notice that the case manager has given her extra time at the end of the day. You witness this more experienced male social worker hugging this client at the end of the workday when most of the staff have left for home. You don't feel quite right about what you saw but don't want to jump to conclusions. This male social worker is well respected by all of his colleagues in the clinic and well liked by his clients.*

   What are your ethical responsibilities to this client?

   What are your ethical responsibilities to your colleague?

4. *A social worker has his own private therapy practice. He needs a new office manager. One of his clients has good office skills. She is unem-ployed, having trouble finding a job, and is having trouble paying her bills. He offers her a job. She takes it.*

   Is there anything wrong with employing the client?

5. *You are a school social worker. One of your clients is a 15-year-old girl who lives with her mother and younger brother. You have been able to establish a good relationship with her in spite of her many disruptive and problem behaviors at school. Late one Saturday night, she comes to your house. She asks you if she can stay with you. She has had a fight with her mother. You see a red area on the girl's face.*

   What should you do?

   What are the issues?

6. *You are a social worker in a university counseling center. Your client is a 25-year-old gay male graduate student. He is depressed and has a history of violence. It has been hard to establish a relationship with this man. He doesn't seem to trust people very easily. There is no consulting psychiatrist at your agency so you refer him to the psychiatric outpatient clinic at University Hospital for a medication evaluation. You see the client the week after the medication evaluation, and the client is enraged. He complains*

that the psychiatrist called him a fag. The psychiatrist gave him a prescription for an antidepressant, but the client doesn't want to go back there and instead wants to go beat up the psychiatrist for insulting him. The client is angry at you for sending him to this psychiatrist. You don't know the psychiatrist.

What are the issues?

What do you need to do?

7. *You are a community practice student, and your field placement is a Neighborhood Service Center in an inner-city neighborhood that is struggling against urban decay. Your supervisor is a charismatic social worker who is well respected in this neighborhood for his advocacy work with city hall. One of your responsibilities is working with a tenant's organization that is preparing a rent strike to pressure a landlord into making needed repairs. This building has been sighted for many code violations. As you begin to work with the tenant's organization, you accidentally discover that one of the tenants in your building is carrying on a sexual relationship with your supervisor. In fact, you discover that he has had several sexual liaisons with single mothers in this building.*

   What are the issues?

   Is a resident of a tenant organization the same thing as a client in a therapy group?

   What would you do?

8. *You work in a rehabilitation center for people who have closed head injuries. You and one of your social work colleagues from the rehabilitation program are members of the same church. One Sunday, you notice one of the patients from the rehabilitation program is in church with your social work colleague. During the coffee hour after the service, your colleague comes over to you and introduces the patient to you. During the next week, this patient joins one of the groups you are running in the rehab program. After the group ends, you speak to the patient alone and ask him about his experience at the church last Sunday. The patient volunteers that your social worker colleague wanted him to come with her because she felt he needed to find God in order to get well. He said that he explained to her that he was raised Jewish, but she insisted that he go with her.*

What are the issues?

What would you do?

9. *You are a social worker in private practice. You have a client who owes you a significant amount of money. You see this client and his wife for marital therapy. You raise the issue of the bill with the client and his wife. They say that they cannot pay the bill right now because the husband is laid off, but they want to continue to see you for marital therapy. The husband suggests that he do carpentry work for you in your home as a way of paying the bill.*

   What should you do?

   What are the issues here?

10. *You are a female social worker in a nonprofit counseling collective. You interview a female client for the first time. She tells you that she has been abused as a child and is very isolated and lonely. She appears to you to be quite depressed. During this session, the client tells you that her previous therapist held her often during sessions when the client felt sad or needy. The client wants to know if you would be willing to do this with her also. In as kind of a manner as possible, you tell her that you do not hold clients and don't feel that holding is an appropriate part of treatment. It is clear to you that the client feels upset and rejected even though you do your best to explain your policy. Shortly after the client has left the session, the agency gets multiple, repeated hang-up calls for several hours. You are able to determine that the calls are coming from the client. You call the client and ask her to stop making the calls and that you and the client may talk about this issue at her next scheduled appointment. The calls do not stop and are now upsetting to you and your colleagues.*

    What are the issues in this case?

    What do you do?

11. *Agency Context: This Department of Social Services (DSS) office is located in a rural, farming community that raises beef, hogs, corn, and soybeans. DSS has successfully recruited a number of farm families to become Adult Foster Care (AFC) homes for many deinstitutionalized and disabled clients after the regional state hospital closed.*

> ### Mary Trueheart
>
> *Mary Trueheart, a recent master of social work (MSW) graduate, accepted a position as case manager with responsibilities to recruit new AFC homes, to monitor the needs of 44 clients in the existing 12 homes, and to provide resources to AFC providers in caring for their clients. In the first 2 weeks of her probation, Mary successfully visited all of her homes, introduced herself to her clients, and met all of the providers. She was concerned about one home because the clients were so noncommunicative, well behaved, and sitting quietly on the front porch. She noticed large welts on two of the clients' arms, which the provider dismissed as "deer fly bites."*
>
> *When she started to leave, an elderly man in a wheelchair suddenly shook her hand and thanked her for coming. In her hand, she found a note with the words cattle prod. When Mary returned to her office, she talked to her supervisor about this experience at this home. The supervisor informed her that this was the home of a centennial farm family who was one of the first families to agree to become an AFC home. Because of the family's reputation, they were highlighted in a local newspaper article promoting AFC homes as a supplementary source of income. The supervisor dismissed Mary's concerns as the reactions of an inexperienced worker. Mary was still concerned about her experiences at the home, so she went to the agency director with her questions. The next morning, Mary was summoned to the director's office and was informed that she was being released for failing to conform to agency procedures while on probation.*
>
> *What are the issues in this case?*
>
> *What should Mary Trueheart do?*

● SUMMARY

In this chapter, we have explored the ideology, values, and ethics that underlie social work in the contemporary world. We have looked at the documents that reflect the norms that are the foundation for social work practice. These norms are codified and written down as laws and regulations. Many of the laws in the United States have their roots in Judeo-Christian religious traditions. The United Nations' UDHR (United Nations, 2010) is another set of guidelines. The UDHR specifies 30 rights that concern economic, political, and individual civil rights.

The profession of social work has explicitly articulated its ideology in its policy statements of 63 contemporary issues (NASW, 2009). Many of these issues are politically contentious, such as affirmative action; immigration; capital punishment; workplace discrimination; and rights of lesbian, gay, bisexual, and transgender people. The underlying theme of these policy statements could be characterized as "liberal" and "progressive." The social work profession is rooted in a set of core values.

These core values, embraced by social workers throughout the profession's history, are the foundation of social work's unique purpose and perspective: service, social justice, dignity and worth of the person, importance of human relationships, integrity, and competence. The core values, as they are written in the NASW *Code of Ethics*, are discussed in detail. These values are a specific guide for social work practice that has been laid out by the NASW.

The chapter ends with situations that present value dilemmas from practice. Social workers are routinely faced with ethical dilemmas that challenge the values and core beliefs of the individual and the profession. The practical case situations present an opportunity to think about the issues that might arise in social work practice.

CHAPTER 4

INTERPERSONAL PRACTICE BEYOND DIVERSITY AND TOWARD SOCIAL JUSTICE

The Importance of Critical Consciousness

BETH GLOVER REED, PETER A. NEWMAN,
ZULEMA E. SUAREZ, AND EDITH A. LEWIS

> *Diversity is the one true thing we all have in common.*
>
> —Anonymous

This chapter originally appeared in the 2nd edition of this book and has been slightly revised for this 3rd edition. One of the authors of this chapter (Beth Glover Reed, or BGR) has contributed to an addendum that brings in the contemporary issue of "intersectionality" into the discussion of critical consciousness. We have added more content about sex, gender identity, gender expression, and sexual orientation that should enhance students' understanding of these concepts. We have also edited the original chapter for clarity and removed some of its redundancy.

This chapter presents an opportunity for readers to explore a series of constructs that are critical to an understanding of working with people in their social environments. For an analysis of the complexity of gender and sexuality see Figure 4.1.

| Figure 4.1 | The Complexity of Sex, Gender, and Sexual Orientation |

Diagram of Sex and Gender

BIOLOGICAL SEX

(anatomy, chromosomes, hormones)

male _____ *intersex* _____ *female*

GENDER IDENTITY

(psychological sense of self)

man _____ *two spirit or third gender* _____ *woman*

GENDER EXPRESSION

(communication of gender)

masculine _____ *androgynous* _____ *feminine*

SEXUAL ORIENTATION

(romantic or erotic response)

attracted to women _____ *bisexual or asexual* _____ *attracted to men*

Biological sex, shown on the top scale, includes external genitalia, internal reproductive structures, chromosomes, hormone levels, and secondary sex characteristics, such as breasts, facial and body hair, and fat distribution. These characteristics are objective in that they can be seen and measured (with appropriate technology). The scale consists not just of two categories (male and female) but is actually a continuum, with most people existing somewhere near one end or the other. The space more in the middle is occupied by intersex people (formerly, hermaphrodites), who have combinations of characteristics typical of males and those typical of females, such as both a testis and an ovary, or XY chromosomes (the usual male pattern) and a vagina, or they may have features that are not completely male or completely female, such as an organ that could be thought of as a small penis or a large clitoris, or an XXY chromosomal pattern.

Gender identity is how people think of themselves and identify in terms of sex (man, woman, boy, girl). Gender identity is a psychological quality; unlike biological sex, it can't be observed or measured (at least by current means)—only reported by the individual. Like biological sex, it consists of more than two categories, and there's space in the middle for those who identify as a third gender, both (two spirit), or neither. We lack language for this intermediate position because everyone in our culture is supposed to identify unequivocally with one of the two extreme categories. In fact, many people feel that they have masculine and feminine aspects of their psyches, and some people, fearing that they do, seek to purge themselves of one or the other by acting in exaggerated sex-stereotyped ways.

Gender expression is everything we do that communicates our sex or gender to others: clothing, hairstyles, mannerisms, way of speaking, roles we take in interactions, etc. This communication may be purposeful or accidental. It could also be called "social gender" because it relates to

(Continued)

(Continued)

interactions between people. Trappings of one gender or the other may be forced on us as children or by dress codes at school or work. Gender expression is a continuum, with feminine at one end and masculine at the other. In between are gender expressions that are androgynous (neither masculine nor feminine) and those that combine elements of the two (sometimes called gender bending). Gender expression can vary for an individual from day to day or in different situations, but most people can identify a range on the scale where they feel the most comfortable. Some people are comfortable with a wider range of gender expression than others.

Sexual orientation indicates who we are erotically attracted to. The ends of this scale are labeled "attracted to women" and "attracted to men," rather than "homosexual" and "heterosexual," to avoid confusion as we discuss the concepts of sex and gender. In the mid-range is bisexuality; there are also people who are asexual (attracted to neither men nor women). We tend to think of most people as falling into one of the two extreme categories (attracted to women or attracted to men), whether they are straight or gay, with only a small minority clustering around the bisexual middle. However, Kinsey's studies showed that most people are in fact not at one extreme of this continuum or the other but occupy some position between.

For each scale, the popular notion that there are two distinct categories, with everyone falling neatly into one or the other, is a social construction. The real world (nature, if you will) does not observe these boundaries. If we look at what actually exists, we see that there is middle ground. To be sure, most people fall near one end of the scale or the other, but very few people are actually at the extreme ends, and there are people at every point along the continuum.

Gender identity and sexual orientation are resistant to change. Although we don't yet have definitive answers to whether these are the result of biological influences, psychological ones, or both, we do know that they are established very early in life, possibly prenatally, and there are no methods that have been proven effective for changing either of these. Some factors that make up biological sex can be changed, with more or less difficulty. These changes are not limited to people who change their sex: Many women undergo breast enlargement, which moves them toward the extreme female end of the scale, and men have penile enlargements to enhance their maleness, for example. Gender expression is quite flexible for some people and more rigid for others. Most people feel strongly about expressing themselves in a way that's consistent with their inner gender identity and experience discomfort when they're not allowed to do so.

The four scales are independent. Our cultural expectation is that men occupy the extreme left ends of all four scales (male, man, masculine, attracted to women) and women occupy the right ends. But a person with male anatomy could be attracted to men (gay man), or could have a gender identity of "woman" (transsexual), or could have a feminine gender expression on occasion (cross-dresser). A person with female anatomy could identify as a woman, have a somewhat masculine gender expression, and be attracted to women (butch lesbian). It's a mix-and-match world, and there are as many combinations as there are people who think about their gender.

This schema is not necessarily "reality," but it's probably closer than the two-box system. Reality is undoubtedly more complex. Each of the four scales could be broken down into several scales. For instance, the sex scale could be expanded into separate scales for external genitalia, internal reproductive organs, hormone levels, chromosome patterns, and so forth. An individual would probably not fall on the same place on each of these. "Biological sex" is a summary of scores for several variables.

There are conditions that exist that don't fit anywhere on a continuum: Some people have neither the XX (typical female) chromosomal pattern nor the XY pattern typical of males, but it is not clear that other patterns, such as just X, belong anywhere on the scale between XX and XY. Furthermore, the scales may not be entirely separate: If gender identity and sexual orientation are found to have a biological component, they may overlap with the biological sex scale.

Using the model presented here is something like using a spectrum of colors to view the world, instead of only black and white. It doesn't fully account for all the complex shadings that exist, but it gives us a richer, more interesting picture. Why look at the world in black and white (marred by a few troublesome shades of gray) when there's a whole rainbow out there?

Source: Center for Gender Sanity. (2001, August 16). *Diagram of sex and gender.* Retrieved from www .gendersanity.com/diagram.shtml.

The focus will be on concepts such as age, race, sexual orientation, ethnicity, gender, social class, and disability status. These are all characteristics that define our membership in various social groupings. Unlike many approaches to these topics, this chapter emphasizes that these group memberships apply not only to "the other"—the target of our concern and services, usually designated as the client or client system within social work—but also to ourselves, as social work practitioners and citizens.

This chapter has four goals:

1. To present and discuss key concepts that help to define competent practice with diverse populations and are important for a social work practice that promotes social justice

2. To describe the concept of multiple identities formed across the life span, the relationship of these identities to social group memberships, and their importance to the outcomes of social work practice

3. To assist the reader in understanding the role of critical consciousness development in social work theory and practice, how critical consciousness influences both service consumers and social work practitioners, and some consequences of the failure to apply critical consciousness while developing working alliances and contracts within social work practice

4. To provide some ways that you, the reader, can develop, sustain, and deepen your own critical consciousness and apply it in your social work practice

Knowledge about how social workers can work for social justice in ways that respect and build on people's social group memberships has grown markedly during the past 3 decades (Gutierrez & Lewis, 1999; Gutierrez, Lewis, Nagda, Wernick, & Shore, 2005; Lewis, 2009; Newman, Bogo, & Daley, 2008; Suarez & Lewis, 2005; Suarez, Newman, & Reed, 2008). Empirical studies and conceptual frameworks have identified many problems that arise from the absence of attention to this knowledge: for instance, the indiscriminate use of standardized testing instruments in diverse populations (Lewis, 1995), the heterosexist nature of family counseling and its impact on gays and lesbians in families (Comas-Diaz & Greene, 1995; Greene, 1994), and the impact of "class blindness" on group interactions in the United States (Thurow, 1994). Knowledge has also exploded about how to acknowledge and build upon people's group memberships and identities, often by delineating key characteristics of a group and the practice implications for working with members of that group (Lum, 1992, 2005; Sue & Sue, 2007).

Less well developed are approaches that attend to power differences and that address the effects of direct and indirect discrimination within different forms of practice, although literature on empowerment is beginning to fill this gap (Gutierrez & Lewis, 1994, 1999; Gutierrez et al., 2005; Levy-Simon, 1994). Even less available is work that is transformative that creates alternative models and processes toward a multicultural and socially just world.

Social work literature proposes complex models that encompass the multiple characteristics of both clients and workers and the contexts of practice (Chau, 1991; Green, 1995; Lewis, 2009; Lum, 1992; Swigonski, 1994). In this chapter, we have chosen not to emphasize only specific problems in our knowledge *and* practices arising from a lack of attention to human differences and oppression, although you, the reader, certainly need to learn to recognize and correct these. Instead, we present what we believe to be the most salient thinking about these multiple dimensions of group membership and how they interact, the importance of critical consciousness, and the implications of these for practice. Any discussion of social group memberships and how they have been reinforced or denigrated within societies must occur within an understanding of their historical, social, and political contexts; in other words, discussion must be contextualized. In addition, we add suggestions about how to develop your own skills and to scrutinize practice theory and methods to identify their biases and strengths. These are essential if we are to work toward a socially just world and a society that acknowledges and respects multiple differences among people.

At a minimum, learning to recognize and understand multiple aspects of diversity and oppression and how they work is important because they are central in shaping who people are. They affect client–worker relationships and contribute to clients' strengths, problems, and styles of coping. Moreover, an awareness of difference and oppression may help you to recognize when experiences meant to be therapeutic may be inadvertently harmful because they are not culturally compatible or they invoke or reinforce existing power imbalances.

A fundamental assumption in this chapter is that recognizing and building on people's differences is important and necessary but not sufficient for a practice that has social justice as a primary goal. For the types of practice emphasized in this chapter, both *difference* and *dominance* dimensions must be recognized and addressed. Developing and using individual and collective critical consciousness are primary tools for understanding differences, recognizing injustice, and beginning to envision a more just society. We define these terms and give examples of their application to practice in the sections that follow. Throughout, we use examples from our own lives and practices to illustrate ways we have struggled to develop our own critical consciousness and to provide practical examples of the definitions and conceptual models that follow.

Just as there are multiple social contexts, there are multiple experiences of these contexts. We demonstrate later in the chapter how one's positionality (group identities and life experiences), standpoint (outsider/insider status), or both influences life expectations and informs the development of critical consciousness. Because we are aware of the potential for capturing only one "lens" or version of reality in any chapter, we have been cautious here to include many of the multiple contexts that we as individuals have experienced.

This chapter was written as the collaborative effort of four individuals from different multiple identities that include most of the group memberships we will discuss. Through the exercises, case vignettes, and dialogues that follow, we present some of the multiple lenses through which we construct and pursue our own work and provide opportunities for you to explore your own. Unless a footnote indicates another source, the personal examples throughout the chapter are drawn from the lives of one of the authors.

WHAT IS CRITICAL CONSCIOUSNESS? ●

Critical consciousness can have many meanings. We define it as a process of continuous self-reflection coupled with action to discover and uncover how we, our approaches to social work practice, and our environments have been and continue to be shaped by societal assumptions and power dynamics. Critical consciousness is an essential tool to help us recognize, understand, and work to change the social forces that shape our societies, ourselves, and the lives of our clients. Without critical consciousness, social work practice too often does not recognize and build on important differences among people, and it perpetuates or at least does not challenge dynamics that perpetuate societal injustice. Working to develop and deepen our critical consciousness also allows us to practice the skills we need to move toward a socially just society that embraces and builds on our varied cultural backgrounds.

Critical consciousness incorporates and gives us a greater understanding of power relationships and commonalities and differences among and within people. People create multiple identities based on their life experiences that are shaped by these forces. We need to work to understand people through *their* construction and enactment of their multiple identities—that is, people must be understood in terms of the social, political, and historical macro forces influencing their lives and the meaning they as individuals make of these forces. We can also apply our critical skills to understanding the social environments around us—our families, organizations, communities, and governments.

Much of our current understanding and challenge to critical consciousness is based on the work of Paolo Freire, the Brazilian educator, philosopher, and visionary. Freire calls the movement from simply experiencing to analyzing and reflecting on one's life, history, and environment "becoming the subject rather than the object of one's own history" (Freire, 1973). An example from one of us illustrates this process:

> *I was raised in the era of the civil rights movement of the 1950s and 1960s. Throughout, as an African American, I was defined by others with a number of terms: culturally disadvantaged, minority, colored girl, and so forth. In the late 1960s, however, I began to access documents on the African continent, the period before the slave trade and biographies about the contributions of African Americans within the United States. I suddenly began to realize that I was a part of a larger increment that defied a limited definition and was, in actuality, contributing to the larger movement. I moved from object to subject—that is from being acted upon to acting.*

Freire termed the process of moving from object to subject, from victim to empowered social agent, *conscientization*. This requires "discovering one's presence within a totality, within a structure, and not as imprisoned or stuck" (Freire, 1973, p. 16). We explore these aspects of critical consciousness and other related definitions and processes in the remainder of this chapter.

Addendum to 3rd Edition

Much of what has been discussed in the previous and next sections is still current in 2011, but with some new language, which has some implications for both how to think about critical consciousness and working for social justice. The term *intersectionality* is now being used to indicate "mutually constitutive relations among social identities" (Shields, 2008, and a special edition of *Sex Roles*). Mutually constitutive means that occupying one social category helps to shape how other social categories are experienced and reacted to by self and others. Intersectionality approaches define ways that all people simultaneously occupy *multiple* social locations within society. Social locations mean positions within a social matrix that are associated with different levels and types of power and influence and imbued with different social meanings. These meanings have both widely understood cultural components *and* personal elements, including components of identities—awareness of self, self-image, self-reflection, and self-esteem.

The concept of intersectionality arose initially from cultural studies and feminist scholars endeavoring to address criticisms that focusing primarily on one social category at a time obscures important differences *within* that category. These patterns of differences shape people's lives frequently in divergent ways even though they may share one or more important social locations, like race or gender. All of this is very consistent with perspectives presented in this chapter as written more than 10 years ago, although now the term *positionality* would be used mostly in its plural form of *positionalities*, since there is more consistent awareness of how we simultaneously must negotiate multiple positions and associated identities simultaneously.

Other key elements of intersectionality approaches also were introduced in this chapter initially but are addressed much more fully in current scholarship and practice (e.g., Hulko, 2009):

- Different social categories are associated with different types and levels of power.
- Immediate and more distant social contexts influence which social categories are noticed or focused upon (cued) and how they are experienced and perceived.
- Much of this may not be conscious and thus not actively processed or "controlled" by the person exhibiting the behaviors or thoughts.

In terms of power, most people *simultaneously* occupy positions associated with different levels of status—some that are associated with disadvantage and others more likely to confer unearned privilege. Interactions among social categories and related identities with very different levels of societal status creates complex opportunities and challenges as we learn to focus on multiple social categories simultaneously. For instance, a white person may have relative advantage in terms of race but have this tempered by a physical disability *and* a lower socioeconomic status.

To complicate this further, social contexts help to determine which social categories are most salient in any given time and location and shape how they are experienced and perceived. For instance, a white person (and others) are likely to be much more aware of race, and race will be understood quite differently in an obviously multiracial social situation or when one is the only white person in a predominantly African American group compared with being white in a largely white environment. Gender norms and age will be enacted and understood differently in a formal dinner party primarily of young people than they will in a community meeting focusing on the safety of seniors in their homes.

Finally, much more is known today about the impacts of what is called identity-based motivation and how our actions and cognitions (thoughts) are "cued" and shaped by our social positions and identities associated with these (e.g., Oyserman, 2009). These identities are stable but highly sensitive to situational cues and thus are often triggered by subtle forces in our environments without conscious awareness. Thus, our various positionalities shape many things in our behaviors and thoughts in ways we often do not recognize and thus are less able to monitor or change because we are not "processing" them.

(Continued)

(Continued)

All of the previously noted items suggest that negotiating intersectionalities in practice must be an ongoing continuous journey, both in terms of understanding ourselves, in working with others, and in examining the motivations informing our actions. Since contexts and mixes of categories are always changing, a practitioner must focus less on achieving competence or mastery of particular facts or knowledge and more on exploring ourselves with humility, emphasizing complex thinking, and engaging with and learning quickly about social contexts and from those with whom we work.

In order to clarify and apply the concept of intersectionality and power, we present the following case example. This is a real case example, and the person involved is used as a case example in Chapter 17 in the discussion about advocacy.

Case of a Rural, Disabled, Elderly Farmer

When we moved to our present farm in rural Michigan, we found ourselves near another farm that from an outsider's view was in need of many repairs from years of neglect. Living in part of the farmhouse was an elderly, disabled (missing one leg), swarthy, short man of Armenian descent. It was clear that he was a "loner" who was used to surviving on his own. He did not respect women in roles of power. We had been warned by others in the community that he was hostile to outsiders and prone to violence. He lived alone and survived on disability payments, a small garden on which he grew many variety of fruits and vegetables, and the gifts of relatives and friends who brought him old clothing. He ate carp that was caught in a nearby river. What was not obvious to outsiders was his ability to survive and thrive in spite of his disability and lack of resources.

We found him to be very intelligent and an observer of the natural world around him. He had developed many "varieties" of vegetables over the years by carefully selecting the seed of vegetables that had characteristics that he wanted to enhance. For example, he had developed a seedless watermelon, potatoes the size of footballs, and green peppers the size of grapefruits. He had managed to master the secrets of "grafting" onto various wild apple trees a number of other varieties of fruit. On one tree he had pears growing on some limbs, three kinds of apples growing on other limbs, and apricots growing on other limbs. He was able to re-engineer the handed down clothes from others to fit his broad physique and one leg. For example, his jackets and shirts all had strips of cloth from other clothes down the back that increased the breadth of these items. To outsiders his clothes looked strange, but his resourcefulness created a functional wardrobe. He had mastered the art of canning the many vegetables that he grew and even developed some innovative products, such as eggplant jam. He had also developed the knowledge of how to make various liqueurs from the peelings of his grapes, pears, and apples. In his workshop, he had the knowledge to work with various kinds of machinery and rebuild various junked parts that he had retrieved from various nearby dumps. For example, he had re-engineered an old VW transmission into his "doodlebug," which was a personal transportation device that allowed him to get around his gardens and farm. This doodlebug looked something like a golf cart but was powered by pumping a lever with his right arm that moved the vehicle forward and backward.

In his living area of the farmhouse, he had one lightbulb, an old oil burning furnace that provided heat in the winter, and water that was supplied by a 19th-century windmill that pumped water out of the ground. In terms of our modern concerns about environmental sustainability, our neighbor had developed ways of surviving and thriving by reusing the materials left over from others and by living with the resources that Mother Nature provided.

Over the years, our relationship with this "neighbor" developed into a strong, reciprocal relationship in which he would help repair our farm machinery, and we would advocate for him with the welfare department to get him emergency oil in the winter or to clarify letters regarding his benefits that enraged him. This "neighbor" became a "foster grandparent" to our daughters by making various toys (origami) out of scraps of paper. We would invite him over to our home on holidays, though he was reluctant to eat our food because it had not been raised and prepared by him—even though all of our meat and vegetables were raised organically.

One day when Barbara (BHS) was getting ready to leave his home after bringing our neighbor some salt and sugar from the store, she explained that she had to go home and get ready to "go to work." We had been very careful never to tell our neighbor that both of us were social workers, because we knew of his contentious history with welfare workers and medical social workers during the amputation of his leg decades earlier. Our neighbor asked, "What kind of work do you do? You don't look like you like your job." BHS responded that she liked her job but she wasn't sure he did, because she understood the kinds of past experiences he had with social workers. She stated that she was a social worker and worked with families who were struggling. His reply to this disclosure was "I have never been helped by a social worker before!" Fortunately in his mind and ours we continued to be "good neighbors" and not the instruments of social welfare institutions that had oppressed him in the past.

This example demonstrates the complicated web of roles and identity issues that emerge in human relationships and how dimensions of power are played out in these relationships. It also demonstrates how outsiders and authority figures may "view" oppressed clients without taking into account their amazing strengths and resilience in the face of adversity. We would often tell our neighbor that if the world economic system collapsed, we would come over and move in with him because he would teach us how to survive off the land.

MAJOR DIMENSIONS OF MULTICULTURALISM ●
AND SOME TERMINOLOGY

The tasks needed to develop a critical consciousness are to identify, to learn to see, and to name a number of dimensions and processes that are usually "nonconscious" and operate outside of our awareness (Bem & Bem, 1970). All people have things that are unique about them that arise from their individual temperaments, family, and socialization experiences. We also have many elements we share with others because of the groups we belong to—some of which we choose and some of which are assigned to us by law or the assumptions of others. These group identities affect how we perceive ourselves and how others perceive us. We have to take different routes to develop critical consciousness depending on our histories, how we were raised, and how many insider or outsider characteristics we inhabit. We can use our knowledge in one category to help us to see and understand more about another and by sharing our understandings and perceptions with others who occupy similar and different categories.

Two major dimensions underlie our definitions of multiculturalism:

1. those that are related to *differences* among people and groups

2. those that arise from past and present patterns of oppression, discrimination, and privilege—factors often described as markers of *status*

Each dimension has commonalities and differences across elements of our multiple group identities. A number of concepts and definitions are extremely important to know for multicultural work and to help you develop and deepen your critical consciousness. The concepts and social group memberships of most concern in this chapter affect our relative ease of access to societal resources and our mobility within the society.

In your other courses, you should have been exposed to many relevant concepts in more detail than we can cover in this chapter (Greene, 1994; Longres, 1990; Queralt, 1996). We will list primarily key terms here with only enough discussion to frame a context for critical consciousness and its application to practice. Be sure that you understand those terms and know how to use them. If you are not encountering them in other course work, seek them in the library or in references we cite in this chapter. Urge your school and other professors to include more of this important material.

Differences or Diversity Perspectives

People naturally develop categories to enable them to understand and make sense of their world. We identify different cues that help us to anticipate and react to people and events without having to gather information and problem solve at every step. Sorting people into categories by recognizing similarities with others can help us decide how to interact in a first encounter with someone, but developing categories also creates limitations. We may attend to some cues and miss others that would lead to different conclusions. We develop *stereotypes*, which are sets of assumptions about who people are and how they will act. These stereotypes are usually based on some aspect of the social groupings that the person represents, but they tend to oversimplify and overgeneralize since they are based on limited information. Stereotypes help us to make sense of a complex world but are often rigid, incomplete, and inaccurate. We must remain open in order to question and revise our incomplete stereotypical impressions.

One way to learn about our stereotypes is to pay attention to the language that we use and the way in which it shapes our understandings. For example, the umbrella term *Hispanic* helps to mask significant differences between the different nationalities of people who were colonized by Spain. It also omits Native American and African influences on Latin Americans. Those who are the targets of stereotypes also must work to discover the ways they have incorporated aspects of those stereotypes into their self-perceptions.

When I was growing up, I bought into the "Golden Exiles" stereotype ascribed to Cubans by mainstream society. The early Cuban migration waves were treated much more favorably than Puerto Rican or Mexican migrants for reasons too many to discuss here (Suarez, 1993). For years I held the unconscious notion that Cubans were indeed "special" or "golden." It was not until entering graduate school when I began thinking more critically that I realized that this was a stereotype and that even though it appeared to be positive, it was actually discriminatory and oppressive. It led to my feeling superior to those who came later and other groups of Latinos or Latinas and interfered with my ability to see the similarities among us and the limiting cultural expectations that were acting on me and undermining my self-confidence.

The most common set of concepts related to difference perspectives are those related to culture. Culture usually refers to the ways in which various groups and societies define themselves, how they live, what they value, how they believe people should behave, child rearing practices, communication and interaction patterns, group rituals, and important societal symbols (Marger, 1994; McWhirter, 1994).

There are at least two ways to think about culture: categorical and transactional approaches (Green, 1995). A *categorical* approach focuses on key characteristics of a cultural group emphasizing those things that make the group distinctive (i.e., within-group commonalities and between-group differences) and that help define the overall norms, values, and practices in that group. Categorical approaches deemphasize the often rich and important differences within groups, commonalities across groups, and the many ways that culture and other group memberships are negotiated, change, and conflict with each other. In this chapter, we also discuss other dimensions of groups (e.g., gender expression, social class, or age) that emphasize key within-group characteristics and differences between groups.

A *transactional* approach to understanding culture is more complex and mutable than a categorical approach. Although a transactional approach also seeks to understand social identity groups, how they form, and how they influence their members, the formation of these affinity groups is conceptualized as an ongoing process that takes place within a political and economic context. Transactional approaches emphasize how people manage and manipulate the symbols of their group membership as a resource for building satisfying lives. In practice, this means that what one person sees of another's culture is at least partially determined by the situation and the characteristics of those with whom the person is interacting. For instance, an African American woman may behave differently in a group with other African American women (both in what she says, how she says it, and her body language) than in a group with white women or with African American men. A social worker's characteristics will similarly help to shape how a client acts. More about this issue will be discussed in the relationship chapter.

The "melting pot" metaphor in this country arises from categorical definitions of culture. "American" culture is perceived as a melt of the cultures of various immigrant groups; new immigrants are expected to shed their previous cultures and adopt their new culture. Rather than conceptualizing this as yes or no and unidirectional phenomena, a transactional view suggests that the processes underlying assimilation and acculturation are strongly based on situational and contextual cues. The complex ways in which people learn what behaviors are expected in different milieus and relationships and how people negotiate conflicting cultural expectations has been termed *identity work*. The newer "salad bowl" metaphor acknowledges that individuals and groups maintain elements of their cultures while also being mixed with others, but this metaphor still misses the complex dynamics that occur within and between members of different cultural groupings and their contexts.

I am often conscious of my affect and level of expressiveness when I'm with a dominant culture group that is more reserved and less effusive. I also stopped wearing makeup when I first entered predominantly white academia because that was the norm, and I was afraid of standing out more than I already did. I had become ashamed about something that is characteristic of me and other Latinas in general. Latinas are most often expected to be feminine within Latino or Latina culture, and wearing makeup is an expression of that femininity.

People generally learn to operate within many cultural and social contexts and will usually adopt whatever style protects or advantages them the most. This style may not be the most comfortable for them—especially if they feel threatened or have little trust for others in the situation. When they are in a more culturally comfortable and compatible environment with members of their own ethnic or affinity group, however, they are likely to behave quite differently because they are with "us" rather than with "them." This shifting of behaviors to fit social expectations and comfort levels is sometimes called "code-switching," meaning that we "put on" and "take off" particular behaviors and styles according to our understanding of the "behavioral code" (i.e., what is expected) for that situation.

I had been living in the Castro—a predominantly queer district of San Francisco—with my partner of 5 years, and visiting relatives from the East Coast were over for cocktails before we headed off for dinner. They commented on what wonderful hosts we had been and the artful hors d'oeuvres. I gesticulated rather lavishly and loudly exclaimed, "Well, thank you." They looked at me strangely and studied the floor assiduously for several minutes. I realized that in my comfort with my home environment I had not switched codes; I had enacted behavior culturally appropriate to the milieu but unfamiliar to (and not comfortable for) my guests.

People may learn how to behave in different contexts through experience, or they may be explicitly taught how to behave by their families or by a mentor. For instance, in addition to learning about their own culture and accepted behaviors within that culture, most African American families actively teach their children how they should behave when among whites. Learning to behave differently in different contexts is an important survival tactic if behaviors that are comfortable and acceptable in the home setting would bring disapproval or danger outside one's ethnic group. One can be unprepared, however, when neither context is operating.

My family did a really good job of teaching me that most whites would misinterpret behaviors and language that were common among blacks. I learned that I needed to follow "white" rules in school if I was to succeed and stay out of trouble. Since I mostly lived in a "black" context and went to school in a "white" context, these instructions were easy to follow when I was a child. Years later, when I found myself in an environment that included members from different Asian groups, the Middle East, different Latin American countries, and whites from many parts of the United States, I had no idea how to behave. This was both exciting and frightening.

Often one learns about cultural expectations when one changes locales or contexts.

When I moved to another city for graduate school, I first felt like a "blow off" because I didn't want to work all the time the way other students did. I was used to working hard and then playing hard, but no one else seemed to do this. At first, I tried to emulate the others—I worked all the time and didn't take time to take care of me or to enjoy my friends and family. I was miserable and felt like an impostor. Then I got angry that I couldn't be myself and at others for making value judgments about different ways of working. Eventually, I worked out a reasonably comfortable balance between work and some play, but I was still careful about how I presented myself to my new professional colleagues.

Many concepts related to culture and other ways of defining differences among people are relevant for this chapter and social work practice. The following definitions provide some examples. The terminology presented can also be applied to other categories of difference (such as gender identity, class, and sexual orientation).

Definitions Related to "Difference"

- *Acculturation*: processes necessary to learn enough of the new culture to operate effectively and to "translate" and move successfully between the old and the new
- *Assimilation*: process emphasizing leaving one's "old" culture and blending into the new
- *Critical consciousness*: includes not only culture but other dimensions of difference and dominance; the need to continuously challenge and expand to move beyond our current knowledge and awareness toward multicultural knowledge and practice
- *Cultural competence*: beyond cultural sensitivity, it includes having the skills necessary to assess situations and work across differences in culturally relevant ways
- *Cultural consciousness*: includes cultural competence as well as a recurring critique, monitoring, and scrutiny of our theory, language, thinking, and actions as they are culturally grounded
- *Cultural relevance*: the degree of "fit" that a service or approach has to key aspects of another's culture
- *Cultural sensitivity*: levels of knowledge and skills that help people to understand cultures—especially those other than their own
- *Transnational communities*: (McArdle, 1995; Rouse, 1991) many immigrant and refugee groups may work in one country and/or travel between that country and their home country, have ties in both locations, and may or may not intend to return to the country from which they came

Perspectives That Incorporate Dominance

We all have much to learn even to negotiate and be respectful of differences among people. Unfortunately, many of these differences are also differently valued within societies so that members of more valued groups have more social and economic power than members of less valued groups. The history of differential access to resources and influence is as important as the patterns of interactions that advantage some members over others.

Sociologists have used the term *status* to describe key differences in power and influence (Berger & Zelditch, 1977; Ridgeway, 1992). They differentiate statuses that are *achieved* and through effort and talent (e.g., educational degrees) from those that are *ascribed* or inherited. Ascribed status is related to the conditions of one's birth (such as the economic and social class of our family of origin) and other social categories such as age, gender, and ethnicity, which one cannot easily escape. Other types of ascribed status are invisible but are stigmatized or marginalized when they become known (such as sexual orientations or transgender expression). One's position in the social structure is dictated by the assigned value of those categories. Often, different statuses conflict, and statuses that are earned often conflict with those that are ascribed— for instance, when a man is interacting with a woman corporate executive who is his boss and he has been socialized to hold the door for a woman and walk behind a boss.

Definitions Related to "Dominance" and Power

- *Colonization*: when more powerful countries take ownership of and impose cultural standards and lifestyles on the people of another country, often making money off the labor of the indigenous people and resources; refers also to current remnants of these histories and the dynamics of privilege and oppression between groups with markedly different levels of societal power
- *Discrimination*: how lower status and power in society lowers economic and social progress and success by interfering with a person's or group's ability to earn or by affecting the criteria by which success is determined
- *Dominance* and *subordination*: what occurs when more powerful groups impose their will on less powerful groups
- *Insider group*: lives according to the values, expectations, and styles of the dominant culture and derives status and advantage from that position
- *Institutionalized discrimination* (Feagin & Feagin, 1986) or *oppression*: discriminatory practices embedded within our customs, procedures, policies, and social structures
- *Internalized discrimination or oppression*: when members of outsider groups may adopt the standards of the dominant group and evaluate themselves according to those standards; can lead to self-hatred and disempowerment
- *Outsiders*: fall outside the valued group, by attribute, because of the position of one's birth family, or key aspects of identity values, or lifestyle
- *Prejudice*: negative beliefs a person holds about members of other groups
- *Privilege* and *oppression*: members of more powerful groups have access to many advantages within society; those with less ascribed power may even be blocked from access to basic needs or overtly persecuted
- *Resistance and agency*: how subordinate groups have fought being oppressed, either covertly or directly, or taken steps to improve their situations and maintain strong sense of self despite cultural devaluations

Discrimination can be overt and blatant or covert and subtle. It can also be deliberate or inadvertent (e.g., when we devalue key aspects of a group's culture and believe that particular ways of expressing oneself mean that one is less intelligent). It can be formalized within the society through laws that do not allow some groups of people to marry legally, such as gay couples. Discrimination can be carried out through uncontrolled or "informal" mechanisms (such as the overt violence of hanging, gay bashing, or rape, or the passive inaction of not speaking up when someone makes an ethnic slur). The effect of all these mechanisms is to convey who has more power, to create obstacles to the progress and success of those with less status, and ultimately to threaten their lives and well-being.

Institutional discrimination can result from rules and procedures carried over from times in which discrimination was deliberate and overt—for instance, through promotion processes that give priority to seniority, when people of color were not eligible to be hired until recently, or to veterans, when most women were not allowed into the military until recently. Institutional discrimination can also arise through mechanisms that reward particular kinds of experiences and knowledge—for instance, intelligence tests that use examples that are far more likely to be experienced by those from particular social class backgrounds.

These concepts focus not only on relative power and status but also on *marginality* and *centrality* within a culture, which illustrates the linkage between dynamics of difference and those related to dominance. One's status as an insider or an outsider influences many things. Insiders have knowledge of how the dominant cultural and political systems work as well as access to centrally controlled resources, although they may not be cognizant of this privilege. Key elements of the culture's values, processes, and benefits may be so taken for granted that they have become invisible, unmarked, and unnamed.

I'd had African American friends most of my life and had already seen how many of them entirely changed their choice of words, syntax, and body language when they talked to other African Americans from those they used when they talked to me. I was still totally unprepared for how little I understood when I was the only white person in a room entirely filled with African Americans. I had no idea how to act and felt awkward and uncomfortable even though people were kind and welcoming.

Whites in the United States rarely identify first as white, and many are unable to articulate key elements of their culture(s). Often white people are more able to identify how they differ from those who are "outsiders" (i.e., those in the "they" category, such as African Americans, Latinos). They are unable to identify how elements of their own culture may differ from those of other whites with very different ancestries but who are included within the "we" category of "whiteness."

Members of outsider groups usually *have* to learn about the rules of insider groups to gain goods and resources needed for survival or because they may be punished if they do not play their roles as expected. As we address later in our discussion of standpoint theory, those in "outsider" positions often are aware of key elements of an inside culture *because* they are outside. They may be especially able to develop unique perspectives on many subjects because they are exposed to alternatives to the dominant ways of understanding the context of that topic. Such perspectives are especially important to articulate and understand as part of the process of developing one's critical consciousness.

Those within an insider group often have little knowledge of cultures with less status than their own, except through the lenses of their stereotypes. Without knowledge of other cultures, they are likely to believe that their way of life is normal and proper and that other styles are lesser or more deviant than their own. Some immigrants, for instance, are judged to be unclean or lazy by their new neighbors if they do not manicure their lawns or if they leave equipment and bicycles on their front porches. These neighbors do not notice the care that is given to sweeping the dirt from sidewalks or understand the cultural contexts in which lawns were hard to sustain and families learned to keep their possessions close and observable.

Most often, different mechanisms of discrimination operate in tandem, such as blaming a woman who is raped rather than the perpetrator. Some states do not compile statistics on ethnically based violence or gay bashing as hate crimes. In these situations, the laws and government procedures are influenced by societal attitudes and then lead to mechanisms and procedures that allow inequities and violence to continue.

The concept of internalized oppression is important but problematic as it can contribute to blaming those discriminated against for colluding with their oppression. It can obscure and overlook the ways people actively resist and fight against the oppression they experience. It is difficult to resist being affected by dominant values about behavior and appearance, especially if characteristics you don't have are rewarded and those you do have are devalued. Common examples are the valuing of lighter skin color among some African American and Latinos or Latinas or the tendency among some gay men, bisexuals, and lesbians to perceive heterosexuality as more natural or desirable. Such processes certainly must be recognized and addressed, but assessing and building upon the agency (i.e., resistance) of those who experience oppression is the basis of empowerment practice and is also transforming our knowledge of the dynamics of discrimination.

KEY SOCIAL GROUP CATEGORIES AND ● RELATED TERMINOLOGY

Many group memberships contribute to the development of our multiple identities. In the following chart, we list key groupings that are commonly linked with patterns of dominance and privilege in U.S. society, with a brief definition or discussion.

Term	Definition
Age	the relationship between age and status varies across cultures
Religion	an important element of culture: affects our socialization, belief systems, relationships, and rituals
Ethnicity	used to mean a cultural grouping within a larger culture or a cultural grouping with outsider status within a dominant culture
Race	has no biological basis and is constructed differently across societies
Gender	used to make biological distinctions but is socially constructed
Sexual orientation	refers to identities constructed around sexuality as well as one's choice of sexual partner
(Dis)Ability status	visible or invisible physical, mental, or developmental conditions that create barriers to full participation in society as currently structured
Socioeconomic status	an indicator of relative power and influence within societies that is based on income, wealth, education, and legacy.

These social group membership categories define many differences among people, which are important for multicultural practice. Previously, we noted that power mediates the formation of multiple identities in the social context and that identity negotiation is also influenced by historical and political forces. Within each category, some identities are legitimated or valued while others are devalued or punished or defined as deviant.

In the following table (Table 4.1), we present key terminology about difference and dominance for several group membership categories. The column labeled "Difference" contains language associated with the category that does not indicate social value. In the "Dominance" column are some of the words used to indicate discrimination or privilege in that category.

Before we move to further discussion of these concepts and their interrelationships, complete Exercise 4.1. This is a reflective exercise that will help you understand how the concepts in this chapter are relevant to your own life experiences. We hope that you will complete this exercise, and share your various identity groups with small groups of your classmates. This exercise will disclose a lot of information about who you are, and you may not want to disclose all of the various identity groups that you identified. In your sharing and discussion with your classmates, observe how these different identities impact who you are.

Social Identity Groups

Social Grouping	Your Member-ship	You Are Most Aware	You Think About Least	Gives You Privilege at Work or School	You Would Like to Know More About	Makes You Most Comfortable	Has Strong Effect on Ways You See Yourself	Has Greatest Positive Effect on How Others See You	Has Greatest Negative Effect on How Others See You
Gender									
Race									
Class									
Ability									
Religion									
Sexuality									
Ethnicity									
Age									
Other									
Other									

Table 4.1 Group Membership With Differences and Dominance

Category	Difference	Dominance
Age	Life span (child, elderly)	Ageism
Religion	Different beliefs & rituals	Anti-Semitism Religious persecution
Ethnicity	Different cultures	Ethnocentrism Ethnic cleansing
Race	Differences in appearance (a flawed biological concept)	Racism
Gender expression	Men/women/transgender	Sexism Binary oppression
Sexual orientation	Gay/lesbian/bisexual	Heterosexism Homophobia
Disability status	Differently abled	Able-bodied-ism
Socioeconomic class	Lower/middle/upper class	Classism

● HOW DO MULTIPLE IDENTITIES WORK?

The process of identity development and negotiation must occur within the larger contexts of an increasingly global environment and within the smaller contexts of our own lives. Aspects of our identities influence elements that are important for social work practice and the ongoing development of who we are. Our identities do not operate independently. Each connects and interacts with our other identities. Some configurations (poor African American lesbians) are qualitatively different from other combinations (poor white gay male).

Sometimes we consciously choose a single identity because of some internal or external situation confronting us. Most often, however, we are constantly negotiating, either consciously or unconsciously, our multiple identities each day. In addition to our negotiations, our environments make multiple attempts to force us into one or more identities. When we are treated with disrespect or encounter barriers related to some identity, our environments can shock us into becoming aware of that identity. For instance, if a woman of color enters a department store with no awareness about her multiple identities, she may be forced to recognize some of them by the behaviors of store clerks, who may choose other patrons to serve although she was first in line, or store detectives, who may follow her expecting her to shoplift.

The early women's movement called our shocks of awareness "click" experiences, where one's experience and perception of that experience suddenly click together with insights about how the experience was gendered, racialized, or otherwise affected by culturally shaped forces. Often these click experiences diminished self-efficacy, self-esteem, or impeded our forward progress. This new level of understanding is an important ingredient and one means of developing critical consciousness.

Identity negotiation processes are more intense in some life periods, although they are ongoing processes. They can be triggered by internal issues, such as health changes (e.g., acquiring a disability), cognitive changes (e.g., achieving a new insight), life course changes (e.g., a birth or a death), or external issues (e.g., a change of job or locale or an inflammatory incident in the community). These triggering events are all affected by the value judgments and power and status dynamics that occur in a society. Some categories are more valued than others and other categories are actively discriminated against.

To consider these forces in your own life, think of times that you have been particularly aware of one or several of the group identities you explored in Exercise 4.1. What about the situation created this enhanced awareness? We shall explore these relationships more in the next section of this chapter.

Positionality, Standpoint, and Critical Consciousness

In this section, we will build on the previous discussion to gain more of an understanding of critical consciousness and its particular relevance for social workers. We will begin by discussing positionality, which is an integral part of critical consciousness. We will present concepts that emerge from poststructuralism, feminist theory, and cultural studies.

Positionality and Standpoint

Each of us comes to the present moment with our own history, our own subjective understanding of our lives and the world. Indeed, we cannot "live as human subjects without in some sense taking on a history," a means of understanding ourselves in the world (Weiler, 1994, p. 34). We are each shaped by our experiences in terms of race, ethnicity, class, gender, sexual orientation, and other socially defined categories. Some of these identities give us, almost automatically, and certainly at times unconsciously, certain privileges and stakes in power. Alternatively, some of these identities work to produce us as oppressed. Oppression can be profitably understood as the limiting and restricting of one's options in the world. "Being oppressed means the absence of choices" (hooks, 1984, p. 5). Oppression born of one's position for example as working class, as woman, as African American, as Latina or Latino, as gay man or lesbian (and these categories are neither exhaustive nor mutually exclusive) places barriers toward one's becoming an active and empowered agent in the world. Positionality underscores the necessity that each of us locate himself or herself along the various axes of social group identities. We must begin to articulate and take responsibility for our own historical and social identities and interrogate (i.e., challenge or question) how they have helped to shape our particular worldviews.

In failing to account for one's positionality, one is likely, despite the most noble of intentions, to participate in the perpetration and perpetuation of oppression. There are definite ramifications and consequences of either being blind to one's own positionality or, moreover, failing to take responsibility for that positionality in how it informs one's world view.

> The claim to a lack of identity or positionality is itself based on privilege, on the refusal to accept responsibility for ones implication in actual historical or social relations, or a denial that positionalities exist or that they matter, the denial of one's own personal history and the claim to a total separation from it. (Martin & Mohanty, 1986, p. 34)

Earlier, we described Freire's concept of "conscientization." Essential to this process is an investigation of one's own positionality. Freire writes of discovering and identifying oneself as part of a whole, a larger structure, but not as imprisoned or immobilized within it (Freire, 1973). This understanding is a critical aspect of positionality. Several points demand elucidation in Freire's rich analysis. First, positionality is at once an inward process of self-examination and self-exploration, and an outward process of understanding and situating oneself in the world. These two processes are dialectical and inextricable: They are two faces of the same phenomenon (i.e., they interact and each changes the other, they are mutually contingent). In abandoning either aspect of investigation, one is liable to remain mired in one's own insular world view or alternatively to jump toward premature evaluation of other's positions without having adequately explored and critiqued one's own.

Second, probing one's positionality involves a dialogue between thought and action, knowledge and experience. This joining of critical reflection and action is known as *praxis*. Third, and founded on the first two points, the union of inner and outer movements, of thinking and action, requires engagement. *Engagement* can be understood as an active process of involvement and commitment, enjoining emotion and cognition. Engagement requires one to bear responsibility for oppression when interacting with other individuals both similar to and different from oneself across various social categories and identities.

Engagement is sometimes counter to what social science and, perhaps to a lesser extent, what social work may teach us. "Traditionally, social science has defined emotional engagement as an impediment to objectivity" (Anderson &

Collins, 1995, p. 8). In delving into positionality, we can begin to interrogate (i.e., actively question) the notion of an objective point of view, a grand or all-encompassing theory. When we work through and with positionality, we begin to see that what may be defined as objective, often by the dominant culture, is often imbued with racist, sexist, and homophobic ideation and subjectivities.

Those who have had to survive in a hostile and oppressive environment have often been forced to recognize their positionality—at least on those dimensions that help to create that environment. Without this incentive, it is often more comfortable not to recognize one's positionality, especially if that recognition challenges the view that one had earned all of his or her advantages. Thus, some of us are far more aware of our positionalities than others, and we will know more about some dimensions than others.

Although some people suffer a great deal more than others, positionality implies that each and every one of us, in our varied positions and identities as privileged and oppressed, are both implicated in and negatively affected by racism, sexism, heterosexism, homophobia, classism, and other oppressive dynamics. It is crucial for individuals of both dominant and subordinate groups to recognize our positionality, or we all contribute to perpetrating oppression.

People with different positionalities acquire different *standpoints* (standpoint theory is summarized for social workers by Swigonski, 1994). From one's standpoint, some features of "reality" become prominent, although others are obscured. Like positionality, standpoint is defined as a position in society from which one develops a level of awareness about his or her social location. Standpoint theory posits that the less powerful members of society experience a different reality as a consequence of their oppression. Because life experiences structure one's understanding of life, members of the most and the least powerful groups will potentially have opposed or at least very different understandings and constructions of the world. To survive, most often those who are subordinate must be attentive to the perspectives of the dominant class in addition to their own. Thus, they have the potential for "double vision" or double consciousness, which leaves them with the potential for a more complete view of social reality than those with more socially valued group identities. Standpoint theory discusses ways that these "outsider" perspectives develop from people's daily activities and then become more fully conceptualized through their sharing of knowledge and through regular reflection and education. Thus, members of marginalized groups within the larger society are valuable "strangers" to the dominant social order and have much to contribute to increasing everyone's understanding of that social order. Those "outsiders" who also have formal education and who live and work in "insider" roles may experience considerable tension in these roles, but they also can contribute unique perspectives to overall knowledge from their "outsider-within" roles.

● ROUTES TO CRITICAL CONSCIOUSNESS AND MULTICULTURAL COMPETENCE

In this section, we discuss briefly some common patterns experienced by people who are working to develop multicultural competence and consciousness. We will highlight some ways paths may differ. Most of us are both advantaged and disadvantaged by some of our group identities. The issues we face when we attempt to develop critical consciousness differ when we work on dimensions in which we have experienced discrimination or oppression, which are outsider categories, from those we experience when we work on dimensions of privilege, which are insider categories. First we discuss some basic principles.

1. The processes for gaining knowledge about the workings of discrimination and oppression and for guarding against bias must be ongoing and lifelong. Cultural and institutionalized biases are subtle, often hidden, and very difficult to recognize, transcend, and change. All of us have learned discriminatory language, cultural metaphors, assumptions about intelligence and competence, and other reflections of long histories of injustice and monocultural assumptions. We cannot change these all at once, nor can we fix them and then stop worrying about them. We also cannot learn all about ourselves at once. One set of insights and areas of knowledge enables us to move on to another, and much of what we must learn will vary from situation to situation. In addition, the forces that create barriers because of differences and that perpetuate inequities and privileges become more subtle as the more obvious ones are removed. As we remove one layer, another emerges that we need to learn to see and confront. It helps to have a vision of what a multicultural and socially just world could be and to develop relationships that help you to realize some of this vision.

2. We must learn about our own culturally shaped assumptions so we do not impose them on others unknowingly, and we need to have core values and standards that allow us to act as social workers. It can be confusing to view everything as socially constructed while we are becoming aware of our biases. It is not always easy to distinguish between well-informed professional judgments and culturally biased and oppressive views. Our personal and professional knowledge also must change and grow as we learn more about how this knowledge has been shaped by cultural and limiting assumptions.

3. We have to work harder to recognize how bias is structured into policies, practices, and norms about social interactions that reflect institutionalized racism than we do to perceive individual prejudice. For example, you may be acutely aware of your boss's disparaging and flippant remarks about people of color, but you may be uninformed about differential wages and hiring practices for people of color or be unable to see the way in which the overtly neutral hiring criteria at your agency may be contributing to these patterns.

4. We must question the knowledge base and theories that underlie our practice. Theories are only as informed as the awareness of those who developed them. One way to address both of these challenges is to work to become aware of your own and others' epistemologies. An epistemology is a theory about knowledge, a framework for apprehending, perceiving, and making sense of the social world of "reality." Our understanding of what knowledge is and who the "knowers" are can help us to critique that knowledge. We need to think regularly and consciously about our beliefs and others' beliefs about relevant knowledge and the language we use, to talk with others about how they understand the world, and to read what is being written about these issues.

5. We have to acknowledge and manage the strong feelings connected with our incomplete understandings, our identity negotiations, and the interactions we must develop in our critical consciousness. If we aren't able to acknowledge these feelings and thoughts, those feelings and thoughts can block our progress and create barriers to critical consciousness. Anger (even rage), joy, defensiveness, shame, guilt, and excitement about new horizons opening up can fuel our progress or shut us down if we cannot work with these feelings and do not have safe spaces in which we can express them.

6. We must use our feelings and reactions and the feedback of others to help us recognize our nonconscious thoughts and feelings that have been shaped by oppressive societal dynamics. We may begin the initial work of learning about our differences and how power dynamics are affecting a situation. We need to become aware of our offensive behaviors when someone points them out to us. Eventually, we learn to recognize more layers of difference and dominance dynamics by ourselves. We will get more comfortable using new language and skills needed to deepen and monitor our critical consciousness. Alertness to subtle cues and regular examination of our interactions always remain important, however. Most people have experiences like the one that follows, although many never recognize or address them.

I once had strong uneasy feelings when first meeting an unfamiliar African American man although I could not say why. Later I learned from an African American friend that many people had had bad experiences with my new acquaintance. I was right to trust my uneasy feelings but was dismayed to realize that my ominous feelings had shaped my perceptions of this man: I described him as much darker than he actually was, probably because of my feelings about his "sinister" motives. I had to accept that racism still profoundly shaped how I thought about and perceived the world despite years of work I had spent examining my socialization and attitudes.

7. You have to be yourself and be genuine while you work on your critical consciousness. No matter how hard we work, we cannot prevent or suppress all the ways we have incorporated negative assumptions and perceptions without

suppressing our potential for learning and making connections with others. We should feel guilty if we fail to challenge oppression, cease to strive to improve our ability to understand and use our differences, or continue to repeat offensive remarks or behaviors. Feeling guilty or angry about who we are, however, affects our self-esteem. Working to adopt key aspects of another's culture to become more culturally competent is also not usually useful. For example, trying to be "black" in style and language if you are white or "gay" if you are heterosexual can be very offensive to those who are insiders to this language and style when these behaviors are new to you and you are not accepted and trusted by these insiders. Many things about ourselves we cannot change, and in fact, we may value them. Who we are and knowing and accepting who we are is important.

8. To reduce communication problems and destructive power-related dynamics, you can use your knowledge about how your characteristics are likely to affect a range of others who are similar to and different from you. If you are a tall and muscular white man, for instance, you cannot change your size, but you can learn to understand how your size can intimidate others. You may then use techniques for minimizing that intimidation by naming the fact that you do not wish your size to create issues of power or by sitting down rather than towering over someone with whom you are having conflict. If you are a Latina who wishes not to suppress her emotional reactions, you can explain to others about the importance of emotional expressiveness in your culture so they will not overreact to your expression of feelings.

9. It is also important to incorporate your knowledge of the contexts of different identity categories. You can anticipate and work to minimize some of the negative consequences that often occur in interactions in which there have been historical problems or current issues.

Walking home from work at night pretty much carefree in the college town in which I live, sometimes I become aware that a woman is walking alone ahead of me. As I realize that having a man walking behind her on a deserted street in the dark might be frightening, even though I know she has nothing to fear from me, I cross the street to make it clear that I am not following her. With the recent series of rapes in my town, I have become even more aware in this situation.

10. The development of our understanding and competence about the many dimensions of concern in this chapter tends to move in cyclic patterns. Periods of increasing personal insight and knowledge, periods of strong emotions, periods of challenging old theories and knowledge and learning new ones, and periods of consolidation and integration of old and new knowledge, thoughts, skills, and feelings will probably all occur.

When One Has Experienced Discrimination and Oppression

When you occupy a category that means you face discrimination, you really have no choice but to develop your awareness of that category if you are to survive. This awareness may not incorporate a larger societal understanding or any knowledge about how discrimination on the categories you are aware of is related to discrimination on other categories. Critical consciousness can give you a larger view and also help you to resist internalized oppression because you have more ability to distinguish or at least examine, how societal dynamics and your own efforts may contribute to the experiences you have.

Especially if your family has prepared you for encountering discriminatory experiences, as many ethnically "different" families do, you may have been aware of them from an early age and have had some coaching about how to handle them. Support from one's family and friends is an enormous help in developing our consciousness about societal discrimination.

Families are not particularly good at preparing or supporting their members to address discrimination on many dimensions of concern in this chapter, however. Many families re-create patterns of gender inequities, for instance, and even more families are unsupportive of and threatened by any violation of the proscriptions for compulsory heterosexuality. Learning to recognize discrimination on dimensions your family doesn't teach you about usually requires accumulating your own experience, or it happens through contacts with and the support of others who are experiencing the discrimination. As a result, this awareness is likely to come later. Sometimes families of origin will join in these struggles, and sometimes the family contributes to the pain of discrimination and oppression.

The emotional tasks that are common in the recognition of dimensions of oppression include managing your anger (even rage) about the unfair things that happen to you. You often have to maintain self-esteem and self-efficacy in situations that make this difficult. Sometimes the assaults you experience are overt, but more often they are covert. You may need to decide repeatedly whether to spend your finite energy confronting distasteful or insulting situations, such as not being waited on repeatedly in a store or listening to homophobic comments in a dentist's office. It is important to develop self-protective mechanisms but so is the struggle to stay open to new experiences and other interpretations of experiences, so as not to become distrustful and paranoid in harmful ways. It can take a lot of intellectual work to distinguish what elements of events are related to discrimination and what arise from other factors.

The periods of anger and rage can be especially difficult for others to understand because to them the anger often seems way out of proportion to the event that apparently triggered it. In fact, it may be an overreaction to that particular situation and may reflect years of pent up, often unrecognized, unsafe feelings we are expressing for the first time. Although often expressed as anger or pain, the intense feelings are usually much more complex, including hurt, grief, fear, and outrage. In multicultural work, we often find that these intense emotions erupt across group boundaries when people begin to feel safe with each other and that one function for the anger is to test everyone's commitment to working together even if things become difficult. We believe that it is important and necessary, both for individuals and for groups, to feel and express these often upsetting but potentially empowering feelings and to find safe spaces for this expression. It is important to get feedback from people you trust, who will support you but present enough diverse opinions so you can reality test and learn from your experiences.

It is often necessary to constantly monitor ourselves and our interactions in order to succeed in a less familiar culture in which we feel vulnerable and scrutinized because we are different and less valued. Achievement within the rules and contexts of the insiders who still dominate most of our social institutions thus takes a great deal of physical and psychological energy. How can we do this without losing valued aspects of ourselves? Emulating insiders does not necessarily lead to acceptance, no matter how hard we work to fit in. We have to learn what is expected but also to preserve valued parts of ourselves. We have to stay aware of alternatives in the hope that we can create more culturally diverse options later.

Those who have experienced oppression, and who thus see those dynamics when others do not, find themselves having to point them out and explain them to others. This process takes energy and can generate anger and resentment about the extra burden, even when others are making a sincere effort to understand and are not resistant. Too often, however, those from outsider groups must challenge situations when others are not necessarily receptive, or they must find ways to live with demeaning and difficult dynamics if the consequences for challenging them are too great. The work of educating others often seems to be never-ending; it can feel rewarding and satisfying, or onerous and tiring, or both, but always it consumes resources that could otherwise be used to sustain the self or accomplish other tasks. A major reason for outsider groups to gravitate to each other in large diverse settings is to find a space in which a person can relax and does not need to sustain the work of environmental and self-monitoring and the need to constantly educate those from other groups.

Think about the previous situations while managing your anger about unfairness, sorting out what may be useful feedback from unfair reactions, and managing your energy when you need to stay vigilant about how you are being perceived, plus educating others about oppression. How often do these situations happen for you? How are you handling them now? Are there ways you can handle them better? Are there people who could provide support? Are you learning from these situations?

When One Has Been Privileged by One's Location

We have noted already that it is difficult to accept and see how one has been privileged or our progress expedited when one's conscious experience is of working very hard for what has been gained. Thus, we may resist perceiving patterns of discrimination that help us to succeed; as a result, we cannot take responsibility for changing them, even though we believe in concepts of social justice and equity. It takes special efforts to understand that others may have to work harder than you for the same accomplishments because they encounter more barriers or haven't started from the same place.

People struggling to recognize and understand the ways they have been and are privileged often feel defensive, guilty, and angry. We may feel blamed for events that happened long before we were born, or we may be blamed today if we say something that is offensive to someone. How can we learn how dynamics of privilege have made our routes easier but not feel overwhelmed by guilt? If relevant, we can make amends for past actions if possible. We can also learn to accept and understand others' anger without feeling personally blamed for the events that have angered them.

It is a major task to learn *how* to learn about other groups and what they have experienced. One way to gain this knowledge is to envision yourself in another's position in order to recognize situations they have to contend with that you do not. Peggy McIntosh has written about her efforts to identify her own privileges as a white heterosexual person (McIntosh, 1995). She generated lists of experiences she has and doesn't have because she is white, including being able to find flesh-colored bandages and not wondering whether a sales clerk expects her to shoplift. Her second list addresses sexual orientation. She suggests that once such lists are made, you can cluster them to discover different types of privilege and define those that should be challenged as unfair.

The acknowledgment that distrust is a reasonable reaction in an oppressive world can form a basis for working and learning together, despite culturally and historically based differences. We will never understand the experiences of another, no matter how hard we work, and this is more difficult if one is an insider on a particular dimension. You can understand and accept the reasons why outsiders may distrust you at least initially and be prepared to earn their trust by being open to and soliciting information about their positionality.

Learning about privilege and reducing the barriers to that learning require that we communicate clearly, exchange information about our histories and perspectives, and ask for feedback about how we are perceived and experienced. During periods in which we are feeling blamed, we may be afraid to say anything for fear we will offend someone. We can learn about privilege by examining our feelings if we feel forced to behave in ways that feel unnatural. For multiculturalism to work, it is probably important for all to feel some disease, since the rules and norms are changing. In this age of concern about political correctness, however, it is difficult to know how to handle these dynamics.

Learn how to ask for feedback and tell people you want to learn about the issues of concern in this chapter. There is a great need for environments in which we can learn from mistakes and express our anger, surprise, and lack of knowledge, with some sense of safety and knowledge that we will not be pilloried for our mistakes. Such interactions can help us to learn how to monitor our own progress, to watch our language, and to learn alternatives. In a recent situation, everyone learned a great deal when a white male asked for feedback at the end of an important meeting. His words allowed others to review the meeting, to note how he had responded to an administrator's first query in a way that precluded others with less power from exerting leadership. He had been unaware of these initial interactions in the meeting, despite his continuing efforts not to be the perceived leader of this group. The discussion also allowed a woman in the group to understand how complicated power-related dynamics can be. She had assumed he had engaged in the behavior deliberately, had *not* seen how the administrator's cues had initiated the sequence of events, and was so angry she would not have said anything to him. The chance to talk about it led to agreements about how this group would handle such situations in the future and a renewed commitment to work together.

In the exercise that follows (Exercise 4.2), we want the student to think more about the experiences of others and how dominance and difference factors influence peoples experiences.

Exercise 4.2

Put Yourself in Another's Place

Try putting yourself in another's place, and walk yourself through a day in their shoes. If you are heterosexual, keep a diary for several days to notice all the incidents where your sexual orientation might have created issues for you—to disclose or not, to challenge a remark or not. You can also try to imagine a world in which the power dimensions are reversed: Most people in power are people of color, have a disability status (and the able-bodied experience discrimination), or are gay and lesbian. Envision yourself within such a world. Think of common events and what they'd be like if other rules governed what was the norm. What would it be like?

Working Multiple Issues at Once

We not only experience multiple group identities within each of us but we also have to negotiate complicated relationships and feelings among us. Work with others is important. The development and sustaining of critical consciousness is enhanced by two sets of relationships: group support among people with similar characteristics and intergroup dialogue and negotiation with people different from us. These interactions can be very complicated, however, as people tend to be in different phases of development in their understanding of each dimension. In addition, what each category of people need so they can move ahead can also be threatening, painful, or both to members of groups working on their development in different ways. In particular, the periods of anger, elation, defensiveness, vulnerability, and guilt that occur often don't coincide. The rage about oppression that some need to express and feel can trigger anger and defensiveness from those who are beginning to understand areas of privilege in their lives. Their guilt and defensiveness can trigger more anger and resentment. We may get stuck in these reciprocal dynamics and stop learning.

Somehow, we need to create spaces in which we can manage the complicated analyses and expressions of emotion that are required. And this space has to have some safety for everyone—or at least everyone needs to feel similarly uneasy, unlike the usual situations in which those with less status feel the bulk of the disease. Skills in negotiation and in strategies for constructively addressing differences and conflicts can be very helpful to support work toward critical consciousness.

THE APPLICATION OF CRITICAL ● CONSCIOUSNESS TO PRACTICE

We end this chapter by presenting some principles for applying critical consciousness to social work practice.

First, we must regularly interrogate (question) the knowledge and theories that underlie our practice and strive to keep up with how theory is changing.

Here, we present several examples of how the application of critical consciousness has substantially changed our ways of thinking about critical arenas for practice. The first area we present is about families. The second focuses on organizations.

Allen suggested that earlier scholarship on families has illustrated three perspectives on diversity (Allen, 1978). The first of these is the perspective of *cultural deviance*, in which dominant cultural values, behavioral expectations, language, and assumptions are the normal standard against which everyone is evaluated. For instance, most early research and theories on families assumed that the norm was a nuclear family with a mother, father, and several children living in a separate household, usually, with a particular division of labor determined by gender in a heterosexual couple with little attention paid to single parents or clan-based family structures. Other families were studied in relation to this norm, which set up a we–they dichotomy. Power (normality) is ascribed to the "we" set of values, structures, and processes. Differences from the norm are emphasized, which often obscures similarities among individuals, families, or groups.

A second perspective, *cultural equivalence*, contrasts different values, structures, and processes exhibited by individuals and groups but does not value one over the others. We–they frameworks remain, however, with little attention to similarities and overlaps between and among groups.

Cultural variance addresses directly the commonalities and differences among different group values, processes, and structures, and then attempts to build bridges across these. There is an assumption of collective strength through the development of a more inclusive "we" group, with expectations of behavioral and structural changes both within and across the original groups. In this perspective, one might investigate the functions that all types of families perform, plus the strengths and struggles that differ among alternative family forms. A cultural variant perspective does not assume, however, that the initial "we" groups are irrelevant. Instead, it recognizes the necessity for a periodic "return to home base" for the purposes of grounding, nurturance, and support while also expanding one's perceptual options.

In a similar progression, this time at the organizational level, Judith Katz proposed that there are stages in an organization's efforts to become more diverse (Katz, 1988). First, the organization usually works to get more people who are different into the organization. An emphasis is placed solely on hiring "qualified" persons, assuming that their presence alone will sufficiently diversify the organization. Although different in terms of outward physical or other characteristics, those worthy of hire are assumed to share the values of the dominant culture, organization, or both and will fit readily into that organization. Later, the organization becomes more concerned with helping individuals succeed. With their dispersion in different categories through the organization, the emphasis on counting positions may obscure problems in turnover, unhappiness, and organizational climate.

Katz suggests that the goal, a multicultural organization, is one that almost none of us has experienced. She does propose, however, that such an organization would encompass a concern with the organizational processes that either foster or restrict diversity. It attends also to the climate of the organization and the subjective experiences of its members. Jackson and Hardiman believe that most organizations striving to become multicultural are in various stages of transition, with new and older forms of norms, procedures, structures, and relationships coexisting, often in confusing and uncoordinated ways (Jackson & Hardiman, 1994).

These developments and transformations of theory have important implications for practice. The first case has implications for how we think about families, how we formulate goals for families, and what research questions need to be asked. The second example has implications for all our workplaces and for various forms of organizational practice and research.

Practitioners must work continuously to understand the multiple contexts of their practice and how these are shaped by differences and patterns of oppression.

Practice must take into account the historical, social, and political antecedents for yourself, the client system(s) with which you work, and the context(s) within which you and your clients live and work.

Developing and using your knowledge about your own positionality, in general and in relationship to a particular practice situation, is fundamental for a multiculturally competent practitioner.

To begin where the client is, one must be able to consciously situate oneself. Positionality, then, is fundamental to good social work—to communication, empathy, and the formation of an alliance—and is all the more important when working across differences. We cannot build on our own experiences without imposing our assumptions on others, unless we recognize these assumptions and have a context for understanding and interpreting them.

We must also interrogate (question) our practice regularly. For instance,

- *How might cultural and gendered assumptions be affecting our assessments?*

It is not uncommon for clients who tend to be more emotionally expressive to be labeled as pathological because their affect differs from that of the helping professional's.

- *Are there organizational or programmatic issues that your client's reactions lead you to notice that you need to address?*

It is often easier to perceive a client as unmotivated or not "psychological enough" when she stops coming for appointments than it is to recognize that a mostly white (heterosexual, middle class, etc.) agency may not be a comfortable environment for her.

Similarities between a client and worker on key social identities can help establish trust and safety but are not absolute. Clients and workers who share characteristics that are very important to them and on which they often feel embattled in relation to the rest of the world can also have high expectations for each other. Those expectations may be impossible to meet.

When in my 20s, I arrived at work one morning in the counseling department of a Hispanic social service agency and was told that a Latina woman was there without an appointment and needed to be seen right away because she was visibly upset and appeared to be in crisis. When I greeted her, she denied that she had a problem. Perplexed by her sudden change, I stayed with her for several minutes trying to identify why she was suddenly no longer in need of help. After gentle questioning, the woman confided that her problems were with her husband and that they were sexual in nature. She was hesitant to talk with another Latina about them because I was so young (the author looked considerably younger than her age) and I was not married. From her traditional worldview, she assumed that I was a virgin since I was single and that she should not expose me to the intimate details of married life out of respect.

The practitioner should expand definitions of trust and safety.

Social work with individuals, groups, and communities is predicated on the building of mutual trust. The formation of an alliance with one's client that is constituted on the micro or macro level is foundational: An alliance is fundamental to change and growth.

Trust must include some confidence that one's social identities will be respected and that the relationship will challenge and not re-create dynamics of inequity and privilege. Thus, it is important to work to create norms and a climate that provides *sociocultural safety* (i.e., some confidence that differences will be respected). This trust can be greatly enhanced if a client recognizes that the worker shares some important experiences and perspectives, and it is possible across important differences as well if the potential issues are acknowledged and addressed. The acknowledgment of differences and issues signals that societal processes and group identities are relevant at the personal and interpersonal levels.

Learn about others' cultural backgrounds and learn how to learn from others and be responsive to cues from those with whom you work.

It is clearly impossible to learn enough about all social group identities and histories that will be relevant for the different people we will encounter. However, it is certainly our responsibility to learn as much as we can about the groups that help to shape our own social group identities and about groups different from our own.

Clear expression of a desire to know someone else and what is important to him or her is a beginning in the development of trust. As trust develops, most clients will convey what they believe you need to know and how they prefer you to be with them. As you become more familiar with different customs, you will adopt some of them naturally or your clients will teach you what is appropriate. One of the authors, for instance, decided not to try to change his style of dress or language when he began to work with youth in a settlement house as a young practitioner. One day, he was gratified when several of the young men decided they should "teach him how to dress." This led to a series of meaningful interactions in which the youth were able to share their own knowledge and expertise, which also altered the power dynamics among them and between them and the practitioner.

Remember that there are many "ways of knowing"—of understanding one's world, of learning and changing. The practitioner who recognizes this concept develops a repertoire that uses many approaches to practice.

These approaches can include use of the arts—poetry, stories, drawing, crafts, drama, music, film—in addition to more traditional modes of talking, planning, and goal setting. Many creative amalgams are evolving that combine traditional cultural practices with Western therapeutic approaches (e.g., Native Americans' combining the 12 steps of Alcoholics Anonymous with sweat lodges and vision quests or women adapting hierarchical management approaches to incorporate some collective processes). As these combinations evolve, we often discover practice principles that broaden our options for everyone, not just the groups who developed them.

The multiculturally competent practitioner recognizes that therapeutic alliances and worker–client relationships will re-create patterns of privilege and oppression unless we are actively working to recognize, challenge, and change them.

The absence of action that identifies, challenges, and undermines injustices and their effects is a major barrier to multicultural social work practice. You contribute to social injustice if you do not work to combat it. The worker must take responsibility to create safety and opportunities for both the worker and the client to constantly monitor their interactions, naming the ways that cultural- and power-related dynamics may be shaping assumptions, interactions, the language used, and the goals established. Both parties have a responsibility, but the worker has the primary responsibility for creating conditions of safety because the worker has more position power in the relationship.

Goals must include developing strengths, preventing problems, creating social change, and addressing the multiple ways that oppression and privilege have been incorporated and are being re-created.

Because what occurs in all forms of social work intervention reflects societal patterns, it is important to incorporate activities that allow us to recognize these larger, institutionalized patterns. This recognition on the part of the worker is necessary to help the client resist unwarranted self-blame if negatively affected by institutionalized dynamics. It also enables the worker and the client to realistically assess abilities if the client is advantaged by these processes. This recognition is essential if people are to work to change institutionalized patterns. Sometimes our tendency is to overly psychologize what are more profitably understood as societal factors, which in turn impedes opportunities for empowering the client, in part through the client's working for social change. Practice must be "less rooted in the social and economic status quo. As such, it is less a potential tool for exploitation of those who are less powerful due to unquestioning passivity, false unchallenged beliefs, or ignorance about causes of problems" (Jackson & Hardiman, 1994).

Practice must also continuously recognize and challenge the multiple dichotomies in thinking that characterize many of our social categories and behavioral options.

Such dichotomies as "black" and "white," "male" and "female," "gay" and "straight" create an oversimplified, fixed (i.e., unchangeable), and "naturalized" (i.e., biologically determined) false construction of reality that limits personal options and blocks our ability to see how oppressive dynamics interact and constrict our lives. Regular examination of the relationships between either–or formulations can lead us to uncover the ways our categorized thinking limits human potential and options in our practice. Scrutiny of the language we use is one way to identify, explore, and change false dichotomies.

Creating new words and labels can help us to think and perceive differently.

Language helps to create social categories and perpetuate hurtful and discriminatory ways of thinking and behaving. Attending to how theory, actions, and thoughts are named and expressed is one way to uncover and change cultural assumptions and patterns of privilege and oppression. For instance, the language that different groups have used to refer to themselves has changed in complex ways as each group works to change how they are perceived and perceive themselves. Thus, we have seen a progression from colored, to Negro, to Afro American, to Black, to African American; the multiple terms that different Latin American groups have used to refer to themselves; and to people of color to refer collectively to the many groups affected by assumptions about skin color and ethnic group characteristics.

Everything previously listed require regular and recurring scrutiny of the processes through which we work, act, and think as well as the outcomes for which we strive.

Critical consciousness and working for individual and social change as a social work practitioner are continuous processes. We usually develop goals that we strive to reach, but most of our work is about getting to these goals. The process is inseparable from outcomes, especially for the practitioner concerned about multicultural practice. Regular examination of who we are and how we work, interact, conceptualize, and monitor our work is an essential ingredient of critical consciousness; regular examination is also essential for the application of critical consciousness to our practice. As noted earlier, we also must examine regularly the theories, knowledge, and concepts that we use.

Engage in praxis regularly with other practitioners and activists; seek feedback from those similar to and different from you on key dimensions.

Note that exploration of one's positionality must occur within the particular context of one's life and when concerned about social work, one's practice. The process of moving to critical consciousness requires taking active steps with those with whom one is practicing within the complex, often contradictory contexts of our lives and multiple realities. It is also likely to need at least consultation and mutual action with other practitioners and others who know you well. You can also identify organizational or societal issues, which affect your clients that need action at a macro level. You can also engage with your colleagues in such actions and in creating new knowledge from your shared practice experiences.

SUMMARY •

This chapter has presented an opportunity for readers to explore a series of constructs critical for working with people in their social environments. We focused on the concepts of age, race, sexual orientation, ethnicity, gender expression, social class, and disability status as characteristics that define our membership in many social groupings. We emphasized the development of critical consciousness as a vehicle for working with dimensions of difference and dominance. We described and discussed key social group categories, relevant definitions, and terminology. We analyzed the relationship between multiple identity development, identity negotiation, and dimensions of dominance and oppression. We emphasized the importance of understanding positionality and intersectionality in the development of critical consciousness. We then presented routes to critical consciousness, emphasizing common strategies and difficulties. Finally, we discussed principles for the application of critical consciousness to social work practice. We summarize our basic assumptions as follows:

1. Our group memberships and identities are critical components of who we are; they influence what we value and how we view the world. To develop our critical consciousness, we must identify our group identities and learn about the roles they play in our lives, including ways we contribute to and benefit from others' oppression.

2. Critical consciousness gives us an understanding of power relationships and commonalities and differences among and within people. These understandings all help us to form and recognize multiple identities based on our life experiences.

3. Dynamics of difference and dominance affect our worldview and our practice. We must learn about them in order to work with important differences, to resist and change destructive patterns of dominance, or both.

4. Being who you are and accepting who you are is important, as is knowledge about how your characteristics are likely to affect others who are similar to and different from you.

5. The more social identities we occupy and have consciously and actively explored, the more likely we are to be able to perceive the world through multiple lenses.

6. Critical consciousness is neither a passive nor a solely intellectual undertaking. Action and engagement are crucial. Critical consciousness can perhaps best be viewed as more than just a point of view or state of mind; it is an ongoing and engaged process, entailing the fostering of critical and self-reflective thinking in tandem with action.

7. It is important to work to understand how differences and dominance affect ourselves and others and how others and our clients understand discrimination and oppression from their own perspective.

8. We will probably need to work hardest on areas that privilege us or in which we hold deep beliefs about social values.

9. We must take responsibility for who we are and for working to improve ourselves but resist internalizing self-blame if we are negatively affected by institutionalized discriminatory dynamics.

10. We must also learn how to assess our abilities realistically and recognize how we are advantaged by our social identities that have higher societal status in this society. We usually recognize more easily how we are disadvantaged.

11. Exploring and critically assessing one's own positionality is a crucial aspect of fostering critical consciousness. In failing to account for one's positionality, one is likely, despite the most noble of intentions, to participate in the perpetuation and perpetration of oppression.

12. The forces that create barriers from differences and that perpetuate inequities and privileges become more subtle as the more obvious ones are removed. Thus, resistance to oppressive dynamics has to be an ongoing and recurring process.

13. The development and sustaining of critical consciousness is enhanced by the identification of and reflection on shared experiences and group support among persons with similar characteristics.

14. We can develop knowledge about our positionalities and deepen our critical consciousness by teaming with persons with different experiences and standpoints and by regularly negotiating differences.

The exercises and personal and practice illustrations we've included in this chapter provide some specific ways you can work to understand your own positionality and develop and deepen your critical consciousness. We hope you have worked with them as you have read this chapter and will revisit them periodically, as our understandings evolve with experience and new knowledge. We also encourage you to continue to pursue deepening your personal and political knowledge through action and reflection with others you trust or from whom you can learn. Interacting regularly with others whose positionalities and standpoints are similar to and different from yours in multiple ways will be important if you are to move beyond the limits of this chapter.

CHAPTER 5

VIOLENCE AND TRAUMA

I object to violence because when it appears to do good, the good is only temporary; the evil it does is permanent.

—Mahatma Gandhi (Dalton, 1996)

It is part of being human that in the course of life we experience trauma in one way or another. Some traumas may be small, others big. Just turn on the nightly news and you will hear about car accidents, earthquakes, floods, terrorist attacks, rapes, kidnapping, murder, death, war, tornadoes and you become a witness to someone's trauma. Just watching the nightly news gives us some distress on a daily basis.

Social workers must learn to recognize and deal with violence and trauma. Violence and trauma are closely related concepts, and in this chapter, we take the view that acts of violence are extremely stressful events that may lead to the trauma experience. The root of the word *trauma* is the Greek word for wound. A physical trauma is defined as a serious bodily injury. A psychological trauma is an emotional or psychological experience that is emotionally painful, distressful, or shocking usually resulting from an extremely stressful or life threatening situation (Everstine & Everstine, 1993).

● RECOGNITION OF VIOLENCE AND TRAUMA

It is easy to deny violence and its consequences. It is unpleasant to experience the reality of physical and sexual violence. Television images of the airliners hitting the World Trade Center towers or the people in New Orleans standing on their rooftops waiting for help as the flood waters rise are etched in our minds. It is difficult to sit with someone struggling with the painful aftereffects of horrible events that they have experienced. It is difficult to know that bad things happen in life and that the world is not always just. It is cleaner and neater to deal on an intellectual level about theories of psychopathology. To quote Judith Herman, an expert on psychological trauma, "To study psychological trauma is to come face to face both with human vulnerability in the natural world and with the capacity for evil in human nature" (Herman, 1992, p. 7).

Early in my (Barbara H. Seabury, or BHS) social work career in a family agency, I did an initial interview with an 11-year-old girl and her mother. According to the notes from the intake interview that had been done on the phone by the intake person, the presenting problem, as defined by the mother, was that the girl "didn't talk much." When I read the intake notes, my first thought was that the girl was shy and socially phobic. I began the interview by talking with the girl and her mother and then talked to each of them separately. When I talked to the girl alone, I asked her about the problem as her mother had defined it. I was shocked at the girl's answer. She said that she didn't talk much because her mother's live-in-boyfriend "frequently held a gun to her mother's head."

Bruce D. Perry, MD, PhD, is the Senior Fellow of The ChildTrauma Academy (CTA), a not-for-profit organization based in Houston that promotes innovations in service, research, and education in child maltreatment and childhood trauma (The ChildTrauma Academy, 2010). Dr. Perry has consulted on high profile incidents, such as the Branch Davidian siege, the Oklahoma City bombing, the Columbine school shootings, the September 11 terrorist attacks, and the Katrina and Rita hurricanes. He tells the story of his experience with an institutionalized 8-year-old boy, which reflects the impact of severe sexual trauma on the child's development. He makes the case that trauma needs to be acknowledged.

I first saw him in the basement cafeteria-style lunchroom at the Residential Treatment Facility. T.—small, wiry, herky-jerky, nose running, dirty shirt sleeves, always out of [the] chair, run-on speech—sat with six other young boys at a round table covered in an institutional plastic, red checkerboard tablecloth. It was lunchtime, and all of the children were eating hot dogs, beans, and potato chips[—a]ll except him.

I was a new consultant to this Center. Sixty children, the majority "in the system" after being removed from their abusive families and failing in an escalating series of "least restrictive" placements—foster family to another foster family to a psychiatric hospital to a therapeutic foster home back to the hospital to a residential treatment center for six months to a different foster family to this Residential Treatment Facility. Failed placements, failing system.

T. stood out because he was loudly demanding that someone "cut my hot dog, cut my hot dog, cut my hot dog." A chant, a pressured, almost psychotic chant. A staff member came up to him and chided him for being "a baby" about not eating the hot dog without it being cut. The staff member, with some good intentions, felt that this was the time to take a stand and make T. "grow up."

"T., it's time you act your age. See all the other kids are eating without me cutting this up. I won't cut it up." T. escalated, shouting louder, frantic. The staff member stood his ground. T. rose from his chair, the staff member commanded him to stay at the table. The confrontation ended with T. a sobbing, hysterical, out of control, child being physically restrained by two staff. He was led off to a quiet place—to re-group, re-organize and, in some sense, to re-develop, emerging from his primitive, terrified, disorganized state through various levels of psychological, cognitive, and emotional organization back to his most mature level of functioning.

"You can't indulge this kind of demanding behavior." The staff member said [this] to me as they carried T. from the cafeteria. The other children seemed familiar with these confrontations—and with the resulting physical restraint. They kept eating. One of the children at his table looked at me and said, "This always happens when we have hot dogs."

Over the years I worked there, I came to see that T. would cut his bananas [and] he would take popsicles off of the stick and eat them with a spoon. He had a number of other "unusual" or bizarre eating habits. He had a host of swallowing "difficulties." He needed to eat soft food—rarely eating foods that were solid. He chewed forever and frequently gagged. While T. could tell anyone what these habits were, he had no idea why he had to do things that way.

"I just have to."

" And if you don't ?"

"I just get angry"

"Angry ?"

"Well, I guess. Maybe scared. Mixed up . . . I don't know."

T. was an 8[-year-old] boy. He had been forced to fellate his father from birth. And later, other men. Many other men. He was very young when this happened—from birth on—at age 6 he was finally taken from this life of pervasive, socialized abuse.

Normal oropharyngeal "patterns" of stimulation during development (primarily from eating) are associated with the development of normal eating and swallowing capabilities. Furthermore, these patterns of oropharyngeal stimulation take place in association with caretaker's soothing touch, and gaze, and smell and warmth and the satiety of being fed. This should be one of the most soothing, comforting positive sets of experiences an individual will have—and it follows us through life. Eating involves 'trainable' neuromuscular events—motor memories, if you will,—and these motor memories are linked to positive emotional, olfactory, gustatory and cognitive memories.

But for T., the development of oropharyngeal stimulation was associated with other things—fear, pain, gagging, suffocating in the flesh of a pedophile. No satiety, no calm, no comfort. Rather than the soothing warmth of the maternal breast, his brain internalized the confused, inconsistent, painful states associated with his abuse. Solid food in his mouth, his throat, evoked the state memories ingrained during the critical formative stages of his first six years. Eating for T. evokes fear and confusion—he has to eat to survive—there is some positive effect of eating but often enough, the evocative nature of the meal can erase these positive effects. With each meal, some small part of T. relives the abuse of his early childhood, some set of deeply burned-in state memories are accessed. These rarely, if ever, come to his awareness as a "cognitive" memory—he will likely never be able to have the insight to make the association between his eating habits and his early abuse.

Each meal scratches at the slowly healing scars of his childhood.

He remains small for his age.

Source: Perry, B. D. (1999) Memories of Fear: How the Brain Stores and Retrieves Physiologic States. In: Goodwin J. and Attias R., *Splintered Reflections: Images of the Body in Trauma.*

Social work education has begun to focus more systematically on violence and trauma. There is an increasing recognition that violence and trauma need to be a part of the social work curriculum (Hsu, 2010). It is a relatively new development that questions about abuse are included in a standard psychiatric history. The probable effects of childhood sexual victimization are many: high rates of anxiety, depression, dissociation, self-destructive behaviors, substance abuse, etc. In a study of nonpsychotic patients in a psychiatric ER, the entering patients were randomly divided into two groups. The first group was given the usual screening interview, but the screening interview of the second group included direct questions about sexual abuse. In the group that received the "usual" screening interview, sexual abuse was only noted 6% of the time. In contrast, the second group, who were asked directly about molestation, had a rate of 70% admitting to a history of child sexual abuse (Briere & Zaida, 1989).

● TYPES OF TRAUMA

Primary trauma is associated with the individual experience of overwhelming events, such as war, rape, child sexual abuse, domestic violence, etc. Trauma, however, is defined by the experience of the survivor and how it is appraised. Two people may undergo the same violent event, and one person might be traumatized while the other person might remain relatively unscathed. It is not possible to make blanket generalizations such that "event X is traumatic for all who go through it" or "event Y was not traumatic because no one was physically injured" (Giller, 1999). "In addition, the specific aspects of a traumatic event will be different from one individual to the next. You cannot assume that the details or meaning of an event, such as a violent assault or rape, that are most distressing for one person will be the same for another person" (Giller, 1999).

Secondary trauma, also sometimes referred to as a vicarious trauma, can seriously impact the mental health of social workers, first responders, critical care nurses, and others in health care professions involved with treating those exposed to traumatic events. Secondary trauma includes experiencing symptoms similar to posttraumatic stress, such as having nightmares or flashbacks, being easily startled, and avoiding situations that remind one of the original trauma (Adams, Figley, & Boscarino, 2008; Boscarino, Charles, Figley, & Adams, 2004; Science Daily, 2008).

Historical trauma is the cumulative emotional and psychological wounding over the life span and across generations, which emanates from massive group trauma (www.historicaltrauma.com). Such massive group trauma was the experience of genocide of Native Americans and the experience of slavery for African Americans throughout the history of the United States. In our contemporary times, the genocide in Darfur and Rwanda will have severe consequences for the survivors of this kind of ethnic cleansing.

ASSESSMENT OF TRAUMA ●

The interpersonal practitioner needs to assess for traumatic experiences in the client's present and past. The easiest way to begin is to ask the client to talk about traumatic experiences in their life as a part of history taking. As part of a client's history, it is important to assess for violence they may have experienced in the past and in the present. Was the person psychologically, physically, or sexually abused as a child? Is there a history of domestic violence? Is the person experiencing abuse in the present? Is the person a veteran of war or refugee from ethnic cleansing? Did the client grow up in a violent context? Do they live in a dangerous place in the present? Is there substance abuse in the present or past?

It is most important to determine whether or not the client is safe in the present. It is my experience (BHS) that if the client has experienced abuse in the past that they may also be being abused in the present. It is essential to assess for ongoing child or adult abuse. If there is a reasonable suspicion that a child or adult is being abused, social workers are mandated to report abuse to either child protective services or adult protective services so that there can be further determination and protection if necessary. If there is ongoing domestic partner abuse, the client should be given resources to help her or him get safe shelter. Later in this chapter we present screening protocols to help the interpersonal practitioner explore the likelihood of violence and abuse.

While asking about violence or abuse is a place to begin, it is often not so easy to determine whether or not there is abuse in the present. The client may not be forthright for many reasons, such as dissociation, denial, shame, and fear. Dissociation is a perceived detachment from the emotional state or even from the body. Dissociation is characterized by a sense of the world as dreamlike or unreal and may be accompanied by poor recall of the specific events or even total amnesia. In order to continue to function on a daily basis, the client may need to deny what is happening to her. If the client is not in contact with reality, she might be unable to assess her own safety or talk about her situation. It is often shameful to recount details of degrading abuse. A victim of domestic violence may not want to testify in court about the abuse she experienced because she is so ashamed of what happened. The client may be afraid of the consequences of telling what is going on in her life. I (BHS) have treated clients who were controlled by boyfriends or perpetrator groups who risked great harm to themselves if they told the truth. Patience and empathy may be needed in order to let the person's story unfold.

In my (BHS) experience, victims of violence often minimize their experience. I remember asking one woman, who was a highly educated professional, about her experience with her live-in boyfriend over the weekend before our session. She said that he had just twisted her arm. When I asked for more information about the incident, she quietly said that she had gone to an ER for treatment and that he had actually broken her arm, but she felt "it wasn't that bad."

Various screening and assessment scales can be used to further screen and assess for violence, child abuse, and dissociation associated with violence and domestic violence. I would use those when I thought they would be helpful to the client or to make a more complete diagnostic assessment.

It is my (BHS) experience that just talking about past abuse may raise the client's anxiety so that they experience significant distress. I thought at one point that if I developed a history questionnaire for the client to take home and fill out privately it might be easier to get a history. I rethought that decision after I used it for the first time with a new client who had experienced significant abuse. I handed the questionnaire to her at the end of the first interview. She returned it to me in the second interview with no history filled in and only black ink marks slashed all over the pages. I didn't use that questionnaire again. When I have used a questionnaire or scale, I have done so in the context of the interview so that I could gauge the client's reaction.

I have learned that some clients cannot give a full history at the beginning of service. With some clients, the history needs to unfold as the therapeutic relationship develops. While various clinical assumptions might be made, it is always best to ask and get the client's understanding of their history. As an interpersonal practitioner who has interviewed many victims of abuse—both children and adults—I have learned that it is important to take a careful but respectful history. It is important to develop a trusting relationship with the client so that he or she is able to share their history. People who have been abused or traumatized have most often had their own sense of control taken from them in the process. An aggressive, pushy interviewer is further traumatizing the already traumatized person.

It is also my experience that clients often do not express their trauma through words. It is often actions and behavior that tell their history. Less direct ways of communication are sometimes more comfortable for the client. It is often helpful to encourage the client to draw or write a journal.

Children often either do not recognize they are being abused or are afraid of the consequences for them if they talk about abuse. Children often do not know what they are experiencing is not "normal." If they are isolated and only have their family as a reference point, they may think all children are hit, screamed at, or used sexually. Children are also often afraid of the consequences of telling about abuse. They may be threatened if they talk or worried about losing their family if they tell. I have seen many adults who were abused in childhood, who told a teacher or another helper in their life at the time. The helpful person then confronted the parent with what the child had revealed. The parents then abused the child further for telling family secrets, and the child learned not to tell again.

CONSEQUENCES OF TRAUMA: SYMPTOMS OF ● PSYCHOLOGICAL AND EMOTIONAL INJURY

There are physical, mental, emotional, and behavioral consequences to traumatic events. There is a range of intensity of reactions depending on the individual, age at the time of trauma, duration of the trauma, and social and cultural supports. The type of trauma may also determine how an individual reacts. Table 5.1 gives an indication of the range of consequences.

The long-term consequences for an individual can be disabling. Traumatic events can severely limit an individual's ability to trust people. There is a sense of lack of control and predictability that can make it difficult to maintain relationships and work. People experience high levels of anxiety and depression. Chronic pain disorders, such as fibromyalgia, are often associated with trauma. In order to deal with the intensity of emotion and arousal, people often resort to substance abuse to self-medicate. Sleep disturbance is also common.

Table 5.1 Some Common Reactions to Traumatic Events

Physical Reactions	Mental Reactions	Emotional Reactions	Behavioral Reactions
Nervous energy, jitters, muscle tension	Changes in the way you think about yourself	Fear, inability to feel safe	Becoming withdrawn or isolated from others
Upset stomach	Changes in the way you think about the world	Sadness, grief, depression	Easily startled
Rapid heart rate	Changes in the way you think about other people	Guilt	Avoiding places or situations
Dizziness	Hyperawareness of your surroundings (hypervigilance)	Anger, irritability	Becoming confrontational and aggressive
Lack of energy, fatigue	Lessened awareness	Numbness, lack of feelings	Changes in eating habits
Teeth grinding	Disconnection from yourself (dissociation) Difficulty concentrating Poor attention or memory problems Difficulty making decisions Intrusive images	Inability to enjoy anything Loss of trust Loss of self-esteem Feeling helpless Emotional distance from others Intense or extreme feelings Feeling chronically empty Blunted, then extreme feelings	Loss or gain in weight Restlessness Increase or decrease in sexual activity

Source: Rosenbloom & Williams, 1999, p. 19.

There are many psychiatric diagnoses associated with trauma, such as a variety of anxiety disorders, dissociative disorders, borderline personality disorder, somatoform disorders, depressive disorders, substance abuse disorders, eating disorders, etc. The psychiatric diagnosis probably most associated with trauma is PTSD. Some of the criteria for this diagnosis are that the person was exposed to a traumatic event that involved actual or threatened death or serious injury to self or others. The event is re-experienced persistently in thoughts, dreams, and images. There is sometimes a re-experiencing of the event in flashbacks or hallucinations. Intense psychological distress and physiological reactivity occur at the exposure to internal or external cues that resemble the original event. There is an avoidance of stimuli associated with the trauma. People often become numb, avoiding anything that would remind them of the event. There is often a feeling of estrangement from others and a sense of hopelessness. Symptoms include sleeping difficulty, irritability, difficulty concentrating, hypervigilance, and an exaggerated startle response (American Psychiatric Association, 2000).

TREATMENT OPTIONS •

The most important first step for the interpersonal practitioner who is concerned with someone who is experiencing trauma symptoms is to assess for safety. If the assessment reveals that the person is in an ongoing violent and abusive situation, the first step is to help get the person out of the situation as soon as possible. It is common sense that if someone is in an ongoing, physically or sexually abusive situation, their chances of healing are much less than if they can be in a place that is free from harm.

It is my experience that people can recover from traumatic experiences with treatment. What kind of treatment is appropriate needs to be decided on an individual basis. Some of the recognized and effective treatment options are individual psychotherapy, group therapy, cognitive behavioral therapy (CBT), psychiatric medications, self-help 12-step groups, eye movement desensitization and reprocessing (EMDR), and family therapy. Some people may require psychiatric hospitalization.

It is beyond the scope of this introductory text to go into the details of treatment options, but instead we feel that interpersonal practice students can learn how to apply various screening protocols with clients so they can help clients get appropriate services. The next section of this chapter concerns risk screening for assault and violence, suicide, child abuse, domestic abuse, and substance use. Screening protocols are shorter and less extensive than assessment procedures and we believe can be implemented by beginning practitioners. We have chosen these five types of violent events because they are closely related to trauma and occur frequently in the caseloads of interpersonal practitioners.

RISK SCREENING PROTOCOLS •

The various issues presented in this section of the chapter all involve legal and ethical issues in interpersonal practice. The laws in many states demand that interpersonal practitioners must take seriously threats of suicide, threats of violence toward others, domestic violence, and suspected child and elder abuse. The NASW *Code of Ethics* also is clear that in situations involving violence, the social worker has a responsibility to break confidentiality and act to protect potential victims by involving proper authorities such as protective services, the police, and other professionals who have the authority to hospitalize or incarcerate individuals making threats (Reamer, 2006).

Screening for Assault and Violence

In the literature on risk assessment of assault and violence, there are disclaimers that such behavior is so unpredictable that any set of measures must be taken with caution. There has been a great deal of effort to develop risk assessment scales that will predict violence in both youth and adult offenders (Scott & Resnick, 2006). The Legal Dangerous Scale (LDS) was an early attempt to develop a risk assessment measure that was based on a legal history of violence. The LDS considered three factors: (1) presence of a juvenile record, (2) number of previous arrests for violent crimes, and (3) number of convictions for violent crimes (Steadman & Cocozza, 1974). This basic scale reflects the most basic predictor for whether a person will resort to violence and assault in the future. A past history of violence is the best global predictor whether someone will engage in violence in the future.

In the past 20 years, there have been attempts to develop reliable and valid scales to predict violence—for example, Violence Risk Scale (VRS), Dangerous Behavior Rating Scale (DBRS), Historical Clinical Risk Management Scheme (HRC-20), and Violence Risk Appraisal Guide (VRAG; Dolan & Doyle, 2000). Most of these scales involve 20 or more items and require training in how to implement them. Instead of presenting any of these scales, we will present a discussion of the many variables that have been associated with violence, which may be included as questions in an interview screening process.

Many of the discussions of risk assessment divide factors into several categories: personal history, demographic characteristics, clinical factors, and situational factors (Dolan & Doyle, 2000; Galloway, 2002; Harris & Lurigio, 2007; Hoff, 2001; Scott & Resnick, 2006). Besides an adult or juvenile criminal record, personal historical factors in childhood may include child abuse and witnessing child abuse of siblings, school problems such as truancy, fighting with peers, and personal behaviors such as enuresis beyond age 5, fire setting, and cruelty to animals. The individual may have grown up in a family in which violence was used as a problem solving method, such as corporal punishment, marital conflict involving domestic violence, and even criminality.

Demographic factors include youth (ages 18–34) and maleness, which means that young adult males are more likely to engage in violent behavior than are women, older men, and children. The problem with demographic factors is these are not powerful predictors of violence in a particular instance and women and youth may engage in violence. Here in Michigan, the last murder of a social worker was carried out by two women with a hammer on a child welfare worker, who was making a home visit in order to help them regain custody of the children.

Clinical factors may include misuse of drugs and alcohol, and serious psychiatric symptoms, such as specific preoccupation with violence; delusions of control with a violent theme; and agitation, excitement, overt hostility, or suspiciousness. Other serious clinical signs may include antisocial, explosive, or impulsive personality traits. Situational factors may include lack or loss of social supports, possession of a lethal weapon, and recent threats of violence.

When an interpersonal practitioner is interviewing a client who has a past history of assault and violence and the threat of homicide appears in the interview, the practitioner should question the client about his relationship to the victim and whether the client has a detailed plan and a lethal weapon to carry out the threat. Has the client recently increased use of alcohol or drugs? Have there been any recent conflicts in significant relationships or negative life events? Is there a threat of suicide following the violent act? (Hoff, 2001). The practitioner should realize that many individuals who make homicidal threats have many antisocial characteristics and may lie significantly about what they are planning.

In most states if there is a serious threat of violence, the interpersonal practitioner is required to warn the victim of the threat and to notify police. "Duty to warn" or "duty to inform" is a professional and legal responsibility of the social work profession and is based on the Tarasoff case. Some states do not have the duty to warn statutes, and students need to ascertain what the specifics are in their particular state (National Association of Social Workers [NASW], 2010).

Issue of Safety in the Workplace

Because violence in agencies, communities, and home visits seems more prevalent in social work practice, we want to talk about the safety of the interpersonal practitioner. There are a number of precautions that practitioners can take to make their work space safer in the event the client or applicant erupts in the interview situation. The interview space should not have any objects that could be used as a weapon, such as a desk lamp, large ashtray, or a small potted plant. The physical arrangement of furniture should not place the client between the practitioner and the door to the office. Such an arrangement would make it impossible for the worker to exit the office without first approaching the client before gaining access to the door. If a client is in the process of escalating toward an assault, the practitioner's approach may be interpreted as a threat. Generally, the assault cycle seems to have four phases: trigger, escalation, assault, and recovery (Hoff, 1989). If the practitioner has said something to trigger the episode, then approaching the client in order to leave the office may provide an escalation to attack the practitioner.

Some agencies have installed elaborate electronic devices that may involve a hidden button that when pushed will turn on flashing lights on the receptionist's desk. This would seem like a secure way to protect staff, but rarely does the agency perform drills to test that the system is working. When the agency hires a temporary receptionist, she may not be informed about the emergency warning system, and if it goes off, it may be ignored or the receptionist may have stepped into the bathroom for a brief moment. The most secure method is for the interpersonal practitioner to alert their supervisor and/or a colleague that they will be interviewing a potentially dangerous client. This support person can listen outside the door or make a prearranged phone call to the office to hear what is going on. Sometimes the caller may have a prearranged code to find out what is happening in the office. For example, the caller may ask the colleague about an unexpected visit from another client. Depending on the answer of the practitioner in the office, the response may reflect what needs to happen—for example, "I will interrupt this interview and talk with the other client right now!" "Tell the client I will see her after this interview!" "Tell the client I can squeeze her in after lunch!" For students in their field placement, we encourage students to ask their field supervisor about safety issues in the agency.

There are also things that a practitioner can do to make home visits safer in dangerous neighborhoods. Some agencies require female staff to take along another staff member (usually male) to the interview.

In my (BAS) second year of field placement in a community psychiatry placement, I went on a number of home visits with female colleagues. I was not expected to be a bodyguard and I did not carry a self-defense weapon, but my presence was assumed to be a deterrent.

The practitioner should drive by the client's house or apartment building to make sure that there are no gang members hanging around on the street. Once inside the house, the practitioner should not sit down unless the client sits down and should sit nearest the exit door. If the client has an object that is a potential or real weapon, the practitioner should quickly and politely leave the home and say that she will make another appointment at a more convenient time for the interview. As a school social worker in the South, I (BHS) went to a home visit in a rural area. When I arrived at the house, I was greeted at the screen door by the mother, but I could see a man sitting in plain sight through the screen door in the kitchen with a shotgun on his lap. I did not enter the house, told the woman that I would meet the family later, and quickly left the community.

In the present context of managed care, the home visit may become obsolete.

In concluding this section on screening for violence and assault, we present a practice case of BHS that has been carefully disguised to protect the confidentiality of this client. Read through this case example and see how many risk factors for violence you can recognize. What would you do if you were the interpersonal practitioner in this case?

Risk Factors for Violence

You are a social worker in a family agency. You have a client, Jim, who is a 45-year-old single white male. He has been your client for about 3 months. He got angry with the last social worker he had in the agency and stopped attending. Jim is your client because he was ordered by the court as a condition of his probation to be in counseling. He was arrested for assault and battery in a bar fight, which seriously injured another party. He is depressed and angry at the world. He laments the fact that he never killed his abusive father, who died recently. At times, Jim talks about wanting to kill himself but imagines setting up a "suicide by cop" scenario in which he attempts to rob a bank and then is killed in a shoot-out with the police. He is very isolated. His only real friend is his dog. Jim has a high school education but has few job skills. His work experience has been primarily in seasonal jobs in the tourist industry. As another condition of his parole, Jim is to be gainfully employed. For many reasons, Jim has not been able to find a job. There is an economic downturn, and many people have been laid off in the area. Before he became your client, Jim began working with two different male employment counselors. He still meets with them periodically. It is his feeling that those men have not helped him in the way they should have because he has not found a job. He has verbalized his anger toward them in past sessions with you. Since you began seeing Jim, you have watched him go downhill. He has little money, no friends, and seems more and more hopeless.

In the latest session, Jim seems more depressed than usual. He is angry and agitated. He seems belligerent and does not seem to want to take any of your suggestions for what he might do to feel better. Suddenly, he says to you that he is going to kill both of the men who should have found him a job. He stands up and abruptly leaves the session. You cannot stop him.

Screening for Suicide

In spite of decades of social science research into suicidal behavior, the prevention of suicide, like the prevention of homicide, is as much art as science (Bongar et al., 1998; Fremouw, De Perczel, & Ellis, 1990; Hawton et al., 1998; Maris, Berman, Maltsberger, & Yufit, 1992; Shneidman, 1985; Shneidman, Farberow, & Litman, 1970; Simon & Von Korff, 1998). For students interested in completing an online tutorial about suicide assessment, the following web address is recommended: www.ssw .umich.edu/simulation/rube-introduction.pdf. In order to present what is known about the risk factors in suicide, we first need to clarify some of the jargon that exists in the suicide literature:

- **Completed suicide** is an intentional, self-inflicted injury that causes death—sometimes called "successful suicide."
- **Attempted suicide** is an intentional, self-inflicted injury that does not result in death.
- **Suicidal gesture** is an intentional, self-inflicted injury usually not lethal enough to cause death and often accompanies a suicidal threat.
- **Suicidal threat** is a verbal or written statement or warning threatening self-harm or suicide.
- **Suicidal ideation** is thoughts or ruminations about killing oneself.
- **Presuicidal state** is when the suicidal person is contemplating and planning suicide—often in response to tragic and painful life events.
- **Suicidal crisis** is when a person is actively engaging in self-injurious behavior—for example, overdosing, cutting, locating and loading a weapon, or driving too fast.
- **Acutely suicidal** is a recent, sudden onset of suicidal thoughts, threats, and gestures.
- **Chronically suicidal** is a long history of suicidal ideation, threats, and gestures.
- **Accidental suicide** is when a person has no intention of dying but miscalculates seriousness of self-injury and dies (or rescuers do not appear in time).

There is no *explicit* statement in the National Association of Social Workers (NASW) *Code of Ethics* about a social worker's responsibility to suicidal clients. There are, however, indirect references to suicide under a practitioner's responsibility to promote client self-determination, yet there is a limit imposed when clients seek to do harm to themselves and others. There is also a limit placed on confidentiality. Workers are expected to break confidence when clients express an interest in harming self or others. In NASW policy statements, there is also a discussion of assisted suicide. Regardless of a client's condition, social workers must not help a client commit suicide—that is, they cannot help a client obtain the means to die and cannot pull the plug on a client's life support system no matter how much a client begs the worker to help him or her die. Social workers should help family members participate in any end of life decision regarding a terminally ill client.

While some philosophers may endorse some forms of suicide, such as among the terminally ill or chronically suffering, there is no debate or disagreement among the mental health community that acting to preserve life is an ethical responsibility and an activity consistent with the ethical values in the helping professions. (Fremouw et al., 1990, p. 3)

Malpractice claims arise when practitioners do not take time to assess and take actions to prevent suicide in their clients. Suicide assessment and intervention must be carefully documented at the time they first arise with a client—not in after-the-fact case notes. Suicidal ideation by any client in a practitioner's caseload must be taken *very* seriously. Dumping clients who express suicidal ideation does not remove the practitioner's responsibility.

The ratio between those who attempt suicide and those who complete suicide is about 10 to 1, which means that many more people attempt suicide, but few of them succeed. Women are 2 to 3 times more likely to attempt suicide than men, and men are 2 to 3 times more likely to complete suicide than women. One explanation for why men are more likely to succeed is that men choose "precipitous methods" that cannot be undone once started—for example, shooting oneself or jumping from high places. Women, on the other hand, tend to choose methods that once started can be undone—for example, ingesting pills or cutting. The average profile for a completer of suicide is a white male who is 50 or older. The most likely method is by gunshot, and the most likely motivation is death. The primary affect is depression and hopelessness. The average profile for an attempter of suicide is a white female in her 20s. The most typical method is taking pills or cutting, and the most likely motivation is a change in situation or a cry for help. The primary affect is depression and anger.

In general, the ethnicity of the client may be a risk factor in suicide. Suicide among whites is significantly greater than non-whites. In urban settings, the suicide rate among young African American males is twice the rate for young white males. Native American suicide rates vary dramatically by tribe (Gould & Kramer, 2001). Tribes on reservations in the West and Northwest have suicide rates that are four times the national average. Tribes in the Midwest have suicide rates that are below their state averages. Practitioners must be careful to realize that ethnicity is a complex factor in determining suicide risk and must be taken into account when other risk factors are present.

Besides ethnicity, there are many other factors that appear in suicidal clients. Major, negative life events, such as recent deaths of loved ones, unemployment, eviction, and discharge from a psychiatric inpatient unit, elevate the risk of suicide. Clients with little social support and who are unmarried or divorced and live alone are at higher risk for suicide. Clients who come from families with a history of suicide and who have attempted suicide in the past are at higher risk. Clients who are well educated and have poor health due to recent serious illness or injury are at higher risk. Clients who are abusing drugs and alcohol and have a diagnosis of depression or schizophrenia are at higher risk.

There are so many risk factors that have been identified in suicidal behavior that the difficult task for practitioners is to sort out which factors are most critical in a particular case. Practitioners do not have the luxury of time to explore all of the potential factors and must make decisions based on the information they have available. In a given case, some risk factors may be more critical than others. For example, a young African American woman (low demographic risk) who recently lost her child in a neighborhood shooting and has thought about suicide and how she might kill herself is probably at high risk. On the other hand, a 55-year-old white male widower who lives alone (high demographic risk) who has no suicidal ideation, no symptoms of depression, and no recent negative life events is at low risk for suicide. Demographic factors alone are probably least predictive of suicide. Suicidal ideation along with a carefully thought-out plan is a high risk factor even in the absence of other risk factors. Risk of suicide is a judgment or conclusion reached after exploring many factors.

In an interview with a client who expresses suicidal ideation, we believe an interpersonal practitioner should apply a SLAP Scale to determine the seriousness of the suicidal ideation. The acronym SLAP stands for *specificity, lethality, availability*, and *proximity*. Specificity of the plan can be determined by the following questions: How detailed is the client's plan? Has the client thought of a place or time or deadline for the act? Has the client made special arrangements to make the plan work? Specific, detailed plans are more lethal than vague and ambiguous ones! Lethality of the plan concerns how "precipitous" is the method of self-harm. Once started, can the method be reversed? Shooting oneself in the head, jumping from tall buildings, and jumping in front of a moving vehicle are highly lethal because recovery is unlikely. Taking an overdose and cutting one's wrist are less lethal because clients can change their mind and still have time to get help. Precipitous methods in a plan are more serious and more lethal! Availability has to do with how accessible is the means or weapon of self-harm. Does the client have a gun, knife, pills, etc., in his or her possession? Do they have to steal, borrow, or purchase them? How easily can the means of self-harm be obtained? Means of self-harm in the client's possession are most risky! Proximity has to do with significant others who are nearby in the client's life. How isolated is the client? Are there any significant others around who might be potential rescuers and interfere or foil the client's plan? Can others be encouraged to actively diffuse the client's plan (e.g., hide guns or confiscate pills)? Clients with few significant relationships are at high risk. The SLAP Scale is not predictive when psychosis and substance abuse are present in the client. Alcohol, drugs, and severe mental illness so distort judgments that the risk of committing suicide increases dramatically.

There are several suicide scales that a client can complete that have been tested for their reliability and validity. One of the most effective is the Beck Hopelessness Scale (BHS), which can be read or taken as a paper and pencil quiz. The adult version has 20 items that are scored as either true or false. For example, the 12th item is "I don't expect to get what I really want." Copies of this scale can be ordered from http://psychcorp.pearsonassessments.com.

It is beyond the scope of this book to go into the various interventions that an interpersonal practitioner may do when a client is deemed to be suicidal. For the beginning student, we strongly suggest that you get your supervisor or another staff member in your field placement to reassess the client and decide whether to violate confidentiality and contact significant others who could disrupt suicide plans or whether the client should be escorted to a Psych ER for further evaluation. For students interested in learning more about suicide assessment and intervention, we suggest they go online and view the interactive tutorial and simulated interview with a suicidal client. See www.ssw.umich.edu/simulation/.

In order to review the various risk factors for suicide, we present three brief cases. Look at these cases and locate various risk factors. Do you see any of these cases as very risky? Share what you have discovered with your classmates.

- It is your day to cover intake at a family service agency. Two sisters call in about their 55-year-old widowed father who lives alone. He was recently laid off from his job, and he has begun to drink more heavily (a 6 pack a day). Yesterday, he threatened to kill himself with his shotgun on his next birthday, which is tomorrow.
- You are a social worker in a pediatric unit of a general hospital. Your 22-year-old female secretary returns from a 2-day sick leave, and you notice a miniature bandage on her wrist. You ask how she is feeling, and she bursts into tears. She explains that she cut her wrist 2 days ago after she and her boyfriend had a "big fight." She wants to get married, and he wants to wait. He has moved out until she "gets her act together." She is still upset and has been staying with a girlfriend.
- You are a social worker at Travelers Aid at an airport. You notice a commotion at one of the security gates. The guards are wrestling with a middle-aged woman who is shouting, "I'm the angel of death!" The guards have removed a gun and a hand grenade from her purse. You recall that she was at the Mutual of Omaha vending machine purchasing flight insurance before approaching the gate.

Screening for Suspected Child Abuse

Even though domestic violence is considered a form of child abuse and substance abuse issues are often central to domestic violence, we have separated these three issues in this chapter for educational purposes so that we can focus on each one. For the interpersonal practitioner in the real world of practice, child abuse, domestic violence, and substance abuse will be interrelated and much more difficult to unravel. The profession of social work has a long history of involvement and commitment to child welfare. In schools and programs of social work, students can take whole courses devoted to child welfare issues, and it is beyond the scope of this part of the chapter to do much more than present some of the "facts" about child abuse and some of the ways in which screening can take place.

In 2006, more that 1.25 million children were abused and neglected in the United States. More than half (61%) of these children (771,700 children) were victims of neglect, which meant a parent or guardian failed to provide for the child's basic needs. The forms of neglect include educational neglect (360,500 children), physical neglect (295,300 children), and emotional neglect (193,400). Another 44% were victims of abuse (553,300 children), including physical abuse (325,000 children), sexual abuse (135,000 children), and emotional abuse (148,500 children; Child Welfare Information Gateway, 2010a).

The National Child Abuse and Neglect Data System (NCANDS) reported an estimated 1,760 child fatalities in 2007, which adds up to about four child deaths per day. With the exception of fiscal year 2005, the number and rate of fatalities have been increasing over the past 5 years. Research indicates that very young children (ages 3 and younger) are the most frequent victims of child fatalities. NCANDS data for 2007 demonstrated that children younger than 1 accounted for 42.2% of fatalities, while children younger than 4 accounted for more than three quarters (75.7%) of fatalities. These children are the most vulnerable for many reasons, including their dependency, small size, and inability to defend themselves.

Fatal child abuse may involve repeated abuse over a period of time (e.g., battered child syndrome) or it may involve a single, impulsive incident (e.g., drowning, suffocating, or shaking a baby). In cases of fatal neglect, the child's death results not from anything the caregiver does but from a caregiver's *failure to act*. The neglect may be chronic (e.g., extended malnourishment) or acute (e.g., an infant who drowns after being left unsupervised in the bathtub; Child Welfare Information Gateway, 2008).

There is no single profile of a perpetrator of fatal child abuse, although certain characteristics reappear in many studies. Frequently, the perpetrator is a young adult in his or her mid-20s, without a high school diploma, living at or below the poverty level, depressed, and who may have difficulty coping with stressful situations. In many instances, the perpetrator has experienced violence firsthand. Most fatalities from *physical abuse* are caused by fathers and other male caregivers. Mothers are most often held responsible for deaths resulting from *child neglect* (Child Welfare Information Gateway, 2010a; U.S. Department of Health and Human Services, 2008).

No group of children is immune from being a victim of child abuse or neglect, although girls are more often the victims of sexual abuse than boys. For all other types of abuse and neglect, statistics are about equal for boys and girls. Children of all races and ethnicities can be victims of child abuse. In 2007, nearly one half of all victims of child abuse and neglect were white (46.1%), one fifth (21.7%) were African American, and one fifth (20.8%) were Hispanic. Children whose parents are unemployed have about two times the rate of child abuse and two to three times the rate of neglect than children with employed parents. Children in low socioeconomic families have more than three times the rate of child abuse and seven times the rate of neglect than other children. Living with their married biological parents places kids at the lowest risk for child abuse and neglect, while living with a single parent and a live-in partner increased the risk of abuse and neglect to more than eight times (Iannelli, 2010).

For those interpersonal practice students working with children and placed in schools and hospitals, here are general signs and symptoms of child abuse that may be helpful in screening:

Physical Abuse

1. Unexplained burns, cuts, bruises, or welts in the shape of an object
2. Bite marks
3. Antisocial behavior
4. Problems in school
5. Fear of adults

Emotional Abuse

1. Apathy
2. Depression
3. Hostility or stress
4. Lack of concentration
5. Eating disorders

Sexual Abuse

1. Inappropriate interest or knowledge of sexual acts
2. Nightmares and bed-wetting
3. Drastic changes in appetite
4. Overcompliance or excessive aggression
5. Fear of a particular person or family member

Neglect

1. Unsuitable clothing for weather
2. Dirty or unbathed
3. Extreme hunger
4. Apparent lack of supervision

Source: http://www.childhelp.org/pages/signs-of-child-abuse.

Screening for Domestic Violence

Domestic violence concerns homicide and various nonfatal forms of violence, such as aggravated assault, simple assault, rape, emotional abuse, etc. Women are the overwhelming victims of domestic violence in marriage (84%) and in dating violence (86%). Males were 83% of spouse murderers and 75% of dating partner murderers. Even in violence committed against men, the perpetrator is likely to be male, though recent reviews suggest that women may be perpetrators of domestic violence more than is reflected in the literature (Robbins, 2010). Intimate violence has declined dramatically for men and less so for women over the past decade, and two thirds of violence for women and men occur in the home. Domestic violence in the United States occurs in all racial and ethnic groups, and even in gay and lesbian relationships (Domestic Violence Resource Center, 2010).

In the literature on domestic violence, partner abuse is conceptualized as having a number of dimensions—that is, psychological and emotional abuse, physical abuse, and life threatening violence. Psychological and emotional abuse involves swearing, threats to leave the relationship, screaming, stomping out of the room, forcing or withholding sex, etc. Physical abuse involves shoves, slaps, burns, thrown objects, reckless driving, etc. Life threatening violence involves choking, strangling, threatening with a knife or gun, etc. (Braham, Furniss, Holtz, & Stevens, 1986; Straus, 1979).

When an interpersonal practitioner is interviewing a potential victim of domestic violence, questions should be asked in the practitioner's own words and in a nonjudgmental way. Here are some examples of suggested questions:

- Are you in a relationship in which you have been physically hurt or threatened by your partner? Have you ever been in such a relationship?
- Are you (or have you ever been) in a relationship in which you felt you were treated badly? In what ways?
- Has your partner every destroyed things that you care about?
- Has your partner ever threatened or abused your children?
- Has your partner ever forced you to have sex when you didn't want to? Does he ever force you to engage in sex that makes you feel uncomfortable?
- We all disagree at home. What happens when you and your partner disagree?
- Do you ever feel afraid of your partner?
- Has your partner ever prevented you from leaving the house, seeing friends, getting a job, or continuing your education?

- You mentioned that your partner uses drugs and/or alcohol. How does he act when he is drinking or on drugs? Is he ever verbally or physically abusive?
- Do you have guns in your home? Has your partner ever threatened to use them when he was angry? (D. Saunders, personal communication)

Another way that screening for domestic violence can occur is to give the potential victim the Internet address for the Domestic Violence Screening Quiz (Psych Central, 2006) and encourage her to take this self-assessment measure on her own. If the potential victim is not Internet savvy, then the interpersonal practitioner can help the individual to complete this test by going online with her. This online version has 18 questions with three basic responses: "No, Sometimes, Regularly." Here are two sample questions from the quiz: "Does your partner keep you from going out or doing things that you want to do?" and "Does your partner criticize you or embarrass you in front of others?" The online version will automatically score the quiz and give the respondent some ideas about the results of their test—that is, how their score relates to others who have taken the test. The value of this online screening measure is that it empowers clients to make their own assessment of their situation, and it is responsive to many of today's youth who are familiar with Facebook, Twitter, and text messaging on their cell phone. In earlier studies of computers that were programmed to do intake interviews, results demonstrated that because the computer is viewed as "neutral" by the respondent, much more sensitive information could be collected that might not be collected in a face-to-face interview with another human being (Seabury, 2001).

Screening for Substance Use

In 2003, the Drug Abuse Warning Network (DAWN) estimated that 627,923 ER visits were drug related. Overall, drug-related ER visits averaged 1.7 drugs per visit, including illicit drugs and inhalants, alcohol, prescription and OTC pharmaceuticals, dietary supplements, and nonpharmaceutical inhalants. Substance Abuse and Mental Health Services Administration (SAMHSA) estimates nearly half (49%) of these drug-related visits involved alcohol or a major illicit drug:

- Cocaine was involved in 20% of ER visits.
- Marijuana was involved in nearly 13% of ER visits.
- Heroin was involved in nearly 8% of ER visits.
- Stimulants, including amphetamines and methamphetamine, were involved in nearly 7% of ER visits.
- Unspecified opiates were involved in nearly 4% of ER visits.

Other illicit drugs were involved less frequently than those previously listed, such as ecstacy, PCP, nonpharmaceutical inhalants, GHB, LSD, and ketamine (National Institute on Drug Abuse [NIDA], 2005).

The *Diagnostic and Statistical Manual of Mental Disorders* (4th ed.) (*DSM–IV*) recognizes two levels of substance use, which are problematic for individuals. The more severe level is *substance abuse*, which is a maladaptive pattern of substance use leading to clinically significant impairment or distress. This level is manifested in failure to fulfill major role obligations at work, school, or home or repeated substance use in situations in which it is physically hazardous, such as driving a car or operating machinery. Other manifestations may involve recurrent substance-related legal problems (such as arrests for drunk driving) and persistent interpersonal problems caused or exacerbated by intoxication. The other level is *substance dependence*, which is also viewed as a maladaptive pattern of use which also results in significant impairment and distress. The criteria for this level requires several consequences of use, such as *tolerance*, which is demonstrated by the need to take more of the substance in order to achieve intoxication; *withdrawal* symptoms when substance use is halted; *unsuccessful efforts* to cut down or control substance use; a great deal of *time* spent in activities necessary to obtain the substance; important social, occupational, or recreational *activities given up* or reduced because of substance use; or substance use *continued despite knowledge* of having persistent physical or psychological problems caused by the substance use (American Psychiatric Association, 2000).

In 2007, an estimated 19.9 million (8%) Americans aged 12 or older were current users of illegal drugs. Nearly 20% of those 18 to 25 years old were current tobacco or binge alcohol users. The consequences of this drug use can be far-reaching and plays a significant role in the cause and progression of many medical disorders, including addiction. Drug abuse also plays a role in many major social problems, such as drugged driving, violence, stress, and child abuse. Drug abuse can lead to homelessness, crime, missed work, or problems with keeping a job. It harms unborn babies and destroys families. There are different types of treatment for drug abuse. Yet only a fraction of people who need addiction treatment receive it. The best treatment is to prevent drug abuse in the first place (Medline Plus, 2009).

There are screening tests for substance abuse and alcoholism. The Drug Abuse Screening Test (DAST) is often used to screen for nonalcoholic substance abuse. The DAST has three versions—a 28-item test, a 20-item test, and a 10-item test that can be taken online. As we stated earlier in screening for domestic violence, we believe the online test of DAST is an effective way to help clients complete a self-assessment of their own substance use. For clients who cannot access this online test, the interpersonal practitioner can complete this test with the client on an agency computer. The 10-item online DAST is organized as a yes or no response test. Here are two examples of questions: "Do you abuse more than one drug at a time?" and "Does your spouse (or parents) ever complain about your involvement with drugs?" The test is scored, and suggested actions are recommended. The test can be accessed at http://archives.drugabuse.gov/diagnosis-treatment/DAST10.html (NIDA, 2010).

In regard to a screening test for alcoholism, there are many examples. We present some of the short tests that involve four questions that can be inserted into an initial interview. Acronyms are used in naming the test so that practitioners will be able to remember the four questions:

The CAGE test is one of the oldest and most popular screening tools for alcohol abuse:

C—Have you ever felt you should **cut down** on your drinking?

A—Have people **annoyed** you by criticizing your drinking?

G—Have you ever felt bad or **guilty** about your drinking?

E—**Eye opener**: Have you ever had a drink first thing in the morning to steady your nerves or to get rid of a hangover?

Because denial usually accompanies alcohol abuse problems, the CAGE test, like most alcohol screening tests, asks questions about problems associated with drinking rather than the amount of alcohol consumed. Two "yes" answers to the CAGE test indicate problems with alcohol. The disadvantage of the CAGE test is that it is most accurate for middle-aged white men and not very accurate for identifying alcohol abuse in older people, white women, and African and Mexican Americans (T, 2010).

The T-ACE test is also only four questions, including three found on the CAGE test, but it has proven to be more accurate in diagnosing alcohol problems in both men and women:

T—Does it **take** more than three drinks to make you feel high?

A—Have you ever been **annoyed** by people's criticism of your drinking?

C—Are you trying to **cut down** on drinking?

E—Have you ever used alcohol as an **eye opener** in the morning?

Again, "yes" answers to two of these four questions is an indication of possible alcohol abuse or dependence (T, 2010).

The RAPS4 test has been found to be highly effective in detecting alcohol dependence in the past year across gender and ethnic groups—white, black, and

Hispanic. Research has also shown that the RAPS4 is more effective than the CAGE test, which has traditionally been the most widely used test in clinical settings. The RAPS4 gets its name from the questions it poses to the patient, which pertain to remorse (R), amnesia (A), performance (P), and starter drinking behavior (S). Each question pertains to the patient's behaviors in the past year.

The RAPS4 Questions:

1. Have you had a feeling of guilt or remorse after drinking?
2. Has a friend or a family member ever told you about things you said or did while you were drinking that you could not remember?
3. Have you failed to do what was normally expected of you because of drinking?
4. Do you sometimes take a drink when you first get up in the morning?

A "yes" answer to at least one of the four questions suggests that drinking is harmful to the client's health and well-being and may adversely affect work and interpersonal relationships. If the client answered "no" to all four questions, this drinking pattern is considered safe for most people, and the results do not suggest that alcohol is harming the client's health.

Source: Buddy T. (2010, May 1). *The RAPS4 Alcohol Screening Test: Proven More Effective Than CAGE Test.* Retrieved from http://alcoholism.about.com/od/tests/a/raps.htm.

The Michigan Alcohol Screening Test (MAST) is one of the oldest and most accurate alcohol screening tests available. It contains 22 yes or no questions with six positive responses indicating a drinking problem. The disadvantage to the MAST test is its length and time required to score. One advantage of this test is that it can be employed with adolescents. If a client scores high in one of the previous short tests for alcoholism, it may be useful to have the client go on line and take the Alcoholism Quiz. This online quiz was developed by the Office of Health Care Programs, Johns Hopkins University Hospital. If the client consumes alcoholic beverages, this quiz may help the client realize that they have a drinking problem (About.com: Alcoholism, 2010).

In this chapter, we have presented a number of screening measures that can be used by the interpersonal practitioner to help clients understand various problems of social functioning. Clearly a practitioner cannot do all of these screening measures in an initial interview with an applicant. The interpersonal practitioner should decide which screening measures might be useful from the clues and hints that the applicant presents in the initial contact. Professional responsibility requires that the practitioner follow up on ideation about violence toward others and self-harm. But the interpersonal practitioner must skillfully find a way to integrate these screening measures with the applicant's view of problems of social functioning.

In order to emphasize the value of using online screening procedures, we end this chapter with an exercise that encourages students to go online and complete an assessment that rates the potential threat of domestic violence in an intimate relationship. We offer this exercise because when teaching the undergraduate social work course at the University of Michigan School of Social Work (UMSSW) and covering the unit on domestic violence, students often shared problem indicators in their dating experiences as well as other family relationships. This exercise involves MOSAIC: Threat Assessment System, which is a sophisticated program created by Gavin deBecker and Associates. MOSAIC has several threat assessment protocols, but you will only be able to access the two domestic violence protocols (one for men and the other for women). (See Exercise 5.1.)

Exercise 5.1

Mosaic Threat System

Go to the MOSAIC website and sign in (www.mosaicmethod.com). Because MOSAIC is an encrypted site, it may take your browser longer than usual to open. You may use ficitious names in order to complete the threat assessment for domestic violence. Think of an intimate relationship in your own family or extended family or a dating experience, and complete the threat assessment for domestic violence. The MOSAIC system is complex, thorough, and will take at least 30 minutes to complete. You will also be able to access explanations for the various questions and information that MOSAIC covers. Because of the nature of this exercise, we would not expect students to be willing to share this experience with their classmates.

SUMMARY ●

This chapter discussed violence and trauma and how debilitating these experiences are in the lives of our clients. Case examples were used to highlight the impact that trauma has on people's lives. The chapter focused on many screening procedures that involve threats of violence and assault, suicide, child abuse, partner abuse, and substance use. The authors believe that these dimensions in our clients' lives permeate practice in the 21st century.

CHAPTER 6

ENGAGEMENT AND RELATIONSHIP

Cross-cultural studies confirm that women everywhere are considered more empathic than men, so much so that the claim has been made that the female (but not the male) brain is hardwired for empathy. I doubt that the difference is that absolute, but it's true that at birth girl babies look longer at faces than boy babies, who look longer at suspended mechanical mobiles. Growing up, girls are more prosocial than boys, better readers of emotional expressions, more attuned to voices, more remorseful after having hurt someone, and better at taking another's perspective. When Carolyn Zahn-Waxler measured reactions to distressed family members, she found girls looking more at the other's face, providing more physical comfort and more often expressing concern, such as asking, "Are you okay?" Boys are less attentive to the feelings of others, more action- and object oriented, rougher in their play, and less inclined to social fantasy games. They prefer collective action, such as building something together.

—Franz DeWaal (2009, p. 114)

The need for emotional connectedness and intimacy is basic to human beings. Even before we are born, we are dependent on others for our survival. Though this need changes and takes on a different shape as we mature and develop, as adults we do not need our mothers and fathers as we did when we were infants and children. Though parents continue to play an important role in our emotional life, so do many other relationships with significant others, such as siblings, friends, lovers, spouses, bosses, etc. Social workers have recognized the centrality of relationships in people's lives and have promoted relationship as a basic principle of social intervention.

Mary Richmond, who almost a century ago wrote the first methods text on social casework, defined social work as "the intensive study and use of social relationships" (Richmond, 1922). For Richmond (1922), the focus of casework was the caseworker's

> skill in discovering the social relationships by which a given personality has been shaped; an ability to get at the central core of the difficulty in relationships; and power to utilize the direct action of mind upon mind in their adjustment. (p. 101)

Several decades later, Gordon Hamilton, an influential teacher and writer in the evolution of casework practice theory, wrote, "Our most fundamental considerations lie in the concept of human relationships—their importance, their dynamics, their use in treatment. Casework, group work, and community organization are alike grounded in the art and science of relationships" (Hamilton, 1951, p. 27). Decades later, Florence Hollis would define psychosocial casework as the study and uses of social relationships and argue that "all social work processes require the establishment of a social relationship in order to be effective" (Hollis, 1964, p. 149).

In this chapter, we present our own conceptualization of this central practice principle in social work. We borrow dimensions from many of these earlier texts. Whole books have been devoted to this concept (Biestek, 1957; Keefe & Maypole, 1983; Perlman, 1979; Rubenstein & Bloch, 1982). In this chapter, we shall present the most salient and basic dimensions of this concept to help interpersonal practitioners guide their practice.

Relationship is a difficult concept to define operationally. Historically, there have been numerous metaphorical descriptions offered to explain what this concept means in practice. For example, relationship has been described as the "soul" of practice, the "bridge or channel," the "flesh and blood" of practice (Biestek, 1957). Other descriptions rely on such terms as "mutuality" (Leonard, 1972), "acceptance, expectation, support, conscious purposiveness" (Perlman, 1957), and "working alliance" (Strean, 1985). Some authors say it is the sine qua non and most essential element of practice (Perlman, 1979), whereas others are more circumscribed in what this concept means to interpersonal practice. This latter perspective is more in line with our position. Relationship is one of many important dimensions of interpersonal practice with individuals, families, and groups. Yet just having a good relationship with clients does not assure that clients will achieve significant changes in their lives.

● DEFINITION OF THE SOCIAL WORK RELATIONSHIP

Though it is possible for individuals to establish a relationship through the mail or through a computer conference or computer network, significant social relationships can only be developed in face-to-face encounters. These encounters teach individuals what to expect when interacting with others. Though there may be a genetic imperative that drives individuals to seek encounters with other individuals, this imperative does not determine the quality of human relationships nor the expectations that individuals may have when they encounter others. In a simple dyadic encounter, there may be two individuals interacting face-to-face, but the quality of their social relationship will be determined by a number of factors. When social workers work in multiperson encounters with groups or families, the number of factors that need to be taken into account is even more complex.

Each person has a set of expectations that raises many questions about the other in the encounter. For example, will this person be friendly, talk to me, and listen to what I say? Or will this person try to harm me, threaten me, or simply ignore me? The potential number of expectations and concerns that individuals may have about another person in encounters are staggering and the result of past socialization experience with others. For example, if an individual has been exploited or cheated by individuals like the one in the present encounter, the prior experience may set up negative expectations and may make the individual who has these negative expectations behave cautiously and be extremely guarded in the encounter.

When these prior experiences are with parents and significant others in our early childhood and these early experiences shape our encounters with individuals in the present, psychodynamic theory refers to these factors as *transference elements*. When clients bring such expectations to an encounter with the interpersonal practitioner, these expectations and relationship patterns are called *transference*. When the interpersonal practitioner brings such expectations to the encounter with the client, they are called *counter-transference*. From a psychodynamic perspective, all present relationships are composites of transferred elements from earlier, significant relationships, and this is congruent with a symbolic interactionist perspective that also considers past relationships to be important socialization experiences.

Symbolic interactionism, however, does not hold those earlier, primary relationships to be as sacred as psychodynamic theory. Experiences in the present and future can also have a marked influence on a person's relationship capacities and expectations. In fact, individual's expectations in relationships can be powerfully shaped and influenced by the relationship and reference groups that one associates with in the present. This position can be readily observed during adolescence when the primary influences of parents moderate, while the influence of peer groups increases dramatically.

Not only do expectations determine how individuals behave in encounters with other individuals but so do the *conceptions* that individuals have of what they are expected to do in the encounter. These conceptions are similar to expectations, except they represent an individual's "guesstimate" of what the other individual in the encounter will be expecting of them as well as what they expect of themselves. We are always being socialized to what others think is appropriate behavior in encounters, and there are many books on etiquette designed to teach us what is expected in various kinds of social encounters—weddings, funerals, a date, or even how to run a meeting (Post, 1992). The problem with etiquette books is that they cannot begin to cover all of the "ritual order encounters" (Goffman, 1967, p. 42) that individuals experience in their lifetimes nor all of the variations that exist in these ritual orders.

There are many ritual orders we take for granted in public encounters with others. For example, when we get into a crowded elevator, we turn toward the door and cast our eyes upward to the numbers at the top of the door because this is the "usual" ritual order for such encounters. Now to test the power of this convention and how important expectations are even in fleeting public encounters, try the experiment in Exercise 6.1.

Exercise 6.1

Importance of Expectations and Conceptions

The next time you are last to enter a crowded elevator, stand with your back to the door and face the back of the elevator. Casually scan all of the occupants of the elevator and look into their eyes. Notice how uncomfortable and possibly anxious you will feel as you stare into the eyes of the other occupants. Some of the other occupants may also feel uncomfortable about your stance and will deliberately avoid your gaze. You may even be asked to turn around or asked to leave the elevator at the next stop. If you do not comply with this request, you may find that you have the elevator to yourself. The importance of this little experiment is how expectations of others and conceptions of our own behavior in encounters is critical to how individuals will feel and respond to the encounter—even in casual public encounters.

Because there are so many variations in ritual orders, misunderstandings may easily arise in social encounters when individuals come with *different* life experiences and have different conceptions about what is appropriate behavior in a given ritual order. An example from one author's practice experience will make these notions more salient and underline the problems that individuals may have in forming social relationships when they come from different ethnic experiences. The ritual order in question involves the expected behaviors of individuals when an outsider comes to the doorway of a family's house and attempts to gain access to the family for a legitimate purpose:

In my growing up years, whenever an outsider came to my (Brett A. Seabury, or BAS) family home with a legitimate request to come inside (to try to sell or repair something), my mother would inquire about the purpose of the visit, and if she was agreeable, she would then invite the outsider inside. She would always politely offer that individual a cup of coffee. The outsider, however, was not expected to accept the offer for coffee but instead was expected to politely refuse and go directly to the business at hand. In my family's conception of an appropriate encounter, the outsider was not there to be fed but to get on with "business." I can even remember my mother's face (i.e., displeasure) when an outsider accepted the offer of coffee and the irritation she felt (but never expressed) in fixing a total stranger a cup of coffee. I do not remember specific situations, but I can imagine that those strangers trying to sell something were unsuccessful in their efforts after accepting the cup of coffee my mother offered.

On one of my first home visits as a second-year student in social work, I was assigned an ethnic family with very different conceptions about this ritual order. I had called the day before and set up the home visit, and my knock on the door was greeted by the mother/wife of the family, who proceeded to say she was expecting me and asked if I would like something to eat. Immediately (without thinking), I politely refused the offer and stated that I had just eaten lunch before making the visit. And almost immediately, she stopped opening the screen door and responded that maybe I would like a nice cup of coffee instead. Unfortunately, I wasn't yet thinking, so I politely turned down this offer, too. This was then countered by another offer, and her husband appeared at the door and suggested several other food items that I might eat. This round of exchanges (their offering and my politely refusing) went through several iterations before I suddenly realized that they were not going to let me into their house to conduct my business unless I agreed to eat something with them first. In fact, on every home visit I made to this family, we would start in the kitchen and eat some food that had been carefully prepared before we would move into the living room where I could carry out the purpose of my home visit with them.

This example is presented to point out how important our conception of ourselves and our expectations of others is to the social relationship that may or may not be allowed to develop. In a diverse, multiethnic, and multiracial society, it is likely we will be encountering many individuals, families, and groups that have diverse conceptions and expectations about others in the encounter. Unless social workers are careful to account for these differences in expectation and conception, there may be many lost chances to form relationships with our clients. It is also important to point out that even though I (BAS) was raised in the dominant and privileged ethnic group (WASP) of American society, there is nothing inherently better or superior to the ritual orders of my ethnic group when compared with others. Throughout this chapter, we refer to expectations and conceptions as essential concepts in understanding social relationships.

The literature on relationship in social work makes a distinction between *personal* relationships and *professional* relationships. One way of understanding this distinction is to consider the professional relationship as a subcategory or subtype of the large category of interpersonal relationships. Unfortunately, there is considerable overlap between aspects of personal relationships and aspects of a professional relationship, yet there are important differences that need to be identified. For example, in a personal relationship, we expect both parties to gain something or have personal needs met, yet in the professional relationship, the needs of the client take priority and precedence over the needs of the worker. Furthermore, a personal relationship may be indefinite and last a lifetime, whereas a professional relationship is more circumscribed, usually time limited, and ends once its purpose has been fulfilled. The professional relationship also prohibits various kinds of behavior (such as sexual relationships) that may be legitimate in personal relationships but are taboo in professional relationships.

The professional relationship is bound by a code of conduct that clearly limits the kinds of activities (no sex, no violence, no exploitations) that worker and client may pursue together. This code, much like etiquette books, spells out the expectations and conceptions that guide the behavior of professional social workers and was spelled out in greater detail in the values chapter (Chapter 3).

POWER DIMENSIONS IN ● PROFESSIONAL RELATIONSHIPS

To practice effectively and competently, social workers must be able to recognize the power dimensions that exist in professional relationships with clients as well as collaborative relationships with other helping professionals. A professional relationship between social worker and client is not a relationship between equals as often characterizes friendship relationship. The social worker, by virtue of his or her position in an organization or by the education and credentials required to gain a license to practice social work in a given state, starts from a one-up position of greater power in the relationship with the client. Even though in feminist literature this kind of power or status difference is viewed as undesirable and often problematic (e.g., Cohen & Mullender, 2003; Garvin & Reed, 1994); also review the discussion of power in the diversity chapter (Chapter 4). The power differential cannot be ignored in the professional relationship (Toren, 1973).

A worker enters a relationship with a client with four of six power bases that have been identified in the social psychology literature (Feld & Radin, 1982). By virtue of the worker's position in an agency and registration/license in a given state, the worker is granted the *authority* and is legitimated by social institutions to practice social work. By virtue of workers' connection to the resources of social agencies, workers have the power to *reward* clients with various desirable resources, such as shelter, food, clothing, or transportation. By virtue of these same connections, workers can *coerce* and punish clients by denying resources or even taking actions that may be undesirable to clients, such as taking children into protective custody, initiating action to terminate parental rights, or revoking parole. Based on a worker's education and past experiences with other clients in similar circumstance, a worker may be perceived as having some special *expertise* that will help the client.

The only power base that a client brings to the relationship is *informational*. The client has control over much of the information that makes up his or her situation, yet this base may be weakened when a worker enters the situation after consulting with significant others who already know the client. The most important power base that both client and worker must develop is the *referent* base. This base refers to the attraction that develops between individuals in a close relationship and based on this attraction and identification with the other, the possibility of influence in the relationship. This referent power base is easiest to see operating when friends go out of their way for each other when asked, with no expectation that they will get something immediately in return.

What's important to recognize about power in the professional relationship is that different kinds of interpersonal power bases are experienced differently when used in a relationship. Some of these power bases produce negative feelings in the individual who is being subjected to the power base. For example, coercive power is experienced negatively, and reward power may also be viewed in the same way when the higher power person withholds a desired reward. The use of these two power bases to influence clients will be perceived negatively by clients, as it is by children when parents force children to behave or attempt to bribe children to do something they don't want to do.

Expertise, authority, and referent power bases are less likely to be perceived negatively by clients when workers use these power bases to influence clients. For example, a client may solicit and follow through on advice that a worker offers (expertise), or a client may tolerate the worker's unpleasant questions about a client's painful experiences because the client likes and trusts the worker (authority and referent power). Unfortunately, in practice, a worker cannot always avoid the use of coercive power. For example, a worker is required by law to report a client's abusive behavior toward other family members. Clients who are reported to protective services will usually view this responsibility of their workers as coercive and undesirable. Likewise, a very suicidal adolescent may not like it when a worker breaks confidence and informs the adolescent's parents about the suicidal risk. Even though the worker is acting responsibly in each of these situations, the clients will probably find the worker's behavior coercive.

We want to point out that clients are not always as powerless as we have indicated. Sometimes clients do not pay for services rendered, or they refuse to attend sessions in voluntary situations. Clients may become openly hostile and angry with their workers, yet workers do not have the same privilege to retaliate when they are upset with client behaviors. In agency practice, clients may start grievances or complain to a worker's supervisor about matters they find disagreeable. Clients may also sanction workers for unethical and unprofessional behavior by taking their complaints to the National Association of Social Workers (NASW), state licensure boards, or court.

STAGES OF THE ● PROFESSIONAL RELATIONSHIP

It is instructive to think about how relationships begin by looking at the very first moments of an encounter between two dogs. Many dog owners have experienced what happens when they are walking their dog and they meet another dog owner with a dog. The two dogs approach each other with tails wagging but in a high state of alertness as they begin to "check out" the other dog. Usually they will sniff each other's mouth—presumably to determine what the other dog may have recently eaten. They will then move around to the rear end of the other dog to sniff the private parts of the other dog, presumably to determine the sex of the other dog. With this preliminary information about the other dog, the two dogs then have three choices. They can (1) flee, (2) fight, or (3) fornicate. At this point in the encounter, the dog owners will usually intervene in this beginning relationship and pull the dogs apart. Now in human encounters between strangers we, too, will spend time checking each other out, but obviously we have many more options than dogs.

We do not view professional relationships as a static dimension of practice but one that is constantly developing and changing throughout the service episode. The relationship that emerges in the beginning phases of service is different from relationship in the middle and termination phases of service.

Relationships grow and develop over time, and there are distinct differences in the phases of a professional relationship. In the beginning phases of a professional relationship, there can be a lot of checking out and sizing up that can lead to guardedness, reserve, yet hope and expectation (Garland, Jones, & Kolodny, 1965; Lennard & Bernstein, 1970). We cannot wag our tails or raise our ruffs like the two dogs, but we experience similar feelings. In the beginning, parties may not be open until they have had a chance to warm up to each other. There is often noticeable anxiety in this new encounter with the "stranger" (Lenrow, 1982, pp. 41–57). This kind of anxiety is very obvious in the first sessions of groups when members are beginning to get to know each other. Usually this beginning anxiety and guardedness gives way to more serious attempts to test or find out more about each other. In some encounters, because of the special circumstances of service (when applicants are forced to accept service or the worker is very different from the applicant), this testing might be severely provocative and often critical to the further development of the working relationship. If the worker fails the test, then it is unlikely that a mature, working relationship can develop, and in fact, if the applicant has a choice about attending, the risk of discontinuance (dropping out) is high. Research on continuance has demonstrated that if the worker is not perceived by the client as caring (wanting to help) and competent (able to help) then it is likely that clients will discontinue or drop out (Kounin, 1956; Maluccio, 1979a).

So, in the beginning of the professional relationship, it is critical that the interpersonal practitioner takes responsibility for initiating the relationship with the applicant. This kind of reaching out to the applicant can take many forms, depending on whether the worker is establishing a relationship with an individual, a family, or starting up a treatment group. "Starting where the client is" (Marziali, 1988) as a practice principle reflects one important strategy that not only embodies social work's value of client self-determination but also prescribes the importance of discovering why the applicant is seeking help at this time.

The interpersonal practitioner should discover what the applicant wants and needs and also what the applicant expects from the worker and the agency. The interpersonal practitioner should be facilitative in the beginning encounter so the applicant can tell his or her story and can express his or her druthers first, before launching into a discussion of the various possibilities that the worker and agency may offer the client. It may well be that what the applicant is seeking in the way of service is not appropriate to the agency, and the applicant will have to be referred elsewhere; but the applicant's view is expressed first. This is not only the beginning of the relationship but also the beginning of the service agreement. These issues are elaborated more fully in the clienthood chapter (Chapter 7).

Another important strategy for the interpersonal practitioner is advanced preparation (Cowan et al., 1969; Pincus & Minahan, 1973, pp. 184–193). Because it is likely that the worker and client will differ from each other in significant ways (such as gender expression, age, race, social class, ethnicity, etc.), it is important that the interpersonal practitioner enter the service process with as much background information about the applicant as possible, so that few surprises will erupt in the first encounter. Advanced preparation is accomplished in many ways. Simply reading the record or face sheet or talking with others who have worked with the client within your own agency can be helpful. Many treatment groups do not allow members to even reach the first session without first going through a prescreening interview in which the group leader meets the prospective member and also helps the prospective member prepare for what is expected in the group (Budman & Gurman, 1988, pp. 253–259; Corey & Corey, 2006). More about this issue is discussed in the group assessment (Chapter 14) and change in groups (Chapter 15) chapters.

Another kind of advanced preparation at a more general level is the worker's training and experience in working with particular clients. Courses, in-service training, and workshops designed to raise a workers' "critical consciousness" (Keefe, 1980) about particular clients are other important forms of advanced preparation. We encourage practitioners to participate in training experiences designed to increase the worker's ethnic, racial, gender, and sexual sensitivities (Cohen & Mullender, 2003).

Critical consciousness, as we discussed in the diversity chapter (Chapter 4), is much more than empathic understanding that focuses mostly on the immediate feelings and content of the client's story. Though empathic understanding and responding are important skills for building relationships, critical consciousness is important because it embodies the intersectionality of class, sexuality, gender expression, and ethnic consciousness. It is so important for interpersonal practitioners who may be middle class yet working with poor and oppressed groups whose history and life experiences are so dramatically different from the workers' life experiences. As we also discussed in the diversity chapter, it is important for interpersonal practitioners to understand how privilege impacts on their understanding of and ability to work with oppressed clients.

Most practitioners at some point in their practice will experience a demoralized client's sigh and comment, "You just don't understand!" Though the worker may clearly understand what the client is feeling at that moment and has listened carefully to what the client has said, the misunderstanding and expressed exasperation of the client reflects the gap in the worker's critical consciousness— the worker's ability to understand and appreciate the highly personal, cultural, and class perspectives of the client's life experience. A significant way of working on critical consciousness is for workers to join consciousness-raising (CR) groups (Kravetz, 1987, pp. 55–66) or to facilitate CR groups for themselves (Sherman & Wenocur, 1983) and their clients (Longres & McLeod, 1980).

Sometimes this beginning relationship develops into a honeymoon phase in which the interpersonal practitioner is perceived by the client as the greatest worker who ever existed and one who will finally save or help the client solve all his or her problems (Mann, 1973). Though it may be flattering to the worker to be perceived as so powerful and helpful, it is important that the worker recognize the honeymoon as a passing phase filled with transference impressions and not based in any mature, realistic appraisal of the worker's abilities. The interpersonal practitioner may use this phase of high client motivation to get a number of preliminary goals established.

Unfortunately, this phase of high expectation often gives way to a stormy transitional phase in which the client begins to have many ambivalent feelings about the worker's abilities and the direction service is going. Often, the client will challenge the worker's authority, and many power and control issues may emerge. For example, the client may not like some of the terms of service the worker or agency has prescribed, or the client may want to make major changes in the service plan. This phase in groups is sometimes referred to as "revision" and is a precursor to a mature working relationship for worker and members.

The worker's role during this phase is to help clients express their disillusionment, to mediate interpersonal conflict, and to move onto revising those elements of the therapeutic contract that can be reasonably revised. It is important to realize that not all revisions are possible and some service arrangements fall apart at this point. For example, a worker in an institution cannot help an incarcerated patient escape, or some groups dissolve when they cannot agree on norms that deal with the level of interpersonal conflict expressed.

Much of the literature on relationship focuses on the mature, collaborative, working relationship that takes some time to develop. This kind of relationship emerges when all parties to the relationship are clear about their expectations of others, their conceptions about themselves in the relationship, and when a high degree of mutual agreement has been achieved about the purpose of their work together. This mature, collaborative, working relationship is the bond of cohesiveness that is experienced among members in a successful group (Forsyth, 1990, pp. 471–483) or is reflected in a family's trust and acceptance that allows the worker to temporarily enter the intimate, personal, and interpersonal space of the family (Kantor & Lehr, 1975, pp. 23–35).

This kind of understanding, trust, and mutual agreement—whether in a family or group—emerges more by what the interpersonal practitioner does through modeling than through what the worker says. Trust does not develop by asking someone to trust you but by observing how trustworthy the actions of a person are. For example, if the interpersonal practitioner has agreed with a group that one ground rule will be that no member will be forced to participate in group discussion or activities, and the worker later coerces or pushes a member into participating in a discussion or group activity, the worker will lose whatever trust may already have developed. With families and groups especially, interpersonal practitioners must be consistent with different members and follow through on any verbal agreement they have made with their clients.

Modeling is an important aspect of the helping relationship. Through modeling, the client may not only learn about actual problem solving by watching the worker or other member of a therapeutic group but also how one behaves in a positive, interpersonal relationship. It is common for people to try to imitate people (models) they admire, respect, and trust.

When service is coming to an end, both the worker and clients may have all kinds of misgivings and negative feelings about the ending of their relationship. In spite of the success of services, clients may feel abandoned by the worker or truly sad that the relationship is coming to an end. Clients may feel anxious, angry, or hurt by the termination. The worker may also have all kinds of feelings stirred up by the ending, yet the worker must take responsibility to point out to clients that these feelings are the consequences of the termination and may not reflect what was or was not accomplished in service. For example, sometimes the least committed, most marginal member of a group may weep profusely during termination and beg that the group not be ended. This termination reaction is in stark contrast to their reluctance to participate fully during the life of the group.

One way that workers can soften the intensity of termination feelings is to stagger sessions as termination is approached (biweekly or monthly meetings instead of weekly sessions) or to plan a ritual or ceremony that acts as a transition marker (Laird & Hartman, 1987) to the end of the relationship (e.g., a graduation ceremony). Another strategy is to plan a follow-up session at some later point in time (e.g., group reunion after 6 months to see how members are doing) or to request permission from the client to "haunt" them at some later time in a follow-up phone call. More of these strategies are discussed in the chapter on endings (Chapter 18).

The purpose of this developmental description is to point out that relationship is an emergent phenomenon and cannot be described or characterized simply at one point in the service process. The appearance of negative feelings or sentiments does not mean that the relationship is in trouble. On the contrary, it should be expected by workers that a variety of expectation and sentiments, both positive and negative, will emerge as the relationship unfolds. The honeymoon is not the only phase to a successful marriage, and if that is all that is expected, as in so many Hollywood marriages, then the marriage is doomed to failure.

TRANSACTIONAL NATURE OF ● THE PROFESSIONAL RELATIONSHIP

Not only are relationships constantly changing but they are also "transactional" phenomenon in which all parties participate in either the successful or failed attempts to form a working relationship. The experiences, perceptions, and sentiments of the worker, as well as client experiences, perceptions, and sentiments, mutually shape and influence each party in the development of the professional relationship. Relationship is not something workers do to passive clients, but there is a mutual interchange and interplay in how the relationship develops and matures. All parties are active as well as reactive. It may be common to blame the client for failed relationships in practice (e.g., it's *always* easy to blame the victim), yet both parties usually have been actively involved in the success or failure of the relationship (Gitterman, 1983).

Positive feelings between client and worker will not flow easily if the worker does not like the client—or in transactional terms, if either party does not like the other. Studies have shown that clients who remained in treatment were those who felt liked and respected by their therapists (Garfield, 1994). This kind of respect is extremely important to oppressed minority clients seeking help from a white privileged worker (Mizio, 1972; Sue, 1981).

The importance of a transactional perspective of relationship is that when things are not going well in the professional relationship, we must look at both the client and the worker for sources of the difficulty. We must also look at the transactional factors (such as the commonalities and incongruities) that emerge when any two or more individuals are put together and expected to form a relationship. It is possible that the interpersonal practitioner and client have noble intentions and desire to build an effective relationship, yet their differences and incompatibilities are so great that such a match would be very, very difficult.

In order to explore these issues in greater depth, we offer the following exercise (Exercise 6.2), which explores how diversity issues can become major obstacles to a social work relationship. This exercise is best performed in small, heterogeneous groups of five or six students in your practice course. Students need to be warned that this is a CR exercise that requires honesty and will result in some anxiety that is generated in the discussion of these case vignettes. We want to be clear that there are no "right or wrong" answers to these discussions but what students learn about themselves and other students in the class.

Exercise 6.2

Critical Consciousness About Relationship Issues With Clients

We hope that you and your instructor will develop many other case vignettes than the five we offer here. There are so many ways that intersectionality and differences between interpersonal practitioners and their clients can be explored that students should develop their own cases to explore these issues.

Again, this is a CR exercise that is best accomplished in small, heterogeneous groups of five or six students. The exercise involves the student's feelings and perspective of working in a case situation, and also feedback about how the student might be perceived by the applicant in the case situation. The instructor may want to use the "Cloverdale process" (Plionis & Lewis, 1995) of staying out of each of the small groups and moving the process along by letting students work for a time in the small groups on a case and then moving back to a discussion of the class as a whole. That way what is learned and experienced in each of the small groups can be shared with the whole class in feedback to the whole class. We recommend the Cloverdale process because it is designed to help the class deal with sensitive issues and avoid some of the negative outcomes that often follow discussions about diversity issues (e.g., all of the majority students are "racist" or all of the white males in the class are "privileged, sexist chauvinistic pigs" or all of the people of color in the class are "enraged, disempowered victims").

Once the class is arranged in small, heterogeneous groups, the students will read each of the case vignettes and focus on each one at a time. The following questions are offered as a starting point for the discussion of each case:

1. What are the identity differences and similarities between you and the applicant in the case?

2. How would you feel about working with the applicant(s) in the case?

3. How familiar are you with the major issues that you see that would arise in the case?

4. How do you think the applicant would perceive you as their practitioner?

After each of the students in the small group has self-shared what they believe to be their responses to the applicant in the case situation, the small group process will shift to group members giving each other feedback to other members. In turn, the small group will focus on each member who will be in the "hot seat." Group members will share how they think the applicant will react to the student in the hot seat. This feedback will all be speculative because group members are only making suppositions about how an applicant will feel about the student in the hot seat. This will help to reduce some of the tension and anxiety that will be generated in this part of the exercise. The final part of this small group process will be to discuss what the students can do to help to manage the issues that have been raised in the feedback process. In the Cloverdale process, one of the early steps is for each group to work out their own ground rules for how they will behave in their small group discussions. This early step, which we recommend, will help each group decide what kinds of information they will want to share with the whole class.

Case Example #1. You are an interpersonal practitioner who is employed in a family service agency. A 25-year-old white mother of two daughters ages 5 and 7 has come to your agency extremely distressed about her abusive ex-husband, who is now threatening to go back to the court and ask for custody of their children. Since the divorce 2 years ago, she has been living in a lesbian relationship with an older woman. Her ex-husband recently found out about this relationship and now believes he has a chance to gain custody of their children. He has also threatened to go to her father, a pastor in a Fundamentalist church, and share the information about her lesbian relationship.

(Continued)

(Continued)

Case Example #2. You are an interpersonal practitioner who is a member of a nonprofit collective made up of social workers, psychologists, and a psychiatrist. This organization contracts with the state department of mental health and the VA to provide counseling services to their patients. You have been assigned to lead a support group for returning veterans of the Iraq and Afghanistan wars. Group members will be struggling with PTSD, readjustment to civilian life, and several to adjustment to civilian life with missing limbs. The group is composed of men who have all been discharged from active duty, between the ages of 22 and 28, some with three tours of duty in a war zone.

Case Example #3. You are the school social worker employed in a large, urban high school in which 65% of the student body is African American, 25% is Latino, and 10% are Caucasian. In the school's administration, 100% are Caucasian, and 90% of the teachers and service staff are African American. The assistant principal has referred a 17-year-old African American male who has been cutting classes, leaving school early, and "mouthing off" to the principal and assistant principal when they have threatened this youth with disciplinary action. In the 9th and 10th grades, he was a straight A student and was assigned to the college preparatory track.

Case Example #4. You are an interpersonal practitioner at Catholic Social Services who has been covering intake for the agency. You receive a call from a frantic mother who demands to be seen today. She explains that she has called your agency after talking with her parish priest. She explains that her family is in turmoil because her 16-year-old daughter has disclosed that she is 3 months' pregnant and wants to get an abortion so she can finish her high school classes. The family is already under many stressors because her husband has been unemployed for 6 months and cannot find another job. She has not told her husband about their daughter's "condition," but she knows that he would be adamantly opposed to an abortion because he is from a large Italian American family.

Case Example #5. You are an interpersonal practitioner at Lutheran Social Services. A 52-year-old pastor of a small, fundamentalist Lutheran church has come to your agency because he is depressed, has been having trouble sleeping, and is upset with his wife for her plans now that their four children are grown and have departed the family home. For 25 years, his wife has been a good homemaker and performed the duties of a "pastor's wife," but now she wants to return to college studies and complete her bachelor's degree. He is concerned that this choice will reverberate negatively with his small congregation.

When forming a group, a worker may spend a great deal of time and effort exploring commonalities of potential members before inviting them to join (Reid, 1997). It is unlikely that members of a group could develop a good working relationship if extreme differences existed between them. For example, we would not put members of the Klan together with members of the Black Panther Party nor expect such a group to develop cohesiveness. It is important that prospective members of a group have some kind of commonality (usually around such descriptive attributes as race, gender expression, age, class, and type of problems) so that some kind of positive feeling and working relationship can develop (Bertcher & Maple, 1996). These issues are discussed in more detail in the group assessment chapter (Chapter 14).

Compositional issues must be accounted for in casework and family encounters, too. The interpersonal practitioner must be aware of the critical differences between herself or himself and the individual client or family. What's important is not that these differences may exist but the implication of these differences in the development of a professional relationship. Any one of a number of significant differences can be problematic in the formation of a professional relationship. For example, major barriers may emerge in gender expression, sexual orientation, race, ethnicity, social class, age, or disability. A worker and client may find they do not share many demographic attributes and that these differences are a major source of strain and misunderstanding of the expectations and conceptions they may have of each other in the professional relationship.

In some situations, these differences may be so problematic for worker and client that only by providing a more careful "match" will worker and client have a chance to form a professional relationship (Palmer, 1973). In some service situations, it may be critical that workers and clients are of the same gender. For example, it may not be appropriate for a male social worker to be working in a domestic violence safe house with women who have recently left a violent marriage. Trotman and Gallagher (1987) made a good case that some groups should be highly homogenous before some issues will arise and be discussed. For example, they suggest that some women's groups should be composed exclusively of African American women in order for significant issues to arise that are the exclusive concern of African American women. The presence of African American men or white women has a dampening effect on the discussion and cohesiveness of the group. Even though these attributes may be critical in some situations, there is research to suggest that clients value competence over commonality when it comes to working with a social worker (Kadushin, 1983).

Social work students are often concerned that their race, age, and gender may limit the variety of clients they can work with effectively. Caucasian students may worry that they may not be credible to minority clients because they are members of the dominant group and have not experienced daily oppression. Students of color may fear that they will be dismissed by Caucasian clients as being inferior because of the color of their skin. Still others worry that they may be too old or too young to be accepted by their clients. We do not want to ignore the very real problems of racism, sexism, and ageism that exist in American society, and we do recognize that some clients will capitalize on these fears that students may have. However, it is important to keep in mind that the beginning of a relationship is plagued by some degree of anxiety both on the part of the worker and of the client. It may be that the clients' challenge of gender, race, or age may be more a manifestation of their own fear of whether they can be helped or not. Though the manifest question may be "Are you capable of helping me?" or "Can you understand me?" the underlying question the client may be asking is "Is there any hope for me? I feel hopeless." If the worker feels vulnerable and self-conscious about his or her personal attributes, she or he may not hear what the client's latent concerns are and may even become defensive. The client then will feel misunderstood and even more helpless and hopeless, and it is more likely that the client will not return to the agency.

When forming relationships with families, the worker is faced with special considerations that do not present themselves in casework or group work. When working with a family in a family session, the worker will have to be able to form a working relationship with parents, children, and sometimes grandparents or other significant family members. The relationship skills necessary to reach one generation may be very different from another generation. The relationship skills involved in reaching a disgruntled adolescent are different from those needed to reach the adolescent's controlling parents. Sometimes social workers will meet individually with family members to establish some kind of beginning relationship with each significant member of the family; however, these tentative, beginning relationships will be severely tested when the family is seen as a whole and all sides are trying to co-opt the worker. The family as a small group breaks most rules of group composition by throwing together in one place different genders, generations, and ages. It is no surprise to practitioners that conflict is much more prevalent and intense in families than in groups.

Because of the nature of long-term relationships in families, families are able to tolerate much more interpersonal conflict than formed groups in which the relationships are much more transient. For formed groups to survive, they must be composed of members who have strong commonalities (such as similar ages and problems) so that cohesion can develop quickly. Too much interpersonal conflict will tear formed groups apart, yet families can survive even in the face of fairly intense and frequent interpersonal conflict.

Besides the difficulty of maintaining relationships with different generations, the social worker must also walk a careful tightrope of not forming too strong a relationship with any one family member. The relationships between family members always take precedence over the relationship that the worker might have with any family member (Budman & Gurman, 1988). The worker must not allow his or her relationship to become stronger or more significant with a family member than already exists within the family structure. The worker needs to behave like a transient though trustworthy guest whose stay is temporary in the family and will not replace existing family relationships but instead will work to improve whatever relationship problems may already exist. In families with needy individuals, this is a trying balance for the worker to establish in the working relationship with the whole family.

WHY IS RELATIONSHIP SO IMPORTANT? ●

Initially, social workers discovered the salience of relationship through the observation of the social environment and of their own work with clients. Some research has shown just how critical relationship is to service outcomes. Studies comparing different types of therapies have shown that while therapy produced positive effects for clients, there were essentially no differences in effectiveness between selected therapies. This was the case even though these therapies varied widely in theoretical background and treatment approach (Smith, Glass, & Miller, 1980). These results suggest that professional helpers, whatever their training and theoretical orientation when they interact with clients, are accomplishing similar things (Lambert & Bergen, 1994).

There have been many studies conducted on the efficacy of therapy in order to understand what factors account for treatment success (Lambert, 2004; Nathan & Gorman, 2002; Orlinsky, Grawe, & Parks, 1994). Studies have compared the amount of training, the types of training, and theoretical orientation of the helpers and the kind of techniques employed in therapy. These factors, however, do not seem to account for the efficacy of the treatment process, and in some studies, these factors seem to make no difference—or very little difference—to outcomes. Outcomes seem more determined by the relationship developed in treatment. These relationship factors have been called "therapeutic bond" and may be found in many types of helping relationships. In some studies, they have been more influential on the treatment outcomes than the type of interventions employed (Orlinsky et al., 1994). This evidence suggests that effective helping cannot take place without the existence of a significant interpersonal relationship between the help seeker and the helper.

The significance of relationships to outcome is clearly evident in group leadership functions. Successful group leaders must pay attention to *task* as well as *maintenance issues* (Forsyth, 1990, pp. 211–229). A group leader employs leadership moves to help the group accomplish its agreed upon goals, while trying to respond to the individuals' needs, wants, and the feelings of members in the group. These socioemotional leadership activities are designed to facilitate positive working relationships between all members of the group. A group in which individuals cannot form and maintain working relationships is a group destined to suffer severe loss in members and ultimate dissolution. Of course, such a group will not achieve its goals.

CONSCIOUS USE OF SELF ●

The professional relationship is one of the primary tools for social intervention. Carpenters, surgeons, and cosmetologists have instruments such as hammers, scalpels, and combs that they use in their daily work; the social worker's tool of the trade is herself or himself. Other occupations and professions may sharpen, fine-tune, and clean their instruments; social workers must regulate, adjust, and fine-tune themselves to the specific needs and situation of the client. This is often referred to in the profession as "conscious use of self." According to Hollis, the worker must keep a conscious balance between the head and the heart, distance, and closeness (Hollis & Woods, 1981, pp. 311–313). This balance enables the worker to be objective enough to assess realistically the client's situation without becoming personally and emotionally involved and at the same time having the empathy that will help the client feel understood and less alone in his or her predicament.

In the past, social workers were trained to maintain a fairly formal and detached relationship stance with their clients. It was taboo to share personal information. Studies of self-disclosure have demonstrated that both client and worker need to engage in this process as the relationship is developing (Jourard, 1971). Genuineness is also an important factor in the development of an effective relationship (Truax & Carkhuff, 1976). There has been a shift toward a more relaxed, freer, open client–worker relationship. This change has resulted from the understanding that a client's need for distance and involvement on the part of the worker may vary according to the client's identified problem, needs, age, race, ethnicity, and gender (Hollis & Woods, 1981, p. 299).

For example, the need for interpersonal distance in relationships varies according to ethnicity. Some ethnic groups that are highly individualistic and independence-promoting may require greater space than other ethnic groups who are traditionally more interdependent because of their communal worldview. Therefore, a worker's formal and distant demeanor may feel comfortable to some clients but may be perceived as cold, indifferent, and suspect by other clients who expect more personalismo and platica in relationships (Sue, 1981, pp. 38–39).

Warmth, caring, and concern by the worker have been identified as nonspecific factors that contribute to effectiveness in treatment. Recent writings have also shown that women are more likely to pay attention to relationship factors than men (DeWaal, 2009; Garvin & Reed, 1995). With these imperatives in mind, workers should modulate their interpersonal demeanor and professional persona according to the specific needs of the client. This kind of chameleon-like adjustment is an ongoing and difficult task for interpersonal practitioners.

IMPORTANCE OF HOPE ●

The offering or instilling of hope has been recognized in the practice literature as a significant global strategy for building relationships and enhancing the effectiveness of helping interventions (Forsyth, 1990, pp. 471–483; Golan, 1978). Effective therapeutic support and self-help groups actively instill hope in their members. Workers who encounter clients in various types of crisis (suicidal, domestic violence, etc.) are encouraged to approach their clients with a firm sense that no matter how bad things are now that they can be better in the future. This sense of hope and optimism are essential to establishing relationships with the client in active crisis.

Medical and psychological studies of the "placebo effect" have demonstrated that when people are told that treatment has begun and they believe in the interventions, about 30% will immediately respond positively and begin to heal even when the intervention is a placebo (Jones, 1977; Rossi, 1986). When clients or patients have a strong sense of hope, confidence, and optimism that the intervention will be effective, the outcomes of the intervention will be more positive. These perceptions can be influenced by workers in the beginning of relationship building by offering hope and sharing the belief that the client can transcend his or her situation. When workers instill a sense that change is possible, client motivation to participate in service will also be enhanced (Miller & Rollnick, 2002).

The caveat to offering hope is that interpersonal practitioners do not make promises to clients in the beginning that everything will be OK. Workers are usually not psychic, nor do they have the power to guarantee outcomes. Offering hope that a more positive future is possible is very different from a guarantee that it will come to pass. Hope can go a long way toward the amelioration of the despair and disempowerment that many clients experience. Hope can turn around low motivation and apathy. Hope should spring eternal in the social work relationship.

This section of this chapter has presented the complexity of relationship as an important concept in social work practice. It has also described some studies and arguments emphasizing the importance of the professional relationship to social work practice and how complex and difficult professional relationships can be in a multicultural world. To underline the importance that relationships have in human experience, we remind readers of something they already know. In the history of cruelty and punishment, the most devastating and dehumanizing tactics are those that deny one individual's access to other human beings. Remember a time in your own life when you either committed or received the silent treatment from others for some social transgression. Remember how dehumanizing and cruel such a process can be. Think how cruel and depersonalizing solitary confinement is to prisoners and the impact exile has on the individual who must leave an important reference group. For many organized groups, exile was a punishment worse than death. The deliberate withdrawal, disruption, and elimination of social relationships are some of the cruelest punishments devised. On the other hand, the conscious and deliberate efforts of one human being to engage and relate to others can be a most healing and affirming experience. In the next section of this chapter, we discuss strategies that interpersonal practitioners employ to engage their clients in the helping process.

● THE INITIATION OF RELATIONSHIPS

Although the relationships between workers and clients contain many subtle elements created out of the unique nature of each person, there are five common elements that are sought in social work helping relationships. These elements have been extensively researched and consist of the following elements:

1. Social workers seek to attain *accurate communication* of thoughts and feelings between themselves and their clients.
2. Social workers seek to achieve *full communication* of pertinent information between themselves and their clients.
3. Social workers seek to communicate *feelings of warmth and caring* to their clients.
4. Social workers seek to create worker and client *complementary roles* so that each facilitates the other's contribution to the purposes of the interaction.
5. Social workers seek to create a *trust* that they and their clients will honor commitments made to each other.

Accurate Communication

We take for granted that human communication is a fairly simple exchange of information from the speaker to the listener, when in fact this process is fraught with many potential problems. In order for two individuals to share information,

| **Figure 6.1** | Human Communication—Transfer of Meaning |

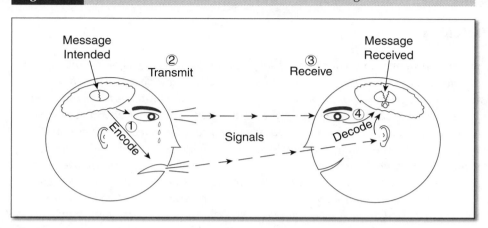

the communication process is a complex series of steps in which many problems may emerge (Seabury, 1980).

In a simple dyadic exchange, one person (the sender) transmits a thought or idea to another person (receiver). The idea is encoded into a set of signals, such as words, facial expressions, and hand gestures. These signals are sent out and received by the other person through sense receptors, such as eyes and ears, and then are decoded and understood by the brain. In human communication, it is unlikely that the idea sent will completely resemble the idea finally received. The process of (1) encoding, (2) transmitting, (3) receiving, and (4) decoding will inevitably change the information sent. In order to reduce these errors, human communication often involves continuous feedback between the two persons in the dyad, which helps to reduce these inevitable distortions. See Figure 6.1, which portrays human communication in a dyadic exchange.

Most people assume that words have meaning, when in fact meaning is in the users of words and in the context of the encounter (Scheflen, 1974). Some researchers of human communication suggest that words convey about 7% of the meaning in an encounter, vocalization conveys about 40% of the meaning, and posture and gestures convey over 50% of the meaning (Mehrabian, 1972). One of the essential skills that social workers must learn is "active listening," which not only involves paying careful attention to what clients say (i.e., words) but also listening to how the words are spoken (i.e., vocalization, tone, and volume) and also observing the nonverbal behavior (i.e., posture, gestures, and facial expressions) that accompany the words. Active listening is an intensive process and is a tiring process. In order to demonstrate how difficult this skill actually can be, we offer Exercise 6.3.

Exercise 6.3

Active Listening

This exercise can be performed in small as well as large classes. Students are organized into triads (i.e., groups of three). Each student will have the opportunity to play three different roles in the triad— speaker, listener, and observer/evaluator. The speaker role involves sharing with the listener what the speaker did over the past weekend. The speaker is given 3 minutes to share what they want to share. The listener may not take notes but can ask the speaker for clarification or elaboration if needed. The observer may take notes on what the speaker says. When the 3 minutes is up, then the listener states back to the speaker what they remember about the speaker's weekend. The observer can take notes at this point in the process, too. When the listener has finished, the observer then gives feedback to the listener about two errors that often enter this simple exchange. Errors of omission involve information that was missed in the listener's response, and errors of commission involve informa-tion that was added in the listener's response and was not in the speaker's original communica-tion. Sometimes students, because of years of oppression in the student role, like to give each other "grades" about the listener's accuracy, but this is not necessary to the success of this exercise. The students in the triad then exchange roles so that the process continues with a new speaker, new listener, and new observers. Students will realize that in a short 3-minute exchange with a fellow student, many errors may be introduced. In an hour interview with a new client, many more errors may appear.

For purposes of analysis, we divide accurate communication into transmission and reception of *thoughts* and *feelings*. By accurate, we mean that what the speaker intends to communicate has been "mostly" understood by the listener. We believe that accuracy in human communication is much more enhanced when the people in the encounter have known each other for a long time and have a lot of life expe-rience in common. When people are meeting for their first encounter, and they are from different life experiences, the chance of misunderstanding is much greater. As in Exercise 6.3, accuracy can be enhanced when the listener shares what they have understood of the speaker's communication. In most cases, however, social work-ers do not engage in such repetition because such responses can be experienced as mimicry, which has unpleasant connotations. Hearing our own words repeated back to us may also indicate that the listener has memorized our comments and is "parroting" them back rather than understanding them.

A concept relevant to what we have just been discussing is *empathy*, which is a central, biological feature of our humanity as social beings (DeWaal, 2009). For the interpersonal practitioner, empathy is the act of experiencing another person's responses as if one were that other person. The phrase "as if" is important because the concept of empathy relates to the act of experiencing something in a manner similar to another person while still retaining a sense of who one is and what one's separate responses may be. After a worker experiences another person in an empathic way, the worker may provide an empathic response in which he or she communicates what was understood.

The literature on empathic responding does not consistently make a clear distinction between responses to another's thoughts and feelings. Because these are two different types of reactions, we refer to a communication regarding another's feelings as an *empathic response* and another's thoughts as a *reflective response*.

Particularly in the beginning of a social work relationship, it is important for the interpersonal practitioner to provide empathic and reflective responses. The interpersonal practitioner is not yet sufficiently familiar with the client to be sure that his or her understanding of the communications of the client are correct. In addition, the client may not yet be sure that the worker is listening or that the worker correctly understands the client's communications. The worker must also facilitate the client's exploration of his or her situation and beginning of problem solving efforts. Empathic and reflective responses are softer, subtler, and less directive ways of reinforcing these client efforts than are direct questions.

Much research has been done on the relationship of empathic responses to therapeutic outcomes (Beutler, Machado, & Neufeldt, 1994). The initial research findings supported Carl Rogers's hypothesis (Rogers, 1957) that the so-called *facilitative conditions* of empathy, genuineness, and unconditional positive regard were necessary and sufficient conditions for desired therapeutic outcomes. As more research was done, however, the findings became mixed. We agree, therefore, with the following conclusion:

> Researchers of process and outcome of psychosocial interventions have accepted the wisdom of pursuing a more complex model. The importance of the "therapeutic relationship" is not dismissed but is included as one of a number of important factors to be considered. (Parloff, Waskow, & Wolfe, 1978, p. 251)

Because empathic and reflective responses are at least one important component of many helping processes, interpersonal practitioners should understand how to apply them and to identify those situations when they are required.

A complete empathic response has several components: One is a restatement in the worker's own words of the feeling the person experiences. In fact, empathy training programs have been devised (Milnes & Bertcher, 1980), and one of the first tasks is to train the student to recognize "feeling" words and their synonyms. A second component of an empathic and reflective response is a reference to the situation that elicited the feeling. For example, if a client says, "I was pissed off when I came home for supper and my wife was out," one possible empathic and reflective response may be "You were angry because your meal wasn't ready when you came home and because your wife wasn't there." The word *angry* is synonymous with "pissed off," and the situation was specified as the lack of a meal and the absence of the wife.

Work has also been done on rating levels of empathic and reflective responses. One such scale has five levels (Eisenberg & Delaney, 1977; Truax & Carkhuff, 1976).

The *first level*, the poorest response, is assigned to worker responses that demonstrate little awareness of the client's feelings, and the situational reference is also vague. An example of such a first level response to the previous statement ("I was pissed off when I came home for supper and my wife was out") might be "And what do you do at work?" Such a response does not reflect either the feelings or the situation. The *second level* connotes a misunderstanding of the intensity of the feeling, and the situational reference is not specific. For example, the workers response to the statement might be "You were irritated with your wife." The clients feelings of "pissed off" are more intense than irritation, and only the "wife" is specified when there is much more information in the client's statement. The *third level* is deemed the minimum facilitative one. Obvious feelings are correctly identified, and at least some aspects of the situation are specified. The response of "You were angry because your meal wasn't ready when you came home and because your wife wasn't there" reflects a third level response because it captures the intensity of the feeling and the situation that has caused the anger.

Fourth and fifth levels are reserved for worker responses that refer partially or fully to client feelings that are "deep" or not clearly expressed. This occurs when the situation in which the feelings are embedded is a highly personal or painful one. These levels assume that there are underlying feelings and issues that are not expressed in the manifest message. For example, in the previous example, the husband may have been extremely upset and anxious to find that his wife was not home when he arrived back from work. There may have been a "big fight" when he left for work in the morning and his wife threatened that she did not have to put up with him. A fourth level response might reflect his anger about her absence but also push the client to disclose more about the situation. For example, "I understand that you were angry that your wife was not there when you returned home from work, but I was also wondering if there wasn't something else going on in this situation?" There is a certain amount of "hypothesizing" that goes on with fourth and fifth level responses, and the interpersonal practitioner should be careful not to try to "mind read" what may be going on in the client's mind.

Many empathy training programs for volunteer and other "lay" helpers direct the trainees to restrict themselves to third level responses because of the risk of causing pain or confusion to the client through using the higher levels incorrectly or inappropriately. Fourth and fifth levels require advanced training in therapeutic communication. In the beginning stages of the social work process, it is wise to utilize third level responses so as not to prematurely direct the client into dealing with painful feelings. As Eisenberg and Delaney (1977) stated,

> Additive responses offered too early in the process can have a disruptive influence on the counseling relationship. Such responses may go beyond where the client is at the present time and thus threaten or intimidate the client. At the least, the client will become very self-conscious and monitor what he or she says. At worst, the client might become so threatened as to terminate. (p. 95)

Empathic and reflective responses at the third level primarily have the effect of letting the client know that his or her thoughts are understood as well as helping the worker to check out whether this understanding is correct. The effect on clients is to induce them to reflect further on the situation or to reconsider their points of view. The worker should be clear that this is what is desired, as too frequent use of empathic and reflective responses can be unpleasant to clients. After a trusting relationship has been established, workers can directly ask clients to elaborate on a discussion, examine a feeling, or reconsider a point of view. Reflective and empathic types of responses at the third level can then be reserved for times when support is required or when the worker is unclear about his or her understanding of the client's ideas and feelings.

Full Communication

When a honeybee returns to the hive after discovering a source of pollen, the bee engages in a dance. The other bees observe this dance and—depending on the direction of their dancing comrade—the hive learns in what direction and how far the source of pollen exists outside the hive (Wilson, 1973). It never occurs to the returning bee to "deliberately" make false moves in the dance and send his fellow bees on a "wild bee chase."

For humans, however, we often deliberately engage in deception when communicating with other folks. Paul Ekman (2001) has conducted research on human deception, and there is even a TV series based on this research called *Lie to Me*. There are many kinds of deception in human communication, such as hyperbole, omission, and falsifying; in some forms, the sender is not even aware that they are sending false information, such as confabulation.

There are also times when deception serves a positive social good (Kursh, 1971), such as telling a friend that her new hairdo looks attractive when in fact we think it looks atrocious. The relationship is more important than the ugly hairdo. The importance of this discussion is that full communication is more often an ideal than a reality in human communication, but it is still an ideal that the interpersonal practitioner should try to achieve in the relationships with the client.

By full communication, we refer to an interaction in which the worker and the client communicate *all* the thoughts and feelings they are aware of that will help them to attain their mutual purposes. Full communication incorporates two dimensions: *genuineness* and *self-disclosure*. Since our emphasis here is on worker responses that serve to build the helping relationship, we shall focus primarily on the worker's genuineness and self-disclosure.

By genuineness, we mean the interpersonal practitioner should be honest with clients and not deceive the applicant or client in any way about the service process. The interpersonal practitioner should not try to project a phony image of themselves or their professional role. We believe it is important that the student intern should state that they are an intern and are in training. They may also add that they are supervised by a person with a masters in social work (MSW). Clients may not want to hear this, but it is required by the ethical principle of informed consent, which was discussed in the values chapter (Chapter 3).

When asked a direct question by a client, there is a reluctance to sometimes admit that you don't know the answer. This may anger the client and seem to reduce the expertise of the practitioner, but we believe it is the correct response. When pressed by applicants who want a guarantee that service will produce a positive outcome, we strongly believe that interpersonal practitioner should never promise an outcome. We do believe that instilling hope in the service process is an important part of all helping relationships, but "hope" and "promise" are not the same thing. These issues will be discussed in greater detail in the contracting and group assessment chapters (Chapters 8 and 14).

There are many situations that arise in practice when the client does not engage in full communication, and we want to mention one that is common in human communication. Whenever people are asked to convey feelings or experiences, it is likely that the person will express themselves in "metaphors" (Barker, 1985). For example, a person may describe an intense, personal experience as "drowning" or "sinking into quicksand" or may even refer to a childhood story: "I felt like Goldilocks being discovered by the three bears!" These metaphors and allusions are not to be taken literally but to convey the threat the person experienced.

Because feelings and the subjective experiences of clients is an important aspect of interpersonal practice, interpersonal practitioners must carefully explore the meanings embedded in the metaphors and allusions that clients use (Barker, 1996; McAdams, 1993). For example, in some American Indian tribes, metaphors are frequently employed by adults to express themselves (Lum, 2005). In these tribes, a child's communication is direct and to the point, whereas adult communication is expected to rely heavily on metaphors to convey experience. When a white, Euro-American practitioner asks these adult clients for information about their experience, it will seem odd when the client replies with a story about the animal kingdom. The Euro-American practitioner should not view the response as tangential and possibly reflective of a thought disorder but instead should carefully listen to the themes and moral of the story. The psychiatric conclusions of the diagnostic worldview may miss the point of the client's communication, and the interpersonal practitioner may have to ask the client for help understanding the symbols and thematic meanings of the story.

In my (BAS) undergraduate education, I took Chinese language courses in order to be able to read and write Mandarin. In 1962, there were no textbooks for Mandarin printed in the United States, so our texts came from Communist China. Whenever the stories in the text referred to the United States, the two characters for the United States ("beautiful country") were always preceded by two modifier characters that translated to "capitalist pigs." At the time this seemed amusing, until our Chinese became good enough to translate newspaper articles written in Chinese. We learned that modern Mandarin was full of metaphors from classical Chinese that would appear routinely in the articles we were reading. For example, the concept of dilemma requires four characters that literally translated would be "difficulty getting off the back of a tiger," and the concept for confusion also required four characters, which literally translated would be "John's hat on Lee's head."

The point of this discussion is that different ethnic traditions have metaphors, allusions, and idioms that may seem strange to someone who does not share the linguistic and cultural experience. Full communication across an ethnic divide requires the interpersonal practitioner to work diligently to understand client's metaphors and the meanings these metaphors are conveying about the client's experiences.

Because of the controversy surrounding the issue of self-disclosure, this response has been the subject of a number of research efforts. Weiner (1978), who has reviewed this research as well as the therapeutic literature, has concluded that self-disclosure can be a useful worker response if careful judgment is exercised as to the nature of the therapeutic situation and the needs of the client. He discusses the use of self-disclosure, for example, in reference to a number of therapeutic strategies. When the strategy involves training the client, the worker's own experience with the training plan may help the client to follow the plan (Weiner, 1978).

Weiner (1978, p. 87) summarized the major occasions for self-disclosure as follows:

1. Enhance reality testing by defining the therapist as a real person and by defining the real patient–therapist relationship.

2. Heighten self-esteem by conveying respect, thus facilitating identification with a respected person (the therapist).

3. Provide feedback about the impact of the client on others.

4. Promote identification with positive aspects of the worker—for example, his or her calmness, reasonableness, and interpersonal skills.

5. Sufficiently gratify the client's transference and object needs to establish and maintain a therapeutic alliance.

6. Resolve certain transference resistances.

Weiner has developed a similar list of occasions when self-disclosure is very undesirable. Occasions include those when the therapist seeks to seduce a patient into a situation, including therapy, to which the patient is seriously opposed; those who primarily meet therapist needs; those who reinforce the patient's pathological patterns; and those who perpetuate the patient's dependence (Weiner, 1978, p. 102).

In conclusion, we believe that there are some occasions for the interpersonal practitioner to reveal personal experiences, attitudes, or feelings. Within some of the constraints described, there are times in most social work interactions for the interpersonal practitioner to engage in such self-disclosure.

Feelings of Warmth and Caring

The next dimension of the social work relationship we shall discuss is the communication of positive feelings from worker to client. This dimension is a subject of controversy as some social workers view it as overinvolvement. They argue that workers who care too much for clients are unable to remain objective and may seek to use clients to meet their own needs. We do not believe that caring for clients leads to these negative dimensions. Worker feelings that are harmful to clients do, of course, occur, but we believe that these do not stem from positive feelings toward the client but rather from feelings that workers have toward themselves and their own problems. In fact, caring for the client in the way we conceive is the opposite of using the client to meet one's own needs.

Evidence from a number of studies exists to support communication of the worker's caring feelings. Ripple, Alexander, and Polemis (1964), in a study of people who had good outcomes from casework service, found "the most important single variable was service and concern, not the skill in specific activities, but rather the amount of encouragement given the client during and immediately after the initial interview" (p. 199). Discouragement did not mean negative attitudes on the part of the worker but rather a "bland, seemingly uninvolved eliciting and appraisal of the client's situation, in which the worker appeared neutral in affect, left the client's discomfort untouched, and offered no basis for hope that the situation could be improved" (Ripple et al., 1964, pp. 201–203).

The dimension of caring is also closely related to the third of Rogers's (1957) facilitative conditions, which has been called "unconditional positive regard" or "nonpossessive warmth." These terms connote the idea that the worker maintains a spirit of warm goodwill toward the client regardless of what the client says, values the client as a human being, treats the client as a person with dignity, and "expresses continuing willingness to help no matter what the behavior of the client and no matter whether he approves or disapproves the client's behavior" (Shulman, 1978, p. 231). Finally, the worker takes interest in the client's concerns and pleasure in the client's achievements (Shulman, 1978).

Complementary Roles

This dimension of the social work relationship reflects the idea that in a functional interaction, each person facilitates the goal attainment of the other person. The role of the worker in this respect is to support the problem solving of the client individually or as a member of a family or other group. The role of the client is to engage in the work of solving problems and to provide the kind of information to the worker that will permit the worker to be helpful. These roles facilitate rather than hinder each other. At times in the social work process, however, roles emerge that require a more specific reciprocal response from the other person so that a constructive relationship can continue, and we shall discuss some of these.

At all times in a multiperson system, as we pointed out earlier in this chapter, the system has task requirements and social–emotional requirements. The task requirements relate to the phases of the problem solving effort. The social–emotional requirements relate to the management of tensions that threaten the system. When one person attends to the task requirements, others can complement this by attending to the social–emotional requirements. Frequently, in the social work process, the client engages in the task activity of problem solving. When this occurs, the interpersonal practitioner often attends to social–emotional requirements by responding to client feelings so as to reduce tensions. The reverse can also occur. A client and a practitioner may be intensively engaged in a problem solving activity as tensions mount. The client may then play a social–emotional role, for example, by using humor to reduce this tension. In these examples, the client and interpersonal practitioner are fulfilling complementary roles.

Another type of complementarity occurs through raising and answering questions. If both the interpersonal practitioner and the client see each other as only raising questions rather than seeking answers, conflict rather than complementarity may occur. There is no general rule for such issues; rather, the worker and the client should recognize when they are functioning in a conflictual manner, and the interpersonal practitioner should search for ways to resolve the conflict. In the chapter on clienthood, we discuss ways that the interpersonal practitioner and the applicant can reduce role conflicts in the beginning of the service process.

Another common example of complementarity involves one person in the role of speaker and the other in the role of listener. When interpersonal practitioner and client are from different ethnic and community backgrounds, there is likelihood that clients and practitioner may vie with each other to speak or even to remain silent. In some ethnic groups, there is a "chain rule" that expects the listener to be quiet and observant of the speaker and to wait for the chance to respond (Byers & Byers, 1972). To interrupt or speak while the other is speaking is viewed as rude and disrespectful, while in some ethnic groups the speaker and the listener are expected to be engaged in conversation simultaneously. It is expected that the speaking and listening functions are carried on simultaneously. In fact, when there is a lull in the conversation, each party will wait for someone to break the silence so they can go on communicating. These communication patterns can be demonstrated by the following classroom demonstration:

Find out who in the class has grown up in families "where everyone speaks simultaneously at family gatherings" and who has grown up in families "where only one person speaks at a time" and all others in the family gathering are listening. Pair up two class members from these different experiences, and have them try to have a conversation about what they did last weekend. Instruct each of the members of this dyad to stick to their comfortable pattern of conversing. The likely outcome of trying to "match" these two styles of communication will involve awkward starting and stopping of the dialogue. For example, when the "only one" starts to speak and then the "everyone speaks" starts to join the conversation, this joining will be viewed as interrupting and the "only one" person will stop speaking. When the "only one" stops speaking, the "everyone speaks" person will stop speaking because there is no one to speak with. What usually happens is the interchange will be difficult to maintain, and the two members of the dyad will find the experience unsatisfying.

Trust

The last component in our discussion of relationship is trust that interpersonal practitioners develop with their clients. In a relationship based on trust, both parties represent themselves honestly, and each honors commitments made to the other. Trust, therefore, is closely related to the full communication dimension we have described, but it also touches on additional issues.

One of these issues is the competence of the worker. The worker has represented himself or herself as being able to undertake the kind of helping activities the client requires. It would be naive to assume that workers are ready for all exigencies. Workers will at times confront client problems for which they lack competence. The broader issue regarding worker competence is that workers should know the limits of their abilities and should seek consultation, bring in other workers, or even refer a client to others when they have reached such limits. This is required by our professional code of ethics.

The client should be able to trust the worker's commitment to this principle. When asked, workers should answer questions honestly regarding their abilities. Some clients will use this issue to express hostility to workers (i.e., to question their competence), but this type of client reaction should be discussed and explored.

Another component of trust is confidentiality. The commitment that an interpersonal practitioner makes to all clients is that nothing will be revealed about the client without the client's knowledge. This implies that the type of records the worker and the agency keep will be confidential and available to the client. Recent legal decisions have often required workers to make the client's case records available to the client. This poses problems for some workers who use technical jargon to describe clients or who record conjectures regarding the meaning of client behavior. In some cases, the client's knowledge of this will not harm the client as much as some workers fear. In other cases, it is clear that workers will have to refrain from placing such material in records. We feel that this change will not have the dire effects some practitioners predict. In fact, benefits may accrue in terms of a reduction in the number of unsubstantiated inferences and labels attached to clients.

An issue that is more crucial than the client's *knowledge* of dissemination of information about them is their *consent* to this. The ethical rule is that nothing is revealed about the client without the client's consent. We accept the idea, however, that there can be exceptions to this rule—exceptions that are explained to the client in advance. Social workers do not promise to keep information confidential when this will endanger the lives of clients or others. In general, social workers do not commit themselves to keep their knowledge of illegal acts confidential but will report this to the appropriate authorities. The usual approach, however, is to help clients to take this responsibility themselves. This situation usually occurs when the offense is serious: Social workers are not in the business of reporting minor traffic violations but will take seriously the offense of a client who was a "hit and run" driver by urging the client to report the event or ultimately by reporting it themselves.

Some clients, such as young children, acutely psychotic, and the severely developmentally disabled, may not be capable of making decisions regarding confidentiality. The worker in such situations will secure releases from family members or others responsible for such clients or from people who represent the interests of the client.

The issue of confidentiality, in addition to the worker's provision of information to others, includes securing information. The client is always regarded as the primary source of information about himself or herself, and the worker should ask the client's permission to obtain information from others. The client has the right to have that information shared with him or her, and the informant is told when the client wishes to exercise this right.

● RELATIONSHIPS IN GROUP SITUATIONS

In group work, workers seek to develop among the members as well as with themselves the relationship dimensions we have previously described.

1. *Accurate Communication.* Workers will describe the processes of empathy and of reflective responses to members and will seek to model these. Workers can train members to make empathic responses through role plays, tapes, and reinforcement of these responses when they occur naturally. Workers will, at times, use such exercises as asking members to repeat the statement of the member who had previously spoken before making additional remarks. This has the effect of both providing feedback to the previous speaker and ensuring that members listen carefully to one another. When this is done in groups, it is after the group has identified inaccurate communication as a problem and has agreed to handle it in this way.

2. *Full Communication.* The issue of disclosure is a very important one in groups, as many persons express anxiety about sharing personal information in group situations. This issue, therefore, is often discussed with the group at the

first meeting. Sometimes, exercises focused on this problem are used. For example, members are asked to think of an issue they are reluctant to discuss in the group. They then are asked to imagine sharing this information as well as the reactions of other group members to this. The kinds of anticipated reactions (not the actual sensitive topic) are then discussed in the group. This usually has the effect of encouraging the members to take greater risks in sharing information about themselves.

With regard to full communication, we previously also discussed the importance of correspondence between verbal and nonverbal communications. Members are usually not confronted in early meetings about a lack of correspondence between these aspects of communication as this will often be too threatening. After early meetings, however, this represents an important kind of feedback in groups devoted to helping members resolve problems in interpersonal communication.

3. *Feelings of Caring.* Members will work on their problems in group situations when they ascertain that the other members care for them; otherwise, they will be reluctant to give or take help from them. The worker, therefore, will reinforce expressions of caring among the members and will seek to resolve interactions that prevent this type of caring from emerging. In the chapter on group assessment, we will talk more about the importance of "altruism" as an important therapeutic variable in groups.

At times in groups, the members will express such caring for a member who, because of self-concept problems, will be unable to recognize or accept it. The member may even declare that the others are not honest in that expression. Helping the member to recognize this type of perceptual distortion can be invaluable in enhancing that member's relationships. Ultimately, expressions of caring among members in the group will be one of the most treasured aspects of the experience because it cannot be discounted, as it may be from the worker, on the basis of "that's her job!"

4. *Complementary Roles.* The role structure in groups is more complex than in one-to-one situations because of the number of individuals involved. Members will initially have to be helped to understand what the role of member is—namely, each individual has a responsibility for the welfare of the group and the other members in it. The role of the worker must also be understood as one who facilitates the way in which *members* take responsibility for the group. Beyond this, in ways that we discuss later in this book, the worker helps members to complement each other in the way they share leadership roles, task roles, and other group facilitation roles, such as mediator, negotiator, spokesperson regarding norms, and provider of emotional support. A good distribution of roles helps each person to

feel that he or she is important to the group. An exercise used by workers to enhance this is for the group to list the roles needed and compare this with the roles that each member has fulfilled.

5. *Trust.* Of equal importance with these dimensions is trust. This aspect of relationships among members includes expectations that all will attend regularly, come on time, and maintain confidentiality. Trust presumes a desire to help rather than to harm one another and a commitment to be truthful in giving feedback.

Each of these dimensions of one-to-one relationships as well as group relationships takes time to develop. The worker, however, must understand the nature of relationships, help the clients to understand them, and, from the very beginning, find ways of facilitating the development of each dimension. The relationship dimension is important because, in addition to the fact that it provides support for problem solving, clients invariably seek help with problems in relationships. The learning that comes from working on relationships with the worker, and in groups, with other members, is a prototype for skills to be employed in life beyond the social work situation.

● RELATIONSHIPS IN FAMILY SITUATIONS

The relationship that the worker seeks with family members, when the worker is interacting with an entire family (or with several but not all family members), differs from the one that the worker seeks in group and one-to-one helping situations. This difference is due to the fact that the family members have had long-standing relationships with each other well before the worker has entered the scene. In addition, the worker's target is usually the family, as a system, rather than the behavior of each family member singly. These relationship differences relate to the following propositions:

1. The family "problem" often lies in the kinds of relationships that exist among some or all family members. Thus, some members may be rejected or scapegoated by others or, in contrast, may be the ones most frequently approached for solutions to problems or for nurturance. Families frequently act to draw the worker into these patterns, particularly when the pattern is dysfunctional for the family. The worker, therefore, must be very aware of the kinds of relationship patterns the family seeks to establish with him or her.

2. Another kind of pattern families may seek to establish with the worker is for the worker to have closer relationships with some family members than with others. Again, this pattern may not be a desirable one for the family, and the worker must then avoid this. The worker, particularly in the beginning, seeks to establish relationships with *all* family members. These can be initiated by referring to each family member by name and interacting, however briefly, with each person. The worker must make extra efforts to initiate interactions with the members of the family who are most passive in the family session. The worker may also first seek to establish a relationship with family members (e.g., the mother, father, or grandparent) who can influence the family's decision to return for subsequent sessions.

3. The list of relationship dimensions with which we began this section of the chapter can be used to assess relationship patterns within the family that are either related to the presenting problems of the family or the family's strengths for problem solving. The worker will use this knowledge to seek to change some family relationship patterns or to reinforce others. We do not deal with this topic extensively here as it will be a major one when we consider family assessment later in this book. A few illustrations, however, will help to clarify this point.

In reference to *accurate communication*, family members as well as those in any group often distort their communications to each other to maintain dysfunctional roles or power positions. In *one* family, the husband failed to express any empathy with his wife's anger about his neglect of family responsibilities because he did not wish to increase these responsibilities. In another family, a father did not reflect any understanding of his son's school difficulties, even though the son discussed these, because the father did not believe he had the skills to intervene on behalf of his son.

In regard to *full communication*, a wife did not tell her husband about some of the difficulties that were occurring in her life for fear that he would be angry with her for her presumed incompetence. The husband, in turn, did not describe some relationships he had with nonfamily members for fear his wife would be jealous of these. The *feelings of caring* dimension is a crucial one, also, with respect to family relationships, as the family is one of the main institutions in society for receiving and offering caring. The worker noticed in one family that when a child approached the father, the father responded in a bland, mechanical, and uncaring manner. The worker subsequently learned that the father did not believe he was the biological father of this child, and his unresponsiveness was an important dimension of his relationship with both the mother and the child.

● SUMMARY

We want to remind the reader that whole texts have been devoted to relationship issues, whereas we presented a chapter that highlights the many ways that relationship has been conceptualized in social work practice. This chapter is loaded with terms and issues that arise when interpersonal practitioners relate to their clients. Many of the processes we point out are taken for granted by all of us when we form relationships. For example, we know intuitively that if you do not listen to someone else, are not particularly friendly and attentive, and do not try to get to know the other person, it is unlikely that a relationship will develop.

We also know that it is difficult to relate to people who have vastly different life experiences from ourselves. In the professional relationship, though, it cannot be left up to chance that the relationship will develop, and the interpersonal practitioner must take responsibility for creating the relationship with the client. For this reason, an interpersonal practitioner must know what steps and procedures are most likely to produce an effective working relationship.

In summarizing this chapter, we present an exercise that reviews main points we have presented. Exercise 6.4 can be completed alone; however, it will be even more meaningful if you compare your experiences with a classmate. You do not have to disclose the actual relationships being reviewed, only the various principles operating in each scenario.

Exercise 6.4

Dimensions of Positive and Negative Relationships

Recall a significant relationship in your life that was close and positive, and also recall a significant relationship in your life that was problematic and full of conflicts. These relationships may involve family members, close friends, or relationships that you formed at school or work. Using these two relationships as comparative reference points, assess each relationship on the following dimensions. These dimensions have been discussed in this chapter and represent basic principles of relationship formation.

1. How similar were you to the other person in the relationship? What were major differences— gender, race, ethnicity, age, religion, social class, sexual orientation, etc.—between you and the other person?

2. How did these relationships develop over time? Did they seem to bloom or dissolve as you and the other person got to know each other better?

3. *How much warmth, genuineness, and empathy developed in these relationships? Were you and the other person able to understand each other, to share important information about yourselves, and to communicate openly any affection that you might have felt for each other?*

4. *Did you and this other person care about your relationship? How much did these relationships matter to you? How much kindness, consideration, and respect was shown in these relationships?*

5. *Did you and this other person develop trust? Were you able to communicate fully with this other person and share intimate details about your life yet realize that what you shared would be held in confidence?*

When comparing these two relationship experiences on these five suggested dimensions, you may find dramatic differences in these relationships. Check to see what your classmates' experiences have been with positive and negative relationships.

CHAPTER 7

BECOMING A CLIENT

When seeking urgent care for "walking pneumonia" in a large university hospital, I (Brett A. Seabury, or BAS) was told by the urgent care receptionist that in order to be seen in the urgent care unit, I would need a "blue card." My university ID, Blue Cross Blue Shield (BCBS) card, and my Visa card were not enough credentials to get me services. I was told to follow a "blue line" on the floor until I reached the registration area where I could receive my blue card. I was feverish so I did not hear the nurse explain that I had to follow this blue line on another floor of the hospital. In the hallway outside the urgent care unit were blue, red, and yellow lines on the floor. I proceeded to follow the blue line on the floor, and it came to a locked door in the hallway. I returned to the urgent care unit and told the receptionist about the locked hallway door. She questioned me about which floor and explained that I needed to go down to the second floor. When I finally arrived in the reception area, which had a large waiting area that was completely empty, I went to the counter and started to explain that I needed to register for the blue card. The receptionist told me to take a number and go sit in the empty waiting area. This seemed like a foolish request, but I docilely complied realizing that I did not want to antagonize the receptionist and jeopardize my chance of getting that important blue card. After about 10 minutes in the waiting area, my number was called and I was told to go around the reception desk to an area with a number of partitioned work areas that contained a table with a chair and computer on the other side from my chair. I sat down and waited for someone to appear in my partitioned area. Another person looked around the partition and told me that I was sitting in the wrong area and would have to move over one cubicle so she could complete the information for the "essential" blue card. By now my fever had climbed because it was late in the afternoon so this information interview was difficult for me to handle. She began typing information into the computer and asking many questions, as well as asking for documents to "prove" the information I was giving her. She asked me for my date of birth, but unfortunately I only heard the word date and I responded with today's date. She proceeded to type in this date and then became angry. She asked, "Are you trying to be funny? I've had a long day and don't appreciate your humor! Now tell me what is your date of birth?" My date of birth was on my driver's license, which she had already made a copy of, but I did not point this out to her. Instead I docilely complied and gave her my date of birth. She told me to return to the waiting area and wait for my card. After a long wait (i.e., from my perceptions as someone with a high fever) my name was announced over the intercom to return to the receptionist to pick up my card. There were still no other patients in this area. When I returned to the desk to pick up my blue card, I was again asked to show ID before it was given to me. I returned to the urgent care unit only to discover that it was closed, and I then had to go to the ER for service. I knew better than to go to the ER because I would probably have to wait all night before being seen. Instead I went home, took a bunch of aspirin, and hoped I would be alive in the morning to start my journey all over again in the urgent care unit. This is a true story.

We begin this chapter with an exercise (Exercise 7.1) that will help social work students understand the experience of becoming a client in an agency. Hopefully this experience will raise the students' consciousness about some of the feelings that are associated with entering the client role. Students who have completed this exercise as an assignment in our courses are sometimes reluctant to complete it because they do not believe they are eligible for these services. They are also worried that a friend might see them going into the local welfare office, which brings home the stigma many clients feel when they become recipients of service. Some instructors may find this exercise somewhat controversial because it involves a real agency in the real world. Our response has been to point out that any citizen has the right to approach a public service and see if they are eligible to receive benefits. In some cases, students have actually been eligible for the services for which they applied.

Exercise 7.1

Applicant Experience

In this exercise, you are to go to your local Department of Public Welfare (DPW) and apply for food stamps. When you arrive, carefully observe the demeanor of the security guard (if there is one) and the receptionist when you enter the building. Look around the waiting area and observe the kinds of furniture, decor, magazines, etc. Are there long lines poorly marked? Are folks milling around or just sitting in chairs waiting to be served? How did you figure out where to start? How long was the form you finally received? Were the questions clearly stated? Did anyone offer to help you fill it out? How did you feel about answering these questions? Did you have to make a special appointment with a worker to see if you could receive benefits? How much time did you spend in the agency waiting, filling out forms, talking with personnel, and trying to come up with documentation? How did this application process make you feel? Share your experiences with your classmates and see what their experiences were.

This chapter describes how individuals in the society become the recipients of social work services. The term *client* is customarily used to refer to such recipients and is defined as the person or persons who come for help to a social agency and who expect to benefit directly from it; who determine, usually after some exploration and negotiation, that this was an appropriate move; and who enter into an agreement—referred to as a contract—with the social worker with regard to the terms of such service.

In this chapter, we discuss some of the details of how people become clients. There are many reasons why individuals seek help. Some individuals are pushed or dragged in by significant others, some individuals are mandated by courts to appear, and even some of those who seem to come voluntarily have little motivation to make changes in their lives. In the initial interview, an interpersonal practitioner may also have contact with others on behalf of clients, which also creates special obligations to these significant others.

● DEFINITION OF A CLIENT

Although the word *client* is widely used in social work practice, there is some controversy that surrounds the use of this term. Lawyers, engineers, and architects all refer to those whom they serve as clients. Opponents of the term *client* insist that the social work relationship is different (Galper, 1980). Clients in many other professions are manipulated in some way (a surgical operation), are given a product (a building), or are represented before a third party (a law court). In social work, in contrast, the major task of the worker is to facilitate the work of clients on their own behalf. Some opponents of the term *client* also believe that the status and power differences between professionals and clients in other professions should not be present in social work relationships. An alternative term, however, has not gained acceptance, although terms such as *service user* or *service recipient* have been suggested.

A notable exception to the use of the word *client* in social work is the use of the word *member* in group work. Many group workers prefer this term because the vehicle of service is the group, and if any entity is the client, for them it is the entire group. There are models of group work, however, in which the individual member is viewed as the client.

Although social work relationships are not identical with those in other professions, we still choose to use the word *client* in this book because of its wide acceptance. We believe the use of this term has not prevented recognition of the special aspects of the social work client role, including those noted by the critics of the term.

In the formative years of the social work profession, casework was the prominent modality, and the term *client* was understood to mean a single individual. With an increase in work with groups and whole families, the term has been extended to include more than one person, as when several people seek help for themselves as a family, a group, or even an organization (Pincus & Minahan, 1973). To avoid some confusion, the phrase *client system* was introduced in Chapter 2, and we shall employ *client* and *client system* interchangeably.

OVERVIEW OF THE CLIENTHOOD PROCESS ●

There is no guarantee that an individual or family who approaches a social agency for help will be accepted for service. Even when individuals are captured or mandated for services, these individuals may not end up receiving the services mandated. This chapter looks carefully at the many issues and steps in the process of becoming a client in a social agency. To clarify this entry level process, we present a visual metaphor that will help the interpersonal practitioner conceptualize what is going on in the context of becoming a client.

There are four dimensions reflected in this metaphor (see Figure 7.1). At the top are the potential users who might seek services. The distinctive characteristic of potential users is their diversity. Look around a room full of people (such as a large classroom), and you will see many different shapes, sizes, colors, ages,

Figure 7.1 Model of the Service Delivery System

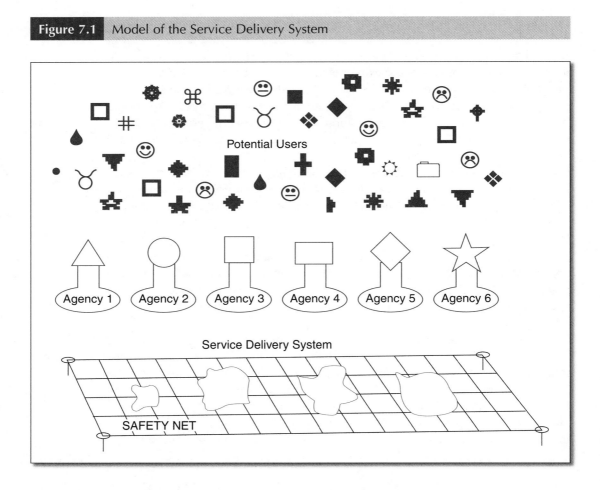

hairstyles, and clothing styles. In fact, it is often difficult to see what a group of folks have in common, such as studenthood. Individuals may have common needs, but they have multifaceted lives and are faced with many different kinds of problems and troubles. Some individuals may be struggling with several problems, such as substance abuse, unemployment, and depression; others may have only one major issue they are trying to resolve.

The next dimension of this model are the "jugs," or "pots," that represent the various service agencies that might be located in a community or geographical area. These agencies are designed to serve particular kinds of users with particular kinds of problems. For example, some agencies would be designed to serve potential users with mental illness, others with substance abuse problems, others with domestic violence, others with financial planning or job placement needs, etc.

In large urban areas, there are many different kinds of agencies serving many different kinds of clients with different problems, and service directories often resemble large phone books with information about each organization.

In an ideal service delivery system, there would be no overlaps and no gaps. Each agency would serve or reach potential clients with a particular social problem. The third dimension of our model is reflected in the mouth of each jug, or pot. The entrance to the agency allows some potential users to pass through, whereas others are screened out and expected to be served by other agencies designed to meet their particular needs. The mouth, or entrance, of each jug is usually controlled by some kind of intake person who is employed as a gatekeeper for that agency. In many agencies, this gatekeeper is a social worker whose job is to screen applicants as they come to the agency and decide whether to accept them for service or to refer them to other agencies in the service delivery system.

Studies of communities have demonstrated that there are several layers to the service delivery system, with some agencies acting as frontline agencies and others acting as feeder agencies to other agencies (Cummings, 1968). Recently, these second- or third-line agencies have been called the "safety net" that is designed to catch potential users who do not fit into the frontline agencies. Examples of agencies in the safety net are homeless shelters, soup kitchens, and— unfortunately in today's world—jails and prisons. Some services are connected to neighborhood agencies or churches, and in most cases they represent the last chance—the fourth dimension of our model—for users to get help. Unfortunately, in the real world, there are holes in this safety net, and some folks fall all the way through the service delivery system to the "streets" and "Dumpsters," eking out an existence living in abandoned buildings or under thruway overpasses and panhandling for change.

When individuals or families seek help in this imperfect and complex service delivery system, there are many chances to fall through the cracks, to be screened out by various agencies, or to become exhausted in a "referral fatigue" process of being passed from one agency to another (Lantz & Lenahan, 1976). When applicants enter an agency, they must be able to build a good case with the intake worker so that they fit the agency's definition of whom the agency serves. Some applicants who come with multiple problems are told they cannot get services in one agency until another agency tackles the applicant's other problems. For example, dually diagnosed clients may be told they have to deal with their substance abuse problem before they can receive help for their psychiatric or marital problems, even though these problems may be significantly interrelated. The tendency of the service delivery system to specialize in problem areas means that some potential users may get passed back and forth between agencies and little service gets delivered.

We discuss in the individual change chapter (Chapter 11) how the interpersonal practitioner can help clients to navigate the maze of services in a community so that applicants have a better chance of being accepted for service and a better chance of continuing in service until some kind of help has been realized. The point we want to emphasize here is that many more people may be eligible for services than actually receive them and that many individuals and families are lost or screened out when trying to become clients in human service agencies. Some studies of the screening process have suggested that as many as half the applicants seeking services are not able to attain them (Kirk & Greenley, 1974). Even when these clients are followed through several steps of the service delivery system (see Figure 7.2), only about half receive the services they are seeking. A baseball batting average of .470 may be a good average, but it is a terrible fielding average and probably would get a child benched in Little League.

Case loss is a serious service delivery problem. It is made even more problematic when frontline agencies "cream" and accept only "ideal" clients. In today's world, an ideal client, according to some, has the ability to pay (insurance or wealth), has problems that can be addressed quickly and solved (no chronic or complicating situations), and is strongly motivated to work on his or her troubles. Unfortunately, many applicants who arrive on the doorsteps of agencies are poor, have serious and complicated social problems, and feel apathetic about their chances of resolving their problematic situations.

Another complicating factor is the lack of support for public social services and the cutbacks in support for human services. This limits the availability of service and further makes it more difficult for applicants to find services for their problems. For example, when substance abuse programs are cut back or

Figure 7.2   Applicant Loss in the Service Delivery System

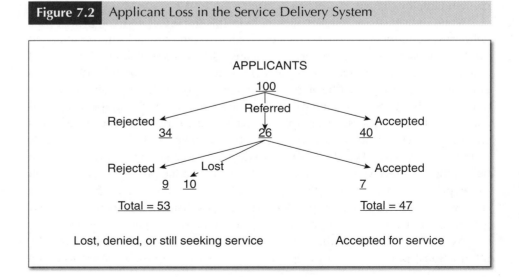

eliminated, the waiting lists at remaining clinics get longer and longer. When applicants are placed on waiting lists—especially long waiting lists—the likelihood that they will drop out of service is increased significantly (Talmon, 1990). We discuss these and other complicating issues in more detail in the rest of this chapter.

PATHWAYS TO CLIENTHOOD ●

Voluntary Clients

Some clients voluntarily seek out the services of a social worker or social agency. These are frequently people whom the community considers to be "normal" and whose problems may well occur in the course of socialization into such life phases as adolescence, parenthood, or retirement. They may, for example, seek help in making crucial decisions relevant to their role transition. Another group of people seeking help on a voluntary basis are those who experience an event beyond their control, such as a natural disaster.

Other voluntary clients are those who wish to improve their social skills or who wish to resolve identity or relationship concerns. These clients often come from social or educational backgrounds that are supportive of psychologically oriented services and are usually the more affluent members of the community. Such potential clients are unlikely to seek services from public agencies because they associate these with poor or otherwise stigmatized groups. They may, however, seek private, possibly sectarian (on either a religious or ethnic basis) agencies or private practitioners.

Voluntary clients usually hear about services from publicity disseminated by the agency or are told about services by other professionals (school personnel, physicians, employers). Agencies will often distribute news releases about such services as parent education, support groups for single parents, preparation for retirement activities, and programs to facilitate career planning.

Nonvoluntary Clients

There is a category of clients who fall between the voluntary and involuntary client—ones that we call nonvoluntary (Garvin & Glasser, 1974). If they do not accept services, these clients do not face legal or other serious social sanctions, but they are pressured to do so. Examples are people whom others see as having problems, such as a wife who views her husband as causing their marital stress, a teacher who assesses a student as having emotional problems that interfere with learning, and an employer who believes that an employee's substance use causes job-related difficulties.

In these types of nonvoluntary situations, clients are not legally required to accept services, but they may suffer unpleasant consequences if they refuse: The wife may leave her husband, the teacher may not promote the student, and the employer may fire the employee. We believe that a large proportion of social work clients are nonvoluntary and that this fact must be dealt with if the client is to benefit from services.

Involuntary Clients

The third type of client is the involuntary one, who is either legally required (i.e., mandated) to utilize services or subjected to some unpleasant social sanction for refusing services (Rooney, 2009). Examples are people who have been placed on probation or parole and are required to see a social worker as a condition of their liberty or people who are caught driving while intoxicated and must attend substance abuse treatment as a condition of getting back their driver's license. Protective service situations in which one member of a family has abused another may also fall in this category. In this latter situation, the protective service agency must investigate certain categories of abuse, such as child abuse, and may institute court proceedings against a family member.

In a sense, there is no such thing as an involuntary client, as we defined a client as a person or persons who accept a contract for social work services. In addition, as we discussed earlier, a major value in social work practice is self-determination and client empowerment. The value, however, that social workers place on individual life and growth induces them to encourage and even pressure many involuntary persons to accept services. In any case, the fact that the referral for social work services has been made despite the individual's preferences has profound implications for how the worker will initiate contact.

In order to dramatize the experience of being forced to see an interpersonal practitioner, we present an exercise that we have used in our classes that reinforces how nonvoluntary individuals may feel and behave when they are pushed or dragged into counseling. Because it involves sharing sensitive information from a student's past, this class exercise is voluntary for students and is not shared with the whole class. See Exercise 7.2.

● THE ENTRY PROCESS

Whether individuals enter the agency on a voluntary, nonvoluntary, or involuntary basis, the worker must consider the applicants' feelings about this entry as well as their perceptions of it and the events leading up to it. We turn now to a consideration of these phenomena and the worker's responses to them.

Exercise 7.2

Empathizing With Nonvoluntary Applicants

Think of a time in your life when you were forced by someone more powerful than you (e.g., parent, guardian, or teacher) to have an interaction with someone who was supposed to help you, but you did not want to talk with this "helper." Recall how you felt about being pressured to see this "helper." How did you behave in this session? Were you open about your feelings, and did you supply much information to this "helper"? What did this helper do to facilitate or not to facilitate the initial encounter? Generalize from this personal experience to the kinds of lessons that interpersonal practitioners should understand when they work with applicants who do not want to be seen.

We want to be clear that it is not just about the applicant's motivation or "resistance" that determines whether the applicant will be able to become a client in an agency (Miller & Rollnick, 2002). There may be some sources of reluctance that come from within the client, but, from a systemic point of view, there are also sources within the agency and the social worker that contribute to the failure of the applicant's entry into the agency. The classic article "Hard to Reach, Client or Casework Agency," which was written over 50 years ago, warns the social worker not to blame the client for the failure (i.e., discontinuance) of service (Lindenberg, 1958). The bureaucratic processes in the agency may deter clients from receiving help. Remember the case example that was presented at the beginning of this chapter.

Not only do agency procedures cause trouble but sometimes the applicant and the interpersonal practitioner are a poor match (Palmer, 1973). In the initial impression of the applicant, the interpersonal practitioner may appear too young or too old, too white or too Black, too casual or too formal, the wrong gender or ethnicity, etc. We have discussed how these mismatches occur in practice, and the chapters on diversity and relationship (Chapters 4 and 6) present these issues in great detail and suggest how the interpersonal practitioner may become more effective in bridging these issues.

Feelings About Clienthood

People are likely to approach a social agency with mixed feelings—even those who do so voluntarily (Miller & Rollnick, 2002). Positive feelings will derive from the idea that the agency may be of help and will create new opportunities, that the staff will be enjoyable to interact with, and that burdens may be shared. Negative feelings are likely to be present because the service may be seen as doing no good or even doing harm to a person. Clients may have heard stories about incompetent staff, or they may even have had negative experiences with such people.

Because some applicants suffer from the stigma associated with their troubles, they may be viewed by friends or relatives as "crazy." Others may believe that only inadequate, poor, or other undesirable types of people use social services. There are psychological costs when one asks another, particularly a professional, for help. One often feels that this places the helper in a superior position because the helper learns the ways in which the client is vulnerable. Because the interpersonal practitioner works within the auspices of the agency and is granted professional status, there is a significant power differential between the applicant and the social worker. The applicant or client is in the low power position, and we discuss approaches to dealing with these concerns later in this chapter and later chapters on individual, family, and group change (Chapters 11, 13, and 15).

Perceptions of Agencies

The way in which the agency is perceived by the applicant may have an impact on the person's approach to services. There are both subjective and objective components to the applicant's views. The subjective ones relate to the applicant's unique history—whether the applicant has received social work services before, what outcome was produced, what other ways the applicant has sought help, and how strongly the applicant now feels that help is necessary.

In addition, the agency may affect the perceptions of applicants by virtue of the services it has previously provided. Former clients may speak about their agency experiences in the community, and these stories may be repeated and sometimes magnified. The agency may also have contemporary effects based on its location and its physical appearance. Some agencies are housed in storefronts, some in converted churches, some in impressive buildings, and some in old, rundown structures. All people may not be affected in the same way: An affluent person may be uncomfortable *in* the rundown structure, whereas a poor person may be uncomfortable in an extremely elegant one. We speak here of extremes— few, if any, people will wish to remain in a setting that does not communicate respect for clients through adequate maintenance and furnishings.

Applicants may be affected by how they are greeted when they enter the building. Some receptionists are courteous and respectful; others are unfriendly and aloof. Confidentiality may or may not be observed by what is asked in the waiting room and how it is asked. Applicants' names may be called out over a public address system in a crowded waiting area that their intake interview is ready. The waiting area may be pleasant and comfortable or stark and in disrepair (Seabury, 1971).

Events Leading to Clienthood

The individual's way of experiencing the agency will also be affected by the events leading up to the application. A crisis in the life of the client constitutes one type of event. A crisis is a sudden occurrence that is experienced as overwhelming. Individuals who experience a crisis are often very receptive to help from a professional and may even feel desperate for it. More about crisis theory and crisis assessment is presented in the chapters on individual assessment and individual change (Chapters 10 and 11).

Not all applicants who appear in social agencies in active crisis will fall into the "voluntary" category. It is also possible that the circumstances leading up to an involuntary referral (e.g., arrest or psychiatric commitment) may have precipitated the crisis.

Because of the likelihood that some resolution of the crisis will take place within several weeks of the event and motivation for help will then drop, it is important that people in crisis receive an appointment soon after calling. For this reason, many agencies that previously maintained waiting lists abandoned this practice. People who called for an appointment were either seen immediately, if staff were available, or were referred to other resources. Studies demonstrate that if clients are not called back within 24 hours of contacting an agency and an appointment scheduled promptly, the likelihood is great that the client will not appear for the intake interview (Talmon, 1990).

Many clients, however, are not in a crisis when they apply for social work services. This, then, raises the issue of why the client has appeared in a social agency at this time. What events may have occurred or what situations changed that have lead to this encounter? In systems terms, something must have shifted in the equilibrium within the individual or between the individual and other individuals and objects in the environment. The worker will seek to understand the nature of these events because these events can—and usually do—have profound effects on subsequent work with the client. For example, the client's motivation to accept help may have changed because of changes in the family, such as separation, economic hardship, death, etc.

The client's motivation to involve himself or herself in social work services will be a function of the client's perceptions about his or her life situation. If the client perceives this situation as having so seriously deteriorated that change is hopeless, motivation will be low. The client must either believe that a previous situation can be restored or that a tolerable substitute can be found (Miller & Rollnick, 2002; Stotland, 1969). An example of this is an applicant who was divorced from her husband. She wished to either explore the possibility of a reconciliation with him or learn ways of rebuilding her social life. Because she believed that one of these two outcomes was possible, her motivation for becoming a client was high. Another woman, however, whose husband had died, believed she would never reestablish that kind of relationship and that she was doomed to a lonely existence. Her motivation for service, consequently, was low. This does not preclude working with the poorly motivated client, but it indicates that steps must be taken to heighten motivation in those who lack it, for example, by reducing the ambivalence for coming to the agency (Miller & Rollnick, 2002).

The client's motivation will also be related to his or her feelings about the event or situation that led to seeking service. The feelings to assess are the degree of discomfort the client experiences and the degree of hope the client has that change will occur. When the costs of not changing are high and the expectation that change is possible, the intrinsic motivation to participate in service will be enhanced (Miller & Rollnick, 2002).

The immediate events or situational changes that lead to seeking services will have effects on what the client seeks to modify—namely, the targets of change. Some clients seek to change their environments, some themselves, and some both. The client is likely to select some aspect of the environment when the environment has recently undergone some change, whether or not this will substantially reduce the problem. Thus, a youth who came to an agency, after being expelled from school, immediately sought help with selecting a new school rather than with looking at his behavior that led to this expulsion.

People actually make contact with agencies in a variety of ways. Some hear about a service that relates to their needs through newspapers, radio and television announcements, and other communications of the mass media. Others are approached through community outreach efforts of agencies. At one time, agencies assumed that people who needed their services would either know of these or be referred by those who did. This was not true of many people who most needed services because they were the poorest, the least educated, and the newest to the community. In the 1960s, when concern for such people was high in the United States, agencies considered new ways to reach out. This included engaging in door-to-door contacts (Bush, 1977); placing staff as speakers in churches, schools, barber shops, bars, and other indigenous institutions (Weiner, Becker, & Friedman, 1967); and having staff approach people living in at risk situations by reason of exposure to poor housing, health hazards, economic hardships, and similar stresses.

The issue of access to social agencies is a crucial one for members of many ethnic groups. Some of the most necessary services are not available in many Asian

American, Latino, Native American, and African American communities. Even when these services are located there, they are likely to be staffed by people who do not come from the ethnic groups in the community. The agencies may appear strange to such potential clients because of language, norms, procedures, and even decor.

Examples of this were a hospital program for elderly Chinese patients that did not serve the familiar foods, speak the language, or understand the family situations of the Chinese Americans in its neighborhood. Another example was an alcohol treatment program that did not understand the history and meaning of alcohol consumption to the Native Americans in its locale. When members of these groups were referred to these culturally insensitive programs, applicants failed to follow through on the referrals.

Potential clients may be referred by interpersonal practitioners, and several tasks are essential to assure that a successful referral will occur. First, the interpersonal practitioner must have sufficient knowledge of the needs, aspirations, and capacities of individuals to know that these needs and aspirations will be met by the referred agency. Second, the interpersonal practitioner must know enough about the agency to know that it can and will likely meet these needs and aspirations. Third, the individual (or family or group) to be referred must be prepared for the referral. This includes giving information about the reason for the referral and what may be expected from the agency. The feelings that the person(s) has about the referral must also be handled, including fears about acceptance or rejection in the new agency. Fourth, the agency to which the person has been referred should also be prepared. Ideally the person being referred can ask for a specific staff member with the assurance that he or she is expected. In some cases, the interpersonal practitioner will accompany the person to the agency, will meet with him or her until the referral is established, and will advocate on his or her behalf if services are not appropriately offered. More about referral and linking strategies is presented later in the chapter on individual change (Chapter 11).

In this chapter, we have used the word *client* to refer both to the person who has entered into a contract with the worker as well as the one who potentially will do so. Many writers usefully distinguish between these two sets of persons, and we now discuss this issue using the word *applicant* to denote a potential client (Perlman, 1960).

THE WORKER'S TASKS WITH APPLICANTS ●

When the individual comes to a social agency, he or she has not necessarily made any commitment to solve problems with the help of the agency. In fact, as we have discussed, many applicants may arrive on a nonvoluntary or involuntary basis. Until this commitment is made and is reciprocated by the worker and the agency, it is appropriate to speak only of the individual as an applicant. The only obligation on the part of the applicant is to explore whether the service is of potential use and whether he or she wishes to use it.

Constraints are placed on the worker also because of the individual's applicant status. The interpersonal practitioner has an obligation to present the relevant aspects of the agency's service in a manner that the applicant can understand. Agencies have often prepared written materials for this purpose, but some also have audio or audiovisual presentations that illustrate agency services. Some will even invite applicants to view actual agency services, such as group meetings, with the permission of the other individuals involved.

The worker should identify clearly for the applicant the information that will be required for both the applicant and the agency to make a decision as to whether the service is appropriate. We believe it is unethical and intrusive for the interpersonal practitioner to engage in an extensive inquiry into the applicant's history or to elicit any personal data that are not relevant for the purpose of reaching a decision to become a client.

The worker also has no right to begin any process of change of the applicant or the applicant's situation until the applicant accepts agency services and becomes a client. This is not to deny the dictum that help begins with the first interview, and a discussion of the move from applicant to client status can have beneficial consequences for applicants whether or not they become clients. They can feel understood, they may gain an awareness of aspects of their situation of which they were unaware, and a decision to seek or not to seek service or to seek it elsewhere can represent a greater degree of clarity than they had prior to such an exploration.

The applicant also may have doubts about whether the choice to come was correct or whether his or her energy could have been employed in a more productive way. This feeling will be even more intense if, as is likely, the applicant has had to miss work or school, or hire a babysitter, or arrange for travel to attend the session. This is not to imply that the feelings of applicants will be all negative. There may also be an expectation of help and relief from pain and comfort in knowing that a burden will be shared.

The interpersonal practitioner throughout the helping process, as we discussed in the relationship chapter (Chapter 6), must communicate to the applicant that his or her ideas and feelings are perceived and understood (i.e., accurate empathy). This serves the function of reassuring the applicant of the worker's understanding of the client's situation. This process begins with the first interview when the worker reflects an understanding of what it may mean for the applicant to ask for help.

In this application process, the interpersonal practitioner helps the applicant to express his or her reasons for coming, and the response is usually in the form of a general statement of the problem. The following are a few examples:

- I'm failing in school.
- My wife and I argue all the time.
- I've just lost my job.
- Ask the judge—I don't want to be here!

The interpersonal practitioner's next task is to ask the applicant about the range of concerns or problems that the applicant may be experiencing. Sometimes applicants will dwell on what is later identified as a lesser problem because of fears about the worker's reaction to more severe problems. This is a complex issue for the worker to confront because some applicants will be best able to tackle more severe problems after they either test out the worker's competence or experience some success with minor ones. The worker may have to assess some aspects of the client's situation to make this decision.

In a case situation in which the applicant is being mandated to attend service and does not want to be there, there is still a lot of information that the practitioner needs to understand. What is the nature of the mandate? Does the applicant understand the consequences of not accepting service? Does the applicant realize that he can refuse service and experience the consequences of the court mandate? Even with mandated clients, it may be possible to help them decide to try out service, and a preliminary contract may be negotiated. We will talk more about preliminary contracts at the end of this chapter.

A central value in our system of practice is that the problem to be worked on should be chosen by the applicant or client. This does not restrain the worker from suggesting that the applicant or client work on other problems but the worker should respect the applicant's right to make the final choice. Some workers will utilize a problem inventory to help in this process. Such an inventory includes questions about how the applicant is functioning in various roles, such as employee, parent, spouse, or friend. Even this type of procedure should be engaged in only with the permission of the applicant.

One typical issue arises when the applicant has been referred for one problem yet has another view of the problem and wishes to work on another. An illustration of this is a child referred to a school social worker for failure on numerous occasions to follow the teacher's instructions. The child refuses to acknowledge this as a problem. Instead, the child states he is being picked on by classmates and the teacher because he is the only Chaldean in an all "white" class. This raises a social justice issue that needs to be explored by the interpersonal practitioner.

We believe it is the responsibility of the interpersonal practitioner to take the applicant's view seriously, even when the applicant is a child. As a starting point, the interpersonal practitioner should acknowledge that this would be a stressful situation for the child and offer to help the child find ways to cope with being an "isolate" in the class. After several sessions with the child to establish rapport, the interpersonal practitioner—with the child's permission—may decide to share this perspective of the problem with the teacher and "recruit" the teacher to find ways to change the classroom climate so that the child does not feel so isolated.

Interpersonal practitioners should also remember that the word *problem* is aversive to some applicants. Synonyms such as *concerns*, *issues*, or *stressors* can be used as substitutes. Based on the many considerations we have presented earlier, we offer the following list of worker tasks that may be undertaken during the application process. This long list is offered as suggestions to help the interpersonal practitioner achieve one outcome in the initial encounter—that is, to help the applicant make the decision to become a client.

1. The worker may inquire of the applicant how he or she arrived at this agency or service.
   a. Was this a voluntary, nonvoluntary, or involuntary process?
   b. Was this a result of a crisis or a new force brought to bear on an ongoing situation?

2. The worker may explain to the applicant the nature of the agency and its programs insofar as they may be relevant to the applicant.

3. The worker may identify and reflect an understanding of the applicant's feelings about coming to the agency. If these feelings are angry ones or in other ways reflect resistance, the worker may indicate an acceptance of these feelings and should not proceed to the next phase until the applicant is ready to do so.

4. The worker may elicit the applicant's view of the problems that have led to coming to the agency. Other problem areas may be explored with the permission of the applicant. Some ranking of problems may be attempted.

5. The worker may explain, at least in general terms, what will happen at the next stage if the applicant becomes a client. Although this will be discussed later in this book in more detail, it consists of greater specifications of the problem, assessment of the client and his or her situation relevant to the problem, and selection of a plan for beginning to work on a solution to the problem.

6. The worker may explore any values or worker characteristics that will influence or hinder the offer of service (e.g., ethnic, religious, and gender differences).

7. The worker may describe potential members of the action system who may be involved in bringing about a resolution of the problem situation.

8. The worker should determine on the basis of the foregoing whether the applicant desires to become a client. If this is not agreed on, a referral process to another resource may be offered. The feelings of the applicant about not becoming a client may be elicited and responded to.

The following case example is presented to operationalize and clarify these tasks:

The Applicant Process

Mrs. W, age 69, had recently been hospitalized for a heart problem, but her medical condition has now been stabilized. Because she is a widow and lives alone, her doctor referred her to the hospital social worker to consider whether this living plan will still be feasible for her. She made the appointment but questioned at the beginning of the interview why she should see a social worker. The worker indicated that one of the functions of medical social service is to help people make plans that are supportive of their health needs. The worker asked Mrs. W if she was willing to discuss this further to see if Mrs. W could use such services. Mrs. W asked what this would involve. The worker indicated that they could go over the doctor's recommendations to see if Mrs. W needed any help in planning how to follow them, such as those regarding climbing stairs, lifting, or doing heavy work. Mrs. W said she could see this discussion might be helpful.

The worker asked Mrs. W if she had some concerns about talking to a social worker. Mrs. W said that she had a friend who was also a widow and who had fallen and broken her hip. She was now in "one of those homes for old people," and Mrs. W said that a social worker and the friend's son had "put her there." Mrs. W thought that once you became involved with a social worker, the worker might find some way to force you to do things you didn't really want to.

The worker replied that she couldn't answer for what another worker had done as she didn't know anything about the situation. She was aware of Mrs. W's concerns about losing her freedom, however. She could promise Mrs. W that she would help her only to think through what she wanted to do in her situation. Mrs. W was fully capable of making her own decisions, and the worker said she would respect that. The referral from the doctor said that Mrs. W might wish some help in deciding whether she wanted to try to keep up her large family home by herself or to make another arrangement. This, the worker reiterated, was completely up to Mrs. W.

We can identify, in this example, many of the characteristics of applicant situations just described. Mrs. W did follow through on her obligation as applicant to find out if the service could be of use by asking for the purpose of a medical social service department. The worker observed the principles we have referred to in that she gave a simple explanation of the service relevant to Mrs. W's needs. The worker did not ask many questions but sought permission to explore Mrs. W's functioning as it was affected by her health. The worker was also careful to explain that her questions would be relevant to Mrs. W's situation. The worker exhibited empathy with regard to Mrs. W's fears of losing her freedom and sought to reassure her that this would not be infringed upon by the worker.

● TASKS WITH NONCLIENTS

The ethical responsibilities of the social worker cover all professional encounters, although issues arise with people who are not clients who differ from those with clients. When the individual is an applicant, the principles of confidentiality, self-determination, and respect for people apply to the same degree they would if the person were a client. In addition, the interpersonal practitioner has the responsibility to help the person secure the best possible service. This means that she must not attempt to push her own service if it appears that another agency's services are more appropriate. The interpersonal practitioner also must consider whether even another worker in the same agency should be utilized. This requires considerable self-awareness on the part of the interpersonal practitioner, as well as courage, as she must admit fallibility on her part as well as the agency's.

● "SIGNIFICANT OTHERS" IN THE CLIENT'S LIFE

We believe that everyone who "enters" the agency must be regarded as a potential client and given the same rights as an applicant. Thus, for example, if an interview is arranged with a family member, the worker must maintain a dual focus. On the one hand, the worker interviews the family member on behalf of the client and focuses on the needs of the client. On the other hand, the family member also has needs, and these should at least be acknowledged to prevent the family member from becoming an "object" manipulated for the benefit of the client. In addition, the family member may wish to utilize the agency's services, or that of some other resource, to attain his or her own goals, and, as with any applicant, the social worker has a responsibility to help that person contact the appropriate facility.

DEFINING THE CLIENT IN A ●
MULTIPERSON CLIENT SYSTEM

As we have noted, several people can jointly constitute a client system in which the contract represents a consensus between members of the system and the worker, the goals of service are expressed in terms of the "group" rather than the individuals, and attainment of goals is measured in "group" rather than individual terms. Such client systems are found in family treatment, some approaches to group work, and work with "natural" groupings, such as people assigned to cottages in residential treatment centers.

One issue in practice is whether the interpersonal practitioner and the people who receive service have the same view about who is the client. The interpersonal practitioner, for ideological or theoretical reasons, may view the group as client and may seek changes in it that are not expressly agreed on by the service recipients. The concept of "group as client" is a fairly abstract one and one that even practitioners may find difficult to utilize. Some even insist that the individual is always the "client."

Because few families, or other natural groups, come for service with a presentation of their problems in systemic terms, the worker who thinks in this way has an obligation to explain this perspective and to secure informed consent to the implications of this view. If the family or other group is provoked into taking measures to protect the way in which it has been functioning as a system, this is their right. We believe that people have the right to define their difficulties in either individual or group terms. The worker who has an intellectual or ideological commitment to a perspective that is different from the applicant's also has a right to pursue this but also has a responsibility to inform applicants of this perspective and to help them to consider seeking help elsewhere when perspectives clash. Although there is some evidence that supports family perspectives as being more effective than individual ones under specified circumstances, one cannot make an across the board claim of the superiority of family approaches under all circumstances (Alexander, Holtzworth-Munroe, & Jameson, 1994). Whenever research suggests this kind of uncertainty of outcomes, we believe that emphasis should be placed on client preferences. This is a complex issue, however, and we shall discuss it much more thoroughly later in the family change chapter (Chapter 13).

In some practice models, both the individual and the group are considered "clients," and contracts are made with both regarding goals and means of achieving them (Shulman, 1979). In one of these models, the worker functions as the mediator between systems and seeks to help each system to negotiate with the other so that, through a recognition of their interdependence, they may attain desired objectives.

It is also possible for changes in the definition of the client system to occur with the same people over time. Thus, one might start out by working with an entire family as the client and ultimately shift to working with individual family members as clients—or the opposite might also occur. The same can happen in work with groups of unrelated people. The important issue in the concept of the client is not that the use of the concept directs the interpersonal practitioner as to who is the client but rather that it forces the interpersonal practitioner to be explicit about whom he or she is working with and on whose behalf the worker's activities are conducted.

● AGENCY CONDITIONS AND DEFINITIONS OF CLIENT

The alleged purpose of a social agency is to serve its clients. Without the presence of people who need the services of the agency, it would disband and its resources would be reallocated. Despite this idealistic rationale, other agency purposes exist because of the objectives of others who are associated with the agency. Some workers may seek particular experiences, such as collecting research data. Some board members may seek the prestige that comes from membership. Legislators and influential members of the community may seek the political support of those who favor programs and policies. Thus, despite the best of intentions, clients are in a low power position, and their needs can be subverted by those of other groups. A number of organizational conditions affect the client's position and consequently, how client needs, in comparison with those of other groups, are met.

One of these is whether the clients, staff, and agency policy makers come from similar ethnic, social class, and cultural backgrounds. When they do, client needs may be respected because of the linkages among these groups. One must consider all the variables that affect social distance, as similarity on one dimension does not mean similarity on another. For example, earlier in the 20th century, services were established for Eastern European Jews by German and other Western European Jews who had emigrated to the United States much earlier. These service providers recognized a social obligation to clients yet viewed the newcomers as inferiors "who must be Americanized in spite of themselves" (Howe, 1976). This led to pressure on clients to relinquish their cultural patterns, a process that must have taken its toll in low self-esteem and cultural impoverishment.

In recent years, there has been pressure on agencies to invite representatives of client groups to join agency policymaking bodies. When this is done, the way in which it is done, who is chosen, and who has ultimate power will also affect how clients are seen in the agency. The concept of clients as indigenous workers has been proclaimed as a way of changing the status of the client, but this, too, has been an idea surrounded by controversy about the influence and role of such staff.

A radical idea regarding the position of clients was espoused by Bertha Reynolds (1951) over half a century ago. She recognized the limitations on client autonomy posed by the powerless role of clients in most agencies. As an alternative, she developed the idea of social workers as employees of an organization controlled by clients and implemented this through the United Seamen's Services of the National Maritime Union. She believed that when social services are established in this way, clients would not be stigmatized, would trust the service, and would ultimately benefit more than from services under other auspices.

We suggest, therefore, that interpersonal practitioners examine carefully how clients are viewed and treated by other groups in the agency. Are there members of the staff, professionals, administration, and board who come from similar identity groups as the clients? Do others in the agency view clients as constituents, creators, or partners in the service process, or, as inferiors, pawns, or necessary nuisances? The results of this examination will include working for agency changes that will reduce discrepancies between agency and client perspectives on problems. In the chapter on organizational change (Chapter 17), we discuss ways that interpersonal practitioners can work to change their agencies so they are more responsive to clients.

CONTINUANCE AND DISCONTINUANCE ●

Even when applicants are accepted for service by the agency, there is no guarantee that the client will be able to make use of the service. In this beginning stage of service, the client role is not well established, and a number of factors may contribute to the premature dropout or termination of the client. In the early studies of the 1950s and 1960s in social work before managed care, discontinuance was considered a serious service delivery problem, and a considerable amount of research went into discovering the causes of these beginning "spoiled" helping relationships (Kounin, 1956; Levinger, 1960; Rosenfeld, 1964; Shyne, 1957). Figure 7.3 is a composite summary of several studies conducted in the 1960s and 1970s in family service agencies and community mental health agencies of how long clients remain in service.

Because the dominant casework paradigm of that time was an open-ended, long-term treatment model, clients who did not continue in services were viewed as dropouts. During the past three decades, however, research on short-term, time-limited models has clearly demonstrated that many clients who have appeared to drop out may actually have achieved the implicit goals they set for themselves when entering service. Bloom's (1981, 1988) analysis of dropouts has

Figure 7.3 Discontinuance Rates of "Voluntary Clients"

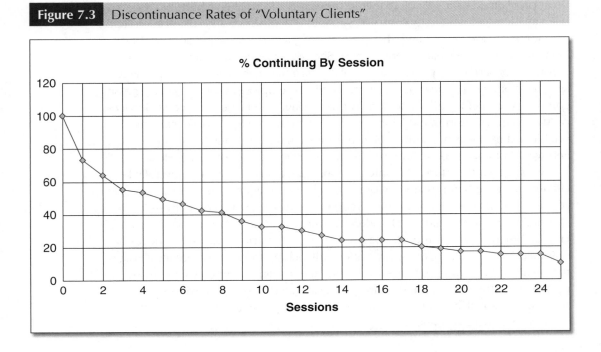

demonstrated that many clients who appear to drop out early are not dissatisfied with service and feel that their brief contact with the social agency was helpful.

But even with this paradigm shift and the realization that service can be delivered in shorter sequences, the entrance into clienthood is fragile and can be influenced by a number of factors in the agency, in the client's environment, and in the demeanor of the worker. The remaining sections of this chapter focus on those factors and also describe some of the techniques that the interpersonal practitioner can employ to reduce the premature dropout of clients.

Much of the research on continuance and discontinuance seeks to compare people who continue with an interpersonal helping process with those who do not. An early social work study bearing on the issue of continuance was that of Ripple and her colleagues (Ripple, Alexander, & Polemis, 1964). In looking at client outcomes, the investigators divided the clients into two groups: those who had "external" and those who had "psychological" problems. Factors associated with the discontinuance of the individuals in the former group were that the responses of their social workers were discouraging or their environmental conditions were restrictive and unmodifiable. Clients in this category, those who had low motivation and capacity, continued to seek service if they received encouragement from the very beginning of the intake process (Ripple et al., 1964, pp. 198–199).

For clients with psychological problems, the factors of motivation and capacity were crucial for continuance in casework—at least casework of the traditional variety. Clients in this category also must have experienced support from other people in their lives. Limitations in regard to motivation, capacity, and such support were overcome, and clients continued to make use of service when supplied with strong encouragement by caseworkers. These variables were very potent as they enabled the researchers to predict accurately continuance and discontinuance for 93% of the clients with external problems and 86% of the clients with psychological problems.

Encouragement from workers was crucial with both groups of clients. It is interesting to note that the investigators defined discouragement as "a bland, seemingly uninvolved eliciting and appraisal of the client's situation, in which the worker appeared neutral in affect, left the client's discomfort untouched, and offered no basis for hope that the situation could be improved" (Ripple et al., 1964, p. 203). It is worth noting that similar issues are presented in the contemporary model of motivational interviewing (Miller & Rollnick, 2002). The other kind of discouragement was the placement of the client on a waiting list, often for an indefinite period.

Garfield (1994) has reviewed a number of studies of discontinuance in psychotherapy that are also relevant to social work services. He concludes, from a representative group of studies, that a majority of clinics have lost one half of their therapy clients before the eighth interview. The median length of treatment was 3 to 12 interviews, but there was a clustering around 6 sessions.

A number of variables have been identified that discriminate between continuers and discontinuers in psychotherapy. One of these is social class: more middle-class than lower-class clients remain in psychotherapy. Other variables related to social class also produce the same kinds of findings. For example, education also has been found to be associated with continuance. Race, a variable that is hard to separate from social class, is also predictive of continuance in that black clients are more likely than white clients to terminate early from psychotherapy. This finding should, however, be viewed in the light of another finding that black clients remain in treatment longer when matched with a therapist in regard to both race and social class (Garfield, 1994, pp. 197–200).

Another issue that complicates our understanding of the effects of social class is the reactions of the worker to the client's social class. Workers often seek to avoid lower-class clients because they predict that such clients are not amenable to therapy: Predictions of this sort are undoubtedly turned into reality, actually a self-fulfilling prophesy.

This is not to deny that lower-class clients have different expectations of therapy than do middle-class ones. Several research studies have shown that lower-class clients are likely to expect therapists to be active, whereas middle-class clients do not have the same expectation. Lower-class clients are also more likely than middle-class ones to expect advice. Nevertheless, we suspect there is a continuum of these variables among all clients and that therapist expectations about social class are strong determinants of how much clients are encouraged to continue (Garfield, 1994, p. 199).

We also should note that age, sex, and psychiatric diagnosis are not associated with continuance. There may be prejudices among practitioners regarding the effect of these dimensions on dropout rates, but this is not supported by research findings.

This presentation of research findings is not meant to discourage students from serving groups that have high discontinuance rates but rather to seek ways of working with these clients, such as approaches that are action oriented rather than primarily verbal so that they find social work a useful service. This conclusion is one we consider throughout this chapter because interpersonal practitioners' clients are likely to be the ones who tend to drop out of psychotherapy: They are often people who are poor, who have less education, who are members of oppressed ethnic minorities, and who, therefore, are not likely to be as oriented to investing their time in long-term, verbal, introspective procedures as are middle-class clients.

Somewhat different forces may well be in operation in relationship to continuance in groups because group members' reactions are directed at other group members as well as at the worker. Yalom (1995), in his examination of data on group dropouts, cited nine reasons for such discontinuance. Some of these are related to "traits which the patient brings with him to the group, whereas others are related to problems arising within the group" (Yalom, 1995, p. 255). Those related to the former are categorized by Yalom (1995) as *external factors*, *group deviancy*, and *problems of intimacy*.

The category of external factors incorporates several dimensions. One is conditions, such as lack of transportation and scheduling conflicts. These factors may actually be rationalizations for discontinuing group membership, or they may be costs that outweigh benefits, but, in either case, they are frequently cited by dropouts. Another external issue is when events in the life of the group members are so disturbing that the individual cannot tolerate attention to anyone else's problems than his or her own. Under this circumstance, individual approaches are more appropriate than group ones.

Group deviancy, as used by Yalom, refers to a situation in which a group member's behavior differs substantially from that of other members—for example, disruptive behavior or nonparticipation. Such people, according to Yalom (1995), also may have "a lack of psychological sophistication, a lack of interpersonal sensitivity, and a lack of personal psychological insight manifested in part by the common utilization of denial" (p. 231). These group members are often of a lower socioeconomic status and educational level than others.

The issue of group deviance is very much a product of the purpose of the group and the characteristics of all of the members and this issue is further considered in the group assessment chapter when we discuss group composition. At this point, however, we should take note that the attributes of some individuals may be so extreme in regard to those of other members of a group that their dropping out of groups is assured.

In addition, we see in Yalom's (1995) conclusions the same social- and class-related expectations that are referred to in the individual treatment literature—that is, continuance is strongly associated with a conception of treatment as primarily a cognitive and verbal process. It is our conviction that interpersonal practitioners, with the mission of the social work profession in mind, will not limit themselves to sets of procedures that depend primarily on psychological mindedness. In the chapter on group change (Chapter 15), we introduce a number of structured activities that the interpersonal practitioner can employ in groups that are more action oriented and will more likely meet the needs of less verbal and psychologically minded clients.

The third variable emphasized by Yalom (1995), problems of intimacy, refers to two sets of individuals: those who are reluctant to share personal concerns in groups and those who shock other members with the rapidity with which they reveal themselves. The likelihood that the client will act in these ways will predict an early dropout from group psychotherapy, but, again, social work groups that utilize nonverbal program activities more than verbal interactions may not have this effect.

In regard to working with families, there are other factors that may affect dropouts of either individual family members or the entire family from family treatment. Individuals may drop out if they are extensively scapegoated by the other family members or if they perceive the worker as biased against them. This is a highly complex issue, as we shall see later, as families usually enter treatment with one member labeled the "patient." Even more complex an issue is the reluctance of the entire family to participate in family sessions, which is due to the refusal of influential members to attend or the way they may influence others to drop out. In the present era of managed care, it is also difficult to be reimbursed by third-party payers for family sessions. Many insurance panels do not recognize family treatment as a legitimate charge. Some insurance companies require that each member of the family be diagnosed on a *Diagnostic and Statistical Manual of Mental Disorders* (4th ed.) (*DSM–IV*) axis, and each family session counts toward each of the individual member's number of allowed sessions.

The information on discontinuance from individual, group, and family situations should provide a backdrop to the rest of the chapter in which we consider the role of the worker in engaging the client in problem solving efforts. The worker should take from this review of research the ideas that the process of engagement must relate to the client's motivation, capacity, and expectation that change is possible. The client's expectations of the helping process are influenced by education and culture and the kinds of supports required from the worker to create bonds between worker and client, in one-to-one, and among clients, in group situations.

In the process of clarifying the problem, engaging in an assessment, and determining goals, the worker and the client must also clarify their respective roles. This clarification process is the subject of the following discussion.

● ORIENTATION TO THE CLIENT ROLE

There are several ways of clarifying roles that can be used to help the applicant move into the role of client. This process, referred to as *role induction*, has been well researched. Findings from this research show that training of clients for the client role is associated with better outcomes (Orlinsky, Grawe, & Parks, 1994). Inducting the client is a cognitive process in which the worker and client together examine the expectations that clients and workers have of their respective roles. What follows is a description of one approach to this process.

A Role Clarification Procedure

When interpersonal practitioners and clients interact, four sets of role expectations must be clarified: (1) the client's and (2) the worker's expectations for the client's role and (3) the client's and (4) the worker's expectations for the worker's role. We discuss each of these in turn and then describe a specific procedure for clarifying such expectations.

The client's expectation for his or her role is a product of the client's previous experiences with helping processes, both professional and informal, as well as of the client's concept of what the social work process is. Some clients believe that their major responsibility is to indicate the problem and the social worker will prescribe a solution. Some clients think they will carry out the prescribed solution, while others assume they can play a passive role. Still other clients will either assume they should play a cooperative role in problem solving or that they will do most of the "work" with minimal help and support from the social worker.

The worker's expectation of the client's role will be a product of the worker's theoretical orientation as well as of the worker's assessment of the client's motivation and capacity. Most theoretical orientations to practice require the client to participate in solving their problems and in implementing solutions. An exception is behavioral procedure in which the worker prescribes a behavioral change activity that has been proved effective for the type of problem presented. Even in this case, the client is expected to cooperate by complying with the recommended procedure. Any theoretical orientation must take into consideration that clients, such as young children or people with severe developmental disabilities, will not be as active in their own behalf as otherwise well-functioning adults who face situational difficulties.

Problems arise when the worker and client hold conflicting expectations for the role of the client. A very frequent type of conflict is when workers expect clients to participate actively, and the clients expect the workers to solve their problems for them. The reverse pattern, as we have implied, is much less likely to occur, as in most cases the practitioner's objective is to encourage the clients' activity on their own behalf.

The worker's and the client's expectations of the role of the worker should fit with the expectations of the role of the client. Workers will have the self-expectation that they should act in a competent manner to assess the client's problems and recommend ways of reducing or solving them. They will also hold the self-expectation that they should be able to secure the participation and cooperation of the clients in their own behalf. Clients will also expect the worker to have these competencies.

A conflict may arise around the workers' self-expectations regarding securing client participation. Many clients will expect the worker to be much more active on their behalf than the workers will expect themselves to be. These contrasting expectations grow out of the fact that the worker's expectations are largely a product of worker professional training, whereas client expectations are a result of the client's previous experience with authority and helping figures, such as their parents, combined with whatever previous exposure they have had to professional helping.

The role clarification process involves three steps: (1) *explicating various expectations*, (2) *comparing and identifying discrepancies in expectations*, and (3) *negotiating agreements on expectations*.

1. *Explicating Various Expectations.* In this step, clients are asked to state specifically (orally or in writing) what they expect or want of the worker and what they expect their own responsibilities in the service process to be. When these two sets of expectations are fairly complete, the worker also states what he or she considers are the worker's role responsibilities and the client's role responsibilities. It is important that the clients state their expectations first, or at least independently, so that worker's expectations do not contaminate or shape the client's.

2. *Comparing and Identifying Discrepancies.* In this step, the worker's and client's expectations of the worker are compared, and the worker's and client's expectations of the client are similarly examined. This will indicate any conflicts or ambiguity that exists between the two sets of expectations.

3. *Negotiating Agreements on Expectations.* In this final step, workers and clients seek to come to terms with the discrepant or conflicting perspectives. This process should also reinforce the areas where no conflicts exist.

With some clients, there will be a tendency to accept the worker's perspective on roles and to deny their own. To prevent such premature closure on discrepancies and to keep clients from "selling out" in the face of worker authority, workers should tell clients there can be legitimate differences and that they will attempt to reach agreement. The worker and client should see differences as constructive, as they can lead to a clarification of many distortions in relationships that prevent the client from interacting effectively with others.

In order to clarify the role clarification process, we present the following real case example:

A Mother's Expectations of Her Role and the Social Worker's in Counseling

The case involved a single mother and her 10-year-old daughter, who the mother believed was becoming uncontrollable. In the initial interview with the mother, the mother stated that she would bring her daughter to the clinic and drop her off for me (BAS) to see (her responsibility). She would give me a list of incidents that happened during the week (her responsibility), and I would discipline the daughter for these incidents (my responsibility). My view of the mother's responsibilities was somewhat different, and my view of the role as a disciplinarian was completely out of the question. At the time, I was not a parent nor did I have a course in my master of social work (MSW) program on how to discipline children except that I knew in social work corporal punishment was seen as taboo. The mother had expressed a desire that I use corporal punishment to sanction her daughter's "bad" behavior. I explained to the mother that I was glad to see that she would be willing to bring her daughter to counseling but that I wanted to meet with her and her daughter in each session. I felt that seeing both of them would be more helpful. I also explained that I did not see my role as a social worker to be a disciplinarian and to punish her daughter for naughty behavior. I further explained that my role would be to help each of them find ways to solve their interpersonal problems so that they would not have to come to counseling. The mother was not particularly excited about my explanation. She questioned me about what "social workers" do and also about how counseling could change her daughter's behavior. After this discussion, she agreed to a "preliminary contract" to try out several sessions with both her and her daughter.

When the client system is a family or group, this role clarification procedure can be repeated for each person, or all individuals can discuss role issues and reach a common perspective. The former process is utilized in therapy groups in which individual goals are established and in which each individual with the help of other group members works toward his or her goals. When there is more of an emphasis on the group, such as in family treatment, the members also can work together to clarify their respective responsibilities.

Role Training

Another approach to role clarification is to provide role training. Yalom (1995) describes an interview procedure for group therapy clients that he found led to better outcomes than outcomes for those clients not prepared in this way (pp. 278–292). Yalom's approach included an explanation of what group therapy is, the results that can be expected from it, the reasons why it presumably works, and the difficulties encountered in initial sessions that may tempt some clients to terminate prematurely.

Yalom (1995) reported on the effectiveness of his training procedure only for long-term group psychotherapy. We have proposed that analogous procedures for other forms of experience can and should be developed and tested (Garvin, 1996). The basic components of such procedures are a description of what is likely to occur in the individual, family, or group experience; what *will* be expected of clients; what the rationale for the particular approach is; and what the outcomes have been.

Another approach to role training for clients is to provide them with examples of client behaviors. This can include the tape recording of interviews or group sessions, written descriptions, or even observation of sessions with the permission of the observed clients. A variant of this is to ask previous clients to share some of their experiences with new clients. This last approach has been utilized in such situations as preparation of adoptive parents, foster parents, and persons newly admitted to residential settings.

Undoubtedly, these procedures are even more essential when class or other cultural differences produce expectations and perceptions of social work processes that are discrepant between worker and clients. Research findings bear out the value of role training with disadvantaged populations. Preparation of such clients, however, is only half the requirement for successful outcomes. Training workers to work with lower-income clients is of great importance. Such worker preparation includes recognition of feelings and attitudes toward lower-income clients and understanding of the lifestyles, needs, and expectations of members of these groups. The chapter on diversity (Chapter 4) in this book is especially relevant to these issues.

When role induction experiences have been completed, the interpersonal practitioner may begin the problem solving process. Simultaneously, the interpersonal practitioner may begin to create the kind of worker–client relationship that will support this process. We now consider these topics.

THE INITIATION OF PROBLEM SOLVING ●

Specifying the Problem

During the process of deciding to become a client, applicants define problems they and their workers believe fall within the purview of the agency. When these problems are expressed in general terms, as is often the case, the interpersonal practitioner helps clients to specify the problem in concrete terms, by asking the clients about the details of events related to the problem. Workers will typically ask about recent events as these are likely to be clear to the clients, and clients may also be motivated to reveal them.

After the client has described one problem, other problems are usually identified. The worker should help the client who has multiple problems to order them in terms of importance and to choose one on which to begin. Some questions that help clients and workers to do this are

1. Which problem is the most distressing to the client?

2. Which problem is most distressing to others?

3. Which problem can be most readily solved or, if solved, will reinforce the motivation and capacity of the client to solve other problems?

4. Which problem, if solved, will simultaneously reduce other problems?

5. Is there a logical order to take up problems such as when the solution to a problem requires solution to an antecedent problem?

Problem Specification in Family and Group Systems

When the interpersonal practitioner interacts with a family as a client system, unique components to problem specification arise. One of these is whether to approach a definition of the problem in terms of individual or family conditions. This issue is also problematic because families who come for help often define one member as the "problem." This person is referred to in the family therapy literature as the "identified patient." Differences exist among family practitioners about how to respond to this. Some accept an individual definition of the problem because rejecting this definition may lead to premature termination as the family's reality has been denied. Others quickly move the family to a statement of the problem in terms of the whole family.

We prefer to operate flexibly in this situation. If the family strongly presents the problem as an individual one, we accept this. If the family, on the other hand, is likely to see the problem in family terms, we work from that perspective. We believe there is a difference between a definition of the problem and an assessment of it. We can accept a statement of the problem as "Johnny does not go to school" and an assessment of it as Johnny remains at home to prevent his father and mother from fighting. We do not insist that the family must define this problem as, for example, having poor ways of resolving family conflicts—although some families are prepared to think in such terms.

An important dynamic in many families, in addition, is that different members may define the "problem" in different terms. When this occurs, it tells the interpersonal practitioner a great deal about how the family functions and will ultimately be used by the interpersonal practitioner to help the family reconcile their differences and work toward common goals.

In group situations, the specification of problems is different from what transpires in work with individuals and families. With support and treatment groups, it is common for the group's purpose to be clearly established in advance, *and* usually this purpose is clearly related to some client problem. For example, groups may be formed to help individuals cope with particular losses (e.g., death of a spouse or child), or to cope with a severe and debilitating illness (e.g., cancer or bulimia), or to teach individuals particular social skills (e.g., assertiveness or anger management). When interpersonal practitioners compose groups, the general convention is followed that all individuals placed in a group will be struggling with the same or similar problem. This is an important form of commonality and universality that groups build in from the start. The interpersonal practitioner may help the individuals in the group to specify the particular circumstances of their problem by encouraging and allowing each member to share his or her story. The worker may also help the group members recognize similarities in their life situations and in their struggle with the social problem that has brought them to the group. Much more about these issues will be presented in the group change chapter (Chapter 15).

THE PRELIMINARY CONTRACT ●

Our approach to practice incorporates the idea that the worker should interact with clients on the basis of a "contract." We discuss the reasons for this in detail in the chapter on contracting. Because a "preliminary contract" is essential to the completion of this phase of service in which the applicant finally accepts the role of client, we introduce this concept now. A contract in social work is not a legal document and, in fact, may not necessarily be written down.

It is a concept that directs the worker to have as clear an agreement as possible with the client about what they are doing together, why they are doing it, and what their mutual responsibilities are. Clienthood will be firmly established if the worker and client can agree on the following preliminary points:

1. The worker and client agree on the problem(s) they will seek to solve together. This may change later, but nevertheless, an agreement exists for the present.

2. The worker and client agree they will continue to work together on these problems because this appears to be the appropriate agency and worker for this effort.

3. At least a minimum, if not maximum, amount of time for work together has been agreed on. For example, the client will meet with the worker at least three times or attend at least three group meetings or family sessions.

4. The client and worker agree that the next phase will include the gathering of information about the problem, the client, and the situation. (In this book, we call this *assessment*.) Assessment is necessary for the worker and client to agree on short- and long-term goals and means for achieving them. The client will cooperate in supplying the information required for the assessment, and the worker will be responsible for identifying the information required and will be able to justify the need to secure such information.

5. Additional requirements of the client and worker, such as fees, the time for appointments, and where and with whom appointments are to take place, may also be identified.

● SUMMARY

We began this chapter with an exercise that demonstrates how the clienthood process unfolds and what this experience feels like to an applicant who approaches a human service agency. This chapter then discusses the term *client* and its meaning in social work. We justified our use of the term, although we recognized some of the controversies related to power and interactional issues implied by its usage. We also noted that in social work the client may be an individual, family, or group. When individuals or families seek service in agencies, clienthood is not automatic, and a screening and sorting process occurs in which some applicants are rejected or sent on to other agencies. Even when applicants accept the offer of service, some do not stay long and drop out of service for a variety of reasons.

The major portion of the chapter was devoted to describing the factors that influence an applicant's decision to become a client and the interpersonal practitioner's responsibilities in helping the applicant make that decision. Role clarification and role training procedures, as well as problem specification procedures, were outlined, which would help the applicant begin on a positive note with the agency. The implications of working with others in the client's environment and issues that arise when the client is a family or group were discussed. The completion of a preliminary contract marks the end of this phase of service.

CHAPTER **8**

CONTRACTING

If you don't know where you are going—any road will take you there!

—The Cheshire Cat in *Alice in Wonderland* (Carroll, 2008)

The concept of "contract" has been extensively discussed in social work literature (Collins, 1977; Maluccio & Marlow, 1974; Seabury, 1976). Contract is a generic term and applies to work with individuals, families, and small groups (Compton & Galaway, 1979; Hartman & Laird, 1983; Kravetz & Rose, 1973; Pincus & Minahan, 1973). Contract has appeared as a central concept in a number of models of social work practice (e.g., task centered [Reid & Epstein, 1972], cognitive–behavioral intervention [Rose, 1977], life model [Germain & Gitterman, 1980], and solution-focused [O'Hanlon & Wiener-Davis, 1989]). Contract is an important concept that prescribes a useful framework for worker–client interactions.

COMPONENTS OF A SOCIAL WORK CONTRACT ●

In practice, contract has been viewed in two ways. First, it has been defined as a product (the service contract) in the form of a written or verbal agreement between worker and client. This agreement is usually negotiated in early sessions and spells out major terms of service (e.g., goals, duration of service, fees, or responsibilities of parties). The contract may also be seen as an ongoing, decision making process (i.e., contracting) in which worker, client, and other service providers continuously negotiate and renegotiate terms as service progresses. From this perspective, contracting is a circular process of negotiation, implementation, evaluation, and renegotiation involving client, worker, and possibly other service providers in the action system.

In both perspectives, contract may be defined as a working agreement among parties (worker, client, others) about the terms of service. This definition of contract has three basic elements. In interpersonal practice, the parties are usually the people involved in the service process, such as the client(s) (individual, couple, family, small group), the interpersonal practitioner, and the other service providers in the action system. The working agreement prescribes that each party is expected to have input into the agreement, to understand it, and to accept it. The terms are the specific conditions or particular decisions that determine how service will proceed.

In practice, there is no end to what can be negotiated as terms in a social work contract (e.g., seating arrangements, length of sessions, or refreshments). The literature, however, does suggest that there are several basic terms to a social work contract: (1) *purpose*; (2) *target problems*; (3) *goals or objectives*; (4) *time limits*; and (5) *specific actions, activities, and responsibilities*.

Purpose refers to the "why" or "rationale" for service in the first place. Purpose is usually the first issue that is raised in an encounter between parties. For example, "I came in today to get some help with personal problems" or "I'm here to tell you about our services and see whether there are things that we can do to help." The practice of social work involves many potential purposes. Social workers may be engaged in prevention, rehabilitation, protection, treatment, education, and sometimes these purposes seem so obvious to the worker that a particular purpose is not made explicit in the first encounter. Purpose is the most important term, and it should be recognized and agreed to early. Purpose shapes all other decisions, and without understanding and agreement, it is risky for parties to continue service. If parties cannot agree on a purpose for their encounter, there is no reason for them to continue. In later chapters on individual, family, and group change, we elaborate how important purpose is when working with these different size client systems.

"Corrupt" contracts can emerge in practice if purpose is not clarified or honestly addressed. For example, students are sometimes assigned "learning cases." In these cases, there is no expectation that the client will be helped by the student, but the student is expected to learn from the interaction with the client. Should a student, then, in his or her first encounter with such a client, say "I've been assigned to you because you will be a good learning experience for me"?

Similarly, clients can propose corrupt purposes. Prisoners may attend a group therapy session not for any benefits in self-understanding or improvement they may obtain but to interrupt the boredom of prison routine or to secure "brownie points" toward parole. Sometimes the purpose stated by one party is not believed by the other. A child welfare worker may state that she wants to help parents solve family problems to return their child, yet the parents may believe the worker is involved with them to collect evidence to remove their other children.

Target problems are identified, deleterious conditions facing clients that must be changed to improve their social functioning. As discussed in earlier chapters, a client may want help with personal problems (alcohol or substance abuse, physical disability, serious emotional or mental disturbances), interpersonal problems (marital, parent–child, role performance), or situational problems (housing, money management, social isolation). In our contractual approach to service, the client's choice of problem is valued and encouraged. Clients are not expected to be passive recipients of service nor is the worker expected to decide unilaterally what is wrong. The choice of target problem is a mutual decision. The client must want help with it, and the worker must be willing to work on it, too.

Negotiation of the target problem requires an approach that encourages the client to participate in the search for that problem. Such an approach does not mean that the worker is nondirective and inactive in the search. The ideal is a balance between worker and client input. In a contracting process, the worker actively engages the client in assessment procedures to help facilitate the client's selection of a target problem. Problems that can only be perceived or inferred by the worker ("oedipal conflict," "narcissistic wound") are not chosen as target problems in our approach.

Goals or objectives are future, desired end states for the client. Sometimes goals flow directly from target problems as when the "opposite" of a problem defines the goal: unemployment–employment, truant–school attendance, depressed–happy, etc. Goals at this level of generality are not useful, and the worker's task is to help the client's goals become more concrete (Maple, 1977). A goal such as "happiness" may be desirable but not concrete enough to clarify what behaviors must occur for the client to be successful. For example, a client may achieve happiness by completing a number of specific objectives such as (1) to secure child care, (2) to enroll and complete a training program, (3) to locate a job, (4) to apply for it, and (5) to be hired.

While all these steps are specific objectives that may be stated in a social work contract, each of these objectives in turn can be specified further. As the contract process unfolds, the terms become more and more specific and reflect actions and responsibilities of all parties. Figure 8.1 graphically presents this contract sequence.

Because the objectives of a service contract are expected to be achieved during the service period, time limits are essential for all goals and objectives. In the example given earlier, worker and client agreed to spend 2 weeks to secure child care arrangements and then move on to locate a job training program. It is impossible to predict with perfect accuracy how long it will take to attain a goal or objective. Time limits are not strict do-or-die requirements, but they do serve to

Figure 8.1 Contract Sequence

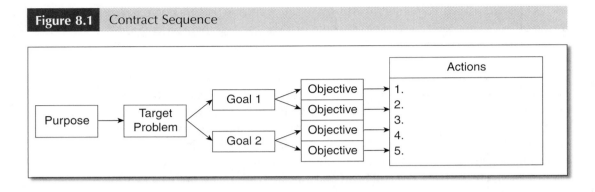

motivate clients. This popular quote represents a basic truism: "Without deadlines, noting would ever get done!" Deadlines have other positive effects on goal achievement (Reid & Epstein, 1972, pp. 78–93). One is that they help people rank the life tasks that face them. Students usually know weeks in advance when term papers are due, yet most term papers are tackled in the last weekend or a few days before a deadline.

Goals and related time limits are terms in a social work contract that raise a thorny issue about the nature of contracting in social work. Contracts are promissory arrangements (Croxton, 1974) that hold parties to certain conditions or actions, yet in a social work contract, goals, objectives, and time limits cannot be conceptualized as promissory in a binding sense. When worker and client establish a goal of employment, the worker does not guarantee the client a job. When a worker establishes a goal with a couple to resolve marital problems, the worker does not promise the couple marital bliss.

This caveat about goals and deadlines in a social work contract concerns a basic dimension of contract negotiation. It is easy to think of all kinds of idealistic goals or desirable objectives; however, it is the pragmatic, reality-based goal that is most likely to be achieved in practice. One way of making goals more pragmatic is to avoid vague global goal statements that promise too much. Happiness, mental health, assertiveness, etc., are global goals that may emerge in practice but are unlikely to be achieved unless they are specified and partialized with reference to particular events that are salient to the client's life. For example, a disabled, returning veteran from the Iraq War with only one leg and moderate PTSD may want to take up his life where he left it before his deployment. A more realistic goal upon discharge from active duty may be to locate a structured living arrangement close to a VA hospital, to work on rehabilitation of his mobility, to plan carefully for his finances, and to locate a part-time job in a protected work environment.

Other time limits that may be negotiated in a social work contract concern the overall length of service (10 sessions, 3 months), the length of sessions (50 minutes, 2 hours), or the frequency of contacts in a given time period (daily, weekly, monthly sessions). Many of these time limits are established by agencies and third-party insurance companies and are not in the client's and interpersonal practitioner's control. The economics of contemporary social work practice determine the length of service and not the needs or wants of clients and interpersonal practitioner.

When goals, objectives, and time limits have been clearly articulated, the interpersonal practitioner and client will focus on the specific actions, activities, and responsibilities that each party will perform to achieve the goals. Such a range of actions and activities is wide in practice, yet it is limited by several considerations. Obviously, the worker and client's knowledge and skill will affect the possible actions. Ethical considerations will also affect what the worker can and cannot do in a particular situation. Interpersonal practitioners cannot engage in sexual intercourse with clients no matter how willing clients may be. They also cannot engage in violence with members of the client's social network who may be oppressing clients. But even with these limits, the worker and client have a wide range of actions that can be taken to achieve their goals.

In an ideal world, those actions and interventions that are most effective in achieving goals with a particular client will have been empirically validated so that the negotiation of actions in the contract can be guided by empirical knowledge. But this level of technical, prescriptive knowledge often does not exist except to a limited degree in social work. Even if this kind of systematic knowledge did fully exist, actions, interventions, and responsibilities will also be shaped by other variables in practice, such as the client's values and preferences, agency policies, and worker expertise. Some clients may refuse to take actions that research demonstrates are important. For example, parents may refuse to visit their child who has been removed to temporary foster care even though visits are important to restoration (Fanshel, 1971).

A major value of contracting is to ensure that all parties are clear about what is expected of them. Such clarity is especially important when several professionals are involved with one client. When good coordination exists, duplication of effort can be avoided, actions are consistent and supportive of each other, and clients are not caught in the middle of conflicting agency agendas. Coordination of service is discussed in greater detail in the chapter on individual change (Chapter 11).

In some writings, references are made to "behavioral contracts" (Rose, 1977), "tasks" (Reid & Epstein, 1972), or "secondary contracts" (Seabury, 1979). Whichever term is used to describe these activities, it is important that all individuals engaged in the service process have an understanding and acceptance of what each person is expected to do. This level of contracting becomes even more critical as the numbers of members of the action system increase.

● CHARACTERISTICS OF A SOCIAL WORK CONTRACT

There are four basic characteristics of a social work contract: (1) *explicitness*, (2) *mutuality*, (3) *flexibility*, and (4) *pragmatism*. A service contract is explicit and clear so that all parties (worker, client, other professionals) understand all terms and little is taken for granted. Preferably, the terms of the contract are expressed in concrete, specific, and simple language. Professional jargon and legalese are avoided, and the client's own words are used so that ambiguity, vagueness, and confusion between parties are minimized.

To assure explicitness, some agencies use written contracts (Knapp, 1980; Stein, Gambrill, & Wiltse, 1974). However, a written contract does not ensure that it will be understood by all parties. Many people sign legal contracts (loan agreements) without reading or even comprehending what they are signing. But simple contract forms have been developed that require workers to compose contracts in the client's own words. (See the written contract in Figure 8.2.)

It is not necessary, desirable, or possible to use written contracts with all clients. With some clients, an informed agreement can be achieved verbally, and a written contract is redundant and unnecessarily time consuming. With other clients, a written contract is threatening and intimidating because it resembles legal devices that have placed them in jeopardy with other agencies or authorities in the past. Still, with other clients (illiterate, psychotic, severely developmentally disabled, small children), a written contract would be meaningless as well as impossible to complete.

Written contracts can be valuable, though, with impulsive clients who should be held accountable for decisions they have reached. Written and signed contracts allow parties to hold each other more accountable for following through on agreements. Some social workers have also used written contracts to hold other professionals accountable for services they have promised their clients (Bush, 1977).

Ideally, a social work contract is mutually established between worker and client and other parties. Not only must contracts be *understandable*, but they must also be *acceptable* to all parties. All parties participate in negotiating terms and should be given an opportunity to participate in decision making. The client's opinions and perspective are seriously considered and solicited, and the worker does not intimidate the client into accepting the worker's "wisdom." This is most likely to occur if the idea of a contract is fully explained to the clients and they are given oral or written examples.

Although mutuality is clearly consistent with the social work value of client empowerment and self-determination, in practice mutuality can be difficult to achieve. For some clients, service is imposed by a higher authority, such as a court, parent, or spouse. In these situations, the client may enter service reluctantly.

Figure 8.2 A Written Contract

Agreement With Natural Parents or Guardians

THIS AGREEMENT is a contract between ___Nancy Dunham___ , Social Worker, Hampton Department of Social Services, and ___Robert and Sally Smith___ parent(s) of ___Alvin and George Smith.___

The purpose of this Agreement is to make permanent plans for ___Alvin and George Smith,___ whose custody is with the Hampton Department of Social Services. It is the wish of the parent(s) to have the child(ren) ___returned to their custody___ .

to accomplish the above goal the following conditions must be met:

1. Parenting skills must be improved.
2. Mr. Smith's employment must be maintained.
3. Household bills must be paid up to date.
4. Household furniture must meet children's needs.
5.

The parent(s) and the social worker will be responsible for doing the following things during this part of the Agreement:

Parent(s)
1. Buy baby crib by 1-27-94.
2. Mrs. Smith will attend weekly parenting class through 3-14-94.
3. Mr. Smith will continue present employment through 3-21-94.
4. Household bills (rent and utilities) will be paid on time through 3-21-94.

Social Worker
1. Register Mrs. Smith for parenting class by 1-24-94.
2. Arrange weekend visits between parents and children every other weekend from 1-20-94 to 3-21-94.
3. Make home visit every other Friday until 3-14-94.

This Agreement will be reviewed on___3-14-94___ to plan the next stage in the completion of the goal. The total period of time for the accomplishment of the goal ___of return of custody___ is from ___1-17-94___ to ___3-21-94___

1-17-94	Social Worker

A court may remove a neglected child from a parent and order the parent to seek services before the child can be returned, or the parents may force a youth, who is having problems at school and home, to come to an agency. Although mutuality may seem unlikely on these occasions, both youth and parent can be engaged in service with a chance to shape it so that the individual's willingness to participate emerges.

A worker may establish a trial contract with some clients, such as adolescent clients and family systems. This is an agreement to try out service for a few interviews (Hartman & Laird, 1983). For example, the interpersonal practitioner may ask an adolescent if she would agree to return for two more sessions and to explore "what's going on" in her life before deciding whether she wanted service. During the few trial sessions, the interpersonal practitioner has the opportunity to explore the client's situation in greater detail and convey to her the value of the service. During trial sessions, the interpersonal practitioner also has an opportunity to provide services, and in some trial periods, clients will constructively use the time to make changes. For clients who come in with crises, one or two sessions may be all that is required to elicit adequate coping behavior.

Not all clients decide they need or want services; thus, at the end of the trial contract, some clients will decide not to return. This decision should be respected by the interpersonal practitioner, who closes the case with the understanding that clients can always return if they change their minds.

Parents who are ordered to use a service by the court can be offered a dual contract approach (Fusco, 1977; Rooney, 2009). The worker offers to help the client separate court-mandated terms from terms negotiated with the worker, and the worker explains that court-mandated terms cannot be renegotiated with the worker and can be changed only through a legal proceeding. But even court mandates may give the client some discretionary power about agreements they may make in the service contract (Seabury, 1979). For example, the court may demand improvements in child care arrangements but not specify what these improvements are or how they are to be accomplished. In this situation, the worker and client will discuss a range of alternatives (e.g., day care, involvement of relative, or child care classes). While contracting with the worker, the client has had a chance to determine alternatives that were not stated by the court.

A social work contract is flexible and dynamic so that decisions may be renegotiated as service progresses. Unlike a signed legal contract that is static and binding, a social work contract usually is tentative and represents a plan rather than a set of rigid rules. Most social work contracts may be renegotiated when the client or worker concludes that the terms are unfair, unacceptable, nonproductive, or missing important issues. When contract terms are not achieved, worker and client will evaluate the impasse and plan alternative terms.

The following dilemma arises concerning flexibility: How much flexibility is appropriate? Too much leads to a meaningless contract that is always changing, and, thus, there are no boundaries, deadlines, or limits to service. Too little flexibility creates a contract that may rapidly become outdated.

Some clients fall into a pattern in which they agree to a responsibility but then fail to follow through. Verbally they agree to a particular action, yet behaviorally they do not comply. This lapse between intention and action is common to us all. It is much easier to agree to do something than it is to apply the time and energy actually to carry it out. This kind of common failure to follow through on a particular task or responsibility is a problem for a contractual approach.

How much flexibility is to be permitted in the service contract? When client and worker do not follow through on terms, should these terms be automatically renegotiated or should some form of sanction or remedy (pressure) be applied to encourage compliance with the original terms? How can a worker judge when terms should be enforced and a client not allowed to renegotiate prior agreements? When is enforcement or pressure unproductive and renegotiation a more plausible solution?

Some clients need the limits provided by a contract to produce significant changes in their lives. When these clients do not follow through, the worker should firmly encourage the client to try again until the action is completed. An excellent procedure has been developed that workers can employ to help clients follow through on tasks they have trouble completing. The Task Implementation Sequence (TIS) is designed to help clients discuss, plan, and practice a particular task, or responsibility, before attempting to carry it out. The TIS procedure effectively increases the likelihood that a client will follow through on an agreed-on task or action (Reid, 1975). The TIS procedure is a motivational strategy, but it cannot produce compliance when a client opposes the task. In fact, it is impossible to complete the TIS when clients are under this constraint.

Developing the TIS is not a time-consuming procedure. It may be completed in as little as 15 minutes, although it can require a full session. It is important that all steps be completed even though the order of the sequence may be rearranged. In order to empower clients during the first three steps, it is best for clients to generate their own examples or ideas first; then the worker may suggest other possibilities. The steps in the TIS are

1. *Enhancing Commitment.* The worker asks the client to consider the potential benefits of carrying out the task, or action, in question. "What good will result from doing this?" "How will you benefit?" The worker gently pushes the client to think of as many benefits as possible. After the client has exhausted ideas, the worker may present positive consequences that have not been discussed. "Think how good you will feel to finally have this task behind you!"

2. *Planning Task Implementation.* The client is helped to specify the task and develop a detailed plan for carrying it out. The worker may ask questions that

enable the client to spell out exactly when, where, and with whom the task will be carried out. For example, the client will decide the day, time, place, main actors, and specific actions that will be involved in completing the task. The worker also helps the client explore alternative ways of doing the task. When the task is carefully planned and specified, sometimes it is obvious that the original task must be broken down into several individual tasks. Some clients may think it is silly to set aside a day and a time to work on the task (e.g., "You really expect me to work on this before I go to bed on Sunday?"), yet this specificity is often missing when homework is assigned to clients between sessions.

3. *Analyzing Obstacles.* The worker asks the client to consider problems or barriers that may be encountered in carrying out the task. If the client has trouble identifying obstacles, possible contingencies can be suggested. For example, "What if this happens?" or "What if that occurs?" Psychological barriers, such as fears or procrastination associated with the task, may be discussed. For example, "Are you comfortable meeting with this person?" or "Would you consider yourself a procrastinator?" The worker should also explore possible negative consequences that the client may face if the task is carried out. Sometimes significant others in the client's social network would not be supportive of the task.

The reason for talking about obstacles is not to give the client excuses ahead of time about why they did not complete the task but to give the interpersonal practitioner and client a chance to make contingency plans if obstacles arise. For example, "If a friend does call and ask you over for pizza, can you tell the friend you will come over after you write an important letter?" Sometimes obstacles cannot be countered in the plan, and it is then best to agree to move to another day or time of day.

4. *Modeling, Rehearsal, Guided Practice.* In this step, the worker helps the client in the interview to practice parts of the task. Usually those aspects that are practiced involve interactions with others or difficult parts of the task. The worker may model possible task behaviors by demonstrating what he or she might say and do in the task situation, or the client may rehearse what to say or do. Modeling and rehearsal may be carried out through role play, and situations may be role-played several times until the client feels some mastery. Practice can also be accomplished by having the client imagine or practice "in their mind's eye" (Lazarus, 1977) in the interview the actions of the task. This is usually the longest part of the TIS procedure.

5. *Summarizing.* The worker restates the task and the plan for carrying it out. This review helps assure that the client has a clear idea of what is to be accomplished, and the worker completes the sequence with a strong expectation that the

client will complete the task. For example, a worker might say, "I look forward to hearing how the interview went at next week's session." It is also helpful to ask the client to summarize the points that are raised in each step of the procedure as they are completed.

As good as TIS is as a practice procedure to encourage clients to complete tasks, some clients will simply fail to complete them even when TIS is employed. When repeated noncompliance occurs, it is not productive to push the client. Clients should not be pressured into situations of failure; on the contrary, successful situations are much more desirable. Renegotiation of terms is more sensible so that clients can plan actions they are likely to accomplish. When the worker has carefully involved the client in decisions and planning and the client fails to complete negotiated responsibilities, the worker should question the client's desire to continue service, and the original purpose of service may be discussed.

A social work contract is pragmatic and realistic. The terms of a contract do not demand actions, tasks, or responsibilities that are beyond the capacity of either worker or client. Workers do not make promises that are beyond their own expertise or agency resources, and clients are not pushed or intimidated into accepting terms that demand more than their skills and resources can deliver. Unrealistic goals, no matter how desirable, may lead to failure and frustration. A contract based on false hope or intimidating demands may be more harmful than no contract at all.

How can a worker and client know in advance how realistic a given term is? One technique to test the reality of terms is for the worker to take a conservative stance. For example, after an objective and deadline have been planned, a worker might say to the client, "Fine, we've agreed to get you enrolled in a training program in 2 weeks, but honestly tell me how far will you really have gone on this in the next 2 weeks?" And the client may answer, "Well, if I have even located a training program in 2 weeks, I'll feel I've done something!" Such a question helps clients consider the objective realistically in the light of their own knowledge of their capacity to complete the objective. The client may then be in the position, also, of pushing the worker toward a more difficult goal instead of the worker doing so.

Another tactic that the worker may use to test the reality of terms is to play the devil's advocate. Once the client and worker have agreed on a term, the worker may deliberately raise doubts or question its value. The worker might say, "I can't see why you would really want to do that." This allows the client to express doubts that he or she may not have raised and also tests the client's commitment to a term. Playing devil's advocate is not intended to talk the client out of a given term but rather to help the client consider all aspects of what is being agreed to in the contract.

● VALUE OF THE CONTRACT APPROACH

The contract approach is valuable to interpersonal practice for both empirical and ethical reasons. Ethically, a contract approach is clearly consistent with social work's professed value that all clients have worth and deserve to be treated with dignity. A contract approach requires that the worker deliberately encourage the client to participate in decisions about service. Even though a worker may not agree with the client's input, the client's opinion is important, and the worker has a responsibility to cultivate it.

Contract approaches thus reflect the professional ethic of client empowerment and self-determination. Contract approaches encourage clients to be active participants in service, not passive recipients. This supports and demands client self-determination in the service process. When a client is not aware of what is being planned or is not in agreement with it, there can be no self-determination or contract as described in this chapter.

Contract approaches also provide a mechanism for accountability. When parties have reached agreement on a given arrangement, each individual is clear about what is expected of him or her and others. This allows parties to question actions that are inconsistent with objectives and to hold others responsible for what they have agreed to deliver. This kind of accountability is double edged and can be used by both workers and clients.

Because the social work profession is committed to serving all people in need, social workers are concerned not only about providing effective service to those they serve but also about developing services for those who have trouble finding and using services. Discontinuance, as discussed previously, is seen in the high dropout rates of clients who seek service and who fail to remain long enough for service to have much effect. Some evidence suggests that discontinuance rates can be lowered by employing a contract approach to service. Because contracting helps to clarify expectations about service, clients feel less anxious and confused about what to expect and therefore are more likely to continue (Perlman, 1968, pp. 172–176).

Research on contract approaches suggests that contracts have a positive impact on both the process of service and its outcome. In a controlled study, patients who were given a special interview to orient them to service and explain what to expect were judged to have a better relationship with their therapist, a better attendance record, and a more favorable response to treatment than did those who did not receive *this* orienting interview between intake and treatment (Hoehn-Saric et al., 1964; Liberman et al., 1972). In child welfare services, contracts have been demonstrated to reduce significantly "foster care drift" by facilitating planning and the restoration of children to their natural parents (Stein & Gambrill, 1977). Contracts help workers to be more systematic and organized in their approach with clients and to be more responsive to clients' needs. Contracts also strengthen the worker–client relationship and encourage clients to be more actively involved in service.

LIMITS OF CONTRACTING ●

Contracting, as any approach to practice, does not work in all situations with all clients. There are some practice situations in which contracting is impossible because it is unlikely that worker and client will reach an agreement about the terms of service. Contracting is primarily a verbal enterprise, whether spoken or written, and it requires that all parties be competent and rational at the time of negotiation. Therefore, extremely disturbed, brain-damaged, or intoxicated people are not fully able to engage in a contract process. Usually, in these situations, a worker will establish a contract with a close family member or friend on behalf of the client.

Contracting is also impossible when a client seeks an objective that violates the values of the worker. Violence against others is not allowed in a worker's code of ethics even though there are clients who view violence as a way of solving problems. Although it may be desirable to be nonjudgmental in a social work relationship, there are limits to how much a social worker can be (Hardman, 1975). For example, a Catholic worker in a Catholic agency might find it impossible to work with a client who seeks help to terminate an unwanted pregnancy.

When there is a fundamental clash in values, the worker has a responsibility to inform the client of the conflict. When there is no chance that the conflict can be resolved, the worker has a responsibility to help the client locate another worker or service that can be responsive to the client's perspective.

Besides impossible situations, there are times when contracting is *contraindicated* because a contractual approach will be detrimental to clients or to others. Although contracts are intended to facilitate service, with some clients in crisis, time is critical, and the worker does not have the luxury of discussing each decision to gain the client's acceptance of it. In fact, to clients who are in suicidal or homicidal crises, it may be absurd for a worker to say, "I'm here to talk you out of blowing up yourself and your family any way I can. By the way, while we are talking, the police are sneaking your family out the back door!"

Life and limb considerations must always take precedence over a client's desires or perspectives, and a worker may have to overrule a client's decision and even act against a client's will. For example, a mother in an intake interview wanted help with her "blackout spells." The worker then learned that the client had an infant at home who had had severe vomiting and diarrhea and a high fever for several days and had not received medical attention. Even if the mother does not want help for her infant, the worker cannot ignore the risks in such a situation and must act to protect the child. In another practice situation, an individual client and worker agreed that information the client shared with the worker was not to be told to family members. When that client became severely suicidal, this agreement was broken by the worker to protect the client, and the family and the client were told this.

Because contracts are impossible or contraindicated in some practice situations does not mean that service cannot be delivered. The reason for discussing these situations is that the worker should attempt other approaches rather than waste time and energy struggling to apply a contract approach.

There are practice situations in which contracting is *problematic*, and the worker and client achieve only a marginal working agreement. Although there are numerous problematic situations in contracting, this discussion will focus on three common problems: the hidden agenda, the corrupt contract, and sabotage.

The Hidden Agenda

Either client or worker or other service providers may engage in contracting while maintaining a hidden agenda. When parties have a hidden agenda during contract negotiation, they deliberately withhold information, an opinion, or a perspective. Even though the term is not fully discussed, secretly the party hopes that some kind of implicit agreement on the hidden agenda can be achieved. For example, a worker may agree with a client that the target problem is social isolation from family and friends, yet the worker may secretly believe the problem that should be addressed is the client's low self-image. In this situation, the worker may never have shared the view that self-image is important to the client, yet the worker may subtly try to direct service or interventions into this area. The confusion that may arise with such a hidden agenda is that the client may be working on the agreed-on agenda, but the worker is working on the hidden agenda. The client and worker end up working at cross-purposes.

Individuals may engage in contracting with hidden agendas for a number of reasons. Sometimes clients are simply too embarrassed, anxious, or threatened to share honestly what is important to them. The client may want service to begin with a safer agenda before moving into heavier issues. Worker and client sometimes can make this kind of entrée into service work—that is, move from simpler to more serious issues. But this is a risky way to proceed because some clients do not remain in service long enough to fulfill serious goals because insurance providers will not support such long-term service.

Sometimes individuals use a hidden agenda as a power tactic when contracting. Instead of discussing the hidden agenda openly and risking having it rejected outright, the hidden agenda is withheld so that it can be subtly employed as time goes on in the hope that the other party will be persuaded that it has merit. For example, in some family treatment situations, the child may be seen as the target (and having the problem) by the parents, yet the worker may view the parents as the targets because they contribute to the problem. To work with the whole family, the worker may contract with the parents to participate as "information givers" yet maintain a hidden agenda that as parents become more involved their problems will emerge, and they will accept the need to change.

The dilemma with hidden agendas is that they do not always work out the way parties intend. As the hidden agenda becomes clear, the other parties may feel outraged at the deception and break off contact without considering the merits of the hidden agenda. The decision to hide the particular agenda for later discussion only dooms it to failure: A more open discussion in the beginning may have produced the desired response by the other party. In the example just presented, if parents had been informed from the beginning that they, too, must be a part of the change if they are to help their child, they might not have liked the idea, but at least they could have negotiated a trial contract to test this out. Even if parents reject the idea that they are to change, time is not wasted manipulating them into accepting something they will later reject. It is difficult enough to change people when they agree to change. It may be impossible using social work approaches to change people against their will—especially when they recognize that they have been deceived.

The Corrupt Contract

Another kind of contract problem arises when several individuals (several clients and several professionals) are involved in the service process. A corrupt contract (Beal, 1972) may emerge when the various agreements among different individuals are not coordinated or are deliberately negotiated to be inconsistent. With some couples who experience marital problems and blame the other, a worker might have both spouses agree to come in and help the other spouse with his or her problems. Both spouses then enter service with the worker with two conflicting contracts—each believes it is the other who is to be changed.

Workers are not the only ones who engage in this kind of corrupt contracting. Some clients who use different services may engage in a similar duplicity by making agreements with one professional who contradicts agreements with the other. The results of this behavior can be disastrous as agencies work at cross-purposes, and the client is caught in the middle (Hoffman & Long, 1969).

The problem with a corrupt contract (as with a hidden agenda) is that sooner or later the contradiction in agreements is discovered. Parties may terminate their relationship together, and the progress already gained may be quickly destroyed.

Corrupt contracting can be avoided if all significant individuals in the service process are brought together in the beginning and periodically thereafter to discuss their various impressions, intentions, and responsibilities in the case. If face-to-face discussion is not possible, then someone (preferably the worker) must take responsibility for monitoring and coordinating the service process.

Even with face-to-face coordination, corrupt contracts occur when some or all of the people involved fear that explicitness will lead to conflict. Some individuals avoid conflict at all costs because they view interpersonal conflict as "bad," "unpleasant," or "unresolvable." There is nothing inherently bad about interpersonal conflict, and attempts to avoid conflict during contracting are usually self-defeating. Expressing differences early in the contract process requires parties to be honest so that each has a better chance to engage in a frank negotiation of contract terms (Chaiklin, 1973; Halleck, 1963). When contracting goes too smoothly, it may be a sign that one party is "selling out" to the other too quickly.

Sabotage

Another problem is sabotage. This involves actions that are designed to keep contract terms (especially goals and objectives) from being realized. Sabotage can be active and deliberate (e.g., a team member may disagree with a discharge plan and actively encourage the patient to act out so that the discharge plan will fail) or it can be subtle, such as in passive resistance or marginal compliance (e.g., parents may periodically "forget" to bring a child to a scheduled appointment).

Workers, clients, other service providers, and significant others in the client's world are all capable of engaging in sabotage. Whenever individuals are strongly committed to a position (e.g., they believe they know what's right or best), sabotage may appear when they are overruled in the negotiation of a service plan. Sabotage may also result from being left out of decision making or in other ways ignored. The point of this discussion is that anyone may engage in sabotage and that, when sabotage occurs, it does not mean that the person is evil—although this is often how sabotage is viewed by those it affects.

Sabotage can be prevented or at least minimized by carefully involving all parties who will be participating in the service plan in the planning and negotiation process. It may be time consuming to encourage maximum participation, yet such effort is invaluable if sabotage is to be avoided. This means that people are not just invited to participate in a conference or session, but during the meeting, their opinions and perspectives are elicited; the final plan takes into account what all parties bring to the session. Although it may be difficult to involve a particularly contrary individual in some case conferences or planning sessions, deliberately leaving the contrary individual out may invite disaster if the plan is implemented and the contrary individual sabotages it.

CONTRACTING WITH FAMILIES AND GROUPS ●

This section focuses on selected issues of contracting with families and small groups. These issues are singled out because they represent contract issues that are particular to multiperson client systems.

The first issue involves *time* and applies to both families and small groups. When there are several people in the client system, negotiating contract terms will take longer than it will with an individual client. It takes more time to hear everyone, share perspectives, and agree to a common ground. Another reality is that the greater the number of people involved, the greater the chance for differing perspectives and the longer it takes to work toward a consensus or compromise. Because of these realities, the worker may spend too much time negotiating terms; individuals may feel that service is dragging because too much time is spent on planning service rather than receiving it.

One way of avoiding these feelings of frustration is for the worker to structure these first sessions to facilitate contracting. For example, with some formed groups, it is possible to have pregroup interviews with each prospective member (Bertcher & Maple, 1996). These pregroup interviews are not only useful as a screening mechanism in selecting group members, but they also can be used to discuss with individuals what they want from the group and what they can expect from the group. When members arrive at the first session, they have completed some preliminary contracting. The groundwork has been laid for the group's efforts to reach an agreement. This approach can be applied with families. Each member of the family may be seen in individual sessions before a conjoint session with the whole family is planned, although this is, for reasons to be discussed later, not typically how family treatment begins. This issue will be discussed in more detail in the chapters on family and group change (Chapters 13 and 15).

Another way of speeding up contracting in early sessions is to assign some of the tasks involved in contracting as "homework" between sessions. For example, members of a family may be requested to think about what they hope family sessions will do for them and the family, to write these thoughts down, and to bring them in to share at the next session. Group members can be assigned similar tasks that relate to contracting, such as deciding how the group might help them or what things they might do in the group to help other members. By using the homework structure, individual members are given a chance to do some of the preparatory thinking, and this will be helpful to facilitate contracting.

There are also activities that a worker can employ within the session to facilitate contracting. For example, individuals can be asked to write on cards what they think is important about a particular contract term (e.g., target problems or goals). The cards are collected and the worker reads or paraphrases each card (Hill, 1960). This activity facilitates contracting because it encourages maximum participation, individuals are more apt to listen to what the worker says, and it is easier for all participants to see commonalities or patterns in what the worker reads because the participants are not focusing as much on their own perspectives.

Another way to minimize the feeling that nothing is happening in early sessions is for the worker to use early sessions for a broader array of activities that includes contracting. Workers may include group activities or experiences that make participants see that service has begun. For example, in an early group session, time may be set aside for one individual to bring up an issue that he or she hopes the group will help to resolve. If the worker can facilitate the ensuing discussion so that other members share information or at least give moral support, all members of the group experience how the group can be helpful to individuals, and thus they will feel that something more than planning has been accomplished.

There are many other procedures that workers employ to facilitate contracting with families and small groups. Contracting can be time consuming in a group. To avoid losing members who drop out in frustration because "All we did was talk about what we were going to do but never did it!" a worker must take responsibility for speeding up the process.

An issue that occurs when contracting with families involves the basic elements of contracting itself. Good contracts require honest sharing and mutual agreement, yet some families seek help with problems that do not lend themselves to successful contracting. Families may be unwilling to share or exchange information honestly or are incapable of listening or responding to information offered by other family members. Some families cannot reach mutual decisions involving all family members. Therefore, contracting with the worker to reach mutual agreements is incompatible with their way of relating. When a worker asks such a family what it considers its biggest problem, chaos may break out as each family member presents a different problem and argues with the others about it.

When families have problems communicating and making decisions as a group, the worker should structure the early sessions to help the family formulate a contract. The structured family interview (SFI) offers a way of building structure into these early sessions. Although the SFI was developed as a diagnostic procedure, elements of SFI can be adapted to help families make decisions about contract terms (Watzlawick, 1966). For example, the *exercises* in SFI require the family to talk to each other in pairs or other subgroups and then regroup to discuss what was accomplished. This patterning interrupts the usual communication patterns that such families use. The process of helping these families contract with the worker about service may be, in fact, the most important technique the worker uses. Once the family has reached a mutual agreement with the worker, it may have accomplished a fundamental and essential change.

Another family contracting issue relates to the approach to family treatment chosen by the worker. In some approaches, the family is told that problems of individuals are maintained by family conditions. The worker contracts with the family to seek a change in such conditions as family communications, family consensus on goals, or family structures. In other approaches, the problem, such as delinquency, psychosis, or depression, of an individual is assumed to be legitimate, and a contract is made in which individual change is a goal. More discussion of this issue is presented in the chapter on family change (Chapter 13).

An issue that is particular to formed groups relates to the dual responsibility of group members to be both helpee and helper. This responsibility must be clearly understood and accepted by them. There are many ways in which a group member can be helpful to other members by giving feedback, support, or being a model. Each member must not only take from the group but also give to it. When the "self-help therapy principle" (Reissman, 1967, pp. 217–226) works, it is often the giving that means the most for a member.

There are five types of contracts in work with families and groups. To clarify this range of contractual possibilities, we list each type with appropriate examples of some contractual terms (see Table 8.1).

This range of possibilities may appear confusing at first to workers, but it should be recognized that each one has its value. When used at the appropriate time, each type of contract can help to unify the efforts of workers and family or group members toward the achievement of mutual, desired goals. Work with multiperson client systems is a complex matter, and devices such as contracts help to make it efficient and effective.

We end this chapter with an exercise that hopefully makes contracting salient to social work students. When students are entering their field placements, they are usually expected to negotiate an educational agreement with their field supervisor. Basically these educational agreements spell out the learning objectives and various activities that the student will complete in their internship. This contracting process with your field instructor places you, the student, in the "low power position," which is the position that clients occupy when they are negotiating a contract with their social worker. Here at the University of Michigan School of Social Work (UMSSW), this is a written document that holds both the student and field instructor accountable for the quality of the field experience. Exercise 8.1 will help you to reflect what contracting as a process is like when you are in the low power position.

Table 8.1	Various Contracts in Multiperson Client Systems

1. Between the family or group and the agency

Examples: The group members agree to pay a fee for 12 sessions, even if a session is missed. The family members agree that all will take responsibility to see to it that all family members are present at sessions.

2. Between the family or group and the worker

Examples: The group members agree they will try to complete homework assignments made by the worker. The family members agree to discuss among themselves the worker's recommendations.

3. Between a member of the family or group and the worker

Examples: Frank, a group member, agrees to make no suicide attempt without first discussing this with the worker. Alice, a single parent, agrees to call the worker when she feels so angry that she will not be able to restrain her violence toward her daughter.

4. Between one member of the family or group and another member

Examples: Two group members agree to become "buddies" and to call each other when they need support. The spouses in the family agree to discuss with each other how they will discipline their child before imposing the discipline.

5. Between one member of the family or group and the entire family or group

Examples: Carol, a group member, agrees to take notes of conclusions reached in the group and use them to provide feedback to the group. Bob, a teenage son, agrees to discuss his plans to leave home with the entire family, including parents and siblings.

Exercise 8.1

Negotiating Your Learning Agreement in the Field Placement

In this exercise, we want you to reflect on this experience with your field instructor and apply the principles we have discussed in this chapter to the experience with your field instructor.

1. Did your field instructor encourage you to express and develop your learning goals for the field placement? Were you empowered to state what you wanted out of the field experience? Or were you handed a document that stated what you could expect at the agency with a "take it or leave it" attitude?

2. *Was your field instructor clear about the kinds of learning experiences (e.g., working with groups, families, children, or the elderly) the agency offered, or were learning opportunities left vague and unspecified?*

3. *Did your field instructor schedule weekly sessions with protected time to process your field activities, or was supervision left up "to catch as catch can" and squeezed in whenever?*

4. *If your field agency employed group supervision, was this process carefully explained to you? How do you feel about group supervision and sharing your work with other students?*

5. *What percentage of the learning agreement reflected your wants, and what percentage reflected the agency and the field supervisor expectations?*

6. *The field experience is an expensive part of your educational experience in social work. Do you feel that you got your "money's worth" in this educational experience?*

SUMMARY ●

We began this chapter with a brief discussion of the origins of the contract concept in social work and the value of contract in practice. We indicated that many different terms can be negotiated in a contract, but the basic components of a social work contract include the purpose, the problems to be worked on, the goals or objectives of the service, the responsibilities and actions of all parties, and time limits.

In developing effective contracts, the worker must help clients to create terms that are explicit, mutual, and pragmatic. A desirable degree of flexibility must also be assured. One procedure termed *TIS* was presented as a way of securing this type of agreement. Such approaches to contracting were described as leading to both more effective outcomes and more ethical practices.

At times, a contracting approach is contraindicated. This occurs when the client is in crisis, when the worker does not seek to demystify service, and when the client is not competent to negotiate a contract. Some common problems in contracting are hidden agendas, corrupt agreements, and sabotage. Ways of identifying these problems as well as solving them were presented.

The chapter concluded with a discussion of issues for workers and clients when the client system is composed of several individuals as in family and group services. The contract differences in these situations stem from the fact that contracts must achieve a degree of consensus among participants and must occur between clients and workers singly or collectively as well as among the members of the client system. This complexity may at first appear to make work with such client systems more difficult, but contracts actually reduce such complexity when used appropriately and skillfully.

CHAPTER 9

MONITORING AND EVALUATING CHANGE

If we don't change direction soon, we'll end up where we're going.

—Comedian Irwin Corey

The modest objective of this chapter is to introduce the reader to the topics of *monitoring* and *evaluation*. This chapter will not present all of the issues in measurement and evaluation that social work students cover in their research and evaluation courses. Instead, this chapter will focus on various evaluation methods that can be incorporated into service with client systems. There are books that present evaluation scales for many of the problems that clients bring into service (Corcoran & Fisher, 2000; Hudson, 1987; WALMYR Publishing Company, 2002), but the actual practice of social work seems to demonstrate that these evaluation scales are not being utilized. In the first chapter of this book, we discussed the importance of empirically based practice and the responsibility of social work practitioners to understand evidence-based interventions. This chapter will not teach practitioners how to do this kind of practice research. We intend for this chapter to describe how selective methods of evaluation can be operationalized in practice with individuals, families, and groups.

We introduce two separate but related topics when we refer to monitoring and evaluating. We define monitoring as identifying and recording events that occur during social work helping. These include the activities of the worker as well as of the client. If the action and client systems include a family, group, or organization, then monitoring also includes a record of events in these multiperson systems. We define evaluating as the determination of whether or not the client has attained his or her goals and whether changes can be attributed to the help offered. It is easier to determine whether changes have occurred in the client than to ascertain what has "caused" the change. We elaborate further on this issue in this chapter.

Our approach to monitoring and evaluation is consistent with a growing commitment in social work to empirically based practice. Siegel (1984), in his definition of such practice, stated that it

1. makes maximum use of research findings;

2. collects data systematically to monitor the intervention;

3. demonstrates empirically whether or not interventions are effective;

4. specifies problems, interventions, and outcomes in terms that are concrete, observable, and measurable;

5. uses research ways of thinking and research methods in defining clients' problems, formulating questions for practice, collecting assessment data, evaluating the effectiveness of interventions, and using evidence;

6. views research and practice as part of the same problem solving process; and

7. views research as a tool to be used in practice.

We believe that practice should be empirically based for the following reasons:

1. To determine and report to the clients whether they have been helped to attain their goals. The clients should use this information to decide whether to terminate the service, continue with the service for other reasons, or seek a new service.

2. To engage in a self-correcting practice—that is, to continue to act in ways that are effective and to discontinue acting in ways that are ineffective. This kind of information should be used not only by workers for themselves but should be shared with colleagues so that the entire profession moves toward more effective practice.

3. To supply effectiveness data to the agency so that the agency can determine whether it is accomplishing its purposes. The evaluation of work done on each case, therefore, should be accumulated so that the agency's program can be evaluated. The agency, in turn, has the obligation to

inform its funding sources of its effectiveness so that public funds are spent in a responsible manner.

● MONITORING

Process Recording

The traditional way to monitor what the worker has done and what the immediate effects of worker activity are has been the process recording. In this record, the worker indicates the individual or group of individuals that constitute the system, who were present in the session, as well as other identifying data such as the date and location of the session. Workers also record their goals for the session. In group situations, these goals are expressed in terms of both the individual members and the group. For example, a process recording of a session may begin as follows:

This interview took place on May 16th in my office. Mrs. Jones and her son Robert were present. The interview was divided into three parts. Mrs. Jones was seen alone for about 20 minutes, Robert was seen alone for about 20 minutes, and the two together were seen for about 15 minutes to plan activities that will take place between this session and the next. The goals of this session were to monitor changes to Robert's defiant behavior toward his mother and to plan other activities that this family may try in the succeeding weeks.

The bulk of the process recording presents a chronological narrative recounting the events of the session from the worker's perspective. The worker indicates her part in these events but does not record every word spoken or action taken. Instead, the worker selects those events that appear pertinent to the purposes of the session. The recording ends with the worker's reflections on the events and plans for further work. This recording may take up several single spaced pages, and the reality of supervision is that students find the writing of process recordings to be tedious and the bane of their field experience. It is also an onerous task for agency supervisors who are overburdened with many demands that are placed on them by their agencies. The reality is that process recordings often are not written nor read, yet if remains one of the most direct ways of monitoring what a social work student is doing in an interview with her client system.

One difficulty is to determine what material to place in the process recording so that it does not become overly burdensome. Carel Germain's (1968) classic article clearly articulates the dilemma of how much information about clients should go into a record. In 19th century casework practice, caseworkers collected "everything" about the client. These early records were several inches thick—like metropolitan phone books. During the 20th century, the profession refined and reduced the recorded information by first only collecting information that was "significant" and then only what was "relevant" and then only what was "salient." You may have noticed that these three criteria (i.e., significant, relevant, and salient) are basically all synonyms. As various theories of practice entered the profession, these theories were used to guide the information and recording process. Today in the age of managed care and time limited models of practice, record keeping is at its minimalist.

Writing the process recording has value as it forces the social work student to reflect on the events of the session and to assess their relative importance. The main beneficiary of the process recording is therefore the student. Training and experience in the writing of process recordings should be included in professional education, as practice makes the preparation of such a recording progressively easier. Process recordings are used in supervision of students because they provide the supervisor with information on the student's use of self as well as on the dynamics present in the session.

Supervisors often will ask social work students to write at least one process recording a week to train the student in the preparation of such recordings and to promote self-awareness. Some years ago, supervisors required workers to prepare process recordings on all their contacts, but this practice is rare today.

Critical Incident Recording

The critical incident record is a modified form of process recording in which only a portion of the session is recorded. The portion referred to as a critical incident is one during which either an issue presented by the client or an intervention of the worker demands thorough analysis. The recording of the incident must be sufficient to indicate all the relevant information about the client's and the worker's behaviors. For example, members of a group became upset as they participated in a structured activity introduced into the session by the leader. This activity generated much more anxiety than members were able to handle in the session, and the group went overtime in order to debrief the incident. Careful review of this incident revealed that the leader put members under too much pressure to participate and did not honor the group's ground rule that there would be no forced participation in group activities.

Electronic Recording

We live in an age of surveillance in which we are surrounded by recording devices (e.g., in banks, stores, parking lots, and street corners). Social workers may use small, portable tape recorders or digital recorders that create highly compressed audio files. Many agencies also have audiovisual equipment that may be used to record client sessions. Unlike public surveillance, clients must be informed and asked for written permission to record sessions. Before clients can give permission, the written agreement must be clear what the purpose of the recording is, who will see it, how long and where it will be stored, and that the client has the right to terminate the permission at any time. In some family treatment sessions, the recordings may be played back and used therapeutically for the family to see themselves interacting.

Electronic recordings provide a more comprehensive view of the session because the recording device does not selectively remember or distort the events of the session, which happens in process recordings. The misconception about electronic recordings is that they are more efficient than process recordings. Whether the recordings are stored in their original form or are transcribed, it takes many hours to review them. The general convention is that the ratio is 1 to 4 between recording and review—that is, a 15-minute recording will consume an hour when played back and discussed in supervision. These electronic recordings are most useful, therefore, immediately after the session to identify events for training purposes.

An advantage of electronic recordings is that the worker may monitor them to see if they have followed the protocols that have been developed in evidence-based practice regimes. It is also possible for beginning practitioners to review sessions with rating scales to get a sense of their style in interviews. Almost 50 years ago, Hollis (1968) developed an empirically based system of social caseworker interventions with individuals and couples. Her theoretical framework was long-term, ego–psychological; she discovered six basic interventions: sustaining procedures, direct influence, exploration and promoting catharsis, reflecting on person/situation, reflecting on personality dynamics, and reflecting on developmental and early life experiences. At about the same time, Reid (Reid & Epstein, 1972) develop a similar, empirically based framework of caseworker interventions from his work on a time-limited, problem-oriented model. In this task-centered model, there were five primary interventions identified: exploration, structuring, enhancing awareness, encouragement, and direction. These two early pioneers set the groundwork for looking carefully at what social caseworkers did inside sessions with individuals and families.

Today there are many rating systems that code and teach beginning social work students about interventions with individuals, families, and groups. Students may use these various rating systems to see if they tend to be active in their session by giving advice, promoting catharsis, and structuring the sessions or are more reflective in exploring, pacing, use of silence, and encouragement. Table 9.1 presents a composite coding system of verbal interventions of the worker. It has been used in method courses to increase social work students' self-awareness. This composite of many interventions is not designed as a typology, as some categories overlap, nor is it comprehensive of all possible interventions. In order to complete this assignment, students must have a basic knowledge of what these various interventions entail. This assignment required students to get permission to record a third or later session with their client system.

| Table 9.1 | Coding Worker Interventions From a Recorded Session |

Date of Interview:	*Number of Interventions*	*Percentage of Total*
Exploring	4	16
Giving Advice	1	4
Clarifying	1	4
Perception checking		
Promoting catharsis	2	8
Interpreting	1	4
Confronting		
Encouraging	3	12
Structuring		
Giving feedback	1	4
Using silence		
Empathizing	3	12
Empowering	2	8
Focusing	1	4
Logically discussing	2	8
Pacing		
Partializing	1	4
Reframing		
Self-Sharing		
Engaging in small talk	1	4
Summarizing	1	4
Teaching		
Universalizing		
Totals	25	100%

Just a cursory review of an electronic record of a session will also give a student feedback about such basic interviewing skills as the use of open-ended, leading, or closed-ended questions; how many times the student interrupts the client; and the use of "why" questions that may be perceived as interrogation questions by clients. Video recordings may also reveal many unconventional nonverbal behaviors, such as ear scratching, nose picking, lip licking, hair preening, etc. It is a "corrective emotional experience" to see oneself in practice whether a teacher, practitioner, or group leader.

Look over the coded interventions in Table 9.1, and decide how you would summarize the social worker's style in this interview. Do you think the style is nondirective and reflective, or do you think the worker was more interactive and directive in this interview? Though this assignment is seen as tedious by social work students, it is an excellent way for students to build self-awareness, and we recommend that interpersonal practice students try out this exercise at some point in their training.

A related approach is observation of the session by others through a one-way window. These observers, whose presence is always known to the clients and approved by them, can perform a number of functions. The observers can code the actions and reactions of worker and clients, and they can advise the worker on desirable interventions during or after the session. Some workers have received such feedback during sessions through a telephone line to the observers or through consulting with them in person. This kind of "live supervision" is often used in teaching students to work with families (Kaplan, 1987). This supervision experience is intrusive and anxiety provoking for social work students, and some students have found it much too difficult to manage (personal experience as a faculty liaison). It seems best employed with experienced workers who are comfortable with each other and willing to share time in the hot seat.

Coded Recording Forms

Forms have been developed that enable workers to utilize coded categories to record client and worker behaviors during sessions. Decades ago, Seaburg (1965, 1970) reported a general framework that is still relevant today. The form indicates the following data about the session in addition to case number, date, and who the client and worker are:

- The persons present and their relationship to the client
- The kind of contact (office visit, home visit, telephone)
- The modality (individual, family, group)
- The problem situation discussed (categories include goals, self-concept, social control, social interactions, personality characteristics, norm violations, each category divided into subcategories)

- Intervention techniques (examples of one-to-one techniques, such as confrontation, clarification, advice giving, logical discussion; examples of group techniques, such as structured activities, making connections, refocusing the discussion)

Agencies today often employ brief forms of problem-oriented record keeping. The SOAP notes found in hospitals include a system of "Subjective data, Objective data, Assessment, Plan" (Beinecke, 1984). This type of information is recorded for each problem discussed. The point of these recording systems is that they are brief and can be quickly used as an ongoing record of the sessions with clients or patients.

Wilson (1980, p. 138) provided the following definitions of the SOAP categories:

Subjective data: The worker would write *S* and then describe the subjective data. Subjective data refers to the client's statement of the problem as he or she sees it. The viewpoint of significant others may also be included. . . .

Objective data: This section asks the worker to record factual data and observations. The client's behavior and/or personal appearance are described but not analyzed or assessed. Details concerning the client's living arrangements, financial situation, and so on can also be included if they are relevant to the particular problem area being discussed.

Assessment: This is where the worker analyzes the meaning of the factual observations he [*sic*] has recorded and the client's perceptions of the problem that he [*sic*] has written down. Do the client's and worker's perceptions of the problem agree?

Plan: Based on the gathering of facts, awareness of the client's feelings, and assessment of what all this means, the worker states what he or she plans to do to work on the problem that has been identified.

Whatever form workers use for recording, the opportunity to store records in a computer offers other advantages. Once case notes have been entered into a computer, it is possible to use the "search" function to locate patterns in the information. One example of this was a worker who thought that each time a client brought up issues concerning her mother, she was entering a period of depression. The worker "searched" for any references to depression and to mother and did confirm this relationship.

Other Monitoring Techniques

There are other techniques for monitoring changes in individuals; for example, behavioral counts between sessions are commonly used when clients are trying to eliminate undesirable behaviors or increase desirable behaviors. These counts may include all kinds of behavior, such as compulsive hand washing, binge eating, crying, attending school more regularly, eating less empty calories and instead eating more fruits and vegetables, etc. The worker will suggest a chart to the client and will negotiate the time period for recording events. Clients may keep track of these counts themselves, or significant others may be recruited to monitor changes in behavior.

Another common monitoring scale is SUDS—Subjective Units of Discomfort Scale. This scale was developed by Wolpe (1958) in his pioneering work with desensitization and today represents a scale from 0 to 10. The scale is a self-rated scale of the client and can be used to reflect many kinds of internal states of the client—for example, pain, anxiety, frustration, confusion, fear, sadness, cravings, etc. A SUDS score of 0 or 1 will represent an absence of the target emotion, and a score of 9 or 10 would represent an extremely high level of the emotion. SUDS is used by triage nurses in ERs to get some sense of how much pain a patient may be experiencing when entering the ER. SUDS is often used in sessions both pre and post a specific intervention to see if a targeted emotion has changed. For example, feelings of stress may be monitored by SUDS before and then after a meditation exercise, or feelings of pain may be monitored by SUDS before and after a yoga session. Trauma models, such as eye movement desensitization and reprocessing (EMDR), developed by Francine Shapiro (2001), use SUDS to monitor the effects of their procedures. For example, when the worker and client are evaluating an incident to be processed by using EMDR, the client is asked to rank the level of their distress about the incident at the beginning of the session and then throughout the processing. The scale is used by the client and the therapist to quantify the client's feelings about the incident. The aim of the processing is to reduce the SUDS to zero if possible or to get it as low as possible. A SUDS of 0 or very low would indicate to the worker and the client that the incident has been resolved.

We believe monitoring that includes the client is important because it empowers the client to participate in the change process, and it provides direct evidence to the client that changes may be taking place. We recognize that SUDS is a subjective scale and cannot be used to compare one person's pain or anxiety with another person. The SUDS score is meaningful when it is used to compare changes in an individual's internal states from one point in time with another point in time. A worker may want to use another corroborating measure with SUDS, such as an observed change in the client's behavior. Ideally, the case notes should reflect both the changes in SUDS as well as the workers observations of behavioral changes in the client.

The amount of time spent on monitoring activities will always be an issue—at least for full-time staff. Students, in contrast, will spend time on monitoring during internship experiences as part of their training. We estimate that workers who take monitoring seriously will spend about 20% of their time on a case on monitoring, which may explain why so many workers who are overburdened in today's practice settings, do not use monitoring and evaluation scales in practice.

As we noted earlier, an important aspect of monitoring is to determine whether the planned intervention did, in fact, occur and included both the actions of the worker and the client. The worker's actions can be demonstrated by a log of worker activities or an electronic recording of the same. Client activities, such as homework assignments, should also be noted in a log or journal. In some cases, these client activities should be attested to by another person. This does not necessarily mean that the worker distrusts the client. Clients, themselves, often want this as a stimulus or reinforcement to their completing tasks. An example of this use was the case of a client who assumed the task of writing a letter to his estranged father. He promised to show the letter to his wife before it was sent to see if he had expressed the ideas and feelings he hoped to communicate.

EVALUATION ●

The Design of the Evaluation

The design of the evaluation refers to the overall strategy utilized by the worker to ascertain what changes have taken place in the client and whether such changes are likely to have been brought about by the service offered. We now shall consider some approaches to the design of such an evaluation, and later in the chapter we shall indicate some ways in which the worker can measure change.

Interpersonal practice in social work has long incorporated the idea that workers should determine whether clients have achieved the purposes for which service was offered. The traditional means of accomplishing this was to use the case record to describe qualitatively the changes in the client. For example, a record indicated that Johnny, who did not attend school, was now doing so, or that Mr. and Mrs. Jones, who were dissatisfied with their marriage, were now happier together. This approach had several deficiencies. First, the judgments of the worker are often subjective and unreliable because of the stake the worker has in looking successful in practice. Second, the time frame was imprecise in terms of the sequence of events that took place related to the worker's intervention. Third, it was unclear what the status of the client was prior to the intervention and, therefore, whether any change had taken place at all.

In recent years, a number of changes have improved this evaluative process. First, workers have strived to employ valid and reliable measurement procedures, and many agencies now require workers to utilize such instruments. Agencies, often utilizing coded forms, also may require workers to indicate client goals as well as the techniques that were employed to help the client. In large agencies, research departments utilize these data to aggregate information and to show overall agency effectiveness with different types of clients and with different treatment approaches.

These kinds of agency-wide data may or may not be shared with workers and subsequently used by them to improve practice. In addition, the categories utilized on agency forms may not have been developed cooperatively with workers and may not correspond with how the workers themselves view their clients and their work. In this event, workers sometimes complete forms in a perfunctory way, and the resulting data consequently are not particularly helpful to anyone. Such agency data systems can be made more useful when they are devised jointly with workers and provide the information that workers would like to have about their practice and its consequences.

Although agency systems for the evaluation of practice have their use, they often obscure the meaning of events in the particular case because data from so many cases are combined. This problem can be prevented by the introduction of means for careful scrutiny of events that occur with each client. Careful preparation of case studies still has an important role in the evaluation of practice because the availability of this kind of narrative allows the worker, as well as colleagues of the worker, to generate alternative hypotheses about changes in the client and the forces that contributed to such changes. This preparation is a time-consuming process and often is not done because case records often contain so much data and data of such dubious reliability and validity as to pose strong barriers to rigorous case study. The alternative that has been introduced into interpersonal practice is the single subject design.

The central idea of the single subject design is that it encompasses a series of measurements before, during, and after an intervention (Nurius & Hudson, 1993). An example is that of a student who has been truant from school. The worker measured how frequently the student attended school by an examination of attendance records prior to offering an intervention. The student in each 2-week period that term missed an average of 4 days. The worker's intervention consisted of planning with the student how to complete his homework. During the intervention, the amount of homework done increased, and after the intervention, for a 3-month period of follow-up, the student averaged 1 day absent during each 2-week period.

An important feature of all single-case designs is the "before" measure, referred to as the *baseline*. The purpose of this measure is to determine what the situation is prior to any intervention. This information then facilitates both goal setting and the evaluation of change. The former emerges because when the worker and client know exactly what exists in the present, what will constitute improvement can be seen. Changes from the baseline both in the direction of improvement as well as deterioration can be measured using the same approach as that employed to secure the baseline.

As Nurius and Hudson (1993) pointed out, "The initial intake interview with a client is one of the single most important devices for collecting many different types of baseline information" (p. 176). This kind of information may be drawn from agency questionnaires, social histories, and intake interviews. We agree with Nurius and Hudson (1993), moreover, that in practice situations this type of data collection must not be protracted to the extent that the client does not receive help in a timely manner. If handled skillfully, the securing of information can be empowering. To further quote from Nurius and Hudson (1993), it is empowering

> because that information helps them understand the severity of the problem, variation of the problem in relation to life events and, later the extent to which changes have been made and to which they have made changes. By involving clients in assessment and progress monitoring, they obtain more control over the problem itself and can, work more effectively toward using assistance given them by the practitioner. (p. 185)

The practitioner also may wish to help the client examine changes in the problem condition over a longer period of time to assess various circumstances that were likely to contribute to the problem. Some practitioners, therefore, gather retrospective information by asking the client to estimate the extent of the problem at various points of time in the past.

A number of different single-case designs have been utilized to evaluate the effectiveness of interventions (Jayaratne & Levy, 1979). One of the simplest is the AB design, in which a baseline is established (A), an intervention is carried out, and a measurement is made of the problem behavior after the intervention (B). Similar to the AB design is the ABC design. This represents a practice situation in which the worker utilizes more than one intervention. A baseline is established (A), after which an intervention occurs, the behavior is measured (B), another intervention occurs, and another measurement of behavior is taken (C). This sequence is potentially continued until the clients attain their goals or terminate for other reasons. Again, by incorporating before, during, and after measurements, this type of design combines monitoring and evaluation components. By using multiple measures throughout the course of service, the social worker can demonstrate that change in the target problem has occurred.

A design less frequently used in social work practice is the ABAB design. In this situation, a baseline is established (A), an intervention occurs, and a subsequent measurement is taken (B). In the event that the behavior has improved, the intervention is withdrawn. If the behavior returns to its preintervention level, this provides some evidence that the behavior is under the control of the intervention.

For example, a child might do his homework when he is awarded "stars" and discontinue doing homework when the "star" system is discontinued. A decision might then be made to continue the star system or find some other means of sustaining attention to homework. The design has the advantage of demonstrating causality, but in the "real world," the existence of many "causes" together with the possible risks in reestablishing undesired behavior makes this design of less use to social workers. There are times, nevertheless, when the factors that control behavior must be ascertained in this way.

As can be seen, single-subject designs are very helpful in determining whether the intervention was likely to have produced the outcome. By establishing a baseline and subsequent measurements, the practitioner can determine the magnitude of changes at different points of time. The careful timing and monitoring of the intervention identifies the time sequences of intervention and change. The monitoring of changes throughout the helping process serves to draw attention to other causal events, although the careful worker will make other efforts to learn of these. The precision of measurement will allow for determinations to be made of the magnitude of changes as related to interventions.

The single "case," can be utilized in groups, families, and organizations as well as individuals. When this is the situation, however, the worker will utilize measures of systems change rather than measures of individual change. For example, the number of affectionate messages in a family, of reinforcing communications in a group, or of ratings of a positive organizational climate can be recorded before and after interventions and analyzed through the single-case approach.

The Measure of Change

The following are some of the approaches currently employed to measure changes in individual clients, and they can be adapted to families and small groups. These evaluation measures are selected here because they can be incorporated into practice without overburdening the practice session and can be quickly scored to produce a number that can be compared at various points of the service process. We will focus on three measures: (1) the visual analog scale (VAS), (2) Hudson scales, and (3) goal attainment scale (GAS). We will also present a measure that will give the worker feedback about their service efforts. Client satisfaction questionnaires (CSQs) provide the client's retrospective perspective of service, which can be useful to agencies and workers about changes they may consider in order to provide more responsive service to their clients.

The VAS (Gift, 1989; Wewers & Lowe, 1990) is a "quickie" measure that can be easily adapted to the problems and goals that emerge in a case. It does not rely on the client's ability to read and can be employed with young children and clients who are illiterate. The scale represents a 100 mm line on a page (about 4 in), which is anchored by words or symbols, such as worst–best, least–most, or ☹–☺. Depending on the problem that is targeted or the goal that is planned, the client places an *X* on the line that represents her judgment of where things stand. The time frame for the judgment can be today, or a past week, or some other short time frame, and the worker will use this time frame whenever the client is asked to complete the scale. Figure 9.1 provides an example of the VAS, which is tailored to reflect a client's perspective of "her depressed feelings." The VAS is simply scored by measuring the distance from the left end of the line to the *X* with the millimeter side of a common ruler, which is rarely used in the United States. For this example, the score is 71, which would be a fairly high score and reflects a significantly depressed perspective for this individual client. This was an initial session, so there are no case notes except to signify that this was the initial interview. This score of 71 now represents the baseline for this measure. In subsequent sessions, the case notes of the VAS may record tasks that the client has completed between sessions, any significant events or changes in the client's life that may be increasing stress on the client, or any major changes in the goals or plans of the service episode. Because the VAS is so quickly rated and scored, it can be used at the beginning of each session to monitor changes in the client's mood from session to session. It is hoped that the client's rating will be moving farther and farther to the left as the service unfolds. When the agreed upon end of the service is reached, the VAS will hopefully be somewhere below 20 on the scale. To add corroboration to the VAS ratings, the worker may also ask the client to complete the Zung screening scale (Zung, 1965), or the Beck Depression Inventory (Beck, Steer, & Garbin, 1988), or the Hudson generalized contentment scale (WALMYR Publishing Company, 2002) in the first contact and in the last session to see if similar changes have occurred on one of these scales. These measures will take up more time in the initial and final sessions and require the client system to be literate.

Figure 9.1	Sample Visual Analog Scale

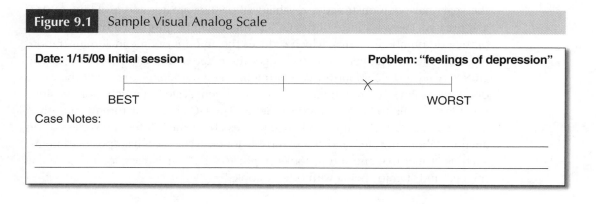

Hudson scales were developed to reflect the types of problems that social workers were likely to see in practice. The scales that have been developed thus far fall into four categories. One is personal adjustment problems, such as self-esteem, stress, anxiety, alcohol involvement, peer relations, sexual attitudes, and homophobia. Another is problems with a spouse or partner, such as marital satisfaction, sexual satisfaction, and partner abuse. A third category is family relationships, such as parental attitudes, child's attitudes toward mother or father, and sibling relationships. The last category includes multidimensional scales for child behavior, global screening, and multiproblem screening. Over the years, these many scales have been tested for reliability (i.e., consistency as a measure) and validity (i.e., scales reflect what they claim to measure; WALMYR Publishing Company, 2002). These scales have been produced so they can be presented either to clients in a standard paper and pencil format or in a computerized version, which can be scored by the computer. The latter version will also generate graphs to portray changes over time.

To demonstrate how a Hudson scale might be used to corroborate the scores on the VAS, we will explain how the generalized contentment scale (GCS) could be used in the previously given case. We are presenting and promoting the use of Hudson scales in this book because they are consonant with our perspective of practice presented in Chapter 1. The following caveat is presented by the folks at WALMYR (2002):

> It is very important to understand that our assessment scales are not measures of psychopathology. We regard all of our client assessment scales as measures of personal and social functioning. They also can be regarded as measures of problems in living but they are not designed as measures of psychopathology.

The GCS is a 25-item scale, which is designed to measure the severity of nonpsychotic depression. The scale is constructed so that scores range from 0 to 100, and higher scores indicate greater levels of depression. Tests of this scale over the years have demonstrated a reliability of 0.90 or greater and a validity of 0.60 and greater. The advantage of the GCS is that it can be shortened by selecting all of the odd numbered items, which reduces the amount of time in administration. Selecting this shorter version also changes the range of the scale from 0 to 52. The GCS is really a scale about "discontentment" (i.e., the higher the score the more discontentment), but reframing it as a contentment scale is a much more positive way for the scale to be presented to clients. The GCS has a mixture of "negative" items, such as "I feel that nobody really cares about me," "I feel powerless to do anything about my life," and "I feel terribly lonely." The GCS has "positive" items, such as "I feel that the future looks bright for me," "It is easy for me to enjoy myself," and "I enjoy being with other people."

We will not go into the rationale for reversals and how reversals are scored in the GCS because we expect this content to be part of a student's research and evaluation courses. We would expect that if a client had a VAS score of 71, that they would also probably score somewhere in the 60s or 70s on the GCS in the initial session.

In order to become more familiar with Hudson scales, we suggest that students acquire two copies of the GCS and take and score the GCS at two points in the semester—preferably one near the beginning and one near the end. We would hypothesize that the GCS taken at the end of the term would be higher than the GCS taken at the beginning of the term. The end of the semester brings all kinds of added stress on the student to complete papers, tests, and other assignments, which would raise the student's sense of discontentment. Try it and see!

The GAS (Kiresuk & Garwick, 1979) is another evaluation measure that has been developed for social workers to account for the changes that clients are able to achieve in service. Like the VAS and Hudson scales, the client is centrally involved in developing these scales with the worker acting as coach to get the scale into the desired framework. The GAS is a way of measuring a client's goal achievement. A chart is developed in which each column in the chart represents a different client goal. Each row of the chart represents a different level of possible attainment of the goal. Five levels of attainment are generated: (1) most unfavorable outcome thought likely, (2) less than expected success, (3) expected level of success, (4) more than expected success, and (5) most favorable outcome thought likely. Kiresuk and Garwick (1979) have developed statistical approaches to generate goal attainment scores for clients. Questions have been raised as to the validity of these statistics, yet we believe that this issue does not preclude the use of GAS to evaluate changes in individual clients. These criticisms are more likely to apply to the uses of the goal attainment scores to compare intervention approaches.

The value of the GAS in practice is that it makes goal statements much more "realistic." Goals are central to our contract-oriented model of practice, and many goals and objectives may be developed over the course of service. Just stating a goal or writing it into a contract does not mean that it will get accomplished. The world is full of good intentions that have never been realized. The GAS can be used to make good intentions fit realistic outcomes.

Unlike the VAS and Hudson scales, the creation of a GAS requires more effort on the worker and client's part because the scale has to be generated for each goal that the client and worker agree to pursue. Most folks tend to think of goals in absolute terms—that is, they are either accomplished or not, but there are many shades of gray. Charting the scale is fairly straightforward, but anchoring each of the points on the scale takes a little creativity.

Let's use a goal that often arises in practice and present how it might be scaled on the GAS. The goal is stated, and a time frame for completing the goal is planned.

For example, a client was an autoworker who was laid off in tough economic times. This event has caused much distress for the client and his family, which is why the family sought services. The client wants to pursue training in another field and take advantage of the buyout money. The goal that emerged was pursuing training in preparation for another job. The client agreed to work on this goal for the next three weeks. The client and worker then discussed how this goal would unfold. This table is the GAS that they developed together for the goal of "pursuing training for another job" (See Table 9.2):

Table 9.2 Goal Attainment Scale for Job Training

Goal: Training for another job	Time Frame: 3 weeks
Most Favorable Outcome:	Enrolled in a training program
More Than Expected Success:	Completed applications to a training program
Expected Level of Success:	Decided on a training program
Less Than Expected Success:	Collected information on various programs
Least Favorable Outcome:	No effort to pursue information on programs

In order to develop this array, the client and worker need to start with the middle point of the scale. The client and worker need to decide on realistic expectations of what can be achieved in 3 weeks. Once this anchor has been established, it is possible to figure out what the other points on the scale might look like. By applying the GAS to goals, it clarifies the reality that many goals involve intermediate steps or tasks that must be realized before the most ideal outcome can be achieved.

With other goals, the GAS can be developed to focus on behavioral counts, such as school attendance or participation in family events, which might be scaled as follows (See Table 9.3):

Table 9.3 Goal Attainment Scale of Family Participation

Goal:	Family participation:
Most: 5 days/week	Most: Participate in 5 family meals/week
More: 4 days/week	More: Participate in 4 family meals/week
Expected: 3 days/week	Expected: Participate in 3 family meals/week
Less: 2 days/week	Less: Participate in a weekend family outing
Least: 1 day/week	Least: No participation with family

The upside of VAS and GAS as evaluation mechanisms are that they can be tailored to each case situation. The downside of GAS is that it will take up more time in each session to complete than the VAS.

The best way to learn how to create a GAS around a goal is to do it yourself. Think about something you want to accomplish in the next 2 weeks. It may be a school requirement like papers due or a social responsibility like completing a task for a student organization. Think about what you can realistically accomplish in the next 2 weeks. This will be the middle point on the GAS. Now think about the other four points of the scale, and what you will be able to accomplish. By creating this GAS, do you feel more motivated to accomplish the goal?

Rating Problem Solving Skills

Cognitive dimensions also exist in relationship to the client's problems, and one such dimension is whether the client uses logical processes to solve problems. We assume that in some cases the goals may involve improving the client's problem solving capacities. If the worker has taught or helped the client to learn an approach to problem solving, the client's problem solving skills can be measured. The client can tell the worker (or in a group or family, can tell the other members) how he or she approached the problem. A rating scale, such as the following, can then be used to evaluate problem solving skills:

1. Has the client sought information relevant to the problem? For example, if the problem is finding a job, has the client found out about the types of jobs most available for persons with his or her training or abilities?

2. Has the client identified the alternatives available to him or her? Do these alternatives include all the most important or relevant ones? Has the individual used the information generated in Question 1 to identify alternatives?

3. Has the client evaluated the alternatives using criteria, such as the following?
   a. the alternative with the most likelihood of helping the client to achieve his or her goal to the optimum degree
   b. the alternative with the fewest disadvantages or costs
   c. the alternative most consistent with the client's values

4. Has the client chosen the alternative that he or she evaluated most favorably?

5. Has the client developed or begun to develop a plan to implement the alternative? (Garvin, 1996, p. 196)

This five-point scale is similar to the GAS and can be simply scored by giving a 1 for each "yes" and a 0 for each "no." A score of 4 or 5 will demonstrate to the client that they are successfully implementing their problem solving skills, whereas a score of 1 or 2 would suggest that more work needs to be done on increasing the client's problem solving abilities.

Rating Interpersonal Behaviors

As we have mentioned earlier, the practitioner can draw on a large array of instruments to measure virtually all the interpersonal behaviors that serve as the focus of social work interventions. Besides the Hudson scales available at WALMYR (2002), Corcoran and Fisher (2000) have edited a two-volume set of scales. The first volume covers scales that can be used with families, couples, and children, and the second volume focuses on scales that can be used with adults. They have also chosen instruments that do not require much time for either completion or scoring.

When practitioners implement evidence-based practice models, there are often scales that have been used in the research on these models to measure baseline and end points. For example, in interpersonal psychotherapy (IPT), a time-limited model for treating depression in adults (Klerman, Weissman, Rounsaville, & Chevron, 1984), the Hamilton rating scale for depression (HRSD) is used to establish the severity of depression and also to engage in an educational discussion of how depression manifests itself in individuals. In the integrative model of practice used in the Case Example at the end of this chapter, the Center for Epidemiological Studies-Depression scale (CES-D) from the National Institute of Mental Health (NIMH) is used to establish depression in clients. The point we want to make here is that there are numerous scales that have been used in clinical research, and the practitioner should become familiar with what is available when applying the protocols of an evidence-based practice model.

Client Satisfaction Questionnaires

CSQs are not designed to measure change, but they are an important source of information for the practitioners. We believe it is the responsibility of the social agencies to collect feedback from clients after service is completed, to collate this feedback, and to share the results with their practitioners. Because CSQs ask for information about the performance of staff and the responsiveness of service, as well as questions about agency procedures and setting that may impact the client's experience in getting service, we also believe it is best if practitioners are involved in the creation of the measure. There are examples of CSQs that can be found in *Measures of Clinical Practice: A Sourcebook* (3rd ed.; Corcoran & Fisher, 2000) and in the Hudson scales, which can be adapted to the needs of a specific agency.

Social work students routinely complete comparable forms at the end of each semester when they complete their course evaluations. These evaluations ask for information about the performance of the instructor, the content of the course, the grading mechanisms, the reading assignments, etc. These data are used as a quality control by the school to ensure that the course fits with the curriculum and also are used as part of the evaluation of faculty for raises and promotions. They are also returned to the individual faculty member so that faculty can use this information to improve future iteration of the course.

Because these measures evaluate the performance of line personnel (i.e., practitioners, instructors, and staff) in organizations, we believe that line personnel should be involved in the creation of these measures. This is a social justice issue that impacts practitioners and clients. For example, in my (Brett A. Seabury, or BAS) own 38 years of experience in academia, student evaluation of instructors existed for 3 decades as a performance measure of faculty expertise. It was a major struggle to get similar evaluations of assistant and associate deans, deans, provost, chancellors, etc., which were only instituted in the last 5 years at the University of Michigan.

Evaluation of Family Change

Some family practitioners will measure changes in individual members of the family and will employ the standard approaches that are used when one-to-one help is offered. When family practitioners seek to measure family-level changes, measures are more problematic. This is because there are no generally agreed-on criteria as to what a good outcome is for the family as an entity. One Hudson scale that is close to a system-wide measurement is the Index of Family Relations (IFR). There are other Hudson scales that have been developed that may be used to evaluate various aspects of changes in a family: index of parental attitudes, index of brother relations, index of sister relations, index of marital satisfaction, nonphysical abuse of partner scale, partner abuse scale: nonphysical, index of sexual satisfaction. Like the GCS discussed earlier in this chapter, these scales are 25-item scales that can be completed by family members to evaluate the various relationships, such as marital, parental, and sibling, that exist in nuclear families.

In the chapter on family assessment (Chapter 12), we present an extensive discussion of the kinds of data that can be gathered to assess families. The ecomap, for example, can be used to compare changes in the family's relationship to external systems at various points in the service episode. The worker may gather information about problem solving, communication, decision making, and affection at various points in time to see if family conditions are improving. It is important that the family be involved in these measures because this creates a kind of "face validity" for the family when they see how their family situation has changed.

Evaluation in Groups

In the chapter on group assessment (Chapter 14), we portray many ways of assessing group conditions. Many of these variables can also be used to evaluate changes in these conditions by comparing the specified data at two or more points in time. For example, the group leader may monitor several of the effectiveness variables, such as group cohesion or self-sharing, to see that they emerge as the group matures. The crudest measure for group cohesion is attendance, and changes in attendance may reflect the level of cohesion in a group. For example, highly cohesive groups will have all members attending every session, while groups that struggle with attendance problems may reflect low cohesiveness. As for self-sharing, it is expected as members get to become more familiar with each other that they will also feel more comfortable self-sharing and communicating with each other. The tendency to communicate with the leader will be shifted to more examples of member-to-member communication.

The VAS and Hudson scales can also be used to evaluate change in groups when applied to the goals and problems of individual members. For example, in a treatment group for adolescents working on self-esteem issues, the Hudson scale for self-esteem may be used in the preliminary screening interview, at several points during the group, and in the final session of the group to demonstrate to individual members that they have accomplished a goal to improve self-esteem. The Hudson scale for alcohol involvement may be used to evaluate individual change in a substance abuse treatment group, and the Hudson scale for stress may be used to evaluate change in a stress reduction group. The VAS can also be used to measure individual client conditions at several points in time. The group leader will have to create individual VAS forms for each member in advance of the sessions in which the VAS is applied. The GAS takes much more time to develop for individual goals and therefore is not easily adapted to groups. But it is possible to employ it in the prescreening session with potential members and then save the scale for a later session of the group.

Leaders of groups can also develop simplified "client satisfaction" measures that can be employed in the debriefing phase of each group session. The measure can be as simple as the example in the elder group in the group intervention chapter (Chapter 15), such as asking members for a "thumbs up or down" on the session. The leader can create a brief form that asks members anonymously to make two judgments about the session: Did the session achieve its goals? How satisfied were you with the group process? Each of these questions can have a simple five-point scale from "not at all" to "a little bit" to "somewhat" to "mostly" to "completely."

Table 9.4	Worker's Evaluation of Session

Did today's session achieve its goals?				
0	1	2	3	4
Not at all	A little bit	Somewhat	Mostly	Completely
How satisfied were you with today's session?				
0	1	2	3	4
Not at all	A little bit	Somewhat	Mostly	Completely

Hopefully, when the group leader collates the results after the session, the mean for both judgments will be above 3. If not, the leader can share the results of this measure and discuss with the group how they might go about improving the group experience.

SIDE EFFECTS ●

An evaluation of change should have two major components: (1) whether the planned intervention accomplished what it set out to do and (2) whether it caused things to happen that were *not* part of the plan. These unanticipated consequences can either be desirable or undesirable. An example of a desirable but unplanned consequence was the work done with a woman to help her leave a mental hospital. A major component of this work was to change aspects of her marital relationship that were stressful for her and that were associated with her "breakdown." Her behavior as a parent was not focused on, yet the worker observed in a follow-up that the wife's skills in negotiating with the husband were now also being used by her with her children, and this resulted in a better relationship between mother and children.

An undesirable consequence, in another situation, was seen when work was done with a wife to help her reduce her periods of severe depression. Although this work was successful, her marriage was terminated. A later interview with the husband indicated that he wanted to be more adequate than his wife, and her improved functioning created a great deal of anxiety in him. He desired an end to the marriage, but his wife did not.

The worker should be aware, therefore, of the effects of intervention that are not anticipated—particularly those that may be viewed by the client or others as undesirable. These "side effects," as they are called in medicine, can be avoided under some circumstances and in others at least anticipated. What follows is a list of major categories of side effects:

1. *The client improves in regard to some behaviors but deteriorates in regard to others.* In one case, a client became more assertive toward her employer but afterward had bouts of anxiety; in another, the client began to work on problems that she previously had denied but became so dependent on her social worker that she felt she had to consult her before making major decisions.

The worker should understand that these types of difficulties can often be predicted. A treatment situation that can create anxiety for the client sometimes requires changed behaviors that are unacceptable to others. Another requires testing out new ways of coping with situations, yet the client risks a great chance of failure. Revealing one's problems in front of others can also produce anxiety even when the "other" is a social worker. A client may also become anxious when discussion of a problem forces the client to confront material about herself that the client has not been aware of or that the client has "repressed." Whenever these events are likely to occur, the worker will watch for the occurrence of client anxiety and will be prepared to help with it.

An increase in client dependency can occur in interpersonal helping under several circumstances. Clients will often feel vulnerable because of the problems that brought them to the agency. Work on problems can increase this sense of vulnerability. Under these circumstances, the client may revert to a form of coping with this feeling that was used earlier in life—namely, to turn to a more powerful figure, such as a social worker, for help. In addition, the emergence of the kinds of anxiety we noted may also cause the client to become dependent on the worker as a way of warding off this anxiety. The social worker needs to proceed in a way that empowers rather than infantilizes the client.

Other kinds of deterioration of behavior can also occur as a result of helping. The worker's attention to some client problems may cause the client to maintain, rather than to change, problems as a way of retaining the worker's attention. The client may also generate problems as a way of avoiding the termination of the worker–client relationship. Later in Chapter 18 we discuss means of dealing with these issues.

The reader should recognize that there are many reasons why the client might suffer negative outcomes in addition to the association of some negative outcomes with positive ones. Stuart (1970) has reviewed the range of events that can occur to produce negative outcomes for clients, which he calls *iatrogenic illness,* a term used in medicine to denote an illness that was created as a result of treatment. Stuart deals with negative outcomes that result from psychiatric hospitalization, diagnosis, labeling, and psychotherapy itself.

2. *The client improves in regard to the targeted behaviors but then suffers from the reactions of others to this change.* This is a phenomenon that is predicted by a systems approach to practice, which sees behavior of an individual as contributing to the maintenance of some system. One example of this is the treatment of a wife whose phobic behavior was a fear of going outdoors. When this behavior was changed, her husband became anxious about what would happen to her, and he sought to prevent her from leaving the house. Another example is a child who had a heart condition and who refrained from social activities with other children to a greater degree than was required by the disability. When the child was helped to plan an appropriate activity schedule, the parent became overprotective of the child.

The implication of such responses of others is that they must be anticipated or at least monitored. The worker should identify those who will be affected by changes in the client and should discuss with the client how they are likely to respond to such changes. The client should be helped to cope with his or her reactions. Often the most desirable plan is to involve these other people in the helping process—either together with or separately from the client as the situation requires.

3. *Another set of side effects are the client changes may affect other people even when these others do not retaliate.* We believe to a reasonable degree the social worker has a responsibility for the effects of his or her work with the client on others. Obviously, there are limits to this responsibility because in at least a theoretical sense a change in the client may be like a stone thrown into a pond that produces ever-widening ripples. We are concerned with serious or immediate effects on those closest to the client. An adult daughter, for example, was helped to see her duty to herself to lead her own life and to move away from her widowed mother. The mother did not resist this move, as she understood her daughter's wish to become more independent. Nevertheless, the mother was very lonely and was likely to become depressed when the move occurred. The worker anticipated this "side effect" and offered services to the mother.

The worker, therefore, should think about the consequences of client changes on other people who interact frequently with the client and should discuss these with the client. In cooperation with the client, decisions can be made as to the likelihood these people may need social work or other services and what the worker's and the client's responsibilities may be to facilitate obtaining services for such people.

In this chapter, we have described many ways that workers can incorporate measures to monitor and evaluate their practice. We now present a case example that demonstrates how several of these measures can be integrated into practice.

"Case of Graduate Student Funk"

The case involves Mary, a 24-year-old gay single white female who is a graduate student in the School of Public Health at a large midwestern university. The University Counseling Center offers individual and group counseling to enrolled students on a time-limited basis (i.e., 10 sessions). The center runs many support groups for students struggling with their transition to university life.

In the first screening session with the social worker, Mary stated that she came for help because she is having trouble being motivated to attend classes and complete her class assignments. She feels lonely, isolated, and has not made any new friends since moving from California and breaking up with her ex-girlfriend. She feels tired most of the time and is worried that the depression that she experienced during part of her undergraduate studies is returning. Mary refused psychiatric consultation and the opportunity to receive medication and instead wants support turning her life around without taking medication. She agreed to the suggestion of her social worker to work on her present "funk" for the next nine sessions by following the "prescriptions" in James Gordon's (2008) Unstuck. This model of practice was attractive to Mary because it is an integrative, holistic model that encourages depressed individuals to take control of their own lives. Mary agreed to weekly sessions with the social worker, and she completed a VAS and GCS. The baseline score on the VAS was 61, and the score on the GCS was 58. Mary agreed to obtain Gordon's book and read the introduction and first chapter before her session next week. She was also encouraged to begin to act on some of the suggestions in this book.

In the second session, Mary acknowledged that she had purchased the Gordon (2008) book and actually read the introduction and first two chapters. She completed the CES-D scale that was suggested in the book for a score of 22, which is in the moderate range for depression. She also started doing the meditation exercise of "soft belly breathing" (Gordon, 2008, pp. 34–37), which she found relaxing and easy to slip into her daily routine. She also completed her "Prescription for Self-Care" (Gordon, 2008, pp. 105–107), which included working on her eating habits, meditating at least once a day, locating a yoga group she could join, jogging at least 30 minutes every day before classes, attending all of her classes, and participating in class discussions. Mary also talked more about her experiences with depression in her freshman year at college, her struggle with her sexual orientation in a small Christian college, and the undesirable side effects of the medications that were prescribed during that time in her life. She completed the VAS with a score of 42, and decided the next things she would do: (1) make an appointment at the student health services for a complete physical and (2) regularly attend the yoga class, which was something she had not done since her sophomore year in college.

In the third session, Mary was noticeably distraught. Her VAS had rebounded to 65. She had not gotten much sleep during the week because she had three papers due, and she had slacked off in jogging before class and was again eating junk food late at night while trying to stay awake to complete papers. She was able to make an appointment at student health services for a physical, but that appointment was not for 2 weeks. She did not have time to attend regularly the yoga class and was not doing her daily soft belly meditation. The only good thing, which happened during the week, was that she had completed all of the papers on time. She felt guilty about not keeping up the routines in Unstuck (Gordon, 2008) but recommitted to them in the coming week. She also agreed to take a careful look at her eating habits and to attend the yoga class she could join. (Note: Students need to recognize that change does not always come in a straight line, and it is important to document what was going on in the client's life that would account for the rebound in her VAS score.)

In the fourth session, Mary had been much more disciplined in doing her meditation and jogging before classes. She had also looked at her eating habits and was appalled by how poor her diet of junk food and snacks had been. She was trying to eat a more balanced diet. She had looked at the recommendation for vitamins and located a multivitamin that was recommended for women her age in an organic health food store.

She had visited two different yoga classes and located a class for gay and transgendered folks that seemed supportive. The class was made up of students, met twice a week in the evenings, and was reasonably priced. Her VAS in this session was down to 46.

In the fifth session, Mary had completed her physical at the student health services, and her blood tests were in normal ranges. The only recommendation was that she is overweight and should find ways to lose weight through more exercise and changes in her diet. The physician's assistant had suggested that she see a nutritionist in the health center, and she scheduled an appointment for the following week. Mary continued to practice meditation and regular jogging. She also read two more chapters in Unstuck (Gordon, 2008) and liked the exercise of "shaking and dancing," which she found very energizing. She found the chapter on finding inner guides difficult to do and wondered if there were groups on campus that she could join that would help her with this part of the program. The social worker and Mary did an Internet search for groups in town but could not find any listed, and the counseling center had not yet composed such groups. The counseling center did have an open-ended lesbian, gay, bisexual, and transgender (LGBT) support group that Mary could consider joining. Mary noticed that she was more positive about her studies, had been keeping up on the readings, and had been participating more in class discussions. Her VAS score for this session was 38, and Mary also agreed to take the GCS again because this was the halfway point in their work together. Her score on the GCS was 28.

(Continued)

(Continued)

In the sixth session, Mary was excited about her appointment with the nutritionist, who gave her all kinds of practical advice about improving her diet and avoiding empty calories and the kinds of vitamins and supplements she might consider. She was surprised that many of the issues raised by the nutritionist dovetailed with one of her classes that covered the impact of diet, food additives, and environmental toxins on public health issues. Mary continued to perform daily meditation and jogging and had joined the LGBT support group, which put her in contact with other student members in the gay community. Mary's VAS score had dropped to 32 in this session.

Mary did not show for her seventh session with her social worker. In the follow-up call, Mary explained that she was feeling much more motivated and connected to activities and new friends. She wondered out loud whether she still needed to come to the counseling sessions. She agreed to come in for one final session to review the changes that she had accomplished and talk about how she could maintain the gains that she was experiencing.

In the eighth and final session, Mary and her worker reviewed the changes she had accomplished over the past 2 months. Mary acknowledged that it was important for her to maintain her jogging, yoga, meditation, and balanced eating routines. She recognized that it was difficult to maintain some of these activities during the times in the semester when she was expected to be writing papers and taking tests. She felt much less isolated because of the new friends she had met in the LGBT support group. Mary felt positive about the changes she had made in her life, and she planned to continue attending the LGBT support group. Mary's VAS score had dropped to 18, and her GCS score was 24. Mary was given the option to return to individual counseling, if in the future she felt she needed more support. Mary agreed to ask the receptionist for a copy of the agency's client satisfaction form, to complete it, and give it back to the receptionist on her way out

The narrative presented in the case notes demonstrates the changes that Mary accomplished in the 2 months of service. The VAS and GCS scores reflect the impact of her accomplishments on her presenting problem. See Table 9.5.

Table 9.5   Graph of Mary's Changes

Intrv	1st	2nd	3rd	4th	5th	6th	7th	8th
VAS	61	42	65	46	38	32		18
GCS	58				28			24

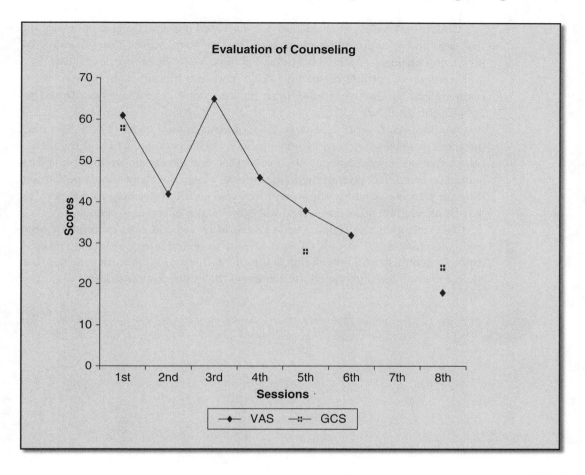

SUMMARY ●

In this chapter, we have stressed the idea that an evaluative plan must be generated at the beginning of the social work process rather than at its ending so that clients and workers alike know how service will be evaluated and collect information throughout the process to produce a valid assessment of it. Two interrelated procedures were described: monitoring and evaluation. Monitoring consists of those activities that provide information on the actions of the worker, the client, and other relevant systems. Under this heading, we described process records; critical incident recording; recording by code, such as SOAP, SUDS; and electronic recording.

Under the heading of evaluation, we discussed possible designs of evaluation that also incorporate monitoring, such as the "single-case" designs. Ways of measuring changes—such as behavioral counts, VAS, Hudson scales, and GAS—and ratings of problem solving skills and interpersonal behaviors were enumerated. We discussed how these measures and others can be adapted to families and groups.

An important topic that was also discussed was "side effects" because interpersonal change processes may produce effects on the client and significant others that are undesirable. To the extent that side effects are predictable, plans should be made to cope with them or, at the very least, the client should be warned they are possible. At times, the worker may also seek to offer help to people who may be affected by procedures used with, or changes effected in, clients.

We concluded the chapter with a session by session case example of how evaluation measures (VAS and GCS) can be incorporated into counseling. The case example demonstrated how events in the client's life and homework activities that the client completed impacted the scores on the evaluation measures.

CHAPTER 10

ASSESSING INDIVIDUALS

Assessment is a perpetual work in progress.

—Linda Suskie (2009)

his chapter presents issues that are germane to all assessment procedures as well as a framework for individual assessment. Assessment and intervention are both continuous processes, and successful intervention depends on a holistic assessment. Assessment processes are designed to help the worker and the client understand the client systems interaction with its environment. This, however, does not require a comprehensive understanding of all aspects of the client system and its environment. A worker does not have sufficient time for that nor is it desirable to understand everything there is to know about other human beings and their situations. Therefore, our approach to assessment will be bounded by both ideological and pragmatic considerations.

PURPOSES OF ASSESSMENTS ●

Pragmatic considerations concern how much information is required to make a sound intervention plan. In earlier models of practice, workers were encouraged to collect massive amounts of information about their clients (Germain, 1968). No piece of information was too trivial, and agency records resembled metropolitan telephone directories. Now, however, we instruct workers to be selective of the data they collect in the assessment process. Salience, as related to the issue at hand, should influence the data collection process (Germain, 1968). Although some agencies continue to put their applicants through a long series of evaluation procedures (social histories, medical histories, psychological tests, psychiatric evaluations), this kind of comprehensive data collection is an unnecessary luxury in these times of shrinking resources and managed care.

Extensive evaluation procedures often seem more designed to meet the needs of professionals or agencies than the needs of clients. Such lengthy evaluations also rarely draw the client into the assessment process. At their worst, they may make the client a passive object rather than an active partner in a process that enhances both the client's and the worker's understanding of the client's problems. The worker, during assessment, should encourage, include, and value the client's participation in exploring his or her problems and life situation.

Obviously the most important source of information is the client system itself. The client is central to the problems and issues to be explored and, therefore, is an essential source of information about it. As with all sources, the client is biased, and information may be distorted. Because information from any source has some built-in distortion, it is the worker's responsibility to identify biases that may require balancing when other information sources are tapped.

Common distortions that clients bring to data are the tendencies to look either too much at external causes for their problems or at causes of their own doing (Jones, 1972). Some clients may be most influenced by emotional factors associated with their problems, and others may be most affected by cognitive issues. The consequence of these common distortions is that data collected will be skewed in the direction of the client's bias. Therefore, an individual client who focuses on external causes will have trouble considering internal factors and vice versa.

Another important source of information about the problem is the "significant others" in the client's life who know the client and the particular problem situation. These may be relatives, close friends, neighbors, peers at work or school, supervisors or bosses, or anyone with knowledge about the client's problem. As does the client, each of these sources will bring biases, which may depend on how involved they may be in the client's problems. For example, a relative had negative feelings about a client, and information that was gathered from him showed he blamed the client for his trouble. Another common bias of significant others is a tendency to "gossip" and share hearsay information about which they do not have firsthand knowledge. A worker will have to sort out carefully information about which others have direct knowledge or experience from that which is hearsay or secondhand.

ISSUES IN USE OF SOURCES ●

The worker cannot simply approach significant others and collect information about the client's problem. The rules of confidentiality require that the client be consulted before others are contacted and written permission must be granted for this contact. In most situations, the client should know who is to be contacted and the purpose of the contact, and a written release should be signed by the client authorizing the worker to contact the significant other (Wilson, 1978). The client has a right to control information collected about him or her as well as to control information that is released. Although it may seem that such a requirement is unnecessarily time consuming, we support these procedures because they show respect for the clients and ensure that they will be involved in decision making. Such protection of the client's right to confidentiality also allows the worker to check out the appropriateness of other sources before they are contacted.

Another source of data about the client's problem is other professionals who have had contact with the client. As with the other sources, there are biases in the information collected by professionals and agencies. Professionals tend to be specialists, and therefore, the information they collect often is focused in the area of their specialization. A doctor may have information on a client's physical health and know nothing about a client's social or job skills. This kind of narrow approach to the client can be misleading when trying to understand the client. Another common bias in data from other professionals is their tendency to focus on the client's weaknesses and to ignore strengths and capabilities. This bias is the inevitable consequence of such roles as "client" or "patient" in which weakness, defect, or incapacity are so often associated with these roles. The records from professionals and agencies make poor source materials for a balanced biography.

Issues of confidentiality are also involved in data collected from other professionals and from agency records. Some agencies require clients to sign a blanket release form at the beginning of service so that information can be released or sought from other professionals or agencies later. A blanket release does not protect the client's confidentiality. Each time a worker intends to seek or release information about the client, the client should be informed and a release obtained.

The issues presented in this section of the chapter point out that the worker cannot simply collect data from any source or accept the data at face value. When information has been collected from a variety of sources, the worker should be able to sort through this information and understand how accurate and reliable the information is. When information is inaccurate or the source is very unreliable, the chances of jumping to false conclusions are great (Berman, 1962).

Generally, information can be conceptualized along a continuum from extentional to intentional. Information may be factual, observational, or primarily inferential (Campbell, 1962; Haney, 1969). Factual and observational information is extentional and is central to law and science, which take great care to determine the reliability of information. For example, in a court of law, hearsay information is not allowed, and in science, serious efforts are made to make sure that any measurement technique is both reliable and valid. Intentional information represents the subjective world of perceptions, judgments, intuitions, and conclusions. For example, in social work practice, we are interested in a client's feelings, perceptions, personal experience, and reactions to events. Both extentional and intentional information can be found in professional records. Both types of information have their place, but they must never be confused. Inferences are not facts but rather conclusions or subjective reactions of the individual presenting the information. Good inferences can be supported by evidence (facts or observation), and the worker should be able to see when data contain weak inferences and are not supported by facts or observations.

To clarify these issues in data collection, an excerpt of case material is presented next. The first few paragraphs of the material present mostly observational and factual data; the last paragraph presents the inferences that have been drawn from this situation. The major inferences have been identified, and the analysis that follows points out those inferences that are poorly supported by the data from those that do seem to have some support.

Case Example of an Elderly Widow

Mrs. X is a 62-year-old widow. Since her husband's death 2 years ago, she has lived alone in a two-room apartment. Her two daughters are both married and live in another state. Mrs. X receives a small pension and survivor's benefits from Social Security. She lives in a section of town that is scheduled for urban renewal. The three-floor walk up that she occupies is on a block that has more than 80% abandoned buildings. Her building is in the process of being condemned and is scheduled to be torn down in 3 months.

When the social worker from the Urban Gentrification Program contacted Mrs. X to inform her of the condemnation procedures and also help her find other housing, Mrs. X stated that she would never leave her apartment and would kill anyone who tried to make her move. She showed the worker the revolver she had purchased to protect herself from drug addicts that she claimed were breaking into her apartment and stealing her appliances.

Mrs. X's apartment was piled waist deep with 21 sacks of old newspapers. Roaches were visible in both rooms, and her kitchen sink and countertops were covered with dirty dishes. Four bags of trash and garbage were overflowing onto the kitchen floor. When the worker asked Mrs. X if she needed any help managing her apartment, she burst into tears and stated that she had saved every newspaper since her husband's death. She asked the worker if he had any hobbies or liked to collect things.

Mrs. X was dressed in a frayed cotton dress that had food stains and several holes in the front. The apartment smelled of urine, and there was soiled underwear strewn in the corner of the room. Mrs. X stated that she had not been to a doctor in more than 2 years. Her eyesight was poor, and she had misplaced her glasses. She was not worried about her poor eyesight and assured the worker that she could shoot straight if attacked by addicts. She explained that she had been taught to shoot a pistol by her husband, who trained in a paramilitary unit of the local militia group. Mrs. X opened the closet door and showed the worker her husband's uniform. The worker noticed that the brass was shiny, the uniform pressed, and the leather straps highly polished.

Mrs. X stated that she felt the uniform would fit the worker and then called the worker by her husband's first name and asked the worker if he planned to spend the night. The worker explained that he would have to go now but would return to help Mrs. X with some of her problems. Mrs. X burst into tears and pleaded with the worker not to "leave again." The worker reassured Mrs. X that he would return and quickly left the apartment. On his way down the stairs, the worker was mugged by two assailants. His wallet and briefcase were stolen, and his nose was broken in two places.

Diagnostic Impressions and Recommendations

Mrs. X is an elderly widow who is incapable of caring for herself. She has created numerous health hazards in her apartment. Her paranoid ideation, incontinence, and flat affect are all manifestations of a psychotic, involutional melancholia. She is depressed and has an unresolved grief reaction from her husband's death. Mrs. X is a danger to the community. She needs immediate hospitalization at the regional psychiatric hospital.

The following inferences seem to have supporting data from what transpired in the interview with the relocation worker:

- "elderly"—Mrs. X is 62 years old.
- "created numerous health hazards"—This inference has some support because her poor eyesight and piles of old newspapers could represent a fire hazard. The garbage and dirty dishes may also attract vermin that could bring disease. The inference "created" might be challenged because it not only seems like blaming the victim but also ignores the reality of her environment. There may be no garbage or trash collection for her building, and she may not want to leave the apartment for long because of the risk that it might be ransacked.
- "depressed"—There is some evidence for this inference because she broke into tears at several points in the interview and has experienced a significant loss in the death of her husband, but more information should be collected.

- "unresolved grief reaction"—There are several pieces of information that support this inference. She maintains her husband's uniform, continues to collect papers since his death, and confuses the worker's identity with her hope that he is her husband. She pleads with the worker not to leave again.

The following inferences do not seem to have much support and, instead, appear to represent the worker's subjective reactions and feelings about his experiences in this interview:

- "incapable of caring for herself"—This conclusion seems to be contradicted by the reality that she has lived for 2 years by herself and somehow managed to pay her bills, feed herself, and handle her pension and benefits, all accomplished in a hostile and inadequate environment.
- "paranoid ideation"—This inference seems contraindicated by the evidence that she lives in a very dangerous environment (the worker was mugged), and one would expect her to feel threatened by a worker who tells her she will have to move.
- "incontinence"—Soiled underwear and the smell of urine do not prove incontinence. Her toilet facilities may be malfunctioning.
- "flat affect"—This inference is contradicted by her crying outbursts.
- "psychotic involutional melancholia"—The worker did not perform a mental status examination or do psychological testing. This is an outdated diagnosis not used in the *Diagnostic and Statistical Manual of Mental Disorders* (4th ed.) (*DSM–IV*). Much more investigation by other professionals is necessary before such a conclusion can be drawn.
- "danger to community"—The community is a danger to her well-being. The worker can attest to that.
- "immediate hospitalization at the regional psychiatric hospital"—There are many other options that should be explored besides this drastic one. For example, most large mental hospitals have been closed down, and alternative resources would have to be found for this elderly widow. Unfortunately, this recommendation seems to meet the needs of the worker to get Mrs. X removed from the building and does not really address some of the problems she may experience at the present.

● INDIVIDUAL ASSESSMENT FRAMEWORK

This section of the chapter presents the framework for our approach to individual assessment. Social work has traditionally taken a bio-psycho-social-approach to understanding the human condition. More recently, this perspective has added "spirituality" to this holistic approach (i.e., bio-psycho-social-spiritual; Canda, 1988; Russel, 1998). Spirituality not only includes traditional, organized religions, such as Christianity, Judaism, Islam, Buddhism, Hinduism, etc., but also shamanic spirituality, Wicca, agnosticism, and atheism. All of these forms of spirituality have an impact on an individual's and family's worldview and value system.

To understand how social problems appear in an individual's life, the two dimensions previously discussed in the "nature metaphor" (Chapter 2) need further elaboration. Social functioning and social problems are the product of two fundamental processes and can be conceptualized as the dislocations and necessary changes that these processes demand of individuals. Individuals are caught in the unfolding changes of development from conception to death; and they are also stressed by the continuous balances that must be established between themselves and their surrounding environments at each stage of this development. To understand the confluence of all these forces, the worker must have an understanding of the basic developmental issues that individuals experience and how these stages are significantly shaped by various ecological balances that must be maintained for the individual to grow and develop (Longres, 1990).

A Developmental Perspective

Because our model focuses on social problems and social functioning as the starting points for individual assessment, our developmental conception is concerned with how people, in relation to their environment, change over time. In the behavioral sciences, there are numerous developmental models that explain systematic changes in the growth of individuals. Freud's psychosexual model of developmental, Piaget's developmental model of childhood cognition, and Erikson's psychosocial model of human development are all examples of developmental conceptions of individual growth and change. Erikson's model has merit because it focuses on the total life span, but our focus here is on the stages of social development that are reflected in the roles that individuals experience in their lifetimes.

Role transitions are a useful way of conceptualizing development because social workers are familiar with the "role" concept, and roles are salient for all individuals. In the same way that an individual cannot "not communicate," an individual cannot be without a role. Roles are an inherent part of an individual's social being, and even efforts to isolate oneself result in the adoption of yet other roles such as hermit or recluse.

Another advantage of the role concept is the ease with which individual roles can be identified. In some developmental models, the boundaries between different stages are blurred and difficult to differentiate; therefore, individuals may appear to be struggling with issues from different stages. It is difficult then for the worker to decide which stage the client may be attempting to achieve. Because role boundaries are much more differentiated, transitional struggles that the client is experiencing are much easier to identify.

Development can be conceptualized as a long time line drawn down a sheet of paper. On the top of the line is birth and on the bottom of the line is death. All along the life line, individuals are faced with transition after transition, from one role to another. Role transitions are a continuous process for individuals, and later life has as many transitions as does infancy and childhood (Brim & Wheeler, 1966). Although role transitions may differ in different cultures, the reality of continuous transitions is present in all cultural contexts. In our complex, pluralistic, American culture, there are numerous roles that individuals may achieve or adopt. Many roles and the transitions that individuals must accomplish are fairly predictable, and most individuals can expect to move through these various role transitions. (See Figure 10.1 for such roles and transitions in schematic form.)

In early childhood, an individual must learn to become a son or daughter and oftentimes a brother or sister, a niece or nephew, a cousin, a grandchild, and so on. Family life brings numerous role possibilities. Family roles are not the only transitions that children must learn to handle, and a number of cultural and organizational roles will require mastery. A child must learn to make the transition to student (whether in nursery school or in kindergarten); to member of teams; to member of organizations, such as the Scouts or 4-H; to member of religious groups, such as Catholic, Muslim, or Jew; and to citizen of the dominant culture in which he or she grows up, as well as a member of the ethnic subgroup to which they belong. Childhood may be conceptualized as constant socialization for individuals to prepare them for membership in various social groupings. This socialization to various roles and membership in social organizations continues throughout life.

During adolescence, an individual will have to make transitions to different schools, clubs, first employment experience, etc. With the biological changes that arise during adolescence, individuals will have to transition to gender expression and gender identity roles and sexual orientation roles (heterosexuality, homosexuality, bisexuality, etc.). A transition to young adulthood also begins with changes in the expectation of old roles that need revision. For example, the former roles of daughter and son *will* need revision as biological maturity stimulates growth in size, sexuality, and interest in independence from parental supervision.

In young adulthood, an individual may make transitions to being independent and living away from home for the first time. This transition may occur by becoming a recruit in the military, a student away at college, or a renter in one's own apartment. A young adult may experience his or her first career or employment roles and the roles associated with creating a family, such as spouse and new parent.

Figure 10.1 Roles and Transitions

SITUATIONAL/STIGMATIZED ROLES   MATURATIONAL/TRANSITIONAL ROLES

                                    BIRTH

                                    CHILDHOOD
                                                                   Infant

                                                                   Son/daughter
Disabled   Sister/brother
                                                                   Grandchild
                                                                   Friend/playmate
Handicapper   Student
                                                                   Brownie/scout
Patient   Member of religion
                                                                   Team member

                                    ADOLESCENCE
                                                                   Middle/high school student
Status Offender   Member of clubs/cliques
                                                                   Sexual being
Dropout   Date/steady
                                                                   Trainee/employee
Delinquent   Driver

                                    YOUNG ADULTHOOD
                                                                   Military recruit
Lesbian/gay   College student
                                                                   Roommate
Victim   Leasee
                                                                   Neighbor
                                                                   First career role
Unemployed   Lover/spouse
                                                                   Parent
Recipient   Taxpayer
                                                                   Credit card holder
                                    MID-ADULTHOOD
Substance abuser   New career roles
Prisoner   Member in clubs/associations
Prostitute   Den mother/coach
Inmate   Separated/divorced
                                    LATER ADULTHOOD   Remarried

                                                                   Career/promotional shifts
Ex(roles)   "Empty nest"
                                                                   Reenter studenthood
"Bag Lady"   Parenting parents

                                    OLD AGE
                                                                   Retiree
                                                                   Widowhood
Recluse   Loss of independence
                                                                   Disabled/incompetent
                                    DEATH   Deceased

During middle adulthood, individuals continue to face a number of role transitions through career shifts, changes in location, membership in clubs and associations, membership in organizations their children may be active in (den mother, coach), as well as some stressful transitions, such as becoming separated, divorced, or remarried.

In later adulthood, individuals will continue to make career transitions either through promotions to new positions within their professions or in totally new career adjustments. Individuals may have to handle the role reversal of "parenting" their aged parents at a time when their own children are "emptying the nest" and becoming independent. This is a time when many women seek to reenter the job market or return to school for more education on the way to a second career beyond motherhood.

During old age, there are still many role transitions that an individual must handle: retirement, widowhood, loss of independence or greater dependence on adult children, and patient in medical facilities and nursing homes. In our own culture, these are fairly normative and expected role transitions that individuals will make in their lifetime.

All role transitions in an individual's life are stressful. Some transitions are potentially overwhelming and may create serious social dysfunction for the individual. Research has demonstrated that some role transitions are much more stressful than others (Dohrenwend, Krasnoff, Askenasy, & Dohrenwend, 1982). For example, death of a child or spouse, divorce, and marriage are much more stressful transitions than are promotions or shifts in employment.

Besides these common transitions, there are also a number of role transitions that are situational or idiosyncratic. All individuals run the risk of becoming disabled or handicapped by accident or disease (Thomas, 1967). Some individuals may find themselves caught in negatively valued roles that society either stigmatizes or considers deviant (Becker, 1967). For example, an individual may adopt a deviant lifestyle or be incarcerated in a prison or mental institution or find himself or herself relying on a welfare program during hard economic times. Such negatively valued roles are not only stressful as transitional roles but they are also made more stressful because of the stigma, embarrassment, and shame that individuals may feel in finding themselves in such roles.

Role transitions are related to social problems, because these transitions are not always successfully accomplished by individuals. There are many reasons why an individual may fail to make a successful transition to another role. An individual may take on too many transitions at once or have so many role responsibilities that adding a stressful transition may overload the individual's capacities to cope with all role demands (Atherton, Mitchell, & Schein, 1971; Spiegel, 1974; Thomas & Feldman, 1967). Role overload is common in graduate students who may be enrolled full-time in a graduate program, working part-time to pay for their studies, and struggling to maintain some semblance of family responsibilities to spouse, children, relatives, and so on. Some role transitions are stressful enough without adding them to an already overloaded set of role demands.

Another reason that role transitions may be overwhelming for individuals is that the individual may not be properly prepared (sometimes even ill prepared) for the role transition (Biddle & Thomas, 1966; Nye, 1976; Spiegel, 1974). For some roles in society, there are few presocialization experiences to help an individual make the transition to the new role. In American society, parenthood is a role transition that has few presocialization experiences. In some ways, the role is even idealized as a special, fulfilling experience, and the responsibility and hard work are underemphasized. Parenthood is not a role that can be easily discarded once it has been adopted, and for most individuals, it lasts the rest of their lives.

Another problem that individuals face with some role transitions is they do not have the skill or capacity to handle the responsibilities and expectations placed on them in the new role. Sometimes, the skills can be acquired, and sometimes, the individual lacks the basic capacity to handle the role successfully. For example, in some practice situations, a worker may help a neglectful mother improve her parenting skills, whereas in another situation the worker might work to terminate parental rights when parents are unwilling and incapable of caring for their children.

Another source of difficulty with some role transitions is the confusion, ambiguity, or lack of clarity associated with the role. Some societal and organizational roles are unclearly perceived, or there is a great deal of confusion and disagreement about how individuals should behave when they occupy the role (Katz & Kahn, 1966; Schein, 1971). Our society has a difficult time, for example, deciding what to expect of individuals with disabilities and how even to understand and accept some disabilities. Sometimes, the disabled are infantilized and expected to stay in their homes and are not given a chance to participate in the job market or act as a consumer in society.

People using wheelchairs have had to struggle for a barrier-free society; the blind have had to push for special resources, such as talking calculators; and the hearing impaired have had to struggle to have sign language institutionalized into television programming. Society is not sure whether individuals with various disabilities should be normalized or mainstreamed and allowed to compete with the rest of the citizenry, or whether they should be treated specially and segregated into smaller, homogeneous communities by themselves. This kind of expectation is stressful for the individual because it ignores the reality that disabilities often affect only one area of functioning, and the disabled may need special attention only to this area of their functioning.

To understand how the stress of role transitions contributes to the social dysfunction of individuals, we return to the case of Mrs. X, the widow facing removal from her apartment. Mrs. X faces several stressful role transitions. She is a widow and has obviously not adjusted well to this role transition that was forced on her by the death of her husband. Because her children do not live nearby, her husband's death has isolated her from family supports. She is also facing another forced transition in that her apartment building is scheduled for demolition and she is being required to relocate. This threat may be the final blow in a series of realities that she has had to face in her attempts to continue to live and survive in a deteriorating neighborhood.

The threat of removal should not be taken lightly by the worker. Such transitions for elderly individuals are extremely stressful and can result in various forms of health deterioration or even death (Blenkner, 1964). Mrs. X also faces another stressful transition—that is, the consequence of losing her status as an independent adult. If the worker's recommendations are to prevail, Mrs. X will have to cope with the likelihood of being placed in a group living situation and having to adjust not only to the demands and expectations of that role but also to giving up the special privileges of an independent person. On the surface, her threats to shoot anyone who tries to make her move may seem extreme. When we account for the stress in all these transitions, it seems understandable that she would react this way, even though the threat is dangerous and cannot be allowed to happen.

An Ecological Perspective

An individual must not handle only the stresses of life transitions but must also balance a variety of individual factors with environmental realities. Stress not only emerges at transitional interfaces but also at the transactional interfaces between the individual and the surrounding environment. For an individual, three critical exchanges must be balanced for the individual to grow and thrive. Individual needs must be balanced by environmental resources, individual wants and aspirations must be balanced by environmental opportunities, and an individual's skills and capacities must be balanced by environmental demands and expectations (Ripple, Alexander, & Polemis, 1964). These three fundamental transactions cannot be perfectly balanced in any situation because both the individual and the environment constantly change. Figure 10.2 reflects these basic environmental transactions.

An individual's needs can be conceptualized as existing on several levels (Maslow, 1954). Survival needs are at the most basic level and must be immediately attended to in order to maintain basic biological functioning. A biological organism must obtain oxygen, water, food, and shelter and be able to expel waste to grow and develop. When the environment cannot provide these resources, the organism will die or be severely damaged. A social worker might be involved in improving these transactions for an individual client by helping a client link up with better housing

Figure 10.2 Ecological Transactions

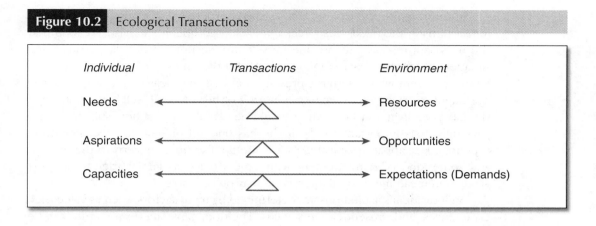

or by providing the client with an emergency grant to pay for fuel oil or by helping a client apply for food stamps or meals-on-wheels to improve nutritional intake.

An individual also has safety needs that somehow must be met by environmental resources. All of us have a need to be secure and protected from the various dangers and violence of the world around us. In some inner-city neighborhoods, the incidence of violence is so prevalent that it is difficult to imagine how families can protect themselves from muggings, larceny, and theft. Sometimes, the home itself is a place of violence and danger.

An individual has a need for belongingness and love in close, intimate relationships. Some relationships allow for sexual expression as well as for mutual caring and support. Life for individuals who are isolated from family and friends and who lack close human support systems is highly stressful. Social functioning may suffer severely. Social workers can be involved in improving these transactions by developing self-help groups for isolated clients or by encouraging clients to reengage significant others in their social context or by encouraging others in the client's environment to be more supportive when a client is passing through a particularly difficult transition.

Finally, an individual has a need to be respected and valued by others. Self-esteem is an important need of individuals. When an individual's environment is belittling or continuously disqualifying, severe social dysfunction may occur. When individuals begin to internalize and accept negative messages sent to them, they may withdraw from meaningful social contact and develop any number of negative traits or behaviors that fulfill the negative images sent to them by their environments. Social workers may be involved in improving these transactions by trying to change the client's internalized negative images as well as trying to move the client into more supportive environments or changing the sources of the negative messages.

In returning to the case of Mrs. X, she is experiencing a number of stressful transactions in the needs–resources dimension. Although she has a weapon that she uses as a resource to provide herself with security in her dangerous living situation, her present environment is clearly hostile, and some serious efforts must be made to remove the hazards present. It also seems clear that a woman of her age ought to have more careful monitoring of her physical well-being. Although she has been living on her own, it would be useful to know how she shops and pays bills. It is important to see if she has enough income to meet her living expenses. Her apparent social isolation should also be a concern to the worker, and some kind of reinvolvement with others (such as family, friends, support groups) in meaningful social interaction may be desirable.

An individual's aspirations are determined by many factors, such as values, life experiences, and present circumstances. The dominant American culture can be viewed as materialistic, competitive, hedonistic, and youth oriented. Within such a context, it is understandable that individuals want to accumulate more things than their neighbors; want to spend their income on leisure and recreational activities; and want to be slim, attractive, and youthful by running, exercising, and eating properly. These dominant values will not necessarily appear in all individuals, and some clients may have aspirations that contradict the dominant culture. For example, Latino or Latina and Native American values tend not to promote materialism and competition but instead promote cooperative relationships with others in the family, tribe, or community. Thus, aspirations of minority clients may reflect different underlying values (Lum, 2005).

The number of aspirations that an individual may have are almost unlimited. The distinction between need and want is significant for individuals. Aspirations and wants do not carry the same imperative that needs do for the individual, yet a great deal of an individual's behavior and striving are tied to wants and not needs. Maslow's (1954) higher-level needs (self-actualization, knowledge, and aesthetics) reflect the kinds of aspirations that motivate individuals to pursue all kinds of enterprises—sometimes at great expense.

No social work student *needs* to be in graduate school, and the power of aspirations to motivate individuals to achieve should never be underestimated. But aspirations do not just happen; they require the environment to provide the opportunity to be realized. The opportunity structures surrounding individuals is never ideal. In the real world, opportunities are either blocked or underdeveloped by the "isms." Sexism, racism, classism, and ageism are just a few of the barriers that limit opportunity structures and keep individuals from achieving their aspirations. Social workers become involved in these dysfunctional transactions when they advocate for clients to open up blocked opportunity or when they work to develop opportunities not available in the client's environment.

Racism and sexism are common in the human services as well as in societal institutions (Knowles & Prewitt, 1969; Seabury & Foster, 1982), and the worker is ethically bound by the code of ethics to work to eliminate discrimination in the workplace. In the case of Mrs. X, we see a common occurrence in practice: From the record, we know very little about Mrs. X's wants and aspirations. The only "want" we do know about is her adamant desire to remain in her present apartment, and the only reason this is reported is that it directly contradicts the worker's purpose in contacting Mrs. X. Regrettably, too much of practice focuses on what clients need at the expense of what clients want. Aspirations and wants are a powerful source of motivation that can be mobilized to help clients make significant changes in their lives (DeJong & Berg, 2002).

The final ecological transaction that workers should understand in a client's life is how well balanced the expectations of significant others are to the client's capacities and skills. All of us have basic capacities to perform various life tasks, and as our life unfolds, we constantly add to our skill repertoire. At different ages and with different experience, our capacities and skills may vary greatly and therefore so must the expectations and demands that our environments place on us as individuals.

An individual's capacities exist in three basic areas of functioning: intellectual, emotional, and performance. Individuals have a capacity to think, solve problems, understand, make decisions, and be rational. Individuals also have a capacity to be emotional and express their feelings. Some individuals are limited in their ability to express their feelings to others, some are easily overwhelmed by their feelings, and others are able to handle their emotions appropriately for the context in which they are being expressed. Individuals also have a capacity to perform or act appropriately with regard to what's expected of them in various roles. Whether it's tying a shoe, driving a car, or making love, an individual is constantly acting or behaving in relationship to others' expectations.

Many social workers have used concepts from ego psychology to identify client capacities. These concepts enable the worker to generate an ego assessment related to such ego functions as reality testing, perception, and logical reasoning. Such an assessment also includes the types of defenses—such as projection, denial, and reaction formation—utilized by the client. Workers who draw on this framework do so in terms of how the ego functioning of the client facilitates or hinders the way the client copes with the environment. For example, in the case of Mrs. X, her collecting of newspapers, her maintaining the appearance of her husband's uniform, and her confusing the worker with her deceased husband can be understood as poor reality testing and the operation of denial (defense mechanism) as a way of coping with the loss of her husband.

If an individual is not pushed, coaxed, and encouraged to take advantage of skills and capacities, these personal resources will not develop and may actually atrophy from disuse. This kind of imbalance can be dramatically seen in mediocre classrooms that do not recognize or provide special learning opportunities for gifted or bright students. Students caught in such a mismatched environment may end up causing trouble simply to cope with boredom and the meaninglessness of the educational experience.

On the other hand, environments can place unrealistic demands on the capacities of individuals, which may push them into situations of constant failure that may seriously hurt their self-images. Expecting too much of an individual may be as harmful as expecting too little. Sometimes clients cannot handle the responsibilities that are given to them, and they need help to improve their skills in order to meet others' expectations.

Sometimes individual environmental imbalances are internalized by individuals, and an individual will develop unrealistic expectations of his or her capacities. Individuals may believe they do not have the capacity to pursue a venture, or they may be unnecessarily hard on themselves when their performance is less than perfect. These internalized kinds of imbalances may be as stressful and dysfunctional as those that occur between the individual and significant others in their environment.

Workers may be involved in a number of ways to improve imbalances in these transactions. A worker may help a client to increase or acquire the skills to meet the expectations of others (e.g., a neglectful client may attend a parenting group to improve parenting skills so that a court-ordered removal of her children can be rescinded). A worker may try to modify expectations with a significant other to remove unrealistic demands on the client (an anxious mother may be encouraged not to worry that her 3-year-old child is not yet reading). The worker may also be involved in increasing the demands that others place on clients in order to help clients work up to capacity. For example, a worker might suggest to parents that they set firmer limits on a problematic child so that the child is clearer about expectations and will acquire a sense that the parents are sincere.

In the case of Mrs. X, we have a confused picture of her capacities even though the worker attempts to build a case that Mrs. X is incapable of caring for herself. She cries easily and confuses the worker with her husband, yet she has successfully managed to survive on her own since her husband's death. If the worker had not entered her life space, there is no indication that she would not have continued to survive. Obviously she could use support and services to improve her living situation, but she should not be denied a chance to continue in an independent living situation.

Although this ecological assessment framework presents these three kinds of transactions as distinct exchanges, in real life these three are interdependent and closely interrelated. Recent attempts to build barrier-free structures and facilities has not only been a change in resources (people with disabilities can now use bathrooms away from home) but this restructuring of resources has also opened up the opportunity structure for people with disabilities so that many can return to school, seek employment outside sheltered workshops, or use public facilities as nondisabled citizens do. This opening of opportunity may encourage people with disabilities to aspire toward new careers and to reach out and develop latent capacities dormant in an earlier, more restricted opportunity structure. Furthermore, this growth in capacity and skill may help society to reevaluate its expectations of the disabled. This kind of rippling back and forth among these three transactions demonstrates their interdependence and the reality that change in one area may promote change in others. And in the long run, these changes will permit a greater chance for individuals to achieve their maximum potential.

We have tried to demonstrate that stressors have a dramatic impact on the social functioning of individuals, but stressors also have a deleterious effect on an individual's biological functioning as well. Stress research has demonstrated that our modern lifestyle choices (e.g., tobacco, fatty foods, empty calories, sedentary routines in front of monitors, and lack of exercise), pollution in the air we breathe (e.g., mercury from coal-fired power plants and incinerators), heavy metals in the water we drink (e.g., lead, arsenic, mercury, and PCBs from industrial waste), toxins and chemicals in our processed foods (e.g., antibiotics in meat and fungicides, herbicides, and pesticides on vegetables and fruit), and the pharmaceuticals and drugs that we take to buffer the stressors in living (e.g., prescription and OTC medications, alcohol, and recreational drugs) are having debilitating effects on our immune system, cardiovascular health, and the rise in chronic diseases, such as diabetes, high blood pressure, autoimmune diseases, and cancer (Adelman, 2007).

Social workers are not expected to be trained as pharmacists, nutritionists, or medical doctors, but we do believe that social workers need to understand that good nutrition, exercise, caution in taking prescribed medications, and periodic physical exams are good practices for our clients as well as ourselves. Bad habits like smoking, drinking to excess, taking recreational drugs, and being a "couch potato" have debilitating effects on a person's physical and mental health. We believe it is reasonable for social workers to explore these areas with clients and to suggest that clients talk with nutritionists and get periodic physical exams from a medical system.

The very young and the very old need to have frequent, periodic health exams. In societies like Canada, England, Cuba, and France that have nationalized health care systems, this kind of periodic health appraisal is easier to obtain than the health care system we have developed in the United States. Because of prohibitive insurance and health care costs, there are over 45 million folks with no health coverage in the United States.

In the case example of Mrs. X, the elderly widow, there are a number of areas that a social worker needs to explore. She states that she has not had a physical in over 2 years, which is much too long ago for this isolated woman. The case does not explore how she gets food and whether the food she does eat is nutritious. Does she order in junk food from a nearby takeout place, or does she get one hot meal a day from a meals-on-wheels program for shut-in elderly? Does she take any medications for any chronic health conditions, or does she self-medicate herself with vitamins, herbal remedies, or alcohol?

In the earlier sections of this assessment chapter, we outlined how important developmental and ecological perspectives are in understanding social functioning. In the next section of this chapter, we present an "aleatoric" or stress perspective. An aleatoric perspective (i.e., "manure happens") focuses on the events that happen in people's lives and does not emphasize personality or trait variables as significant ways of understanding personal problems (Budman & Gurman, 1988). No matter what the capacities and personality of people, their growth and potential is most influenced by the events that happen to them on their life course. This aleatoric perspective has been heavily researched in the behavioral sciences recently and is consistent with our social functioning focus. Our ideology throughout this book is to avoid perspectives that blame clients for their own problems.

● STRESS ASSESSMENT

This section of the chapter discusses concepts from stress theory relevant to understanding individual social functioning. Over the past 3 decades, there has been an explosion of stress-related research in psychology, medicine, and social work (Billings & Moos, 1995; Brown & Harris, 1989; Figley, 1989; Goldberger & Breznitz, 1982, 1993; Lieberman & Yager, 1994; Meyer, 2007; Miller, 1989; Rosano, Rotheram-Borus, & Reid, 1998).

Much of the research has focused on the relationship between stress and illness and stress and changes in physiological functioning. From this literature on stress a number of concepts have emerged that explain how the stress paradigm operates. One of the major problems with the concept of stress is that it has been defined as both the cause and consequence of changes in a person's life. We will sort out what we mean by the various concepts and how they apply to interpersonal practice.

Instead of "stress" we use the concept "stressor," which more accurately describes the kinds of changes and conditions that unfold as a person moves through his or her life course. There are several ways of understanding these stressors. Some stressors are conceptualized as *events*; others are conceptualized as *conditions*. Events are changes that occur or happen at a particular point in an individual's life. Events are short-lived and have a sudden, immediate impact on an individual. A person's life is filled with a continuous series of events and changes. A person's life is also composed of a series of conditions. Unlike events, these conditions are circumstances or situations that are not so changeable or fleeting but persist for longer periods of time.

Conditions reflect the environmental context that surrounds the individual. Conditions are present in the state of the *physical* environment and the *interpersonal* environment. There may be numerous stressful conditions, such as toxins in food, heavy metals in polluted air and water, lack of material resources, or dangers in the physical environment of an individual. These kinds of stressful conditions are often present in the physical environment of poor people who may have to contend with inadequate housing; a violent, drug infested neighborhood; and shoddy secondhand products (Caplovitz, 1963). Stressful conditions in the interpersonal environment can be conceptualized as the various social roles an individual must perform. For example, single-parenthood can be a significantly stressful role (Glasser & Navarre, 1967) and so are other roles of "caring" or "caretaking," which fall most often to women (Belle, 1982).

There is an interplay between events and conditions in an individual's life. Events may produce conditions (see Figure 10.3), and conditions may have an impact on how events affect an individual. For example, a factory closing (event) may result in chronic unemployment (condition) and poverty (condition), which may severely undermine an individual's ability to cope with a sudden natural disaster such as a flood (event) that destroys the individual's home.

There are a number of ways of conceptualizing stressors. Stressors may be dichotomized as *eustress* or as *distress*. Eustress is experienced by individuals as positive change and distress as negative change. Some typical examples of eustress are promotion, marriage, winning a lottery, and being released from prison. Examples of distress are serious accidents, loss of a job, and death of a significant

Figure 10.3 Interplay Between Events and Conditions

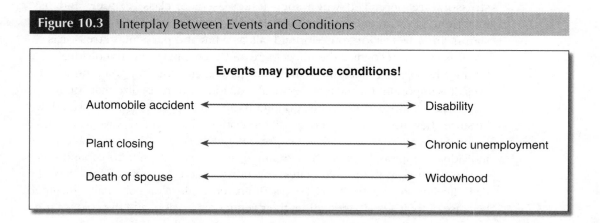

Events may produce conditions!

Automobile accident ←————————————→ Disability

Plant closing ←————————————→ Chronic unemployment

Death of spouse ←————————————→ Widowhood

other. It is important to recognize that positive experiences in a person's life may be just as stressful as negative experiences. Stressors are also conceptualized as existing along a continuum (or range) of severity with, on one end, *traumatic* stressors, such as incest, rape, or terrorism (Everstine & Everstine, 1993) to milder micro-stressors, such as acquiring a pet.

A considerable amount of stress research has focused on identifying the relative stressfulness of various events, and these efforts have resulted in stress scales that rank the impact an event may have on a person's life. The assumptions of these scales is that a given event has an intrinsic amount of stressfulness, and scales are often organized with most stressful events on one end and least stressful events on the other. For example, on the PERI life events scale (Dohrenwend et al., 1982), death of a child is given the highest weight, whereas acquiring a pet the lowest weight. Many different scales have been developed for different stages of the life span. There are scales for children, college students, parents, and the elderly. Each scale emphasizes events that are the most likely to be perceived and experienced as stressful by the group being researched. On child scales, for example, death of a parent is given the most weight, whereas on adult or parent scales, death of child is given the most weight. These scales are tailored to different age groups because research has demonstrated that different groups perceive the same event differently. Research by the Dohrenwends (Dohrenwend et al., 1982) has demonstrated that not only do age cohorts view stressors differently but factors such as gender, class, and race produce different perceptions. For example, men and women do not view infidelity of their spouse the same way. Men are much more distressed by their wife's infidelity than women are by their husband's infidelity.

Though it is obvious that some events are much more stressful than others, this research has highlighted how important *appraisal* is to the stress reaction. There is a significant perceptual difference in the way stressors are perceived when such issues as race, class, gender, and past experience are taken into account. How a stressor is appraised may be as significant a factor for some individuals as what the particular stressor is.

It is easy to recognize the impact stressful events have on an individual's life because people are much more aware of the changes that are going on in their lives. It is important for the interpersonal practitioner to recognize that conditions may be just as stressful as events. Conditions are often overlooked or played down because they are ongoing, and usually individuals have found ways to adapt to them. Stressful conditions may be present but become almost invisible to an individual's appraisal system. For example, in a sexist, homophobic, and racist society, such as in the United States, gay, transgendered people of color face the daily likelihood that they will be discriminated against or personally affronted because of their sexual orientation, their gender expression, and the color of their skin (Meyer, 2007; Rosano et al., 1998). This kind of discrimination can emerge at any time (e.g., service in a restaurant, accommodations in a hotel, evaluations on the job, and grades in school). This kind of continuous vulnerability follows gay, transgendered people of color around in all their daily activities. It is always there, and one never knows when homophobia and racism will raise its ugly head. The privilege that heterosexual white people have in the United States makes it difficult to understand and experience this kind of continuous stressful condition.

There are many other kinds of stressful conditions that individual clients face besides homophobia, racism, and sexism. Poverty is a severely stressful condition that has many negative consequences for an individual. Poverty increases the risk of many health problems, such as infant mortality, heart disease, and even life expectancy. Poverty places families in poor neighborhoods where the risk of gang violence is great, where it is likely that toxic wastes have been dumped, and where it is likely that schools will be inadequate. Poverty is associated with child neglect and abuse, alcoholism, drug abuse, violence, and dropping out of school. The lack of money and the inability to purchase the numerous resources that abound in our consumer-oriented society is a stressful condition. The continuous advertisements on television, in newspapers and magazines, and on public transportation are a constant reminder of what one does not have.

Most of social work's clients come from various oppressed groups. The concept of oppressed group reflects the stressful conditions that individuals in these groups face. Oppression takes many forms (i.e., racism, sexism, ageism, classism, and homophobia) in American society. What is important for the interpersonal practitioner to recognize is that these oppressive and stressful conditions surround individual clients on a daily basis. This continuous background has an insidious, undermining effect on an individual's social functioning, and it is just as important for the practitioner to address these issues as to address the sudden, stressful changes and events.

In the same way that events can be ranked from extreme to mild, so can stressful conditions. For example, there are extremely stressful roles that individuals may find themselves in. Refugees in Rwanda, Bosnia, and Darfur who are leaving their homes and fleeing tribal genocide or ethnic cleansing experience extreme distress. Individuals who are members of cults that routinely use sexual and physical abuse to terrorize and control members experience an extremely stressful role. Not as extreme but also distressful are roles such as widowhood, single-parenthood, unemployment, homelessness, and disability. These roles are distressful because of the kinds of losses associated with them. Some of these roles not only involve the loss of loved ones or close relationships but also loss of status and resources, ability, and function.

Other distressful roles are tied to institutional arrangements and the accompanying stigma that society attaches to these roles. For example, the roles of welfare recipient, inmate, ex-con, mental patient, and unwed mother are all made more stressful by the stigma that is attached to them by the rest of society. Sometimes the stigma is so oppressive that members of society may actually persecute individuals who occupy these roles by discrimination in employment and housing or even referring to them with derogatory labels, such as "welfare queen, psycho, baby mama."

There are a number of experiential ways that educators have tried to raise the consciousness of students about the stressful conditions that people may experience when they occupy various stressful roles. For example, in some classes on aging, students are required to wear earplugs that muffle their hearing and glasses that blur their vision and weights tied to their arms and legs that inhibit mobility. In poverty classes, students may be instructed to spend the allowance for food over a week that a welfare recipient receives (and only that allowance). The kinds of food and the amounts that can be purchased do not allow for the snacks or goodies or balanced meals or eating out that students may be accustomed to normally. Even for a week, some students cannot stick to the food allowance for welfare recipients. Those that do know they can return to their often privileged allowance when the experiment is over—something that the welfare recipient cannot do. These exercises are intended to enhance the critical consciousness and empathic understanding of students about the stressful conditions that many clients experience on a day-to-day basis. To enhance your critical consciousness about these kinds of stressful conditions, we have proposed an exercise (see Exercise 10.1) that is aimed at those students who have come into social work from relatively privileged backgrounds. As we have discussed in Chapter 4, privilege in the United States accrues to those who are male, white, heterosexual, physically healthy, educated, and wealthy. Some folks have all these privileges going for them, whereas others may have some but not other privileges.

Exercise 10.1

Critical Consciousness

In this exercise, you are to visit a context in which you are surrounded by people who do not share some of the privileges that you may take for granted. You can decide which "privilege," such as race, class, sexual orientation, etc., you want to experience. We warn you that in some situations, you will be putting yourself in considerable risk when you enter the context. There are many ways (some safe and others risky) that you can use to operationalize this exercise. For example, if you want to experience the meaning of a physical disability, you might get permission to attend a local support group for amputees or paraplegics, attend a consciousness-raising (CR) performance put on by a disability troupe, or visit an institution that takes custodial care of disabled individuals. You should observe and listen to the daily struggles of disabled individuals. You should observe and listen to the daily struggles that disabled individuals face in performing commonplace activities. You might decide on a more risky experience in which you want to experience the impact that race and class have on an individual's social functioning. For example, if you are white and middle class, you and a friend might go into a poor inner-city ethnic/racial community. You and your friend should go during the daytime and spend time shopping in the stores, eating in the restaurants, and wandering around the parks and playgrounds. You will probably feel out of place and somewhat uneasy. You may be stared at by community members or even accosted about what you are doing there. You will probably feel vulnerable and at some risk. This is the kind of daily stressors that people of color feel when they try to make it in dominant society's white institutions. The caveat for this experience is that there are some inner-city areas that are simply too dangerous for any "outsider" to wander around in (even police avoid these areas), and you must carefully avoid these areas.

In this section of the chapter, we have presented how developmental theory, ecological theory, and stress theory inform the assessment of an individual's social functioning. Various stressors have a major impact on an individual's social functioning, and we now turn to specific assessment frameworks (crisis and network) that can be utilized by interpersonal practitioners to understand their individual clients.

CRISIS ASSESSMENT •

This kind of assessment has been mentioned in other places in this book, but here it is described in considerable detail so that the interpersonal practitioner will be able to recognize the indicators of active crisis and be able to understand the precursors that led to the client's present situation. This crisis paradigm is consistent with a stress framework, and it can be readily utilized by students. The crisis paradigm also fits well with our assumption that most service is brief, time-limited, or of an episodic nature.

The model of crisis presented in this chapter is a distillation of several models of crisis theory that have informed social work practice for years (Aguilera, 1990; Golan, 1978; Hoff, 1989; Roberts, 1990, 2005; Seabury, 2005).

The interpersonal practitioner needs to discover the *hazardous events* and *conditions*, how the individual coped during the *vulnerable state*, and what seems to have been the *precipitating factor* that finally pushed the individual into *active crisis* (see Figure 10.4).

Figure 10.4 Crisis Assessment

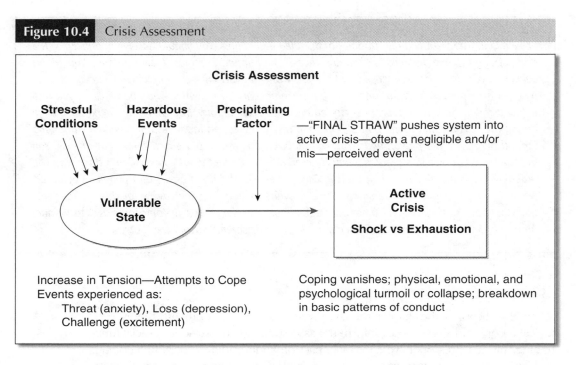

Active Crisis

Though individuals may behave bizarrely and way out of character during active crisis, active crisis is a normal state and not pathological. It may occur to anyone at any stage in his or her life span (Golan, 1978). We cannot emphasize this point enough. Some individuals in active crisis may hallucinate, be delusional and emotionally uncontrollable, or engage in bizarre behaviors in which they appear acutely psychotic, yet within 24 hours all of these extreme symptoms may disappear. For example, look at how disturbed the behavior was of the individual in this real case example:

Transient Nature of Disturbed Behavior During Active Crisis

A 45-year-old woman with severe burns on her scalp and shoulders was dragged into a hospital ER by her husband. Before coming to the hospital, she had poured lighter fluid over her hair and lit it in an attempt to "get the bugs off me!" She was shouting obscenities at her husband and the hospital staff and had to be physically restrained in order to treat the burns on her head and shoulders. Because she was making suicidal and homicidal threats, she was placed in the psychiatric ward of this hospital. Within 2 days of her hospitalization, her "psychiatric symptoms" had completely disappeared. She had no past history of psychiatric problems and was an active and successful member of her rural community. She was extremely embarrassed and ashamed of her behavior in the ER and thanked and apologized to the medical staff.

One way to understand the difference between crisis and psychopathology is that everyone gets to experience active crisis in his or her lifetime—and some at several points— whereas extreme forms of psychopathology, such as schizophrenia and bipolar depression, are reserved for only a few members of the population (less than 5%).

Active crisis is a time-limited state. Some books state that individuals cannot stay in active crisis much more than 6 weeks (Caplan, 1964). For most individuals, active crisis may last for a few hours, several days, or a week but rarely more than a month. From an equilibrium perspective, the individual will seek or find some kind of readjustment or resolution to the active crisis state. The active crisis state is so distressful for the organism that some kind of resolution will have to occur. The graphic in Figure 10.4 reflects this equilibrium perspective.

The active crisis state may reflect two common responses that individuals seem to adopt when they enter this state. Some crises can be characterized as *shock* and others as *exhaustion*. In shock crisis, the individual displays a dramatic shift or change in behavior, affect, and cognition. The individual may suddenly appear distraught, agitated, confused, and so on. In exhaustion crisis, the changes may be gradual and sometimes subtle. For example, individuals may quietly start sleeping more and more until they make a complete retreat to their bed, or they may slowly start to show signs of deteriorating social functioning, such as not relating to others or shirking routine responsibilities. It is much easier to recognize individuals in shock crisis because they are making their distress so obvious to others in the social environment. Both shock and exhaustion crisis reflect the basic characteristic of someone in active crisis. That person is no longer functioning, and the interpersonal practitioners must be careful to recognize exhaustion crisis when it is occurring.

There are three basic dimensions to the active crisis state. First, the individual's basic social functioning is impaired. The normal expectations and demands of others are not met, and social obligations and responsibilities begin to slide. For example, individuals may not go to work or school, may not perform routine child care or parenting responsibilities, or may not even take care of themselves in the most basic patterns of conduct—they may stop bathing, combing hair, performing basic hygiene, etc. Second, the individual's ability to cope with normal demands and life stressors vanishes, or the individual adopts self-destructive or dangerous coping patterns. For example, an individual in active crisis may feel helpless and hopeless and withdraw or, on the other hand, may respond violently and lash out in response to a simple demand from a friend or family member. During active crisis, suicide, self-inflicted violence, substance abuse, and antisocial behavior may appear as coping strategies. Third, the final characteristic of active crisis is that it is "ego dystonic," and subjectively the individual thinks that the crisis state is strange, uncharacteristic, even alien to how he or she usually acts. When individuals look back on the crisis state, they may describe it as a bad dream and may find some of their thoughts and behaviors embarrassing and out of character (see Figure 10.5).

Figure 10.5 Time-Limited Nature of Active Crisis State

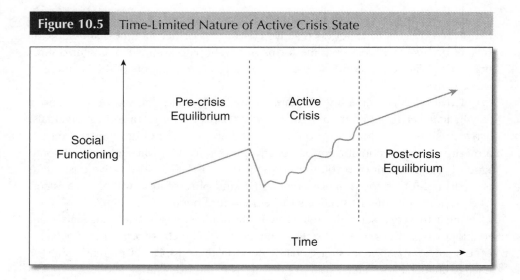

When an individual is in active crisis, there are many ways that the individual will display his or her distress. These cues or symptoms can be discovered in four areas of individual functioning.

1. Some individuals will have all kinds of physiological distress. Individuals may feel fatigued or have no pep or energy. They may notice changes in their sleep patterns, such as sleeping much more or much less, and changes in eating patterns, such as loss or gain in appetite. They may be experiencing diarrhea, cramps, indigestion, headaches, vomiting, numbness, or dizziness. They may feel weak, numb, and describe themselves as physiological wrecks.

2. Individuals may also experience many kinds of emotional distress, such as uncontrolled crying, rage, and fear. They may feel hypersensitive or overreactive to the slightest environmental stimulus. They may experience a rapid range of feelings or feel completely affectless, empty, or hollow.

3. Various cognitive distortions and distress may appear. Individuals may not be able to focus or concentrate on a topic. Their thoughts may "race" uncontrollably from one idea to another. On the other hand, their thoughts may get bogged down, and they may obsess about one idea. Problem solving is burdensome, and even solving a simple problem may seem overbearing. Information from the environment may be misinterpreted or even ignored.

4. Individuals may also display a number of behavioral signs of distress. They may appear agitated, fidgety, and engage in repetitive behaviors that seem to have no purpose. They may be performing activities that seem aimless and unnecessary, or they may be immobilized, withdrawn, and isolated. Often, individuals will

engage in self-destructive behavior, such as suicide attempts or dangerous activities that may include abusing drugs, alcohol, or other chemicals. Individuals may be so distressed that they threaten other's lives and even try to act on these threats.

The point of this discussion is that individuals will display a wide range of signs and symptoms when they are in active crisis. There is no characteristic set of signs and symptoms that reflect active crisis in individuals. Individuals can have a few of these cues or many of them, or they can be subtle or extreme, and that will depend on who they are and their life circumstances. For example, during my (Brett A. Seabury, or BAS) experiences as a social worker on a U.S. Army training base during the Vietnamese War, many Puerto Rican trainees were seen for a seizure-like disorder that was termed by clinic psychiatrists as "the Puerto Rican syndrome." These attacques, as they are called in the Puerto Rican community, were a culturally common way of responding to stress. Basic training for draftees during wartime is an extremely stressful experience, and these trainees were expressing this distress in a manner that looked similar to an epileptic seizure. From a crisis perspective, these "fits" were a response to a stressful experience that kept the individual from performing his expected role as a trainee. Anglo trainees never displayed this seizure-like response to their stressful circumstances, but they were more likely to make suicide gestures of ingesting shoe polish, swallowing brass cleaner (serious gesture), or cutting themselves. African American trainees were more likely to go AWOL or to turn their distress into passive resistance by refusing to train.

Many clients who seek help or are brought to an agency for help are in active crisis or very near to active crisis. From a research perspective, it is difficult to identify clearly the referents for "active crisis" (Lukton, 1974) because individuals seem to have so many idiosyncratic ways of expressing this state. In some cases, it is difficult to differentiate between the vulnerable state and the active crisis state. In many cases, there is no dramatic shift or change, but the individual gradually slips into the active crisis state. From a research perspective, there is no objective way to differentiate between "big" crises and "little" ones. To the person experiencing the crisis state, "a crisis is a crisis," and subjectively there is no reliable way of quantifying the meaning of the crisis. In spite of this absence of objective criteria, the crisis concept is useful to practitioners in understanding how individuals' social functioning may be compromised at various points in their lives. This paradigm also provides a number of potential ways of resolving as well as preventing various kinds of social dysfunction. These will be discussed in the chapter on individual change (Chapter 11).

There are three general paradigms for understanding how an individual is "pushed" into active crisis. In the *stochastic* model, it is not so much what events or changes are occurring but the inability of the individuals to continue functioning when their capacity to cope with stressors is simply overloaded (Golan, 1978; Roberts, 1990). As stressors pile up in a person's life, a final threshold is reached in which even a small event can push the individual over the edge. The metaphor that is used in this model is "the straw that breaks the camel's back." Each individual has a different capacity to cope with life's stressors; however, when these stressors begin to pile up and the demands get too large, anyone can be pushed beyond his or her breaking point by even the slightest event. For example, when someone is coping with a number of significant life changes, such as death of a loved one, job changes, moving, or serious illness, it may only take a micro stressor, such as being cut off in traffic, to push him or her over the edge. He or she might respond to this common hassle with road rage by chasing down the car, ramming it, and running it off the road.

In the *dynamic* model, it is not so much the accumulation of stressors that is important but the "meaning" that events have for an individual. Some individuals are not overwhelmed by some events that to other individuals are extremely overwhelming. This individualistic response to events is explained by the personal past history (Hoffman & Remmel, 1975). All individuals face struggles and events in their lives—some of which are mastered and resolved and some of which are not resolved and become overwhelming. When these old nemeses rear their ugly heads again, the individual is unable to cope. For example, some individuals may have experienced many losses in their lives and will therefore be "vulnerable" to events they interpret as losses. A child who has been separated from her parents and is then shuffled from one foster home to another in childhood may be extremely susceptible to interpersonal rejection or loss. Thus, during adulthood, this individual may be pushed into active crisis when even normal life separations, such as graduation, changes in employment, or moves from one place to another, take place.

In the *systemic* model, it is not necessarily how much stress or what meanings are attached to the stressor that is important, but it is a combination of factors that interact to push the individual into active crisis (Aguilera & Messick, 1984). These factors relate to the awareness that people have about their stressful situations and how successful they are in coping with the events. When individuals become aware of the changes and demands that are being placed on them, they will try various coping strategies to deal with these demands or will turn to support systems and resources to help with the demands. When individual coping strategies fail and attempts to try new coping strategies also fail, and the usual resources and supports are also not able to help, then the individual is likely to he pushed into active crisis. In this model, it is the realization that the individual does not have the resources and supports or the coping capacity to resolve the stress that pushes the individual into active crisis. A common example of this kind of crisis often occurs when a graduate student moves away from friends and family to a new program in a new city. The stressors of coping with the demand of graduate studies and the demands of the field placement may require new coping skills that the student has not developed.

Isolated from the support of close friends and family and challenged by new demands in graduate school, the student may feel isolated, incompetent, and overwhelmed. If the student cannot find the resources to help with these demands and the skills to accomplish the task and demands of the class and field, the student is likely to enter active crisis.

In many crisis situations, all three of these paradigms are operating. The individual is experiencing too many stressful events, many of these events reflect unfinished business and past failures, and the person's resources and coping repertoire are not able to cope with the demands of the situation. Unfortunately, for the poor and oppressed clients of social workers, all of these factors may be operating in the crisis situation. A poor single mother may be facing eviction, loss of welfare benefits, threat of removal of her children, inadequate resources to cope with debts, dangers from her gang-infested environment, poor physical health, lack of transportation to reach potential resources, and threats of violence from her abusive ex-husband.

Vulnerable State

The vulnerable state is the period of time that precedes active crisis. It is important for the interpersonal practitioner to assess this time period in order to understand how the individual client has appraised the stressful events and conditions, how the individual has tried to cope with the hazardous events and conditions, and what resources the individual turns to when he or she begins to feel overwhelmed by life circumstances. Many clients come to social agencies for help when they are in this precrisis state, and the act of reaching out for help is an example of how they are trying to cope with the stressful events and conditions in their lives.

Throughout an individual's life, there are constant changes and circumstances that place stress on the individual. Stressors are a necessary part of human growth and development, and they challenge individuals to adapt and grow to new situations. There are times, however, when the normal stress and strain begin to overtax the individual's coping repertoire. During the vulnerable state, the individual may begin to experience many kinds of dis-ease. Individuals may use many metaphorical analogies to explain their subjective reactions to the vulnerable state: "I felt like I was going to explode." "Even little things seemed overwhelming." "I felt like I was losing control." Some individuals do not seem to have these kinds of internal feelings, and they will recognize that they are in this vulnerable state by the feedback they begin to get from significant others. For example, some of this feedback may include "Boy are you in a picky mood!" "Why are you biting my head off?" "Sounds like it's nap time for you!"

During the vulnerable state, the individual is usually aware of this rise in tension, and various appraisal mechanisms begin to operate. Individuals may experience a number of different subjective reactions to the events and conditions that surround them in the vulnerable state. Some folks may interpret the stressors as a *threat* that may result in feelings of anxiety, nervousness, and sometimes anger. Other folks may interpret the stressful events as *losses*, and they may feel sadness, despair, grief, and sometimes anger. For some folks, the stressors of the vulnerable state will be perceived as *challenges*, with accompanying feelings of excitement, anticipation, hopefulness, or even anxiety.

In Exercise 10.2, three individuals are experiencing the same stressful transition—graduation from college—yet each appraises this event differently and therefore seems to feel and react differently to it. See if your answers agree with your classmates on these three vignettes. Remember what it was like when you graduated from college. How would you characterize your reactions to this transition? Was your reaction one of loss, threat, challenge, or some mixture of these three?

In response to the rising tension, individuals will begin to cope with the pressures and demands associated with the stressful events and conditions. If these coping efforts are successful and they can muster the resources to meet the various stressors that they are experiencing, then the tensions will subside and active crisis will be averted.

Exercise 10.2

Reactions to a Common Stressful Transition

A. Sherry is becoming more depressed as graduation approaches. She has been active in student government, an active member in her sorority, and leader in several campus groups. She will miss many friends she has made at college. How would you characterize Sherry's reaction to graduation?

Loss   Threat   Challenge

B. Sam is becoming more anxious as graduation approaches. He is having trouble concentrating on his studies and completing his course assignments. He worries about getting a good job after graduation so he can pay off student loans. He hopes that he will be able to do what his future employer will expect. How would you characterize Sam's reaction to graduation?

Loss   Threat   Challenge

C. Raul is so excited about graduation that he can hardly contain his pride. He is the first member of his family to graduate from college. He looks forward with great anticipation to attending law school next fall. How would you characterize Raul's reaction to graduation?

Loss   Threat   Challenge

Many individuals do have the skills and capacity to resolve the demands they are facing, or they are able to find the resources and social supports to help them cope with the demands. Unfortunately, oppressed clients may not have the personal resources or social supports to cope with the many stressors and demands of the vulnerable state. As these individuals try to cope—and efforts to resolve the stressors associated with events fail—then tensions will continue to rise. If the individual cannot locate other resources or learn new coping strategies, he or she may frantically and repeatedly apply unsuccessful strategies. This kind of "deviance amplifying feedback loop" results in a vicious cycle of attempts and failures, which ultimately propels the individual into active crisis.

The interpersonal practitioner should understand the various coping strategies that the individual has tried to use during the vulnerable state. All individuals have a repertoire of coping strategies they have accumulated over their life course. As we experience new events or are given new opportunities or enter new life situations, we are constantly adapting and changing to these new situations. As we gain more life experience, we also have the potential to grow and gain more coping capacities. Obviously, some individuals have more capacity than others. Individuals vary by intelligence, physical ability and prowess, emotional stability, and courage. Individuals also vary by the number and kinds of social supports and resources that they have in their life. Both the coping capacities and the resources and social support that individuals can muster will have a major impact on whether they succeed during the vulnerable state.

The most direct way to understand how an individual has coped during the vulnerable state is

1. to clarify the hazardous events and hazardous conditions the individual has been struggling with over the past year and will have to struggle with into the near future (about 3 months);
2. to explore how the individual has coped with each event and stressor; and
3. to discover the kinds of resources and social supports that the individual has mobilized to cope with the various stressors.

One simple way to collect this information is on a 15-month time line. This time line is constructed to collect only salient information about events and conditions over the past year, the present, and the near future. Anticipation of events in the future may have as much impact on an individual as events in the present and past. Some models collect this information over the entire life span of the individual to uncover significant anniversary phenomena (Budman & Gurman, 1988), but that is a much longer assessment process than is proposed here.

The time line (see Figure 10.6) is placed on the middle of a piece of paper in the "landscape" orientation and has 15 spikes evenly divided across the line. It can have more or fewer spikes depending on how many months you want to cover on the time line.

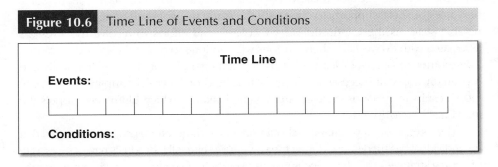

Figure 10.6 Time Line of Events and Conditions

The underlined segment of the time line near the right end of the line represents the present month for which the interpersonal practitioner and client are completing this assessment tool. The first mark that should be placed on this line is a large X that represents the present (today's date) somewhere within this underlined segment. This X becomes the temporal reference point for all other marks on the line. Above the line, the practitioner and client will locate all significant stressful events that have already or will be occurring in the next 3 months. Below the line, all stressful conditions or life strains will be noted. When this assessment procedure is completed, the line will represent a temporal graphic of all the stressful life events and conditions that are going on now in a client's life.

When each stressor has been identified—and this may take several sessions, as clients will often think of other stressors they forgot to mention—the practitioner will inquire what the client's reactions were to the various stressors and how they tried to cope. Though there are three common reactions to these stressors (loss, threat, challenge), there are many ways that clients may have tried to cope. Sometimes, a successful strategy is simply to ignore the stressor and its demands. Sometimes, ignorance is bliss, and the tension is reduced when an individual no longer worries about a particular demand. Sometimes, the clients have the personal resources to cope with the demand; other times, they may ask for help from their social support system. Sometimes, clients have to improvise and try out new coping responses that are not in their repertoire. In situations where clients are simply overloaded with conflicting role demands, clients sometimes cope by meeting the minimal expectations of each role or organizing their time so that different roles take precedence at different times (Thomas & Feldman, 1967). In some situations, clients may leave the most stressful roles, such as walk out of the marriage or try to drop out of life altogether by turning to drugs and alcohol to anesthetize the pain. In Exercise 10.3, you will have a chance to assess how various stressors have affected your life over the past year.

Exercise 10.3

Graphic Representation of Stressors

Before you attempt this procedure on an individual client (it can also be completed with families, though it is a much more complex line), you should try this out on yourself. You will find as a student in social work that you have experienced a number of stressful events over the past year and are struggling with a number of stressful conditions. For example, you may have moved several times, given up a job to go back to school, incurred large debts to pay for your education, and be struggling with many demands in your role as student both in class and in your field placement. You also may have experienced changes, such as deaths of loved ones, separation, or the breakup of a romantic relationship in your interpersonal life, that will all add to the stressors you are experiencing now in your life. You may also have to be coping with some lifelong impairment, such as dyslexia or physical disabilities, that make your educational experiences even more demanding. You may also find that you are experiencing some "cultural" stress if you are from a particular ethnic or racial group that is underrepresented in the student body or faculty of your school. For example, you may be the only Chaldean or Native American or one of a few Latinos or Latinas in your program.

Clients will have an easier time coping with stressors during the vulnerable state if they have support and resources they can fall back on when their own coping efforts fail. One way to understand an individual's social support system is to complete a "Social Network Support Map" (Tracy & Whittaker, 1990) with the client. This graphic assessment procedure is similar to ecomapping, which will be described in Chapter 12 on family assessment. This visual graphic (see Figure 10.7) is designed to tease out the various social support systems that are available to the client and also to determine the kinds and amount of support these various systems provide. The map provides seven sectors that social support may be explored with clients. These sectors are

1. household members;

2. extended family;

3. work and/or school;

4. clubs, churches, and/or associations;

5. friends;

6. neighbors; and

7. professional or formal services and programs.

Figure 10.7 Social Network Support Map

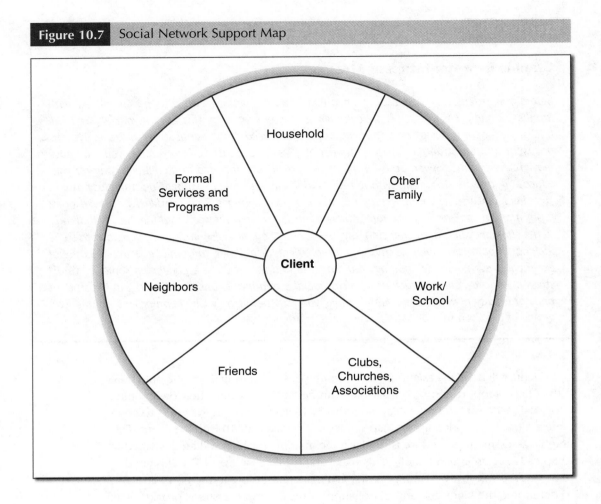

Interpersonal practitioners may want to improvise and add other sectors that seem to fit their particular case.

Clients are encouraged to write in the people in their social network that fit in each sector. This can be accomplished by drawing in small circles with names to represent women and small squares with names to represent men or the gender expression symbols for male and female may be used.

Along with this map, the interpersonal practitioner writes the names of all the significant others that the client mentions (see Table 10.1) on a table with 10 dimensions including the name of the significant other.

In the first column is the name of the significant other. The next column reflects the sector that the individual falls into, and the next three columns reflect the kinds of support that this person provides: Concrete Support, Emotional

Table 10.1 Quality of Social Support From Others

Name	Area of Life 1 Hsehld 2 Oth Fam 3 Wrk/Sch 4 Clbs/Chr 5 Friends 6 Neighbr 7 Prof Svc other	Concrete Support 1 Hardly Ever 2 Some-times 3 Almost Always	Emotional Support 1 Hardly Ever 2 Some-times 3 Almost Always	Informatn /Advice 1 Hardly Ever 2 Some-times 3 Almost Always	Critical 1 Hardly Ever 2 Some-times 3 Almost Always	Direction of Help 1 Goes both ways 2 You to them 3 They to you	Closeness 1 Not very close 2 Sort of close 3 Very close	How often Seen 0 Doesn't 1 Few X/yr 2 Monthly 3 Weekly 4 Daily	How Long Known 1 Less than 1 yr. 2 1–5 yrs. 3 More than 5 years
1									
2									
3									
4									
5									
6									
7									
8									
9									
10									
11									
12									
13									
14									
15									

Support, Information/Advice. The next column reflects the quality of this relationship and is designated as Critical. In research on social support, this term is sometimes conceptualized as "undermining." Each of these four columns is coded on a three-point scale: 1 = Hardly Ever, 2 = Sometimes, and 3 = Almost Always. The next four columns concern the Direction of Help (whether it flows back and forth in the relationship or just one way), Closeness, How Often Seen, and How Long Known. When the map and the table are complete, the interpersonal practitioner has a comprehensive overview of significant relationships in the client's life. Because the table also quantifies the kinds of social supports in a client's life, the practitioner can use this information to analyze and study how a client's social support may relate to case outcomes and effectiveness. In a case by case comparison, it is possible to compare how various supportive relationships with significant others affect the service process. Exercise 10.4 gives you a chance to try out this assessment procedure on one of your classmates.

Exercise 10.4

Social Network Map and Grid

Before you try this assessment procedure on a client, we want you to practice it with one of your classmates. If your instructor is willing, your class could be broken up into dyads. Each of you will then complete the network map and grid on the other. If this is not possible, you can still get practice by doing this assessment procedure on yourself. To complete this exercise with a classmate, each of you will need a blank piece of paper and a copy of the network grid. On the blank piece of paper, draw a large circle and divide it into the seven sectors of the network map. As your partner identifies individuals in various parts of the social network and places them on the map, simultaneously ask questions about these people and complete the information in the grid. After you have each completed the map and grid on each other, talk about the experience. Does the map really reflect your social support system? How did you feel disclosing this information to a classmate? Do you think some parts of this procedure are more useful than others? Do you notice any patterns that seem to emerge on the map or grid? In experiences with our own classes, the most useful and salient information from the grid is the information compiled in the three columns that identify the kinds of social support. Another curious pattern that often arises is that people who are most likely to be critical are often those who are most supportive.

The Precipitating Factor

The precipitating factor is the last event that occurs in the vulnerable state before the client enters active crisis. The precipitant is an event that demarcates the vulnerable state from active crisis. From a stochastic view, this is the final straw.

From a psychodynamic view, this may be an event that is simply too overwhelming and threatening because of what it symbolizes; and from a systemic view, it represents the last event with which the individual tries unsuccessfully to cope.

The precipitating factor in many crisis situations is an insignificant or minor event. To a third party, this event hardly seems a justification for going into active crisis. Often the precipitant is misperceived by the client, or the client will read into the event all kinds of "doom and gloom."

In the assessment interview with the client, it is essential that the interpersonal practitioner attempt to locate the precipitating factor, because this event is pivotal in the crisis situation. In many crisis situations, the individual can be helped to regain control quickly over his or her life by focusing on the precipitating event. Unfortunately, it is not always easy for a client to identify the precipitant, and in some cases there simply is none. Other clients seem to drift into active crisis and there is no clear-cut, single event that precedes their shift from the vulnerable state to active crisis. In spite of these realities, the interpersonal practitioner must determine when the client entered active crisis and if there were any events that occurred around or just before this time period. Clients may not be able to recall any changes, but if they are pressed, they may be able to remember the precipitant. Even when they have recalled the precipitant, they may not see any connection between this event and how they reacted during active crisis.

In the case example of the 62-year-old widow presented in the beginning of this chapter, it would be unlikely that Mrs. X would recognize that the worker's visit to her apartment and offer to help her relocate would be the precipitating factor. She might be unable to connect this visit and her confusion about the worker and her statement that she would shoot anyone who threatened her. We have analyzed this case from the perspective of supportable *inferences* and now want to use it to review the major concepts of crisis assessment that we have presented in this chapter.

A critique of this worker's impressions and recommendations can be summed up in one comment. The worker enters this case with a strong psychiatric bias that causes him to focus on the particulars of her behavior in the interview and not the particulars of the social conditions and events with which this 62-year-old widow must cope. It is possible that his labeling of her behavior would have some merit if he did a mental status exam and also got her to agree to some psychological tests, but these activities would only further ignore what is going on in her life space. The crisis/stress paradigm brings its own bias that the situation of the client must be understood.

Mrs. X has experienced several *hazardous events*. Her husband died 2 years ago, she has experienced break-ins to her apartment, and her apartment building has been condemned and scheduled for demolition. She has lost her glasses and has not kept her kitchen clean, which is in direct contradiction to how carefully she has maintained her husband's uniform. We can only speculate about other possible events she may have experienced. Because of where she lives, the city may no longer be providing trash removal services, we do not know how long ago her daughters moved out of town, and we do not know how she gets food into her apartment and whether her utilities (i.e., water, power, gas, and sewer) are still working.

Mrs. X is experiencing a number of *stressful* conditions. She is a widow and lives alone. She lives in a deteriorating neighborhood with many dangers and must constantly be on guard for her safety and the safety of her belongings. We know that her eyesight is poor, and she may have other physical conditions that are the consequence of the aging process or possibly the consequence of inadequate nutrition. If various utilities have been cut off to her apartment, then she will be living under the constant stressor of not having adequate resources to keep warm or cook or have water, sewer services, and light at night to see around her apartment.

With all of these stressful events and conditions, it seems amazing that Mrs. X has been able to survive in such a hostile environment. Her purchase of the gun to protect herself from her hostile environment is not a *coping strategy* that a social worker would recommend—especially with her poor eyesight. But the knowledge that she has this gun and is willing to use it in the surrounding community may have provided her with some security. It is not clear what kinds of *social supports* she has on which to rely. Are there neighbors, old friends, or programs that help her to get food, cash her pension checks, and pay her bills? We know that her two daughters do not live nearby, but we do not know how much contact and what kind of support they provide her. We know that the most recent event (relocation) that confronts her has several negative consequences. Not only will it push her into active crisis but moving her out of her apartment at this age will increase her risk for health problems and even death.

● ASSESSMENT AS A "LABEL"

In many practice models, the assessment phase is often completed with a diagnostic impression of the client's trouble (Hollis & Woods, 1981). This professional judgment or diagnosis is intended to inform the treatment process that follows, and in certain ideal situations it does. The diagnostic label is supposed to specify the client's primary and sometimes secondary problems, and the diagnosis itself is a shorthand label for the essential problems of the client. We are uncomfortable with some diagnostic systems, and we do not believe they serve the profession of social work. Diagnostic labels are inferences, conclusions, or judgments that professionals make about a client's behavior.

Sometimes, these labels take on a life of their own, and agencies and professionals treat them as though they were fundamental "truths" about the client. When labels are revered in this manner, they are hard to change and may remain with a client for the rest of the client's organizational career—even though the client's behavior and attitudes may have changed dramatically. Another shortcoming of diagnostic labeling systems, such as *DSM–IV*, is that it focuses on individual behavior and states of being. Thus, they pay little attention to interactive problems that clients may be having with other individuals or organizations in the client's environment. Some proponents of the *DSM–IV* system would argue that axis IV and "V codes" attempt to reflect these dimensions; however, these axes are rarely used in practice. With some insurance carriers, a worker may be required to diagnose each individual member of the family, even though the worker is seeing and working with a systemic problem that involves the whole family.

PIE—THE PERSON-IN-ENVIRONMENT SYSTEM ●

This final section of the chapter introduces PIE, or person-in-environment, which we consider to be an important step forward for the profession of social work. The PIE system (Karls & Wandrei, 1994a) is a significant alternative to the *DSM–IV* classification system that has come to rule so many service agencies (Kirk, 1992; Wylie, 1995). To be reimbursed or to be accredited, the *DSM–IV* nomenclature has been adopted as a classification standard in health, mental health, and social service settings. The PIE system is much more consistent with a social work rather than a psychiatric paradigm because it focuses on the client's social functioning (Karls & Wandrei, 1994b). The focus of the PIE system is on role problems and problematic transactions that individuals may be having with their environments. The present PIE system is designed for use with adults, and later iterations may be developed that focus on children and adolescents. Though PIE was designed to be integrated with the *DSM–IV* system, we view it as an important way of classifying the work of social workers. The difficulty of integrating PIE into this assessment chapter is that it is a complex problem system with many categories and modifiers. We do not intend to teach students how to master this system (that is beyond the scope of this chapter); however, we do want students to understand the basic framework of the system and to gain an appreciation of why PIE is important to social workers.

In this chapter, we will focus only on the first of the two dimensions of PIE. Dimension I focuses on role problems. Dimension II focuses on environmental problems and will be discussed later in the chapter on organizational and community change (Chapter 17). One way to understand these two dimensions is to view them like a grid, similar to the table that was presented for the social support network map. On the left-hand side of the network table, the names of the individuals who made up the client's support system were listed. Instead of names of individuals, the left-hand column of dimensions in PIE lists the names of significant roles.

In Table 10.2, four major categories of roles are identified in column one: (1) family roles, (2) other interpersonal roles, (3) occupational roles, and (4) special life situation roles. Each of these four major role categories is further broken down into specialized roles. *Family roles* are further subdivided into six categories: (1) parent role, (2) spouse role, (3) child role, (4) sibling role, (5) other family role, and (6) significant other role. *Other interpersonal roles* are further subdivided into five categories: (1) lover role, (2) friend role, (3) neighbor role, (4) member role, and (5) other interpersonal role. *Occupational roles* are further subdivided into six categories: (1) worker role—paid economy, (2) worker role—home, (3) worker role—volunteer, (4) student role, and (5) other occupational role. *Special life situation roles* are further subdivided into nine categories: (1) consumer role, (2) inpatient/client role, (3) outpatient/client role, (4) probationer/parolee role, (5) prisoner role, (6) immigrant role—legal, (7) immigrant role—undocumented, (8) immigrant role—refugee, and (9) other special life situation role. The first two columns of the PIE grid contain these categories and their associated numerical codes.

Therefore, if a client's problem was associated with the role of parent, it would be coded as 11. If the problem was associated with a neighbor it would be coded as 23. If it was associated with the student role it would be coded 34. Each of these roles is described and defined in the manual, and each subcategory has a miscellaneous cell (usually named "other") for roles that do not fit in any of the other categories. If we apply PIE to the case of Mrs. X, she seems to have three major role problems that are impacting her social functioning. The unresolved death of her husband could be classified as 12, the debris spread around the house might be categorized as 32, and the looming problem of being evicted by the Urban Gentrification Program might be categorized as 49. See if you agree with our classification of these three role problems.

Exercise 10.5

Applying PIE to a Practicum Case

Take one of your practicum cases and categorize some of the major role problems that impact your client's social functioning. The more you try out the PIE system, the easier it will be to use. We move on to the next two columns (or codes) of this dimension.

The next column describes the kinds of role problems likely to exist in the particular role identified in the first two columns. This column is labeled Interactional Difficulties and is subdivided into nine categories: (1) power type, (2) ambivalent type,

Table 10.2	PIE Role Categories

1 = Family roles:	1 = parent role
	2 = spouse role
	3 = child role
	4 = sibling role
	5 = other family role
	6 = significant other role
2 = Other interpersonal roles:	1 = lover role
	2 = friend role
	3 = neighbor role
	4 = member role
	5 = other interpersonal role
3 = Occupational roles:	1 = worker role—paid economy
	2 = worker role—home
	3 = worker role—volunteer
	4 = student role
	5 = other occupational role
4 = Special life situation roles:	1 = consumer role
	2 = inpatient/client role
	3 = outpatient/client role
	4 = probationer/parolee role
	5 = prisoner role
	6 = immigrant role—legal
	7 = immigrant role—undocumented
	8 = immigrant role—refugee
	9 = other special life situation role

(3) responsibility type, (4) dependency type, (5) loss type, (6) isolation type, (7) victimization type, (8) mixed type, and (9) other type. Both the role description and interactional difficulties are descriptive of the client's problem, not the other person in the relationship. When we add this column to the PIE grid, we now have three codes (See Table 10.3).

If we consider the three problematic roles identified in Mrs. X's case, how would we categorize the role problems? In her role as spouse (12), we consider the main problem to be loss type (5), so this problem would be coded as 125. In her housekeeping role (32), we might consider this problem to be both an isolation (6) and a victimization type (7). If we cannot decide which problem type is paramount, we would use the mixed type code (8), and this problem would be coded 328. If we thought the problem with this role was more one of victimization, we would code this role as 327. In the final role, we identified as her looming eviction and relocation (49); we probably would categorize this problem as victimization and thus her code would be 497.

The Interactional Difficulties column is one of the most difficult to apply because there is some overlap among categories, and it requires a judgment call on the part of the interpersonal practioner. In future iterations of PIE, this area may have to be significantly revised. Now, return to the cases that you coded from your practicum and try to code the Interactional Difficulties column. You now know how to code the first three columns of Dimension I.

The final three columns of Dimension I are common codes in many classification systems. The fourth column concerns the *severity index*, the fifth column concerns the *duration index*, and the sixth column concerns the *coping index*. There are six subcategories (codes) for the severity index: (1) no problem, (2) low severity, (3) moderate severity, (4) high severity, (5) very high severity, and (6) catastrophic. There are six subcategories (codes) for the duration index: (1) more than 5 years, (2) 1 to 5 years, (3) 6 months to 1 year, (4) 1 to 6 months, (5) 2 to 4 weeks, and (6) 2 weeks or less. There are six subcategories (codes) for the coping index: (1) outstanding coping skills, (2) above average coping skills, (3) adequate coping skills, (4) somewhat inadequate coping skills, (5) inadequate coping skills, and (6) no coping skills. When we add these three columns to the grid, Dimension I has six columns and therefore six codes when classifying role problems (see Table 10.4).

If we now add these last three codes to the three problems that we have identified in Mrs. X's life, we end up with the following codes. On the spousal role characterized as loss (125) we consider her as high severity (4), the duration is from 1 to 5 years (2), and her coping skills seem to be inadequate (5). This role problem then is coded as 1250.425.

You are probably wondering where the zero comes from in the fourth position. The interactional difficulties column is given two spaces instead of one. This

Table 10.3 Addition of Interactional Difficulties

Major Role Categories:	Role Subcategories:	Interactional Difficulties:
1 = Family roles:	1 = parent role	1 = power type
	2 = spouse role	2 = ambivalent type
	3 = child role	3 = responsibility type
	4 = sibling role	4 = dependency type
	5 = other family role	5 = loss type
	6 = significant other role	6 = isolation type
		7 = victimization type
2 = Other interpersonal roles:	1 = lover role	8 = mixed type
	2 = friend role	9 = other type
	3 = neighbor role	
	4 = member role	
	5 = other interpersonal role	
3 = Occupational roles:	1 = worker role—paid economy	
	2 = worker role—home	
	3 = worker role—volunteer	
	4 = student role	
	5 = other occupational role	
4 = Special life situation roles:	1 = consumer role	
	2 = inpatient/client role	
	3 = outpatient/client role	
	4 = probationer/parolee role	
	5 = prisoner role	
	6 = immigrant role—legal	
	7 = immigrant role—undocumented	
	8 = immigrant role—refugee	
	9 = other special life situation role	

Table 10.4 Complete Variables of Dimension I of the PIE System

Major Role Categories:	Role Subcategories:	Interactional Difficulties:	Severity Index	Duration Index	Coping Index
1 = Family roles:	1 = parent role 2 = spouse role 3 = child role 4 = sibling role 5 = other family role 6 = significant other role	1 = power type 2 = ambivalent type 3 = responsibility type 4 = dependency type 5 = loss type 6 = isolation type 7 = victimization type 8 = mixed type 9 = other type	1 = no problem 2 = low severity 3 = moderate severity 4 = high severity 5 = very high severity 6 = catastrophic	1 = over five yrs. 2 = one to five yrs. 3 = six mos. to one yr. 4 = one to six mos. 5 = two to four wks. 6 = two wks. or less	1 = outstanding coping 2 = above-average 3 = adequate coping 4 = somewhat inadequate 5 = inadequate coping 6 = no coping skills
2 = Other interpersonal roles:	1 = lover role 2 = friend role 3 = neighbor role 4 = member role 5 = other interpersonal role				
3 = Occupational roles	1 = worker roles—paid economy 2 = worker role—home 3 = worker role—volunteer 4 = student role 5 = occupational role				
4 = Specific life situation roles:	1 = consumer role 2 = inpatient/client role 3 = outpatient/client role 4 = probationer/parolee role 5 = prisoner role 6 = immigrant role—legal 7 = immigrant role—undocumented 8 = immigrant role—refugee 9 = other special life situation role				

recognizes that this category will have to be expanded in future iterations of PIE. On her housekeeping role—the interactional difficulty we categorized as mixed (3280)—we consider her as moderate on severity (3). The duration scale is difficult to judge, depending on which pile of trash we focus on. We consider that her problems have existed for at least several weeks (5). The coping index on this problem we judge to be inadequate (5) for a complete code of 3280.355. On the relocation issue and her code as an evictee (4970), we judge the severity as catastrophic (6), the duration as two weeks or less (6), and the coping skills as inadequate (5), for a complete score of 4970.665. You have now learned all of the codes for Dimension I of PIE, and we hope you can try it on one of your cases. Go back and see Exercise 10.5 on page 284. The value of trying to apply PIE to your own cases is that this classification system will force you to think like a social worker. You will begin to understand how role performance impacts on an individual's social functioning.

To really learn how to master the PIE classification system, it will be necessary for you to purchase the manual and applications books (Karls & Wandrei, 1994a, 1994b). These two books give explicit descriptions for each of the various categories and many examples of how these categories relate to social work practice. In the same way that *DSM–IV* has hundreds of categories describing how various forms of psychopathology are classified, PIE has dozens of categories of social problems that may be classified. In some schools of social work, an entire course would be devoted to teaching the student how to use these classification systems. Unfortunately the *DSM–IV* classification system with all of its problems (e.g., labeling; focusing on behavior, signs, and symptoms; and ignoring situational factor and contextual issues) has supremacy over PIE in practice because the *DSM–IV* system is required for insurance reimbursement. Until social work practitioners begin using PIE in case recordings to challenge the reductionism of the *DSM–IV* system, it seems reasonable that PIE can be implemented as a parallel classification system in most cases as we have demonstrated in this chapter with the case example of the elderly, isolated widow who is facing eviction.

A final note about classification systems: PIE—like *DSM–IV*—is not a perfect classification system and has its own problems. Though it does include many of the roles that clients may occupy that cause trouble, there are others that the system does not cover, such as lesbian, gay, bisexual, and transgender (LGBT) roles; disabled roles (e.g., amputee and developmentally disabled); and very special roles, such as a terrorist, serial killer, self-mutilator, suicide seeker, etc. Though the most valuable and central part of the system presents categories of "interactional difficulty," these categories are hard to operationalize reliably because some categories overlap and with some roles there may be several of these difficulties present.

Another issue that arises with PIE, when it is taught to social work students, is it does not have jazzy, jargon-filled labels like the *DSM–IV* system. Students entering a profession have to master the jargon of the profession, and the *DSM–IV* provides students with a sense that they have a professional (i.e., secret to outsiders) nomenclature that they can use to describe their clients to other members of the "club." Students in social work method classes will describe their clients as "borderline" or "bipolar" or "narcissistic" with a sense of pride that they can use the jargon of the psychiatric world. As they become more experienced in their field experience, they begin to realize that these labels are not as useful in describing the social work they do with their clients.

For us, the PIE system is much superior to *DSM–IV* because it is focused on social functioning and not just a label. To a psychiatrist, it may be useful to diagnose someone as schizophrenic and therefore plan what kind of medication to prescribe. To a social worker, however, the concerns in the case are much broader for the patient labeled as a schizophrenic. How will this patient handle the transition from inpatient to outpatient? Can this patient find a self-help group that will be supportive and employment that will pay him a living wage? How will the patient be helped to deal with all of the stressors that he faces upon discharge?

● SUMMARY

This chapter has discussed a number of general issues about assessment, such as the sources of information, potential biases in these sources, and the ethical considerations that guide data collection. This chapter has presented a number of assessment procedures that are useful in understanding an individual's social functioning—social support network map, the use of time lines, and the PIE classification system. The focus of this chapter has been on social problems and how these emerge as the individual travels over his or her life course. The chapter has deliberately focused on environmental factors that influence an individual's social functioning. The major underlying theories used to explain individual assessment have included stress theory, role theory, social systems theory, and a life span perspective. Stressors such as events and conditions are discussed as they impact on individual well-being. Crisis assessment is presented as a practice framework that explains how stressful events and conditions lead to social dysfunction in individuals.

11

INDIVIDUAL CHANGE

When we are no longer able to change a situation, we are challenged to change ourselves.

—Victor Frankl (1984, p. 135)

This chapter presents the various roles that interpersonal practitioners engage in when working with individual clients. Because of our social problem focus in this book, we discuss the "boundary roles" of enabler, trainer, broker, mediator, resource developer, and advocate, which social workers are traditionally known to perform. Each of these roles will be operationalized and specified at the knowledge and skill levels. This chapter is closely tied to the individual assessment chapter (Chapter 10) and elaborates the steps of crisis intervention, as well as how the interpersonal practitioner works to help individuals cope with various role problems and problematic transactions with their environment.

To emphasize the social functioning perspective of this book, we focus on those interventions that help individual clients change their transactions with their environment. Many psychotherapy books place the locus of change within the individual client. For example, clients are diagnosed with a psychiatric label, such as borderline personality disorder or agoraphobia, which exists "inside" the individual. Though with some individual clients it may be useful to adopt such a perspective, we want to emphasize a "boundary" perspective that clearly outlines the kinds of interventions that can be taken that address the client's problematic transactions with his or her social environment.

● THE CONTEXT OF INTERPERSONAL CHANGE

Because interpersonal practice is *social* work, we do not expect the client alone or worker and client together to be the only actors involved in the change process. Even when the primary intervention involves dyadic counseling of an individual client, most practice involves a network of resources, opportunities, and other helpers that are enlisted, orchestrated, and encouraged to work on the client's behalf to achieve the change objectives. In this book, we consider these "others" to be part of the "action system."

In many practice contexts, resources are scarce, and in others, even though ample resources exist, the individual client may not be able to utilize them effectively. Rural social workers often lament the lack of resources in rural areas (Ginsberg, 1993) but overlook the reality that even a broad network of services does not guarantee that resources will be employed effectively. Social work literature abounds with case examples of clients who are caught in dysfunctional networks of uncoordinated and competing service programs (Hoffman & Long, 1969). This chapter emphasizes how important it is for client and worker to develop a coordinated plan for the various resources to be called into action. Without a coordinated plan, the actions taken may be jeopardized and may be ineffective.

The Treatment Plan

In social work practice, the most common action plan is referred to as a *treatment plan*. There is no universal treatment plan in social work practice. Wilson (1980) has suggested that a treatment plan should contain (1) the ideal means of meeting the client's needs, (2) what can realistically be done to meet these needs, (3) the client's willingness and ability to carry out the plan, (4) progress made since the plan was first developed, and (5) what about the plan needs to be revised. Most agencies develop their own form.

In spite of the many variations, there are, however, common elements of treatment plans that do appear in most agency treatment plans and in most treatment plans of third-party vendors. Treatment plans are written down or often entered on a form. Ideally, the worker and client develop the plan together so that the various terms of the plan have been mutually established (see the chapter on contracting—Chapter 8). Most treatment plans involve the following specific terms: (1) an identified target problem; (2) clearly stated objectives that relate to the target problem; (3) the various actions that the client, worker, and others will be taking in order to help the client achieve the objectives; (4) the obstacles that may interfere with the plan; and (5) a specific time frame—when actions are expected to be completed.

The importance of the treatment plan is that it clarifies and specifies what is to be done, when things are to be completed, and by whom. The central element of most treatment plans is the objectives that are developed by the worker with the individual client. Objectives should be explicit and clearly identified so that all parties understand what they are trying to accomplish. Explicitness helps to minimize confusion and hidden agendas that may develop in the planning process. It is also important for objectives to be specific and focused on a particular aspect of the target problem. "Partializing" (i.e., focusing on only one or two problems or goals at one time) is an important practice principle that should shape the plans that worker and client develop (Perlman, 1957; Reid & Epstein, 1972). Objectives should also be realistic and feasible. Although in the beginning, it is not always possible to know for sure what is feasible, highly idealistic or extremely unlikely suggestions should be avoided in planning. Remember Aesop's fable of "Belling the Cat" (Jacobs, 1966):

Long ago, the mice held a general council to consider what measures they could take to outwit their common enemy, the Cat. Some said this, and some said that; but at last a young mouse got up and said he had a proposal to make, which he thought would meet the case. "You will all agree," said he, "that our chief danger consists in the sly and treacherous manner in which the enemy approaches us. Now, if we could receive some signal of her approach, we could easily escape from her. I venture, therefore, to propose that a small bell be procured, and attached by a ribbon round the neck of the Cat. By this means we should always know when she was about, and could easily retire while she was in the neighborhood.

This proposal met with general applause, until an old mouse got up and said: "That is all very well, but who is to bell the Cat?" The mice looked at one another and nobody spoke. Then the old mouse said: "It is easy to propose impossible remedies."

One of the first steps in developing a treatment plan with an individual client is for the worker and client to discuss aspects of the target problem they think can be immediately addressed. The solution-focused models (Cade & O'Hanlon, 1993; Cooper, 1995; DeJong & Berg, 2002; O'Hanlon & Wiener-Davis, 1989) are clear that clients can be quickly mobilized to work on their problems if they are asked to think about the changes they want to achieve. Such questions as "Where would you like to be in 2 weeks?" or "How will we know things are better?" may help the client generate specific objectives. At this point in the planning process, the worker helps the client to specify each objective as concretely as possible. For example, an individual client may want to work on improving his or her relationship with a spouse, parent, or employer. The worker can help the client focus on specific aspects of those relationships he or she wishes to change, such as the amount of time he or she wants to spend together, the topics to be discussed, or the conflicts they wish to reduce. When each objective is finally agreed on, the worker and client should specify how long they plan to work on that specific objective. Pressures from managed care arrangements are continually whittling down how long the client and worker can work together on a specific objective.

To develop an effective treatment plan with the individual client, the interpersonal practitioner should develop an understanding of the many kinds of helping resources that may be mobilized in the client's environment. The worker must discover the various informal and intimate resources available to individual clients, as well as have a working knowledge of both the formal, societal helping resources and the indigenous, alternative resources that the clients may turn to in their particular neighborhood or ethnic community.

Formal and Informal Resources

Formal resource systems are those agencies, programs, and services that comprise the public, voluntary, and private sectors of the service delivery system. These resources are staffed by various helping professionals who have degrees and credentials that have been sanctioned by society. Many other professions besides social work, such as medicine, law, nursing, and psychology operate in these organizations. Hospitals, psychiatric outpatient clinics, substance abuse clinics, public welfare, public schools, family agencies, community action agencies, legal aid programs, courts, and private therapists are examples of the services that are available in the formal resource system.

Most counties or metropolitan areas print a listing of these formal resources to identify and briefly describe the programs in their particular catchment area. Besides the Yellow Pages, some areas have information and referral "hotlines" that can be called. The problem with these printed guides is their inaccuracy. Some of the descriptions in guides are public relations statements of what the agency "would like to do" and are not, in fact, representative of what agencies actually do. Some information in guides is out of date, so that agency location, phone number, and contact person may have changed. Another problem with guides and referral services is that they inevitably overlook and omit potential resources that may be unknown to the authors of the guide or referral service. A final problem with guides reflects the reality that just knowing about a service does not guarantee that a client will be able to make use of it. Information about a service is not enough to assure a successful referral.

Alternative and indigenous helping resources refer to practitioners, groups, and institutions that the formal resources may disparage yet to which individual clients tend to turn first in time of trouble (Golan, 1980; Green, 1982). Troubled individuals often try to solve problems on their own or turn to family and friends for help. If these efforts bring no relief, the individual may move into the indigenous healing system and seek help from a culturally specific practitioner who is not formally recognized or legitimized by society at large (see Figure 11.1).

Figure 11.1 Help-Seeking Journey

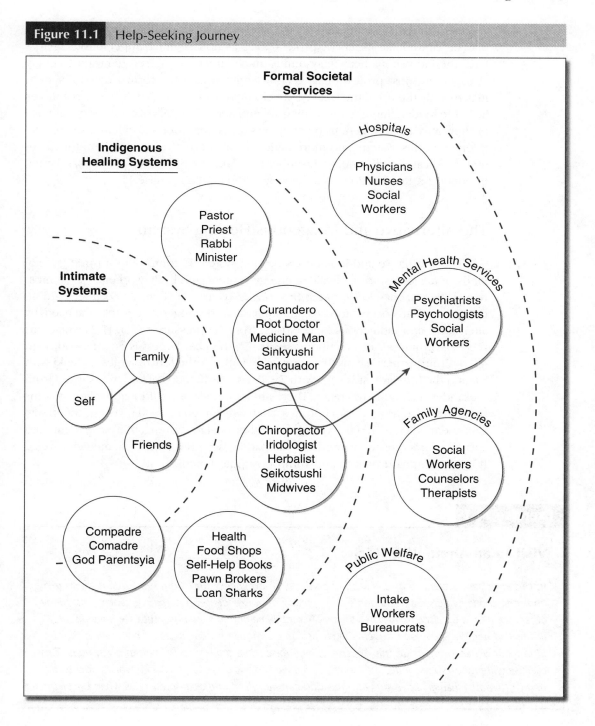

Even though practitioners in the alternative and indigenous healing system may be viewed skeptically by professionals as nonscientific, superstitious charlatans, the indigenous healing system is much larger and more significant to many clients than most professionals acknowledge. In fact, the formal helping system may be only the tip of the iceberg of helping resources, and many more resources lie in the hidden, indigenous healing system. Recent studies of client or patient use of alternative and indigenous practitioners reveal that over $20 billion goes to practitioners in this system, and more patients use alternative practitioners than general medical practitioners (Eisenberg et al., 1998; Foster, Phillips, Hamel, Eisenberg, & Renouf, 2000; Kessler et al., 2001). (See Exercise 11.1.)

The Alternative and Indigenous Healing System

The alternative and indigenous healing system is composed of three general kinds of healers: spiritual healers, energy healers, and body workers. In the most recent *Ann Arbor Holistic Resource Guide* (Crazy Wisdom, 2009), there are 46 categories that cover various techniques and healing procedures practiced by alternative and indigenous healers (i.e., from acupressure to yoga). Massage has the largest number of practitioners with 72, the next largest is energy work with 44, the third largest is spiritual counseling with 37, the fourth largest is Reiki with 31, and the fifth largest is yoga with 27. There are 12 kinds of bodywork listed from Alexander technique to Trager. There are a number of traditional healing systems that have been around for centuries, such as Ayurveda (4,000+ years), traditional Chinese medicine (2,500+ years), and other healing systems that have competed with the emergence of modern, allopathic, scientific, Western medicine (e.g., homeopathy, naturopathy, and anthroposophical medicine).

Exercise 11.1

Visit to an Alternative Healer

In this exercise, we want to give you an opportunity to experience and learn more about alternative and indigenous healers. Some students may already have experienced alternative healers, but many others seem to know little about the various alternative healing technologies that we have discussed in this chapter. We encourage students to choose an alternative healing system about which they are unfamiliar. When students do this exercise, it may raise some anxiety so they often go in pairs. This exercise will probably cost you some money, which we know is a burden for social work students, but many alternative healers have student rates and can be talked into even lower rates when they learn

> *that you are doing this as an educational activity for your professional development. Many alternative healers can be found in the Yellow Pages, and local health food stores and food co-ops may have listings of practitioners in your community. When you visit the practitioner, ask about her or his training and education, typical clientele, and whether she or he ever collaborates with other professionals. Our students enjoy sharing this exercise with their classmates, and we hope you will do that, too.*

For specific ethnic groups, indigenous healing is a healing system parallel to Western, allopathic medicine (Delgado & Humm-Delgado, 1982). There are curanderos in the Mexican American community, espiritistas in the Puerto Rican community, Santeria and Lucumi practitioners in the Cuban American community, shamanic and medicine persons in Native American communities, voodoo practitioners in certain rural and urban black communities, and faith healers in both the urban black and rural white communities.

Most of these indigenous and alternative healing systems have their own herbal system that supplies various herbal remedies, potions, and salves in the same way a pharmacist supplies prescription drugs and medicines. Many of the modern wonder drugs of the pharmacist were once the secret folk remedies of indigenous healers. Many tranquilizers, antibiotics, anesthetics, and even aspirin have their origins in "folk medicine" (Root-Bernstein & Root-Bernstein, 1997).

Table 11.1 is presented as a guide to the many kinds of indigenous helpers who practice in various ethnic communities. The table is by no means comprehensive but does demonstrate a broad range of indigenous practitioners who are often ignored and little understood by professionals (Eisenberg et al., 1998; Gross, 1979).

Self-Help/Support Groups

Communities in the United States are also permeated by numerous self-help groups and associations. Americans are self-help, do-it-yourself people. There are self-help books for almost any conceivable human condition: divorce, sexuality, handicaps, parenting, dieting, nutrition, exercise, and so on. There are also numerous opportunities for individuals to meet in groups with other individuals who face similar problems or life transitions. Social work has recognized the value of self-help and support groups in many communities (Collins & Pancoast, 1976; Kurtz, 1997; Powell, 1976). Not only are there face-to-face groups but also telephone groups for homebound individuals (Meier, 2004) and Internet support groups that individuals can join (Finn, 1999). Many have modeled themselves on the 12-step paradigm of AA.

Research on these groups has demonstrated that they can be helpful to clients who are struggling with personal problems, such as addictions, chronic

Table 11.1 Examples of Indigenous Practitioners

Practitioner	Consumer Population	Common Healing Procedures
Espiritista	Latino (Puerto Rican)	Diagnose spirits; prescribe rituals, ceremonies, herbs
Curandero	Latino (Mexican American)	Diagnose spirits; prescribe rituals, ceremonies, prayers, herbs
Santero	Latino (Cuban American)	Diagnose spirits; prescribe rituals, prayers, animal sacrifice, ceremonies
Santguador	Latino	Treats mostly physical ailments
Yia	Greek American	Advice and counsel
Root doctor	Rural African American	Prescribe herbs, potions, and home remedies
Voodoo practitioner	Rural and urban black	Diagnose spirit; prescribe rituals, prayer, ceremonies, talisman
Sinkyushi	Asian community	Acupuncture, massage, advice
Seikotsushi	Asian community	Skeletal/muscular adjustments
Shiatsushi	Asian community	Skeletal/muscular/energy work
Herbalist	Found in many communities	Herbal remedies, nutritional advice, plant extracts, etc.
Iridologist	Urban/suburban communities	Diagnose organ health; prescribe purgatives, natural foods

debilitating illnesses, as well as life tragedies such as death of loved ones or discovering a severe, life-threatening illness (Call, 1990; Hopman & Werk, 1994; Kabat-Zinn, 1990; Lyon, Moore, & Lexius, 1992; Powell, 1990; Vugia, 1991; Wasserman & Danforth, 1988). Some research has indicated that these kinds of groups can even have an impact on how long one survives a life-threatening illness (Harmon, 1991; Krupnick, Rowland, Goldberg, & Daniel, 1993; Spiegal, 1990). Recent research, however, has demonstrated that these earlier studies are contradicted by more recent studies that show that longevity from cancer is not increased by membership in support groups (Goodwin et al., 2001; Spiegal et al., 2007). These later studies, however, do show that psychological, emotional, and quality of life issues are improved with membership in support groups.

In Table 11.2, a list of typical self-help groups is offered as an example of the many kinds of self-help and support groups that may meet in a given community.

Table 11.2	Examples of Self-Help Groups
Al-Anon/Alateen	Support group for families with an alcoholic member
AA	Support group for alcoholics
Dawntreader, Inc.	Support group for those who have received or presently are receiving psychiatric care
Families Anonymous	Support group for parents of teens with substance abuse and behavioral problems
Gay Alliance	Support group for lesbian women and gay men
Gray Panthers	Advocacy group for the elderly
Hospice	Support group for individuals and family members facing a terminal illness
Informed Birth and Parenting	Educational and support group for new parents
Lamaze International	Educational and support group for expectant parents
Multiple Sclerosis Society	Educational and support group for individuals with MS and their families
New Beginnings	A grief recovery group for persons experiencing a recent loss
Overeaters Anonymous	Support group for overweight people
Parents Without Partners	Support group for single parents
Reach to Recovery	Support group for women who have had a mastectomy
Recovery, Inc.	Support group for former mental patients designed to prevent relapses
Tough Love	Support group for parents with a troubled teenager
Widowed Persons Group	Support group for widows and widowers
Women for Sobriety	Support group for alcoholic women

This list is illustrative and not exhaustive. The American Self-Help Group Clearinghouse (White & Madara, 2009) has information on more than 1,200 national and international groups, and the "Psychology Self-Help Resources on the Internet" (Psych Web, 2008) lists hundreds of groups focused on psychological issues. In some states, there are clearinghouses that provide information on the location of groups throughout the state and will also supply resources and technical support to help individuals start up their own self-help group in their own community. Funding for the

Michigan Self-Help Clearinghouse (2010) has been discontinued as part of the state of Michigan budget cuts, and the online database is being maintained by volunteer staff. Many of the formal information and referral services in communities, such as those published by United Way, may also list self-help groups. Local newspapers may also publish a list of meeting times and contact persons for local self-help and support groups on a weekly or monthly basis. Many dozens of these groups may be meeting in even small towns. Many of the support groups that are meeting may be run by social workers who have targeted a particular client group that is struggling with a particular social problem. For example, social workers can be found running groups for survivors of domestic violence, for women who have had mastectomies, for individuals diagnosed with HIV, and family members who have lost a child to cancer. (See Exercise 11.2.)

Exercise 11.2

Visit a Support Group

In this exercise, we want you to locate a support group in your community or to locate a support group on the Internet. If you decide to visit a support group in your community, contact the facilitator of the group and get permission to observe a session. Many 12-step groups have open meetings in which visitors and newcomers are welcome. You may find that some groups will not allow you to visit and their sessions are closed. If you decide to visit an online group, the two websites previously listed will help you to locate a group.

Choose a group that interests you, could be of support to you, or might be helpful to clients with whom you are working. If you can locate an active, online group, and they will let you sign on, follow the group for several weeks so that you can get a sense of how effective this group might be for its members. In the chapter on group assessment (Chapter 14, we will talk about therapeutic variables that can be found in groups (e.g., self-sharing, catharsis, or altruism). Were any of these variables evident in the group you visited? Whether you visit a community group or an online group, how helpful do you think this group was to its members? What are the upsides and downsides of Internet support groups? Share your experiences with your classmates.

In the individual assessment chapter (Chapter 10), we outlined an ecological framework that suggested that many social problems individuals experience can be conceptualized as imbalances in three areas of social functioning. Social problems may reflect an imbalance in (1) an individual's needs and environmental resources, (2) an individual's aspirations and environmental opportunities, and (3) an individual's skills and capacities and the expectations and demands from others in the client's environment. We will employ this framework to demonstrate how the worker's interventions with individual clients can be organized to help client's cope and resolve these imbalances.

Most of us played on a seesaw, or teeter-totter, as a child and learned that balance is achieved by changing what is happening on either end of the beam. This metaphor of the seesaw is useful in understanding how the interpersonal practitioner intervenes in individual client lives. Efforts can be directed at the client end of the transaction, at the environmental end of the transaction, or at both ends simultaneously.

INTERVENTIVE ROLES ●

We will explore six basic *interventive roles—enabler*, *trainer*, *broker*, *mediator*, *resource developer*, and *advocate*—that interpersonal practitioners perform when they are working with individual clients (Compton & Galaway, 1994). These are traditional roles that have been performed by social work practitioners for many decades. In recent years, some of these roles have been combined under the term *case management* (Anthony, Cohen, Farkas, & Cohen, 1988; Moxley, 1989; Rothman, 1992, 1994). Many large formal service systems now hire social workers into this position of case manager, and the procedures we describe in this section of the chapter will be germane to many of the functions of case managers. We present these six roles as though they were distinct categories; however, in practice, there is considerable overlap between these roles, and often they blend together when a worker applies several strategies at once (See Figure 11.2).

Figure 11.2	Ecological Balance—Individual and Environment

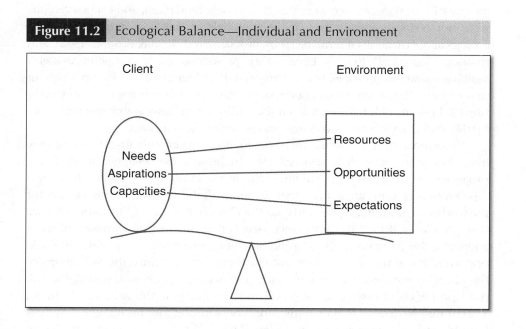

Enabler

In some contexts, the enabler role is viewed negatively because it is used to describe behavior in one person that enables another person to maintain self-destructive behavior. For example, in the substance abuse literature, the enabler is someone close to an alcoholic who helps the alcoholic to maintain his or her drinking behavior by protecting the substance abuser from the negative consequences of drinking. This meaning of enabler is not the one we will be using here. In the early literature of social casework, this role would be described as "supportive" (Selby, 1956). The enabler encourages, motivates, and coaxes the client into *taking actions* that will solve problems. The enabler does not take action for the client but encourages the client to take actions for herself. In some situations, the worker has to take actions for the client, but the ideal of enabling is to maximize client involvement in the helping process. This principle of maximizing client involvement is central to client empowerment and is basic to all the interventive roles described in this chapter. This role is clearly shown in the solution focused literature of the last decade (Cade & O'Hanlon, 1993; Cooper, 1995; DeJong & Berg, 2002; O'Hanlon & Wiener-Davis, 1989).

In early studies of casework practice, social workers spent very little time actively encouraging or promoting client action (Hollis, 1968). Most of the caseworker's interventions involved exploring the client's situation, helping the client express how he or she felt about her circumstances and then helping the client understand the impact various situational dynamics were having in the client's life. Less than 2% of the worker's verbal interventions could be categorized as encouragement. Early models of casework practice were deficit or problem oriented, and client strengths were not seriously encouraged. In later models of casework practice, such as ecological (Germain & Gitterman, 1980), task centered (Reid & Epstein, 1972), and solution focused (DeJong & Berg, 2002), promoting client competence was a significant strategic principle. In comparison to the older psychosocial model, about 18% of the verbal interventions of a task-centered practitioner are encouragement (Reid & Epstein, 1972). We want to emphasize in this discussion that it is important for the worker to involve, encourage, and promote client actions.

Unfortunately, some clients are so demoralized by their life situations that they have little hope that their own efforts can bring about changes in their life situations. Even when opportunities are made available to them, their own aspirations and wants are almost nonexistent. With these clients, it is necessary for the worker to motivate, cajole, and coax the client to pursue opportunities that are being made available. The imbalance between aspirations and opportunities is addressed by increasing client aspiration and motivation to pursue available opportunities. If the worker does not encourage and enhance the aspirations of the client to pursue opportunities, then just making opportunities available will not help the client resolve social problems that emerge in this area. For example, a client may have been told by significant others throughout his lifetime that he is "stupid and will never amount to anything." Even if a worker can locate opportunities for the client to complete his education and pursue advanced training in an area, it is unlikely that the client will be able to follow through without support that enhances client motivation.

Many oppressed clients have such little confidence in themselves and such low self-esteem that the interpersonal practitioner must work to give the client a greater sense of self-efficacy (Maluccio, 1981). Nothing builds confidence like success. If the worker can help the client tackle small, manageable tasks and succeed, the client will be much more confident about pursuing more complicated goals. In this chapter, we want to emphasize how important it is for the worker to develop specific, manageable steps that the client can achieve through his or her own action.

The enabler role is sometimes hard for beginning practitioners to perform because they may know exactly what to do to help a client cope with his or her life situation. The interpersonal practitioner is not supposed to be building up his or her sense of self-efficacy by doing a task for the client. It is difficult sometimes to see the client struggling to complete a task that the worker can accomplish quickly and successfully, yet that is what the enabler role requires. The following real case example is offered to clarify the enabler role.

Promoting Competence in Chronic Psychiatric Patients

In a summer camping program for institutionalized psychiatric patients, one of the units complained they had no way to store wood for campfires in a way that would keep it dry. The members of the unit complained that the camp staff should supply them with a way to keep their wood dry. Instead of complying with this request, one of the camp staff (a social worker) said that he would help the unit build their own wood rack. This suggestion was met with derision from most members of the unit. They complained they did not know how to build a rack, they did not know how to use the tools, and it was not their job anyway—which in their minds was to be lethargic, passive patients. In spite of the protests, the social worker was able to get 8 of the 12 members of the unit to attempt to build a rack. Two members who refused to be involved claimed that the state could not use them as "slave labor," and they were able to convince two other members of their unit to go off to the arts and crafts tent instead of building a wood rack.

For the four who went off to arts and crafts, this was a major serendipitous success, for they had been only marginally involved in any of the camp activities. To make a long story short, those eight institutionalized psychiatric patients planned, designed, foraged in the woods for materials, and constructed a functional wood rack. It was not the most aesthetic wood rack nor the most sturdy wood rack, but it worked. It kept the wood off the ground and offered some protection from the rain.

The value of this experience for these eight patients was dramatic. Not only were they proud of their wood rack, which they showed to patients in other units, but they became the "consultants" to help other units construct their own wood rack. The social worker who "helped" them with their rack did not "do" any part of the construction but instead encouraged each member to take responsibility for some part of the construction process.

Trainer

In some cases, clients will not have the skills necessary to meet the expectations and demands of their environment. In some of these situations, it is possible that the demands coming from the environment are unrealistic or unreasonable, and the worker needs to modify the expectations of significant others in the client's life. For example, some clients with a particular physical impairment may be treated as though they have impairments in other areas of social functioning. Sometimes people will speak louder to blind individuals even though their hearing may be excellent, and deaf individuals are sometimes treated as though they are retarded because they are unable to respond to speech. In these situations, the worker may intervene in the environment by changing expectations of significant others.

Social Skills Training

In some situations, however, the worker may be working directly with the individual to change various skills that the individual needs to develop to cope successfully with demands from the social environment and to perform roles that they occupy. Social workers may be engaged in helping individuals become more assertive, helping parents be more effective parents, or helping disabled veterans from various wars who are returning to civilian life with special needs. There are many specific, social skills programs designed to teach various skills across the life span, and many of these programs are developed for group learning experiences (Alberti & Emmons, 1990; Lange & Jakubowski, 1976; Liberman, DeRisi, & Mueser, 1989; MacKain, Soy, & Lieberman, 1994). It is beyond the scope of this book to present all social skills training programs except to present the basic paradigm that most programs follow (See Figure 11.3).

There are several basic steps to skill acquisition programs. In the first step, the trainer educates the individual members of the group by carefully explaining and demonstrating the skill and also enhancing the members' motivation to acquire the skill. In the next step, videotaped examples of the skills may be demonstrated, or short video and audio vignettes may be used to engage members in discussions of situations in which skills may be employed. In the next step, members may use role playing to practice the various skills they want to acquire, and the group will help members sharpen their new skills by providing feedback and support. The next major step is to plan how the skills can be stabilized and transferred to the real world of the individual members. There may be obstacles that must be addressed and resources that need to be acquired before members are ready to try the new skill in the real world. The next major steps involve practicing the new skill in the real world—sometimes with the support of the trainer or other members of the group. Finally, individual members will apply the skill on their own in a real-life situation. In such programs, the interpersonal practitioner will act as teacher, trainer, coach, enabler, and group facilitator.

Figure 11.3 Social Skills Acquisition Paradigm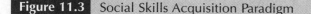

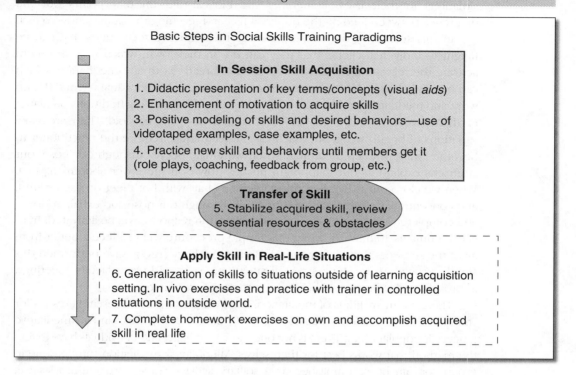

Basic Steps in Social Skills Training Paradigms

In Session Skill Acquisition

1. Didactic presentation of key terms/concepts (visual *aids*)
2. Enhancement of motivation to acquire skills
3. Positive modeling of skills and desired behaviors—use of videotaped examples, case examples, etc.
4. Practice new skill and behaviors until members get it (role plays, coaching, feedback from group, etc.)

Transfer of Skill
5. Stabilize acquired skill, review essential resources & obstacles

Apply Skill in Real-Life Situations

6. Generalization of skills to situations outside of learning acquisition setting. In vivo exercises and practice with trainer in controlled situations in outside world.
7. Complete homework exercises on own and accomplish acquired skill in real life

Stress Reduction Techniques

In the individual assessment chapter (Chapter 10), we presented the impact that stressors have on our physical, emotional, and interpersonal well-being. There are many stress reduction techniques that clients can learn that will mollify the negative impact of stressors and activate the "relaxation response" (Benson, 1975; Benson & Klipper, 2000). The relaxation response is the body's natural, healing response that buffers and counteracts the negative impact of stressors. There are many activities that clients can be taught that will activate this response. We strongly believe that clients who are literate should purchase Davis, Eshelman, and McKay's (2000) *The Relaxation and Stress Reduction Workbook* (5th ed.), which can be purchased for less than $2.00 as a used book online. The interpersonal practitioner should become familiar with the various techniques that are presented in this workbook and use the workbook as a framework to teach individual clients many of the stress reduction activities that clients can perform on their own time. There are dozens of techniques outlined in this clearly written, self-help workbook, and even a chapter on nutrition and exercise. The value of this workbook is that it empowers clients to engage in activities that will manage stressful roles and situations in their lives. Remember the biblical allusion that points out the difference between feeding the hungry a fish and teaching the hungry how to fish!

In this section of the chapter, we will focus on two techniques that can be taught to individual clients that they can do on their own, which will help them activate the relaxation response. The two are breath work and meditation, which can be easily taught by the interpersonal practitioner to individual clients. Breath work and meditation are derived from one of the oldest healing traditions on planet earth. Ayurvedic medicine has been estimated to be 4,500 years old. There are many variations of breath work, but essentially all techniques require the practitioner to become aware of deep breathing. When we inhale deeply through our nose, our stomachs expand as our diaphragm pushes down on the lower abdominal area. When we close our eyes, sit comfortable in a chair with both feet on the ground, and concentrate on inhaling slowly and fully through our nose and exhaling slowly and completely through our mouth, the relaxation response will be activated. In as short a time as 10 minutes a day, this simple procedure will produce a buffer from all of the stressors that fill our lives. I, Brett A. Seabury (BAS), have performed this simple procedure in many stressful situations, such as boring faculty meetings, approaching deadlines, and before an important presentation.

There are many kinds of meditation, and because of positive research results for "mindfulness meditation" (Kabat-Zinn, 1990; Smith, 2005), this kind of meditative practice is popular today. There is not one way to meditate, and individuals have to find the method that works best for themselves. Mindfulness meditation can be done in groups or can be accomplished as a solitary activity. Some yoga enthusiasts will meditate in a full lotus position on the floor, others will meditate to soft music created for meditation, others believe it is best upon waking up in the morning, and others set aside time before going to bed at night. For most folks, meditation can be done while lying down or sitting in a chair—or even walking silently through a labyrinth. The essential ingredient is a space that will be free of interruptions for at least 20 minutes.

Some folks begin their meditation session with breath work to begin the relaxation process. Meditation requires the individual to be focused in "the present" and to ignore thoughts about what happened in the past and also to ignore thoughts about what has to be done in the future. In mindfulness meditation, the individual does not try to stop all of the thoughts that come cascading into consciousness but to act as an observer and let these cascading thoughts pass through consciousness. For those of us who have roots as WASPs and are predominantly future oriented, being in the present is a skill that has to be learned. As a novice, it may be difficult to let go of all of the thoughts about things that have to be done in the future. Meditation may also be impossible for some fundamentalist Christian devotees. Because of its Buddhist roots, meditation may be seen as anti-Christian. For these folks, extended prayer can have similar healing effects (Benson & Stark, 1997) (See Exercise 11.3.).

Breath Work and Meditation

In this exercise, we want you to practice both deep breathing and meditation that has been described in this section of the chapter. Before you begin your practice, we want you to take a moment to think about how "stressed out" you are and to decide where you are on the Subjective Units of Discomfort Scale (SUDS) (0–10). Next take your pulse rate (number of beats per minute). These two numbers will be your baseline to see if deep breathing and meditation lower these two numbers, which would be a positive outcome for these stress reduction techniques. Try deep breathing for at least 5 minutes and check your pulse and SUDS score. Now meditate for at least 15 minutes and again check your pulse rate and SUDS score. You have now built in evaluation into this practice exercise!

Problem Solving

A major part of the time in one-to-one sessions with clients is spent with the interpersonal practitioner enhancing the problem solving and decision making capacities of clients. These processes are not only a significant part of the service process but they are also some of the skills that practitioners hope to transfer to clients. The following guideline is offered as a framework to the interpersonal practitioner and also can be taught to individual clients:

1. *The Problem Is Specified in Detail.* This specification includes the amount of discomfort felt about the problem, how severe the problem is, how frequently the problem is experienced, and in what situations it occurs and in what situations it does not occur. In solution-focused models, exceptions are more important than when the problem occurs because the exceptions form the basis for planning interventions.

2. *Goals to Be Attained Through Problem Solution Are Specified.* For many clients, this step may be a difficult one because some clients do not know what they are capable of attaining. They may not be aware of resources and opportunities in their environment nor able to realize that problems do not occur all the time, and there may be situations in which the problem does not occur.

3. *Information Is Then Sought to Help the Client Generate Possible Solutions.* This includes information about the client's characteristic ways of solving problems as well as situations that relate to the viability of one possible solution compared to others. Clients are made aware of their problem solving repertoire and solutions that they may never have tried.

4. *Alternative Solutions Are Evaluated.* The criteria used for evaluation include the benefits for the client, the costs to the client, and how the alternatives relate to the client's values as well as those of significant others. For some clients, terminating a pregnancy or leaving a marriage may not be options they can pursue.

5. *One Alternative Is Chosen.* The basis for this choice should stem from the evaluation described in Step 4 with special emphasis on whether the solution can be implemented in the light of existing resources. Pragmatic and realistic choices should take precedence.

6. *The Final Stage, Once an Alternative Has Been Chosen, Is to Plan the Details of How to Carry Out the Alternative and Then Act on the Basis of This Plan.* The worker may have to help the client determine these details and secure the necessary resources and support. During the implementation of the plan, the worker may have to provide support and coaching for the client. If major obstacles occur, this may necessitate a return to Step 4 to select another alternative or even the initiation of a new problem solving process.

Many individual clients can be taught these problem solving steps. Other clients may have acquired problem solving skills but are unable to use them. One reason for this may be emotional factors that are getting in the way of problem solving. The client may be too agitated, anxious, angry, or depressed to participate in problem solving. Under these circumstances, the interpersonal practitioner may have to respond to these strong emotions by promoting catharsis—the release of these pent-up feelings. Sometimes the client may be helped to relax if she or he is too tense, or the clients may be helped to recognize how depressed they feel. In some situations, the client may need to address the situation that evoked the depression or anger before continuing with problem solving.

Emotional Freedom Techniques

Instead of relying on pharmaceuticals to control these undesirable emotional factors, we want to introduce a simple technique that interpersonal practitioners can use on themselves and also teach to clients so they can successfully reduce fear, anxiety, depression, grief, anger, guilt, pain, cravings, etc. Though Emotional Freedom Technique (EFT) is a controversial healing intervention, it can be used by clients to control many kinds of unwanted emotional and physiological symptoms. The controversy of this technique is that many of its proponents claim EFT is a miracle cure that can quickly heal many chronic disorders such as MS, diabetes, and many pain syndromes (Craig, 2008; Gallo & Robbins, 2007; Temes, 2006).

There are many testimonials of patients that have used EFT successfully but few scientifically controlled studies of EFT (Brattberg, 2008; Waite & Hodder, 2003; Wells, Polglase, Andrews, Carrington, & Baker, 2003).

We are skeptical of the many claims that EFT can "cure" illnesses, but from our own experience with EFT it can work the way many pharmaceuticals and herbal remedies work to reduce symptoms. EFT can reduce pain after an injury, it can reduce cravings for addictive substances, it can reduce anxiety, but it does not cure the injury, addictions, or anxiety disorder. EFT's greatest asset is it can be taught to clients and students as a self-help intervention technique. We will not go into the details about the underlying mechanism for EFT (e.g., chi, meridians, and energy nodes), but suggest that students interested in more information may go to the website (Pick, 2010). In this section of the chapter, we will present the basic steps, sequence of tapping, and vocalizations for EFT.

1. *The Setup*: In this step, the subject identifies a feeling or issue that they want to change, such as a craving for a cigarette, chocolate, or a cup of coffee; pain in some part of the body, such as a headache, back pain, or pain from a recent injury; or anxiety about a traumatic experience, upcoming test, or class presentation. The subject then rates the intensity of the craving, pain, anxiety, etc., on the SUDS (0–10). The subject then locates the "sore spot" on her or his chest, which is located about 4 in (10.16 cm) below the collarbone and about 2 in (5.08 cm) from the sternum (middle of chest). While gently rubbing this area with several fingers, the subject vocalizes a positive affirmation about herself or himself and the symptom they want to relieve—for example, "In spite of this splitting headache, I totally and completely accept myself!" or "Even though I am very anxious about this test, I am confident in my abilities and capacities as a person!" It is not so important what words subjects choose but that they say them out loud and vocalize them in a way that they mean it! This rubbing of the sore spot (sensitive area on the chest) and vocalization of the symptom and positive affirmation is repeated three times.

2. *The Tapping Sequence*: In this step, the subject begins tapping on various acupuncture points. While tapping, the subject should be thinking about the symptom they want to eliminate or they may softly vocalize it as they move through the tapping sequence. The tapping is done with some rapidity, at least five or more taps, but gently on each of the following points of the body, which is shown in Figure 11.4.

The subject begins by tapping on areas of the face. The first point is the inner edge of the eyebrow, followed by the bone on the side of the eye and under the eye. The fourth point is the area between the nose and upper lip, followed by the area between the lower lip and the chin. The next two areas are on the body—that is, the collarbone and a point on the side about 4 in (10.16 cm) below the armpit. The next five areas are

Figure 11.4 EFT Tapping Points

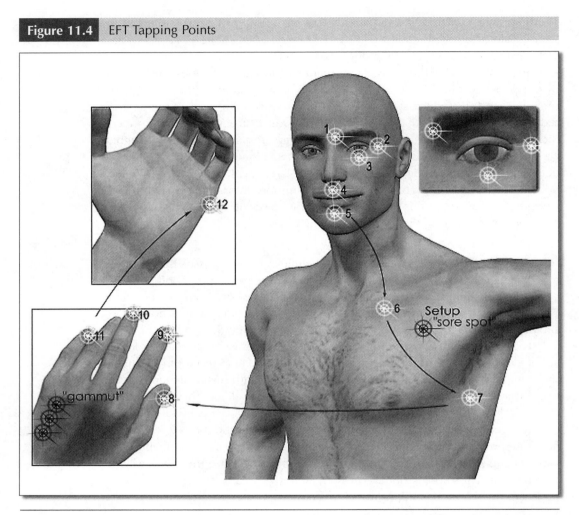

Source: Wieman, M., & Stiehler, G. (2005). *Location of the acupoints used in Emotional Freedom Technique.* Retrieved from http:/commons.wikimedia.org/wiki/File:Eft_punkte.jpg.

on the hand starting with the first joint of the thumb, index finger, middle finger, and pinky. The final point is called the karate chop point on the side of the hand.

3. *The 9 Gamut Procedure*: This is a Neuro-Linguistic Programming (NLP) procedure allegedly designed to reset the mental set of the brain. To beginners, it is even stranger than the tapping sequence just described. To begin, the subject must locate the "gamut point" on the back of the hand about an inch below the knuckle and between the joints of the little and fourth finger. While rubbing this area, the subject completes the sequence shown in Figure 11.5.

Figure 11.5 The 9 Gamut Procedure

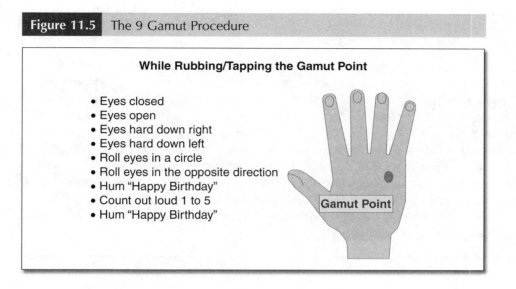

While Rubbing/Tapping the Gamut Point

- Eyes closed
- Eyes open
- Eyes hard down right
- Eyes hard down left
- Roll eyes in a circle
- Roll eyes in the opposite direction
- Hum "Happy Birthday"
- Count out loud 1 to 5
- Hum "Happy Birthday"

Gamut Point

While gently rubbing the gamut point and thinking about the issue, the eyes are closed and then opened. With eyes wide open, look hard down to the right, then hard down to the left. Roll the eyes in a circle and then roll the eyes in the opposite direction. Hum out loud a few measures of "Happy Birthday," count out loud from 1 to 5, and finish by humming a few measures of "Happy Birthday."

After completing this sequence, the subject completes another round of tapping (Step 2 of the protocol) and checks the SUDS level to see how far down on this scale the symptom has moved. For example, if the issue was a headache with a preliminary SUDS score of 7 and now the score is a 3, the entire EFT procedure can be repeated until the SUDS score reaches 0 (See Exercise 11.4.).

Exercise 11.4

Practicing EFT in Your Class

Talk your instructor into setting aside about a half hour in class to learn EFT. Have your instructor bring in a bag of Hershey's Kisses and Hugs. Most folks like chocolate, so you will be able to use the candy to test out EFT as a way of reducing cravings. Pass out the candy and have everyone open the wrapper and smell the chocolate, but don't let anyone eat the candy yet. In my classes, there is always someone who ignores this request and promptly eats the chocolate. Give this person another piece of candy and plead with them to wait. Get everyone to smell the chocolate and then mark down a SUDS rating for "cravings for chocolate." Then complete the EFT procedure. This can be done with students in dyads or small groups. After completing the entire procedure, have everyone reevaluate

(Continued)

(Continued)

their SUDS score for cravings. Repeat the EFT procedure again until most in the class have a SUDS rating at 0 or 1. At this point in class, I take around a wastebasket and get as many students as I can to throw away their Hershey's Kiss. Usually I can get about a third of the class to throw away the chocolate, but there are usually others who will not want to give up their chocolate and will negotiate with classmates to get the unwanted chocolate. In spite of the claims of EFT proponents, it does not work 90% of the time. A variation of this demonstration can also be accomplished by putting all of the cigarette smokers in a small group and repeating this exercise using a cigarette instead of chocolate. I can usually get one or two members of this small group to move their cravings down to 0 and throw their cigarette in the trash. This does not mean that I have "cured" their addiction to nicotine, which is a powerful, addictive substance, but I have given them a tool to forestall cravings when they finally decide to "kick the habit."

Broker

This role refers to one of the most common activities that social worker's engage in—referral. Referral is such a common activity for social workers that it is surprising that this area of practice has not received more attention. Those few studies that have addressed this area show a disturbingly low success rate (Kirk & Greenley, 1974; Weissman, 1976). Less than half of those individuals who are referred to other agencies make it to the next agency or are accepted for service when they get there. "Referral fatigue" (Lantz & Lenahan, 1976) is an unfortunate reality for many clients.

Knowledge of the formal, alternative, and indigenous resources in a community is critical to the success of a broker; however, knowledge alone will not guarantee that a successful referral will take place. The interpersonal practitioner must also be able to establish working relationships with both the individual client and the various resources available to the client. One important aspect of successful referrals is the worker's ability to develop contacts and cultivate relationships with other workers and professionals in community resources. It is easier for a worker to connect a client to a formal or alternative resource when that worker knows somebody in that system. Such a prior relationship between worker and contact person may be critical in some referral situations in which the client does not exactly "fit" the resources' eligibility standards or the client is ambivalent and unsure about pursuing services in the agency. The worker's prior relationship with a contact person in the agency and the worker's present relationship with the client can be used to enhance the process so that a successful referral can be established.

Successful brokers must be able to perform linking and cementing strategies. Weissman (1976) has suggested a number of procedures that a worker can employ to improve the chances of a successful link between client and agency. These procedures are presented in a hierarchy with the most intrusive and active interventions by the worker presented last. We have somewhat modified Weissman's list, but the main ideas are his.

The first level is to write down the critical information about the resource, such as name, address, telephone number, hours of operation, and let the client make the connection on her own. With those clients who have the motivation and capacity to negotiate the linkage with the resource, basic information will be enough to promote a successful link.

With other clients, it may be necessary to provide the name of a particular contact person whom they should seek out in the resource or the name of individuals they should avoid in the resource. In large organizations, there are numerous "gatekeepers" who have a great deal of discretionary power about who is served or rejected, and clients should be helped to locate responsive gatekeepers. In some situations, a written description of the client's particular problem or concern should be sent along. This kind of advanced preparation allows the worker to help the client build a good case with the gatekeeper.

In some situations, it may be necessary to introduce the client to an intermediary who can help to arrange the connection with the resource. Some indigenous healing systems cannot be approached directly by either clients or worker, and the worker will have to connect the client with an intermediary who, in turn, will help the client make contact with the resource. For example, I (BAS) have helped individual clients who believe they are hexed to locate an indigenous healer who can remove hexes. These referrals were arranged through an intermediary who was experienced with this kind of indigenous healing system.

It may be necessary to begin the linkage by phoning the prospective resource and making prearrangements before the client does anything. Such prearrangements allow the worker to initiate the link and also help the resource to understand what to expect when the client arrives. Finally, in some situations the worker will have to accompany the client to the resource to facilitate the client's entry or acceptance into the organization. The Lower East Side Family Union in New York used this linkage strategy to connect poor ethnic families with the large service agencies that would normally ignore or reject such applicants (Bush, 1977).

The worker will have to decide what level to choose to facilitate a successful link. If a linkage does not result from one level, it may be necessary to move to successively more intensive linkage strategies.

Linking only gets the connection started, and often a weak or fragile link can be easily dissolved unless the worker takes further action to strengthen the tentative connection. Weissman (1976) offered a number of *cementing strategies* that are designed to reinforce and maximize the linkages established between client and resource. Essential to all cementing strategies is *follow-up*, which should be built into all referral activities. Not only does follow-up provide information to the worker about the success or failure of the referral but it also provides information to the worker about what various resources are actually doing (e.g., screening procedures or new programs).

There are five basic cementing procedures that we have adapted slightly in this book: *check back*, *haunting*, *sandwiching*, *alternating*, and *individualizing*. In check back, the client is requested to call back the worker and inform him or her how the referral went. The responsibility for the follow-up is placed on the client's shoulders. In haunting, the worker is more active and takes responsibility for the follow-up. The worker asks the client's permission to call either the client or the resource to find out about the results of the referral.

In sandwiching, a follow-up interview is scheduled for worker and client to discuss how the referral process went and to plan other strategies that may be necessary to make a successful connection to a resource. In alternating, the worker and client plan a series of contacts following each contact the client has with the resource. This strategy of alternating interviews is intensive because the client and worker remain engaged while the client receives help from the resource. Clearly these last two strategies are employed when the client's motivation or capacity is limited or the resources are difficult to utilize and the worker must remain involved in supporting the client's connection to the helping resource.

In some situations, the worker will have to be intensively involved in encouraging the client to use a formal resource, as well as working with the resource to help it "bend" to the client's special needs. "Individualizing" (Meyer, 1976) refers to the process of trying to improve the match between the client's individual needs and the agency's requirements. Individualizing requires the worker to engage both the client and resource if a successful connection is to be maintained. As was discussed in the chapter on clienthood (Chapter 7), there are many barriers that applicants face in trying to become clients in a large, formal organization. Workers should be able to educate and even coax clients so that clients can present themselves in the best light. For example, some agencies are reluctant to serve clients who could benefit from their services because the client has an "undesirable" condition associated with the problem the agency is organized to tackle. Therefore, some clients are warned to avoid discussing, at least initially, their alcoholism and instead focus with the gatekeeper on their family conflicts. At the same time, the worker may have to bargain, persuade, or gently push the gatekeeper in the agency to bend policies and procedures to meet the client's individual needs. Workers may make "deals" to accept each other's difficult clients on the promise of future reciprocity.

As Figure 11.6 illustrates, the connection between client and resource is the focus of the individualizing process. Individualizing is both a brokerage and a mediating strategy and will require the worker to be actively engaged with both the client and the agency if a successful link is to be nurtured and maintained.

Figure 11.6	Individualizing Process

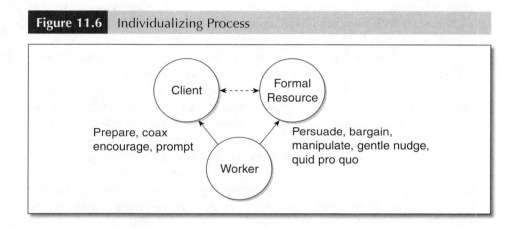

Mediator

The purpose of mediation is not to create a new linkage as in brokerage but to improve existing connections and relationships that the individual client has with resources in the client's environment. As with individualizing, the mediator must be able to work with both the client and the resource whether that is a significant other of the client or an agency. In the chapter on group change (Chapter 15), we will discuss the activities of the interpersonal practitioner in resolving conflicts that arise in group work. These tactics are germane to the interventions of the mediator role.

Successful mediators must accomplish two critical tasks besides establishing a relationship with all parties. First, they must not appear partisan to any side in any conflict that may exist or emerge. Successful mediators must be "neutral" or at least appear to be neutral to all involved (Gallant, 1982). This is a difficult part of this practice role for many social workers to perform. A mediator is not an advocate for the client but takes up a position between the client and the resource to improve the existing linkage. Whatever opinions the mediator may have about what is fair and just for the client in the situation must not be raised. The mediator's task is to facilitate the communication between the various parties so they can reach their own resolution or agreement.

The second element of successful mediating is related to the first but involves more than just neutrality. A mediator must be recognized by all parties as a legitimate authority. If either party feels the mediator is incapable of performing this role or does not have the knowledge or expertise to understand the particular conflict or impasse, then the mediator will have no legitimate basis for bringing the disgruntled or warring factions together. This is a problematic element of mediating because sometimes social workers must mediate between clients and other higher status professionals, such as psychiatrists. The client may feel that the worker is more than legitimate, but the psychiatrist may not feel that the social worker is capable of resolving the dispute and may refuse to give up time to attend a staffing or case conference on the client. Even social workers who have had extensive formal training in mediation, conflict management, and negotiation may not be able to convince a higher status professional to come to the table.

In spite of these critical, underlying dimensions of successful mediating, social workers engage in this role all the time. Not only do interpersonal practitioners mediate conflicts when working with conflicts in families and small groups but they also must take responsibility to mediate conflicts in the service delivery system. In the case that is presented in Figure 11.7, the individual client is caught in a web of connections with many service agencies. The problems that emerge in such a case situation are that service

Figure 11.7　Ecomap of 15-Year-Old Youth

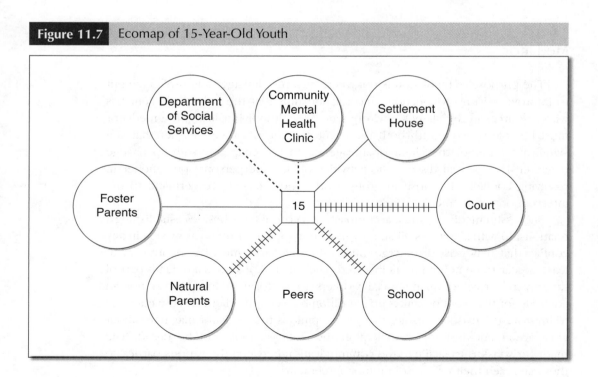

providers are not aware of what other service providers are trying to accomplish. Agencies and professionals may end up duplicating each other's service or working at cross-purposes.

In this figure, not only were some service providers unaware of other services that were involved but there also were interagency hostilities that pitted one service against the other, and this youth was caught between them. The courts did not get along with the settlement house and community mental health clinic, and the latter agency and school had poor relationships with the Department of Social Services. Because of these interagency conflicts, the 15-year-old youth was given mixed messages about what was expected of him, and these compounded his problems with the law and school. As this simple ecomap reveals, this youth has conflicted relationships with the court, school, and natural parents; weak relationships with the Community Mental Health Clinic and the Department of Social Services; and a positive relationship with his foster parents, peers, and the settlement worker.

This case is presented to demonstrate how great the need for *coordination* is in many practice situations. The action system must be planned with coordination in mind, or whatever change strategies are implemented may be neutralized or vitiated in a network of competing services. Another negative consequence of uncoordinated action systems is that lack of communication between professionals may allow some client or target systems to avoid making changes by triangulating (i.e., playing off) one professional against another. Inconsistency in the action system may allow a "system wise" manipulator to pit one part of the action system against another and thus keep services from having any influence or producing any significant change.

Coordination can be accomplished through a variety of processes, but it is essential that someone in the service network take responsibility for these activities. In some settings, these activities are performed by case managers (Bertsche & Horejsi, 1980; Rothman, 1994) whose job it is to oversee all planning and to be responsible for coordinating the various service providers in the action systems. The case manager is similar to an orchestra conductor. No matter how proficient each individual player may be, the conductor must take responsibility for organizing and coordinating each of the individual instruments if a successful "piece" is to be performed.

Some forms of coordination may require telephone contact, memos, letters, or even formal hearings; others may require face-to-face contact between all parties involved. What type of coordination is best will depend on the particulars of the case situation, what is feasible for the resources involved, or what may be required by law or agency routine. In today's practice world, it is extremely difficult to get various professionals together in face-to-face meetings, except in large institutions, such as hospital settings, which may routinely hold team meetings to review progress of patients.

The Case Conference

In this section of the chapter, we discuss the case conference as a coordinating activity that workers use to plan and improve existing linkages in a case situation. The case conference usually occurs at some decision or transition point in service, such as discharge or admission planning. In some organizations, a case conference is required before a change in the client's service plan can be implemented. For example, in some school systems, an Individual Educational Planning Committee made up of teachers, the principal, parents, and the school social worker must meet before changes are made in a student's special education services. In some health systems, a Placement Review Committee made up of hospital staff and community caregivers must meet before a patient is discharged to the community.

Most case conferences attempt to accomplish two tasks. All resources and service providers should understand and agree on an overall objective for the client or target system. Although each provider may be working on a particular piece, each piece must fit together into some general objective. Each provider should recognize how a particular effort fits together with that of others. Second, a case conference should also clarify and attempt to achieve some agreement about the role responsibilities of each member of the action system. Ideally, a case conference should also generate some commitment among members to carry out their respective responsibilities.

There are three parts to a successful case conference: (1) calling the meeting, (2) conducting the meeting, and (3) following up the meeting. What happens in the meeting is only a small part of a successful case conference. In fact, without careful planning and follow-up, a good decision making conference may go nowhere.

The worker must accomplish a number of decisions and tasks before the meeting or case conference occurs. First and foremost must be consideration of purpose. There must be a good reason for calling members of the action system together. The worker should be able to clearly articulate this reason to all who are invited: for example, "We need to meet to discuss the patient's discharge plans"; or "We need to get everyone together to clarify what each of us is doing in this case"; or "We need to get all parties together because it seems that there are several disagreements about what should happen next in this case."

Once purpose has been established and there is a good reason for calling the conference, the client should be informed of the conference. Whether the client or family plans to attend the conference, permission for release of information must be obtained prior to the conference. In discussing the release of information with the client, it may also be useful to discover whom the client feels should attend the case conference. The worker might overlook members of the action system whom the client feels should contribute to the decisions in the conference. For example, in some ethnic families it may be essential to involve a "compadre" as well as a parent in the case conference.

The next step in planning the conference is most critical and is influenced by many factors. Who should be invited to the case conference is a complex decision. Should everyone in the action system be invited? Should the client be invited, or should the meeting be for "professionals only"? Decisions to include or exclude potential members will depend on the purpose of the conference, which is why clarity of purpose is so essential. Obviously, there is no reason to invite a resource person who has nothing to do with the purpose of the conference. There may also be no reason to invite several people from the same service or agency when this involves duplication.

Case conferences should not be too large, or they become unmanageable. In large meetings, it is impossible for everyone attending to have an opportunity to present perspectives and opinions. How large is too large will depend on the worker's skills at managing and facilitating the group as well as the particular issues for the conference. It is easier to mediate highly contentious issues when fewer parties are present (Gallant, 1982). No matter how skilled the worker may be, a case conference with 10 or more members will be unwieldy and allow too little time for each member to present and interact.

A common way of reducing the number of members in the conference is for the worker to contact less essential resources before the conference and to represent their perspective in the conference. The optimal size for a case conference is around five or six members. Full attendance is rare in small groups, and the worker should expect some members to be unable to attend when the conference actually occurs. Attrition is a fact of life in groups.

Because there are many factors that will determine who should be invited to a case conference, it is almost impossible to generate firm rules about inclusion. Our bias is that it seems best to err on the side of inclusion rather than exclusion. Inviting too many members to the conference is a lesser evil than inviting too few.

Our position for inclusion is based on two important considerations. Too often in practice, the client is excluded from case conferences, yet we strongly believe that clients should be included. Clients are not only a good source of information but they have a right and a responsibility to participate in decisions that affect their lives. It may be easier for professionals to meet without clients present, and some professionals may find it discomfiting to share negative information in the client's presence; yet the client's presence will eliminate unsubstantiated character assassination and inferences that cannot be supported by facts and observation.

A problematic issue that sometimes occurs in action systems is sabotage (Seabury, 1979), as when one party deliberately works against the plans of other parties and contributes to the failure of the plan. A way to minimize sabotage is not to overlook any member of the action system who might be opposed to a coordinated plan. Action system members who are left out of the case conference may retaliate by not supporting the decisions of the conference. Even though some individuals may be obnoxious, contentious, or disagreeable in a conference, these are not viable reasons for excluding them. It is better to have a stormy planning session than to have the case conference go smoothly and later have the whole plan defeated by one action system member who was excluded from the meeting.

A case conference that is planned to avoid conflict is an example of faulty decision making. The different perspectives and interests of members of the action system make conflict inevitable, and it is naive (and maybe even impossible) to try to plan an effective case conference that does not have conflict. The worker should expect conflict and be able to mediate differences—not try to avoid them. In fact, if there is no conflict in a case conference, there probably was not much need for the conference in the first place.

Once members have been selected for the case conference, each should be contacted and invited. This step sounds much easier than it actually is. Trying to arrange a common time and an agreeable place in which to meet may require patience and persistence. Individual calendars are usually crowded, and not all meeting places are convenient or desirable for each individual. The worker may spend more time and energy on just this step, such as sending out e-mails and making phone calls to arrange a time and place for the conference than the actual conference itself.

Because of the time demands placed on professionals, face-to-face meetings are often impossible, so that the interpersonal practitioner must be able to arrange a telephone conference call for potential members. This technology allows members who are not physically present to attend a conference and be involved through a speaker phone. For example, in academe, this is a common way for faculty members of a committee to meet with other faculty who are at a great distance from the meeting. This simple telephone technology is also used in small seminars to bring in an outside presenter into the class (Seabury & Burton, 1999). There is also Internet software technology that will allow members to meet online in live chat rooms, but the problem with online meetings is that many clients—and even professionals—need to be educated how to make use of this kind of online meeting. See, for example, www.webex.com, www.gotomeeting.com, or www.freeconference.com.

Once a time and place have been arranged, the worker should follow up the phone call with an e-mail or snail mail. This message should remind each participant of the time, date, place, and purpose of the conference. It is also desirable to include a brief, tentative agenda for the conference in the form of a short list of the major issues or decisions that will be addressed. An agenda will give participants a chance to prepare for the conference, and advanced preparation is an important way in which to increase the efficiency of the meeting (Tropman, 1995). A copy of the message should also go to the clients—whether they plan to attend or not.

The primary responsibility of the worker who called the meeting is to facilitate decision making and group interaction. The basic task of this worker will be to clarify and mediate the various positions and perspectives of each participant. A good mediator should allow each party a chance to present his or her perspective and must keep any one party from dominating the meeting. The best conference plan is one for which everyone has input and can come to some agreement. No one party knows what is best, even though some usually think they do! In practice, some case conferences will not result in a common plan to which all parties can agree, but even this ending to a conference is valuable because the divergent positions of members will have been clarified.

In conducting the meeting, the worker should ensure that all members are introduced to each other in the beginning. Everyone should have a chance to state what his or her interests are in the situation, such as how long and in what capacity each knows the client. As the discussion progresses, the worker should try to identify the common ground between all parties that will form the basis of the conference plan.

When a common plan finally emerges, the worker allows each party a chance to comment on the respective actions each will have to carry out for the plan to be realized. Both the plan (decision) and specific responsibilities of each party should be briefly recorded as minutes. The worker may also take responsibility for arranging a time and place for subsequent conferences if they are deemed necessary by the group.

To assure that decisions reached during the case conference are implemented later in practice, the worker should take responsibility to follow up the conference. A simple way of following up is to send each member of the action system a follow-up letter and e-mail that includes the minutes of the case conference. At a bare minimum, the minutes should reflect the date of the meeting, members present, and all major decisions reached by parties at the conference—that is, major objectives, plans, and responsibilities of each party. In a sense, the minutes become a written contract of what members agreed to in the case conference and can be used by the worker to monitor individual activities.

Workers should have made it clear in the meeting that they will follow up the conference by contacting each member of the action system. Follow-up does not have to be in person, but it should be accomplished by phone, letter, or e-mail. This kind of "haunting" is essential for the worker to reinforce decisions made in the conference and to work out impasses that may arise when the plan is implemented.

At this point in the planning process, both planning and intervention are going on at the same time. Conceptually, the differences between planning and intervention are slight when the operations of the action system are considered.

The point that should be emphasized is that interpersonal practice involves lots of work "in the wings," and this work is essential to successful interventions.

Resource Developer

In some situations, the problem facing the client is lack of resources. As the service delivery system is cut back, this reality becomes more and more likely for underserved and oppressed clients. When existing or available resources are not available, agencies may opt for some kind of triage system to identify the most needy or those who can be helped most quickly (Coulton, Rosenberg, & Yankey, 1981). Triage is an organizational response when the demand for service drastically outstrips the supply of service. Scarcity brings drastic measures. When nursing home beds fill up and hospitals have nowhere to discharge patients, patients may be sent home to extremely risky environments. When extremely cold weather threatens a large metropolitan area, the homeless shelters fill up, and the overflow may be sent into subways. Scarcity may produce all kinds of stopgap measures; however, it is the ability to develop and locate these stopgap measures that is the mark of a good resource developer faced by a crisis of scarcity. Though social workers may occupy long-range planning positions designed to develop human resources, the interpersonal practitioner is more likely to have to perform this role in times of scarcity.

Resource development can be conceptualized at two levels. There is the broad, large-scale program development approach, which attempts to create services and resources aimed at a large number of clients or to address large-scale social issues. For example, the recent growth of domestic violence programs, safe houses, rape prevention services, and service aimed at batterers are all programs that emerged in response to "women's issues." Such broad resource development involves needs and asset assessment, interagency planning and organization, funding, and staffing for resources to become a reality. This level of resource development is beyond the ken of most interpersonal practitioners except that they may support such developments by testifying at public hearings, supplying planners with data about the needs of their clients, or voting for special millages designed to fund such programs.

The other, narrow-scoped level of resource development is more germane to interpersonal practitioners. This level concerns the development, mobilization, or reorganization of agency resources at the case level. For example, an agency may be encouraged to change its hours of operation to provide evening and weekend hours for working clients. An agency may be nudged to set up a "satellite" program in a local church or community center, which will provide better access to a particular geographic population. Interpersonal practitioners may exhort their agency and fellow practitioners to initiate self-help, support, and consciousness-raising (CR) groups for specific high-risk populations of clients.

This role of resource developer requires knowledge of the community and how alternative resources may be tapped during times of extreme scarcity. For example, during natural disasters—such as floods, hurricanes, earthquakes, or tornadoes—schools, churches, and community centers may be converted to shelters and food and water distribution centers. Businesses may donate trucks to transport supplies into the ravaged area. These kinds of large-scale adjustments are necessary to address the public issues; however, in the daily work of interpersonal practitioners, case issues also may be ameliorated in a similar fashion. The same principle applies to the case that applies to the class. If the worker is aware of the community, creative enough to think how other resources may be co-opted, and persuasive enough to get those in control of the other resources to give them up, the worker may be able to match the needs of a client with the creative use of an alternative resource. Churches, synagogues, mosques, civic associations, organized labor, business, etc., may all be approached to help generate resources. At little cost to these other organizations, places to meet, kitchens in which to prepare food, and volunteer labor for service activities may all be extracted from these sectors to tide us and our clients over in these times of Elizabethan retrenchment.

A social work student creatively matched the needs and resources of two of her individual clients. One client was a young boy in foster care who was estranged from his family. He was isolated, lonely, and beginning to get himself into trouble after school. Another client was an elderly woman who had no family and was isolated in her own home. The social work student was able to get these two clients together and successfully created her own "mini-foster-grandparents" program. Her two isolated clients almost immediately formed a bond, and the young boy started coming over to the elderly woman's home after school. Serendipitously, the woman, who was a retired school teacher, started helping the youth with his homework. The youth, in return, began helping the elderly woman with household tasks and repairs around her home. This "match" had a dramatic impact on both clients' sense of loneliness, but more importantly, it also had a major impact on both clients' self-esteem because they were productively doing something to help another human being.

Advocate

Advocacy has been clearly defined as a professional responsibility of social workers (Faust, 2008; Gilbert & Specht, 1976; Lens, 2005; Schneider & Lester, 2001; Schneider & Lori, 2000; Schneider & Netting, 1999; Thursz, 1976). The National Association of Social Workers (NASW) has defined the social work advocate as the "champion of social victims" (Ad Hoc Committee on Advocacy, 1969). In an advocacy situation, the worker takes a *partisan* stand with the client against some powerful environmental system that is perceived as unjustly intimidating the client or denying the client some basic right (Moxley & Freddolino, 1994). Unlike brokerage, mediation, and resource development, the worker takes a firm position with or on behalf of the client and is willing, though it is not always necessary to engage in adversarial tactics to redress the injustice that has befallen the client. In the chapter on organizational and community change (Chapter 17), we discuss in much greater detail the kinds of adversarial tactics (i.e., power tactics deliberately designed to generate conflict) that a practitioner can employ in an advocacy situation. The point we want to make in this chapter is that such tactics as bringing lawsuits, organizing a protest demonstration, or whistle-blowing are perceived negatively by agencies. The worker and client can be in considerable risk when they decide to resort to these tactics. See Figure 11.8, which reflects the basic kinds of advocacy in social work practice.

| **Figure 11.8** | Typology of Advocacy |

	Case	Class
Internal	trying to change a staffing decision on one of your own cases in your own agency	trying to change a procedure in your agency that affects many clients
External	trying to get a client reaccepted at an agency that has denied services to the client	trying to change the laws, public policies, etc., that affect large groups of citizens

In social work practice, there are four basic kinds of advocacy:

Case advocacy (sometimes called client advocacy) is probably the most ubiquitous form of advocacy. In case advocacy, the client system—whether individual, family, or group—is identifiable and therefore vulnerable. In *class advocacy*, sometimes called cause advocacy, the client system is anonymous or represents such a large collective that individual members are for the most part unidentifiable except by some demographic characteristic, such as age, status, clienthood, and so on. There is a clear connection between case advocacy and class advocacy. The "private troubles" of case advocacy often represent the "public issues" of class advocacy. One client's troubles may be systematically experienced by many other clients in a similar situation (Riley, 1971; Schwartz, 1969; Sunley, 1970). Though social workers are exhorted to take case troubles and follow them up as class issues, this happens infrequently because of the time, caseload, and agency demands on the interpersonal practitioner.

In *internal advocacy*, the worker is employed within the agency or in some way is part of the agency to be changed; whereas in *external advocacy*, the worker is not employed or within the target agency. This dimension of advocacy is important because it reflects the sanctioning power that the target system can bring to bear on the worker in various advocacy situations. When social workers advocate against their own agency, they are more likely to be sanctioned, *but* there is a relative advantage that workers have when they engage in advocacy in their own organizations. As an insider, the worker and the client have much easier access to information that may be useful to the advocacy situation. This access to information does not exist in external advocacy. The worker and client may not know a whole lot about agency procedures, grievance mechanisms, and how the agency dealt with similar complaints in the past.

In each box of the advocacy typology, the level of risk to the worker and client varies. In internal case advocacy, both the client and worker are at risk because both can be sanctioned by the agency. Both are identifiable and both have something to lose: The client may lose benefits, and the worker may lose his or her job. In internal class advocacy, the client has minimal risk because of his or her anonymity, but the worker who is identifiable is at risk. The internal guerrilla may have access to agency operations because he or she is on the inside, but the guerrilla runs the constant risk of being passed over for promotion, demoted, or fired.

In external case advocacy, the client is at risk because he or she is identifiable, whereas workers are at much lower risk because they are not employed by the target organization. In external class advocacy (as in social action), the client has almost no risk unless organized with the worker in some kind of protest or political action. The risk in external class advocacy is greatest for the worker and depends on the kinds of tactics the worker is willing to pursue. These issues will be discussed in much greater depth in the chapter on organizational and community change.

Because clients are at risk in the case advocacy situation, the interpersonal practitioner is ethically bound to discuss and weigh these risks with the client before engaging in any advocacy activity. If the client does not want the worker to pursue an advocacy strategy, especially on behalf of the client, then the worker cannot pursue such strategies. Even if the worker is certain that the case advocacy strategy will work, this strategy cannot be pursued. We know of practice situations in which the zeal of the worker to help the client backfired, and the client's welfare was jeopardized when professionals in the agency decided to retaliate by cutting the client's benefits. Unfortunately, there is a great deal of discretionary power that some line workers have in public agencies (Lipsky, 1980), and this power can be used to "punish" clients who make work more difficult. In class advocacy situations, the informed consent ethic (discussed earlier in the values chapter—Chapter 3) does not apply. The worker can pursue the broader issues because the individual client is not in jeopardy when the broader, class issues are being addressed.

Because we strongly agree that the client should be empowered whenever possible, we not only want clients to decide about the use of advocacy tactics but ideally we also want them to participate in the advocacy process. Some clients are reluctant to challenge authority figures or decision makers (DMs) in agencies, but they are willing to let the worker make this challenge on their behalf. When clients can participate in the advocacy tasks, they are more likely to feel a sense of increased self-esteem. When these efforts are successful, this result helps them feel more effective and more empowered to pursue other issues in their lives.

● OVERCOMING BARRIERS

In the individual assessment chapter (Chapter 10), we described the many imbalances that may occur in an individual's life. These imbalances emerge in three kinds of transactions that the individual depends on with the environment: needs<-> resources, aspirations<->opportunities, and capacities<->demands. In each of these imbalances, all four of the boundary roles we have presented in this chapter could be employed to improve imbalances in each of these transactions. For example, brokerage may help a client locate and connect with unused resources and opportunities—a new single parent may be connected to a nutrition program that provides supplemental food for the newborn and also parenting education for the new mother. Mediation may be employed to reduce the unrealistic demands that are being placed on an incapacitated client—bill collectors may agree to a payment schedule that more realistically reflects the economic resources of the client. Resource development may be employed to create an opportunity that is presently unavailable to a client—a local school may be talked into allowing another agency to use the school's gym as a recreation facility for troubled youth in the community.

Case advocacy may be employed to cope with the common "isms" that arise in the aspiration–opportunities transactions. Poor and oppressed clients are often overlooked or denied access to the opportunities that privileged folks gain because of their wealth or status. It is easier for private institutions to actively discriminate against poor and minority clients. American society accepts the notion that private clubs can establish barriers, such as expensive membership fees and membership processes that directly discriminate against various groups. Many private clubs bar women and racial and ethnic minorities from admissions. Unfortunately, this kind of discrimination also goes on in public and commercial institutions. Poor inner-city, minority families have a difficult time getting mortgages; minority applicants for jobs are systematically steered away from some job opportunities by job search agencies; and realtors systematically steer minority families *away* from some neighborhoods. In some public schools, the schools track minority students into vocational or commercial courses instead of college preparation courses, even when an applicant may be intelligent and motivated to pursue a college career. The point we want to make here is that for the privileged members of our society, the opportunity structure is much more open, and for poor minority folks, the opportunity structure is much more closed. Because social workers work with oppressed groups, it is almost a "given" that oppressed individuals will have or be experiencing some kind of barrier that keeps them from realizing their aspirations. We want interpersonal practitioners to realize that these kinds of transactional problems are a significant injustice and that case and class advocacy are legitimate and necessary strategies for dealing with these injustices.

There is nothing wrong with helping a youth work on reading and writing skills, but to overlook the barriers in the opportunity structure and not address these barriers is an incomplete helping strategy. Talent and motivation are not enough to help some of our clients achieve their goals. We believe that the interpersonal practitioner has a responsibility to work as hard to change an unjust environment as he or she does to help the individual client change or adjust to the demands of that unjust environment. If interpersonal practitioners ignore this part of their responsibility and ignore the NASW *Code of Ethics* (National Association of Social Workers Delegate Assembly, 2008) that states it is the responsibility of professional social workers to work to change injustice in organizations, then the interpersonal practitioners are by default a part of the problem and not part of the solution. To ignore injustice and not speak out against it, to join that great silent majority who accepts the inequalities that surround us, is a major form of support for those who systematically practice these injustices. Silence and inaction are interpreted as agreement. In the organizational change chapter (Chapter 17), we will present in greater detail the tactics and techniques of case and class advocacy.

CRISIS INTERVENTION •

In the individual assessment chapter (Chapter 10), we presented a model of a crisis assessment; now we turn to the interventions that the interpersonal practitioner will pursue with a client in active crisis. The Chinese character for "crisis" is a composite of two *other* characters: one meaning "danger" and the other meaning "opportunity" (see Figure 11.9 on page 328).

The Chinese concept of crisis captures the nature of this phenomenon. Crises are a time for potential growth and change, but they are also a time of potential harm and danger. A crisis may further undermine a client's limited coping capacities and make clients feel less confident about themselves and their ability to cope with life changes. The clients may, however, achieve a positive outcome to the crisis situation, which, in turn, may give them the confidence and the necessary skills

Figure 11.9 Chinese Characters for Crisis—Danger and Opportunity

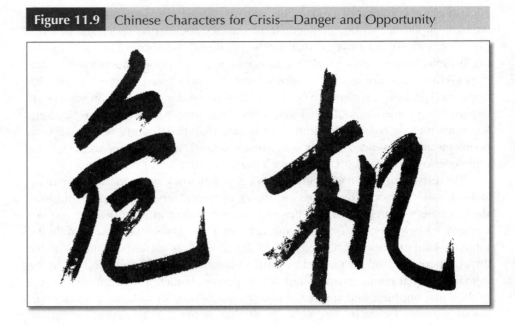

to tackle other life stressors. The worker's objective for intervening in a crisis is to prevent it from resulting in a greater disaster. At a bare minimum, the worker should be trying to reestablish the precrisis equilibrium of the individual client. Ideally, the intervention efforts of the worker will promote growth in the client, and the resolution of the crisis will improve the client's precrisis functioning.

There are five basic steps to crisis intervention: (1) *offering hope*, (2) *promoting catharsis*, (3) *staying event focused*, (4) *reconnecting client to support systems*, (5) *reactivating client's coping mechanisms* (Golan, 1978; Roberts, 1990, 2005). Offering hope is a global strategy that is common to all healing efforts and is not just specific to crisis intervention. The interpersonal practitioner should approach the client in active crisis with optimism and an attitude that reflects the belief and desire that help can make a difference. No matter what the client situation, the worker must try to help the client see that things could be different and that situations can change. The worker does not offer a promise or guarantee that things will get better but the hope that things can change and improve. This is such an important factor in helping that we believe workers should not enter a helping situation in which they believe things are hopeless. For example, the interpersonal practitioners who work in a hospice setting know that their clients are dying, yet they approach each client with the belief that dying can be a growth experience. Even clients who are facing death can do all kinds of transcendent and practical things to prepare for this transition and make it easier for themselves and those they leave behind.

Catharsis is the ventilation or expression of feeling. Some clients in active crisis are already actively expressing feelings, so this step does not have to be promoted by the interpersonal practitioner. Some clients, however, are not actively expressing feelings and may almost be in a numb or affectless state. These clients need to be encouraged to express the underlying feelings to this affectless state. Often, clients cannot do the cognitive tasks that are part of crisis intervention until they have expressed the underlying affect. Clients in active crisis may feel demoralized and overwhelmed and afraid to "let go" of their feelings. Workers will have to encourage clients that it is part of the working-through process that feelings should be expressed.

Workers must, however, be prepared for whatever intensity and kind of feeling the client finally expresses. Whether it is rage, terror, abandonment, or grief, the worker must be ready and able to support and empathize with the client. When catharsis begins, the client must be allowed to express feelings in his or her own way. Sometimes workers are worried about the intensity of affect that gets expressed, and they may prematurely try to get the client to gain control of the affect. This may send a double message to the client that it is OK to express emotion but not too much emotion.

The point of catharsis is not that it is some kind of magical process that heals but that it relieves the pressure so that the worker and client can begin to accomplish the other steps of crisis intervention. Another important aspect of catharsis is that when the client shares these intense feelings and the worker reciprocates with support and empathy, important elements of the helping relationship are facilitated. The client begins to see the worker as a sensitive and nonjudgmental helper who is willing to share in some of the horror the client is experiencing.

To put the crisis situation in perspective, the worker and client must stay event focused. Staying event focused means that the client needs to explore the precipitating factor and other recent hazardous events that have occurred. These events need to be explored, discussed, and realistically reframed. One or maybe two of these events will become the focus of intervention. Often in crisis situations, old wounds or traumas will be reactivated, and the client will recall earlier life events. These earlier life events are not the focus of crisis intervention, even though they may be connected to the present crisis. Interventions must focus on present events—that is, events that have happened within the past few weeks or months. The client must be encouraged to begin the problem solving process by looking at these recent events and understanding how he or she might apply available resources or coping skills to address these issues.

During active crisis, the client may have withdrawn from social supports and significant others who could be instrumental in the client's healing. In this step, the worker needs to begin to suggest how the client can go about reconnecting with these supportive resources. If the client has completed a network map, it will be fairly obvious who the significant supportive people are in the client's life. The client needs to reengage these supports, or the worker needs to remobilize them in the client's life. This can be as simple as a suggestion that the client contact one of these persons or that the first step the client takes will be to talk with one of these significant others. Sometimes this can be facilitated by having the client call one of these supportive people, even before the client leaves the interview situation. In some cases, the supportive person may be called to come and pick up the client as the client leaves the interview. In some cases, it may be necessary for the client to reach out to some kind of support or self-help group, and the worker may engage in the kinds of brokerage strategies that we discussed in the earlier sections of this chapter.

The final step in crisis intervention is a meta-strategy. Though the worker may be doing a number of things to help clients recover from the crisis situation, it is important that the clients begin to do some of these helping tasks for themselves. During active crisis, a typical pattern is that the client will begin to stop coping with any of life's demands. In this final step of crisis intervention, the worker must engage in reactivating client's coping mechanisms in the client. The client must be encouraged to begin to do what he or she had been doing before the active crisis state occurred. In the beginning, these coping tasks might be fairly small. The point is that we want clients to succeed with these small steps so they can realize that they are ultimately responsible for their life and that they must now get on with living it.

Sometimes these coping tasks are planned as "homework" or "next steps" that the client will address in recovery. It is important that the worker and client plan tasks that the client is responsible for carrying out and that are likely to be accomplished. These tasks can be started even from the interview. The client can make a phone call to someone from the interview, or the client and worker may discuss and practice the first step that the client must take on leaving the interview. In many of the time-limited models of practice, this is an important strategy that combines homework with client responsibility (Bloom, 1992; Talmon, 1990). In the chapter on contracting (Chapter 8), we presented the Task Implementation Sequence (TIS) that was developed within the task-centered model of practice. TIS is an excellent procedure that can be employed with clients at this step of the crisis intervention process, and we refer the students to that chapter, which describes the five steps of the TIS procedure.

● ROLE SOLUTIONS

In the chapter on individual assessment (Chapter 10), we presented many role problems that individuals face as they move through life. In this chapter, we have presented a number of interventions (e.g., mediation, social skills training, stress reduction techniques, tapping, and linking to resources) that can help individuals cope with the stressors of role problems. "Coping" is a strategy that we all use to deal with the stress and strain of role problems. There are, however, other specific techniques that individuals employ to deal with role problems. In some situations, individuals can leave the problematic role—that is, an elimination strategy (Thomas, 1967)—which is the source of major stressors. For example, students may drop out of school when the demands of higher education and the associated costs become unbearable. An abused wife may decide to take her children and leave her abusive husband. An employee may decide to leave her job so she does not have to put up with sexual harassment from her supervisor. This strategy of leaving the role may seem like a simple solution; however, the interpersonal practitioner must recognize that this is a major life decision and can only be made by the individual client.

Interpersonal practitioners work with individual clients who are in difficult role situations. The practitioner must avoid the tendency to give the client advice to leave the role but instead must work with the individual client to make such a difficult life decision. The interpersonal practitioner can use the problem solving steps discussed earlier in this chapter to help the client reach a difficult decision. No matter what the ideology of the worker, a pregnant teen must be helped to decide what all the options are when faced with this difficult role. The issue is not simply to have an abortion or bring the fetus to full term. As social workers, we should help clients look at the many situational issues, such as religion, family, emotional implications, and available resources, that are involved in such an important life decision.

Another role solution is "muddling through," which is a temporary strategy that is related to "coping." When individuals find themselves overextended and overloaded with all the role demands that have emerged in their life situation— and they do not want to eliminate roles—they may find ways to compromise and respond to some of the various role demands of the situation. For example, many social work students return to graduate education after establishing many other life roles, such as parent, significant other, wage earner, etc. The demands and transitions to graduate student along with these other major roles are overwhelming. Students recognize that the graduate role is a temporary role so they do not eliminate other roles in order to focus on the overwhelming role demands of graduate school. Instead they will respond to some of the demands of each role by letting some of their responsibilities as spouse, parent, breadwinner slide and simultaneously giving up the idea that they will be able to do all of the assigned readings and write perfect papers and perform well on tests. These kinds of compromises do take their toll on both the individual and other individuals in the role network. Children, spouses, and bosses may notice that the graduate student is not around as much and not as conscientious since entering school. The graduate student may simultaneously feel that they are not conscientious in their studies when they only focus on readings and assignments that meet the minimal requirements.

Another role strategy is role "clarification." We have already discussed this strategy in the chapter on engagement, which helps applicants understand what the role expectations are for them when they come to an agency for help. We will also talk more about this strategy in the family change chapter (Chapter 13) as a way of dealing with role problems that emerge in family conflict.

● SUMMARY

This chapter opened with a discussion of the pivotal place of the treatment plan in work with individual clients. The treatment plan is a routine part of modern practice and represents the organizing structure for the objectives, activities, and interventions that follow from the assessment process. Because of our social problem focus in this book, in this chapter we chose to focus on the various roles that interpersonal practitioners can carry out particularly with oppressed clients. The roles of enabler, trainer, broker, mediator, resource developer, and advocate were presented in the context of changing the client's transactions with his or her social environment. The chapter emphasized the importance of understanding the client's social environment before intervening in the client's life. The chapter concluded with a discussion of crisis intervention tactics and various role strategies designed to resolve many of the role problems raised in the individual assessment chapter (Chapter 10).

CHAPTER 12

ASSESSING FAMILIES

If you don't believe in ghosts, you've never been to a family reunion.

—Ashleigh Brilliant, syndicated cartoonist

P eople live in constant interaction with others in small groups of family and peers and in larger systems, such as places of employment and residence. Behavior is always a consequence of forces present in these groups and organizations.

An understanding of individual behavior involves an assessment of both the individual and these other systems. The only question, therefore, is how extensive this broader assessment will be. When working with the individual, the worker may spend only a moderate effort on a comprehensive assessment of family, peer group, and organizational dynamics. On the other hand, when workers directly interact with these systems, they will assess them in greater detail.

Some workers argue that because of the strong impact of systems—particularly the family—relevant systems should always be assessed in detail, and the worker should invariably seek to work directly with them. We are not doctrinaire on this topic and will remain neutral until more evidence is forthcoming to support such a position. There is insufficient evidence to support the superiority of working with family or peer groups for *all* clients, although this has been established for some limited categories (Alexander, Holtzworth-Munroe, & Jameson, 1994) Our position, nevertheless, is that family, group, and organizational factors should be identified in broad terms for all clients and pursued in detail for some. The greatest amount of detail should be sought when the impact of these systems is a strong force in producing the problem or is a major resource or both for change.

For many beginning workers, as well as for those whose training was oriented only to individual assessment, the idea of an assessment of a system is an unfamiliar concept. The question is often raised whether system characteristics are as real or as measurable as individual ones. Our answer is that system variables represent the interaction among people, and that these interactions can be as stable and measurable as the personality characteristics of an individual. What is even more important is that system characteristics can account for as much—if not more—of the behavior of individuals as their personalities. Changes in systems, therefore, can be sought as a means of resolving individual problems, and it may be easier to influence system variables than personality dynamics.

In assessing systems such as families, groups, and organizations, the worker should remember that these are also embedded in the larger society and that the influence of the society should be identified. Thus the worker who "blames" the family for some family problem, to the exclusion of recognizing relevant societal factors, makes the same type of mistake as the worker who "blames the individual" without seeing family or group situational causes. The worker, therefore, should be able to see how such conditions as the energy crisis; the global, economic meltdown; rising unemployment and poverty; the deterioration of confidence in government; and the depersonalization of the individual in urban communities affect individual, family, and small-group dynamics. Some clients may experience relief when they decide to direct their energies toward societal conditions and not simply toward an inward quest.

● WHAT IS A FAMILY?

When you think of a "family" what image pops into your mind? Do you think of a heterosexual couple with two or more biological offspring called sons and daughters? Social workers do work with families who fit this view of the traditional nuclear family, but social workers also work with many other family forms. Social workers serve gay couples who may have adopted children, three generation families (i.e., children, parent(s), and grandparents), single-parent families, blended (step) families with children from prior marriages, communal families with many children and many adults, and adult couples whose children may have been launched.

In some ethnic families, there may be godfathers (compadres) and godmothers (comadres) who do not live in the household unit but are a central part of the family. In other ethnic families, there may be "woodpile cousins" who appear to be members of the sibling-ship (brother or sister) but have no biological connection to their siblings. In other families, there may be "aunties" who live in the household unit but are actually older siblings who have borne children during adolescence. In some ethnic families, it is true that the "whole community is raising the children." The point of this discussion is that as social workers we should realize that there are many family forms that exist in practice and to be prepared to engage these many family forms in order to help them cope with the stressors, issues, and problems that they face.

MEASUREMENT OF SYSTEM VARIABLES ●

Later we discuss in detail specific instruments that can be used to assess families. There are a number of ways of collecting data about family dynamics. One way is the use of observation instruments by family members and other observers who know the family. These instruments may consist of checklists and records of who communicates and associates with whom under what conditions. Another approach is to ask family members to fill out questionnaires about their interactions with each other, whom in the system they perceive as fulfilling certain roles, and whom they consider to be "members" of the family system. This final question is important in helping the interpersonal practitioner understand the boundary of the family system and what family form she will be engaging.

Still another kind of data is provided by diagrams that represent family variables. These are often created by workers, along with family members, to represent relationships within the family system and with the interactions of the family with systems in its environment. The purpose of this kind of graphic information is to enable workers and family members to consider complex information more easily because it is in a visual form. Examples of these kinds of data are ecomaps and genograms, which will be described later in this chapter.

Last—and often most important—is the worker's observation of what happens in the family system as he or she interacts with it. Active listening is a basic skill that interpersonal practitioners must learn when assessing individuals. When assessing families and groups, the interpersonal practitioner must develop skill in active observation of the behavior of family members in interviews. The nonverbal process of family members' interactions may carry more information than what they say about each other (Mehrabian, 1972). The interpersonal practitioner has to pay careful attention to the movement of family members, their postures, who speaks to whom, facial expressions, vocal expression, and finally what is said. To focus exclusively on what is said in a family interview may be to miss most of the meaning of the interview.

FAMILY ASSESSMENT ●

A family assessment may be undertaken for several reasons. The interpersonal practitioner will *always* assess the family conditions of clients even when other family members are not brought into the action system and even when the client is living alone. This family assessment is done because much of the variance in our behavior is determined by our interactions with our families—no matter how physically distant we may be from them. In addition, historical events in our family life continue to affect our emotions, attitudes, and behaviors through our recollections of them.

When the worker chooses to work with several or all family members, the worker's responsibility for a comprehensive family assessment is even greater, and the worker may have to collect a vast amount of data about the family system. Families usually enter treatment with the idea that the problem is primarily that of one member of the family, the "identified patient." For example, parents may bring a troubled adolescent into service for various kinds of acting out in school. When the worker explores various circumstances with the parents and adolescent, the family may come to realize that there are family circumstances that are contributing to the acting out behavior of the youth. The attention of the family and their worker may then shift to these family circumstances.

In helping the student assess such family circumstances, we describe the process of gathering information about families. We subsequently discuss how this information is organized around a set of categories of family circumstances.

● THE PROCESS OF FAMILY ASSESSMENT

Assessment is seen throughout this book as a process intimately linked to intervention. This linkage varies, depending on the type of system the worker seeks to change. In this section, we discuss some of the relationships between family assessment and family change. One of the important assessment ideas to emerge from the field of family practice is the view of each aspect of a family assessment as a *hypothesis* (Campbell, Draper, & Crutchley, 1991).

The way workers utilize hypotheses is to formulate ideas based on their interactions with the family. These "hunches" are temporary hypotheses that are constructed about the specific family conditions that may be present and that contribute to the problem. The worker proceeds to engage the family members in ways that test these hypotheses. This represents a continuing process of hypothesizing and revising hypotheses, which has been termed *circularity* (Roberto, 1991). This engagement often confirms not only one or more of the hypotheses but also the relationship between the family conditions and the problem(s) for which the family has sought help. The worker is in a position as a result of this activity to plan ways with the family to alter such conditions.

Hypothesizing in a Family Session

An example of this occurred in a family that sought help for severe conflicts between an 11-year-old son and his father. In the initial session with the family, the worker observed that the mother and son pulled their chairs close together and farther from the father. The mother and son also crossed their legs pointing away from the father, and likewise, the father crossed his legs away from the mother and son. When either the mother or father made a statement, they appeared to look to the son for confirmation of the statement rather than to each other. The worker hypothesized that a contributing factor to the presenting problem was a strong coalition between the son and his mother that excluded the father from their interactions. This was also hypothesized to be related to a lack of closeness between the father and mother.

The worker proceeded to test these hypotheses in the next session by asking the family to describe a typical day in the family's life. The mother answered for the family by describing how the father left for work before anyone else arose. She spent the early part of the day shopping for clothes for her son. When he arrived home from school, she helped him with his homework. In the evening, while the father read the papers, the mother and son watched a television program together. Several times during the evening the father criticized his son for watching television excessively and his wife for encouraging it. The father went to bed before either his son or wife as he said he had to get up very early the next morning.

In this example, the worker created a hypothesis about what we shall later characterize as *family structure*. The worker also selected an assessment device, a request for a family member to describe a typical day, as a means of gathering additional data to test the hypothesis. We describe in the next section of this chapter a number of ways workers can collect data about families.

The use of hypotheses has a particular relevance for family work because of the initial difficulty some readers are likely to have in "thinking family." So many of us have been accustomed to think in terms of *individual behavior* that we find it difficult to recognize such a thing as *family behavior*, which is made up of the pattern of interactions among family members. Formulating and testing hypotheses about family behavior reinforces our awareness of family behavior as a reality.

Another issue that confronts the family worker is how to choose hypotheses that will be most useful in helping the family in question from among various possible ones. This type of choice is based both on the experience of the workers as well as their knowledge of the literature that reports both family research and the experiences of experienced family therapists. As yet, these causal ideas have not been organized in any systematic way. The worker, nevertheless, should keep in mind the idea of prioritizing hypotheses as described by Campbell et al. (1991):

> Part of the process of constructing a hypothesis also involves making continual ongoing assessments about which of the family beliefs and relationships offer the greatest possibility for introducing new information. That is, some beliefs organize more of the behavior connected to the problem and others are more peripheral, and these beliefs can be placed in a hierarchy or "prioritized" for the benefit of the therapist. For example, a family may initially present the therapist with a range of beliefs from various sources, such as ethnic background, cultural or religious influences, gender issues, life-cycle stages, and family constellation, but the prioritizing of these beliefs in terms of their influence on the problem behavior can only be accurately done by observing (and assessing) the feedback the family gives to the therapist's questions. (p. 342)

Some experts in family therapy have suggested a sequence for gathering assessment information from families. Roberto (1991), for example, proposed a progression from "macroscopic" to "microscopic" as follows:

> Assessment is meant to capture successively smaller "shells" of context, moving the unit of diagnosis from macroscopic (the extended family system) to microscopic (the identified patient). In between, we move to the level of the nuclear family system and its overall emotional climate. Is it a family of individualistic achievers? Or does it live in an empty home where the members practice phobic avoidance? Has the group become passive and helpless in the face of prolonged distress? The next lower level of fixed triangles and tetrads is explored. Accordingly, levels of assessment move from large familial beliefs and relational legacies; through complex problems of cultural or religious conflicts; to the level of circular reactions; and finally to the unitary level of psychological, somatic, and fantasy symptoms in the individual. (p. 452)

● OBTAINING FAMILY ASSESSMENT DATA

There are many ways that workers can gather information on family conditions and the functioning of individual family members as well as the interactions between the family and its environment. Each one yields unique information about the family and its members and confirms or disconfirms information secured in other ways.

Initial Contact

A great deal can be learned by considering who makes the initial contact with the worker (or the worker's agency). This ensues from what that person says about why she or he has reached out to the agency at this time, who knows about or has promoted the contact, and what the problem is. The worker who has been contacted will note whether this person has been referred to the social worker or has initiated the contact without such a referral. The person making this contact may be the person seen by the family (or others) as "the one with the problem," in which case in family therapy jargon, this person is referred to as the "identified patient."

It is also possible that another professional has suggested that the caller seek family rather than individual help. Whatever the circumstance, knowing about these matters may give the worker valuable clues to how the "problem" is seen by the family as well as the role in the family of such an identified patient.

On the other hand, the caller may be the spouse or the parent or some other relative of the identified patient. The family role of this person may disclose who holds power in the family or who is selected to communicate to outsiders on behalf of the family or who is most affected by the behavior of the identified patient. This information helps the worker begin to map out the structure of the family and the roles of its members.

We discuss in the chapter on family change (Chapter 13) how the worker deals with this person around the issue of bringing the other family members to the session.

Tracking

Another means of gathering data is what Minuchin and Fishman (1981) referred to as "tracking." The techniques of tracking are utilized to help people tell their story. The worker, however, is not primarily interested in the stories, as such, but in what they reveal about the roles of family members and the relationships among these individuals. The worker elicits this information by asking crucial questions:

1. What effect did the behavior under discussion have on other family members?
2. What preceded and followed the behavior?

Tracking in a Family Session

An example of this occurred in a family in which the behavior being discussed was the husband's complaints about his wife's silences. The practitioner tracked this by asking what had happened before a particular instance of such a silence. The wife responded, "My husband had been berating me for not preparing the food he likes for dinner. He threatened to leave and go out to dinner by himself."

The worker asked her how she felt at that time, and she responded, "I felt powerless because he is seldom clear about what he wants for dinner. I'm sick and tired of trying to guess!"

The husband immediately jumped in to say, "My mother always knew what I liked!"

The worker then asked the teenaged son, who was present, what he thought was going on. The son stated, "My father is abusing my mother, and that's why I spend so little time at home!"

This example allowed the practitioner to develop a hypothesis that the family pattern included abusive behavior by the husband and that other family behaviors were related to this abuse. The practitioner continued to use the tracking approach to learn more about the relationships among these behaviors.

Enactments

One of the virtues of family treatment is that the worker often has an opportunity to assess how the family members interact through direct observation rather than through what one or another family member says about their interactions. Members will often have reasons for distorting what actually happens in the family and may not even be aware they are doing so. One of the things a worker must be able to do at times, therefore, is elicit behavior during the family session that is typical of behavior outside the session. "Enactment" is the technique "by which the social worker asks the family to dance in his presence" (Minuchin & Fishman, 1981, p. 78). This kind of situation also has therapeutic possibilities, as the social worker "is not only an observer, but also a musician and dancer himself" (p. 79). This often requires very little activity on the part of the worker, as family members can quickly have an argument, move into antagonistic coalitions, or even provide a great deal of support to each other if these are customary behaviors.

At other times, the worker must do something to elicit an enactment. One of the ways the worker does this is by asking a family member to direct a comment directly to another family member rather than talking to the worker about another family member. Another way is to pose an issue to the family that the worker suspects has been discussed before in the family. At still other times, the worker can ask the family to deal with an issue in a session as they would deal with it at home.

Example of Enactment in a Family Session

An example of enactment occurred in work with the Stevens family. The worker suspected that Mr. Stevens was undermining Mrs. Stevens's efforts to develop a career outside the home, although Mr. Stevens denied this was the case. The worker asked if they would be willing to discuss this topic with each other while the worker "listened in," and they agreed. The worker then prompted them by asking them to begin the conversation where they had left off. Mrs. Stevens said to her husband that she had been looking at courses at the local college that might help her pursue a career in business. Mr. Stevens immediately began to attack the reputation of that college. When his wife mentioned another institution, he criticized that one also as being too expensive. When Mrs. Stevens explained how she hoped to finance her education, Mr. Stevens started raising questions about their financial security at the moment. In this discussion, his tone of voice was loud and strident. Mrs. Stevens, in turn, spoke softly and plaintively.

The case example supported the worker's hypothesis that Mr. Stevens was opposed to Mrs. Stevens's desire to develop a business career for herself, although he denied this; he was, therefore, communicating a mixed message to her. Mrs. Stevens, in turn, did not confront Mr. Stevens. The family circumstances and history that supported this type of interaction were not evident from this episode, so the social worker would need to select other assessment techniques to learn more about this enactment.

Another way for the worker to elicit an enactment is to note how family members interact when an emotionally laden topic is under discussion. Frequently, under these circumstances, the members revert to a typical interactional pattern.

Enactment in Response to a Stressful Topic

An example of this phenomenon occurred in a family when a father and his daughter, Sarah, were discussing when she had to return at night to their home. He accused her of becoming sexually active. She answered that he suspected her of every form of wrongdoing. He said that he was sure she was just like her mother—his former wife, who had left him for another man. At this point, the stepmother stepped in to defend Sarah.

The worker in this case had good evidence on how members of this family interact.

Yet another way of securing an enactment is to ask the family to role-play an incident that recently occurred. A related technique is to pose a situation that is likely to occur in most families and ask the family members to deal with the situation. Examples are to plan a short trip or to make a decision about a specified purchase.

In working with families, the worker is not limited by how the family members describe their interactions but can actually observe these interactions as a way of gathering information about them. This also requires the utilization of appropriate techniques inasmuch as some or all family members may desire to mask their typical interactions in order to appear in a good light in the eyes of the worker.

Tasks

An approach that has some similarity to enactment is "task assignment." In utilizing this approach, the worker asks the family to engage in a task outside the treatment session. Such tasks can be used by the worker for assessment, or change purposes, or both. An example of a task used for an assessment purpose is of a worker who asked a father to take his children to a local park for an afternoon while the mother studied for her college examination. In the next session, the mother reported that she worried constantly that the children would be hurt in an accident while with their father. The father, however, reported that he worried the whole time that his wife was "goofing off" rather than studying. This report gave the worker a great deal of new information on this family. Previous reports from the family had been to the effect that the mother felt unappreciated for all the things she had to do, and the father claimed that he always stood ready to be helpful to her.

Tasks may also be developed with families as part of the change process. This topic is to be dealt with in more detail in the chapters on individual, family, and group change (Chapters 10, 12, and 14).

Collecting Data Directly From the Family

The social worker may directly ask the family for relevant information that can help the family and the worker understand what is going on in the family system. Such information will include the following:

1. *History.* Historical information provides a context in which to place the current family situation and may be essential to make sense out of it. The following historical material is secured in all but the most limited type of service:

    A. How did the partners meet? What was their courtship like? How was the decision made to enter into a committed union?

    B. What were the early days of this relationship like? Did serious problems arise, and how they were handled? If these days were relatively conflict free, what accounted for this?

    C. What were the interactions between the couple and their extended families? Were there cultural/class/religious or other similarities or differences, and how did these affect the pair?

    D. If the couple decided to have a child (i.e., by birth, adoption, or foster care), how was this decision made? How was the couple affected by this before and after the arrival of the child?

    E. What kinds of issues arose for the family during the course of child rearing?

    Historical information is often obtained through the use of a genogram, which is explained later in this chapter.

2. *Relationship to Other Systems in the Environment.* As we emphasize in every chapter of this book, we view all individuals and larger systems as inextricably interwoven. The family, consequently, cannot be understood

without examining its interactions with other systems. These include economic, social, extrafamilial, political, educational, ethnic, gender, and spiritual spheres. The nature of the family and how and why it sought service will determine in how much detail the worker seeks to explore these realms.

Nevertheless, brief information is usually sought on all these dimensions. This casts light on how much support the family secures from the environment, how much tension is produced by the environment, how much the environment demands from the family, and even whether the family is relatively isolated from other systems. The worker will usually ask the family members to talk about their connection with these systems and whether this connection is experienced as helpful or harmful. This information is often portrayed in a network map described in the individual assessment chapter (Chapter 10) or in an ecomap that is explained later in this chapter.

Family Sculpture

It is sometimes difficult for the family members to describe the complex interactions that occur among them, especially since many occur simultaneously. An assessment device that helps the worker and the family members view these interactions in a way that can be very dramatic is by creating a living sculpture of the family. This involves arranging the family members in positions in the room and in body postures that represent ways they communicate with each other (Duhl, Kantor, & Duhl, 1973; Papp, Silverstein, & Carter, 1973; Satir, 1988). The worker starts the process by explaining the procedure. The worker may then choose a family member to do the staging or may even ask for a volunteer.

A major rule is that the sculpture is created without talking. This is because the idea is to reveal aspects of family functioning that are often concealed when talked about. It helps the sculptor to start with a statement as to the setting (e.g., the family as it looks after a meal or during meal preparation). After the family is arranged in the sculpture, the worker will often ask the members how they feel and what they observe. The family members may then sit in their normal seats while a discussion of the sculpting experience takes place. Some of the issues that have been illuminated in sculpting have been power structures, the closeness or distance of a family member to others, and coalitions that exist in the family.

Before students try sculpting with whole families in practice, they should do this procedure in class with other classmates, so they get a chance to practice and get a feel for the sculpting experience. Sculpting can generate a lot of feelings even in practice sessions with classmates, and students should be aware that strong feelings are often elicited with families in practice.

Importance of Practicing Sculpting in Class

For example, a student in an advanced methods course decided to practice sculpting on a very sensitive experience in his own childhood when his parents separated. After choosing classmates to play his father, mother, and two younger sisters, he created a sculpture in which his father was at the classroom door looking back on his family. His mother and sisters, who were sitting on the floor around his mother, were placed near the back of the room, and he was kneeling down between his father and family with one arm stretched toward his father and the other arm stretched toward his mother and younger sisters. Needless to say, this was an emotion-laden sculpture to debrief in class. Many of the classmates who played members of the family were in tears, and other members of the class were also in tears, who in their childhood had also experienced divorce. We will discuss in the group intervention chapter (Chapter 15), exercises borrowed from psychodrama which this example exemplifies.

The Kvebæk Sculpture Technique (KST) is similar to family sculpting, which was just described, but employs wooden figures to metaphorically represent family members. The primary advantage of this assessment tool is that it does not require the whole family to be present in the interview, and it can be employed with individuals as a way of understanding family system dynamics (Thorsheim, 2005).

The KST is a symbolic form of family sculpting to show subjective relationships. This is a quick means to obtain a picture of the internal family system as experienced by each family member. The KST set—"toolkit"—is made up of semiabstract hardwood figures in two shapes and three sizes that the person sculpting selects from to show self and family. Often, the person sculpting will add additional figures to indicate their pet, a close friend, or other significant persons. The KST is an effective tool for conducting a family systems assessment. See Figure 12.1.

• CATEGORIZING FAMILY CIRCUMSTANCES

After we have collected information in one or another of the ways we just described, we have found it helpful to organize this information by using a set of categories. These categories can be utilized to plan ways in which family circumstances can be altered with the family to resolve family problems. The categories are

1. *Phase of the Family Life Cycle.* Various authors have described this differently. Typically, the family life cycle is described in terms of transitions, such as

Figure 12.1	KST Toolkit

Source: Thorsheim, J. L. (2005). *Guide to using the Kvebæk Sculpture Technique (KST)*. Copyright © 2005, KST ASSOCIATES. Retrieved from www.healthyhumansystems.com. Permission granted by Julie Thorsheim, KST Associates.

joining, coupling, procreation, child rearing, launching, and moving on (Carter & McGoldrick, 1988). This conceptualization is useful because it points out potentially significant changes that a family must navigate. It also has weaknesses, though, especially when the family is not a "traditional" nuclear family and instead reflects one of the many alternative family forms. For example, with the prevalence of divorce and remarriage in the United States, how do we fit blended families into these stage models? Where do couples who join and choose not to have children fit in these models? Though these models do offer some clues to how family dynamics may change over time, the interpersonal practitioner has to recognize their limitations.

2. *Family Culture and Tradition.* The family possesses sets of beliefs, rituals, and ceremonies drawn from its religion, ethnicity, and community. The adults in the family may have obtained their sets of beliefs from their families of origin, and there can be conflicts and tensions when the families of origin have different beliefs and

practices. For example, the wedding or union ceremony of a young couple can be fraught with angst and conflict when the young couple being joined is surrounded by their "clans," which have very different ideas about what is an "appropriate" wedding (joining) ceremony.

3. *Family Emotional Climate.* When people are in close interaction, the emotions of some individuals tend to be "contagious," and other members may begin to express similar feelings. Thus when some family members are depressed, the entire family often appears depressed. It is also possible for different subgroups of the family to express different emotions. In either case, it is important to note the pattern of emotions in the family. A depressed and listless family, for example, may not put energy into changing anything, and the worker may have to introduce an intervention directed at the shared feelings of family members. Other families may have such a fearful, closed, and cautious emotional climate that it will be almost impossible for family members to share any information with the interpersonal practitioner (Paniagua, 1998). Because there are ethnic groups who do not believe in sharing family information about family troubles with outsiders, these ethnic families may make very poor candidates for family treatment (Lum, 2005; Spiegel, 1974).

4. *Family Communication Patterns.* This refers to who in the family communicates with whom and about what. This can be a problem, for example, if there are secrets in the family that prevent the family from discussing issues and underlying conflicts (i.e., the proverbial elephants in the room). When some individuals are excluded from family discussions or if clear messages fail to be transmitted, family problem solving suffers. For example, in some families there may be an adult member who is an alcoholic, but this is never discussed or acknowledged by the family. This family secret may have significant implications for the problems in the family, but it is never shared with the worker nor addressed by family members.

5. *Family Boundaries.* "Boundary" is a concept that refers to a metaphoric "wall" that surrounds a system or subsystem. Such a wall may be easily crossed or may, instead, be a major barrier. Boundaries exist between the subsystems of a family as well as between the family and its environment. If family boundaries are too easily crossed, the family may be chaotic as individuals enter and leave the family in unexpected ways. If it is almost impossible to cross them, the family may persist in destructive, undetected internal behaviors, such as child abuse.

From a boundary perspective, child sexual abuse may be seen as a boundary violation between the parental subsystem and the child subsystem. There are many activities and interactions that are appropriate for the parental subsystem with the child subsystem, but sex is not considered appropriate by the dominant values in the United States. There are subcultural groups in the United States (i.e., polygamist cults) that do promote sexual relations with the dominant male and female children of the cult.

6. *Family Structure.* Families consist of subgroups inasmuch as any family member will interact with some family members more than others. For example, there may be a parental subgroup, a sibling subgroup, and various parent–child coalitions that form. Often these subgroups become the client system and target system of family interventions—for example, a mother and daughter relationship may be the focus of intervention, or the marital relationship of the parents may be the focus of intervention. Some of these subgroups have more power than others, thus creating a hierarchy.

Pseudo-Democracy in Family Meetings

For example, in our own family of procreation there were three daughters, and the five of us would meet as a family to decide where we might go on a family vacation. In these family meetings, we operated on pseudo-democratic principles—final decisions were voted upon. This worked well for parental authority until one meeting in which the three daughters were old enough to figure out that their three votes could overrule the two parental votes. This was the last time we engaged in these pseudo-democratic meetings.

The interactions among subgroups might be competitive (e.g., as in the example of the family meeting), hostile (e.g., as in families who argue and fight whenever they try to sit down to a meal together), cooperative (e.g., an ideal that happens much less often than most families realize), or there may be few interactions of any sort (e.g., as in families that spend no time together in meals, recreation, or interaction and the household unit is just a place for individual members to sleep and go about their lives outside the family). Some of these structural arrangements may be problematic to family functioning,

7. *Family Resources.* The family must secure such resources as money, housing, and food to survive. How these resources are obtained and how adequate they are will affect every other family condition. Low income families may have eight or nine individuals living in an inadequate three-room apartment with no

air-conditioning in the hot summers, which may push many of the children to "live on the streets" with gangs, drugs, and violence. On the other hand, some of the Richistan families (Frank, 2007) may have many houses with many rooms so that the family rarely interacts with each other and each of the children are highly programmed to participate in many enrichment activities, such as sports, clubs, music lessons, tutoring, horseback riding, etc. In some families, the resources are tightly controlled by a single family member who exerts excessive force on the other family members in how these resources are doled out. For example, in one heterosexual, nuclear family, the father was the only breadwinner and controlled all of the other family members by not allowing them to work outside of the family nor to have contact with other families. Instead he kept control by paying each family member an allowance for the labor they were to perform inside the family, he controlled what they could spend their allowance on, and he even controlled how much food they could eat at mealtime. From the outside, this family looked very "successful," but you can imagine what happened to this family when the children reached adolescence.

8. *Interaction With Other Systems.* The family interacts with many other systems such as the extended family, schools, workplace, community, and church. These interactions may support and nurture the family when they face difficult transitions and tragic events that unfold in their lives. On the other hand, if these interactions are antagonistic, they may drain the family of energy and create conflicts within the family. For example, families may develop "cutoffs" with members in different branches of the family tree. These cutoffs may develop around many kinds of unresolved issues, and family members will not communicate or interact with each other in the family tree. In spite of this noninteraction, the maintenance of the cutoff drains energy from the families in the family tree. Cutoffs are specific kinds of trouble for families, which can be discovered in the genogram. Another possibility is that the family system boundary may be so "impermeable" and not allow interactions with other systems that will benefit the family and, thus, deprive members of needed resources and opportunities for growth.

Table 12.1 presents this set of categories and examples of behaviors that fit into each category with some of the problems families have related to the category. It is also important to note that the worker should bring to this analysis an understanding of the culture of the family, particularly related to its ethnicity, and how this culture affects these categories of family conditions. Another important issue is how the family interactions are affected by the family's beliefs and practices related to the gender of its members. These aspects of family life are also portrayed in Table 12.1.

In order to demonstrate how the various dynamics and circumstances in families can be operationalized, the case of the Angelo family is presented.

Table 12.1 Sample Behaviors and Problems for Categories of Family Behavior

Category	Sample behaviors	Cultural issues	Gender issues	Problems
Phase of family life cycle	Birth of first child; child rearing behaviors	How does culture view life cycle phases?	What roles are prescribed for men/women at each phase?	Parents argue over how to discipline children
Family culture and traditions	Family observes Christmas; daughters are expected to develop homemaking skills	What beliefs and traditions of the family's culture are adhered to by family?	What are the family's beliefs about roles and behaviors of men and women?	Jewish spouse argues that Jewish holiday should be observed; daughters rebel at being confined to homemaking role
Family emotional climate	Lack of emotional expression is typical of family; family appears to be enthusiastic during family get-togethers	What does the family's culture prescribe re: emotional expression?	What does the family's culture prescribe re: emotions encouraged or prescribed for men and women?	Depressed family member is seldom engaged in activity with others in family
Family communication patterns	All members included in discussion of major family problems	How does family's culture structure communications?	How does family view communications between men and women?	Father resents being excluded from discussion between mother and children
Family boundaries	Family members notify each other when non-family friends are expected to visit; confidences among family members are not violated	How are family boundaries viewed by the family's culture?	How are boundaries established in relationship to gender?	Adults who are not known to the children frequently "stay overnight" and endanger the children's feelings of safety
Family structure	Parents form a subgroup and children form another subgroup	What family structures are prescribed by the family's culture?	What structures are created in the family related to gender of members?	Father and daughter form a subgroup that excludes mother

(Continued)

| Table 12.1 | (Continued) | | | |

Category	Sample behaviors	Cultural issues	Gender issues	Problems
Family resources	Family has adequate income for necessities as well as such "luxuries" such as two automobiles	Are the family's resources expanded or limited by the family's cultural identity?	How do the different levels of access of resources to men and women affect the family?	Family lacks sufficient income to provide for such minimum requirements as an adequate diet
Interaction with other systems	All family members have friends among peers in the community; parents involve themselves in parent activities in their children's school	How does the culture of the family affect its interaction with other systems?	Are different types of interaction with other systems prescribed for men and women family members?	Family members are isolated from others in the community; parents interact with school personnel in a hostile and suspicious manner

The Angelo Family

The Angelos have been referred to a family agency because their son, Robert, is not doing well in school and seems hostile and rebellious to his teachers. The family is composed of Juan Angelo, age 39; his wife, Alice Angelo, age 39; and three children—Robert Angelo, age 16; Mary Angelo, age 13; and Richard Angelo, age 9.

Phase of the Family Life Cycle

The family was at the stage in which some children are in adolescence but none are preparing to leave the house in the near future. Nevertheless, the family must help Robert plan for his educational and vocational future and will have to do this for Mary in a few years. Juan and Alice would like their children to be able to continue their education after high school and are trying to save money for this purpose. They are worried because Robert may have been experimenting with drugs, and he is not doing well in school. He also has a girlfriend, and the parents are worried that he may be sexually active. Robert, in turn, is resentful that his parents worry so much about him. He is worried because he is being pressured by other youths to join a neighborhood peer group in which several boys have been in trouble with the law, yet he craves some of the excitement that these boys are experiencing.

This information indicates that the family is in the stage of the family life cycle in which adolescent children are seeking independence from their parents and in which the parents must relinquish some of the control they have exercised in the past. The environment, however, is introducing pressures that make this transition difficult (pressures around sexuality and drug use). The family must also help adolescent members become economically self-sufficient but this family also experiences financial difficulties.

Family Culture and Tradition

This family comes from a Latino background. Juan's and Alice's parents were born in Mexico. The parents have been raised in the Catholic faith, although Alice is more involved in church activities than Juan. The worker was careful not to stereotype the family based on this information, as people from similar backgrounds do not have identical ways of thinking and acting. The worker, however, used her knowledge of these sources of culture and tradition to ask questions about them. The worker learned that the parents are both proud of their ethnic and religious heritage. They are concerned that Robert appears embarrassed about his Latino heritage and also ridicules the church. His parents recognize that some of this is because of adolescent rebelliousness, and they avoid confronting him about this although it makes them very uncomfortable, and they fear he will influence his younger siblings.

The family clearly has a source of strength in its cultural and religious heritage, although Robert is struggling with his views of this heritage. The worker made note of the value of exploring this with Robert further; she also intends to explore whether the difference in church participation between the parents is a problem to them and to other family members.

Family Emotional Climate

The Angelo family appears to be an animated one in which the members show enthusiasm or other strong feelings when they are talking to each other. The worker saw this as a strength as interventions from the worker or actions on the part of one family member are likely to be responded to quickly and spontaneously by others in the family.

Family Communication Patterns

There appeared to be many communications among all family members, although the parents did not talk with each other often in efforts to develop united approaches to dealing with their children's issues as well as with other family concerns. The worker thought it was vital that these parents be able to do this when deciding how to respond to Robert's behavior.

Family Boundaries

The family members had many friends in the community, and the parents had close and supportive relationships with members of their respective families of origin. All the children expressed fondness for their grandparents, and these feelings were reciprocated. The worker viewed this as another strength of the family as it sought to deal with stress.

(Continued)

(Continued)

Family Structure

The worker failed to detect any significant coalitions across generational boundaries. The two structural conditions the worker thought were problematic were that the parents failed to be a clear and strong subsystem when dealing with their children and that the relationship between Robert and Juan was distant. The worker saw this as a lack of clear executive functions in the family as well as a lack of opportunity for Robert to utilize his father as a role model as he struggled with his own issues of identity and sexuality.

Family Resources

Juan was employed as a skilled worker in a local factory, and his wife was a salesperson in a department store. Their income was adequate for the family's needs and to save for a down payment on a house—an objective the entire family agreed on. This commonality of objectives and the lack of financial stress are additional family strengths.

Interaction With Other Systems

The family had close and nurturing ties with several institutions, such as the church and, in the father's case, his trade union. Both parents liked their work and felt accepted in their work environments. Robert, however, felt alienated from his school, and the Angelos saw the school as antagonistic to their culture and to their use in the home of the Spanish language. This was a source of tension in the family, and the worker saw this as exacerbating the presenting problem of Robert's school difficulties and the peer pressures he was experiencing.

● WAYS OF PORTRAYING FAMILY CONDITIONS

When engaging in a family assessment, the worker will often use one of several ways of graphing or portraying one of the family categories just discussed. These "devices" are needed because of the difficulty one experiences in communicating complex, systemic circumstances through words alone. The devices we describe and the categories are listed here:

Family Category	Device
Phase of family life cycle	Chronological chart
Family resources	Need-resource diagram
Interaction with other systems	Ecomap
Family culture and traditions	Genogram

Chronological Chart

L'Abate described an excellent yet simple means of portraying the family life cycle (L'Abate, 1994). As he described it, the chart tells

how the parents met and lived over the individual and dyadic life cycles, tracing individual development; courtship: marriage ceremony; honeymoon; occupational career; important traumas, such as conditions at the birth of the children, abortions, miscarriages, accidents, illnesses; and pleasant and unpleasant memories. (L'Abate, 1994, p. 119)

Because L'Abate's chart assumes the family unit is a heterosexual couple with biological children, we have applied it to an alternative family forms that were discussed previously in this chapter. The chart of the Arnold-Smith-Wellington family is presented here (See Table 2.2):

Table 12.2 Chronological Chart of the Arnold-Smith-Wellington Family

Mother	Year	Significant Other/Partner
Meets male partner at bar	1983	Meets mother at bar
Moves in with male partner	1984	Moves in with mother
Graduates from college	1985	
Marry each other	1985	
Works part time	1986	Joins U.S. Army and serves overseas
First child born (daughter)	1987	Receives injury and loses arm
Own mother dies	1988	Discharged from U.S. Army with 20% disability Enrolled for college degree supported by military disability
Second child born (son)	1989	Alcoholism and domestic violence
Takes part-time job	1990	Domestic abuse escalates
Separates from partner	1991	Served with protection order
Divorced from partner	1992	Convicted and incarcerated for manslaughter in a bar fight
Move to another city and first child starts school	1993	
Meets new partner in a women's support group	1994	Meets mother in support group
Second child starts school	1995	

(Continued)

Table 12.2 (Continued)

Mother	Year	Significant Other/Partner
Moves into partner's home and begins full-time employment	1995	Begin domestic partnership
First child graduates from school and goes away to college	1995	Surgery and chemo for breast cancer
First child becomes pregnant and drops out of college	1998	Files lawsuit for sex discrimination
	2000	Loses suit against employer
	2001	Treated for major depression
Second child acting out in school	2002	
Second child starts abusing drugs	2004	
Second child enlists in U.S. Army and sent to Iraq	2005	
Mother and partner seek counseling	2005	Partner and mother seek conjoint counseling for partnership issues

The worker, in examining the chart, developed cooperatively with the domestic partner, used it to develop hypotheses about how the family's present tensions are the result of many stressful, hazardous events (i.e., losses) and stressful conditions (i.e., domestic partnership in a homophobic community and gender discrimination in the workplace).

This basic chart of events in the family system does highlight the various stressors that the family has endured over the past 2 decades, but these events only gain meaning in details of the context that surrounds these events. For example, the acting out of the son in school is the consequence of teasing and bullying by his classmates for having "two mothers" for parents. The choices of both children to drop out of school, the decision of the daughter to have the child, and the decision of the son to join the U.S. Army and go to Iraq are extremely stressful for this educated couple who now face an "empty nest" situation and must figure out how to move on together.

Family Resources

As we have indicated throughout this chapter, conflicts emerge at the transactional interfaces between the family and the surrounding environment. For the family and its members to grow and thrive, three critical exchanges must be balanced: Family needs must be balanced by environmental resources; family wants and aspirations must be balanced by environmental opportunities; and the skills and capacities of family members must be balanced by environmental demands and expectations. The following chart indicates one way to make these connections clear. We will use the example of the G family in Table 12.3.

Table 12.3   Family–Environmental Exchanges

Needs	Resources
The family needs more adequate housing.	They need enough money for monthly payments on an adequate house they would like to purchase but not enough for a down payment.
The family needs a special school for their daughter who is developmentally disabled.	A school for children with special needs in this community is of poor quality.
The family needs respite care for a grandparent who suffers from Alzheimer's disease.	There is an excellent program providing a full range of services for families with a member who suffers from Alzheimer's disease available in the community.
Aspirations	**Opportunities**
Mr. G wishes to become active in the political life of the community.	The political leaders of the community have acted subtly to exclude Mr. G because of his religion (Pentecostal Christianity).
Mrs. G wishes to continue to develop her singing talents and join a church choir.	There is no charismatic church in their community that is of their faith.
Their son, Robert, wishes to join a Little League team.	A Little League team practices across the street from where they live, and the team members are actively recruiting players.
Capacities	**Expectations**
Their daughter (Sara) has a developmental disability that will severely limit how far she may go in her schooling.	Mr. and Mrs. G expect all of their children to attend college.
Mr. G is attending school at night to obtain a law degree and is doing well in this program.	Mr. G wishes to become the first lawyer in his extended family as all of his extended family members are employed in blue-collar occupations.
Mrs. G has an excellent voice and musical talents.	Family members are encouraging Mrs. G to locate a choral group to fulfill her ambitions to perform musically and to appear on *America's Got Talent*.

Interaction With Other Systems

Family conditions are also a consequence of the way in which the family interacts with other systems in their community, such as institutions, agencies, neighbors, places of employment, extended family, etc. Two instruments are frequently used to assess these interactions. The *ecomap* presents the relationship of the family to other contemporary systems; the *genogram* emphasizes interactions with the extended family and has the additional virtue of portraying aspects of the family's history that may still affect contemporary beliefs and behaviors (Hartman, 1978).

The Ecomap

The ecomap is described in this chapter, but it can also be used with individual clients, formed groups, and even organizations. The essential quality of the ecomap is the ability to quickly and visually demonstrate the quality of the connections between the unit in the center of the map and the interactions with other units and systems that surround and influence the unit. The ecomap is a slice in time of the family system and is expected to change over time.

We will describe the basic notations of the ecomap as presented by Hartman (1978), but interpersonal practitioners and clients often innovate and create their own notations (e.g., wavy lines, double lines, or color coding) to represent other qualities in the interactions. It is also important to realize that drawing the ecomap is a joint activity of the interpersonal practitioner and the client system (whether individual, family, or group). The interpersonal practitioner may start the process by describing how the system works to the client, but as the map is drawn it becomes obvious to the client system that they are the content experts in the construction of the map. Because the ecomap captures positive—as well as tenuous and stressful—connections, it is empowering to clients when they realize that they are in control of the assessment process and they are not being "interrogated" by the social worker about all of the negative things going on in their lives.

The ecomap is created by placing the names of members of the household in a circle in the center of a large sheet of newsprint paper. A series of large circles and ellipses placed around the family are labeled to represent the institutions, persons, and even abstractions, such as the political economy, natural disasters, career plans, etc., that play a significant role in the life of the family or household. The convention in ecomaps is to represent males as squares and females as circles with names and ages placed inside. Lines are drawn between the members or the family/household circle and the other circles and ellipses in the client's environment. A variety of lines are chosen to indicate supportive (positive) ———, tenuous (weak) -------------, and stressful (contentious) +++++ associations. Arrows are placed on the lines to indicate the flow of energy (e.g., the direction in which support or conflict flows).

In order to demonstrate how the ecomap can reflect information about the family in a visual diagram, the following case description is presented along with the ecomap completed with Liz, the mother in this family system (see Figure 12.2). The ecomap presents her perspective of the various connections to her environment. The information that was collected about this family system emerged while drawing this map with her, and the information has been disguised as presented in this chapter. The interpersonal practitioner should realize that they may not agree with the way clients characterize their interactions with the environment. For example, in the ecomap, Figure 12.2, social workers would not see Roy's drinking alcohol as a supportive connection.

Figure 12.2	Ecomap Example

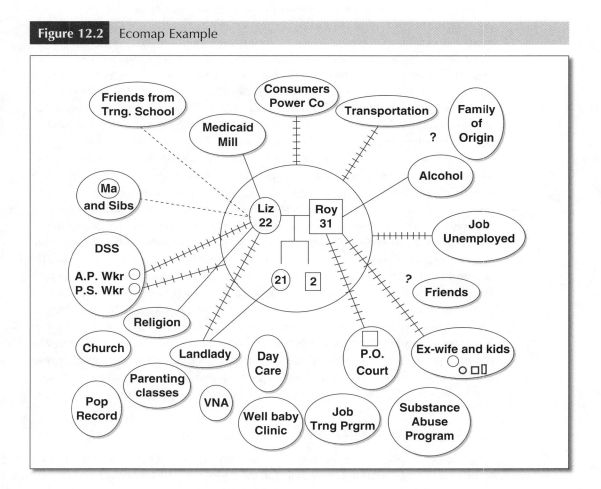

Narrative Description That Corresponds to the Ecomap in Figure 12.2:

Liz is a 23-year-old Caucasian woman who lives with her 31-year-old boyfriend Roy in a small, rented trailer in a rural Midwestern county. Her relationship with Roy has produced two children: Sam, who is 2, and Cheryl, who is 1 year old. When Liz is not washing diapers, she is usually watching TV or sleeping on the couch. Liz and Roy do not have a car, and there is no public transportation near their trailer so they must walk or hitchhike in order to get to town to shop and make appointments. Liz feels isolated and "trapped" in her trailer. Two months ago, she made a suicide gesture by drinking a bottle of her ulcer medicine. A physician's assistant, whom she sees at a local "Medicaid mill," gave her some antidepressant medication (Zoloft) to "remove the blues."

Liz is a product of a "chaotic" family. Her mother never married the numerous men who fathered Liz and her six younger siblings. Because her mother could not handle her sexual, acting out behavior, Liz spent 5 years of her adolescence in a state training school for the developmentally disabled. Since leaving the institution 4 years ago, Liz left behind all of her close friends. She has very minimal contact with her mother and siblings, who live upstate. Her primary relationship is with Roy, who is unemployed, on probation for assault and battery in a bar fight, and separated from his previous wife. He is behind on child support payments and is being threatened by a local court. Roy is a heavy drinker and is physically abusive to Liz, but she would not think of being "without her man." Liz has a strained relationship with her landlady, who babysits for Liz when she goes out shopping, yet this landlady has called protective services twice about her concerns for the two children.

Liz has no desire to work though her assistance payments worker has threatened to cut off her Aid to Families with Dependent Children (AFDC) grant unless she seriously considers some king of job training program. Liz has one big dream: "to cut a hit record." Liz loves to sing and was active in the choir in the training school. At present, Liz does not attend church though she considers herself "very religious," which is her rationalization for refusing to consider any form of birth control. Recently, her power company threatened to shut off her electricity unless she paid up her past due account ($300). Liz states she has poor self-esteem and is embarrassed about her past institutionalization in the training school. She is 50 lbs. (23 kg) overweight and is surprised that Roy still finds her sexually attractive. She is not happy about her present circumstances, nor where her life seems to be going. She has agreed to work with you as her newly assigned social worker in a "homebound prevention" program. The ecomap also reflects a number of resources and opportunities that the social worker has discussed with Liz (i.e., parenting classes, Visiting Nurse Association, well baby clinic, day care, job training program, and substance use program).

Family Culture and Traditions—The Genogram

The genogram is another diagrammatic way of presenting family culture and traditions. The genogram focuses on the extended family as a system and reveals historical information about family members in earlier generations. The genogram looks roughly like a family tree. It, too, is created with the client so that the client's perceptions and reflections can be collected. A genogram usually portrays three generations in the family, though with some issues the worker and family may wish to explore more generations. As with ecomaps, the convention observed in such diagrams is to identify males with squares and females with circles. Names and ages are placed inside the lines, and other pertinent data (e.g., dates of death, geographical location, and significant facts) are placed above this (see Figure 12.3). Lesbian, gay, bisexual, and transgender (LGBT) members have their own symbols. There are symbols for alcoholism, physical illness, and mental illness of members, as well as whether these members are in recovery. Marriages, affairs, separation, divorce, reconciliation, cutoffs, deaths as well as symbols denoting quality of interactional patterns between members may be denoted.

Figure 12.3 Common Genogram Symbols

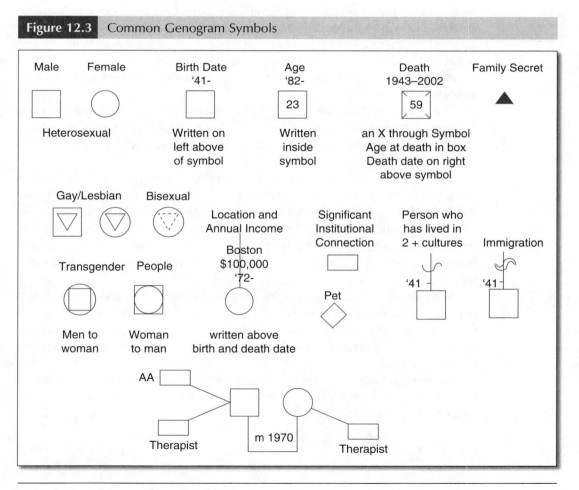

Source: Adapted from www.multiculturalfamily.org/genograms/genogram_symbols.html.

Genograms have developed such complexity that just about every orientation, event, condition, and relationship pattern can be denoted in a person's family tree. There are genograms that focus on attachment issues (Demaria, Weeks, & Hof, 1999), on spirituality and religion (Carroll, 1988; Frame, 2001), on cultural issues (Hardy & Laszloffy, 1995), and even genograms that are designed for solution-focused therapy (Kuehl, 1995). The point here is that a "comprehensive" genogram would be so complex and it would take so much time to collect all of the potential information about three generations in a family that we are only introducing this assessment procedure in this book. The interpersonal practice student should expect to spend much more time on genograms in advanced family treatment courses.

To develop a basic genogram, the interpersonal practitioner along with the family secures facts and events that can illuminate the forces pertinent to the family's problems. These facts may include demographic information, such as date of birth, physical location, religion, ethnicity, and occupation. In addition, other data that the client considers important may include economic status, health, and behavioral characteristics. Traumatic events, such as the causes of death, imprisonment, mental illness, and other catastrophes, in the extended family may be elicited.

The worker may inquire into issues that are significant to the family and that may center on some members of the family. These might be strongly held cultural beliefs or highly sensitive topics that still affect family behavior and may be sources of conflict.

Examples of these topics are alcoholism, abortion, out-of-wedlock pregnancies, elopements, and family conflicts around religion and spirituality issues. In Figure 12.4, we present a sample genogram that was completed in the third session with the Romano family. This genogram will be discussed later in the family intervention chapter (Chapter 13) when the first two sessions with the Romano family are presented in order to demonstrate interpersonal practice with families.

Even though there are software programs designed to create genograms (e.g., www.genogram.org; www.smartdraw.com; www.genopro.com), we decided to create the Romano family genogram as hand drawn. Because we want practitioners to create genograms with the family, it is likely that genograms will be hand drawn in practice.

Once the genogram has been created with the family, it can be used to provide assessment information that may help the worker and family understand the dynamics of present problems:

Figure 12.4 Genogram of the Romano Family

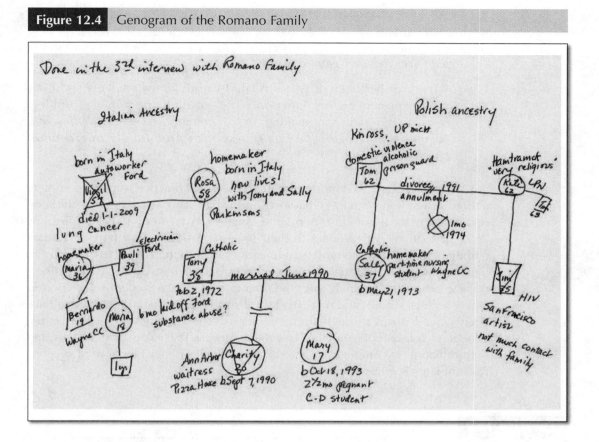

1. What behavioral patterns have occurred in the family system that have per-
sisted through several generations? Are there recurring patterns of substance abuse, domestic violence, or victimization? *Look at Figure 12.4, and
discover any behavior patterns that may be persisting through several
generations.*

2. What are the sources of mutual reinforcement of values in the family
as well as sources of value conflict? Are their cultural and religious
beliefs that run throughout the generations? *Look at Figure 12.4, and
discover any religious affiliations that may appear through several
generations.*

3. What resources exist that are or could be of help to the family? How has the family coped with tragedy over the three generations? *Look at Figure 12.4. Can you see any tragedies (i.e., stressful life events) that they have coped with over the three generations?*

4. What are the kinds of issues related to the family's beliefs and common experiences that function either to limit the family's problem solving and decision making or to enhance it? *These issues will become apparent in the family sessions in the family intervention chapter (Chapter 13).*

We believe that it is important that interpersonal practice students complete a three-generation genogram that focuses on spirituality and religion with themselves as the focal person (Sheridan & Amato-von Hemert, 1999) before they apply genograms with families in their practice. Students may have to contact members in their parents' and grandparents' generation in order to discover the information about spirituality of these ancestors, their struggles, their connections to others in the family tree, and their achievements. Students may uncover family secrets, cutoffs, and tragedies as well as the resiliency and values that have been passed down through the generations. The student will learn that the genogram is a complex family assessment process that takes lots of effort and determination to complete. In practice with families it may take several sessions to complete (See Exercise 12.1).

Exercise 12.1

Spiritual Genogram

This exercise will help students to explore genograms and also make them aware of the impact religion and spirituality has on them. It will also sensitize students to issues that may arise when they work with families who come from very different religious and spiritual traditions than their own. The spiritual genogram should contain basic genogram information about ancestors from three generations, such as age, gender expression, birth dates, marriages, divorces, remarriages, and deaths. Information about adoption, twins, unmarried couples, and quality of family interactions should be included if this information can be obtained from willing informants in the student's family tree. Formal religious affiliations, such as Catholic, Protestant, Muslim, Jew, Buddhist, Agnostic ,etc., are denoted, along with changes in religious affiliations at times of marriage, births, or other events. Major religious and spiritual conflicts between members should be noted. After compiling all of this information, students should consider the following questions that emerge from their spiritual genogram (Frame, 2001, p. 111):

1. *What role, if any, did religion or spirituality play in your life when you were growing up? What role does it play now?*

2. *What specific religious or spiritual beliefs do you consider most important for you now? How are those beliefs a source of connection or conflict between you and other family members?*

3. *What religious or spiritual rituals did you participate in as a child or adolescent? How important were they in your family of origin? Which ones do you still engage in? Which ones have you let go? What new rituals have you adopted as an adult? How do these rituals connect to your religious or spiritual belief system?*

4. *What view did / does your religious or spiritual tradition hold about gender? About ethnicity? About sexual orientation? How have these beliefs affected you and your extended family?*

5. *What patterns of behavior and relationship resulting from religion or spirituality emerge for you as you study your genogram? How are you currently maintaining or diverting from these patterns?*

6. *How does your religious or spiritual history connect with your attitudes toward working with clients' religious or spiritual issues? What new insights or concerns occur to you based on the discoveries made through the genogram?*

SUMMARY ●

This chapter described how the worker engages in family assessment. The first section of this chapter described how assessing a family system may require new skills in observation that are different form the skills applied to assessing individual clients. The chapter presented the many family forms that are found in social work practice. Family assessment was introduced as a process of generating hypotheses about the family, testing these hypotheses, and modifying them if necessary.

Ways of obtaining family data to generate hypotheses were described. These include the way the family members handled their initial contact with the worker, the ways the worker "tracks" family interactions, the ways the worker observes family interactions (enactments), the kinds of tasks workers can assign families to obtain assessment information, the kinds of questions workers can pose to families to secure their perception of family conditions, and "sculpting" the family.

Once information is obtained about the family, workers often find it useful to categorize the information under headings related to different family conditions. These categories were phases of the family life cycle, family culture and tradition, family emotional climate, family communication patterns, family boundaries, family structure, family resources, and family interaction with other systems. All of these family conditions, described in the form of a table (Table 12.1), should be examined as they relate to gender and cultural issues. An example of a family assessment that takes these categories into consideration was presented (the Angelo family).

Because family conditions are often complex, workers find it helpful to present them in the form of charts and diagrams. A variety of these are described in the last section of the chapter. Specifically, such charts and diagrams were presented with reference to phase of the family life cycle, family resources, interaction with other systems (ecomaps), and family culture and traditions (genograms).

CHAPTER 13

FAMILY CHANGE

Other things may change us but we start and end with the family.

—Anthony Brandt

Social work writers, such as Hartman and Laird (Hartman & Laird, 1983) and Janzen and colleagues (Janzen & Harris, 1986; Janzen, Harris, Jordan, & Franklin, 2005), have described social work practice with families in ways that are compatible with our ideas.

We begin with what we believe is the social work mission with families:

1. To support the empowerment of the family to seek the changes that will enhance well-being

2. To enhance the ways families interact with their environments so that families are more likely to obtain the resources they need to meet the needs of the family as well as meet the needs of its members

3. To assist the family in identifying aspects of the environment such as sexism, racism, heterosexism, ageism, and other forms of discrimination that limit the family and its members' access to opportunities

4. To advocate for changes in agencies, communities, and society that enhance the healthy functioning of families

5. To help families address internal strains and conflicts within the family that can be changed by interpersonal practice interventions

● OCCASIONS FOR FAMILY INTERVENTIONS

When an individual's problems are maintained or caused by family conditions, the interpersonal practitioner should consider family interventions. We have repeatedly emphasized our empowerment perspective and believe that individuals and their families should decide how they want to intervene in the stressors that are impacting their lives. We agree with the idea that it is difficult, if not impossible, to separate an individual's behavior from her or his social interactions. Nevertheless, some individuals wish to focus on their thoughts and feelings, and workers should respect this. Workers should explain, however, that even these kinds of purposes may be best achieved if the individual secures feedback from others who are significant in her or his life.

Thus, we believe that even one-to-one practice should have a group and family perspective. Clients' problems should be understood as they are related to social interactions, and goals should be developed regarding changes in these interactions. There are many situations when workers are most likely to think about working directly with several family members:

- The problem is described in terms of conflict among family members. This is especially true in cases of marital conflict, as work with only one individual is likely to harm rather than help the marriage.
- The problem is described as impaired communication among family members.
- The problem is described in terms of the system itself, such as a family that does little together or a family that is disorganized. There also are circumstances when many workers will appropriately avoid working with several family members at the same time. These include the following:
- A family member may be in danger when meeting with several or all family members. Working, for example, with a man and woman together when the man has abused the woman often places the woman in jeopardy between sessions, as the man may punish her for her behavior in the session.
- The family is in the process of dissolution unless the purpose is to help the members deal with this. Examples of this situation are marital partners who have decided to separate; parents and children after the decision has been made to place the children in the care of others. The reason for this is that family techniques tend to support the continuation of the family. When the family is in the process of dissolving, it is stressful to pretend they are not. This is not meant to contradict the practice, under some circumstances, of meeting with divorced couples and others in their new families to help them negotiate such things as boundaries and the respective roles of various family members.
- The session would be too stressful for some family member. An example of this is a session with a family that includes a member with a serious mental

illness when that member cannot handle this experience at the time in question. Very useful sessions have been held with families with mentally ill members when the time is right.

The interventions in this chapter are organized around the stages of family work and the kinds of family conditions that were discussed in the family assessment chapter (Chapter 12). As we discussed in the family assessment chapter, in social work the term *family* has many forms—single parent, multiple generations, gay and lesbian couples, etc. The stages of family work are logically described as (1) prior to the first family session; (2) the initial sessions; (3) the family change stage; and (4) the ending stages (Hartman & Laird, 1983).

PRIOR TO THE FIRST FAMILY SESSION ●

As is true in all forms of interpersonal helping, there are a number of routes through which family work will be initiated. These are likely to be one of the following routes:

1. Another professional, whether from the same or another agency, has reached the decision, usually with family members, that family work is appropriate. The worker, under this circumstance, should receive information from that professional on the reasons for this referral. The worker should, however, inquire—when she or he makes the initial appointment— how the family member perceived the referral and how that family member and others in the family feel about it. Sometimes the referral has been made without sufficient family involvement so that there can be resistance to it that must be addressed. Family treatment may be a new concept to the family who may not understand the reasons for it.

2. An individual family member may contact the worker who, in the course of either a phone conversation or face-to-face session, with that individual prescribes family treatment. The worker should recommend that the family be seen when the problem is expressed in interpersonal terms that involve other family members. One example of this follows:

Appropriate Case for Family Intervention

Sara Jones stated that she wanted counseling because the man with whom she lived refused to discuss whether they had a future together in which they made commitments to each other. He also quarreled with her regarding household expenses and accused her of being a spendthrift.

Here is another typical example:

Another Case for Family Intervention

Robert Gordon phoned to say that he found his family life very stressful. His children argued with each other all of the time, and his wife didn't seem to know what to do about it. He admitted that he also was at a loss how to deal with the many arguments in the family. He had recently lost his job, which added to the pressures on him.

If workers think that family sessions are desirable, they should state this to the family and explain their reasons. The worker should speak positively when asking the individual to bring other family members to the session, with the assumption that the request will be accepted. Inexperienced workers are sometimes apprehensive about the family's response and express the request hesitantly, unfortunately conveying to the family member the worker's own qualms about family work. The family member might sense the worker's hesitation, which can reinforce any reluctance the family member has.

Here is an example of this:

Selling Family Treatment to Family Members

Mrs. Reed told the worker that her father is a widower and had recently come to live with them after suffering a stroke that left him partially paralyzed. Her father and her husband had never gotten along because the father was upset when she married a Jewish man and through their 15 years of marriage frequently criticized him.

The worker asked Mrs. Reed to bring her father and husband to the session (the father is able to walk with the help of a walker). She explained that the problem involved all three of them, and each had a stake in finding a solution. She added that she had found that sessions involving everyone connected to a problem in a family were most likely to lead to a solution that benefitted each one. Family members were also more likely to carry the solution out if they all had a hand in figuring out what the solution was to be. Mrs. Reed said she doubted that her father would come as he had no use for therapy. The worker reiterated the idea that Mrs. Reed should explain to him that she wanted him to have a chance to explain things as he saw them and to have a say in what happens in the family. She added that she had respect for her father's opinions, and the worker thought she should tell her father that.

The family member sometimes calls back to say that a person who was requested to be present still refuses to attend. The worker can offer to call that person. Under these circumstances, the worker should stress the "positives," such as what that person can contribute to the sessions. Some workers will state that they are sure the reluctant family member is concerned about the well-being of the other family members. This kind of comment, however, poses problems if for some reason it is not completely true. There can also be negative consequences if the worker brings too much pressure to bear.

Some ways of minimizing the pressure are to ask for the person's presence at one session and to discuss over the phone the reasons for the person's opposition to attending. When appropriate, the worker can express empathy with these reasons, thus making a tentative bid for a relationship with the family member in question.

THE INITIAL SESSIONS ●

The goal of the first sessions is to develop a contract with the family for service. This includes an agreement as to the problem(s) to be worked on; the changes that are sought to resolve or improve the problem situations; the means, as far as they are known, to work on the problem situation; the worker's and each family member's responsibilities in the treatment process; and any expectations about the length of the service.

When agreement to these terms does not exist, Hartman and Laird (1983) suggested the worker think of a "preliminary contract," and they defined it as follows:

> At a minimum, the preliminary agreement, usually verbal, must include the identification of a shared purpose, even if a very tenuous one, and an agreement to meet together for a specified number of sessions at a mutually satisfactory time and place. The goal during this phase is to determine whether client and worker can together agree on the central issues and concerns which need to be resolved, and formulate some beginning ideas concerning the means by which the resolution might occur The preliminary agreement, without implying or mandating a long-term commitment on the part of either the family or the worker, proposes a testing and study period and defines some of the rules that will be observed; thus, such an agreement is particularly reassuring to the client unsure of her goals or of the amount of time and energy she is willing to commit. (p. 143)

Each of these aspects of the contract requires adaptations for work with families. The problem to be worked on may be seen differently by each family member. One frequently found issue in determining the problem is that of the "identified patient or client." This determination indicates that the family, and even the referring agency, may single out one family member as "the problem" or as the reason for referral. This person can be an individual family member who suffers from a mental or physical illness, from chemical dependency, or from being in trouble with the law or with another system, such as a child suspended from school.

Family practitioners have dealt with the issue of the identified patient in a number of ways. Some "accept" this definition, at least at first, because they reason that when families are motivated to utilize treatment to resolve a problem with an individual member, the family's view of the problem should be respected. Others move quickly to establish the notion that everyone in the family contributes to the condition of the family, and it is how well the family functions to solve problems that is the issue. We do not hold rigidly to either approach and have utilized each when it is consistent with how we think the particular family functions. In either case, however, we seek to establish the idea that all contribute to family circumstances and have a stake in the outcome. We seek to help the family to think beyond the circumstances of individuals to what the family as a system is like.

Each of the other terms of the contract must be seen in the light of different perceptions and beliefs of each family member and the degree to which there is consensus among family members. This issue is a very important one in terms of both assessment and change. The degree of agreement tells a great deal about the family and how the internal workings of the family contribute to its difficulties beyond the contribution of larger systems. Achieving agreement among family members may be an important change goal rather than something that must be achieved before treatment begins.

To create and carry out a contract with the family, workers must establish a relationship with family members and must find out about the individuals in the family as well as about the family as an entity. The following are some of the ways workers do this:

1. Develop contact with each member so that the member sees herself or himself as recognized and respected by the worker.

2. Obtain each member's perception of the family's problems and preferred outcome of the helping process.

3. Determine the amount of agreement on the nature of the problem.

4. Obtain agreement on at least one preferred outcome, even if that outcome is to continue to work toward agreement.

5. Obtain enough information to form at least initial hypotheses about how the family functions and how this contributes to the problem.

6. Obtain enough information to formulate initial hypotheses of how the larger environment contributes to the problem.

7. Identify strengths of family members who will contribute to the initial phase of helping.

8. Determine what actions to take so the family will return for additional sessions, if that is appropriate.

9. Determine how the helping process is likely to be affected by the worker's characteristics, such as gender and ethnicity, and discuss this issue with the family in ways that are appropriate to the family's circumstances.

Some workers prefer to hold the first family session with all members invited. They believe this helps them to develop a relationship with all family members that is not negatively affected by some members thinking that others have an advantage because they had prior sessions with the worker. Other workers prefer to meet with the adults in the family for one or more sessions before they meet with the whole family.

It is useful to have in mind a way of structuring the first (and often subsequent) family session, although one must be flexible and modify this structure as circumstances require. This structure for a first session is as follows (Haley, 1987):

1. The interviewing room is set up so there are sufficient chairs for all family members arranged as much in a circle as the furniture and room sizes allow.

2. The family is met in the waiting room by the worker and brought into the interviewing room, where it is suggested that the family members sit wherever they wish. Their choice of seats is a piece of assessment information.

3. The worker briefly introduces herself or himself by giving his or her name and title in the agency and indicating that part of the job is to help families who are experiencing difficulties. This is also the point at which the worker typically discusses family reactions to the worker's gender as well as any apparent difference in cultural characteristics, such as race, ethnicity, lifestyle, etc.

4. Depending on the circumstances, a brief explanation is sometimes given at this point of ways to work with families. The family members are then asked to introduce themselves. It is important to make eye contact with each one and to acknowledge in some brief way each introduction.

5. The worker asks what concerns or circumstances brought the family to the agency, while not looking directly at any family member, as it is important for assessment purposes to note which family member answers. At times, however, this is not done, as when cultural or other circumstances

dictate that a particular family member be addressed first. For example, with some ethnic families it would be expected and respectful of the authority structure in the family if an "elder" in the family speaks first.

6. Each family member is then asked if she or he wishes to say something about why the family is here, how each feels about being here, and what she or he hopes to get out of sessions of family work.

7. The worker then comments on the degree of consensus regarding the reasons for the family's presence. The comment is often one of the following: (a) noting the degree of agreement; (b) noting the degree of disagreement and labeling this as an issue that the family might want to deal with; or (c) if the agreement is in the nature of defining a member as the identified patient, noting that very often there are problems in which every family member has a role. When these are resolved, the family members can better help one another with the difficulties the identified patient is experiencing.

8. The worker seeks an issue to lay before the family that relates to the problem. An example might be "What have you tried before to deal with (the problem)?" Family members are encouraged to discuss the issue, which also should be seen as part of the process of solving the problem. The worker, however, tries to be an observer of this family discussion so that she or he can obtain information on how family members interact, at least under this set of circumstances.

9. The worker asks the family members to comment on what they would like to see different in the family.

10. The worker states at least a preliminary form of a contract, either to continue examining the question posed in Number 8 or in the form of a more specific goal, if there is a consensus on one at that point.

11. The worker summarizes the major information presented during the session by family members.

12. The worker concludes with arrangements for future meetings, places, times, and other such details. This is the time to clarify whether the next session should include individuals not present in the first one.

In order to apply the principles just discussed, we present an interactive family session that is based on the genogram of the Romano family, which was presented in Chapter 12. Return to this chapter and refamiliarize yourself with this multiethnic family.

Family Sessions With the Romano Family

The interpersonal practitioner in this case is Ms. Ortega, a married 32-year-old Latina with 5 years of experience working with individuals, families, and groups. She is fluent in English and Spanish and was hired by her agency to reach out to the growing Latino community. The agency context is Catholic Social Services, which is supported by local Catholic parishes and United Way funds. Though the agency is sectarian, it hires staff and sees clients from any religious affiliation. Catholic Social Services has community programs for troubled youth; food programs for homeless people; foster care and adoption services; and counseling services for individuals, couples, and families.

From your review of the Romano genogram and what you know about Ms. Ortega and Catholic Social Services, what do you see as potential obstacles and potential commonalities in the relationship between the Romano family and Ms. Ortega?

Obstacles:

Commonalities:

Mrs. Romano had called 2 days before the initial interview and expressed urgency in being seen as soon as possible. She stated that she had heard from a friend that Catholic Social Services had been helpful to them with family problems, and she needed help now with a family problem that she would not discuss over the phone.

The Romano family (Sally, Tony, Mary, and Rosa) arrived on time, and Sally Romano filled out the agency's brief intake form, which collected information about names, address, phone numbers, religious affiliation, insurance information, and a question about the "reason for today's visit," which Sally left blank on the form. Ms. Ortega greeted the Romano family in the waiting room and invited all of them into the interviewing room. Ms. Ortega invited the family to sit wherever they were comfortable in this moderately size room with eight movable chairs that were set up in a circle. Ms. Ortega entered the interviewing room first followed by Sally, Mary, Tony, and Rosa. The family arranged themselves in the following configuration:

(Continued)

(Continued)

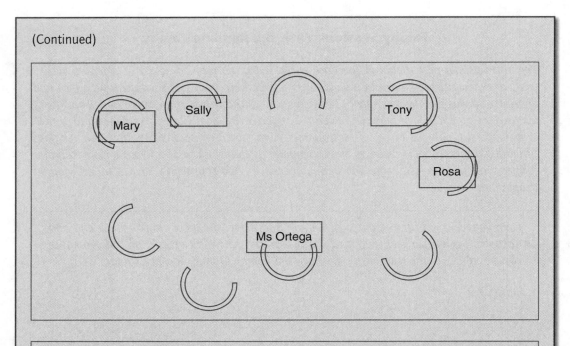

The Romano family had already begun to display family dynamics in how they entered the interview room and how they chose to sit. What kinds of initial "hypotheses" can you make from their behavior?

Ms. Ortega briefly introduced herself and explained that she is a social worker who meets with families who are struggling with family issues. She asked the family to introduce themselves. Sally explained that she is Mary's mother and Tony's wife and that Rosa is Tony's mother, who had recently moved in with the family after the sudden death of Tony's father 3 months ago. Ms. Ortega thanked Sally for introducing her family and asked what was happening in the family because of the urgency to be seen today. Sally began talking about all of the stressors that the family was experiencing—for example, Tony had been laid off for almost 6 months, Tony's father died suddenly, Tony spent most of his time with his laid off buddies in a local bar and did not help around the house, Sally had begun taking part-time courses in a community college to work toward a nursing degree to help with family finances. At this point in her long narrative, Tony interrupted and stated that he was the "breadwinner" and Sally should not be taking classes but instead be taking care of her daughters and his mother. Sally and Tony got into an argument about Sally's aspirations to become a nurse, and Rosa spoke up that it was the role of the wife to focus on the home and not be "running around" getting a degree. At this point in the interview, Mary crossed her arms and turned her chair around with her back toward her family. Ms. Ortega responded to this behavior and asked Mary if "arguments like this happen often in her family." Sally immediately answered and stated that there were many other issues that were going on in the family that needed to be addressed. Ms. Ortega turned to Tony and asked what he thought was going on in his family. Instead of answering, Tony looked at Sally, who then stated, "Tony is hardly ever around to know what is going on in the family!" At this point, Mary moved her chair farther away from the rest of the family.

> The Romano family continued to display family dynamics in the interview. What kinds of new "hypotheses" can you make from their behavior?
>
>
> At this point in the interview, do we know why Sally called with such urgency that the family needs to be seen immediately? What was the issue (potential precipitant) that pushed the family into seeking help now?

Ms. Ortega stated that she would like to go around and ask each family member what they felt was going on in the family that brought them to seek help. Ms. Ortega turned toward Tony and asked him to start. Tony shook his head and looked at his wife. Sally began to answer for Tony, but Ms. Ortega interrupted and explained that she would get a chance, but it was now Tony's time to share. Tony looked puzzled and stated that he did not know why they came today. Tony stated, "All I know is Sally told me we all needed to go to this appointment." Ms. Ortega then turned toward Rosa and asked her what she knew about today's session. Rosa spoke up and stated that she did not like the idea that "family business" was being shared with outsiders and that in the past her generation would resolve family issues on their own. Ms. Ortega thanked Rosa for her honesty and sharing her views. Ms. Ortega then turned to Mary and asked Mary to turn her chair back toward the center of the room and to answer the same question about what was going on in the family. Mary rolled her eyes and pointed to her mother and sat quietly with arms across her chest. Sally stated that Mary had been caught skipping school and hanging around with a "fast" crowd. Tony immediately interjected that this would not happen if Sally was home supervising "her daughter" instead of taking classes for nursing training. Rosa agreed with Tony that Sally needed to take her parental responsibilities more seriously, and added that the oldest daughter, Charity, who was not in the family interview, would never have become a lesbian and moved out of the family home about a year ago.

(Continued)

(Continued)

> The Romano family continued to display family dynamics in the interview. What kinds of new "hypotheses" can you make from their behavior? Do you see any coalitions, ethnic patterns, and who seems to be the "family spokesperson"? Who might be considered the "identified patient"?
>
> At this point in the interview, do we know why Sally called with such urgency that the family needed to be seen immediately? What was the issue (potential precipitant) that pushed the family into seeking help now?

Ms. Ortega reiterated the question about what happened 2 days ago that created the urgency for the family to be seen now. After a long pause, Sally asked Ms. Ortega if she and Mary could speak alone with the social worker. Ms. Ortega asked Tony and Rosa if that would be OK with them and invited them to return to the waiting room. Tony and Rosa agreed and left the interview room.

Sally turned to Mary and ordered her to tell the social worker what she had told her mother 2 days ago. Mary crossed her arms, glared at Sally, and retorted, "You tell the social worker!" Sally then explained that her daughter has missed two periods and tested positive on an OTC pregnancy test. Mary was not sure who the father was because she had been sexually active with several partners. At this point, Sally began to cry and said she did not know how to tell Tony about the pregnancy. Mary's pregnancy brought back all of her old conflicts with her own pregnancy in high school with Charity, the interruption in her education, the rushed wedding to Tony when they were just teenagers, and the conflicts that emerged between Tony's family and her own family. Sally explained that she had gone to her parish priest and asked for his help, and he had suggested that the family come to Catholic Social Services and talk with a Catholic social worker. This was an important point for the priest because abortion was out of the question. At this point, Sally asked whether Ms. Ortega was Catholic and breathed a sigh of relief when Ms. Ortega answered that she was Catholic. Ms. Ortega then asked Mary what she wanted to do. Mary explained that she did not know what to do and was getting conflicting advice from her friends; some had encouraged her to get an abortion, which directly contradicted her own and her family's values. Mary also did not want to get married because she had seen the conflicts that emerged from her mother's decision years ago with her high school pregnancy. It was also out of the question because she did not know who the father is.

Ms. Ortega asked Sally and Mary if they were willing to share this information about the pregnancy with Tony and Rosa and what their reaction might be. Sally explained that Tony would be upset and would blame her for Mary's pregnancy for not being a "good mother." He would use this against her desire to pursue a nursing degree. Ms. Ortega asked Sally if Tony had a temper and would retaliate against her when they got home. "Has Tony ever taken out his anger on you in the past?" Sally explained that when Tony was angry with her, he sulked around the house or went out to be with his drinking buddies. Ms. Ortega then asked Sally and Mary if she could go out in the waiting room and bring back Tony and Rosa so the whole family could begin to work on this issue. Ms. Ortega asked who would prefer to be the spokesperson for this issue when the whole family was together in the interview. Sally stated that she would share the issue of Mary's pregnancy and hoped that the social worker could keep the discussion focused on the pregnancy and not a whole lot of other issues in the family.

What is your reaction to splitting up the family in this initial interview?

Do you think Ms. Ortega explored the issue of potential family violence when this secret is shared with Tony? What other ways exist for broaching this subject with the whole family?

What do you think is the purpose that is emerging for this family seeking help at Catholic Social Services? What are your own feelings about teen pregnancy, abortion, and options for the Romanos in this situation?

When the family was reassembled in the interview in their original seats, Sally explained what happened 2 days ago when Mary came to her with the news of her pregnancy. With all of the recent events in the family, this news was just too overwhelming for Sally, and she followed the recommendations of Father Soprano to come for help at Catholic Social Services. A long, heavy silence followed Sally's disclosure. Tony and Rosa sat stunned with the news. Rosa was the first to speak and stated that she was excited to learn that she would have a new great-grandchild. Tony was concerned that the financial pressures on the family would make it difficult to take on the responsibilities of a new family member. He asserted that Sally would definitely have to spend more time at home taking care of an infant and give up the notion of becoming a nurse. The adults all began discussing plans about the "new arrival," and Mary sat

(Continued)

(Continued)

quietly looking distraught. Ms. Ortega pointed out that Mary was being silent and asked Mary to share how she was feeling about her pregnancy. Sally began to speak for Mary, and Ms. Ortega had to remind Sally that it was Mary's turn to share. Mary looked up at her father and mother and said that she did not know what to do. She knew that an abortion was out of the question, and all adults nodded in agreement with this statement. Mary also shared that she did not know who the father was. Tony gasped in disbelief that his daughter might be sexually active with many partners and glared at Sally for this lapse in her parenting skills. Mary stated that she did not want to get married but also was not ready to be raising a baby. She had thought about adoption, but Sally and Rosa felt that "this was out of the question."

At this point in the interview, Ms. Ortega pointed out that they only had about 10 minutes left and wanted them to think about how she could help the family resolve the many issues that would have to be worked out with Mary's pregnancy. Ms. Ortega offered to see them twice more as a family to help them with this issue and also to address some of the other stressors that were bearing down on the family. Ms. Ortega also stated that today's session had focused on problems, and in the next session, she would like to explore family strengths and resources that the family could bring to bear on stressors. Ms. Ortega disclosed that she was a Latina mother with two of her own children at home. Rosa responded that she noticed an accent when Ms. Ortega spoke and wondered, "How long have you been in the country?" Ms. Ortega smiled and stated, "All of my life!" She explained that she was raised in a large immigrant family with parents who spoke mostly Spanish. It was not until she began grammar school that she began to learn how to speak American English. In the final minutes of the interview, all members of the family agreed to come to another appointment with Ms. Ortega, and an appointment was scheduled at the beginning of the following week.

Employ the crisis model presented in the individual assessment chapter (Chapter 10). What are the major stressors that the Romano family has weathered over the past year? What events and conditions have been stressful for this family? What event can be seen as the precipitant?

Events:

Conditions:

Precipitant:

In the individual change chapter (Chapter 11), we talked about the enabler role. How did Ms. Ortega exemplify this role with the family? How do you see her empowering this family to work on their own issues?

In this initial interview, Ms. Ortega did not ask the family to describe how they would like their family to be different. Is this an omission that Ms. Ortega should pick up on in the next family session?

How would you grade Ms. Ortega's interpersonal practice skills in this initial interview with the Romano family?

A+   A   A-   B+   B   B-   C+   C   C-   D+   D   D-

THE FAMILY CHANGE STAGE ●

As we discussed in the family assessment chapter (Chapter 12), interpersonal practitioners choose different ways of helping families to change based on their assessment of the family and the family's problems. This assessment enables the worker to develop hypotheses about how the family's problems are maintained or how solutions to problems may be prevented or both. This assessment is shared with the family and becomes the basis of their work together. These hypotheses can be categorized as relating to the following systemic processes: (1) family–environment transactions, (2) family–extended family transactions, and (3) transactions within the family among its members (Hartman & Laird, 1983).

There are approaches to helping the family to change related to each of these categories. In most families, workers will use interventions from two or all three categories as these relate to the family's problems and struggles. The following discussion in which each category is explored is meant to clarify the many interventions that can be applied in each of the three strategic areas.

Based on the genogram of the Romano family and the information you have seen in this first interview, can you see issues and stressors that are relevant to these three systemic areas?

Family–environment transactions:

Family–extended family transactions:

Transactions within the family:

Interventions Related to Family–Environment Transactions

The profession of social work in the United States emerged at the end of the 19th century in two approaches to helping poor families—that is, the Charity Organization Society (COS) and the settlement movement. The charity organization movement sent "friendly visitors" into the homes of poor families in order to use "moral suasion" to help families cope with the effects of poverty (Lubove, 1969). The settlement movement helped poor immigrant families assimilate to their new country by teaching American English, advocating for changes in the labor conditions in sweat shops, and lobbying for legislation that protected children from labor abuses (Addams, 1935).

In the past 50 years, social caseworkers developed programs that focused on poor families. Unfortunately, these various models had a tendency to blame these families for their troubles. In St. Paul, Minnesota, in the 1950s, Overton, Tinker, and Associates (1958) developed programs that targeted poor families who were receiving multiple community services. In Boston in the 1960s, Louise Bandler described a casework model that worked intensively with low-income, "disorganized" families (Pavenstedt & Malone, 1967). In the 1970s, in the first book to collect models of social casework practice, McBroom presented a "socialization" model that targeted low-income families (Roberts & Nee, 1970).

A major objective in working with family–environment transactions is to help the family members see their difficulties in the light of these transactions and not solely in terms that "blame" the family. In the organization and community change chapter (Chapter 17), we suggest ways that clients can be engaged to change environmental issues. In this chapter, we will focus on ways of working with families that help strengthen and empower them, that avoid blaming them unfairly, and that help them to be more effective in dealing with their environments. Our experience with such families supports our belief that most of them, in their own words, desire the same.

Very few texts have focused on these environmental issues. A notable exception is the work of Evan Imber-Black (1988). Her book *Families and Larger Systems* is one of the best treatments we have of the family–larger system issue. Imber-Black is especially strong on gender issues, as she discusses the impact on the family of the blame for family problems placed on the woman and the ways that the role of the woman in larger systems has an impact on family functioning.

> *Can you see any gender issues in the Romano family that have emerged around the way Sally performs her role as mother? What are your perspectives on the role of women in families? Can a woman be a mother, homemaker, breadwinner, partner, and daughter-in-law?*

When helping families with reference to their environmental problems, the interpersonal practitioner often functions as a *case manager*. The interpersonal practitioner may help families connect to community resources and services, may mediate conflicts that families are having with organizations, and may advocate with/for families that are being denied services or discriminated against by community agencies. This practice role was discussed in the individual change chapter (Chapter 11) in some detail and now needs to be adapted to working with families. There are a number of considerations that an interpersonal practitioner must take when performing this role with families:

1. The case manager with a family must not only think of linkages to services for individual family members but also must think of linkages required by the family as a whole system. An example of this is a recreational resource for the entire family or the family's connections to churches, schools, neighborhood organizations, etc.

2. When linking an individual family member to a resource, the interpersonal practitioner should consider the impact of that linkage on other family members. For example, helping one child to secure a special educational service may cause tension among siblings who may feel their individual needs are being ignored.

3. When linking a family member to a resource, the interpersonal practitioner should consider how other family members might support that individual to connect with and use the resource. The reverse issue is to consider how

internal family dynamics may deny the use of a resource to an individual. For example, a young woman with a mental disability was discouraged from attending a social program because her parents feared they would be stigmatized if her condition became known in the community.

Another approach is *family preservation services*. It is heavily focused on family–environment transactions, although workers may draw on interventions from all the categories of family work. It has been called by various names such as intensive home-based family treatment, home-based services, and family-based child welfare services. This model is widely employed and has been the subject of a great deal of attention from practitioners, policy makers, and researchers (Schuerman, Rzepnicki, & Littell, 1994; Wells & Biegel, 1991). Its major purpose is to work with families whose children are likely to run away or be placed in substitute care. Such families typically experience frequent crises.

Pecora, Fraser, and Haapala (1991) discussed an evaluation of one model of family preservation services developed by an organization known as Homebuilders, which was founded in 1974 in Tacoma, Washington. They described the program as follows:

IFPS (Intensive Family Preservation Service) therapists who use the Homebuilders model are distinguished from other types of family-centered or child welfare workers by the intensity and diversity of services they deliver. Homebuilders therapists provide a wide range of counseling, advocacy, training, and concrete services to families. They work with families in the home and focus on improving child and family functioning, so that children can be prevented from running away or being placed unnecessarily in substitute care.

Therapists carry small caseloads of two to four families at a time and they use various on-call procedures to provide 24-hour-a-day case coverage. Services are crisis-oriented, intensive, and brief. On average, they are provided for four weeks, and it is common for the workers to spend 10 hours a week with a family during the initial stages of treatment and five to eight hours a week thereafter

The Homebuilders program is based upon Rogerian, cognitive-behavioral, crisis, and ecological theories. The family and its social support system are viewed as the focus of service with an emphasis upon promoting client independence and psychosocial skill-building. In addition to teaching skills, Homebuilders therapists provide or arrange for a variety of concrete services to assist families to obtain food, clothing, housing, and transportation. Other community resources that provide families with food stamps, medical care, day care, and employment training may also be recommended by the worker Therapists also use a variety of clinical methods, including parenting training, active listening, contracting, values clarification, cognitive-behavioral strategies, and problem management techniques. (Pecora et al., 1991)

Wells and Biegel (1991), in a review of many studies, concluded that these kinds of services do prevent the placement of children. Despite this assertion, they noted that the findings may suggest that these services may delay rather than prevent placement. In addition, there may be different effects under varying circumstances, such as the child's age, nature of problems, and exact services offered.

Schuerman and colleagues (1994) summarized their findings as follows:

> There have been a number of well-controlled studies of family preservation. While the results of these studies vary somewhat, they suggest that the effects of these programs in preserving families are likely to be quite limited. A major problem in attaining the placement prevention objective is that of targeting, a problem that we need to understand much better. It is possible that there are inherent limitations in the extent to which programs such as family preservation can be effectively targeted. For some families, the programs do provide important resources and may result in modest benefits in the form of improved family and child functioning but these benefits are likely to be time limited. (p. 25)

Current research and evaluation studies of family preservation programs continue to demonstrate the positive impact that intensive, home-based programs have on poor families. See, for example, Fisher and Chamberlain (2000), Kirk and Griffith (2004), and Child Welfare Information Gateway (2010b). Though evaluation results continue to be positive about intensive, home-based service, it is also a reality that no program can overcome, for some families, the weaknesses of the child welfare service system and the destructive impact of the environments in which poor people live.

A third type of service focused on family–environment transactions is *family network therapy* (Attneave, 1976; Rueveni, 1979). This approach requires the worker to help the family convene its friends and neighbors to help the family solve problems. This takes on a similar character to a Native American practice of bringing family issues to the tribe. In fact, the first phase of family network therapy is referred to as "tribalization," in which the workers use a variety of tools to help this large group become cohesive. This approach is also similar to the healing ceremonies that espiritistas perform in Puerto Rican communities. Families in the community are brought into "el centro" to work on spirit problems that may be problematic for individuals and families in a neighborhood (Delgado & Humm-Delgado, 1982).

Family network therapy is seldom used to its full extent, although family workers do ask individuals in the family network to attend sessions when they see this as beneficial. As we shall point out in the chapter on organizational and community change (Chapter 17), people can be strengthened by enhancing their ties to their communities. Family network approaches can have this effect, and they should be used more frequently than they are. Workers may hesitate to interact with large groups, especially when they have become accustomed to working with nuclear families, and the issue of confidentiality may make it difficult for some families to share their struggles with other families in their neighborhood.

Family members are likely to feel empowered as they are helped to see that their private troubles are actually public issues, and environmental forces have created many of their problems. Interpersonal practitioners can work with families in the following ways:

- Teach family members advocacy skills and tactics such as letter writing, meetings with representatives, etc., that may be useful to effect environmental change
- Help family members link up with organizations that seek to have an impact on the environment, such as consumer advocacy groups
- Help family members connect with other families with the same investment in environmental change, such as self-help groups, neighborhood watch groups, etc.
- Join with the family in confronting an environmental target

Family–Extended Family Transactions

Some family problems are caused by problematic relationships between people and their extended families: their parents, siblings, aunts and uncles, and so on. Examples are a man who has not spoken to his parents for years because of their objection to his having married a woman of a different religion, a woman who has never forgiven her mother for failing to protect her from abuse by her stepfather even though the mother is now divorced from him, or a man who has been angry for many years with his father for divorcing his mother and failing to maintain contact with him while he was growing up.

These kinds of situations can have negative effects in the present for individuals and their family. These include an inability to obtain needed material resources from extended family members, feelings of resentment toward the "family of origin" that interfere with other relationships, and a repetition of dysfunctional patterns because of repressed thoughts and feelings regarding the "family of origin."

As Hartman and Laird (1983) pointed out, the processes of assessment regarding the extended family may also have treatment implications, and the genogram is one of the most useful assessment procedures for uncovering these issues. Couples, for example, are often helped to identify the sources of conflict they experience as stemming from different belief systems with which they were raised that are illuminated through their discussion of their respective family histories. They may have previously falsely attributed these conflicts to their individual values, rather than family of origin, differences. Once clarified, this can help them begin a process of negotiation as to what they want their current family life to be, which will be grounded in a new, more current view of their relationship.

When completing the genogram, the family may uncover repetitious patterns of problematic behavior, such as substance abuse, suicide, separations, cutoffs, etc., that the family is presently facing. This awareness may help the family address these issues in the present and make decisions about what they need to do to resolve these situations in the present.

> *Based on the Romano genogram and the initial interview, can you see repetitious patterns in the family that are playing themselves out in this family? What kinds of cultural/value differences may exist between a Polish American family and an Italian American family?*

Another way of assisting families to deal with extended family issues is to help them plan how they will handle occasions when they will see extended family members. These occasions may be in the nature of holiday visits or of attendance at such events as weddings and funerals. One aspect of such help is to discuss the event before it occurs. The family members may become aware of feelings and thoughts of which they were not aware as a result of this discussion. This new awareness may aid them in freeing themselves from painful memories. It may also aid them in identifying and seeking solutions for problems that they previously had been avoiding.

Sometimes the family members determine, with the help of the worker, that they wish to arrange an interaction with certain family members so they can raise issues that are important to them. This interaction can be in the form of an e-mail, a letter, a phone call, or a face-to-face visit. This interaction may range from obtaining missing information on a genogram to seeking to resolve long-standing conflicts and cutoffs.

As the family member writes a letter or creates an e-mail to her or his extended family, this message often is shared with the worker in either its final or preliminary version. This allows the worker to help the family member deal with thoughts and feelings that arose in the course of writing it. In some circumstances, the family members may decide not to mail the letter or send the e-mail; they may have concluded that either they or the extended family are not yet ready to deal with that content.

When the family wishes to have an opportunity to interact with the extended family but distance or other factors prevent a face-to-face visit, a telephone call may be used. The worker will usually help the family plan for the call and, if requested, be present in the room when the call is made to give feedback afterward. This call also may be preliminary to a visit.

There are two types of visits. One occurs when the family takes a trip to visit the extended family. The other occurs when the extended family is invited to come to the family's location to attend a session with the worker. The latter may be easy to arrange when the extended family members live in the same state.

The interpersonal practitioner has a different role in an extended family session than in a nuclear family session because the practitioner's treatment contract is with the latter. The interpersonal practitioner can indicate at the beginning of the session what role, such as that of mediator or as facilitator, he or she plans on taking. The facilitator role can be one of helping those present determine the purposes of the session and then helping them carry these out by assisting the members to listen to one another, to avoid interrupting each other, and to clarify the intent of their communications.

Transactions Within the Family

The interpersonal practitioner and the family must consider what aspect of family life may be altered. In the chapter on family assessment (Chapter 12), we presented the following dimensions of family life: (1) *phase of the family life cycle*, (2) *family culture and traditions*, (3) *family emotional climate*, (4) *family communication patterns*, (5) *family boundaries*, (6) *family structure*, (7) *family resources*, and (8) *interactions with other systems*. We have already discussed interventions with family resources and interactions with other systems in this chapter, and we now turn to interventions that address the first six dimensions of family dynamics.

● PHASE OF THE FAMILY LIFE CYCLE

In a sense, anything a worker does is with reference to the stage of the family's life cycle. Some stressors, such as the birth of a first child, preparation of children to begin school, conflicts with adolescent children as they struggle with sexuality, feelings about adult children leaving home, and caretaking issues involving children and their elderly parents, are characteristic of one stage and not another. The worker will often use one of the following approaches to help with these types of family life stage issues.

1. *Anticipatory Socialization.* This involves helping the family anticipate and plan for the stage. By helping families to recognize that life stage changes bring new challenges, families can decide for themselves how they want to tackle the stressors that emerge in a given stage. Families may have to change how they divide up their time and labor in order to respond to the stressors in a stage. For example, work schedules may have to be juggled or one of the working parents may have to drop out of the workforce in order to care for infants and small children in the family. Parents may decide to join support groups for expectant parents, for parents of children approaching school age, parents coping with an "empty nest," or parents facing retirement.

2. *Social Skills Training.* The worker may provide the family with literature on skills or may teach the skill through giving information, engaging the family in role play, or offering himself or herself as a model in demonstrating a skill. Such skills may include problem solving, decision making, communication, parenting, and limit-setting techniques. Some of these techniques are discussed in some detail in the individual and group change chapters (Chapters 11 and 15).

3. *Coping.* The changes and associated stressors that families face as they move through their life stages are inevitable. For many families, some stages may be easier to navigate than others. This may be related to family of origin struggles that have been repeated from generation to generation. By helping the family to become aware of these patterns and encouraging them to engage in problem solving and decision making about how they want to approach these issues in the present, families may become empowered to cope with these stages. A family that meditates together may be freed to work in the present on issues that are haunting them from their past. We previously discussed various stress reduction techniques in the individual change chapter (Chapter 11) that can be used to help families cope with life stage stressors that cannot be avoided.

Family Culture and Traditions

In the chapter on values (Chapter 3), we discussed how important cultural sensitivity and cultural competence is in the social work profession. Like "the prime directive" in the earlier episodes of *Star Trek*—that is, this directive stated that the crew of the Starship Enterprise was not supposed to interfere or try to change the alien cultures that they encountered in their explorations—the social work profession is under a similar proscription not to interfere or change the ethnic values of our clients. When working with various ethnic families, it is likely that interpersonal practitioners will encounter families that have different values from the practitioner and different values of the social work profession, which has a secular, progressive, and social justice ideology.

For example, families may have roots in Christian fundamentalism and political conservatism. Sometimes their struggles may be exacerbated by these cultural values. For example, a rural family may be struggling with economic hardship and providing for the needs of its members (i.e., nine children, one with autism, an elderly grandparent with dementia, and one parent in the labor force with a low wage job with no health benefits). The family's fundamentalist values do not accept birth control, do not accept secular public education so that the children are "homeschooled," and do not accept help from "the state" in the form of food stamps, Medicaid, and other public resources to which they are eligible. None of the children are vaccinated against childhood diseases, and none of the family members receive health services such as prenatal care and annual health checkups. Neighbors are concerned that the children look malnourished and are poorly clothed when the children sneak over to their neighbors' houses to ask for food. How does the interpersonal practitioner help this family cope in a way that it does not infringe on their values short of protective services from the child welfare system?

The previous case example exaggerates the value conflicts in working with families but is presented in order to highlight the dilemmas that interpersonal practitioners face when working with families to change their circumstances that are imbedded in cultural values. A feminist social worker may believe that parental authority should be shared with husband and wife in an "equal partnership," yet this value conflicts with the ethnic values of the family. The public stance of the National Association of Social Workers (NASW) is "pro-choice" (National Association of Social Workers, 2009), yet many families that interpersonal practitioners contact are "pro-life." We have presented in the family assessment chapter (Chapter 12) that the interpersonal practitioner has a responsibility to discuss potential value conflicts and obstacles in the treatment relationship with the family and make it clear that the family is the final authority in making decisions about what course of action they might take. The role of the interpersonal practitioner is to empower the family to act within their own values, not to change their values to fit NASW or the worker's values.

Families will differ considerably from one another, and one of the many sources of such differences is their ethnic and cultural background. This is not to say that all families of a particular cultural background are alike but rather that the experiences of the family as they relate to its culture are very important. For any of the statements we have made regarding how to work with families, we must take this into account.

An extensive literature has been evolving on the subject of how work with families should be oriented to cultural differences (Ho, 1987; Lum, 2005;

McGoldrick, Giordano, & Garcia-Preto, 2005; McGoldrick, Pearce, & Giordano, 1982). This literature is a rich one, and we cannot do justice to it here. A few of the major points repeated again and again by these writers are the following:

1. There is a great deal of cultural diversity, as it affects the family, within each ethnic group, and this is often overlooked.

2. The history of the group within the society has had a strong affect on the lives of families, albeit in different ways depending on the families' own experiences.

3. There are many myths about each type of ethnic family in the social science literature that present a negative picture of family life in that ethnic group: a picture that focuses on pathology rather than strength.

4. Many ethnic families are resistant to professional help, and the reasons for this must be understood.

A number of practice principles for work with families that have been oppressed on the basis of their ethnicity have evolved. Some of these are the following:

1. An important goal of work with the family must be empowerment of the family, which means that the family must be helped to see itself as entitled to and capable of working toward a better environment for itself.

2. Environmental forces such as poverty, job discrimination, lack of adequate housing, etc., must be seen as important factors in promoting family breakdown when they are present. The worker must avoid blaming the family for family circumstances caused by these social forces.

3. The strengths of the family must be recognized and reinforced. As Boyd-Franklin stated in relationship to African American families (Boyd-Franklin, 1989).

> The focus on strengths in terms of Black family life-styles began in the late 1960s. Hill (1972) cites strong kinship bonds, strong work orientation, adaptability of family roles, high achievement orientation, and strong religious orientation as important strengths of the Black families he studied. It is important to note here that such strengths should not be read comparatively (i.e., as perceived to be stronger than in other ethnic groups/cultures) but merely as inherent within the Black cultural framework. (p. 16)

4. In joining with the family, the interpersonal practitioner should understand that different cultures prescribe different ways of developing relationships,

and the worker should seek to understand the implications of this for the family in question. This is particularly important with ethnic groups in which the role of the man in the family has been minimized by the larger culture.

5. The assessment of the family should be done in the light of the expectations for families found within the ethnic group rather than the expectations of the larger society. Especially important is for the interpersonal practitioner to be aware of how her or his own family experience in her or his own culture can bias this assessment.

6. The interpersonal practitioner should understand and work with communication styles created by the family's ethnic conditions. Thus, a stereotype of family therapy in which family members politely hear each other out may not be what the family has experienced.

7. The interpersonal practitioner should seek to understand the social networks and resources available *within* the ethnic community. The churches; indigenous healers; local heroes, such as athletes whose origin was in the community; and wise elders in the community may have much to offer the family in solving its problems that are typically overlooked by workers unfamiliar with the ethnic community in question.

8. The interpersonal practitioner must understand how her or his ways of working with families may be perceived in the light of the family's cultural experiences. Some topics may be forbidden, whereas others are expected ones. Some interventions, such as telling family members to change their seating patterns, may be seen as rude. Asking questions of some family members before others are asked these questions may be seen as intentional insults—for example, how will the parents view a worker who asks questions of children that the parents think should be asked?

This list could be an endless one. In summary, we state that there is no substitute for the interpersonal practitioner learning as much as she or he feasibly can about the culture, history, language pattern, and traditions of the ethnic group with which the family identifies. A good idea for interpersonal practitioners, who do not have this knowledge, is to expose her or his work to the scrutiny of other professionals who do have such knowledge and who ideally have grown up in the group.

Family Emotional Climate

By family emotional climate, we mean occasions when family members express similar emotions. Thus, one might observe a family in which all members appear elated or anxious or depressed. The shared emotion may be a product of "contagion" among the family members or may be a reaction to a common stimulus, such as a story told by one family member. One approach to modifying an emotional state, if this is desirable, is to bring the emotional state to the awareness of the family members, if it is not already evident, and then to explore its sources.

On some occasions, the interpersonal practitioner will wish to increase the expression of a "positive" emotion related to caring for or supporting other members. One way of doing this is through an exercise such as "giving and receiving compliments." As described by Lange and Jakubowski (1976), this exercise begins with the worker pointing out behaviors to family members that discourage compliments, such as stating that they are not valid or the member giving the compliment depreciates herself in the process. The worker can demonstrate, and the family members can practice giving brief, unqualified compliments. The exercise consists of each family member giving a compliment to the person on her right and receiving an appropriate response. Each member giving a compliment then expresses something that she liked about how the compliment was received by the person complimented.

The interpersonal practitioner often has the objective of helping family members become more aware of their feelings. This can be accomplished by asking them to share their feelings or their emotional reactions to family events with each other. This can also be accomplished by involving the family in "family sculpting," which has been described in the chapter on family assessment (Chapter 12).

Family Communication Patterns

Very often problematic communication patterns are embedded in repetitive sequences of behaviors among family members. The following are some of the ways workers have used to deal with this type of situation:

Communication Training

Workers use many techniques to help family members communicate clearly with one another. One is to ask members to talk directly to each other rather than "about" each other. Speaking about one person to another is a form of what is termed *triangulation*, and this type of communication prevents family members from solving interactional issues; instead it may intensify them.

Another technique is to ask family members for a short time period to repeat what the previous person has said before making any comment. This technique requires family members to take note of the ways they change the subject or otherwise ignore the previous comment. The first step in the LARA (listen, assess, respond, add information) procedure is to listen carefully to what is being said in a contentious situation. LARA is a technique designed to de-escalate interpersonal conflict and may be used to help families communicate more successfully. LARA is discussed in more detail in the group change chapter (Chapter 15).

Another type of intervention is to ask that the family replace one type of dysfunctional communication with a more successful form of communication, even if the new type of communication still poses problems to the family. This replacement can take many forms as tasks for the family to initiate between sessions. This strategy can have the effect of initiating a change process that culminates ultimately with a set of communications that is appropriate for the family. An example of this occurred in a family in which the husband was underinvolved with a child. A grandparent was critical of the mother in this family. The grandmother was attending sessions, and the worker asked her to care for the child for a day. The father, in turn, was critical of the grandmother's handling of the situation, and this ultimately led to his greater involvement.

Family Boundaries and Structure

We place these two dimensions together, as the same interventions are often used to affect both of these. The first intervention discussed under this section is role clarification, which may help a family deal with role conflicts they are experiencing. The procedure helps each family member clarify their expectations about family roles and to surface role confusions, conflicts, and hidden agendas. By bringing light to these issues, the family has a chance to renegotiate family roles and expected role performance.

The individual assessment chapter (Chapter 10) discussed many role problems that emerged in the lives of clients, and the person-in-environment (PIE) framework was presented as a way of categorizing these role problems. From the first interview with the Romano family, can you see any role problems that they are struggling with presently?

Take each of the family members and think about their role problems. Review the PIE system and categorize the conflict for the following roles:

   Rosa—widow—?

   Tony—breadwinner—?

   Sally—student—?

   Mary—teen mother—?

The role clarification procedure helps family members to share their expectations about various family roles, to surface discrepancies or conflicts in expectations, and then to help members reach a resolution to the conflicts. Many role conflicts in families revolve around complementary roles—for example, mother–father, husband–wife, parent–child, etc.

For example, a newly married couple was experiencing a role conflict about what each expected of the other about "fixing lunch." Every morning, the wife would fix lunch for her husband and put the lunch in a small paper bag for her husband to take to work. This was what her mother had done for her father. The husband would dutifully take the lunch in the brown paper bag and put it in his briefcase. Later at work, he would often throw the lunch away and go out to lunch with his buddies. Tensions arose because the wife thought it was ridiculous that her husband could not make his own lunch, and the husband was irritated that he would have to hide his lunch from his buddies. During the role clarification procedure, they both expressed their feelings and reactions to "fixing lunch" and realized that they had not communicated their expectations of this simple marital issue. They quickly resolved that the wife would not fix lunch for her husband and therefore her husband would not have to throw away his lunch at work. If he wanted to take a lunch with him then he would make it himself.

Reframing helps a family to see things from a different perspective. Families have a view of their situation that was created by their experiences together. Minuchin and Fishman (1981) stated,

> They have made their own assessment of their problems, their strengths, and their possibilities. They are asking the therapist to help with the reality that they have framed. . . . Therapy starts, therefore, with the clash between two framings of reality. The family's framing is relevant for the continuity and maintenance of the organism more or less as it is; the therapeutic framing is related to the goal of moving the family toward a more differentiated and competent dealing with their dysfunctional reality. (p. 74)

Examples of reframing are declaring that a father whom the family labels as overprotective is "caring," that a mother whom the family labels as uninvolved is "working too hard at her job," and a child whom the family labels as a troublemaker is "keeping the number of family rules within reasonable limits."

We take a more general view of reframing and do not like the tone of Minuchin and Fishman (1981) that seems to imply that the therapist's view (or frame) is somehow better than the "dysfunctional" frame of the family. We would prefer to see that there are many frames of reference in which to perceive the world. The interpersonal practitioner's and family's perspectives may be different—and one not necessarily better than the other. From our perspective, we all live by "fictions" that have been generated by our life experiences (Feinstein & Krippner, 1988). The therapeutic value of reframing lies in the sharing of different mythologies so that the family can understand its own fictions and then decide whether they want to modify them.

> A very old Chinese Taoist story describes a farmer in a poor country village. He was considered very well-to-do because he owned a horse that he used for plowing and for transportation. One day, his horse ran away. All his neighbors exclaimed how terrible this was, but the farmer simply said, "Maybe."
>
> A few days later, the horse returned and brought two wild horses with it. The neighbors all rejoiced at his good fortune, but the farmer just said, "Maybe."
>
> The next day, the farmer's son tried to ride one of the wild horses; the horse threw him and broke his leg. The neighbors all offered their sympathy for his misfortune, but the farmer again said, "Maybe."
>
> The next week, conscription officers came to the village to take young men for the army. They rejected the farmer's son because of his broken leg. When the neighbors told him how lucky he was, the farmer replied, "Maybe." (Bandler & Grinder, 1982)

This basic Taoist philosophy points out that meaning we give to events in our lives is heavily dependents on the "frame" in which we perceive it. Reframing is a technique that helps the family to see things from a different frame of reference and possibly change their responses and behaviors to the event.

Restructuring involves a direct manipulation of the family's interactions, physical space, or tasks to change the coalitions among family members (Minuchin & Fishman, 1981). Three examples of this follow:

1. The worker directed the father to speak directly to his son rather than talk to the mother about the son.

2. The worker asked the mother and her son to change chairs so the mother was seated next to the father. The worker then moved the mother's and father's chairs into a position in which they sat facing one another.

3. The worker assigned the father to be responsible for all child discipline for one week.

Task assignment is another important approach not only for providing assessment information but for promoting change in families. A task is an activity in which the family engages to attain a goal. Tasks may be created by the worker and, in this form, are sometimes referred to as "behavioral assignments" or as "homework." They also may be developed out of joint discussions between the family and the worker, and we prefer this latter approach as a more empowering one than the former (Tolson, Reid, & Garvin, 1994). The following reasons are offered for the family to carry out mutual tasks:

1. The task itself may involve a skill the family desires to strengthen, such as the family planning a family outing or several family members engaging in an activity when they do not usually do so.

2. Carrying out the task may help the family change an undesirable family condition. An example of this is a task in a family that has a member with a developmental disability. The family agreed upon the task of helping her function independently outside the home by taking public transportation and making purchases. They will do this by accompanying her to these places and coaching her on appropriate behavior.

In working tasks out with families, the worker and family will specify when and where the task is to be performed and what each member's responsibility is in carrying out the task. If carrying out the task requires skills the family members do not possess, time will be spent in the session to acquire these skills. Some tasks will be carried out between sessions, but some may also be executed during a session. In the chapter on contracting (Chapter 8), we have discussed the Task Implementation Sequence (TIS), which is a motivational technique that can help families follow through on tasks between sessions.

We now return to the second interview with the Romano family.

Second Session With the Romano Family

In this interview, Rosa did not attend but Tony, Sally, and Mary were present. The mood in this second family session was much more relaxed than the first session. The family sat in the interview room in the same configuration as the first session except there was no empty chair between Sally and Tony. Ms. Ortega thanked the family members present for returning and asked them how things had been going in the family over these past few days. Sally explained that Rosa chose not to come to this session, but the whole family had several discussions about Mary's pregnancy over the weekend. Tony stated that his older brother had a similar situation in his family with a teenage pregnancy. His brother's family had decided to keep the baby and raise her as a member of their family. This was a difficult decision, and it dramatically changed

(Continued)

(Continued)

the family when an infant was added to the family. Lots of tension arose between the teen mother and her parents about how to raise this child. In the end, Tony's brother felt it was a mistake to keep the baby. Sally explained that they had reached a decision to put Mary's baby up for adoption. This was a difficult decision because Rosa wanted to keep the baby, but the other family members felt it would be better for the rest of the family members if they considered adoption.

Ms. Ortega complemented the family for working out this important decision on their own and explained that Catholic Social Services has an adoption program. Ms. Ortega explained that she could set up an appointment with the adoption worker, who would explain various adoption procedures and help them decide how they wanted the adoption to occur. The family members agreed and Ms. Ortega left the interview room and returned with Ms. Jones, the adoption worker, with her appointment book in hand. After the introductions, Ms. Jones scheduled an appointment with the Romano family and left the room.

> The chapter on individual change (Chapter 11) talks about brokerage strategies and presents a number of linking strategies. Some rely on client action and some involve worker action. Do you think Ms. Ortega selected a strategy that disempowered the Romanos? Should she have taken a less active strategy and just given the family Ms. Jones's name and phone number with the expectation that they would call and make an appointment later?

Ms. Ortega asked the Romano family if she could explore more of the stressors that were bearing down on them and discuss other ways Catholic Social Services may be of help to the family. Sally agreed to this, but Tony and Mary seemed to be less interested in further exploration of issues now that the decision to pursue adoption had been made. Ms. Ortega explained that she would like to map out on a time line all of the changes and events that the family had experienced over the past year. Ms. Ortega had brought a large newsprint pad and drew a long line across the middle of this pad in "landscape" orientation. About a quarter of the way toward the right-hand side of the paper, she placed an X on the line with today's date. To the left near this X she placed another X with the following note: "Mary discloses pregnancy to family." She then turned the pad toward the family members and asked them to think of changes and events that had happened over the past year, as well as any impending changes that they knew about in the next few months. Sally spoke first and talked about the death of Tony's father and Rosa moving into Charity's old room. Tony pointed out that he had been laid off for about 6 months. Mary added that it had been a year since Charity moved out after disclosing that she was a lesbian. This disclosure caused a big fight with Tony, who vowed he would never have a "lesbo" in his house. In the next 15 minutes, the family members filled up the line with many events and changes, some affecting the whole family and others mostly affecting individuals. When the line exercise was complete, Ms. Ortega held up the pad for the family to see, and they were astonished at all of the events they had to deal with over the past year. Ms. Ortega stated that the line is proof of the strengths in the Romano family to cope with many life stressors. Sally pointed out that many of the events were still playing themselves out with Mary's pregnancy, Rosa's recent diagnosis as pre-Parkinson's, and Tony's need to make a decision to accept a buyout from Ford and get training for another career or hang on and hope to be called back when the economy turns around. Ms. Ortega asked the family members to evaluate and comment on what they had learned about themselves from the life line exercise. All three members felt they were surprised by how much the family had experienced over the past year and that the exercise had been helpful.

Ms. Ortega asked the family if there were any of these stressors that they would want to think about working on now. Sally commented that many of the stressors were "out of our control." Tony agreed and stated, "I can't do anything about the lousy economy!" Sally interjected, "You could stop going to the bar with your laid off drinking buddies and spend more time looking for another job!" An argument ensued between Sally and Tony about her desire to continue her nursing education and her aspiration to get a nursing job, which would help the family finances. At this point, Ms. Ortega interrupted the argument and pointed out that even though some stressors were out of the family's control, it was still possible for the family to plan and take actions that would help them cope with events. She pointed out that the family had successfully found a way to cope with Mary's pregnancy.

Ms. Ortega explained that she would like to engage the Romanos in another exercise that would help them decide whether they wanted to continue to work with her in family counseling. The family members nodded in agreement, and Ms. Ortega handed each family member a 5 x 7 card and a pencil. She asked each of them to write down "things you want changed about your family or things you wish were different about the family." Ms. Ortega explained that she would also write down several suggestions on one of the cards. She explained that she would collect all of the cards and paraphrase various items from each of the cards, and the family could discuss the ideas that were expressed on the card. It is not necessary for members to know who wrote the suggestion, but it is important for family members to discuss each of the items that Ms. Ortega read off the cards.

When all family members were finished writing suggestions on their cards, Ms. Ortega collected the cards and briefly looked over what had been written. She explained that there were many good suggestions, and one in particular had been suggested on all of the cards. She stated, "All of the cards wished that the family could find a way to get along better with less arguing and more cooperation! One card wished that this cooperation could even include Charity." After a brief pause, Sally commented, "Well, that's a nice wish, but I'm not sure that's realistic unless you have some kind of magic wand that you can wave over us!" Ms. Ortega smiled and stated, "I do have a magic wand, but I left it in my office. It is only used on very, very dysfunctional families, and the Romanos are much more capable of solving their own troubles!" The family members looked surprised and then laughed. Ms. Ortega, who was also laughing, suggested that the family talk about ways they could achieve this wish.

(Continued)

(Continued)

The Romano family discussed this goal, and Ms. Ortega helped them to list on the newsprint pad many of the possibilities that emerge from the discussion. When they had exhausted suggestions about what they might do, Ms. Ortega asked them to prioritize the list and see if any of the items could be combined. Sally pointed out that many of the suggestions revolve around issues that she and Tony need to work out in their marriage. Sally wondered out loud whether she and Tony might benefit from some kind of marital counseling, which may help them resolve some of the conflicts and stressors the family is experiencing. Tony frowned at this idea, but did admit that it might bring some more peace to the family. Tony was not sure that marital counseling would necessarily deal with all of the issues that the family was facing at this point in time. Ms. Ortega pointed out that she was willing to meet with Sally and Tony for a trial session of marital counseling. If that session seems to be helpful in reducing some of the conflicts in the family, they could decide whether they wanted to schedule other sessions. Sally and Tony agreed to try out one session, and Ms. Ortega arranged a time for the next week. Mary commented that she was glad that her parents agreed to try marital counseling. She hoped that this would help the family deal with some of the conflicts that were going on inside the family.

In the closing minutes of this session, Ms. Ortega asked Sally and Tony if they could complete an important task before the marital session for the next week. She explained that many couples think that their conflicts are caused by issues in their marriage, when in fact, some of the conflicts come from issues that are related to their respective families of origin. In order to explore these issues, Ms. Ortega asked both Sally and Tony to take a look at three generations in their family tree and to sketch out their family tree with parents, grandparents, and siblings. She handed them a sheet with basic notations for a genogram (i.e., names, gender, age, and date of deaths) and explained that they might make notation about deaths, separations, divorces, personal struggles such as mental illness, alcoholism, substance abuse, etc. When they return the following week, Ms. Ortega will organize these family histories into a genogram, which is a useful tool for understanding families over time. Sally and Tony were curious about this idea and agreed to find out about their respective family trees.

Ms. Ortega ended the session by stating that this might be the last time she would see Mary. She wondered whether there were any questions that Mary had about her two interviews with Ms. Ortega. Mary responded that she was a little nervous about her pregnancy and hoped that the adoption worker would be able to answer all of her questions about birthing and adoption. Ms. Ortega reassured Mary that Ms. Jones was a competent worker, and Mary would be in good hands.

Ms. Ortega then asked all of them to evaluate today's session and whether the two exercises, about the time line of stressful events and the card activity that focused on goals, was useful for the family. The members agreed that the card activity and the discussion that followed helped them focus on next steps for the family. Sally stated that the time line activity was difficult to see because it pointed out so many things that the family has to continue to address.

She was glad that she and Tony had agreed to continue to work on issues. Ms. Ortega reminded them of their appointment with Ms. Jones and the marital session set up for next week. How do you feel about the changing membership in family sessions? How do you feel about Rosa's decision not to attend the second session? How do you feel about the decision to work only with Sally and Tony in the third session? Did Ms. Ortega respect the family members' decisions to leave the action system?

How would you grade Ms. Ortega's interpersonal practice skills in this second session with the Romano family?

A+   A   A-   B+   B   B-   C+   C   C-   D+   D   D-

ENDINGS ●

The ending stage of family work is not basically different from the ending stage in work with individuals and groups. The worker will help the family assess the progress it has made and the goals it has reached and plan for future services it may need. Maintenance of change is an important point for the worker to consider, and she or he should help the family plan ways of maintaining changes and coping with threats to this. The worker and family members are likely to have feelings about their departure from each other, and these should be discussed. The service should be evaluated in terms of its strengths and weaknesses.

A special issue for work with families is *when* to terminate. The worker should remember that the goal of family work should be to help the family become an effective system for assisting its members to cope with their problems. It is not intended to help every member solve every problem. When it appears that the family has become more effective in functioning in this way, the worker should withdraw. This usually means that the time for the worker to withdraw is when some family conditions, such as skill, structure, communication style, or way of interacting with the environment, that stood in the way of family coping have been improved.

At this point in the chapter, we want to review the various interventions that have been employed by Ms. Ortega with the Romano family.

Can you identify the composition of the client system as it emerged in this case?

(Continued)

(Continued)

Can you identify the composition of the target system as it has changed in this case?

Can you identify the composition of the worker system?

What were the in-session structured activities that Ms. Ortega employed?

What is your reaction to the "metaphoric intervention," which involved the magic wand? Do you think this was effective?

What homework tasks did Ms. Ortega assign to the Romano family?

How do you feel about the way Ms. Ortega evaluated the two family sessions?

● SUMMARY

Our approach to work with families emphasizes family–environment transactions, ways of coping with oppressive environmental circumstances such as racism and sexism, family empowerment, and the worker's own investment in working to help create an environment conducive to healthy family functioning. We subsequently examined the occasions when workers will work directly with families. We point out reasons for thinking about families even when working with clients individually.

The next sections of the chapter dealt with the phases of family work, which we divided into (1) prior to the first family session, (2) the initial sessions, (3) the family change stage, and (4) the endings. Specific information on the role of the worker at each stage was presented, and particular attention was paid to the family change stage. Change activities of the worker were described as related to family–environment transactions, family–extended family transactions, and transactions within the family. In order to help students understand how concepts can be applied in practice, we presented two family sessions with a hypothetical family. This case example was interactive and asked students to relate concepts to what was transpiring in these interviews.

CHAPTER 14

ASSESSING GROUPS

Groups are ubiquitous!

—Brett A. Seabury (BAS; 1995)

We begin this chapter by asking the reader to complete a simple self-assessment of her or his membership in groups over their life span. Turn a blank piece of paper on its side (i.e., landscape orientation), and draw a line across the middle of this page. On the left end of this line place an asterisk (*), which represents birth, and on the right end place the omega symbol (Ω), which represents death. This line will represent your life line, and you need to place an X on the line where you think you are now! You now have a visual representation of your life line. The next step is to recall and write down many of the groups that you experienced in your childhood, youth, and young adulthood. Next write down many of the groups that you belong to now, and the next, more difficult, task is to write down some of the groups that you think you will belong to in the future. This exercise is not meant to be a comprehensive statement of all of your membership groups, but most students who complete this exercise can come up with about 25 groups in 10 minutes. We will refer back to this exercise as we discuss the many kinds of groups that social work practitioners lead in practice. Figure 14.1 gives you an example of what this exercise might look like.

Figure 14.1	Groups Over the Life Span

*				X			Ω
Preschool	Elementary	High School	Higher Education	Work	Health/ Recreation	Retirement
Head Start	classes	cliques	clubs	teams	Yoga	Gray Panthers
Montessori	Scouts	teams	sororities	cliques	book clubs	AARP
siblings	4-H	MySpace	SWAA	unions	AA	RNC

Note: SWAA = Social Welfare Action Alliance; RNC = Republican National Committee.

● TYPES OF GROUPS

Social workers may lead, be members in, and refer clients to many kinds of groups. There are many typologies that attempt to organize these groups (Garvin, 1996; Toseland & Rivas, 2008), but for our purposes in this book we will describe the most common groups that social workers encounter. Task groups are the most common groups that social workers will experience in practice. The agency context of social work practice requires that social workers are involved in various organizational groups, such as teams, committees, boards, etc. Many of these task groups are interdisciplinary and involve decision making in agencies. For example, social workers may be members of discharge planning groups in large institutions like hospitals, as well as educational planning groups for struggling students in school settings. Social workers may also be involved in interagency task groups that are surveying and planning programs for specific populations in the community. For example, social workers may be involved in a community task force surveying the needs and available services for homebound elders. Social workers may also participate in various political and social action groups, such as Gay Liberation Front (GLF), Mothers Against Drunk Driving (MADD), National Association of Black Social Workers (NABSW), Social Welfare Action Alliance (SWAA), etc. Task groups are organized to plan and make changes in the environment and are not focused on changing their individual members, though it is clear that membership in social action groups does have an impact on their individual members' sense of community and empowerment.

The other large category of groups involves individual change groups. These groups are focused on helping or making changes in their individual members. There are many examples of groups that reflect this focus—treatment groups, support groups, self-help groups, developmental groups, consciousness-raising (CR) groups, etc. Social workers may lead treatment groups in schools, psychiatric and medical hospitals, VA hospitals, juvenile detention centers, nonprofit agencies, and private practice. For example, social workers may run inpatient and outpatient therapy groups for clients with depression, eating disorders, substance abuse, domestic violence, and PTSD.

Self-help groups are closely related to treatment groups. These groups, however, are not run by professionals, even though they are focused on changing the undesirable behaviors of their members. The classic self-help groups are 12-step groups like AA, Al-Anon, Narcotics Anonymous (NA), Parents Anonymous, etc., which are led by long-term members who are familiar with the 12-step program. Though some of these groups may meet in institutions most meet in churches, community centers, and public settings. These groups are important in social work practice because many clients are referred to and involved in these groups.

In some books (Kurtz, 1997), self-help groups are classified as support groups, but we believe that self-help groups are more like treatment groups because of their focus on dysfunctional and undesirable behaviors. These groups reflect the disease metaphor discussed in Chapter 2. Many of the support groups that are run by social workers and other professionals fit more closely in the life metaphor because they do not view their members as mentally ill or deviant. Instead, their perspective fits the "manure happens" view. People go through life doing the best they can when sudden, tragic events happen that throw individuals and families off their life course. Individuals may suffer debilitating accidents, sudden diseases, catastrophic losses of loved ones, etc. Professionally run support groups, for example, may be designed to help members deal with grief and loss issues, such as the death of a child, partner, or close relative; to cope with a cancer diagnosis; or to cope with the debilitating, emotional effects of natural disasters, such as earthquakes, tornadoes, hurricanes.

The roots of social group work were firmly rooted in the settlement movement of the 19th century (Addams, 1935; Toseland & Rivas, 2008). Social workers in settlements and community centers lead many kinds of developmental groups, such as recreational activities for youth, scouting programs, after-school activity programs, yoga and meditation groups, enrichment programs for the elderly, etc. These groups fit the life model because they are not organized around a deficit model but instead are seen as enrichment and educational purposes that promote character development, healthy lifestyles, and citizenship. Scouts, 4-H, Camp Fire Girls, Little League, soccer leagues, bowling leagues, softball leagues, bicycle clubs, bird-watching clubs, and many other membership groups in adulthood promote ongoing healthy lifestyles. It appears that social workers in recent years have moved away from leading these kinds of groups and instead are leading therapy groups. This change may reflect the economic reality that insurance and managed care companies pay for treatment groups but not developmental groups, which are seen as "voluntary activities."

CR groups often emerge from support groups and may transition into social change groups as group members come to realize that their troubles are connected to injustices or inequalities in the environment. Social workers have led CR groups for prostitutes; depressed women; lesbian, gay, bisexual, and transgender (LGBT) clients; and welfare mothers (Brody, 1987). In a CR group the goal is to help members realize they are not alone and that the characteristic they share in common is the injustice they experience in society's institutional structures (i.e., schools, police, and courts). Social agencies often eschew these groups because of the potential conflict that arises as these groups' transition into advocacy and social change. On a political spectrum, CR groups tend to be on the opposite end from therapy and self-help groups.

Now that we have covered some of the most common groups that social workers will encounter in practice, go back to your life line and look at the groups that you have experienced. Write a "tk" next to task groups, "th" next to therapy groups, "sh" next to self-help groups, "su" next to support groups, "dv" next to developmental groups, and "cr" next to CR groups. You may discover that some of your groups do not fit into any of these categories. For example, family, peer groups, and gangs are referred to in the group literature as "natural groups." You may also discover that by thinking about these groups you have recalled other groups that you have belonged to over your life span. Because you will be running groups as a social worker, you now need to look carefully at the groups you recalled and see if there are any patterns or themes that stand out. As a group leader, you need to know how your past experiences in groups will impact your participation in groups in the future.

● THERAPEUTIC/EFFECTIVENESS VARIABLES

What are the active ingredients in treatment groups that influence members to change their behaviors and perceptions? What elements in groups influence individual members to make changes in the issues that bring them into the group? How does a group leader know that her treatment group is "working"? What are the characteristics of effective support groups that one can observe in a given session? This section of the chapter will discuss the variety of variables that have been identified in effective, individual change groups. These variables are general characteristics, and in the chapter on evaluation (Chapter 9), we discussed more specific measures that are used to demonstrate the effectiveness of groups to achieve their objectives for individual members. The following discussion will borrow concepts from the work of Irving Yalom (1995) and other models of individual change groups (Reid, 1997).

Instilling Hope

Models of therapy and interpersonal practice—whether focused on individuals, families or small groups—all work to instill hope in the client. Hope is a general attitude that is found in successful groups and is instilled by the actions and statements of the group leader and other members. To instill hope is not the same thing as making promises. The group leader cannot guarantee that the group intervention will help the members of the group, even though members often want such guarantees. Instilling hope is more elusive than a promise, because in the beginning of the group it bumps up against the despair and pain that many new members may be feeling. Hope is instilled when members talk about the changes they may have made in their lives and others observe these narratives. Hope is also instilled when the group leader encourages members to develop goals for themselves and describes the achievements of members in earlier groups. In treatment protocols, the placebo effect will positively affect outcomes about one third of the time, and instilling hope seems to be one way to activate this effect.

Self-Sharing

In order for groups to work, members have to feel comfortable to self-disclose the issues they are bringing to the group. This kind of self-disclosure will not only involve personal experiences but also feelings, perceptions, and attitudes that may develop as the group matures. When members are reluctant to share information about themselves or events in the group, the leader may employ a number of structured activities to facilitate self-sharing. Some of these activities will be discussed in the chapter on group change (Chapter 15). The leader may also engage in self-sharing in order to get reluctant members to share. There may be many reasons why members are reluctant to share, such as discomfort about sharing with strangers, concerns about safety, shame about the purpose of the group, etc., and as the group matures, members will be more comfortable self-sharing.

Feedback

As members get to know each other in the group and listen to the narratives of their fellow members, there are chances for members to give each other feedback. This is a chance for members to hear how others perceive them and their issues. Both the leader and members may be giving feedback to each others. The leader is in a position to model how to give feedback, as well as how to respond to feedback when it is given. There are also a number of structured activities that leaders can employ to facilitate the feedback process. Feedback is an important group process because it helps individual members understand things they may not recognize in themselves. Feedback is most helpful when it is solicited. An example of *solicited* feedback is "I would be interested in knowing what members of the group think about my situation," *descriptive* is "I can see in your face that this is upsetting for you," *immediate* is "I want to respond to what you were just saying about your relationship with your parents," and *focused* is "Let's go around and talk about each individual member's experience." Feedback is not particularly helpful when it is about old events, such as "I want to talk about a comment you made three sessions ago in the group" and judgmental, such as "I can't believe that you were that stupid to put up with it." If members are forced to get feedback from the group, ethical issues of self-determination are involved, and member's anxiety may be raised so they decide not to return to the group.

The Johari Window

The concept of the Johari Window (Luft & Ingham, 1955) is a concept that explains how self-sharing and feedback contribute to the success of groups. The Johari Window has four quadrants (see Figure 14.2) and explains how individual members and the group as a whole share information. An individual member of a group has information about herself that she may share (i.e., open quadrant), as well as information that she chooses not to share (i.e., hidden quadrant). The group may give feedback to the individual member, which also increases the information in the open quadrant. This feedback process often involves information that the individual does not know about herself or himself (i.e., blind quadrant). The group may also withhold feedback from the individual members, which is information in the blind quadrant. Both the group and the individual members may have information that no one knows about, which is in the unknown quadrant. Information in this quadrant often involves various group dynamics that the interpersonal practitioner brings to the attention of the group, such as avoiding topics, addressing underlying conflicts, or the scapegoating of members. When groups first meet the open quadrant is the smallest, and as the group progresses, more and more information about individuals and the group will move into the open quadrant.

Figure 14.2 The Johari Window

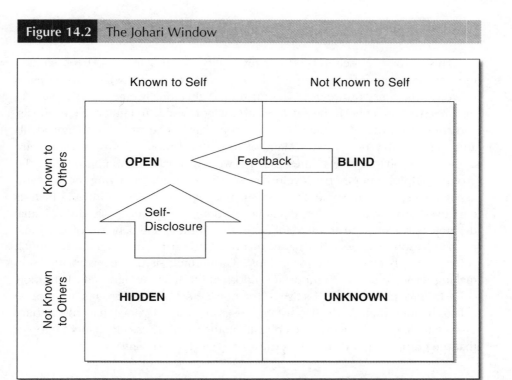

Universality

This factor is not present in family treatment and individual treatment but is an important factor in group work. Members realize that they are not alone in their struggles and that others are facing similar issues and circumstances. The support group offers a context for members to learn how others are coping with the same issue and also to feel that they are not "freaks" or weak for the issue they are facing. Groups may be diverse on demographic factors, such as gender expression, ethnicity, life experience, etc., and the commonality of the issue will help to transcend their differences and promote cohesiveness. Not all individuals will respond positively to universality. Some folks view their problems as unique or highly individualized and will not want to compare their struggle to others. These folks do not do well in groups and are not interested in hearing similar struggles in others.

Cohesiveness

This factor is closely related to universality and probably has been studied more than any other factor of group dynamics (Cartwright, 1968). Cohesiveness is viewed as the sense of "we-ness" in the group that gradually emerges as the group matures. Without cohesiveness, the group will not be able to influence individuals, and attendance will be problematic. The group will not be attractive to individuals and will probably not survive. Many of the interventions of group leaders are designed to enhance cohesiveness, such as working on a common purpose for the group, helping members develop a sense of trust, clarifying norms and expectations, etc. In some groups, such as Positive Peer Culture, which is employed in institutions for delinquent youth, cohesiveness is an essential dynamic that allows the group to influence the attitudes and behavior of individual members. Cohesiveness is a dynamic that needs to exist in moderation. Too much cohesiveness is problematic for groups. "Groupthink" is disastrous for decision making groups because important information may be ignored. Extremely cohesive groups may look positive to the outsiders, but these groups may not be able to handle conflict, which inevitably arises in groups. Groups that stifle or bury dissent are likely to have many "elephants" in the room. These elephants are topics that the group cannot deal with because they will lead to conflict.

Receiving and Giving Advice

Giving advice in social work has a long history of being taboo. For example, when we were trained in the mid-1960s, our method instructor told us that social workers never give advice. "Advice was what Dear Abby and Ann Landers did!" There is a desire of beginning social workers to be helpful by giving advice whenever an opportunity arises in practice. There are many television or radio shows, such as Dr. Phil or Dr. Laura, which promote advice giving. Social workers must be restrained in the kind of advice they give their clients. Advice on *ends* is "bad" advice, while advice on *means* can be useful to clients. Advice on ends concerns advice about major life decisions that a client may be facing, such as whether to get a divorce, drop out of school, get an abortion, change careers, etc. In practice, clients often ask their social worker directly what they should do when facing a major decision. In groups, other members will often offer advice to an individual member about what to do with a major decision. The group leader has to temper this kind of advice giving from other members and make it clear that some decision can only be made by the individual member. Advice on means, however, can be offered once an individual has made a major life decision. For example, suppose a member has decided to leave a violent marriage. There are many considerations that this member needs to take into account when implementing this decision for their own safety and economic well-being. This kind of information can be shared by the leader and other members. Because members want to be helpful to other members, giving advice is a constant activity in groups, and the leader has to help members realize what kind of advice will be helpful and what kind is not helpful.

Altruism

Though some would argue that altruism does not exist and altruistic acts are basically acts of self-interest (Rand & Peikoff, 1943), social workers, who run groups, see and encourage many acts of unconditional kindness between members. When group members enter a group, the group leader needs to clarify the reality that members will be occupying two complementary roles: helpee and helper. Not only will members be getting help from the group but there is the concurrent responsibility of helping other members of the group. Altruism may exist in many forms such as handing another member a tissue or offering to share a ride with another member who is having car trouble. For some very needy group members, this expectation to give as well as receive help may be difficult to do. For example, "I have to pay all this money to be in this group and you expect me to be helping others?" The social work profession has a long history of promoting the self-help principle in practice (Gartner & Reisman, 1984). There is both practice experience and research that demonstrate that helping others has a benefit for the helper. For example, the best way to learn a topic is to teach it to someone else.

Learning Interpersonal Skills

Because groups are composed of several members including the leader, the group can become a microcosm to practice various interpersonal skills within the group before a member tries out the skill in the real world. In assertiveness training groups, members learn the differences between aggressive, assertive, and submissive responses and how these responses appear in various scenarios. Through role play and role reversal, members can practice assertiveness in the group and get feedback from other members before trying out new skills as homework in the real world (Alberti & Emmons, 1990; Lange & Jakubowski, 1976). The group context offers many dyadic, triadic, quadratic, etc., activities that a leader can implement in a group that will help individual members develop interpersonal skills. Family, work, and social situations can be re-created in the group in order for individual members to work on these issues within the safety of the group. In the chapter on group change (Chapter 15), we will discuss some of the structured activities that have come from psychodrama and assertiveness training that are designed to facilitate interpersonal skill acquisition.

Vicarious Learning

The group context allows members a chance to learn about their own issues when another member is expressing her or his narrative. It may seem that being an observer is not a particularly active role in a group. When one member is relating an intense personal experience, the other members will be focused and transfixed by the story. The observing members may be crying and experiencing intense emotions as they relate the narrative to their own life experiences. Even when in the audience, members will be working on their own issues. The leader needs to allow members to express what was going on inside while listening to the other member's narrative. Modeling is another dynamic that takes place within vicarious learning when members share how they have tried to cope in situations. Members can take back into their own lives the examples they have experienced with others inside the group.

Catharsis

Many forms of treatment promote catharsis, and groups are not unique in encouraging this dynamic. The expression of feelings and getting in touch with pent up emotions is viewed as helpful in treatment and support groups. Catharsis is a form of self-sharing, but it is specific to the expression of affect. Catharsis is not an end in itself but needs to be followed by reflection and discussion. It is not helpful to let members just wallow in their despair, grief, or anger. Groups that promote catharsis need to focus on ways that individual members can deal with the affect that is being expressed and experienced. For example, in grief support groups in which individual members may be expressing intense emotions about the loss of a loved one, the leader will reserve time at the end of a session to help members debrief and reestablish composure before leaving the group. Catharsis can be problematic for some individual members who come from ethnic backgrounds that do not encourage the public display of emotions. It may be uncomfortable when these members find themselves in groups in which other members are much more open about the expression of affect.

Humor

Humor is therapeutic. Laughter is a stress reducer and can encourage camaraderie. Humor in groups can help to relieve tension that arises and to smooth over the "ruffled feathers" that conflict may create. The role of group clown may often emerge in groups to facilitate playfully relationships among members. "Clowning around" can also have a deleterious effect on the group when it keeps the group from getting down to business and discussing difficult topics. The group leader may encourage humor but also has to focus the group back on topics when clowning is getting in the way of doing the business of the group.

Socialization

Members need to learn how to be responsible members of the group if the group is to succeed and mature. In a children's group, a lot of the leader's effort will go into teaching the members how to behave in the group. Children may need to be reminded to stay seated, not to interrupt, to wait for their turn to speak, and not to carry on side conversation with other members. In adult groups, this kind of socialization takes place in the discussion of ground rules so that members will know what to expect, how to behave, and what is taboo. Intoxication and violence will get members removed from groups because these conditions endanger the well-being of other members.

The important caveat about effectiveness variables and therapeutic factors is that not all of them will necessarily appear in a successful group. This long list of factors is presented as some of the most obvious group dynamics that can be found in successful individual change groups. Some are more essential, such as self-disclosure, while others may be less critical, such as humor.

Look at the groups that you have been involved in over your life span. Can you think of examples and experiences in these groups where some of these effectiveness variables appeared? Can you think of groups in which members helped each other (altruism) and gave each other advice about how to succeed? If you played on a successful team in the past, you may have had a chance to experience a highly cohesive group. During childhood, you may have been a member of a friendship group in which you shared many secrets (self-sharing) and tears (catharsis).

GROUP DEVELOPMENT ●

Groups are dynamic entities, and even when the membership of a group is stable over time, the group will change and develop. For example, suppose a group meets for eight sessions and all members attend all eight sessions; the group will change (mature) in fairly predictable ways from the first session until the last session. These characteristic patterns have been recognized and described in the literature. There are many different models of group development in the social work and social science literature (Garvin, 1996; Reid, 1997; Schiller, 2003; Toseland & Rivas, 2008), and it is beyond the scope of this introductory text to describe and compare the pros and cons of each. Instead we will summarize some of the common themes in these models and present some of the basic issues that beginning practitioners need to recognize about the groups they have formed. Even though social workers are leaders of task groups, this discussion will focus on individual change groups, such as treatment groups, support groups, and CR groups. We will explore group development in closed groups (i.e., time-limited groups in which no new members are added) and open-ended groups (i.e., new members are entering, and old members are leaving as the group meets over time). We will begin with a discussion of how groups change within a single session, "from opening bell to final buzzer."

In-Session Phases Within a Closed Group

Social workers who lead therapy and support groups recognize three general phases within each session of an ongoing, closed group, such as "warm-up, work, and cool down." These phases are not evenly divided within a session and may be more a function of the actions of the leader to influence the group in each session. In the warm-up phase, the group members will enter the group and find a seat and engage in small talk about weather, news, current events, etc. If there is coffee available, the members may congregate around the coffeepot and fetch a cup of coffee. Latecomers will straggle in during this part of the session. Practice experience suggests that even though it seems that little is going on during warm-up, the group leader(s) should listen to the themes and underlying metaphors that are being expressed in the small talk of the individual members. These themes and metaphors can be the harbinger of things to come during the working phase. For example, if the themes are about storms and contentious current events, the session could turn out to be very lively.

Social work practitioners, who come from ethnicities that strongly believe in getting down to business, need to develop patience during this phase to see how the warm-up plays out. With some ethnic groups and regions of the county, such as the Deep South, it is seen as impolite to jump into business without first getting to chat. It is the personal experience of the authors that these expectations can be so strong that no "business" will be conducted in the group until the members have a chance to warm up. With some groups, it is possible to encourage the members to begin the working phase but asking members to talk about the "homework" they planned to work on in the last session.

The working phase may take up the largest part of the session and reflects the therapeutic variables that demonstrate the group's effectiveness. During the working phase, members will self-share, give each other feedback, and begin to address whatever was planned for that session. For example, in a grief support group, the members may have planned to bring a picture of their deceased love one and share it with the group, or in a therapy group for trauma survivors, the leaders may initiate a structured activity, such as writing poetry or drawing a picture about the event. During this phase in the session, the leader is encouraging members to participate and reflect on the issues that are planned. The leader will also be "watching the time" in order to stop the working phase with time left for the group to "cool down." The struggle during the working phase is to make sure that all members of the group have a chance to complete the activities, while also leaving time for the group to debrief the session.

The cooldown phase may be as brief as 5 minutes, or in an extremely emotional session, it may take up 20 or 30 minutes. If the members have experienced catharsis and expressed some strong emotions, the leader will want to be sure that members leave the group with a chance to talk about the experience in the group. The leader may employ a "round" and go around the group and ask each member to comment on their perceptions and experience in today's session. Debriefing may also involve the planning of between session tasks for each of the members so that they continue to work on issues before the next meeting. In time-limited groups, it is common that members will be completing "homework" between sessions. This homework will be tailored to the needs of each member, and it is important that it be designed by each member and not imposed by the leader.

These in-session phases can be seen in task groups as well. When I (BAS) became the chair of the curriculum committee for the first time, I asked the members of the group if we could implement a time structure in which we would stop the group 10 minutes early in our 2 hour sessions. In this 10 minute time frame at the end of the session, we would each have a chance to discuss how we viewed the session—for example, whether it was productive, a waste of time, frustrating, etc. When I first proposed this structure, there were puzzled looks on the faces of many colleagues and student members. As this activity became routine, this time was a chance for individual members to express feelings about conflicts that may have arisen in the group that could be addressed more personally. When a number of members felt the session had been unproductive, it was also a chance to discuss how we might change the process to make future meetings more productive.

In-Session Phases in an Open-Ended Group

Because members may be entering and departing in a given session, the leader of an open-ended group needs to have a structure that accounts for this constant change in membership. In many sessions, there needs to be time in the beginning to welcome new members and help them get "on board," as well as time near the end of the session to recognize members who will be leaving and help them "launch." There will be sessions in which no new members are added nor are there departing members, and these sessions will have more time to allot to the working phase of the session.

For new members who are entering the group, it is important that these members feel welcome. In practice, AA self-help groups do an excellent job of reaching out to members who are new to the program. Older members will go over and thank the new member for attending and give them an overview of what will be happening in the meeting. In a therapy or support group, the leader must perform this important, welcome function. Because ongoing members are familiar with each other, there is a tendency for ongoing members to talk with each other and to ignore a new member who will feel alienated in a group of strangers. The leader can reduce some of this strangeness by starting the group with brief introductions and getting ongoing members to share some of their impressions of the group. Ongoing members can be encouraged to explain the group's ground rules to the new member, and the leader needs to make sure the new member joins the physical space of the group—for example, no sitting in a back row. The leader may also ask the new member to share any experiences they may have had with groups and to give the new member a chance to ask questions about this group. The group can then move into the working phase of the group session.

For "graduating" members who are attending their last session of the group, the leader needs to save time at the end of the session to recognize this departure. In some groups, the departing member is given a token certificate to show that they have completed the program. The departing member is given space to talk about what the group has meant to her/him and what she/he has learned. Continuing members are also given a chance to express their feelings about the departing member. Before the final session, the leader may have given a homework assignment to the departing member to think about ways that they can continue to change and get support after leaving the group. The results of this assignment can be shared at this point. In some groups in which members have been meeting for several months, the group may develop a termination ritual to recognize the departing member such as a party or celebration ritual.

During the Vietnam War, I (BAS) was stationed as a military social worker in a small mental health clinic on an U.S. Army base in the South. This clinic had about 15 staff members composed of psychiatrists, social workers, and social work technicians. This was a cohesive unit, and periodically we would be assigned new staff, and old staff members would get orders to go to Vietnam. The clinic would have a farewell party for the staff on orders. It became a tradition for this farewell that members would bake a large chocolate cake, filled with

M&M'S and covered with thick chocolate icing. On the cake would be written "Fuck the War," which was our way of protesting the loss of our colleague.

Stages of Group Development in Closed Groups

In a review of the literature on stages of group development, there seems to be five general stages that closed, individual change groups go through: (1) *pregroup planning*, (2) *formation*, (3) *revision*, (4) *maturity*, and (5) *termination*.

Pregroup Planning

In the pregroup planning stage, the assumption is made that the worker has an opportunity to plan, propose, and compose a group from a potential pool of members. In the practice world, not all individual change groups can begin with careful planning, but we will describe the ideal way a group can be launched in an agency. Careful planning even before the group meets can prevent some serious problems that may arise in the first and later sessions of the group, such as member incompatibility, dropouts, etc.

Because most individual change groups are sponsored by the agency, an interpersonal practitioner should seek support and approval from her or his agency. A good way for the interpersonal practitioner to get this kind of agency sanction is to develop a group proposal that can be shared with colleagues for feedback and then forwarded to supervisors, the clinical director, and in some agencies even the agency director. This agency process takes place long before a first meeting of any group.

The Group Proposal. The group proposal (Reid, 1997) should begin with a clear statement of the kind of group that is being considered and who the target population (i.e., expected beneficiaries) will be. This opening sentence should also state whether it will be an open-ended group with members being added and launched as the group develops or whether it will be a closed group that starts with a group of members that will meet for a given number of weeks. The next part of the proposal should present the group's purpose (i.e., why these members should meet) and a rationale (i.e., why this is an important group and what unmet needs are being addressed). The group's goals (i.e., expected outcomes that members can achieve) and any evidence that group interventions are effective with this target population may also be included.

What follows are two examples of proposals that cover these basic aspects. These two examples will be used to highlight the various aspects of a group proposal.

Middle School Group

"The proposed group will be a closed, time-limited support group that will meet weekly and run from the end of September until the Christmas break (e.g., approximately 12 sessions). This group will target youth who are just entering middle school and who have been referred by teachers to the assistant principal for unruly and disruptive class behavior. The purpose of the group is to help students who are struggling with the transition to a new school and with the maturational struggles that preadolescents face. Students at this stage of development struggle with self-esteem issues, peer relationship issues, and the demands and expectations of a new school setting. By placing these struggling students in a group early in their middle school career, more serious problems may be avoided down the road. And in some cases, the group may help the school recognize students who have more serious problems that may need more intensive interventions. Students can expect the group to provide them with an opportunity to meet new friends in a supportive environment where they can discuss issues and concerns. As the term progresses, it is hoped that teachers will see changes in these students behavior—that is, more focused on learning and cooperating with other students.

Outpatient Treatment Group for Veterans of the Iraq War

This open-ended treatment group will be for veterans returning from their tour in Iraq who have been identified as suffering from PTSD. This may be an ancillary treatment option for veterans who are being seen for individual counseling of PTSD. The purpose of this group is to help returning veterans cope with the symptoms of PTSD and with the issues of reentering family roles and returning to civilian life. Because of the massive numbers of veterans returning from Iraq with severe physical injuries (e.g., closed head injuries) and emotional traumas, treatment groups are a way for the military and VA to reach many of these casualties of this war. The goal of these groups is to prevent suicide, domestic violence, and to manage and mollify the symptoms of PTSD. The groups will provide veterans with a supportive environment in which they will be surrounded by other veterans who are struggling with similar problems, and where they will have a chance to learn how others are coping.

Composing the Group

The next section of the group proposal concerns how members will be recruited, screened, and invited to the first session of the group. Composing the membership of the group involves a little bit of planning, a little bit of luck, and a little bit of intuition about compatibility of potential members. In general, there needs to be some fairly large "reservoir" of potential members from which members can be drawn (Sundel, Glasser, Sarri, & Vinter, 1985). This reservoir will reflect the target population of the proposal, and the proposal needs to describe how members will be approached and selected from this reservoir. In many agencies, the reservoir may come from the caseload of the agency, whereas with some groups it may represent a segment of the agency's catchment area or surrounding community.

There are a number of ways that the screening and recruitment process can take place. A worker can ask other colleagues in the agency if they have members of their caseload who could benefit from the purpose of the group. The worker may also go through the case records of active and recently closed cases to see if there are potential members who might benefit from the group. The worker may develop a flyer that can be placed in strategic areas of the agency or community announcing the formation of the group. This flyer may have a contact number or e-mail that a potential member can respond to.

Once prospective members have been identified, the worker may want to prescreen each potential member with an individual interview. Though this requires a significant amount of time and effort on the workers' part, it does provide the group leader with an opportunity to describe the purpose of the group and to find out the motivation and past experiences of the potential member with groups. The prescreening interview also allows the prospective member to get to know the worker and ask questions about concerns they may have with group treatment. If the prospective member also seems like a good candidate for the group, then the leader can also secure a preliminary agreement from the member to try out the group. It may be that some prospective members are not good candidates for the group, such as people not motivated to participate in groups, people who are extremely shy and uncommunicative in groups, people struggling with issues that are different from the purpose of the group, etc. These individuals may be referred to other groups or encouraged to seek individual counseling for their problems.

Another way to prescreen prospective members is to invite all of the identified potential members from the reservoir to a "pregroup workshop." This allows the leader to introduce herself and to explain the purpose and potential benefits of the group, as well as answer questions from prospective members about any concerns they may have. The advantage of the workshop over individual interviews is that it is less time consuming and allows the worker to observe how potential members may actually behave in a group. By the careful use of structured activities in the workshop, potential members can be placed in dyads with the instruction to get to know a little about this person and be prepared to introduce them to the whole group. This simple "introductory" exercise allows the leader to see how potential members will behave in the context of the group. The group leader can also use other basic icebreakers to see how potential members respond to the group context. The toughest part of this way of screening for the leader is the ending of the workshop. The ending requires the leader to be honest with members and to share in the group context who will go on to be members of the group. In some workshops, the leader may have to exclude some members of the group.

Because of the ethical principles that prohibit social workers from discriminating against clients, the exclusion of members from the group can place the worker on shaky ethical grounds. For example, one of the principles of group composition is the "Noah's Ark" principle (Reid, 1997). This principle suggests that it is problematic for groups to have "isolates"—that is, individuals who are very different from the rest of the group. One can be an isolate for many reasons: gender expression, ethnicity, age, disability, etc. It is likely in the workshop that there may be several individuals who are isolates based on identity characteristics, and these differences were played out in the interactions of members during the workshop. These members may have self-shared little information and appeared uncomfortable during group activities. The worker cannot single out these isolates in this workshop session, because pointing out their differences and difficulties will be anxiety provoking for them and other group members. By suggesting to all workshop participants that some may not want to continue and then going in a round to find out who may be interested in continuing, some of these isolates may self-select themselves out of future session of the group.

In some situations, there may be a member who does not self-select himself out of the group. This can be problematic when that member has demonstrated in the workshop that he is a "monopolizer" and the other members of the group are irritated by this individual. The monopolizer is a communication hog and takes up way more than his share of the communication space in the group. It is the responsibility of the group leader to deal with monopolizers. If the leader does not find a way to dampen this behavior, the other members will be irritated with the leader for not controlling this member. When monopolizing behavior emerges in later sessions of group treatment, the leader has time to exert some control and modify the member's behavior. But in a one-session workshop, the leader does not have the time to help this member modify his monopolizing behavior. It may be necessary for the leader to suggest to the prospective member that they will not be invited to join the planned group and they should seek individual treatment for their issues. The leader may suggest that she is willing to meet with the individual monopolizer after the workshop and discuss alternatives. It is important that this gentle rejection of the monopolizer is done in the context of the group, so that other members will see that the leader is responding to the broader needs of the group. This display of leadership may allay the concerns in other prospective members' minds who were considering not to return to the group if the monopolizer would be there.

There is an extensive literature about what is the ideal composition for a successful group (Bertcher & Maple, 1996; Corey, Corey, & Corey, 2010; Davis, 1984; Davis & Proctor, 1989). We have discussed some of the issues that are considered in composition (e.g., isolates and there are other considerations that a leader needs to think about in planning the composition of the group). These considerations involved the attributes of potential members, such as demographics (e.g., age, gender expression, ethnicity, disabilities, etc.) and behavioral responses in groups, such as the example mentioned about monopolizing reflects this consideration. The composition of a successful group should somehow balance homogeneity and heterogeneity of members. Group members need to have some things in common in order to develop cohesiveness, but they also need to have some elements of diversity in order for the group to develop some energy around issues. Too much commonality and the group may become stagnant, and too much diversity and the group may not be able to keep itself together.

It is beyond the scope of this book to go into all of the considerations that go into composition except to give some general considerations about balancing membership. The group's planned purpose is the major factor that should determine membership. For example (Trotman & Gallagher, 1987), if the group's purpose is to give African American women a place to discuss issues that affect them in particular, then such a support group should be demographically homogenous. No white women and no African American men should be included. If, on the other hand, the purpose of a dialogue group is to discuss the impact of racism and sexism, then there could be both men and women and many members representing a range of ethnicities (Gutierrez & Lewis, 1999).

Another important consideration is the motivation of members to be in the group. Members who are strongly opposed to being in the group should be excluded for both ethical reasons (Corey et al., 2010) and for pragmatic reasons. One or two reluctant members can have a negative impact on the group's climate. Another factor to consider is the developmental and social skills of potential members. We would not expect 10- and 11-year-olds to fit into a group of 16- and 17-year-olds, nor would we expect children of any age to fit into an adult group. The final consideration in composition is to exclude extremes in behavioral attributes (Bertcher & Maple, 1996) in the same way that we exclude demographic isolates who have little in common with other members. Potential members who are extremely shy and uncommunicative in groups should be excluded as well as those potential members on the other end of the continuum who are overly talkative and monopolizing.

Though the tendency in composing a group is to focus on the attributes of potential group members, we must also take into account the attributes of the leader(s) of the group. Should a male worker lead a support group for women who have been sexually abused by men? Should a heterosexual woman worker run a group for gay teens struggling with coming out issues? The issue is not whether a professional worker can run such a group when he or she is the demographic isolate, but what will be the impact of such a leader on the group. Sometimes the leadership structure is balanced by having a coleadership structure with male and female leaders or coleaders with different ethnicities. There is some social science research the suggests that group members prefer to have a leader who is like them demographically (Forsyth, 1990), but that does not mean that it is impossible for an experienced leader to work effectively with groups that are poorly matched. In the real world of group practice, there are instances in which there has been no time to plan and compose a group, such as the worker has been "given" a group by their agency that violates all of the principles of composition that was previously stated. In spite of all the mismatches, the leader is able to develop a cohesive and effective group (See Exercise 14.1).

Exercise 14.1

Self-Assessment Exercise: Mismatches and Matches in Leaders

Look again at the groups you have experienced over your life span. Have there been group experiences in the past in which you were a member of a group with a major mismatch between leader and group members? What was the impact of this mismatch? Make a list of the kinds of groups (i.e., purpose and membership) that you believe would be a mismatch for you as a leader, and make another list of groups that you feel confident you could run. List the kinds of groups that you would prefer to have a coleader.

Where, When, and How Many?

The proposal may also state where the group will meet. It is important that the leader check out in advance what rooms are available in the agency for group meetings. Many agencies do not have adequate interviewing space for groups, nor furniture that can be arranged so that members can see and interact with each other. For some groups, it may be necessary to go into the community and locate available space for the group to meet. Local churches and community centers may make rooms available as a service to members in their community. It is also necessary to check out times when the room is available. The leader will have to decide when the group might meet that has the best chance of attracting a large number of potential members. For working adults, it may be necessary for the group to meet in the evenings; for children in school, it may be best to meet during a free period or after school.

How long a group should meet will depend on its purpose and the composition of its members. Groups for young children with short attention spans may only meet for a half hour while groups for adults may plan to meet for about 90 minutes, which is a common length of time for therapy and support groups for adults. Agencies that run many groups often allot a 2-hour time frame for their adult groups so that the leaders can meet for about 90 minutes and have time to wrap up the group and complete any recording. A half hour after the group also allows coleaders to discuss the session's progress and plan for the next session of the group.

The planned size of a group will depend on its purpose. For adult therapy and treatment groups, the convention is that the group should be somewhere between 7 to 11 members for the group to be effective. There are groups that exceed this number such as "network therapy," which requires between 50 to 250 members present for the network effect to take place (Attneave, 1969), but this group model rarely occurs in social work practice. There are other groups that are much smaller, such as children's groups, because it may be necessary for group leaders to maintain control over the members. In some groups, the neediness of members may also require the group to be small so that members' needs can be adequately addressed in each session.

The importance of size in planning a group centers on the issue of attrition. The leader needs to plan the ideal size of their working group and then work backward. If the ideal size of the group is about 8, then the committed members of the group should be about 10 because groups experience attendance attrition. Not all members will show up at every session. In planning for the first session, the leader will have to invite about 12 to 15 prospective members if 8 is the ideal. Some members will change their mind and not show up after the individual interview or workshop experience, and some will drop out after the first session when they have had a chance to meet other members. And looking one step farther back, the reservoir for an 8-session group may require at least 25 or more potential members because the leader will be able to recruit and attract only a small percentage of the potential members in that reservoir. Even with intensive mailings, flyers, and contact with referral sources, there is high attrition in attracting members from the reservoir. The lesson of attrition is that it is unlikely that a group can be developed from a small reservoir. If the worker cannot locate enough potential members in the agency caseload or from reliable referral sources, then it is probably a waste of time to go through all the other steps in recruiting, composing, and making arrangements for the group.

Agency Sanction and Approval

Most of the groups that social workers run take place within an agency or service setting. The social worker should plan to vet their group proposal through the sponsoring organization. There is no guarantee that a well-planned and articulated proposal will be approved in a given setting. A social work intern in her field placement may have to take her group proposal through a number of decision making layers, such as the field supervisor, clinical director, and agency CEO. Even a well-planned and articulated proposal may find resistance when the proposal works its way over all of the decision making hurdles. It is helpful when designing the proposal if the worker shares a draft of the proposal with colleagues and gathers feedback on the plan. A new student intern in the agency may learn that a similar attempt was made in the past to start a group, but the effort failed. The student might also learn that there are some members of the staff who do not believe that groups are a viable treatment modality. These are all potential sources of resistance to the proposal that can be taken into account in shaping the final proposal. For example, if colleagues are apathetic to groups as a modality, then the proposal may need to describe in detail the empirical evidence for why the proposed group is an effective approach to the problems of the target population. It may also be necessary that the proposal's recruitment procedures, size requirements, and possibility of a co-therapist will be modified in various ways before the group can be implemented.

Middle School Group (continued)

This group will be drawn from students who have been identified by teachers as struggling with the transition to middle school. A notice describing the purpose of the group and a permission slip will be sent out to parents of these students. Students, whose parents grant permission, will be interviewed individually to see what their prior experiences with groups have been and if they are interested in joining such a group now. This individual interview will give the leader a chance to introduce herself to prospective group members and answer any concerns the students may have about the group. In order to account for attrition, the leader will prescreen at least 18 potential members in hopes of finding 12 members who seem motivated and likely to form a well-balanced group. These prospective members will be invited to the first session of the group in the school's conference room during the recess break after lunch. The group will be scheduled to meet for 30 minutes. Hopefully about 10 of these prospective members will show up for the first session. It may be desirable for the leader to find the students in the lunchroom and remind them of the first session. Because the group will take place on school grounds during school hours, the group will have to be authorized by the school principal.

Outpatient Treatment Group for Veterans of the Iraq War (continued)

There may be several groups formed to take into account the needs of this large population of returning veterans. Flyers will be placed in the local VA hospital and sent to the local Army Reserve and National Guard units that have supplied troops to the Iraq War. The flyer will describe the purpose of these groups and who to contact if veterans are interested in attending. The flyer will state in what rooms the groups meet in the VA hospital and the times and evenings when various groups meet. There will be no formal screening of members except to make it available only to veterans, which will provide the commonality for the groups. It will not be necessary for prospective members to have been diagnosed with PTSD, but it is expected that many of the prospective members will be referred by the psychiatric staff of the VA hospital. There will be at least two coleaders of these groups, because there is no way to control the size of these groups on a given evening. If a large number of veterans happen to show up (over 20) then it may be desirable to break the group in half and meet in separate rooms. The group will be scheduled in the evening for 90 minutes with the possibility of extending the time to 2 hours. The rooms will have to have the capacity to accommodate a fairly large number of members in a circular or rectangular seating arrangement so that members can see each other. This seating arrangement will promote member to member interaction and sharing. Because these groups will take place in the VA hospital, it will be necessary to get approval from the clinical director. It will also be desirable to meet with psychiatric staff in the VA hospital and the commanding officers of local military units to explain the purposes and value of these groups.

This lengthy discussion of the pregroup planning phase is designed to point out that there is a lot of effort taken by the leader in creating a group. Though there may be input from colleagues and potential clients, the leader is ultimately responsible for most of the decisions made in this stage. In some situations, in practice leaders are not given the opportunity to do this kind of careful planning, in agencies. For example, the agency may advertise various groups in a particular community without surveying potential members. In the initial meeting, the response may be overwhelming and several groups may have to be formed to cover the interest. Workers may be assigned to these various groups without much preparation or chance to meet and prepare group members. "Muddling through" is a common strategy for social workers and does not necessarily mean that the group will fail.

Formation

The formation stage concerns the process that takes place in the first and/or second session of a closed group. In a time-limited group with 10 sessions, it may only take one or two sessions before the group will move into revision. In formation, the members get to meet and learn a little about each other, to learn more about the leader(s) and the purpose and goals of the group, to get a schedule for each session, and to begin the discussion of ground rules. In this first session, the leader makes clear the expectations of members, their responsibilities, and how they might benefit from the group. By the end of the first session, the members will be able to give a commitment to attend the group and work on the issues that have been identified. Because the first session of the group is critical to getting the group started, the chapter on group change (Chapter 15) will present in some detail the issues that a leader must address in the first session.

Revision

There is some disagreement in the group literature about whether this stage is necessary as a group matures. Some authors assert that it does not occur in women's groups but is more common in men's or mixed gender expression groups (Schiller, 2003). Other authors suggest that this stage occurs because leaders trained in groups "expect" it to occur and subtly facilitate its occurrence. We will not attempt to resolve these issues here but instead discuss how and why revision seems to emerge and what the worker's responsibilities are in helping the group move through this phase.

Revision reflects a change in the group's climate from the formation stage with a considerable amount of conflict, tension, and disagreement arising in the session. During revision, the members move beyond their initial, friendly persona to a more critical persona. They may question ground rules that have already been agreed to previously: "Why can't I smoke during meetings?" or "Why can't I tell my friends what goes on in this group?" They may complain about the behavior of members that in prior groups was left unmentioned: "Your whining is starting to get to me!" or "Stop interrupting me when I am speaking!" Members may raise questions about the stated purpose of the group: "The focus of our group is much too narrow and should include a discussion of all relationships not just with our parents."

This contentious phase is a chance for the members to begin to shape how they want "their" group to evolve. It is a chance for members to take ownership of the group. It is a chance for members to learn how to disagree and work to resolve conflicts that inevitably arise in groups. The leader's primary role is to help the group resolve their conflicts, to recognize and respect their differences, and to find a way to work together. Even though a revision session may become quite contentious and look to the members like the group is failing, by going through this process the group has a chance to mature and experience the therapeutic variables that result in an effective group. Because conflict resolution skills are essential for group leaders, we will discuss in the chapter on group change (Chapter 15) these important skills.

Unfortunately, there are some risks that emerge during revision that leaders must recognize and deal with. Some members may find the contentious climate too uncomfortable, and the risk of dropout increases. The leader will try to help the group establish norms about how much conflict group members can tolerate. The ethnic background of members may have prescribed different levels of tolerance and expression of interpersonal conflict. In some subcultures of the United States, even raising your voice is taboo—especially to anyone older—and in others, the tolerable level of conflict expression can include swearing and direct confrontation. For example, the "F" word is absolutely taboo and offensive to some folks, while with others it is a common part of their vocabulary. This kind of conflict is common in heterogeneous groups that include diverse class, ethnic, and gender expression among members.

Revision is also a time when scapegoating may arise, and the group will resort to this dynamic in order to deal with interpersonal conflict. Scapegoating of individual members does reduce the tensions within the group, but it glosses over the underlying conflict that the group is ignoring and avoiding. Group members who are most likely to be scapegoated are the most deviant member of the group, the least powerful member of the group, or the leader of the group. Each of these members in the group is a target for the frustrations that group members may experience during revision. The task of the leader is to help the group look beneath the scapegoating, to recognize the underlying conflict, and to resolve the conflict by changing ground rules or revising prior agreements that may have been made during formation. From the perspective of the Johari Window, the group needs to address what is in the unknown quadrant.

Maturity

Maturity is the ideal stage that closed groups hope to reach in order for the group to achieve the purposes for which the group has been formed. It is the true working stage of the treatment and support group because members will be able to help each other achieve their goals. Members will have a clear understanding of what to expect in the group and how to relate with other members of the group. During this stage, many of the effectiveness variables will appear (e.g., self-disclosure, feedback, altruism, cohesiveness, catharsis, interpersonal learning, and humor). The task of the leader is to stay out of the way of the group and let it function. For the most part, the group only needs the leader to be a catalyst, and the leader's style will be laissez-faire. The dependence on the leader will be greatly reduced, and when the group turns to the leader for input, the primary intervention may be for the leader to suggest that they can figure things out for themselves.

Termination

In a time-limited group, several sessions may be saved for the group to work on "termination issues." During these termination sessions, the group will evaluate the success of their efforts, as well as those issues that still remain as challenges for members. This is also a time to talk about what members found helpful. There are a number of tasks that the leader helps the group complete. Because many of the changes that members may have achieved in the group are easily reversible, during the termination stage, the members need to discuss what they can do to solidify and support achieved goals. The group may plan a reunion session as a way of reinforcing success, or some members may plan to join other groups to go on working on issues.

The termination process also brings up many kinds of feelings in group members that may be related to transference issues, such as experiences of loss or transition that were not easily resolved earlier in their lives. Some members may feel they are being abandoned by the group and leader, others may be angry at the leader for ending the group, and others may have such difficulty saying good-bye to members who will drop out and not return to the termination sessions. These feelings need to be discussed and put in perspective so that members realize they are arising in response to the termination process. Members can be encouraged to find ways to cope with these feelings such as planning a termination party, creating a gift giving system for each member so that they will take something away from the group, and using rituals and ceremonies to recognize the transition out of the group.

Look over the groups you have experienced in your life span. Can you see any of the patterns we describe here? Was there a pregroup planning phase in which leaders made decisions about the membership of the group? Did any of your groups go through some of the growing pains found in the revision stage? If any of your groups were time limited, how did they handle termination and the feelings associated with stopping? As a member of these groups, how did you respond to revision and termination? As a group leader, you need to be aware of your own reactions to conflict in groups and how you handle termination. If your tendency is to withdraw from interpersonal conflict or avoid difficult encounters, you will have to learn how to overcome these propensities. As a group leader, you will have the responsibility to help the group through these contentious stages.

● ASSESSING GROUP DYNAMICS

There are whole courses taught and books written about all of the dynamics that appear in small groups. We have already discussed some of these dynamics, such as effectiveness variables and group development, and now we will focus on some of the basic dynamics that we feel a group leader should be able to recognize when they are leading groups, such as *norms, communication, sociometry, roles,* and *geography*. This is by no means an exhaustive discussion of these dynamics, but it should help the beginning interpersonal practitioner to understand what is going on inside small groups.

Norms

This concept has already been presented in earlier discussions of values and ethics. The discussion here will focus on how important norms are for understanding small groups. Norms involve behavior of members and how this behavior is evaluated by the group. Some behavior will be desirable, such as helping other members in the group, friendly demeanor, being a "team player," etc., while other behaviors will be undesirable, such as verbal hostility, coming late to sessions, monopolizing discussions, etc. Because many of the conflicts that arise in groups involve normative disagreements, a group leader has to be able to make norms explicit and clear to members. In the beginning session of groups, leaders spend a lot of time discussing "ground rules" with members so that certain norms are explicit, such as confidentiality, no smoking, no physical violence, etc. Other norms may emerge over time that the leader may have to make explicit and help members understand, such as no use of foul language, no interrupting when others are speaking, allowing others a chance to speak, etc. In multiethnic groups, there is a good chance that normative conflicts will arise because the cultural values of individuals are likely to clash with the cultural values of others. Different cultures have different norms about sharing information with others, expressing emotions in groups, and handling interpersonal conflict. An ethnically sensitive leader can help the group recognize the source of cultural conflict and help members to develop ground rules that will mollify tensions.

Communication

A group leader needs to be able to keep track of the communication patterns in the group. Who talks the most, who talks the least, and who talks to whom are some of the patterns that a leader needs to be aware of when leading groups. One function of a group leader is "gatekeeping," which involves helping silent members have a chance to speak and suppressing talkative members who are speaking too much. For example, a leader might suggest to a silent member that he has not heard anything from her in the session and wondered if she had anything to add to the discussion. To overactive members, the leader might suggest that an overactive member wait while the group finds out what others have to say. When the group is not directing any conversation toward a member and that member is silent, the leader has to be concerned that this member may become an isolate and needs to be encouraged to join the discussion. There is a tendency in the early sessions of groups for members to address most of their comments to the leader, and the leader will be encouraging members to address each other. Such comments might be "That's a good idea! Why don't you ask others in the group what they think!"

In order to keep track of talkativeness of members, the leader needs to develop a "birds-eye view" of the group as the session progresses. This perspective needs to include the behavior of the leader as well as members. In Figure 14.3, a diagram of such a perspective is given of the communication patterns in a six-person session. The leader is marked with an *L* and members with an *M*. Can you discern who talks the most, who talks the least, and who seems to have most of the conversation directed at her?

The complexity of human communication is that words are only a small part of the interaction between individuals, and there are many nonverbal channels that are simultaneously sending information back and forth between group members. In human communication, affect is expressed in facial expressions, gestures,

Figure 14.3　Communication Pattern in an All Female Group

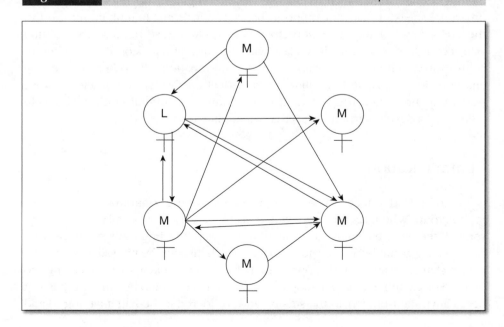

posture, and vocalization (i.e., tone and timber). Members may shake their heads, roll their eyes, smile, or scowl while others are talking. Some members may move their chairs out of the circle of the group or get up and move to other seats when a late member comes in and sits beside them. The leader will have to decide whether to point out these nonverbal behaviors to the rest of the group, such as moving information from unknown to open in the Johari Window, in order to make explicit dynamics that the group may be ignoring. Long silences are problematic for groups and may increase the tension in the group's climate. Long silences may be especially difficult for new leaders, and the group members may be asked to clarify what silence means. Silence is a form of communication. It is impossible not to communicate with others in the group. Even getting up and leaving the group is a statement.

Though it may seem desirable that every member of the group should talk about the same amount of time, as well as with each of the members, this is an unrealistic expectation for leaders to have. In practice, leaders can expect about one third of the members to talk about two thirds of the time. By using "rounds," a leader can go around the group and get each member to share on a particular topic. This basic tactic will provide a structure to control overactive members and also encourage silent members, but this may put shy members on the spot.

Sociometry

This dynamic concerns the attractiveness of members to each other. Do members like each other in the group? There may also be negative sociometry in which some members are disliked by other members (e.g., monopolizers, "know-it-alls," or bullies). The sociogram is a way of diagramming the attraction between members of the group. In Figure 14.4, an example of a sociogram is presented for a six-member group. The sociogram shows that there is a triad, dyad, and isolate in this group: three members are mutually attracted to each other, two members are mutually attracted to each other, and one member is not attracted to anyone in the group. A sociogram can be used to calculate the cohesion of a group by dividing the actual number of mutual attractions by the possible number of mutual attraction. For this six-person group there are 4 mutual attractions out of a possible 15. This would give a score of .27, which would be a low score and would suggest that the leader needs to engage the group in activities that will enhance mutual attraction such as helping members to get to know each other better or engaging in activities that expose commonalities among members.

In the early session of a group, attraction between members is usually associated with demographics—that is, gender expression, ethnicity, age, etc. In Figure 14.4, there are four women and two men, which accounts for some of the

Figure 14.4 Sociometry in a Six-Person Group

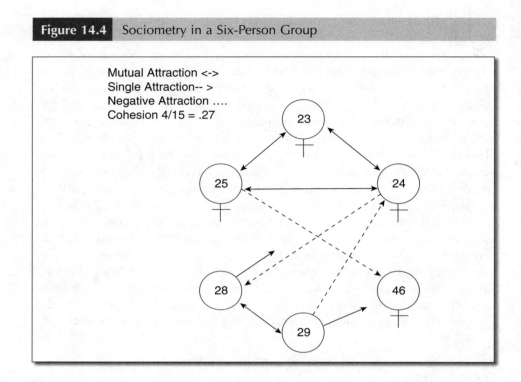

Mutual Attraction <->
Single Attraction-- >
Negative Attraction ....
Cohesion 4/15 = .27

attraction between members. The ages of members seems to account for the lack of attraction to the woman who is the isolate. The isolation of this particular woman would be increased if she was the only Latina or African American in the group. In the beginning of a group, the Noah's Ark principle assures that every member will find someone else in the group who they can see some commonality. Later as the group develops, sociometry may develop around personality characteristic and information that members share with the group. In the previously mentioned group, the older woman may be appreciated by other members of the group as she shares her experiences and becomes a "model" for the other members of the group.

Because sociometry is related to cohesiveness in groups, the leader of a group will be working to increase the attractiveness of members as the group develops. When a leader is composing a group, the decision to invite members who have things in common to join a group is a tactic designed to enhance sociometry and cohesion. When a leader employs an activity that promotes self-sharing and then points out connections in what is shared, this will also contribute to the sociometry among members. When leaders enforce sanctions on deviant members who violate the group's ground rules, this action will decrease the negative sociometry in the group. In the real world, rarely does everyone like everyone else. A group of people who like each other may have a hard time dealing with conflict, which is inevitable in formed groups. It is not necessary that everyone will be liked and like everyone else in the group.

Roles

There are many formal and informal roles that emerge in task, support, and treatment groups. In task groups, there may be formally designated members who are "chair, vice-chair, secretary, treasurer," etc. Besides formally designated roles, there are also a number of informal roles that emerge as groups develop. There are roles that help the group to function, such as task leader, socioemotional leader, mediator, initiator, supporter, observer, critic, etc. There are also informal roles that are dysfunctional to the group, such as character assassin, blocker, scapegoat, etc., and there are special roles that may emerge that sometimes fit the personalities of members such as clown, placater, confessor, junior therapist, etc. In this discussion, we will not cover all of the potential roles but focus on those dysfunctional roles and special roles that a beginning practitioner may have to confront and suggest some tactics that a leader might employ to handle these roles.

Some leadership roles have already been discussed in prior sections of this chapter—for example, gatekeeper or observer of group dynamics. Leaders need to be able to balance two important roles: task leader and socioemotional leader. A leader must work to ensure that the group is achieving its purpose and simultaneously helping members to feel supported. In order to help the group stay on task, a leader may have to point out that the group is off on a tangent and needs to get back to the agenda or topic of today's session. A group leader will help the group develop an agenda for the session. The group leader will keep track of time so that the members will have time to debrief a session and plan homework tasks in the interim between sessions. These actions are some of the task responsibilities that leaders perform.

Leaders must also observe the climate of the group and get a sense of how individual members are feeling about the process of the group. Do some members seem upset about the discussion in the group? Are some members having difficultly dealing with conflicts that may emerge between themselves and other members? The leader may have to be able to mediate conflicts, smooth over "ruffled feathers," and encourage individual members to share feelings about what is transpiring in the session. These socioemotional functions are important because they help individual members to be involved in the group and to recognize that human groups involve feelings as well as just getting the task completed. As groups develop and mature, it is likely that many of these functions will also be picked up and performed by members, but in the beginning, the leader must be the model for these important group roles.

One of the most problematic, dysfunctional roles is that of "character assassin." This role seems to relate to the personality of individual members, and it is a role that the leader needs to address immediately in the group when it arises. It is possible for leaders to prevent this role from appearing by carefully composing a group and assessing potential members who may perform this role, but it may arise anyway in the most carefully composed group. A character assassin is unable to engage in productive dialogue or conflict. Instead of disagreeing with an issue or statement of another member, the assassin attacks the member who raises the issue: "I would expect YOU to raise such a stupid issue!" "I don't know why you are in this group—you are such a misfit!" Character assassins know how to wound and put down other members and unfortunately effectively increase the amount of "self-censoring" that goes on in any group. No one wants to be humiliated in the group so that members will clam up and not share perspectives. This is a disaster for task groups because they will be losing information that may help to inform group decisions.

Character assassins will generate a significant amount of negative sociometry—dislike among other members. If the leader does not deal with this role when it emerges, other members may drop out of the group, the ultimate form of self-censoring. Self-sharing will stop, group cohesiveness will suffer, and the group will struggle to develop. In order to deal with this dysfunctional role, the leader needs to develop a ground rule about the negative value of attacking fellow members. This can be cast as a positive rule to increase the safety members feel in the group by not engaging in attacks on each other. In adolescent groups, this dysfunctional role is likely to appear, and the leader may "socialize" members to understand that "words can wound" and personal attacks are undesirable (Carrell, 2000).

The scapegoat role is another fairly common dysfunctional role, but it is not as dramatically problematic as the assassin role. There are both positive and negative aspects to this role when it emerges in a group. Scapegoating has a group "binding" function (Coser, 1956). Group members have a chance to coalesce and feel camaraderie when they are attacking the scapegoat. The group will have a chance to express explicitly what behaviors they view as deviant or undesirable. This kind of social control function is common in groups. Unfortunately the downside of scapegoating is that it usually emerges when the group is struggling and unable to deal with an underlying conflict. It is easier for the group to attack the scapegoat than address the "elephant in the room." After the scapegoat has been attacked, the tension will be reduced, and the underlying conflict will be temporarily ignored. In the Johari Window, scapegoating is in the unknown quadrant and will have to be addressed by the leader.

The most likely candidates for a scapegoat in the group are the most deviant/different members—that is, isolates, the lowest member on the status hierarchy, "omega chicken," and the leader. It is fairly obvious why the most different and lowest power member would be likely candidates, but the leader is also vulnerable. When the group is unable to deal with internal conflicts or achieve its goals, the leader can be easily blamed for all of the group's troubles. There are also complicating personality characteristics that play into scapegoating. Some needy members may find the negative attention that comes with being a scapegoat better than being ignored. This needy member may engage in behaviors that "ask the group" to pick on them. Some needy members may carry a metaphoric sign on their back with "Kick me!" on it. This situation is difficult for leaders to disentangle because there are both individual dynamics and group dynamics that are reinforcing each other.

Just pointing out this role to the group may be enough to keep the group from engaging in this behavior. It is also helpful if the leader can get the group to recognize the underlying tension or conflict. The leader might say, "I get the sense that members are in the grip of strong emotions that are not being shared!" Group members need to address the underlying issue and honestly share their feelings about the issue. This tactic is easier said than done, and the leader may have to make several attempts to get the group to deal with the underlying conflict. Conflict resolution is a major topic in the later chapter on group change (Chapter 15).

The role of blocker is especially problematic in task groups. Bales and colleagues' (Bales, 1958; Bales & Cohen, 1979) research on small group decision making delineates a dimension that involves the communications of members that help the group to move forward and achieve its purpose or create obstacles that move the group backward so that goals are not achieved. The blocker is able to sidetrack the discussion, raise red herrings, or simply make suggestions that keep the group from making decisions. These delaying tactics can keep a group from reaching conclusions in a meeting. These suggestions are often considered reasonable, for example, "Before we decide, I think we should complete a survey that collects data about how other agencies have dealt with this problem!" When the group agrees to collect data that may take months to organize, often the issue is long forgotten or no longer pressing and the decision is never made.

Red herrings are tangential issues that can easily sidetrack the discussion. When the red herring involves a "worst case scenario," members may be tricked into believing that the worst case scenario is inevitable and the decision will not be made.

For example, I (BAS) was a member of a standing committee in my school of social work who was discussing the idea of allowing master's students to be placed in private practice settings. There were 20 members on this committee, and most members were supportive of this change. Only three of us voiced opposition to this new policy. After writing a short position paper in opposition to this change, which did not convince any of the other members (I was a brand-new junior faculty member), I brought up a red herring. I planted the seed of a worst case scenario by asking members what would happen if a student engaged in unethical behavior in the field placement. Would the faculty liaison for the student also be liable? None of the faculty had any kind of malpractice insurance, and the discussion that followed raised all kinds of concerns about liability. The net result was this policy change was never brought to a vote. This is an example of how a "blocker" can keep the group from moving forward.

The blocker role may also appear in support and treatment groups when a member finds ways to keep the group from addressing issues that are difficult for the member to deal with. For example, some members may be uncomfortable with the open display of feelings. This may relate to ethnic and family background of the member.

For example, my (BAS) Yankee, British American roots taught me to hide my feelings and not express emotions that I was feeling.

This tendency to neutralize the expression of feelings is found in a number of Euro-American groups (McGoldrick, Pearce, & Giordano, 1982). When members are expressing intense emotions that are cathartic and appropriate to the healing process, a blocker may quickly grab a box of tissues and tell the sobbing member to get control of himself or herself. More obvious examples of blocking occur when a member tries to change the subject or bring up tangents. Such a tangent might be "Why do we have to pay for these services?" In the context of treatment groups, this kind of "resistance" or reluctance to address topics is central to helping the individual member deal with issues.

Special roles are not so problematic for the group leader because they do not interfere with the purpose of groups. They do not seem to be tied to group dynamics but instead to character traits of individual members in the group. The clown may help to relieve tension in the group by getting group members to laugh about issues. Through satire or sarcasm, the clown may bring information to the group. This role has appeared in many cultures such as the "holy fool" or court jester in feudal England and the "coyote" or trickster in Native American cosmology. In feudal courts, the jester was able to bring up critiques or add information that would not be tolerated by the leader from other subjects.

The clown and group leader are mutually exclusive roles, and members are uncomfortable when the leader plays the clown. When the "clowning" in the group gets out of hand and the group is not addressing its task, the leader may have to refocus the group on its task. The clown is not as serious a role as the blocker, and the blocker is not interested in relieving tension or being playful.

The placater is another special role that is tied to the personality of a member (Satir, 1972). The placater is hypersensitive about insulting or upsetting other group members. Before speaking or commenting on a subject, the placater will make all kinds of disclaimers about what she is about to say, such as "I would like to make a comment, but I want all to know that I like everyone in the group and would never want to hurt anyone's feelings!" or "Please forgive me if I say something that upsets anyone!" The placater introduces all of her comments with placating, and it is the placater's disclaimers that often irritate the group, such as "Don't worry about our responses. Just say what's on your mind!" The placater may be a shy member of the group who often is self-censoring. Only by placating can she muster the courage to speak up. Placaters may also come from ethnic subcultures in which self-assertion or speaking up is not valued. With Asian American clients, who are minorities in a group, Confucianism proscribes deference to others, especially those who are older and have higher status (Lum, 2005).

The confessor is a role that seems to fit well within support and treatment groups. Individual members share painful information about negative events in their lives with which they are struggling. This kind of self-sharing is grist for the mill in treatment groups, but it can be undesirable in task groups when and if it keeps the group from getting to its agenda (e.g., "Before we begin with the budget today, I have to tell you about what happened last night!"). The confessor will then start a long narrative about some terrible life event that the group can do little to change. The narrative may involve catharsis and expression of great emotional pain and despair. The confessor may give graphic details of the event that are disturbing to other group members, and it will be almost impossible for the group to get back to the agenda. The only chance the leader has of avoiding this calamity in a task group is not to grant the space for this narrative when the member asks permission to bring up the issue. The leader says, "We will listen to what happened to you last night at the end of our meeting today, but first we will discuss the budget and other items on our agenda."

The confessor role can be problematic in support and treatment groups when it occurs in a first session and the member confesses to a whole lot of tragic issues. The member will "dump and run" and never be seen again in any other sessions of the group. Sharing personal information is central to support and treatment groups, but this information needs to unfold slowly as the group matures. When a member dumps a whole lot on the group in the beginning, the group cannot be much help, and the member will avoid the other therapeutic variables.

The "junior therapist" is a special role that may emerge in treatment groups. As treatment groups develop and mature, some members may identify so strongly with the leader that they begin to mimic the group leader's behavior. They may move into a seat next to the leader and appear to run the group session. The junior therapist may even use the exact words of the leader when she invites the group to begin working by saying, "OK, folks! Let's get started and go around and share how homework went this past week!" For some members of the treatment group, this may be irritating and seem like a "power move." It is useful to point out to the group that during the maturation stage of the group it is possible and desirable that the group can run itself. The potential downside of this role is that the junior therapist may avoid doing her own work in the group while focusing on the work of others. The potential upside of this role is that when the leader is the brunt of hostility in group, the junior therapist is in a position to mediate and resolve this kind of conflict.

This discussion of group roles is not meant to be exhaustive but instead to present some of the most common roles that will emerge in the variety of groups that social workers lead. The most important roles for interpersonal practitioners to identify are the problematic roles that may keep groups from achieving their goals: monopolizer, character assassin, blocker, scapegoat. It is also important that leaders engage in tactics to mollify these roles when they do appear.

Geography

Group geography includes the physical setting of the group session and how members arrange themselves in that space. The setting and arrangement of space can have an impact on the interaction of members in a group. Some agencies do not have adequate rooms for social workers to run groups. Some rooms may be too small and crowded with many tables and chairs, and some group rooms may be in the damp, poorly lit basement with no windows and musty walls. Some agencies have no space for groups to meet, so they meet in rooms that serve other functions, such as cafeteria dinning areas, hallways, or day rooms for all residents in a facility. These kinds of inadequate group settings set a negative tone for the group. Sometimes there is a paradox in these agencies with inadequate space because there may be a comfortable group room that is reserved for board meetings. This room is rarely used and sits empty most of the time but is off limits to staff. Previously in this chapter we have discussed how important it is for the group leader to plan where the group meets so that space is adequate and that in some agencies space for groups may have to be found outside the agency.

The arrangement of furniture in a group setting is also important in the facilitation of groups. Some seating arrangements are sociopetal (i.e., they encourage interaction), while others are sociofugal (i.e., they discourage interactions; Seabury, 1971; Sommer, 1969). The ideal sociopetal arrangement for a group is a roundtable in which everyone can see each other, and there are more chairs than group members. There should be room for everyone at the table. In a large group, it may be necessary to have a rectangular table to accommodate all members at the same table. Couches, long rows, and members sitting behind members in chairs are sociofugal and should not be used for group meetings. Couches and benches do not allow members on the ends to see and talk to each other. Before members arrive for a group session, the leader should arrange the chairs in a circle and draw an invisible circle in the air around the chairs in the group. As the group members arrive and select seats, and as the group meeting progresses, the leader should be aware of members who sit or move their chairs outside the invisible circle. Leaders can observe how members will interact when they are inside and outside of the circle. When members sit outside the circle, it may indicate the member's lack of commitment to the group.

In the film Anger Management *with Adam Sandler and Jack Nicholson, Sandler is court ordered to attend the anger management group run by Nicholson. When the group starts, he is sitting about 10 feet outside and behind most of the other group members When he is introduced to the group by Nicholson, he communicates verbally to the group that he does not plan to attend other sessions of the group because he does not feel he has an anger management problem. Nicholson invites Sandler to move his chair and join the group. As the group progresses, Nicholson antagonizes Sandler and gets him to express anger (i.e., moving information from blind to open in the Johari Window).*

The group setting should have more chairs than members because who sits next to whom may reflect sociometry. Members who have things in common or have some attraction to each other will often sit next to each other in the group. As cliques form in the group, members will sit next to each other. It is also common in groups that the chairs on either side of the leader will be empty, except when the role of junior therapist emerges and sits in one of these empty chairs. When there are empty chairs in the group, the leader may use these empty chairs to move members around in various group activities. Sometimes a leader may move members away from each other when they are engaging in disruptive sidebar conversations. The leader may also have members count off by two's or three's when planning a group activity in order to break up cliques in the group. The leader can use group geography to impact the climate of the group, and the leader should realize that interventions into geography can sometimes produce anxiety when members are forced to sit in chairs they have not chosen.

SUMMARY •

The chapter began with an exercise to help readers think about groups that they have been in over their life span. Throughout the chapter, these groups are referred back to as examples of what happens in groups. The chapter then moved into a discussion of some of the most common types of groups that social workers lead in practice. The next major topic concerned those elements in groups that lead to an effective group experience for members. Numerous therapeutic variables were described and operationalized. The major part of the chapter discussed how groups develop over time both inside a single session and from session to session. The chapter ended with a selective review of basic group dynamics that a leader can expect to see in the groups they run.

CHAPTER **15**

GROUP CHANGE

Change is inevitable—except from a vending machine.

—Robert C. Gallagher (n.d.)

In Chapter 14, we discussed how group leaders assess the groups they are leading. In this chapter we will present some of the interventions that group leaders may employ in order to help groups achieve their goals. This chapter will be selective of interventions that will be covered. There are many group books (Corey, Corey, & Corey, 2010; Garvin, 1996; Reid, 1997; Toseland & Rivas, 2008) that are more comprehensive than this chapter. We are selecting those interventions that are basic to running groups and can be mastered by beginning social workers when they begin to run their first groups. Though social workers lead task groups, the interventions covered here are focused on individual change groups such as consciousness-raising (CR), psychoeducational, support, and treatment groups.

In this chapter, we will look carefully at the responsibilities and interventions that group leaders perform in the first session of a closed group. The first session is critical for setting the tone and preventing attrition (i.e., dropouts) in succeeding sessions. Because interpersonal conflicts are inevitable in formed groups, the chapter will also look at interpersonal conflict and suggest interventions that a group leader can employ to resolve these conflicts. In this chapter, we will also discuss the use of structured activities, suggest a number of structured activities, and point out the limits and downsides of such activities. We will begin this chapter with a contrived, interactive case example of a support group for institutionalized elders (see Working With Elders in a Support Group). We want the reader to imagine that she or he is the social work student who is composing and leading this support group. The case reflects a number of issues that have been covered in previous chapters in this book—that is, intersectionality, cultural competence, social justice, group screening as well as provide a forum to discuss leadership interventions.

Working With Elders in a Support Group

The setting is an extended care home for elders in a neighborhood of a medium-sized city in a Midwestern state. The residence has about 200 residents of varying social skills. The ethnic composition of the residence is about 40% white, 30% African American, 15% Latino, 10% Asian American, 4% Arab American, and the remaining 1% identify themselves in other ways (e.g., Chaldean, Native American). The city in which the residence is located has a large working-class population who work in factories located in or near the city. There are also a significant number of single-parent families and many of these families rely on some form of financial assistance (e.g., unemployment compensation, supplemental assistance, Social Security). The residence is an older building constructed in the 1930s. It has been expanded with the addition of several wings to house couples as well as singles and to account for the various levels of independent living and nursing care.

As the social work student, fill in your identity characteristic:

Age _____

Gender expression _____

Race/ethnicity _____

Sexuality _____

Ability/disability _____

Marital Status:

Never married/single _____

Cohabitating couple _____

Married _____

(Continued)

(Continued)

Domestic partnership _____

Separated _____

Divorced _____

Widowed _____

Family Status:

No children _____

Number/age of child(ren) _____

Parents' ages (if living) _____

Socioeconomic Status of Family of Origin:

Poor ___ *Working-class* ___ *Middle-class* ___ *Professional-class* ___ *Upper-class* ___

The Field Placement Assignment: You are assigned to work with a support group for single residents who have been struggling with their adjustment to the facility. These new residents are reluctant to participate in programs, are socially withdrawn, and are hostile to custodial staff. Professional and nursing staff made referrals to your group, and the following residents were identified for individual screening interviews:

Mr. Willie Jones is a 72-year-old African American widower. Mr. Jones worked for over 40 years as a janitor in a large Baptist church. Since his wife's death 5 years ago, he had been living in the church basement. Though he is a hard worker, recently the church became concerned about this living arrangement and arranged for him to retire and move to the residence. Mr. Jones is soft-spoken, very religious, and tends to avoid participating with other residents in any of the activities and programs. Mr. Jones has been diagnosed with early stage Alzheimer's.

Mr. Alexi Chekhov is a 69-year-old single man who was born in Russia and immigrated to the United States about 20 years ago. He speaks English well; however, he is muscular, has a large frame, and has been observed bullying other residents and custodial staff who are smaller than he is. He does not do well in programmed activities and irritates other residents who see him as abrasive and a "cheater" at bingo. His room is cluttered, he does not pick up his belongings, and must be reminded to take care of personal hygiene. He identifies himself as Jewish, but he has no interest in associating with other Jewish residents or religious services. Mr. Chekhov has been diagnosed with Parkinson's.

Mr. John Brown is a 67-year-old widower of African American background. He had worked for General Motors (GM) as a line worker for almost 40 years and retired 5 years ago when offered a "buyout" by GM. He and his wife had lived in the same neighborhood for over 30 years until

2 years ago when his wife was murdered in random drug violence. He was seriously depressed by this terrible life event and the police inaction in trying to locate the perpetrators. His four children are all married, have successful careers, and have all left the state. He has little contact with his children and grandchildren. He has not made any friends, is a social isolate, and does not participate in the residence programs. Mr. Brown has high blood pressure and suffers from emphysema.

Mr. Nils Hansen is a 73-year-old Norwegian bachelor farmer who worked all his life on a dairy farm until he was injured in a farm accident that severed his right arm. After the accident, he was forced to retire from farming. He has no heirs to the estate that was created when he sold his dairy cattle and calves, machinery, and farmland. He has bequeathed his estate to the extended care facility with the agreement that they will care for him until his death. Mr. Hansen often complains about the food because it does not agree with his Norwegian palate. He misses lutefisk, smoked salmon, rutabaga, and potato dumplings. The staff is concerned that he often skips meals and may not be getting enough nutrition. He may be showing signs of failure to thrive.

Ms. Bobbi-Joe McCoy is a single 72-year-old white woman. She moved with her family in pursuit of jobs from the hollows of Kentucky after WWII. Her mother died of tuberculosis when she was in her teens, and as the oldest daughter, she took on the responsibility of raising her five younger siblings. She never married and worked intermittently at various waitress jobs. She is in poor health now because she has been a lifelong smoker and alcoholic. She often gets caught smoking in her room, which is a violation of residence rules. Ms. McCoy has been diagnosed with early stages of Korsakoff"s Syndrome.

Ms. Alice Trotter is an 81-year-old heiress of African American heritage. She is the grand-daughter of Samuel Trotter, who made his fortune as an entrepreneur in the peanut butter industry. Most of Ms. Totter's life was spent enjoying the wealth of her family's peanut butter empire, until the company was bilked of millions and left bankrupt by the unscrupulous activities of two accountants. The SEC and law enforcement officials never investigated the illegal activities of the two white accountants, and Ms. Trotter and her family were left penniless. Ms. Trotter has spent several years homeless on the streets. She believes that someday the courts will bring her justice, and she can return to a life of fine clothes, fine restaurants, and celebrity status. She is a social isolate and does not interact with the other residents who she calls "hoi polloi." Ms. Trotter is HIV positive and is beginning to show symptoms of AIDS-related complex.

Ms. Letitia Gonzales is a 74-year-old curandera with a Mexican and Native American background. She had been able to support herself from her thriving practice in the Mexican American community. As her practice and reputation grew as a successful indigenous healer, the AMA filed suit against her for "practicing medicine without a license." She lost the suit and threatened jail time destroyed her practice. She has no family living in the area and has been supporting herself on Social Security. Ms. Gonzales is obese, diabetic, and suffers from decubitus ulcers. She gets around the residence in an electric wheelchair.

STUDENT REFLECTIONS

Diversity Dimensions: What issues may arise in this group because of the various identity dimensions and disabilities that each member brings to the group? Can you predict any of the interpersonal tensions that may arise because of the diversity of this group?

What characteristics of these members will require you to get more information—for example, do you understand the various medical diagnoses, what a Curandera is, and what Medicaid and Social Security are?

How will your own identity dimensions facilitate and present obstacles for you as the leader of this group? How will your age, gender expression, and past life experience with elders in your own family influence your ability to relate to this diverse group of residents, as well as their ability to relate to you?

Other Reflections (Authority Issues) on Referrals to Your Group

- *How will the residents feel about a group that the residence seems to push them to attend? They may already see the institution as a negative force in their lives that does not take their needs and wants into consideration.*
- *Will the residents see you as an extension of the power of the institution? Who is aligned with it?*
- *How will the residents respond to you when you tell them you are an intern from the school of social work?*
- *What have been these residents' previous experiences with authority?*
- *The institution sees the residents' problems as their response to their living situation. What will the residents feel about this perspective? Do they see themselves as having problems?*

In preparation for this group, you will be completing screening interviews with each prospective member. What follows are some suggested issues you might raise in the prescreening interview:

1. *Introduce myself as a student intern and briefly indicate my previous experiences working with support groups.*

2. *Explain who the resident has been referred by (give name of referring person who is on the staff).*

3. *Ask the resident what he or she knows about this referral. Possibly indicate that the resident has been referred to get some help in being more successful in the facility and in dealing with staff. Ask resident's feelings about the referral.*

4. *Ask the resident what she or he thinks about joining a group.*

5. Describe the group: Say something about other residents in general and indicate that it will meet for 10 times on a weekly basis in the mid-afternoon snack break.

6. Indicate that much of what the group members talk about will be determined by them, and the subjects should deal with their thoughts and feelings about the residence. If they find things they don't like about the residence, I will try to help them find ways of changing these. If residents have disagreements with each other or with me, I will try to help them resolve these in peaceful ways.

7. Ask the resident what she or he would like to accomplish in the group or would like to see changed as a result of the group.

8. Ask the resident what she or he might like to talk about in the group.

9. Finally, ask if the resident wishes to join the group. If the resident is reluctant, ask if she or he is willing to try it out for a few times.

Sample Write-Up of
Prescreening Interview with Mr. John Brown

I greeted Mr. Brown at the door of the social work office in the residence. I introduced myself and suggested we sit in the two adjoining armchairs in the room. I asked Mr. Brown if he knew why he was here. He said that Ms. Bennett, the nurse on his hall, had talked to him about his lack of interest in attending activities and making new friends. She would like him to talk to someone about this. I said that I was a social worker and that I helped new residents adjust to the facility. One of the ways I did this was by meeting with groups of residents in which the group members and I could work together on things that stood in the way of their transition to the facility. I wanted to talk to Mr. Brown about joining a group.

Mr. Brown stated that he did not want to be any trouble and was not particularly interested in meeting other residents. He still misses his wife and feels there could not be anyone who could fill her empty shoes. I acknowledged how difficult this tragic loss would be for him and asked whether any of his children lived in the area. He stated that they all are married and have their own lives. None of them live in the state, and he does not want to be a burden on them

I asked whether Mr. Brown had ever been in a support group before. He explained that after his wife was murdered, he joined a grief support group. This was a difficult experience because there was so much crying and sadness in this group that he only attended two sessions. After these two sessions, he felt so much worse, and he decided he would not be able to get over his grief in this way. I explained that this would not be a grief group.

I also asked Mr. Brown what he might want to know about me. He said that he didn't have any questions. I said that he might want to know that I would be working in the facility for 8 more months and that I was doing this to get my social work degree and then work in an extended care facility like this one.

(Continued)

(Continued)

Mr. Brown asked what the group would be like and whether I would be like a teacher. I said that wasn't what I was there for. I was there to help the members talk to each other, and I would give my ideas as part of the discussion. The topics will be picked by all of us together. Mr. Brown asked what we would talk about. I asked him what he might like to see discussed. He said that some staff were mean to residents and even called them names. I asked what kind of names, and he said he couldn't remember now. I thought that what he said about the staff could be something the group would talk about.

Mr. Brown said he needed to go to his room right now to use the toilet. I asked if we could continue our talk tomorrow. He agreed, and we agreed to meet during the lunch hour.

STUDENT REFLECTIONS

Do you think Mr. Brown will be a good candidate for the group? Why?
In your judgment, what is Mr. Brown's motivation to join the group?
Very low . . . . Low . . . . Moderate . . . . High . . . . Very high
Special considerations that you will have to take as group leader if Mr. Brown joins the group:

● FIRST GROUP SESSION

After meeting with each prospective member and getting a preliminary agreement from each to try out the group, I had suggested to the residents that we meet during their mid-afternoon snack break. The meetings would be held in a smaller conference room that is adjacent to the large dining hall and is not used at that time. Before the meeting, I arranged 10 chairs in a circle around a round table so that members could have some choice about where they choose to sit. Mr. Chekhov was the first to arrive; I greeted him and indicated he could sit wherever he wished. Shortly after that, the rest of the members trickled in, except for Mr. Hansen, who did not appear. As members entered the room, I indicated they could sit where they wished. I noticed that the men and women sat near members of the same gender. They looked at me expectantly to begin.

I introduced myself by giving them my first and last name, and I indicated that I was a graduate social work student and leading this support group was part of my training. I thanked them for coming to this first meeting and then suggested everyone introduce themselves by giving their names and telling something they liked to do. Mr. Chekhov was first to speak up; the other men followed and the women were last to volunteer this information about themselves. Here is what they said:

Mr. Jones said he liked to listen to gospel music.

Mr. Chekhov stated that he liked to go out to bars and dance.

Mr. Brown said he liked to read newspapers and watch America's Most Wanted.

Ms. McCoy said she also likes to watch TV and listen to country music.

Ms. Trotter said she does not watch TV but enjoys needlepoint.

Ms. Gonzales said she likes to do readings with some of the other residents and enjoys watching Medium.

I said that they had all been encouraged to attend this group by one of the staff who thought the group could help them make their experience in the residence a better one. I asked if there were any questions. Ms. McCoy asked how the group could help her. She stated that she was happy to have a roof over her head and three square meals a day. I said that they could discuss things that happened to them in the residence that they weren't sure how to deal with and the other group members could make suggestions. I also said they might want to change some things about the residence that made it hard for them. I then asked how they thought the group might help all of them.

STUDENT REFLECTIONS

Do you see any themes in what the members like to do?

Is the student leader clear about the purpose of the group?

How is the student leader encouraging group members to participate in the group?

Mr. Chekhov said that the group could help him find a drinking buddy and change the rule about alcohol consumption in the residence. I asked what the others thought about this idea. Ms. Gonzales said she thought the group might help members to stay healthy and avoid bad habits, and Ms. McCoy and Ms. Trotter nodded in agreement. I commented that I hoped the group could help them make good choices for themselves. Mr. Brown said he hoped the group could do something about the prejudice in the residence. I asked what he had in mind. He said that a lot of the white residents don't like blacks and the same was true of the staff. I asked what the others thought, and Ms. Trotter said that Mr. Brown knew what he was talking about. I agreed that this was an issue the group should talk about a lot more.

STUDENT REFLECTIONS

Do you see any conflict that may be arising between group members?

How do you think the student leader dealt with the issue of racism? What would you have done differently about this issue? Does your own race or ethnicity play a role in what you would do in this situation?

I asked if there were other ideas for the group. Ms. McCoy said that the staff were down on her and didn't like her because of her smoking. Ms. Trotter muttered under her breath that "they had good reason." I commented that sometimes we are likely to have disagreements and conflict in this group, and we should look at ways of resolving these that make the group a safe place to say what we feel.

STUDENT REFLECTIONS

Why is it important for the student leader to introduce the concept of conflict at this point in the group session?

I wondered if we could discuss now how we could make the group a safe place to speak our minds. One idea I had was to promise each other not to repeat outside of the group what anyone said in the meetings. Ms. Trotter asked if that went for me, too. I said yes with one exception: If someone threatened to hurt himself or someone else, I would have to try to find a way to stop this, but I would discuss this with them first if at all possible. I asked the members if they were willing to keep what was discussed inside the group, and they all nodded agreement.

STUDENT REFLECTIONS

The student leader introduced the ground rule of confidentiality. Do you think this was effective—that is, tying it to "safety"?

I said our time was almost up today. I summarized what had been said and suggested that at the next meeting we continue to discuss how the group can help each member and also find ways of making the facility a place that benefits everyone. I asked how the members felt about this meeting by suggesting they indicate this by turning their thumbs up or down. Everyone turned their thumbs up except Ms. Trotter, who turned her thumb sideways. I thanked her for her honesty and to everyone else for their participation in this first meeting. We all continued to finish our "healthy snack," and most agreed that they were sick of tapioca pudding and did not want it to appear as a "healthy snack" at our next meeting.

I asked members if it would be OK if I made name cards for our next meeting so that it would be easier for us to remember names. Because of his failing eyesight, Mr. Brown commented that he hoped the name cards would have large letters, and others nodded in agreement.

STUDENT REFLECTIONS

How might the student's use of evaluation be empowering to the members?

How will the name cards help to facilitate group process?

What should the student leader do about Mr. Hansen, who did not appear at this first meeting?

SECOND GROUP SESSION ●

All the members were present except Mr. Hansen. They had come on time, and I opened the meeting by saying that I was glad everyone had returned. I suggested we begin the meeting by everyone saying a few words about what they were feeling today. Mr. Chekhov said he was in a bad mood because another resident had an "attitude" toward him. Mr. Jones said he felt uplifted by the Lord because he had played gospel music all morning. Mr. Brown said, "Same old, same old." When asked, he said it had to do with particular staff. Ms. McCoy said she felt the same way but in her case it was about other residents who were complaining about her smoking. Ms. Trotter said she was feeling good because she had met a new friend who came from "a long line of good stock." Ms. Gonzales said she was OK and had nothing else to say.

I said this was a good beginning, and I wondered if the members might like to begin meetings in this way. The members all nodded. I then mentioned that at the last meeting each member had brought up some concern with which the group might help. Mr. Brown asked if it was required that they attend every session of the group. He explained that on some days he felt too depressed to talk with others. I stated that this was a good topic and asked what other members thought about attendance. Ms. Trotter reiterated that this was a voluntary choice, and no one should be forced to attend. Several members nodded in agreement.

Mr. Jones acknowledged this choice, but he was concerned that if someone suddenly does not show up, would this be a concern to members: "Did something happen to the member who did not show up?" Mr. Chekhov joked, "You never know when one of us old geezers may have croaked!" The group chuckled at this comment. Ms. McCoy offered the suggestion that if we planned to skip a meeting we might let the social worker know that we planned not to attend. Members seemed to accept this suggestion as a common courtesy to other members in the group.

Mr. Brown commented that he wanted to talk about some of the staff who used racist language when interacting with black residents. He does not mind being called "colored" or "black," but he does not like the "N" word. He does not like it when white staff and even when black staff use this term. A tense silence fell over the group, and no one else picked up on this conversation. After a pause, the members looked at me to see what I would do with this discussion.

STUDENT REFLECTIONS

Describe the conditions present here that promote an openness to discuss issues related to oppression and racial epithets.

I said that I thought this was an important topic and a hard conversation that we should have. I stated that we all may have witnessed these interactions between staff and residents. Members are likely to have strong feelings about this issue, and it might be difficult to bring them out when we are still getting acquainted with each other. The group also had members from different backgrounds and this might make the discussion difficult as they didn't know where others stood. I asked if we should work on getting to know each other better in this session and reserve this discussion for a later session. Members nodded, and Mr. Jones stated that he would like to know more about each member.

STUDENT REFLECTIONS

Do you think the student leader is avoiding the discussion about racism? This topic emerged in the first session and now in the second session. Is the group ready to discuss this issue?

Mr. Chekhov added that it is not just about racial slurs. He feels that staff members make negative comments about his Russian background. Ms. McCoy added that she does not like it when staff members and other residents refer to her as "ridge." Ms. Gonzales noted that there are many examples of intolerance that she experiences because of her Mexican roots. Ms. Trotter commented that it is not just racial slurs but also the way staff relate to residents. Many talk to her in a sweet, maternal voice as though she was a "child." Several members spoke at once—nodding and complaining about this issue. Mr. Brown summarized this discussion by stating he "is not stupid, not a child, and should be respected for his age."

STUDENT REFLECTIONS

It seems that the members chose to move ahead with their discussion of discrimination. What conditions are present in the group that favor their decision to continue?

At this point in the group, I summarized the discussion and noted that everyone has negative experiences with comments about their background. I offered to engage them in an activity that would help them share their backgrounds with other members of the group. I explained that this would involve some simple writing and drawing on a piece of paper. I handed out paper and pencils to everyone and said that they would be creating their own personal coat of arms and sharing it with other members of the group. This activity did not require any artistic skill but did require some careful thought about what was important about their ethnic roots. I suggested that we might include a number of items and comments on our coat of arms—that is, favorite holiday, special foods from our youth, strengths we gained from our background, and how others (outsiders) tend to view our roots. I explained that I would be doing this activity and sharing, too. I also warned them that each must decide how much they want to share with the group about their background.

STUDENT REFLECTIONS

Comment on the student's use of a structured activity at this point in the group's development: How does this activity reflect on the issues raised by the group, and does it fit where the group is in its development?

Members worked diligently on their coat of arms and were surprised that they had some common experiences. This activity took up most of the session; generated a lot of discussion between members; and in the end, members *evaluated it as a positive experience (all thumbs up). The members agreed that in the next meeting we would discuss examples of discrimination that are experienced and what can be done about them. The group finished up the plate of oatmeal cookies that I had provided with the help of the kitchen staff. Once again, the group agreed that oatmeal cookies were much better than tapioca pudding.*

STUDENT REFLECTIONS

Do you think it was important that the student leader respond to the group's request to have a different snack?

If you were leading this group, how would you prepare for the third session of this group?

Mr. Nils Hansen has now missed two meetings of the group in spite of efforts to convince him to attend. What would you do about his absence?

Is it the role of a student intern to address issues of institutional racism in the field placement?

● THE FIRST SESSION OF A CLOSED GROUP

This section of the chapter will present some of the tasks that leaders face in creating a successful experience for members in the first meeting of the group. Some of this work can be front-loaded in the prescreening interviews with prospective members. For example, if the interview indicates that a potential member is a good candidate for the group and the potential member accepts the offer to attend the first session (preliminary contract), then the leader can use the interview to suggest some "homework" that the prospective member may consider before attending the first session of the group. The leader might ask the prospective member to think about things they might share with the group, to think about what they hope to get out of the group, and to think about what will be most difficult for them about attending the group. There are many issues that a leader might front-load in the prescreening interview, which will depend on the purpose and type of group that is planned.

Groups have to deal with a number of issues when they first convene. These issues do not necessarily follow a set order and include the following:

1. Establishing initial relationships with the worker and other group members

2. Determining the purpose and goals of the group

3. Determining group norms and ground rules

4. Dealing with feelings about being in the group

5. Establishing a preliminary contract to continue with the group

6. Ending the first session

Establishing Initial Relationships

If members are to commit themselves to the group and begin the process of mutual aid, they must start to establish a bond with the worker and other members. This bond involves a sense of commonality with other members and a willingness to explore the issues that bring them to the group.

The worker can initiate the creation of bonds among members by helping them begin to learn something about one another. Most groups start by developing a "naming ritual" in which members share their name and some brief information about themselves. Depending on the purpose of the group, the leader can determine the information that is to be shared. For example, members may be encouraged to talk about the reasons that bring them to the group when they introduce themselves. In the case example at the beginning of this chapter, the social work student asked members to share their names and something they like to do. Another simple icebreaker can involve the request that members look in their purse, wallet, or backpacks for something that is meaningful to them. Members take out this item, say their name, and share it with the group. Because members are surrounded by strangers and are likely to be anxious about speaking, this simple activity gives each member control over what they will share. This activity also gives the group leader a sense of how difficult self-sharing will be for the members of the group. For example, some members may share fairly mundane items like a driver's license or credit card while others may share pictures of family members or membership cards in various organizations.

Another icebreaker that generates lots of energy and laughter is "Two Truths and a Lie." In this activity, members are to introduce themselves and tell two things that are true and one thing that is a lie. The leader then encourages the group to try to figure out which piece of information is a lie. This encourages members to interact with each other, and it can generate a lot of surprises and humor when members are fooled by other members. The downside of this exercise is that members often remember the lies about other members and not the truths. Whether these opening naming rituals are done as a round or left up to the group to decide who will go next, it is important that the group leader listen carefully to the name, look at the member introducing herself, and thank the member for sharing. As the members introduce themselves, it is also important that the leader listen carefully for common themes and point them out to the group. For example,

"Mary and Bill both play a musical instrument!" or "Wow, we now have three members of the group named Cindy." It is important that the leader of the group participate in these icebreakers by sharing information, too. It is also important that these naming rituals are not designed to gather a whole lot of information about each member but just a little bit to begin to reduce the strangeness that members feel in this first session. From the perspective of the Johari Window, these exercises are moving information from the hidden areas into the open areas of the group.

Because of the special role of the leader, there are ethical prescriptions that require the leader to disclose her credentials and expertise with leading groups. This disclosure statement (Corey et al., 2010) is sometimes difficult for beginning social workers who are in training and running the group for the first time.

In reflecting back to the group example at the beginning of this chapter, does the social work student present this kind of professional self-disclosure to the group?

Determining Purpose and Goals

In Chapter 14, we discussed the importance of the group purpose when developing a group proposal for the agency. It is important that the planned purpose of the group, its rationale, and how the group may help individual members be discussed in this first session. Even if this information was discussed in the prescreening interviews, it is essential that the members discuss the proposed purpose as a group. The worker needs to clarify the purpose, how it fits with the individual members goals, and whether members agree with this starting point.

It is likely that the group's purpose may expand or contract as the group matures, but it is important that everyone is on the same page in the first session. In the first session, there is a tendency for members to agree with the proposed purpose of the group, and the leader should encourage group members to raise questions or concerns they may have about the purpose. For example, members may nod in agreement and not volunteer any questions. When one or several members raise some questions about the purpose, this allows the group to shape the purpose to their own needs and also gives the leader a chance to support and empower members of the group.

Now in groups where members have been mandated to attend and no one wants to be there, it will be much more complicated to get agreement with the group's purpose. As was discussed in the chapter on contracting (Chapter 8), the leader will have to use a dual contract approach and clarify what cannot be changed by a court mandate and what can be accomplished within the parameters of the group. For example, parents charged with neglect who are court-ordered to go to parenting classes before their children can be returned may be extremely unhappy with the idea of a parenting class. This was the case that Barbara H. Seabury (BHS) described in the first chapter in the book. The leader will have to make it clear how the purpose of the group to improve parenting skills will reflect on the court mandate. The leader, however, cannot change the court mandate nor make any promises that completing the work of the group will assure the return of children. The leader needs to make it clear that parents have the choice not to attend the group, which will probably not help them get their children returned, or to attend and make the most of the services so that a positive report can be delivered to the court. There is a paradoxical issue in such mandated groups—that is, all members clearly have something in common, which is their desire *not* to be in the group. The task for leaders of such "socialization groups" is to begin to change the "involuntary" perspective of members into a more "voluntary" position so that they can benefit from the purpose of the group. Because attrition is a fact of life for voluntary groups, social workers need to realize that mandated groups also face similar issues of attrition.

Take a look again at the support group example at the beginning of this chapter. How much pressure is being put on members by the residence to attend the group? Clearly this is not a court mandated group, but is it fair to say that it is voluntary when members of the staff, who occupy power positions in the residence, are referring members to the group? Obviously Nils Hansen has not responded to the pressures from staff nor the group leader to attend. Do you think this reflects an independent streak that is found in Norwegian bachelor farmers and in the fact that he is paying his own way and does not rely on Medicaid? His role in the residence is that of consumer and not recipient.

Members should also be encouraged to explore their individual goals for the group (i.e., what they hope to achieve by being in the group). In the first session, these individual goals may only be tentative; however, articulating these goals helps the group leader and members select appropriate group activities that will lead to attaining goals. The process of deciding on goals is easier if members have similar concerns. In more diverse groups, workers sometimes have to find ways of helping members select goals without drawing the process out to the point that members find it overly burdensome. In these circumstances, workers may offer members relevant goal statements they can modify to fit their circumstances. Workers may also subdivide the group into smaller groups or pairs, for work on individual goals—that then may be reported back to the full group.

In the support group example with the elders, the leader has been clear about the purpose of the group, but individual members have not worked on individual goals. Mr. Chekhov and Mr. Brown have suggested some goals, but others in the group have not articulated what they hope to get out of the group.

Determining Group Norms and Ground Rules

All groups create norms, which are expectations that members will engage in some behaviors and refrain from engaging in others. Some of these norms, such as expectations about attendance and maintenance of confidentiality, are regularly posed by group leaders. The latter is often a subject of concern to group members who fear that if other group members have sensitive information about them, this information can leak to the community. Members usually contract with one another that they will not repeat outside the group anything said by another member, even if that person's name is omitted. They are free, however, to tell others what they have said about themselves. The confidentiality rule is important to group members because it contributes to a sense of safety in the group climate, and members usually take it seriously. In some groups, the confidentiality rule is an absolute—that is, "what's said in the group stays in the group!"

Some ground rules are imposed by the agency that is sponsoring the group. Some group leaders will bring a list of these ground rules for members to review. For example, there may be rules about paying for missed appointments, no smoking inside the agency, and prohibitions against attending groups when inebriated or high. Social work groups also proscribe physical violence within the group and the use of racial, ethnic, and gender epithets. There are many norms and ground rules that groups may develop as the group matures that are particular to the group. For example, in the Carrell (2000) workbook, which focuses on adolescent groups, the ground rule of "be kind to each other" is offered because of the tendency for this age group to be cruel to members who are different from other members. Later we will talk more about structured activities, and a ground rule that leaders offer members is that no one will be forced to participate in an activity if they choose not to.

What two ground rules have the group of elders discussed and agreed on?

It is unrealistic to expect the group to develop all of their ground rules in the first session. Many ground rules will emerge as the group develops because of conflicts that arise between members. For example, in an educational group of adults composed of men and women and members of different ethnicities and religious affiliations, the group was almost torn apart by the use of swearing and foul language. Some members felt foul language was extremely offensive while others felt it was a form of expressive communication. The group finally reached an agreement that they would not use the "F" word in sessions.

Dealing With Feelings About the Group

Members typically have positive feelings about the group related to their hopes that the group will help them attain their goals. They may also have some anxious feelings about whether they will be accepted by other members, whether the group will do them any harm, and whether the group will be a waste of time and resources. For members to decide to remain in the group, they will have to resolve these mixed feelings so that the positive outweigh the negative.

The worker can be helpful in this process by helping members to express both sides of their feelings. Members may be asked to share past experiences in groups and how they evaluated those experiences. The members' positive experiences and feelings may give some members a sense of hope about the group. The worker would be unwise to give false reassurances guaranteeing that negatives will never occur. In fact, the leader is ethically bound to warn members about the potential risks of participating in a group (Corey & Corey, 2006, pp. 70–74). These risks include the following:

- Members may violate rules of confidentiality that cannot be guaranteed.
- Members may self-disclose personal information that is very sensitive.
- Members may express intense feelings that are embarrassing.
- Members may find themselves in conflict with other members of the group.
- Members may feel that other members of the group are ganging up on them.

Informed consent dictates that these risks be discussed in the group, and having them recognized is often reassuring. The worker may offer reassurances that there are ways of dealing with group problems. Both the leader and members should be vigilant to note problems in group functioning as these emerge and seek ways to resolve them.

Establishing the Preliminary Contract

As with contracts with families and individuals, the contract in group work can range from a written and formal one to a verbal set of agreements. The situation around contracting in groups is complicated because there are really five contracts:

1. Between the group and the agency, for example, members will understand what the agency expects of them and what members' expectations are of the agency. For example, the agency may expect the group members to put away equipment the group has used so another group can make appropriate use of the meeting room. The group will expect the agency to supply it with adequate meeting space.

2. Between the group and the worker, for example, the group will expect the worker to help the members to accomplish the work of the group, and the worker will expect the members to come prepared to do the work that is necessary for the group to accomplish its purposes.

3. Among the members, for example, the members will expect other members to help them and to accept help from them.

4. Between the member and the group, for example, the members will expect the group (the members acting collectively) to develop a set of activities that will help the group accomplish its purposes, and the group will expect each member to contribute her or his "fair share" in making the activities successful.

5. Between the individual member and the worker, for example, the worker may form individual contracts with members related to the goal each one has established. Members may, in turn, individually expect the worker to carry out commitments, such as to contact a teacher, a parent, or other individual, that are important to achieving individual goals.

It is not realistic to expect that all of these arrangements and agreements can be reached in the first session nor that members will be able to understand all of these agreements. Hopefully the first three points can be understood and accepted by members. The third point is sometimes difficult for clients who may have experienced individual treatment. They may not realize that they are not only expected to receive help but also give help to others in the group.

Ending the First Session

As presented in Chapter 14 on group assessment, the leader should plan to leave time (i.e., 10 or 15 minutes) at the end of the session to complete some closing tasks. The leader should summarize the main points of the session and promote member reflection and reaction to the session (e.g., "I'm curious how each of you feel about today's session. Are there any issues that are unclear or questions that you might have?"). In the group example at the beginning of this chapter, the leader asked members to give a "thumbs up or down" to the first session. This is a quickie kind of evaluation mechanism, and the leader may choose to use other, more formal mechanism, such as the visual analog scale (VAS), which was discussed earlier in Chapter 9. The leader also needs to obtain a preliminary, public commitment from members to become a member of the group and to return to the next session. For example, "I would like to go around the group and ask each of you whether you will be able to attend our next session. Some of you may have decided that you do not want to be a member of this group. I am willing to meet with you after our session today and figure out other options."

The leader may also talk about next steps and in time-limited groups may assign "homework" (i.e., between session tasks) for the members to work on. For example, the leader might suggest that members think more about their individual goals and other issues they would like to bring up in the group. The worker should be clear about the date, time, and place of the next session and whether there are members who cannot make it. For example, the leader may say, "If a week from today is a problematic time, we can spend some time trying to find a better time to meet." Members may have to search for a better time in order to assure that most of the members will make the next session.

In the first session, the leader has to maintain a balance between being responsive to the members of the group, yet also being systematic (i.e., task oriented) to make sure certain issues are addressed (Reid & Epstein, 1972). It is important for the leader to encourage member participation so that members feel empowered and a sense of owning the group. "Starting where the members are" is important, but the leader cannot let the group get bogged down in tangents or details that may arise. Too much structure and control by the leader may discourage group participation, yet group structure helps to reduce anxiety in the first session so that members know what to expect. The group leader needs to keep an eye on herself (i.e., conscious use of self) and observe how this balance is playing out with members.

LEADERSHIP INTERVENTIONS ●

There are three general ways that a group leader can intervene to make the group experience successful for members: Vinter categorized worker actions under the headings of *direct*, *indirect* and *extra-group* means of influence (Vinter, 1985). This is not a perfect typology (i.e., overlap between categories), but it is useful as a heuristic schema to organize the many interventions that group leaders engage in. Direct means of influence involve the interactions between the group leader and individual members designed to affect member behaviors. These interventions involve a range of skills and techniques that are not unique to group work but also appear in work with individuals and families. For example, group leaders will engage in exploration, active listening, encouragement, advice giving, empathetic responding, confrontation, clarification, etc. There are whole group books devoted to these techniques (Haney & Leibsohn, 2001). We will focus on some of the most basic interventions that beginning leaders can employ.

Indirect means of influence involves interventions that are directed at the group as a whole that will have an influence on the individual members of the group. In this chapter, we will present a number of structured activities, programs, and intervention models that have been developed to work with various groups with various purposes, such as meditation and imagery techniques designed to reduce stress, social skills training to increase assertiveness, and CR to increase members awareness of common forms of oppression. There are numerous interventions that leaders employ that influence group conditions, and we will only present some basic examples in this chapter.

There are numerous workbooks that present various structured activities that can be used in groups (Barlow, Blythe, & Edmonds, 1999; Carrell, 2000; Dossick & Shea, 1988, 1990, 1995; Leveton, 1992; Liebmann, 1986; Pfeiffer & Jones, 1975). We will present some of them in this chapter that support the effectiveness variables found in effective groups. The caveats with structured activities are that they should be carefully planned to fit the purpose of the group, the stage of the group's development, and the abilities of the group members. They should not be used as "fillers" that are busywork to take up group time and the activity itself is never as important as what process results from the activity. It is important that enough time in a session be set aside to complete the activity, but the activity should not be seen as an end in itself. Sometimes the activity will "bomb," which is a great fear of beginning practitioners. Usually the group will forgive the leader when an activity bombs because they recognize that the leader was trying to do something that will be helpful to the purposes of the group.

Go back and look at the support group example. Can you find a structured activity that was employed by the leader? Do you believe that the structured activity was effective?

We have already discussed some of these indirect means of interventions in Chapter 14 on group assessment. The leader's efforts to plan and compose a group that will be able to build cohesiveness through pregroup interviews or to remove a potential member who will be disruptive to the group (e.g., character assassin) are examples of indirect influence. During a group session, the leader may use "rounds" to encourage silent members to participate or have the group count off by 2s or 3s and break into smaller groups in order to break up cliques.

Go back to the support group example in the beginning of this chapter and locate the use of "rounds" in both of the group sessions.

Extra-group means of influence include a number of interventions that group leaders may employ in order to impact the individual members of the group.

Groups do not exist in isolation from their environments. Social workers who are leading groups in school settings will often maintain contact with teachers and parents of their student members. Group leaders may have to negotiate with their own agency administrators or with other organizations to locate appropriate settings for their groups. As discussed in Chapter 14, group leaders may have to influence colleagues who are skeptical of group interventions so these colleagues do not sabotage the efforts of the leader. Group leaders who are working with parents may have to create child care arrangements so that parents can attend group sessions.

In the case example at the beginning of this chapter, the leader arranged with the kitchen staff to provide oatmeal cookies for the second session of the group. This may seem like a trivial intervention, but it has a positive impact on how the group members viewed the leader.

There is also another way of conceptualizing extra-group interventions. Because of the profession's commitment to social justice, many social work groups may engage in social action, such as action focused on changing oppressive arrangements in the client's environment. There are many support groups that not only focus on helping their individual members cope with life tragedies but also work to change the external arrangements that cause and/or contribute to these tragedies. For example, Mothers Against Drunk Driving (MADD) offers support groups for mothers who have lost a child to a drunk driver. This organization has also worked over the past 30 years to influence laws and courts so that drunk driving is viewed as a serious offense (Davies, 2006). Domestic violence groups not only offer support to victims or survivors of domestic violence but also work locally to change the laws and attitudes of police, ERs, and courts. Theses extra-group interventions are discussed in the two chapters on assessing and changing organizations (Chapters 16 and 17).

Leadership Moves and Structured Activities

In the 1960s when researchers began to look carefully at the effectiveness of interventions in social work, there was practice research that was looked at in regards to what social workers did in interviews to bring about change in their clients (Hollis, 1968; Reid & Epstein, 1972). The most common techniques were exploring, promoting catharsis, encouraging, promoting insight and understanding, and giving advice. Over these 5 decades, the types of interventions and techniques available to practitioners has proliferated with the development of different practice models such as cognitive behavioral interventions, solution focused interventions, strategic family interventions, time-limited interventions, etc. The value of research based models and evidence-based practice is that models must be prescriptive with detailed protocols of what social workers are doing in the interviews. Because there are so many techniques that social workers can employ in their interactions with individual clients and members of groups and families, this section of the chapter will organize techniques by tying common interventions to the effectiveness variable mentioned in Chapter 14. As was discussed earlier in Chapter 14, the effectiveness variables represent the "active ingredients" of successful groups.

Self-sharing is a critical component of group work. Without it, there will be no "work" done in the group session. A most common technique to promote self-sharing is exploration—asking members to "tell their story." There are many variations of exploration that can take place in groups. A leader may ask the group to "brainstorm," "to think of an issue they want to share with the group," "to describe a particular event or experience," etc. In Hollis's (1968) early research on interventions, exploration was the most common technique used by social workers in the first four sessions with individuals and families. Leaders also promote self-sharing in groups by self-disclosing information about themselves. The disclosure statement of the leader is a form of self-sharing that is related to the purpose of the group. It will demonstrate the genuineness and openness of the leader to share with the group members.

Social workers must avoid exploration that slips into the interrogation mode. A simple way to avoid the interrogation mode is not to ask questions of members that start with "why." "Why" questions tend to demand that members justify their actions. Instead, the use of "how" questions can avoid putting the members in a defensive position. For example, "Can you tell me how you got yourself into that situation?" instead of "Why did you get yourself into that situation?" Even though it is desirable that all members should be asked to share, not all members will share the same amount of information. Even when a leader uses a round to encourage each member to share, some will share more than others, and some may decide to pass.

There are many structured activities that leaders may employ in groups to help members self-share. In Chapter 14, we mentioned two structured activities: "Two Truths and a Lie" and taking an item that means something out of one's purse or wallet and then sharing it with the group. In this chapter, we will add two more structured activities that work well with many groups, such as "Weeding Your Garden" (Barlow et al., 1999) and "T-shirt" (Carrell, 2000). Both of these activities require paper and markers or crayons, but a pencil will work as well. Both of these activities ask members to draw on the paper, which is sometimes more difficult for adults than children. Adults will often say that they cannot draw, and the leader may have to suggest that stick figures, symbols, and words are OK, too.

Figure 15.1	"Weeding Your Garden"

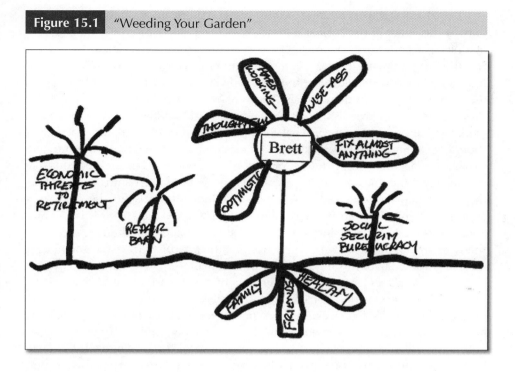

"Weeding Your Garden" works best when the leader demonstrates on the piece of paper how this activity works. All of the symbols can be stick figures. The leader draws a circle near the top of the page and places her name in the circle. The leader then draws five petals shaped like ovals around the edge of the circle. These petals are filled in with personal attributes that the person likes about themselves. The leader then draws a stem from the flower down to the ground and draws several roots under the ground. The roots represent the resources or strengths that support the flower, and the roots are labeled accordingly. Now around the flower several weeds are drawn that represent issues in the subject's life that need attention or must be addressed at this point in time (see Figure 15.1). The leader then shares this drawing with the members of the group and asks for comments and questions. Members then complete their own drawings, and when they all are finished drawing, the members share what they have drawn.

It is important that this activity not be completed in a cursory manner, but as each person shares their drawing, the leader encourages members to ask questions about other members' drawings. The leader also points out similarities and connections in the drawings of the members as they are shared. The value of this activity is that it allows members to point out positives, strengths, and issues in one exercise.

The "T-shirt" activity requires some advanced preparation on the leader's part to copy the figure of the back and front of a blank T-shirt onto the front and back of a piece of paper. This figure can be copied from the Carrell (2000) workbook. On the front of the T-shirt, members are instructed to draw things about themselves that they believe members already know about them. On the back of the T-shirt, they are to draw things that they believe the members do not know about them. This activity is a paradigm of the Johari Window frames of open and hidden. When members share what they have drawn on their T-shirt, the leader should encourage members to ask questions about other members' drawings and to make connections between the drawings of different members. It is curious that this activity sometimes produces reversals in the sides of the T-shirt. For example, the group may say they did not know something that was on the front of a member's T-shirt but did know something that was on the back of the T-shirt. Sometimes members may draw on both sides of the paper, but then decide not to share what they have drawn on the back of their T-shirt. Thus the member is choosing not to share this hidden piece of information.

Giving feedback is another dimension of the Johari Window that can be promoted by interventions of the leader. Both leaders and members may give individual members feedback. Leaders may give feedback by pointing out the nonverbal behavior of members when they are talking. The leader might say, "I notice you rolled your eyes when you said you agreed!" or "You moved your chair back when you started to explain what you expected to get from this group!" Feedback can come in many forms as confrontation, interpretations, and personal reactions. The general guidelines for feedback to be an effective technique are that it should be

- solicited by the member not imposed by the leader or other members of the group,
- descriptive (what was observed) and not evaluative (judgmental),
- immediate (given close to the event) and not days or weeks later, and
- intended to be helpful not hurtful (avoid words that wound).

Some groups rely heavily on confrontation as a technique, such as Gestalt groups, Positive Peer Culture, domestic violence groups for perpetrators, etc. This technique, however, seems to have fallen out of favor because it can increase the defensiveness and resistance of members to change their behaviors (Miller & Rollnick, 2002). It should never be done by a leader when the leader is angry with the member because only the anger will come across in the communication.

Interpreting is a technique used in psychodynamically oriented treatment groups because insight is expected to be the "active ingredient" for behavioral change (Pines, 1985). When a member comes to understand the etiology and history of their problems, this unconscious knowledge should help them break the cycle of their psychological problems. Other group models also use interpretation but conceptualize it more broadly as education and building awareness (Garvin, 1974). Our bias is that beginning students should view interpretation broadly as helping members gain awareness about themselves that fits the purpose of the group. For example, a group may help members understand how others perceive them and how they relate interpersonally to others and not uncover unconscious material.

Instilling hope is a central part of all therapeutic methods. Many clients come into service after trying many attempts to resolve their difficulties. Newcomers to groups may be skeptical that the group will help, and the leader will offer hope directly by establishing expectations that members can be helped to change. The leader's demeanor is important in conveying hope. Leaders who are "burned out" will not be able to convey a sense that groups can be helpful. The best intervention a burned out leader can offer a group is not to be a leader. In open-ended groups, there are members at different stages of the healing journey, and long-time members can be encouraged to explain how the group has helped. For example, in AA groups, a newcomer will meet members who have been sober for months and even years. In support groups, the leader may deliberately compose the group of members who still feel victimized by a traumatic life event with other members who have moved into the survivor role. The survivors will be models to help newcomers experience how groups can be helpful. Some leaders may take an educational approach and give newcomers homework such as articles to read that describe how similar groups have helped their members. There is evidence that the practitioner's expectations of an intervention is a factor in the success of the intervention. Leaders who do not believe their groups can help members should not run groups.

Building cohesiveness and a sense of "we-ness" is important in all groups in order to avoid attrition. For members to continue to attend, they need to feel that they are not only being understood but also getting something out of the group. There are many interventions that the group leader does throughout the development of the group that are designed to increase the cohesiveness and attraction of the group. A common intervention is pointing out connections and common themes that arise in group sessions. Universality is automatic when all of the members of the group are struggling with the same issue, such as a natural disaster, death of a child, losing a job, etc. When the leader points out successes that the members of the group achieve, this increases the attractiveness of the group. In children's groups, the leader may help the members to decide on a name for their group. When the leader encourages members to take risks and share sensitive information or try out new things, this will increase the cohesiveness of the group. We will describe two structured activities that build cohesiveness in small groups, such as "Singing in the Rain" and "The Group Story."

These activities are not done in a first session but when the group has had a chance to mature.

"Singing in the Rain" (Barlow et al., 1999) is an activity that prompts members to take risks in the group. It also helps the leader understand how much comfort the members have with each other and whether they are willing to do something in the group that makes them vulnerable. The activity does not require any advanced planning or materials. The leader explains that this activity is designed to help the group take risks and that risk taking can sometimes be fun. The leader asks the group to stand and then explains that he wants everyone to sing a verse from a song. This can be anxiety provoking to members, so the leader reminds the group that they will not be forced to sing. The leader also explains that members can tell a joke to the group if they do not want to sing.

The leader should go first (and hopefully will not be a good singer) so that members can see singing talent is not important to this activity. Because of my (Brett A. Seabury, or BAS) Yankee background, I usually choose "Yankee Doodle Dandy," which gets chuckles from the members of the group. The leader should then wait until someone else decides to break the ice. Sometimes there will be long silences as a few brave members sing or tell a joke. This activity is best done without the pressure of a round, and the leader should make sure that everyone has had a chance to go before debriefing this exercise—that is, the leader needs to be comfortable waiting out long silences. This exercise will generate a lot of anxiety but also some surprises and laughter when the group hears some of the songs that are chosen and the fact that some members have very good singing voices. When I do this exercise in my class on groups, I always tell students who are not native speakers of Standard American English that they can sing in their native language. The songs that young adults choose range from songs they learned in nursery school to songs of their favorite pop group. It is also delightful that some students will ham up their singing much to the pleasure of other members in the class. I once had a young man drop down on one knee and take the hand of a woman next to him and begin to sing a love song. The caveat with this structured activity is that it can bomb and no one will try to sing. This will be a dramatic sign to the leader that the group does not feel safe to its members and that the leader needs to consider incremental activities that will build trust. You should not expect all members of the group to sing, but if at least half of the group can sing and then debrief the exercise, you will see a dramatic impact on the cohesiveness of the group. They have survived an anxiety provoking experience as a group and survived!

"The Group Story" does take some advanced planning. The leader needs to bring a small tape recorder and a blank tape that can be placed in the center of the group so that the story will be recorded. The group leader explains that the group is going to tell and record a group story. After the story has been told, the group will listen to the story and have a chance to react to the story and debrief the experience. The structure of the storytelling activity is fairly simple. The story will be told in a round with each member of the group adding a piece to the tale. If a member cannot think of anything to add, she may pass. The leader explains that stories have a beginning, middle, and end and that usually the group will go around four, five, or six times before they will all sense that the story is told. The leader primes the group by stating that the more fictional and fanciful the story, the more fun it will be for the group. The leader states that she will begin the story and is very excited about this activity because the group will be creating a story that has never been heard nor told before today. The leader can decide with the group in which direction the story will be told and then begins: "Once upon a time, in a far off place, long, long ago there was a . . ." and turns to the next person in the round, who is often surprised to be getting the story so abruptly.

The underlying dynamic of therapeutic storytelling is that the story is a metaphor for the group. The group will project their issues into the story's characters, plot, and theme, which should be analyzed by the group during debriefing. This group activity generates a lot of laughter while the story is being told. When the story is debriefed and analyzed for themes, it also lets the group realize that they are an entity capable of producing something together. Some of the dynamics in the story often reflect the dynamics in the group—for example, if there are members who are often in conflict in the group, this conflict will enter the story metaphorically in the story's plot. If one member introduces a rabbit into the story, the other member may introduce a hungry wolf into the story when it is their turn. The theme of the story often reflects the purpose of the group—for example, if the group is dealing with losses or self-esteem issues, these themes will emerge in the story. We will be discussing conflict resolving techniques at the end of this chapter, but this structured activity can be used to defuse interpersonal conflict in groups.

Several years ago I (BAS) was driving a van from Ann Arbor to St. Louis with a group of seven students to attend a conference. This was a long drive in a crowded van, and one of the students was particularly obnoxious and getting on the nerves of other students. When we arrived near Indianapolis and stopped for lunch, two of the students asked me if we couldn't trick the obnoxious student into using the restroom and then abruptly drive away leaving him at the rest stop. I was flabbergasted at this suggestion coming from social work students, but I promised them that I had another way of dealing with these tensions than what they had suggested. After lunch, when we *all* returned to the van, I explained that we would engage in an activity that would help us cope with the long drive to St. Louis. When I explained the group storytelling activity, many of the students groaned, but I was able to get them to try it out. As we continued on our journey, we created a complicated and enchanted story with much laughter and many surprises. As luck would have it, the obnoxious student was an excellent storyteller and really captivated the reluctant students to join in the storytelling process. The scapegoating of the obnoxious student subsided, and we drove on to St. Louis in much better spirits.

There are many books that describe how metaphoric interventions can be employed in treatment with families, children, and adults (Barker, 1996; Leveton, 1992). It is beyond the scope of this chapter to describe all of these metaphoric interventions, but this group storytelling exercise embodies how these interventions work with clients.

Catharsis is a common experience in many therapeutic methods. There are many ways that the leader can promote the expression of feelings in members of the group. Direct questions such as, "How did that make you feel?" or "Can you remember what you were doing when you found out about the death?" will probably generate catharsis in clients. Leaders may engage in empathetic responding by reflecting back emotions and the issues that members are sharing. Sometimes leaders may respond to members' emotions by suggesting that there may be hidden emotions or issues behind the affect that is being expressed—for example, the leader may help a member recognize that the member's obvious anger and irritation with the discussion may actually reflect underlying anxiety about the topic.

Besides direct interventions by the leader, there are also many structured activities that will create ventilation in group members. For example, writing a letter to a deceased member of one's family will activate feelings of loss and sadness. The feelings are even more intense when the member reads the letter out loud to the group. A similar intervention from psychodrama can produce affect in group members. The group member sits across from an empty chair and imagines that the deceased relative is in the empty chair and carries on a conversation with the imagined relative, even though there are various cultures that use the empty chair in celebrations (e.g., ghost suppers in Native American tribes to honor deceased relatives and the empty place at Passover for Elijah). The empty chair activity is more difficult for some members to accomplish than the letter writing activity. These activities can also generate vicarious learning because the intense feelings of some members will dramatically impact other members who listen to the letters and observe the conversations with the deceased.

Eva Leveton (1992) described many activities that are derived from psychodrama that can generate catharsis in group members. She describes several simple warm-up techniques that will generate catharsis and can be used in many support and treatment groups. The two paired activities that follow require no advance preparation or materials. The leader explains that these warm-up activities are designed to share interpersonal issues that can be explored in more depth by the group. In the first activity, members are asked to think of someone with whom they are close and recall something that you wish they would *not* say to you. The members will have a chance to share these thoughts with the group by saying who the person is and exactly what they say. It is probably best for the leader to go first, because often members paraphrase rather than share the direct quote, and the leader can model this activity—for example, "I am thinking about my wife, who often says, 'You are not going to this party dressed like that, are you?'" The activity can be completed as a round with permission for members to pass if they so choose. This activity will generate some laughter and comments from other members who respond vicariously to what is shared. When the round is complete, the leader will then invite the group to complete another, similar warm-up.

In this activity, members are to think of someone they are close to (can be a different person from the first activity) and now think of something they wish this person *would* say to them. Again the leader ought to model this activity by going first—for example, I am thinking of my daughter-in-law, who never says, "Thank you, Pop, for babysitting the grandchildren." This activity—though similar to the first—will be much harder for members to complete and will not generate laughter as the first activity often does. The emotions that may be expressed are more about feelings of pain or being ignored and not appreciated. It is important that when completing these two activities in the group that the leader keeps track of the relationships that are mentioned and the effect and themes that are expressed in the quotes. These simple warm-up exercises will generate feelings in members. When these exercises are debriefed, the leader should bring up the commonalities that are expressed—for example, "I noticed that most of you mentioned conversations you had with parents. I was wondering if we shouldn't focus on our relationship with parents today!"

Though catharsis occurs often in support, CR, and treatment groups, it is not an end in itself. When emotions are expressed, there may be some sense of relief for the member, but the emotions have to be put into perspective. Members can be helped to see that emotions are shared by other members of the group. Members can also work on discussing ways to handle emotions and get advice from other members what they do when experiencing intense emotions: "I find that when I have had a really bad day at work, because of my domineering supervisor, I feel much better when I get home and have a chance to split firewood for my wood stove." "When I have had an intensely stressful morning at work, I find that sitting and meditating for about 15 minutes will help me get through the rest of the day!"

Beginning interpersonal practitioners have to be aware of their own abilities to handle emotions that are expressed by members in groups. When a rookie leader encourages catharsis in a group by employing a particular structured activity, that leader must be ready to deal with the reactions of members to the structured activity. In Chapter 14, we discussed how important it is for leaders to save time at the end of a group session to allow members to reflect on the session and talk about any unresolved feelings they experienced in the session. This "cooldown" time is especially important in a group that has raised many intense feelings in the members of the group.

Interpersonal learning is a major advantage that groups have over individual treatment. Because there are other members in a group, members have available a microcosm in which to practice and work on interpersonal relationship issues. One of the most common techniques that groups may use is role playing. There are many ways that members can use role playing to work on interpersonal issues. They may play themselves in a scenario (i.e., role rehearsal) or play another person in a scenario (i.e., role reversal). They may sit on the sidelines and watch other members of the group play out a scene from their own life (i.e., vicarious learning). The other members of the group can be recruited to play out multiple family members in a particular scenario. Role playing can be used to re-create situations in a member's past, present, and even future. Moreno called this ability for group members to play out these re-created role scenarios as "surplus reality" (Fox, 1987). The reality is that some members will find it difficult to enter surplus reality and play a role in another member's life (Blatner, 2004; Blatner & Blatner, 1988). These members may not be able to play a role from their own life, nor to play a complimentary role in their life (Blatner, 1996). The only way to help these members gain something from role playing is through vicarious learning, such as watching other group members play out various role scenarios.

There are two letter writing activities that group members can do to work on interpersonal relationships. One involves writing a letter to someone who has victimized the group members. For example, in support groups for members who have suffered sexual abuse or other forms of abuse, members can be encouraged to write a letter to their perpetrator. Members should share a draft of their letter with other group members, and discuss what they might say in this highly charged letter. It is important that members know up front that this letter will *not* be sent to the perpetrator. The letter writing activity is designed to be an expressive technique and not designed to be shared with anyone outside of the group. This activity will generate a lot of self-sharing, catharsis, and feedback from group members. The interpersonal context of sharing these traumas will be helping individual members to deal with whatever crippling consequences the abuse may have produced on members' abilities to relate interpersonally with others. This corrective emotional experience is a therapeutic activity that combines several of the therapeutic factors in groups. Members may have an easier time writing the letter than sharing it with the group.

The second letter writing activity involves an internal dialogue with oneself. In this structured activity, members are primed for the letter writing by creating a table of contents for their autobiography. They are asked to write the chapter headings for their autobiography and then share it with the group. This journaling technique (Goldberg, 1986; Kelley, 1990; L'Abate, 1992; Progoff, 1975) in itself will start to raise members' self-awareness. The next step in the process is to write a letter from your present self to a past self or a future self. When the first letter is complete, the member then answers the letter as though they were writing from either their past or future self. Like other letter writing activities mentioned earlier in this chapter, reading the letters is often more emotional than the private activity of writing them. In order to make this activity therapeutic for the members of the group, the leader needs to help the members recognize and reflect on the themes of their two letters. There is a tendency to focus on what is said in the letters (the plot) and not to "read between the lines" and understand the themes and underlying issues. The themes in the letters usually reflect the struggles that members are facing in the present. The leader should encourage each member to look at the themes. As the creator of the letters, the member should make the first interpretation. After each member has reflected on their own themes, then other members and the leader may gently offer some other possibilities, such as giving feedback. This activity can be very meaningful to members and often gives them ideas about how they might cope with whatever challenges and issues they are facing in the present. Sometimes members are surprised with the good advice that they get from their self at another point in time!

INTERPERSONAL CONFLICT IN GROUPS ●

Social work students tend to view interpersonal conflict as "bad." It is true that some forms of interpersonal conflict are negative, such as violence and abuse. Interpersonal conflict in groups is inevitable, and resolving these conflicts is an important responsibility of the leader in social group work. In order to be an effective group leader, the student must understand how conflict emerges, what their own learned responses are to interpersonal conflict, and how a leader intervenes to resolve interpersonal conflict when it arises in the group.

Game theory (Rapoport, 1974) is often used as a way of understanding conflict. Conflict is viewed as a contest between parties that can result in three outcomes: (1) a positive sum game in which both parties win, (2) a zero sum game in which one party wins and the other party loses, and (3) a negative sum game in which both parties lose. Most games that we play are structured as zero sum games such as checkers, chess, poker, Monopoly, etc., because they end when someone has taken all of the pieces or has all of the chips or money. Negative sum games are destructive to all parties and all parties lose in the outcome—for example, nuclear war is seen as a negative sum gain because it will be followed by a nuclear winter and all life on earth is destroyed, except maybe cockroaches.

Social workers often end up mediating interpersonal disputes in marital counseling and custody disputes. These disputes sometimes end in negative sum outcomes when children are kidnapped or either parent is murdered or the two parents end up using the children to make the life of the other parent miserable. Ideally a successful resolution will bring all parties to a win-win situation, but this outcome is not always possible when social workers mediate disputes.

Social workers need to understand their own personal response to interpersonal conflict. Our ethnic background, family experiences growing up, and personal life experience have influenced how we tend to respond when we find ourselves in conflict situations. We are hardwired to either fight or flee when confronting a dangerous situation. In an interpersonal context, this may appear as withdrawing (i.e., fleeing) or trying to force the other party to take our side of the issue (i.e., fighting). Other responses may involve denying the conflict exists, smoothing over the conflict by minimizing it, denying any responsibility for the conflict, or blaming others for it. It seems that most of us are taught to engage in conflict aversive behavior than to address the conflict and resolve it. The training of social workers and group leader must involve training that teaches the practitioner how to ignore their built-in propensities and instead address interpersonal conflict with conflict resolving strategies.

In the group example at the beginning of this chapter, how would you assess the leader's response to potential conflict in this newly formed group? Did the leader ignore conflict that arose in the group, or did the leader address conflict issues in the group?

In Chapter 14, we discussed many of the sources of interpersonal conflict that can emerge in groups. Some members may adopt roles such as monopolizer, character assassin, and scapegoat, which are problematic for group functioning. In heterogeneous groups, which are diverse in ethnic background and social class, there are many potential problems that may emerge in how the group communicates and how members may feel about each other, such as sociometry. As groups develop and mature, conflict will emerge in the revision phase that is often tied to group norms, and conflict may emerge in the termination phase because of transference issues that departing members may have to leaving the group.

Look again at this group of elders, and see if there are any potential sources of conflict for this particular group.

In the mediating model of social group work (Schwartz, 1976), the central role of the group leader is mediator. In order to be a successful mediator of interpersonal conflict, the leader has to demonstrate two attributes to members of the group who are in conflict. The leader must be seen as a legitimate authority to resolve the conflict. The leader's skills, knowledge, and behavior in the groups should demonstrate to members that she is able and willing to help members resolve the conflict that has emerged. The leader as mediator must also be perceived as "neutral" in the dispute by the parties. The leader cannot be seen as taking sides or having a vested interest in how the conflict will be resolved. If the group feels that the leader has "favorites" or "pets" in the group, this perception will undermine the ability of the leader to act as mediator. Neutrality and legitimacy are essential in the Schwartz model but also reflect good leadership practice in all groups (Schwartz, 1994).

Go back in your own experience as a child in school. Do you ever remember an experience in which one of your teachers had "teacher's pets"? If you were the teacher's pet, you may not realize how the other members of the class felt about your special role.

There are specific and fairly simple techniques that a leader can perform when interpersonal conflict emerges between members of the group. These techniques are intended to produce a win-win outcome for the group, but in some situations the best outcome that members may be able to reach is a win-lose situation. For example, one member may apologize for their behavior toward the other member. Though apologies have their place in a dispute, they are a win-lose outcome. One side concedes that they were wrong and the other side was right. The danger of one side offering an apology too soon in a dispute is that it may gloss over and cover up an underlying issue that needs to be examined and resolved by the group. Apologies cut off exploration of the issues, and from the perspective of the Johari Window, information in the unknown pane will not be brought out into the open for the group to examine.

The techniques that are presented in the next section of this chapter should be employed by the leader to produce a win-win outcome or at least a win-lose outcome. We need to remind the students that lose-lose outcomes are extremely undesirable to the group, and the leader must exert her authority to avoid this kind of interpersonal conflict. When members stop talking about the issues of the dispute and instead start to bring up personal attacks, the mediation process runs the risk of becoming character assassination, and members may start "wounding" the other party with no desire to resolve the dispute. When the conversation takes this turn, the leader must redirect the parties away from words that wound and revert back to the issue. If there is a ground rule about "being kind" and "not attacking other members" this is time for the leader to remind members of this rule and also remind them why the group has this rule.

When conflict appears between members and even when there is a hint of tension, the first step is *not* to ignore, minimize, or avoid the issue but address it directly. The leader could say, "I sense that the two of you do not agree with that decision!" The leader should then ask each member to express their perceptions of the issue: "Tell the rest of us what you think is going on with your disagreement!" When each party has had a chance to express their views, the leader may then open the issue up to other members in the group so that they can comment on the conflict. The leader could say, "Now that we have heard from each of you, I was wondering what other members of the group are thinking about this issue?" The leader now needs to normalize the perspectives and opinions that have been shared. "It is not unusual for members of a group to have different opinions and legitimate concerns about what is going on in the group!" Finally the leader needs to appeal to the goodwill of members and search for common ground and suggest that the group needs to focus on resolutions for the conflict. The leader could say, "Let's talk about what is common to each side of this dispute and think of ways that we may be able to resolve this issue." By opening up the discussion of the conflict to the whole group, the leader has demonstrated her faith in the group to solve a conflict when it arises. When the group as a whole is empowered to develop the resolution, it is much more likely to be sustained than one imposed by the leader. Conflict resolution does not always unfold in the orderly way presented in this paragraph, but each of these steps may be pursued to help members resolve disputes.

What does a leader do when the conflict that arises is between the leader and several members? How can a leader mediate a dispute when they are not a neutral party to the conflict? The steps are similar to disputes between members but with the added skills of LARA (listen, assess, respond, add information). LARA is an interpersonal method developed by American Friends Committee to diffuse angry counterdemonstrators in peace rallies (Koyama & Medve, 2003; Pelz & Remley, n.d.; Rendleman, 2009). The method is similar to what social workers do when they are responding empathetically to clients, but in this case, the purpose is to diffuse a verbal attack. In order to be capable of employing LARA in a dispute, leaders must be aware of what happens when they are feeling defensive. It is normal for individuals to become defensive when they are engaged in interpersonal conflict. Instead of retaliating by arguing or rationalizing her position, the leader responds with the four steps in LARA:

- Listen: Actively listen to what the member is actually saying. Listen for the underlying moral principle, feelings, or issue. Listen for something that you share with the member's complaint or dispute.
- Assess: Assess any common feeling, experience, or principle that you share with the member.
- Respond: Answer the question, or respond, to the issue raised by the member after completing the first two steps of LARA. Point out with the member where you agree with their concern.
- Add Information: Share additional information that you want to give the member about the concern that is being raised.

When the leader has responded with LARA, the steps can be continued, and the leader can open up the discussion to other members. The other members can be included in the discussion, and often the leader may discover that other members are not in agreement with the concern raised by the original member. At this point, the leader can normalize the perspectives and opinions that have been shared, appeal to the goodwill of members, and suggest that the group needs to focus on resolutions for the concern that was raised.

CONCLUSION ●

In conclusion to this chapter on group interventions, we want to raise the following question: Under what circumstances should a social worker choose to work with clients in groups rather than seeing clients individually or with their families? In the present context of evidence-based practice, there are many group models that demonstrate their effectiveness with particular client populations. There are cognitive behavioral models (Rose, 1977), psychoeducational models, social skills models (Alberti & Emmons, 1990), stress reduction models (Davis, Eshelman, & McKay, 2000), and meditation and support group models for individuals struggling with chronic health conditions (Kabat-Zinn, 1990). There is such a proliferation of evidence-based models of groups. A beginning social work practitioner will have to consider taking advanced courses in group work in order to continue to develop knowledge and skills in working with groups. Many of these models are treatment models with a focus on health and mental health populations. The focus of the two group chapters (Chapter 14 and 15) in this book is broader; more generic; and presents basic, foundational knowledge of group work.

We are not convinced that the question posed in this conclusion can be answered by looking only at evidence-based practice. Reviews of the research literature on treatment effectiveness (Garfield, 1994) point out that specific intervention only accounts for about 15% of the many variables that contribute to successful outcomes. There are many other factors in treatment, such as client motivation and nonspecific factors such as the relationship between worker and client that contribute more to treatment outcome. Groups are so often offered as an ancillary service in agencies that clients must be willing to try out groups. If clients are unwilling to work in groups to help themselves and other members in the group, they will drop out of the group. If a client decides not to return, the superiority of an intervention becomes irrelevant to the outcome.

In general there are some circumstances in which groups have clear advantages over work with individuals and families. These include helping members realize they are not alone with their problems, helping members work on ways of improving their relationships with others, reinforcing reality testing, providing an opportunity to practice social behaviors, and offering a context for engaging with peers in nonverbal ways through the use of structured activities.

● SUMMARY

In this chapter, we presented a detailed example of group work in a residence for elderly clients. This case was used to highlight questions about diversity and social justice issues and also to raise questions about the group interventions of the social work intern. The chapter focused on the responsibilities of a group leader in the first session because this session is critical to produce a climate in which members will want to return to the group. The chapter looked at many interventions and structured activities that leaders may employ in order to enhance the effectiveness variables of successful groups. The chapter also looked at interpersonal conflict, which is inevitable in groups, and suggested ways a group leader helps group members resolve these conflicts when they emerge.

CHAPTER 16

ASSESSING ORGANIZATIONS AND COMMUNITIES

One is a member of a country, a profession, a civilization, a religion.
One is not just a man.

—Antoine de Saint-Exupery (1986, p. 76)

In our discussion of assessment thus far, we have given a great deal of attention to individuals, families, and groups, which are the client systems of interpersonal practitioners. The worker must also be concerned with the quality of the environments with which these client systems interact. In many ways, individual and small system assessment is artificial if it is not done simultaneously with an assessment of the individual's environment and the interactions between the individual and the environment. People live in constant interaction with others in their extended family, with peers and classmates in schools, with coworkers in the workplace, and with neighbors and shopkeepers in their community. From the ecological perspective presented in the chapter on individual assessment (Chapter 10), behavior is influenced by forces present in the larger systems that surround us all.

There are times when these larger systems are target systems—that the worker becomes actively involved with one or more of these systems and will need to assess them in greater detail. From the ecological perspective, the worker must be concerned with these interactions and, consequently, must seek to understand and help clients understand relevant aspects of their environments.

In order to demonstrate how system variables influence individuals, please complete the following questionnaire in Exercise 16.1. This questionnaire was adapted from a questionnaire in Irwin Epstein's (1969) doctoral dissertation that focused on social workers' participation in advocacy. There are no right or wrong answers, and you will be forced to take a position on a number of general practice situations. If you compare your responses with those of your classmates and talk about the reasons why you have taken a given position, you will see that social workers are influenced by many forces in their social environment.

Exercise 16.1

Influence of System Variables

Indicate on the scale after each question how strongly you feel a social worker should or should not do what is suggested by each of the following statements. Even though none of the choices may completely reflect your views, circle the number on the four-point scale that comes closest to your position.

1 = ABSOLUTELY MUST (AM)
2 = PROBABLY SHOULD (PS)
3 = PROBABLY SHOULD NOT (PSN)
4 = ABSOLUTELY MUST NOT (AMN)

	AM	PS	PSN	AMN
1. A social worker should act to meet the needs of clients even if a particular act differs from explicitly stated agency policies.	1	2	3	4
2. A social worker should act to carry out the policies of the agency even if doing so differs from what influential segments of the community think should be done.	1	2	3	4
3. A social worker should act to meet the needs of clients even though a particular act is considered "unprofessional" by colleagues.	1	2	3	4
4. A social worker should act to carry out the policies of the agency even if doing so differs from what the social worker's own professional judgment leads her or him to think should be done.	1	2	3	4

5. A social worker should act to meet the needs of clients even if a particular act conflicts with the social worker's personal convictions.	1	2	3	4
6. A social worker should act according to his or her personal convictions even if a particular act differs from explicitly stated agency policies.	1	2	3	4
7. A social worker should act to meet the needs of clients even if doing so differs from what influential segments of the community think should be done.	1	2	3	4
8. A social worker should act to support the decisions and positions of colleagues even if doing so differs from what influential segments of the community think should be done.	1	2	3	4

As this questionnaire demonstrates, social work practitioners do not make decisions in isolation but are influenced by colleagues, professional ethics, agency policies, client needs, and community standards.

The reality of practice for social workers is that there are often competing or conflicting demands from various forces (see Figure 16.1). For example, even though the National Association of Social Workers (NASW) has a position that supports choice, social workers with a strong religious conviction against abortion may struggle with clients who come into service seeking information about ending an unwanted pregnancy. This situation creates a conflict between the personal convictions of the worker with the position of the profession and the wishes of the client. Another common example of conflict occurs in agencies with procedures that do not always meet the needs of applicants or clients. When social workers take the side of the client they may end up engaging in "banditry" or internal advocacy, which may put their own job in jeopardy. We will talk more about these activities in the chapter on organizational and community change (Chapter 17).

ORGANIZATIONAL ASSESSMENT •

Need for Understanding Organizations

Before we launch into a discussion of organizational assessment, the term *organization* needs to be defined. In social work practice an organization is a social agency that

Figure 16.1 Competing Demands on Social Work Practitioners

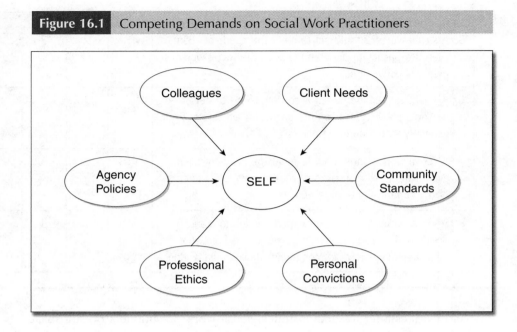

delivers social services under the auspices of a board of directors and is usually staffed by human service personnel (including professional social workers, members of other professions, paraprofessionals, clerical personnel, and sometimes indigenous workers). It provides a specific range of social services for members of a population group that has (been) or is vulnerable to a specific social problem. The agency may be funded by combinations of philanthropic contributions and privately solicited donations, by governments, by fees paid by those served, or by third-party payment. (Barker, 1995)

There are many kinds of organizations found in social work practice. Social workers are employed by large formal organizations, such as hospitals, schools, public welfare departments, the military, sectarian social service agencies, etc. Some of these settings are referred to as *host* settings (hospitals, schools, military) because the social work function is ancillary or secondary to the primary mission of the organization—that is, medicine is central to hospitals, education is central to schools, and maintaining national security is the main task of the military. These host settings are different from those agencies such as family service agencies, child welfare agencies, settlement houses, etc., that have a primary social work mission.

Sometimes social workers in host settings find themselves working at cross-purposes to the mission of the host agency, and in some cases the profession of social work may actually go on record as opposing the mission of the host setting. For example, during the Vietnamese War, NASW passed a resolution opposing the war, yet many social workers who were in military uniforms were also members of NASW and voted for this resolution. In the 1940s, after the bombing of Pearl Harbor, the social work profession opposed the activities of the relocation services, whose job it was to remove Japanese Americans from their homes in West Coast cities to inland relocation centers in Arizona and New Mexico. This massive relocation was accomplished by trained social workers as well as opposed by many social workers in that era (Glenn, 1944; Nickel, 1942a, 1942b).

It is not only in host settings that social workers have to work to change organizational policies and procedures when they impact negatively on clients. Even in settings where social work is the primary mission, organizational arrangements may have to be challenged. Procedures and routines in social work agencies may discriminate against particular groups of clientele. Agency hours of operations that are inflexibly arranged from 9:00 a.m. to 5:00 p.m. discriminate against working clients. Some agencies do not have barrier-free entrances to accommodate the physically disabled, and few agencies have staff who can sign for the deaf client. Some agencies are far from public transportation, making it particularly difficult for poor clients to attend scheduled appointments. Other agencies may be centrally located in a particular community but make no effort to reach out to potential clients. No matter how well intentioned the staff and mission of the agency, in the world of practice, there are no perfect agencies. Social workers have a professional responsibility to work on improving their service delivery system (National Association of Social Workers [NASW] Delegate Assembly, 2008).

How to Assess an Organization

There is a large, dated literature on "changing an organization from within" that explains how workers in low power positions can go about understanding and influencing the agencies that employ them (Resnick & Patti, 1980). Our discussion will borrow concepts and principles from this literature and bring them online as the 21st century begins. To improve the social agencies that employ them, social workers need a framework for understanding how a social agency operates. In this section of the text, we explain the key dimensions of organizational behavior that may be taken into account when trying to understand how agencies impact their employees and clientele.

In order to "case" an organization, a social worker must know where to collect the kind of information needed to assess that agency. A great deal of information about organizations is written down in annual reports, minutes of working task groups, mission statements, operations guidelines, procedural manuals, personnel and case files, etc. Some of this written data is considered confidential (i.e., case files and personnel files) but most is public information that can be accessed by an interested party. In this age of Google, it is possible to access most organizational information from a laptop. With some information, it is easier to access information when one is employed by the agency than when one is an outsider trying to understand what is going on. Accessibility is greater for insiders than for outsiders, and the more privileged the information, the harder it is to access.

Besides written materials (or electronic, as the case may be), another major source of information is from people working in the organization or agency. Most agencies have a "historian," which is not an official title. This informal role may be held by members of the organization employed for a long period and who have a good memory for details. Such members can be a useful information resource. Another useful and informal role is the "agency snitch." The snitch is more difficult to find in an agency than the historian. Snitches have usually been around for a while, but their major characteristic is their willingness to disclose compromising and privileged information that the historian is often unwilling to disclose. Snitches are willing to divulge agency secrets because they do not have the same kind of allegiance to the agency that other members do. The historian and the snitch can be useful resources for gaining information about an agency. For students in a field placement, the easiest place to start is with their supervisors (See Exercise 16.2).

Exercise 16.2

Locating "the Snitch"

In this exercise, we want you to try to locate the snitch in either your school of social work or in your field placement. You may be lucky and discover that your classroom instructor or field supervisor is a snitch. Keep track of how you went about trying to find the snitch, and share your experiences with your classmates. You will need this information when you read the chapter on organizational change (Chapter 17) and decide to use your school or field placement as the target system for change.

Norms and Operating Rules

As we have discussed in the chapter on group assessment (Chapter 14), all groups, including large groups such as an organization, develop a normative system. In small, interpersonal groups, these norms may never be written down and sometimes are not even verbalized, but in agencies, norms are often formalized and written down in some kind of formal rule system. Many agencies give new employees a handbook that states what the SOPs of the agency are. These SOPs can be detailed descriptions of what is expected of each employee (such as a job description) and the operating procedures and processes of given programs in the agency.

Some organizations have massive tomes that incorporate all possibilities and contingencies an employee in the organization is likely to encounter. Large bureaucracies such as the military and public welfare organizations have volumes of regulations that have been developed to guide the actions of all employees and the services that clients are expected to receive. For example, the U.S. Army has a manual that describes how many sections of toilet paper soldiers are supposed to use when relieving themselves. Women are allowed twice as many sections as men. This kind of detail is codified so that supply officers can figure out how many rolls of toilet paper to requisition for a given size unit for a given period of time.

There are a number of ways of conceptualizing the kinds of norms and rules that can be found in a social agency. The *formal* rules will be written down and clearly explained to new employees or applicants as they enter the organization. The *informal* rules are left to be clarified as situations or events arise. Agencies vary about the ratio between formal and informal rule systems. An overly extensive formal rule system is likely to be found in bureaucratic organizations, whereas a small formal rule system is likely to appear in smaller, "younger" organizations. The consequence for workers in such agencies is that when there is a small, formal rule system, the organization relies on the professional judgment of its worker, whereas in the large bureaucratic organizations, the organization does not give as much discretionary power to its workers. But even in large, bureaucratic organizations, there is some discretionary decision making power for line workers (Lipsky, 1980).

The consequence for decision making and change in each of these agencies is different. In the bureaucratic agency, to change the behavior of the organization, it is usually necessary to change the formal rule system. Changes to written rule systems can be a cumbersome and time-consuming process. In the agency with a more informal rule system, it will be necessary to influence and change the decisions of individuals. The major differences between these types of organizations is that in the bureaucratic system, more weight is placed on the written rules, whereas in the less bureaucratic agency, more value is placed on the judgment of the decision maker (DM). Sometimes, it is possible in large bureaucratic agencies to get DMs to ignore the rule system and make a decision that violates written policies. This kind of "banditry" will take place when the DM is convinced that the rule system is inflexible and not responsive to the individual case (Seabury, 1983, 2001).

Look at questions 1 and 4 in the questionnaire you completed at the beginning of this chapter, and see how much of a "bandit" you might tend to be.

Did your responses support client needs and professional judgment over agency policies?

Another useful way of conceptualizing the normative structure of organizations is that some norms may be *prescriptive* while others are *proscriptive*. Prescriptive norms suggest what is desirable or expected of workers and clients in the agency, whereas proscriptive norms refer to what is taboo behavior—behaviors that individuals are not supposed to do. Prescriptive rules are not as specific as proscriptive rules because they cover a much larger domain of possible behaviors. For example, the NASW *Code of Ethics* is clear that sexual relations between worker and client are taboo. The code proscribes that sexual behavior *must not* occur. The code, however, is more general when it exhorts workers to respect client self-determination. This is a prescriptive norm and reflects a long-standing value position of the social work profession. This statement of what is ideal, however, leaves open the possible ways that workers may do this and the kinds of behaviors that clients are encouraged to pursue. Obviously, a social worker cannot support all kinds of self-determined behavior by the client, and in some situations in which a client may be engaging in abusive behaviors with another person, the worker has an obligation under state law to report that abuse to authorities.

Another usual way of understanding the normative structure of organizations is that some norms are *pivotal* and others are *relevant* (Schein, 1971). A pivotal norm or rule is one that is essential and critical to the agency. When an individual violates a pivotal norm in a social agency, the organization will react quite strongly and *sanction* the rule breaker. The sanctions or remedies administered to a rule breaker are often harsh and obvious so that all in the agency are reminded that this norm is to be taken seriously. When pivotal norms are violated, the sanctions often include the termination of the client's service, or employees may be fired or put on some kind of probationary status. Clients, for example, may be thrown out of detoxification programs if they are found to have drugs on them or in their urine screening, and residents of homeless shelters who are discovered to have weapons are not permitted to remain in the shelter.

Relevant norms are desirable but are not critical rules. Clients and workers may violate relevant norms fairly often, but these are not severely sanctioned the way pivotal norms are. In a sense, relevant norms are the "unenforced rules" of the organization. They may be written in the manual, but the agency will not take the time and effort involved in enforcing them. For example, in some agencies, there is a dress code. This dress code can be pivotal and absolutely required as in the military, or it can be relevant and generally accepting of a wide range of ways of dressing. Sometimes students struggle with dress codes when they go into their field placement for the first time and discover that the casual and relaxed dress code of the classroom is different from the requirement to look "professional" in the agency setting. The pivotal and relevant norms of one setting may be very different from those norms in another setting. As we move from setting to setting, we must understand the norms of the present setting and be ready to respond accordingly.

Decision Making Structure

Social agencies are constantly involved in a process of making decisions and then acting on those decisions. Agencies develop structures so that the constant need to make decisions is manageable. Large agencies may divide themselves into departments or sections and assign these departments to different decision domains. For example, in a hospital, there are many kinds of specialized areas with responsibility for making decisions in that area. Pediatrics focuses on children, geriatrics on the elderly, oncology on cancer, accounting on billing, building maintenance on custodial services, etc. Some agencies do not have so many decision domains and have a more generalized decision structure. In fact, in small, grassroots organizations, the entire staff may be involved in *all* decisions with no delegation of decision making. In some co-op agencies, all decisions and actions are made by all members of the co-op, which includes clients and staff. When students are placed in such agencies, they are sometimes upset that they are responsible for taking out their own trash, sweeping snow off the agency walkway, and delivering food baskets to homebound elders.

Not only do agencies divide up decision domains that are responsible for particular decisions but agencies also develop an *authority structure* to manage the flow of decisions. In social work agencies, the authority structures can be primarily *hierarchical*, *collegial*, or a mixture of these types of structures within decision domains. In hierarchical decision structures, there is a chain of command with progressively higher levels of DMs having progressively more power and responsibility for decisions. In social work agencies, there may be different departments focused on different services (foster care, adoption, family services, child advocacy, school consultation), but within each of these services there may be levels of authority, such as line staff, supervisors, or a director.

Even within hierarchical structures, not all decisions will have to be passed up to the top. Some decisions can be made at each level of the hierarchy; others may have to be passed up the chain of command to progressively higher levels of the authority structure. Each agency will develop its own kind of decision process about what decisions are at the discretion of what level in the hierarchy. In large, bureaucratic organizations, these decision processes may be formally specified in written procedures, whereas in smaller agencies there may be a lot of discretion about what decisions are made, by whom, and when someone in the hierarchy needs to pass on decisions to progressively higher levels of the authority structure (See Figure 16.2).

Figure 16.2 Hierarchical Decision Structure

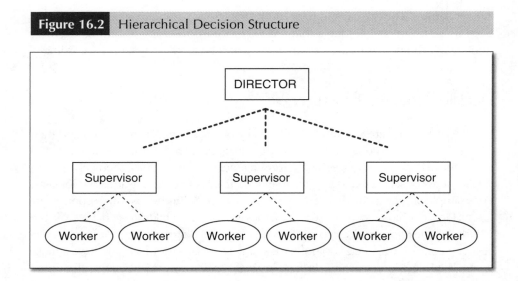

Collaborative decision making structures in social agencies are reflected in teams, committees, staff meetings, retreats, etc. In these kinds of decision structures, several and sometimes many people are convened to make decisions for the agency. In an ideal collaborative structure, all members of the group have input into the decision making process, and the decision represents some kind of consensus or at least a majority of the group members. Often this ideal is not realized, and what looks like a collaborative decision making structure is just "hierarchy in collaborative clothes."

Unfortunately in some team or committee processes, the chair may ignore the input of group members and unilaterally make decisions for the group. For example, students will discover that in some interdisciplinary teams those made up of many professionals, such as doctors, nurses, psychologists, and social workers, the team decisions will be dominated by *status* issues. High status members of the team may ignore and not listen to information from lower status members and then produce a "team" decision that reflects only their limited perspective. Though feminist writing clearly decries these kinds of status hierarchies in groups and organizations, it is important that social workers recognize how these status hierarchies work and impact on decision making when they appear in practice.

Exercise 16.3 is offered to help you understand how hierarchies might emerge in social agencies and what factors may account for the kinds of status and power that individual team members may wield in team decisions. This example may encourage you to think about some of the factors that influence member status in groups. Some of these factors, such as age, race, or gender, are outside a person's control, but other factors, such as credentials and experience, an individual may work to achieve. Deliberately missing from this exercise are behavioral factors, such as assertiveness and task-oriented communications that also have an influence on status (Forsyth, 1990). These immediate factors can be under an individual's control and can have an ameliorating effect on those demographic factors that are not in an individual member's control. For example, a high-status person, such as the psychiatrist, will quickly move downward on the pecking order if he or she frequently skips team meetings, does not offer many comments when he or she is there, or tends to distract the team from making clinical decisions.

Exercise 16.3

Factors That Influence a Status Hierarchy–Pecking Order

Imagine that you have just arrived in your field placement, which is a psychiatric inpatient unit of a large urban hospital. Your team is composed of the following five individuals besides yourself. From the little information given about each team member and the extensive information you know about yourself, create a plausible pecking order or status hierarchy that might exist. This exercise has no right or wrong answers but is designed to make you think about those factors that influence status in groups. Put a 1 by the individual you think will most likely occupy the top position (the alpha chicken, so to speak) in the pecking order, a 2 by the second in order, and so on until you have decided who will be on the bottom of the pecking order.

Yourself (taking into account your education, age, gender expression, ethnicity, length of service)

Mrs. Jones, master of social work (MSW), your supervisor, an African American, 40-year-old woman with 10 years of service

Dr. Gupta, a psychiatrist (MD), an East Indian, 38-year-old male with 2 years of service on the ward

Ms. Ratchet, a psychiatric nurse (RN), a Euro-American, 50-year-old woman with 20 years of service

Dr. Sanchez, a counseling psychologist (PsyD), a Latino, 30-year-old male with 3 years of service on the ward

Mrs. Joy, an art therapist (MS), a Euro-American, 25-year-old woman with 2 years of service

Compare your rankings with several of your classmates to see how they evaluate the various impacts that different demographic factors have on status hierarchies. Remember that there are no right or wrong answers to this exercise, though most folks who complete it usually believe their rankings are the best. For those students who are placed on an interdisciplinary team, you may want to share information about your team and how status and decision making takes place in the real world of your agency.

In the real world of practice, most agencies have some mixture of both hierarchy and collaboration. There is a defined authority structure as well as various kinds of teams and committees making decisions in various areas of agency operations. In order to understand what these decision making structures might be, students should locate the latest agency "table of organization." Such graphic representations of the authority structure are constantly changing in most agencies but can reflect the way decisions are delegated and made in the organization. The table of organization also will show how many hierarchical levels of authority exist in the agency. Large bureaucracies may have many levels and domains, whereas smaller agencies may actually have only one or two levels of hierarchy.

The reason it is important to understand the decision making structure of an agency comes down to time and effort. Anyone wanting to influence the decisions made in an agency needs to know where particular decisions are most likely to be made. It is a waste of time and effort to take an issue or request to a DM or task group who does not have responsibility for that decision. An effective change agent must case the organizational structure and know who, where, and how various kinds of decisions are made. For example, in a large school of social work, there are many kinds of standing committees, such as executive; curriculum; admission and financial aid; multicultural affairs; and recruitment, promotion, and tenure, that make decisions about various operations of the school. Many of these committees refer their decisions to either the dean or the governing faculty that is finally responsible for the decisions. Some decisions must even be referred to outside committees or officers in the larger university.

Decisions that involve many layers of decision making will be more difficult to influence than those in which only one layer or individual is involved. This is referred to as *depth*: how many levels of hierarchy must be involved, how many steps in the decision process must occur, and at what level of the hierarchy can the decision be actually made and implemented. Decisions that involve many people or layers in the agency take longer to bring to a conclusion and will require the change agent to move from one layer of the decision process to another until the decision is finally realized (Patti, 1974). For example, in a social agency, a given decision might have to go from line staff, to supervisor, to supervisory committee, to clinical director, and finally to an executive committee before a final approval is achieved. At each stage in the decision process, the ball may be dropped and no action will be taken on the proposal.

To underscore the importance of knowing how decisions are made, the following exercise is presented (Exercise 16.4). Because most of the readers of this text are students in social work programs, we have provided examples that will allow you to check out your school to see what seems to be the best answers.

Exercise 16.4

Who Is Responsible for What Decisions?

There are no exactly correct answers to this exercise, though some answers are probably incorrect in some situations. To check out your decisions, you will have to compare your results with your classmates and ask your classroom instructor for her perspective, too. What level of decision making in your program will be responsible for responding or modifying the issues presented in the following three scenarios?

1. *You and your classmates are upset about a 50-page midterm paper assigned in one of your classes. You consider this to be an "unreasonable length" for one assignment.*

   - *Regents/Board of Governors*
   - *Chancellor/President of the University*
   - *Dean/Director of Social Work Program*
   - *Curriculum Committee*
   - *Academic Advisor*
   - *Faculty member teaching class*
   - *Other*

2. *One faculty member in your program consistently flunks African American students, though these students do well in other classes. Students of color believe that this faculty person is "racist" and something needs to be done.*

   - *State Civil Rights Commission*
   - *Regents/Board of Governors*
   - *University Minority Affairs Office*
   - *Dean/Director of Social Work program*
   - *Curriculum Committee*
   - *Tenure/Promotion Committee*
   - *Faculty member in question*
   - *Other*

3. *Your program has a small social work library, but it is open only from 9:00 a.m. to 5:00 p.m. on weekdays. Students want weekend and evening hours so the resources of the library are more accessible.*

   - *Council on Social Work Education*
   - *Chancellor/President of the University*
   - *Dean/Director of Social Work program*
   - *Curriculum Committee*
   - *Faculty Advisor*
   - *Social Work librarian*
   - *Other*

Organizational Roles

All social agencies have expectations and conceptions about how the various roles will be performed within the organizational structure. There are roles reserved for the users of service, and there are roles reserved for the employees of the agency. These roles have a name or label and often a written description (i.e., for employees this is called a job description). For example, an agency will have clerical staff who fill a variety of roles. The role of secretary is different from the role of receptionist, though sometimes agencies may ask persons in either role to cover the responsibilities of the other.

The label or name given to the "user" of the agency's services is usually carefully considered. Social agencies may refer to their users as "client," or "patient," or "recipient," and these are important distinctions that impact on how the user is viewed and subsequently treated by the agency (Arluke, 1979; McCleary, 1978). Though "client" is a generic, common term that is used often in social agencies and in this text, some homeless shelters have deliberately avoided this label for the more descriptive term of "guest." This decision is consciously made to avoid some of the undesirable consequences (such as stigma and disempowerment) that may flow from the use of the term *client* (Haus, 1988).

It is important to analyze carefully how the agency labels its users and to look carefully beyond the label to see how the agency defines the organizational role of its users. There is a big difference between the roles of *consumer, patient, deviant, victim,* and *survivor*, yet these perspectives may underlie the actual label given to those who use the agency's services (Rein, 1970, pp. 50–53). Different agencies may all refer to their users as clients, yet each agency may have a different underlying role perspective for clients. The role of patient is often used as a label for users of services in medical settings. Implications of perceiving someone in this way is that the individual is sick. Often the patient is disempowered as the passive receiver of highly expert services. The deviant perspective may appear in agencies that have to work with clients *who* have broken society's laws or are engaging in *taboo* and immoral behavior. An agency that is working with offenders may want to treat its clients with respect but may in fact deliver a large amount of moral indignation, stigma, and revulsion for whatever problem the client is struggling to resolve. Many domestic violence agencies started out viewing their users with the victim lens (i.e., someone who is being traumatized, terrorized, or brutalized by someone more powerful) but have now consciously moved to the survivor perspective, which is designed to empower the user and give credit for latent strength that someone must have to survive in an abusive relationship.

These are not the only roles that an agency may place on its users, and there are many others, such as resident, inmate, perpetrator, rescuer, and codependent, that will affect how clients are treated by the agency. The importance of understanding these organizational roles and underlying perspectives is that they will shape how services are delivered and how clients are treated on their journey through the service process. We have discussed in earlier chapters our support for an empowerment- and strengths-based perspective in social work practice. Unfortunately, some of these stigmatized, organizational roles are anathema to an empowerment- and strengths-based perspective, and students will find them active in practice and agency settings. In fact, many practitioners and students may prefer to view their clients from these stigmatized perspectives and not realize the implication of this view on how people are treated.

Imagine the underlying confusion and conflict when an applicant approaches an intake worker in an agency in which all three parties have a different perspective. For example, if a teen enters a crisis agency feeling completely victimized and terrified by a recent date rape experience and is immediately confronted with a legalistic intake form that asks specific questions about the circumstances surrounding the event, this formal procedure may convey to the teen that she may have, at some level, been responsible or "asked for it." Suppose this teen is then greeted by the intake worker who congratulates the teen for surviving the rape and having the courage to seek help. This kind of confusion can occur often in social agencies because applicants do not always know what to expect, and different workers may adopt different perspectives—even those in conflict with the agency setting.

Though it is not fair to stereotype how a given agency may perceive its users, we have a short matching exercise (Exercise 16.5) that will help you think about how different agencies might approach their users and how the role perspective they take of their clientele may not reflect an empowerment- or strengths-based perspective. Individual social agencies or particular programs may differ from what this exercise suggests. Many of these role perspectives probably represent the kinds of perspectives that the broader community places on the kinds of social problems that clientele bring for help. For example, society may see mental illness as "deviant," though most services to the mentally ill probably treat their users as "patients."

Exercise 16.5

How Do Agencies View Their Users?

Match the social agency or program with the underlying role perspectives likely to emerge when services are delivered to users. Some services may view their users from several perspectives. Draw lines between services and perspectives, and compare your results with a classmate. Our thoughts are suggested at the bottom of this exercise. You and your instructor may not agree with all of our choices.

(Continued)

(Continued)

Service or Agency	Connect Service to Role	Potential Role Perspectives
1. Homeless Shelter		Deviant
2. Department of Public Welfare		Victim
3. Community Mental Health		Consumer
4. School Counseling Services		Recipient
5. Domestic Violence Shelter		Survivor
6. Adult Correctional Facility		Patient
7. Forensic Center		Citizen
8. Hospital Social Services		Client
9. YMCA		Perpetrator
10. Public Library		Guest

Our view: (1) = guest, victim; (2) = recipient; (3) = patient; (4) = client, consumer; (5) = survivor, victim; (6) = deviant, perpetrator; (7) = deviant, patient; (8) = patient, client; (9) = consumer, guest; (10) = citizen.

Role perspectives also have implications for the relationships that go on between members of the staff in agencies. Studies have demonstrated that not all workers share the same perspective of their role as social workers in a social agency (Billingsley, 1964), and it may be even more confusing in interdisciplinary settings, such as a hospital when other disciplines such as physicians and nurses who work with social workers are often confused about what to expect from their social work colleagues. In interdisciplinary settings, social workers are constantly engaged in clarifying their responsibilities and demonstrating their expertise to other professionals and sometimes fighting to maintain "turf" from the incursions of other professions.

Social workers seem to adopt either a *client, professional*, or *bureaucratic* orientation on the job (Billingsley, 1964). Client-centered workers are most responsive to their clients and most likely to engage in advocacy for them.

Profession-centered workers are most likely to be responsive to their professional training and to the ethical practice of their method. Bureaucratic-centered workers are most likely to be responsive to agency rules, regulations, procedures, and to the directions of their superiors in the hierarchy.

If you look back at how you answered the questionnaire in the first part of this chapter, do you see how these orientations might appear in your own answers to this questionnaire? For example, if most of your answers strongly supported client needs over other considerations, you probably would fit the client-centered orientation. If, however, your answers tended to support professional interests over all others, then you have a professional orientation. If your answers tended to support agency policies over other competing demands, then you probably have work experience and a family to feed and realize that without a job none of the other orientations is possible!

Another important perspective on organizational roles is to look at the orientations of various key DMs in the agency. In the same way that clients are *categorized* and diagnosed by agencies, it is also possible to categorize the administrative styles of key DMs in an organization. These administrative typologies are much simpler, though, than *Diagnostic and Statistical Manual of Mental Disorders* (4th ed.) (*DSM–IV*) and much more useful when a worker is trying to influence a DM. The three most common styles are *conserver, climber,* and *professional advocate* (Patti & Resnick, 1972).

The conserver style is prevalent during hard economic times and necessary when support and resources for the social agency are shrinking. The conserver is most concerned with saving money, the efficiency of the agency, and the number of clients served. Conservers have a way of reducing everything down to costs and dollars, which is their primary concern. An extreme example (and a real one, too) of a conserver took place in a moderate-sized, family service agency. On retirement of the executive director, the staff of this agency learned that their retiring executive director had returned ever increasing amounts of budget money to the United Fund (a funding source) at the end of each fiscal year. This "penny pinching" over the years had resulted in a reduction of service and staff and a stagnation in the development of this organization in the service community. The conserver is not so much concerned about what is right or fair unless there is a risk of an expensive lawsuit that the agency might lose. Conservers are not particularly interested in expansionist dreams and are much more adept at "reengineering"—modern business rhetoric for firing staff and trimming positions in an agency.

The climber is a style found in administrators who "are on the way up the hierarchy." Climbers are not particularly committed to the positions they hold because they hope to use the position in the organization as a stepping stone to bigger and better things. Climbers spend most of their efforts trying to make themselves look good or positioning themselves so they get credit for organizational achievements. They are also quick to blame others when things are not going well. Hierarchical agencies are usually full of climbers, and this style can be found in almost any social agency. The climber's greatest terror is to have something go wrong on his or her watch. Climbers will do almost anything to cover up mistakes that might mar their record. This obsession with "image" is the climber's Achilles' heel, which will be discussed further in the chapter on organizational change (Chapter 17).

The professional advocate utilizes a style similar to the client- and professional-centered orientations of line staff. The professional advocate is concerned about delivering high quality, effective services to the people the agency serves. These services must be ethical and represent the highest standards of professional practice. The professional advocate is interested in hiring a highly trained professional staff and in maintaining a highly trained work force. Unlike the conserver, professional advocates are expensive and need to have an expanding resource base to actualize their administrative styles. This style of administrator may be a creative visionary and a risk taker along the lines of the modern image of the business entrepreneur (Tropman & Morningstar, 1989) and adept at helping an agency expand its services and programs. The downside to this style is that fiscal concerns will be secondary to expansionist dreams. This kind of decision making style is most responsive to moral or ethical arguments and what is just and fair for the agency's clientele.

These administrative styles do not operate so clearly in the real world of agency practice. Administrators and DMs are blends and mixtures of these pure types, and some individual administrators are able to move from one style to another as circumstance and agency development dictate. The value of being able to recognize the characteristic of these types emerges when the practitioner is in the position of advocating or trying to promote a change in the organizational structure or process. Effective persuasion should take into account the administrative style of the DM.

The next time you are welcomed to an organization by one or several administrators, listen carefully to the themes and anecdotes each administrator discloses about the organization. Read between the lines! A short speech should reveal the administrative style of the speaker. You can corroborate your assessment by obtaining a copy of the latest "state of the agency" or "state of the department" report compiled by the DM. How would you assess the following speech? Was this man a conserver, climber, or professional advocate? "I have a dream—that one day on the red hills of Georgia, sons of former slaves and sons of former slave-owners will be able to sit down together at the table of brotherhood" (King, 1963).

Organizational Climate

The concept of "organizational climate" has been used in the formal organization literature to describe some of the "softer" elements of organization theory (Morgan, 1986; Ott, 1989). This dimension of formal organizations is critical to social work because it relates to issues of organizational sexism and racism (Roosevelt, 1991). Even though organizational issues such as discrimination on the basis of race, ethnicity, and gender are difficult dimensions to evaluate and change in an organization (Meyerson, 1989), the social work profession is committed to the goal of developing multicultural organizations both in practice agencies and schools of social work (Comas-Diaz & Griffiths, 1988; Edwards, Edwards, Francis, Montalvo, & Murase, 1992; Lewis, 1993).

Climate concerns the "image" that individual members have about the organization (Boulding, 1956). This collective image is usually hidden from members of the organization but is hardly a trivial force in organizational dynamics. Utilizing the psychoanalytic metaphor of the unconscious, we see an individual's action as overdetermined by many forces that are outside conscious awareness, yet these forces in the unconscious play a profound role in determining human behavior. Likewise, the collective "images" of an organization can exert a profound effect on organizational behavior and to overlook these images is to ignore an important force in organizational dynamics (Pondy, 1983; Tsoukas, 1991).

There are a number of ways of studying the "metaphoric images" that exist in an organization's culture (Marshak & Katz, 1992; Trice & Beyer, 1984). One way is to listen carefully to the metaphors that members of the organization use in describing the organization. Another approach, referred to as "narrative technique," is to listen to the stories that people tell about the organization at various points in its birth (founding), growth, and development. Another way to assess climate issues is to explore the metaphors and images that employees rely on when they explain what it is like working in the agency. You should realize that different worker's images of the agency may vary dramatically. In studies of organizational climate, there will be differences of perception of climate that vary across gender and race. The experiences of women in a setting will differ from the experiences of men in the same setting, and the experiences of people of color will differ from white employees (Seabury & Lewis, 1994).

A simple way to get at these out-of-awareness climate images is to ask someone who is a member of an organization to close her or his eyes and relax. Once the person has settled down, ask him or her to imagine what it is like being a member of this particular agency. Then instruct the person to "capture" the first thought or image or memory that comes to mind. No matter how silly or absurd this image might be, ask the person to share it with you. Next, ask her or him to talk about this image and tease out what the various levels of meaning are in this image in relationship to the organization that he or she works in.

For example, after closing his eyes, one social worker described that he felt as if he were in "the French Foreign Legion." He went on to say that he felt isolated from the main office in his satellite setting and that he had little support, resources, and personnel to do the job that his agency expected. He also uncovered a surprising connection when he realized that he saw the French Foreign Legion's primary mission as "colonizing people of color" and that unfortunately this could be applied to what he was doing in his social agency. Another worker described her agency as a circus. She actually heard music and could see clowns and acrobats. Unlike the first example, her associations were positive, with lots of humor and joyousness. These two examples illustrate how dramatically different organizational climates can be, even though both of these agencies were similar and provided services to troubled youth.

What is important about this kind of analysis is that it gets at the "meaning level" of what happens in an agency. One agency may have a new building with complete resources and staff, whereas another agency may reside in a shabby old building with crowded offices, limited resources, and overworked staff, yet the privileged agency could be a "snake pit" to clients, and the struggling agency could be an "oasis of hope."

Information Technology

Most social work agencies employ various kinds of information technology. Many agencies have management information systems that keep track of the agency's financial matters—billing, payroll, budgeting, etc. Some agencies also employ client case recording systems. These systems are designed to reduce the amount of paperwork, forms, and case summaries that presently are the bane of a social worker's day. Instead of completing intake forms, assessment forms, and treatment plans by hand, the data necessary for these forms are directly loaded into the computer by social workers. This information can then be later assembled into various formats or reports for disposition of cases (Jongsma, Peterson, & Jongsma, 1996). Some agencies have even established terminals in the waiting areas so clients can open their own cases and begin the data collection process even before they see an intake worker. This information may even be collected over the Internet, the telephone system, or some other e-mail system before a client gets to the agency.

Besides data collection, storage, and retrieval, the agency of the future may employ decision tools and expert systems. These electronic aids are already used in industry and medicine to help line staff rapidly obtain expert advice about what to do in complex situations. In social work, for example, there are some programs now that help an intake worker weigh the risk to a child who is in an abusive home situation (Oyersman & Benbenishty, 1993). In practice, there are many decisions that social workers make that can be aided with decision tools that determine risk of suicide or homicide or eligibility for services, and computer terminals may be a common part of any intake procedure. Computers help social workers do discharge planning by rapidly discovering what beds are available at what level of care so that patients leaving hospitals can expeditiously locate after-care placements. Referral and information services are going online so that social workers will not have to use the phone or outdated manuals to locate services for clients

Computer and distance technology allows workers to have case conferences without having to leave their offices and even to involve expert consultation without having the consultant come to the agency. Case conferences and case consultations can take place over large distances. Connectivity not only brings staff and consultants together but also allows agencies to bring clients together. Computers may be used to connect homebound clients into various kinds of support groups. At present, some agencies already use telephone conferencing to connect clients into various kinds of support and treatment groups. Even today on the Internet there are hundreds of lists of support groups such as survivors of cancer, AIDS survivors, parents of SIDS victims, relatives of Alzheimer's patients, etc., that clients can join (Meier, 2004).

Along with these positive effects of the information technology revolution come serious concerns. The ease of access and connectivity that computers provide also increases the threat that case material can be accessed by unauthorized personnel. To protect the confidentiality of information that agencies collect on their clients, computer information systems must have multiple safeguards. Agencies must not allow the database that contains client information to be interfaced with other system databases. For example, clerical staff may have access to time sheets and billing information on clients, but they should not have access to clinical information.

Another concern for social work is that these marvelous advances in technology will not be shared evenly across all segments of society or even the world for that matter (Leiderman, Guzetta, Struminger, & Monnickendam, 1993) in the same way that many of social work's clientele are disenfranchised from many of the opportunities and resources of society, such as wealth, jobs, adequate health care, housing, etc. Social workers have to work hard to ensure that clients are not left out of the information technology revolution. Client groups need the opportunities to become computer literate so they can participate in the information revolution.

Geography

Geography is an important factor in the operations of a social agency. Most agencies have some kind of *catchment area* from which they draw their applicants.

This geographical area may overlap with census tracks, city or county boundaries, or even larger areas, such as state or national boundaries. Catchment area is important because it represents who will come to the agency for services. Some agencies successfully attract a broad range of applicants from their catchment area, but others may have procedures, operations, reputation, or personnel that deter applicants from seeking services. For example, an agency that has a mostly white staff may have trouble attracting people of color from the catchment area. In fact, in some agencies, whole sectors of the catchment area will underutilize agency services unless the agency makes a concerted effort to hire staff with a similar cultural background and consciously works to sensitize staff to applicants and clients from these underutilized groups.

The following example focuses on a child and family service agency in an urbanized town close to a large city. The four major racial and ethnic groups in the catchment area are Euro-American, African American, Latina/Latino, and Arab, so these groups are used in the comparison. As Table 16.1 demonstrates, whites and African Americans represent about the same percentage in the catchment area, in clientele, and on the staff. For Latina/Latino and Arab citizens in the catchment area, however, this agency is underutilized, and this may result from the absence of staff from these two ethnic groups. These two ethnic groups might be more likely to use this agency if there were bicultural and bilingual staff who spoke English and Spanish and English and Arabic.

This strategy of *matching* social workers and clients has been advocated for years in the professional literature (Palmer, 1973). It is an important reason why the social work profession recruits students and workers from all racial and ethnic groups in the United States. This strategy does, however, have its limits, and it is unreasonable to think that all agencies will have on staff a worker who can match all applicants or clients or all of the various identity groups of a given applicant (review the relationship chapter—Chapter 6). Though the profession is still committed to recruiting and training a diverse workforce, the profession is also pursuing a broader strategy of training all students and all staff in multicultural sensitivity and competence.

The NASW *Code of Ethics* prescribes multicultural sensitivity and competence. Sensitivity is an easier skill to achieve, whereas competency, which includes

Table 16.1 Comparison of Composition of Catchment Clients and Staff

	White	African American	Latino/ Latina	Arab
Catchment area	64%	25%	8%	3%
Clientele	67%	32%	1%	0%
Staff	70%	30%	0%	0%

intervention, is much harder and more complex to achieve. There are numerous texts in social work that promote multicultural competence (Gutierrez & Lewis, 1999; Lum, 2005; Paniagua, 1998), and we agree that this is an important skill for all social workers to acquire. Multicultural training does not just mean teaching white students and staff to be more sensitive to people of color, but it involves *all* of us in becoming more sensitive to *all* the different groups that social work serves—women; poor; disabled; lesbian, gay, bisexual, and transgender (LGBT); and racial/ethnic groups (Lewis, 1993). This effort is going on in schools of social work and at in-service training and staff development of community agencies.

Another important dimension of agency geography is where the agency is located within its catchment area. This dimension has a major impact on how accessible an agency may be for potential applicants. The location of the agency should be along bus and public transportation lines so the agency is accessible for poor clientele. In large catchment areas, social agencies may place satellite offices in neighborhoods they are trying to reach. During the War on Poverty era of the 1960s, which is different from the war on the poor era of the 1990s, many storefront satellite offices were opened throughout poor urban communities to make services more accessible (Brager & Purcell, 1964). To increase service to these "invisible" population groups, some agencies even developed outreach teams that targeted urban blocks. These teams were bicultural and bilingual to match the ethnic composition of the neighborhoods. These teams would systematically enter apartment buildings and meet with residents to help them connect with underutilized services in the community (Bush, 1977).

To underscore the importance of geography and composition on agency practice, Exercise 16.6 is offered as a way of becoming familiar with your field placement and its catchment area. In this exercise, you will be seeking information about the catchment area of your agency, the demographics of the clientele, and the demographics of the staff who work in your placement and comparing them as we did in Table 16.1.

Exercise 16.6

Comparison of Agency Catchment, Staff, and Clientele

In this exercise, you will need the cooperation of your supervisor or some other administrator in your field placement. Most of this information can be gleaned from agency annual reports and from census tract information found in the reference section of your school library.

(Continued)

(Continued)

1. *Purchase a detailed street map of the community that surrounds your agency or create a map on your computer using one of the mapping programs like MapQuest.*

2. *Ask your supervisor or another administrator to point out the boundaries of the agency's catchment area. Sometimes this information is contained in a graphic in the latest annual report.*

3. *Draw the catchment area of your agency, and also mark the location of your agency on your map.*

4. *In the personnel section of the annual report, find out what the gender expression and racial and ethnic composition is for all the staff. If this information is not available, you may have to ask your supervisor to construct this information for you by going through a list of all agency personnel. If this makes your supervisor nervous, you may have to meet each of the staff and make your own judgments about race and ethnicity.*

5. *Convert raw numbers into percentages by race and ethnicity. This already may be done in the annual report.*

6. *In the services section of the annual report, locate the racial and ethnic composition for all applicants and clients served. If these client data are not in percentages, convert them.*

7. *Now, go to your library and locate the census tracts that fall within your catchment area. If you never have used census data before, ask the reference librarian to show you how to access this information. You may have to do a little interpolating, because your catchment area may not exactly overlap with census tracts. Try to come up with some population totals for the entire catchment area. You will notice that the census tract data has much more information than you need for this particular exercise; however, you may be interested in the socioeconomic factors of your catchment area, and you may also discover small ethnic enclaves or neighborhoods within your agency's catchment area that you might want to draw onto your map. In this age of geographic information systems (GIS), you may be able to find a GIS that covers your agency catchment area and displays much of the demographic information that exists in the census data. The value of GIS is that it presents a visual map of data for a particular geographical area, which is useful to those of us who are "visual learners." (GIS is further discussed later in this chapter.)*

8. *Finally, compare the racial and ethnic composition of the catchment area with the composition of agency clientele and staff.*

9. *Bravo! You are done. Your supervisor and other agency staff may be interested in your results.*

10. *Caveat: In some agencies, this exercise may not be appreciated by administrators. You can explain that you are doing it for a class assignment. This answer will not make the administrator less upset, but it will get you off the hook and maybe your professor in hot water. Don't worry about putting your professor in a little hot water; that's what he or she is paid for. We have been in hot water, too, for assigning exercises like this one.*

This part of the chapter has explored the complex world of a social agency and pointed out the various elements of agency practice that will impact on the social worker and the clients. In the next part of this chapter, we turn to the community and neighborhoods that surround the client and social agency. To restate, our purpose in focusing on these large systems is to help the interpersonal practitioners understand the impact these larger systems have on themselves and their clients and also to give them the tools to understand these systems so they can change them.

COMMUNITY ASSESSMENT •

Need for Understanding Communities

Before we launch into this discussion of community assessment, the term *community* must be defined. The community concept in social work practice has been defined in a number of ways (Warren, 1975).

Community can be seen as a geographical entity such as a neighborhood or a catchment area surrounding an agency. Community can also be defined as an identity group that may share a common ethnic history, such as blacks, Polish Americans, or WASPs. Community can also be defined as a group that reflects their social status, such as the LGBT; homeless; or "Richistans" (Frank, 2007) community. For our purposes in this chapter, we will present the framework that is outlined as Dimension II in the person-in-environment (PIE) assessment system (Karls & Wandrei, 1994a). This framework fits our ecological view and also calls attention to the important aspects of a client's environment that will impact a client's social functioning. This conceptualization tends to blend all of the definitions of community that may be found in social work practice (Karls & Wandrei, 1994a, p. 29), but it takes as its reference point the individual client's necessary interactions with her environment.

In Chapter 12 on family assessment, we presented the assessment technique of "ecomaps." This is a client-centered assessment technique that often will bring up many of the environmental variables that are included in Dimension II of the PIE system. We will describe five of the conceptual categories of Dimension II of PIE but will not be concerned with the coding system for these categories. It is not these numerous and complicated codes that are important but the conceptual perspective of community that is presented in PIE. These environmental categories are (1) economic/basic needs system; (2) education/training system; (3) judicial/legal system; (4) health, safety, and social services system; and (5) voluntary association system. We will not be covering the affectional support system here because we believe this system has been covered in our discussion of individual assessment in Chapter 10 of the network map, which focuses on the issue of social support.

Because the PIE system was developed by social workers for social workers, the system reflects the importance of discovering the social justice issue of "discrimination" in these various sectors that may be impacting individual clients. By contrast, the *DSM–IV* system ignores discrimination as an important factor in the health and well-being of individuals. PIE presents a typology of the most likely bases of discrimination that can be found in these sectors: age, ethnicity/color, language, religion, sex (gender expression), sexual orientation, lifestyle, noncitizenship status, veteran status, dependency status, disability, marital status, etc. For example, some resources may discriminate against LGBT clients for religious reasons, while others may discriminate against poor clients because they only provide services to clients with "adequate insurance." Some agencies do not have a sliding fee scale for low-income recipients. Some agencies may not be barrier free, do not have bilingual and bicultural staff, nor staff members who can "sign." Some agencies do not have evening hours, so they place an extra burden on their working clients to leave work and lose pay in order to attend interviews.

The economic/basic needs system is the largest environmental system with which individual clients and families interact. This system provides for most of the basic needs of clients for food, shelter, employment, and transportation. Poor families may have many problems that emerge in this sector, such as unemployment, poor nutrition, homelessness, and lack of access to transportation to acquire resources. Poor inner-city communities have few opportunities for employment, local "ma and pa" grocery stores charge much more for food than suburban chain stores, and many local shops may be recycling used appliances that break down soon after a poor family purchases them (Caplovitz, 1963). The primary source of income for poor families may come from the Department of Public Welfare (DPW), which provides income grants and food stamps, and from church-sponsored programs, such as food banks, breakfast programs, garden plots, and meals-on-wheels for shut-in elderly citizens.

The goals of the education/training system are "to nurture intellect, to develop social skills, and to foster individual potential to its optimal level" (Karls & Wandrei, 1994a, p. 30). The schools in poor communities may have few enrichment programs, most students are performing below grade level on standardized tests, and the physical plants are old and decaying. There are few opportunities for adult education, retraining, or vocational training. Because schools are often supported by local taxes, the schools in affluent suburbs may receive twice the per pupil support than schools in the inner city (Eitzen & Zinn, 2005). There may be traditional social work agencies in poor communities, such as settlement houses and community centers. These resources provide opportunities for youth to participate in recreational and developmental activities, such as team sports, computer training, and language acquisition.

The judicial/legal system concerns the social control function of the criminal justice systems, which includes the police, sheriff, courts, and jails. In some communities, there may be informal groups, such as neighborhood watches, that are designed to provide some semblance of security in the absence of police and fire protection. In poor communities, problems may arise from inadequate police and fire coverage, "profiling of particular ethnic groups," inadequate defense, and mandatory sentences for various violations that lead to prison overcrowding. In every step of the criminal justice system, poor ethnic minorities are more likely to be arrested, charged, convicted, and incarcerated than more affluent, white lawbreakers (Eitzen & Zinn, 2005).

The health, safety, and social services system includes the community's health, mental health, and social services delivery systems. Besides these formal systems, communities also have an extensive network of alternative and indigenous healers. For example, there may be curanderos, espiritistas, root doctors, acupuncturists, homeopaths, naturopaths, etc., who provide services to folks who are not insured and cannot afford the costs of the allopathic, formal health care system. Poor inner-city communities may have public health clinics with well baby clinics, needle exchange programs, and screening programs for HIV, AIDS, and STDs. It is likely that there are no general hospitals or VA hospitals, no outpatient clinics for either physical or mental health issues, and few social service agencies besides the welfare department. There may be group homes and halfway houses for deinstitutionalized mental patients but no clinics or service providers for follow-up.

The voluntary association system "consists of the common ways people satisfy needs for social support and interaction outside of the family and the workplace" (Karls & Wandrei, 1994a, p. 31). There may be large institutionalized churches, synagogues, mosques, as well as small locally organized religious communities organized around specific belief systems such as Santeria, fundamentalist Christianity, or Native American shamanic beliefs. This system also includes many kinds of self-help groups, such as 12-step programs (e.g., AA, Al-Anon, Narcotics Anonymous [NA], Overeaters Anonymous [OA]) and other support groups focused on specific characteristics of community members, such as Dawn Treaders, Save Our Sons and Daughters (SOSAD), and Recovery Incorporated. These groups were discussed in more detail in the chapter on individual assessment (Chapter 10). A common problem with this sector is that these resources may not exist in some neighborhoods, and transportation resources are not available to allow community residents to access these services in other geographical areas.

When the social worker is completing an ecomap with their client system, the diagram in Figure 16.3 represents the five sectors of PIE that the social worker may keep in mind when thinking about how the environment surrounds and impinges on the client. The value of ecomaps is they do not just reflect problems, deficits, and struggles but also highlight resources, opportunities, and supportive systems.

Figure 16.3 Diagram of PIE Dimension II Sectors

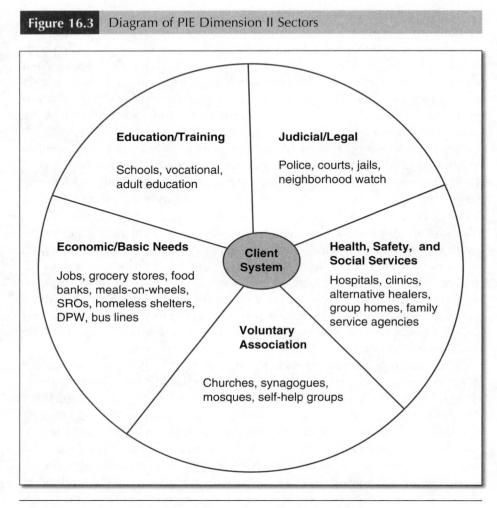

Education/Training

Schools, vocational, adult education

Judicial/Legal

Police, courts, jails, neighborhood watch

Client System

Economic/Basic Needs

Jobs, grocery stores, food banks, meals-on-wheels, SROs, homeless shelters, DPW, bus lines

Health, Safety, and Social Services

Hospitals, clinics, alternative healers, group homes, family service agencies

Voluntary Association

Churches, synagogues, mosques, self-help groups

Note: DPW = Department of Public Welfare; SRO = single room occupancy.

Poor communities have many problems, but they also have resources and strengths that help their members cope and survive.

In order to operationalize this conceptual map of a client's environment, the following exercise is presented that will require the student to do a little legwork in learning about the environment that surrounds their agency's neighborhood and the clients they serve. Exercise 16.7 will be the last exercise that is proposed in this chapter and will piggyback on the data that was collected in Exercise 16.6.

Exercise 16.7

Qualitative Experience of Your Agency Catchment Area

Take the map of your agency's catchment area, and locate the various resources, institutions, and commercial areas that fit into the five sectors that were previously discussed.

You may be able to find some of this information on a GIS that has already been created for your agency catchment. In the next section of this chapter, we present more about usefulness of GIS in understanding communities. Because the GIS map is a metaphor for your catchment, it cannot capture the qualitative experience of the catchment area. The qualitative assessment can only come from walking or driving around the catchment area and seeing what is there. This experience will add to your understanding of the geography surrounding your agency.

Another dimension missing from your map, which you may be able to infer when you walk around your neighborhood, is the history of the community. An ecomap is an assessment framework that captures a snapshot of a client's life, but it does not collect information about the "history" of that environment and how the environment is changing. So many communities are in transition for economic reasons, such as white flight, gentrification, and changes in the composition of ethnic groups that are moving into the area. This history is more difficult to collect and requires the student to contact the local "historians" in the community. Sometimes this history can be gathered in the local library, in a popular barber shop, in a popular bar, or breakfast place that is inhabited by retired members in the community. In the particular rural town in which we (Brett A. Seabury, or BAS, and Barbara H. Seabury, or BHS) live, there is a table in a donut shop that is reserved (informally) for a group of retired farmers, merchants, and first families who meet regularly for coffee and donuts in the morning. This group is a marvelous resource for the history of Manchester, Michigan. Another resource in African American urban communities is the local barber shop. When you try to access these informal systems, you will discover what it means to be in the "outsider" role and the kinds of suspicions and hostility that come with the outsider role.

Geographic Information Systems

GIS have been around for a long time. In Edward Tufte's (1983) *The Visual Display of Quantitative Information*, he presented many historical and contemporary examples of how various types of data can be presented on maps. In one historical example in 18th century London, he demonstrated how a physician concerned about cholera outbreaks was able to locate the well that was responsible for the epidemic. By placing the cases of cholera on a map of London and observing where these cases clustered around public wells, he was able to rule out the safe wells from the contaminated well.

Today GIS maps are used to display various kinds of census data in geographical areas. For example, Professor William Bowen, Department of Geography, California State University–Northridge, has produced a whole series of GIS maps with 1990 census data that takes into account ethnicity and poverty in the United States and various large metropolitan areas. These maps are designed to show the concentrations of ethnic groups in various areas. Figure 16.4 displays the concentration of poverty in the five metropolitan boroughs of New York City.

Presently in social work GIS technology is being used to present information about communities from a strengths perspective (Mowbray et al., 2007). GIS technology is taught to community practice students as a tool for understanding their target communities.

Contemporary Issues in Community Assessment

There is a tendency in social work to focus on the problems in poor communities in order to understand these problems so that the profession can do something about them. There are needs as well as assets in poor communities. Because there are many vacant lots, these lots have been cleaned up by local residents and made into miniparks where children can play and parents can congregate and engage in social interaction with each other. These vacant lots have also been cleaned up and converted into urban garden plots in which community residents can grow vegetables to supplement their diet. Because of the proximity of homes in urban areas, nonprofits have developed local area networks (LANS) so that community residents will have access to the Internet. Other programs have been developed to recycle computers from corporations and universities so that poor families will have computers at no cost. Local schools, libraries, and community action nonprofits provide free training for adults in basic computer usage. All of these activities are designed to bridge the digital divide.

● SUMMARY

The chapter began with a discussion of the reasons why an interpersonal practitioner would seek to assess organizations and community. The next section of the chapter focused on organizational assessment. The concept of "organizations" was defined, and the various kinds of agencies that social workers encounter were identified. The impact of organizations on clients and social workers was highlighted.

| Figure 16.4 | GIS Map of Poverty in New York City: 1990 Census Data |

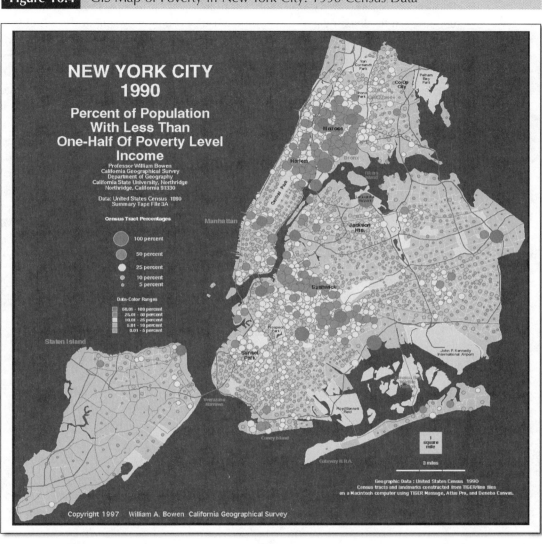

Source: From www.spc.edu/PAGES/1775.asp.

The process of organizational assessment was described. This process relies on knowing where and how to collect organizational information from written materials and organizational informants. The kinds of information concerned norms and operating rules, decision making structures, organizational roles, organizational climate, information technology, and geography. This section of the chapter concluded with a discussion of contemporary problems found in agencies, such as societal diversity and the composition of the agency staff and clientele.

The next section of the chapter focused on community assessment. Consistent with our ecological perspective, community dynamics impact clients and workers alike. In conceptualizing community, we presented Dimension II from the PIE system. Five of these sectors reflect the details of the various dynamics that emerge when social workers draw ecomaps with their clients. The five environmental categories are (1) economic/basic needs system; (2) education/training system; (3) judicial/legal system; (4) health, safety, and social services system; and (5) voluntary association system.

In the concluding sections of this chapter, we introduced GIS and the value of this technology in portraying demographic and public health data on maps of geographic areas. These GIS maps are not only valuable as a descriptive tool but can also be used to analyze dynamics that are inherent in geographical areas. We concluded this chapter with a caveat that social workers should not only be focusing on the problems of communities but also on the strengths and resilience of communities.

17

CHANGE IN ORGANIZATIONS AND COMMUNITIES

The reasonable man adapts himself to the world. The unreasonable man persists in trying to adapt the world to himself. Therefore, all progress depends on the unreasonable man.

—George Bernard Shaw (1957)

I n this chapter, we present ways that interpersonal practitioners can change organizations and communities. We want to restate our position that when working with individuals, families, and groups, it is often necessary for practitioners to be involved in environmental change. Many times, a practitioner must direct interventions at multiple levels, such as the individual, family, and neighborhood, before significant changes in social problems will occur. For example, in working with youth who are in trouble with the law, it may be necessary to work directly with the youth, with the youth's chaotic family system, and with the youth's gang-prevalent neighborhood. Such multilevel interventions *may* involve several workers employing a variety of intervention strategies.

● ETHICS OF ORGANIZATIONAL AND COMMUNITY CHANGE

The ethics and principles involved in changing organizations and community structures are different from working with individuals, families, and small groups. When an interpersonal practitioner is involved in organizational or community change, there are three primary conceptual units—the worker system, the client system, and the target system—involved in the change process. In most cases in which environmental change is taking place, the interpersonal practitioners will find themselves interacting with two distinct parties: the client and some organization or some part of the client's community. These parties are conceptualized as the client system and the target system (see Chapter 2). The relationship that the interpersonal practitioner has with the client system differs from the relationship that the interpersonal practitioner will develop with the organization or community. Even though there are practice situations in which the organization is conceptualized as a client (Googins & Davidson, 1993), from the perspective of an interpersonal practitioner the organization and community are conceptualized as target systems.

Interpersonal practitioners do not have the same ethical responsibilities to target systems that they do to client systems. Unfortunately, the ethical responsibilities to target systems are not spelled out in detail in the National Association of Social Workers (NASW) *Code of Ethics*. What are the worker's obligation and responsibilities to an organization and community when they are the targets of the change interventions?

There are overall values that apply both to client systems and target systems. For example, social workers are prohibited from engaging in activities that endanger the client's life and likewise any activity that will endanger lives in the target system—that is, members of the organization or members of the community. Social workers cannot threaten or use deadly force to influence clients, nor can they use such tactics to influence decision makers (DMs) in agencies or communities. For example, social workers cannot support prison riots and the taking of hostages as a means to transform prisons.

The professional values and the code of ethics are clear that social workers must protect the information they have about clients, and this information can only be disclosed under strict situations. This kind of "privileged communication" is protected by law in many states as part of licensure. Confidentiality, however, does not operate in work with changing organizations and communities. In fact, the threat and even disclosure of information about a target system is a common tactic in organizational change and may even be protected by law. For example, many states have "whistle-blowing" laws that protect workers who disclose compromising information to outsiders, such as the press or funding sources.

These laws are designed to protect the employee from organizational retaliation. The very act of disclosure and deliberately violating confidence is a tactic that is used in organizational or community change, but it would never be sanctioned as a tactic in client change.

In the earlier chapter on values and ethics (Chapter 3), we raised many issues that apply to interpersonal practice with clients, but in community work, community practitioners have traditionally considered their client systems to be "citizens" or "members" of the community or neighborhood in which the practitioner is working. Are the ethical responsibilities that limit the relationship with clients also applied to "citizens"? Are the boundary problems that may arise in work with clients also an issue in work with citizens—especially when the interpersonal practitioner lives in the same community as the clients and other citizens?

For example, can an interpersonal practitioner form a personal relationship with a member of a community group that is helping one of her clients? Can that interpersonal practitioner have a consensual sexual relationship with that community member? Are all of the citizens and members of the community off-limits for the interpersonal practitioner when it concerns personal and intimate relationships? Does the issue of dual relationships apply to members of the community in the same way that it applies to clients?

Another ethical issue concerns the risk and liability that an interpersonal practitioner may face in linking up a client to an informal community resource. For example, as previously stated, a social worker cannot promote or engage in violent action as a change strategy. What happens when an interpersonal practitioner encourages a client to participate in a community group that is promoting changes in a community institution, and the change tactics employed by that community group result in violence in which members of the community are injured? It is important that the interpersonal practitioner understand the tactics that a watchdog group or advocacy group will use before encouraging clients to join these groups.

What happens if an interpersonal practitioner promotes an alternative healing resource for the client and the technology applied by the healer harms the client in some way? For example, herbal remedies, like pharmaceutical drugs, can have negative side effects with some individuals. What is the responsibility of the interpersonal practitioner who suggests to a client that she or he might consider talking with an herbalist in order to get relief for some physiological symptoms? In Chapter 2, we talked about the litigiousness of modern practice, and though physicians are more likely to be sued, social workers also need to have malpractice insurance.

When we engaged in community change, there are often competing interests that may emerge in any change that is proposed. Such competing interests can create dilemmas for the interpersonal practitioner when the client's interests may have a negative impact on other groups within the community. In order to clarify this dilemma, we present a contemporary example in the following case example.

The Case For and Against Walmart

Walmart has begun to expand and build large stores in poor inner-city communities, and in some communities, there have been protest movements and political action to keep them out. The opening of a Walmart store in a poor inner-city community will bring the opportunity for many new, low-skilled jobs and low prices for the many consumer goods that Walmart sells. This store may also increase local taxes for the community and may act as a magnet for other stores to move into the shopping area around the Walmart store. But because of Walmart's predatory model of capitalism, the small "ma and pa" grocery stores, shoe stores, hardware stores, clothing stores, etc., will be driven out of business. So the poor community will gain jobs and inexpensive goods, the working-class members of the community will lose their jobs and family businesses. How does an interpersonal practitioner respond? Do you help to mobilize your poor clients to promote Walmart's request to build the store before the community planning board or do you join the advocacy groups that will be fighting to keep Walmart out of the community?

Another major difference in the relationships between the worker and client and in the relationship between the worker and target system concerns empowerment. Interpersonal practitioners are working to empower clients, yet the opposite is often going on in work with target systems. Because the client is in the lower power position and often the worker is too, in relationship to the target organization or community, the worker's tactics often are to attempt to disempower or diffuse or shift power from the target system to the client. Workers rarely attempt to empower the organizations they are trying to change in behalf of clients unless these are organizations established by oppressed peoples to meet their needs or struggle for human rights. Most of a worker's efforts in trying to change organizations or communities involve mobilizing support for the client's position and simultaneously attempting to reduce the power inherent in the target organization.

Because of the power differentials between clients and organizations, there are tactics that the interpersonal practitioner might use with organizations, yet these same techniques would not be used with clients. For example, such tactics as manipulation and surprise are not considered desirable tactics in the relationship between client and worker because these tactics do not build trust. With organizations, however, trust may not be as essential to the relationship. In fact, in some organizations, there may be little trust between the DM in the organization and the interpersonal practitioner who is trying to influence the organization to make a decision on behalf of the client.

Another ethical difference concerns the primacy of client interests. The interpersonal practitioner must place client's needs and interests ahead of the worker's needs and interests (Reamer, 2006). This does not at all apply to target systems. The worker does not place the needs and interests of the target system over the needs of the client and the worker. In fact, in some situations, the worker deliberately places his or her own needs before that of the organization. For example, when the worker organizes a union or takes a labor action against a social agency to improve procedures in the workplace, this situation may actually cost the organization time and resources and is a direct benefit to workers and clients (See Figure 17.1).

Figure 17.1   Worker's Relationship to Client and Target Systems

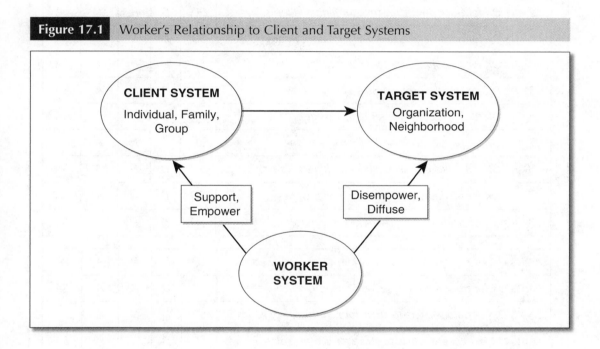

In order to demonstrate some of the ambivalence that many social workers have about unions, the following exercise, Exercise 17.1, is presented here to help social work students clarify some of their concerns about labor issues. The ethics of the social work profession permit members to join various social service unions (Alexander, 1983, 1987). There are no right or wrong answers to this simple questionnaire, but it is important that students and faculty share the results of this questionnaire with each other. The discussion should help class members raise their conscious use of self when they are engaged in working to change organizations.

Exercise 17.1

Attitudes Toward Unionism

Read each of the statements, and circle the response on the five-point scale that best reflects your attitudes.

SD = Strongly Disagree, D = Disagree, N = Neutral, A = Agree, SA = Strongly Agree					
1. It's OK for mine workers to strike for higher wages.	SD	D	N	A	SA
2. It's OK for truck drivers to strike for higher wages.	SD	D	N	A	SA
3. It's OK for auto workers to strike for higher wages.	SD	D	N	A	SA
4. It's OK for schoolteachers to strike for higher wages.	SD	D	N	A	SA
5. It's OK for social workers to strike for higher wages.	SD	D	N	A	SA
6. It's OK for nurses to strike for higher wages.	SD	D	N	A	SA
7. It's OK for physicians to strike for higher wages.	SD	D	N	A	SA
8. It's OK for police officers to strike for higher wages.	SD	D	N	A	SA
9. It's OK for firefighters to strike for higher wages.	SD	D	N	A	SA
10. It's OK for soldiers to strike for higher wages.	SD	D	N	A	SA

A. It's OK for mine workers to strike for health/safety issues.	SD	D	N	A	SA
B. It's OK for truck drivers to strike for health/safety issues.	SD	D	N	A	SA
C. It's OK for auto workers to strike for health/safety issues.	SD	D	N	A	SA
D. It's OK for schoolteachers to strike for health/safety issues.	SD	D	N	A	SA
E. It's OK for social workers to strike for health/safety issues.	SD	D	N	A	SA
F. It's OK for nurses to strike for health/safety issues.	SD	D	N	A	SA
G. It's OK for physicians to strike for health/safety issues.	SD	D	N	A	SA
H. It's OK for police officers to strike for health/safety issues.	SD	D	N	A	SA
I. It's OK for firefighters to strike for health/safety issues.	SD	D	N	A	SA
J. It's OK for soldiers to strike for health/safety issues.	SD	D	N	A	SA

THEORIES OF ORGANIZATIONAL CHANGE ●

There are many ways of approaching organizational change. The model that we propose is a derivative of the "Change the Organization from Within" (COFW) model (Resnick & Patti, 1980). We selected this model because it is most likely that social workers will be working to improve services in some area of their employing agency. Social workers do work to change social agencies and organizations—on behalf of their clients—that do not employ these workers, but it is beyond the scope of our discussion here to get into all aspects of organizational change. We also believe that the principles of the COFW model are clearly spelled out and can be operationalized easily by social workers in their employing agency and that many of the principles can also be applied to changing aspects of the client's community.

The change model we present is basically a problem solving model with a number of phases and guiding principles. There may be many things that should be changed about an agency, but the model reduces the change effort to those things that an interpersonal practitioner can effectively influence in a reasonable amount of time and effort. It is our belief that social workers must be committed to broader issues of social change, but this goes beyond the scope of this book. They must, however, know how to change the more specific, detailed dysfunctions that arise in social agencies.

Problem Solving Framework

There are seven phases to this model of agency change: (1) *identifying the issue*, (2) *formulating a goal*, (3) *identifying the decision making structure*, (4) *assessing the feasibility of the goal*, (5) *implementing the change strategy*, (6) *recognizing and responding to the agency's countertactics*, and (7) *evaluating the effectiveness of the change efforts*. These seven stages serve as a heuristic guide to the social worker; however, in the real world of practice, these seven steps may not unfold in the order presented or in such discreet phases.

When applying this problem solving model, an interpersonal practitioner may be guided by a number of practice *principles* that can be generalized throughout the change process. There are four general principles presented: (1) *documentation*, (2) *low visibility*, (3) *least contest*, and (4) *client participation*. We begin by describing these general principles and practice guidelines.

Social workers are well aware of the demands for "documentation" in practice, though often it is perceived as the bane of paperwork and red tape so common to agency practice. In organizational change, documenting the issue, the decisions, and the actions taken is critical to the effectiveness of change efforts. From the beginning to the end of the change process, the worker must carefully document and get written evidence of all steps in the change process. Verbal agreements, recollections, promises, and hearsay complaints are no substitute for memos, letters, minutes, and written documentation. Interpersonal practitioners as change agents must create a "paper trail" of evidence throughout the change process.

In the beginning, when a complaint or issue is surfaced in the agency, the worker must be sure to verify the existence of the complaint or issue. It is not enough to go on what the client says or thought happened. As the issue emerges around which of the change efforts will be taking place, the worker must collect evidence that the issue did in fact occur. For example, if the client was denied services, was the denial accomplished by a letter (good evidence) or by a verbal statement of some DM (weaker evidence). If there were witnesses to the verbal denial, that will strengthen the case that the issue occurred. Sometimes clients misunderstand agency procedures and may feel they have been rejected when in fact they have not been rejected. Before engaging in any remedy, a worker should be clear that the infraction actually occurred and is not the result of misperception, misunderstanding, or some kind of hidden agenda.

A real example is presented that will demonstrate how ridiculous an advocate can look when this basic step is ignored:

Advocating for a Neighbor

I (Brett A. Seabury, or BAS) had a disabled, elderly, distrustful-of-authority neighbor who lived alone near my farm. I mentioned to this neighbor that I was planning to go to the meeting of the township tax review board to challenge a recent increase in my tax assessments. This neighbor asked if he could go along and also complain about his recent change in assessment. Because he was missing a leg, I agreed to transport him to the meeting and help him up the township hall steps (a non-barrier-free public building). Once through the signing-in procedure, we both had a chance to meet with the tax board. Normally this is a private meeting in a back room, but my neighbor asked me to accompany him through the proceedings. To make a long story short, he began his tirade about how his taxes were being raised precipitously and this was unjust because he was living on a fixed income (SSI). The board looked quite puzzled by this outburst and pointed out to my neighbor that his assessments had actually been reduced that year. We all experience moments in life of looking like a "fool," and this should be avoided when acting in our professional role as a social worker. I still felt very foolish, though I was only acting in the role of "neighbor."

Documentation of decisions should take place as they occur in the change process. For example, if DMs will not write down what remedies they have agreed to take or put it into the minutes of a meeting, the advocate can write a follow-up letter or memo to the DM outlining the decisions that were made. Saved copies of memos can form the basis of documentation of decisions, especially if the DM responds to the memo. Documenting decisions and actions is also important when trying to hold the DM accountable for remedies not implemented.

The principle of low visibility is similar to the confidentiality principle with clients. It is unnecessary and often undesirable to have too many individuals involved in the change efforts, especially in the beginning (Middleman & Goldberg, 1974). The fewer the number of folks who know about the issue and proposed remedies, the better for the change process. The principle of low visibility does not mean that the client and social worker should sneak around and create subterfuges in the change process, but only those who need to know should be informed. There are many things that go on in social agencies that are not everyone's business.

A related principle to low visibility is the corollary principle of "start small." In this model of agency change, the worker does not want to involve any more of the organization in the change process than is necessary to achieve the specific change goal. Social agencies are constantly adjusting and responding to events, and it is neither necessary nor desirable to have everyone in the agency involved in all the many changes going on. Some changes, such as funding sources, press, accrediting bodies, courts, in agencies may have to involve outside groups, but in the beginning, the worker must try to produce a change with the smallest number of DMs. When change efforts have to be expanded to include many DMs in the organization and many outside decision making groups, the change process becomes much more difficult to manage and much more likely to attract "distraction" forces: other change forces in the organization that do not necessarily support the changes proposed (Bennis, Benne, & Chin, 1969; Lippit, Watson, & Westley, 1958).

The principle of least contest (Middleman & Goldberg, 1974) applies to the way in which the social worker adapts change strategies and tactics to the change process. This will be discussed in more detail later; however, the general principle reflects the desire to create change with the least amount of contention or conflict. Whenever social workers are trying to create agency change, they should begin by engaging in gentle nudge, collaborative strategies before moving on to more pressured, adversarial tactics. It is better if change can occur with these softer tactics because the relationship between the change agent and DM will not be put in jeopardy (Mailich & Ashley, 1981; Richan, 1973; Simmons, 1972). This principle recognizes that organizational change is as much an interpersonal process as it is a system process.

This principle does not mean that social workers as change agents should avoid conflict or avoid the use of adversarial, contentious tactics but they should employ them only after more collaborative efforts have been tried. In some organizational change situations in which the resistance is great and the stakes to the client and worker very high, it may be necessary to escalate to more adversarial tactics, but it is important that the social worker begin with gentle tactics. The relationship principle that "you can draw more flies with honey than with vinegar" underlies this principle. In the debate in the organizational change literature between the effectiveness of the "carrot" or the "stick," it may be necessary to use both, but we always start with the carrot.

This principle does not deny the reality that in some agencies it may be necessary to engage in extremely adversarial tactics, such as lawsuits or demonstrations at public hearings, before change can occur. This principle does suggest that there are many consequences that may come from such escalation and that the worker must carefully weigh the risks to self and client. Possible consequences are that clients may be terminated and workers fired. When this principal is ignored, it usually means that the interpersonal practitioner has not done her homework. For example, it would be a mistake for social workers to threaten an administrator in an agency with a strike without first finding out what the position of the DM is on the issue and how the administrator feels about remedies.

The principle of client participation is not important only in organizational and community change but it is a basic principle that underlies almost all actions of interpersonal practice. Social workers have an ethical responsibility to involve their clients in any action they might undertake for, with, or on behalf of these clients. Client empowerment demands that clients be involved in the decisions and actions that practitioners are taking. This book has repeatedly emphasized how central the client is to the change process—that is, self-determination, contracting, etc.—whether that change process involves only the individual client or whether that change process involves others in the client's environment. As we have discussed in the chapter on contracting (Chapter 8), the client must be informed and understand what is going on in the change process.

Unfortunately, it is much easier to operationalize this principle when the target of change is the individual client or close associate of the individual client, but this principle of client participation gets more difficult to practice as the size of the target system increases. Often clients have suffered many negative experiences with social agencies, organizations, and public bureaucracies. This kind of learned helplessness can be found in the expression "no sense fighting city hall" that pervades the consciousness of many of our clients, as well as the consciousness of many social workers. There are many ways to change city hall without having to "fight." There are many situations and aspects of organizations and communities that can be changed, as well as some aspects that are very difficult to change. Taking an "a priori" position that organizational change is impossible is extremely disempowering for workers and clients and may in fact be one of the most empowering forces going for the DMs in organizations.

We have discussed earlier how important consciousness raising (CR) is to working with disempowered groups of clients, and it is important here to realize that in some situations, clients will want to avoid trying to change agencies or organizations because of their consciousness that such change is impossible. The client and the practioner are in the low power position when they seek organizational change, and the risks involved must be openly and carefully considered before the worker and client take action. Clients realistically may be concerned about losing benefits or having services curtailed if they speak up and challenge agencies they depend on for their livelihood. This kind of organizational retaliation is real. Applications can be "lost" or "misplaced," and sometimes decisions can be delayed for months. Likewise, workers also must be realistic that agencies have considerable control over their lives, too, and there can be a number of ways that agencies can retaliate against workers, such as fire them, not promote them, give no raises, or give negative evaluations.

How do we sort out these issues of client participation in agency change when such factors as risk, consciousness, vulnerability, and ethical responsibility are intertwined? We offer general principles that will help guide the interpersonal practitioner about client participation. First, it is desirable that client and practitioner both be involved in any kind of change activities, though it is recognized that in some situations, the practitioner may be acting alone without the client's direct involvement. The most ideal situation involves the practitioner and client going together to the DM and building the client's case. The most ideal scenario is for the client to do most of the talking and expressing, with the practitioner going along as support or backup. In some situations, however, the practitioner might have to do most of the talking, with the client being drawn into the conversation at points. In some situations, it might be all that the client can do to go along to the meeting and not speak but witness what transpires between the practitioner and the DM. And still in other situations, the client might want the practitioner to go alone to the DM and build the client's case—that is, act for the client. Or the practitioner and client may decide that in some situations, the client should go alone and present the issue. In all of these scenarios, the practitioner and client collaborate in planning and practicing what might transpire in the meeting with the DM.

Problem Solving Steps

Now that we have discussed underlying principles that guide the practitioner's actions, we turn to the steps of the problem solving model. The first step or phase is identifying the issue. We prefer to use the word *issue* rather than *problem* because it is broader in scope and does not imply that something must go wrong in an agency before it requires "fixing." Services can always be improved, and innovations can be tried and some form of preventions proposed without waiting for trouble to emerge. In the world of practice, though, much organizational change is generated by problems that emerge in the daily operations of the organization, and here we focus on those issues that involve the client's use of services in the agency. We will not focus on employee–personnel issues or agency-to-agency problems that also may have an impact on our clients.

Because our perspective is client centered, it is from the client that the issue or problem should emerge. Interpersonal practitioners may have their own perspectives about what needs to change in the agency, but these perspectives should not be projected onto clients. Clients should be the source of the issue that is developed so that hidden agendas from practitioners may be avoided. For example, interpersonal practitioners do not organize clients into some kind of protest movement because they do not like the pay increments in their agencies.

When issues first emerge in interviews with clients, these issues are often fairly global and seem to represent a generalized kind of discontent with organizations or agencies. For example, if you ask a group of social work students what they do not like about their program, you will often get a number of general complaints: financial aid process, placement process, high cost of tuition, overcrowded classrooms, or disinterested faculty. Any one of these generalized complaints could be the starting point for making changes in the program, but each issue must be carefully operationalized, developed, and explored. In what situations does the issue occur? Who is involved, and what are the consequences to those involved? Is the issue something that actually happened, occurs repeatedly, or is it something that exists only in the "eye of the beholder"? Can the issue be documented, and do others agree there is a real issue that needs to be addressed?

For example, suppose we were to explore the complaints of social work students about the placement process in their programs. There are many possible examples of these complaints. Some students may think there are not enough agencies to choose from, others may think the placement director is inaccessible, others may want more time to make placement decisions, others may want to have shorter or longer time in their placements, others may want to have paid placements, others may want their agencies to be within walking distance of their residences, and others may want to have placements that fit their particular religious beliefs. The number of particular issues that could emerge around complaints in the placement process is almost as numerous as the number of students that have to be placed in a given term.

Besides specific complaints, it is possible to obtain a list of existing agencies, the numbers of entering students, the number of staff involved in the placement process, the kind of information that students are given about agencies, etc. One way to address this area is to focus on those particular issues that have the best chance of improving the placement process for most of the students. Issues such as the number of agencies to choose from, the amount of time and effort given by the school to help students make the choice, and the number and availability of staff in the placement office are fairly specific issues the program might address.

The important point of this discussion is that the practitioner does not just seize the first complaint a client makes about an agency and charge off to make changes. There is a careful assessment process to decide whether the issue exists and can be clearly identified. In the case of a particular problem, can the problem be clearly identified and verified? During this assessment process, the practitioner does not want to appear as though she disbelieves the client's complaint; the practitioner wants to understand the complaint in detail and see if others have also experienced this problem.

When an issue has been explored and identified, that it clearly exists and can be documented, the next step is to formulate a goal that will address the identified issue. This goal should be specific and particular and represent the change that must be made in the agency's operations or procedures that will resolve, prevent, or keep the issue from occurring. There may be a number of particular goals that could be generated from one issue. For example, in the complaints about the placement process, a school might discover that it is short staffed in its placement office in relationship to the number of students it is trying to place. A particular goal might be to increase the personnel in this office, to change the number of students that must be placed in a given term, or even to allow students to find their own field placements. The school might also recognize that it does not have a systematic way of informing students about potential placements, and this might be addressed by holding a pre-orientation process in which advanced students share their placement experiences with entering students. The placement office might also publish a list, description, and evaluation of all placements it has recently used, and with some situations, students are not placed in their first term until they have had a chance to find out more about social services and what areas they might be interested in pursuing.

Whatever list of potential changes emerges from these deliberations, with each suggested organizational change the interpersonal practitioner and the client must identify the relevant agency decision making structure. As we discussed in the chapter on organizational and community assessment (Chapter 16), the decision making structure of the agency must be understood by the interpersonal practitioner if any kind of successful change is to be undertaken in the agency. For each particular change goal that is developed, the client and worker have to pinpoint the particular DM who is capable of making and implementing the change. Sometimes, the DM is an individual administrator, and sometimes, it may be several administrators and a committee. The practitioner must be able to identify the lowest level of the organizational structure capable of making the desired change. The lower the level of decision making, the more likely the decision can be addressed quickly.

The interpersonal practitioner must know both the formal and informal DMs who would have the power to make and implement the change. With the placement process example previously discussed, it might be possible to get some of the changes implemented by talking about these changes with the director of field placements, whereas in other programs it might be necessary to get the dean of the school or some faculty standing committee involved in charge of field placements. Which decision making structure to use will depend on the particulars of the program being changed, and in one school it might be a very different DM than in another school.

Once the interpersonal practitioner and client have identified the DM in the agency who is responsible for the change goal, it is possible for them to assess the feasibility of the change goal. Before taking actions to change a procedure, process, or decision in the organization, the worker and client must assess carefully a number of factors to determine how much resistance there will be to the proposed change goal. In some situations, there may be great resistance to change, and in others, there may be only minor resistance, depending on the issue and the DMs who are involved. When there is great resistance to the change goals, it is sometimes possible to modify these goals and concomitantly reduce the resistance so that goals can be successfully achieved without an inordinate amount of time and energy required for the practitioner and client.

The Long Waiting List

For example, in a mental health agency with a long waiting list, a few workers had suggested that the agency try out a single-session model with all applicants upon completion of the intake process. A single-session procedure would reduce the number of clients moving onto the waiting list, provide a further screening of inappropriate applicants, and actually help those applicants who could respond to this model of practice. Most of the professional staff and the agency director were opposed to single-session models, so instead of implementing a new procedure, the student interns in the agency agreed to see all uninsured applicants after they were screened through intake. In the past, these clients were constantly pushed toward the end of the waiting list queue because this particular agency "creamed" full-fee and insurance clients before accepting low-fee or no-fee clients. When this modification to the goal was accepted and implemented, students had the opportunity to try out single-session treatment with clients who normally would wait for months on the waiting list before being seen or dropping out in despair. Because single-session models can be effective with some clients (Bloom, 1992; Talmon, 1990), this procedure improved service delivery to the poor clients who were seeking help in this agency.

There are five factors that the interpersonal practitioners should consider in order to decide on the feasibility of the change goal: (1) *position of DM*, (2) *scope of the change*, (3) *sunk costs*, (4) *distraction factors*, and (5) *support and resources* (Patti, 1974). Before approaching the DM, the practitioner must find out how the DM might react to the change goal that is being considered. Basically, a

DM can be in agreement with the goal, opposed to the goal, or indifferent to the goal (Patti, 1974). There will be greater resistance to the change goal when the DM is in disagreement or indifferent than if the DM is in agreement with the goal. Obviously, one way to find out what the DM's position might be is to ask the DM what he thinks about the goal, but—unfortunately—this would be an implementation strategy that might jeopardize the change process. At this point in the agency change process, the practitioner has to infer the DM's position by talking to people who know the DM, such as the agency "snitch," and discover how past decisions of the DM might bear on the present proposed change goal. For example, as we discussed in the organizational assessment chapter (Chapter 16), it is possible to categorize DMs into various "types," such as conserver, climber, or professional advocate. If the DM is a "conserver," and the change goal requires a considerable expenditure of resources to implement, then it is likely that DM will be in disagreement with the change goal; however, if the change goal produces a savings or recouping of resources, then the "conserver" DM is more likely to be in agreement with the goal.

The "scope" of the change concerns how much of the agency will be affected by the change goal. As we previously discussed under guiding principles, change goals should involve only those parts of the agency absolutely necessary to the change. As more and more of the agency is involved, more and more resistance is likely to arise in the change process. If the change goal involves many departments, multiple layers, several programs, or a substantial change in the mission of the organization, the resultant resistance to such broad-scope change is likely to be great. If, however, the change goal involves only a simple procedure or decision that affects few in the organization, it is much more likely that resistance will be lower. For example, changing a decision that involves only a single case is much easier to achieve than trying to get the agency to start up a new program that will have an impact on many cases and on many of the staff.

The sunk costs in the change goal are often hard to tease out in the agency. The sunk costs do not have to do only with how expensive or costly a change goal might be; they have to do with how much of the status quo of the agency may already be tied up in the arrangement the change goal addresses. For example, some agencies have "traditions" that they continue to uphold long after the tradition serves any purpose for the agency. Sunk costs may also arise in other parts of the agency when some procedure or program is overvalued as a "pet" or "showcase" part of the organization, even though this showcase program may be a disaster. For example, in one agency, the director's wife was actively involved as a volunteer in one program that had many problems, but it was extremely difficult to address change in this part of the organization because of the wife's involvement. The director's wife was a "sunk cost."

Sunk costs usually are discovered after the change process is begun, but it is best to try to find out whether there might be some kind of support for the status quo that is beyond any purpose for that part of the organization. One way to get at these sunk costs is to ask confidants and "the snitch" in the agency what areas of operations may be "hands off" to any kind of change. Trying to institute change in an area in which the organization spent a lot of time and energy changing recently will be resisted—for example, "We just changed that program!" Trying to make changes in areas that have been long established will also be resisted—for example, "We've always done it that way!" Bad habits are as difficult for agencies to change as they are for individuals. Remember the opening case in "The Bent Backs of Chang 'Dong."

Distraction or interference force is a concept borrowed from force field analysis (Lippitt et al., 1958, pp. 86–89). See, for example, Figure 17.2. This analysis shows that whenever change forces are being exerted on a system, there are two other forces the will emerge: resistance forces and distraction forces.

In most complex organizations such as social agencies, there are many forces that are pressing on the agency. Sometimes the agency may be under so much "siege" from these outside forces that the agency has no time and energy to pay attention to small, internal changes. Even when these outside forces are in support

Figure 17.2 Force Field Analysis

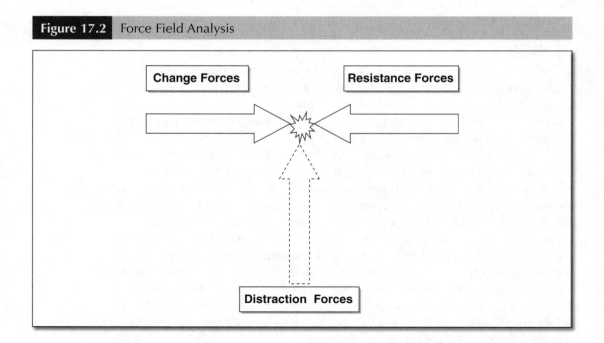

or could be used in concert with the smaller, inside changes, these outside forces are so much more threatening to the organization that all other considerations are put on hold until the external threat is addressed. For example, an agency going through an accrediting process with an outside accrediting body would seem to be an ideal candidate for smaller internal change, yet the accrediting activities consume so much of the agency's time and energy that all other changes get put on hold until the accrediting process is completed.

The final consideration when considering the feasibility of the change goal is whether there is support and what kind of resources the worker can mobilize in support of the change effort. If no one else in the agency supports the change goal, and the worker is alone in addressing the issue, it is unlikely that success will be realized. If the worker can mobilize others in the agency to support that change goal, and some of these other supporters are power persons in the agency, and they agree to speak publicly for the change, then change may be more likely. The intent is not to get everyone to support the change but to garner support selectively for the change from key personnel who work in the area that the change goal addresses. In some cases, it may be necessary to have only one key person involved in the change process for the DM to be influenced positively. Even though students are in a low power position in their field placement, they can effectively make agency changes by mobilizing the support of their supervisors.

The value of reviewing these five considerations before acting on the change goal is to keep the worker from pursuing unrealistic goals and from expending scarce energy and resources on battles that cannot be won. In every case, the worker should decide whether it is worth pursuing the goal after reviewing these five considerations. Each consideration adds potential resistance that may make change difficult. If the DM is likely to oppose the goal, if the goal involves a number of programs in the agency, if the changes will be expensive and tread on hallowed ground, and if there are many other changes going on in the agency and there are few other staff in support of the goal, then such a goal will generate a large amount of organizational resistance (i.e., sum of these considerations = R). When the DM is likely to be in support of the change goal, when the change involves only a procedure in one part of the organization, when the change will save money and does not threaten any sacred cows, when the agency is experiencing a fairly stable environment, and when there are several key staff that also support the change, then such a goal will generate little organizational resistance (i.e., sum of these considerations = r).

This analysis does not mean that workers always back away from goals with a large *resistance* value. Goals with such large resistance to be realized will require more effort, more time, more support, and more complex strategies. Workers may have to engage in more adversarial tactics, and the risks for pursuing such goals may be greater for themselves and their clients.

There are numerous organizational change tactics for advocates in low power positions that have been described in the literature (Buchanan & Badham, 2008; Lens, 2004; Nelson, Netting, Huber, & Borders, 2001; Patti, 1974; Patti & Resnick, 1972; Specht, 1969), and the most common will be presented here and organized into a hierarchy. There are five levels to the hierarchy, but the fifth level will only be mentioned and not be presented in detail because it is outside the realm of professional social work. The highest, most contentious level of these tactics is considered violent and unethical. Professional social workers are barred from engaging in these tactics because they threaten or actually cause harm to individuals. Acts of terrorism, arson, kidnapping, hostage taking, etc., cannot be employed even if research demonstrates them to be effective methods of influencing DMs in organizations (See Figure 17.3).

Level one of this hierarchy concerns the least contentious of the change tactics. These are sometimes referred to as "gentle nudge" tactics and are employed in situations in which the DM and the worker are acting in good faith. The expectation between parties is that whatever the issue, they both have a common interest to try to resolve the problem. This is the point at which the worker begins in the change process, even when the assessment may indicate there will be considerable resistance on the DM's part to the goal that is being proposed. The most common opening tactic is to bring the issue or problem to the attention of the DM. The issue should be clearly articulated so that the DM will understand what is being proposed and presented. The assumption at this point is that when the DM hears about the issue, he or she will be motivated to change the situation.

Depending on the situation, it may also be useful to propose a change in the organizational routine that will rectify the situation but doing this carefully so that the authority of the DM is not challenged or threatened. With some DMs, it may not be possible to make such a suggestion without appearing as though you are making demands. Making demands is not a collaborative tactic but one that is reserved for bargaining and adversarial levels, not this opening level. Another tactic that may accompany this opening move is to offer, before directly confronting the issue, to help the DM carry out any assessment process or data collection the DM may require.

An effective change agent will have worked hard to develop documentation of the issue but may not have to offer this evidence in this opening move unless the DM reacts with a countertactic. *Countertactics* are seen as resistance forces that can be expected to emerge as the change process begins to unfold. There are a number of common countertactics that a DM may employ in order not to have to

Figure 17.3   Hierarchy of Organizational Change Tactics

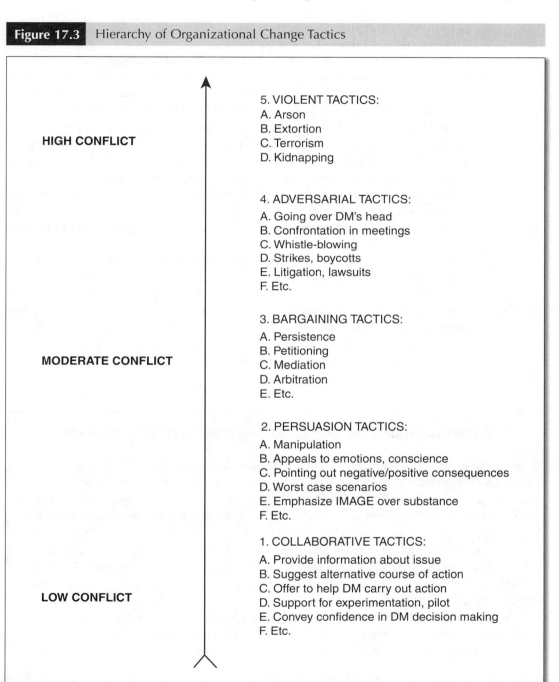

HIGH CONFLICT

5. VIOLENT TACTICS:
A. Arson
B. Extortion
C. Terrorism
D. Kidnapping

4. ADVERSARIAL TACTICS:
A. Going over DM's head
B. Confrontation in meetings
C. Whistle-blowing
D. Strikes, boycotts
E. Litigation, lawsuits
F. Etc.

3. BARGAINING TACTICS:
A. Persistence
B. Petitioning
C. Mediation
D. Arbitration
E. Etc.

MODERATE CONFLICT

2. PERSUASION TACTICS:
A. Manipulation
B. Appeals to emotions, conscience
C. Pointing out negative/positive consequences
D. Worst case scenarios
E. Emphasize IMAGE over substance
F. Etc.

1. COLLABORATIVE TACTICS:
A. Provide information about issue
B. Suggest alternative course of action
C. Offer to help DM carry out action
D. Support for experimentation, pilot
E. Convey confidence in DM decision making
F. Etc.

LOW CONFLICT

address the issue that the worker and client bring up. The most common countertactic is to *deny* that the problem or issue exists and suggest that the worker and client is misinformed. "Why, that couldn't possibly have happened here!" or "You shouldn't believe everything your client says!" or "I know for a fact that you are mistaken!" If the worker has compelling evidence that can document the issue, this should be brought to the attention of the DM. Sometimes, a DM will concede that the problem exists but will employ another common countertactic, and that is to *minimize* the issue or problem. "Well, that may have happened once, but I can assure you that it rarely goes on around here!" or "Well, that affects only a few clients and is unavoidable in a small number of cases!" or "Well, we are only human and occasionally make mistakes, but this is no reason to condemn the whole program!"

In a printed book, it is not easy to show the interchange that might transpire between the worker, the client, and the DM in this opening encounter, but we do want to make it clear that what transpires is interactive and depends on the counter-response of the DM to the worker and client's opening moves. In some cases, the DM is upset about the information that is brought to the session, will take the information presented seriously, and will be responsive to exploring the issue. In some situations, the DM, after checking with staff involved, will take remedial action swiftly and decisively and the change process will not have to be escalated beyond this gentle nudge level.

A Halfway House for Deinstitutionalized Psychiatric Patients

For example, I (BAS) worked with a client who was deinstitutionalized from a large state hospital to a community-based halfway house in a large, bankrupt hotel. This hotel was in a downtown metropolitan area and housed 200 deinstitutionalized mental patients. There were numerous problems and complaints about this setting, but the most serious was the inadequacies of the food service. This issue arose from complaints that the residents were not getting enough to eat, and my particular client had lost more than 80 lb (36 kg) in the past 14 months, had fainted on the sidewalk, and been treated in a local ER. Several residents had died over the past 2 years from a heart condition that is associated with malnutrition.

In order to document the issue, several residents agreed to keep a careful account of what was served to them at all meals over a 1-week period. They also estimated the amount of food served. This documentation was then taken by me to the nutritionist in charge of food services

(Continued)

(Continued)

at a nearby university hospital. The nutritionist was appalled by the imbalance in the menu and the inadequacies of the diet for adults and agreed that she would testify (if it came to that in court or at a public hearing) about the inadequacies of the diet. She also gave me the average monthly food cost of providing an adequate diet to an institutionalized adult. I located a physician in the ER nearby this halfway house who was also willing to testify that they were seeing a number of residents with the heart condition that is associated with malnutrition. With this documentation and the support of experts, I then went to the director of this facility after getting concurrence from my client, who did not want to be present at this meeting.

I went into the meeting with a number of presuppositions about this issue. I knew that this facility was owned by several MDs who had a "chain" of such residences, and I wondered whether they were ripping off the state and feds by receiving Medicaid, SSI, and SSA payments but skimping on the food and other services. I also was concerned about the operations in this particular facility because it had employed three directors in the past 2 years, and the director I was meeting had been on the job for only 2 weeks. In this meeting with the director, I explained who I was and what I was concerned about in this institution. I explained that my client had collapsed on the street and was taken to a nearby ER to have his scrapes and bruises tended to. The ER MD felt that he was not getting enough to eat. I also presented her with the weekly description of meals served, and she compared it with the planned dietary plan for that week. There were a number of discrepancies between the planned dietary plan and what had been served during the week to the residents who collected their data. I also asked her about what amount of money in her budget was allocated for food for each resident on a monthly basis, and the figure that she showed me was more than adequate by the university hospital nutritionist's estimates. The director explained that she was new and had never eaten in the residents' cafeteria in the basement of the building. She was honestly concerned about the information that I had presented to her and decided that she would randomly begin to eat meals in the cafeteria over the next few weeks to learn more about what was being served in the institution. I was confident that she would honestly pursue this matter when she told me that she was a "Jewish mother and no one in her house would go away hungry from a meal."

As it turned out, the facility's cook, who ran a restaurant in town, was taking food purchased for this residence out the back door and serving it in his restaurant. In this situation, the director had responded to the gentle nudge and acted in good faith. The cook was fired, and the food service significantly improved. This was a positive ending without having to escalate to more contentious levels, though this might have been necessary if the problem had been a budgeted lack of funds for the dietary needs of the facility.

This example is presented to reinforce the notion that organizational change can occur without having to resort to a long, contentious contest between change agent and DM. The amount of time taken up in contacting other experts, a nutritionist, and MD in the hospital ER was about 3 hours. The bulk of the effort to document the issue was carried out by the client and several other residents who carefully listed what foods had been served to them over the week. The handwritten entries of the foods served were a powerful documentation of the issue. Their descriptions were often humorous yet poignant: "At lunch today we had a scoop of pinkish food that looked like meat, smelled like meat, and tasted something like meat, but we have no idea what kind of meat it might be!"

When the DM is indifferent to the issue, not responsive to the worker's suggestions, and seems unwilling to explore the issue further, the worker will have to escalate to the second level and engage in persuasion tactics. These tactics put more pressure on the DM to respond to the issue and goals being raised. For persuasion tactics to be successful, the worker should match tactic to decision making style. If the DM is a "conserver," an effective persuasion tactic involves arguments that the change being suggested will *save* money and resources or will make the staff more efficient in delivering services. If the DM is a "climber," the persuasion tactic to use is to appeal to the positive consequences that will come to the DM if he or she adopted your suggestion and resolved the issue. The worker might suggest that resolving this issue will make the DM look good, or in the worst-case scenario tactic that if this issue is ignored and not addressed it could blow up into a really big mess and reflect negatively on the DM. If the DM is a "professional advocate," appeals to emotion, conscience, higher values, and ethical standards will have the most influence. No one likes to feel manipulated, so the worker needs to be careful about what tactic to pursue and not go on "nagging" if the DM does not respond positively.

There are a number of countertactics that might emerge at this level if the DM does not want to respond to the worker and client's pressure. The DM might suggest that he or she is not responsible for the issue and is not to blame for the problem. "It's not my fault that this has happened!" or "This was completely out of my control!" Often, what follows is another common countertactic of blaming the victim (Ryan, 1976): "Well, if the client had followed the instructions carefully, this never would have happened!" or "We can't be responsible for clients when they act irresponsibly!" Sometimes, the DM will even blame the worker and suggest that the worker has some kind of hidden agenda in bringing up the issue: "Do you realize the damage you're doing by bringing up this whole matter?" or "Why are you always causing trouble?" All of these tactics have in common the shifting of blame for the issue from the DM and agency to someone else.

In some situations, persuasion tactics will fail to move the DM, so the worker and client will have to escalate their pressure to the third level, which is bargaining tactics. These tactics serve two purposes. In one way, they put more pressure on the DM to respond positively to the issues. The first two tactics are pressure tactics that worker and client *may* employ when persuasion seems to have failed. Persistence can be a successful pressure tactic. The worker and client should not give up on the first or second or third rebuff by the DM. Let the DM know that you will not be deterred by a "no," and you will continue to pursue the issue. DMs would prefer to have issues resolved or tabled rather than continuously be reminded that something needs their attention. Another pressure tactic is to convince other staff to sign a petition that clearly shows how broad based the support is for the goal being proposed.

Bargaining tactics also serve another important purpose than just the escalation of pressure on the DM, because this level is absolutely necessary if worker and DM escalate to the adversarial level. The adversarial level is the most contentious but in and of itself does not resolve any issues. For adversarial tactics to succeed, all parties must be able to move away from the highest level of contest and move back to tactics that can be used to settle the conflict. These tactics are bargaining tactics such as "quid pro quo" or "this for that," or they may require third-party mediators and arbitration to settle the contest that has emerged between the worker and the DM. In some situations, rather than moving on to the adversarial level, the DM and the worker will realize that it is in both their interests to engage in some kind of process that will bring a halt to the escalation and more compromise and resolution into the process.

There are a number of ways that a DM may resist these pressure tactics. Sometimes the PM will *stall, delay*, or *drag out* the decision making process in hopes that the worker and client will tire in their pursuit of the goal. The DM may offer to set up an ad hoc committee to further explore the issues being raised. However, the true intention of this offer is not to find facts or gather data. Instead this offer is to postpone the decision and to stall in hopes that the client and worker will relent. In some situations, the DM and agency may decide that one way to remove the pressure is to *co-opt the change agent*. Co-optation can take many forms, from pay incentives, promotions, special perks, special rewards, etc., that will buy off the worker. Unfortunately, this strategy may be a win-win strategy for the agency and the worker, but it is a lose strategy for the client who has nothing to gain.

Sometimes, agencies will attempt to influence the client directly at this point in the process by *sending out an intermediary to "cool out the mark."* The purpose of this countertactic is to get the client to accept his or her misfortune as an inevitable error. The agency may express concern about the issue and even apologize for what has happened, but the purpose is really duplicitous: to keep the client from pressing the issue further and to see the agency as primarily not responsible for the issue. Some agencies will go so far as to try to get the client to see that in the complexity of delivering services, there is always some reasonable level of error (Singer, 1978). Some agencies might also *offer a trivial concession* at this point in the process to get the client to back off. This tactic was tried in the case example with the client who collapsed on the street from malnutrition. When he returned with bandages on his face, the food service staff gave him "double portions" for a week—that is, two scoops of mystery meat! These minimal concessions may seem as if the agency is actually taking responsibility, but it may be trying to avoid costly litigation and future lawsuits. This kind of settling quickly an insurance claim in a natural disaster is a common tactic of insurance companies to get money into their clients' hands to avoid more costly claims later on.

When agencies and DMs are opposed to the changes, or the changes can be achieved only at considerable cost and reorganization, it may be necessary to move up to adversarial tactics for the agency to respond. There are a number of adversarial tactics that an interpersonal practitioner and client may employ, and it is important for both to realize that these tactics are negatively experienced by DMs and usually perceived as antagonistic. These tactics often bring various forms of retaliation from the agency, and the risks to client and worker must be carefully considered.

To many beginning practitioners, the first tactic of going over the DM's head to a higher level DM may not appear to be a particularly adversarial act, but it is extremely threatening for the DM whose judgment is being called into question to involve the DM's superior. This tactic is effective only when there are distinct levels to the hierarchical decision structure. Other common adversarial tactics include confronting or challenging the DM in public meetings or threatening to contact agency funding sources or accrediting bodies if the issue is not addressed. This is referred to as "whistle-blowing," and in many states there are laws to protect the whistle-blower from agency retaliation. When the worker or client goes to the media with an exposé, they are likely to be protected by the reporter's ethical commitment to conceal and protect the sources of the exposé.

Many adversarial tactics take energy, organization, and time to implement. Strikes, boycotts, and demonstrations take a lot of work in developing support and mobilizing resources to retaliate actively against the organization. Seeking sanctions against the agency from accrediting bodies and pursuing litigation and lawsuits can be expensive and involve many months and years of effort. These tactics take a strongly committed client, worker, and considerable resources. In many cases, the mere threat of engaging in these adversarial tactics is enough to cause the DM to bargain seriously about the issue and goals. Agencies frequently do not have the resources to fight lawsuits or to explain and defend to funders and accrediting bodies what is transpiring in their operations.

But in some cases, agencies will resist these adversarial tactics and escalate the countertactics they will take against the client and worker for pursuing the contest to this level. One of the most common countertactics is to *delegitimize the change agent* in order to reduce the support for the cause. There are many ways that an agency may try to undermine the worker's base of support, which always is necessary if adversarial tactics are to succeed.

The agency and the DM may appear to be concerned about the worker who is bringing the issue up to this level of contest. For example, change agents may be told by their agency that they look exhausted (and they may be) and need a rest. This is similar to co-optation because the agency is trying to make a vacation more attractive than a fight within the organization. If the change agents do not accept this agency view of their performance, the agency may escalate their delegitimatizing further by suggesting that "We're worried about the strain you are under and the impact this is having on your health."

When this countertactic does not deter the change agent or undermine the worker's base of support, DM may resort to slander and rumor to try to delegitimize the worker. In one agency, the rumor was circulated to other staff that the worker was "drinking while on the job and his judgment was impaired," and in another agency, the rumor was circulated that the worker was engaging in sexual relations with clients. In both of these situations, the rumors were untrue; they suddenly appeared at the point that adversarial tactics were being employed, and they had a chilling effect for the change efforts on the support that colleagues provided.

And, finally, when these countertactics fail, the agency may resort to direct threats against the worker: "Keep this up and you're fired!" The threats may even involve greater harm.

Counterthreats of Violence

When I (Barbara H. Seabury, or BHS) was working in a recently desegregated school system in the South during civil rights activities in the 1960s, a school principal was angered that I had contacted the head of special education about a situation in which an African American youth had been expelled for the offense of "looking at white girls." This principal made it clear that he could get me fired. He also stated that he knew where I lived and that he knew how to deal with "Yankees."

Most agencies have grievance mechanisms that clients and employees can activate, but these procedures are slow, and even if the client "wins" the grievance, the grievance procedure may not be final and may be perceived as "advisory" to the DM. Such grievance mechanisms consume a lot of time and effort and in the end may produce no effective result. If, however, the worker and client plan to engage in litigation against the agency, it will be necessary for them to exhaust all internal grievance procedures before going outside the agency to the courts. This will demonstrate to the court that their lawsuit is not frivolous and that all other mechanisms of redress were tried.

As a final thought about agency change, we need to warn the interpersonal practitioner that it is difficult to remove an ineffective DM from an organization. Even if the worker and others in the agency know that the DM is incompetent and should not be making decisions, any strategy to remove the DM will be almost impossible to achieve. Instead of seeing the organizational problem as one that rests with the DM's competence, it is much more productive to ignore the limitation of the DM and focus only on the decision or goal that is being pursued.

Unfortunately when the agency questions the legitimacy of the worker and uses rumors and dirty tactics to impugn the worker's behavior, it is easy for the worker to allow the contest to sink to a personal vendetta between worker and DM. This kind of conflict is a negative sum game, and both sides are more interested in hurting the other than actually resolving the issue. Instead, it is much more productive for the worker to believe that no matter how tyrannical or deceitful the DM might be, it is possible to get an incompetent DM to make a "good" decision, which will result in a positive organizational outcome.

The final step in the problem solving process of organizational change is evaluating the change effort. This process is usually obvious. In some situations, the client and change agent will give up and not pursue the issue beyond the feasibility step. The reality is that the client and interpersonal practitioners are in the low power position, have fewer resources than the agency, and the risks to pursuing the changes are simply too great in some situations. In other situations, the interpersonal practitioner is simply overburdened with other work tasks, which take on higher priority than the agency change activities. When the change process begins to evolve into an escalation of adversarial tactics and involvement of groups outside the agency, the amount of energy and effort necessary to maintain the pressure simply cannot be sustained. In effect, the interpersonal practitioner as change agent "burns out!" By simply stalling, the agency often wins because the client and worker have to move on to other responsibilities.

This is a most common outcome with many of the productive plans that social work students raise in order to improve their educational experience. Their plans are shuffled off into various school committees in which the overburdened agendas of these committees mean that their plan will probably not be addressed until after the student has graduated. The change process dies a quiet death, buried in committee notes and languishing with no student support.

We do not want to end this section of this chapter on such a discouraging note. Agency change is possible when carefully planned by clients and interpersonal practitioners. The changes may not be as "big or dramatic" as originally planned. Agencies do evolve, and incremental change happens. As a faculty member in two schools of social work over the past 38 years, I (BAS) have seen many changes initiated by students and supported by sympathetic faculty and administrators. I offer this list to show that change is possible:

- Increase in student financial aid with rising tuition costs
- Offer of paid field placements in some agencies
- Availability of night classes to accommodate working students
- Recruitment of ethnic minority students from small ethnic colleges in the South and Southwest of the United States
- Expansion of library hours on weekends
- Scattering of multiple section foundation courses across the schedule so that commuter students with families do not have to attend 8:00 a.m. classes
- Expansion of the function of the student services office to help students find jobs, write resumes, and arrange interviews with prospective employers
- Creation of a support structure for foreign students with faculty, staff, and 2nd year foreign students to help students transition to the culture of a large American university
- Removal of the cigarette and candy machine from the student lounge
- Placement of student representatives on all standing school committees (50% representation)
- Support of student groups with their own office space, funds to support travel to national conferences, and available bulletin boards to announce student activities
- Pre-orientation and preregistration for entering students in the summer before the fall term begins
- Second-year student participation in planning and involvement in the pre-registration and pre-orientation process
- Expansion (double) of staff in the field office in order to help students with their field placements
- Online information about potential field placements and agency requirements to help students make decisions about field placements
- Development of block field placements in foreign countries (e.g., Ghana, South Africa, Costa Rica, Ecuador, Israel) for students interested in international social work

- Curriculum changes to increase content on lesbian, gay, bisexual, and transgender (LGBT); women; racial and ethnic groups; poverty; oppression; and social justice
- Development of e-portfolios for students and encouragement of faculty to create assignments that can be potential artifacts for students' portfolios

Many of the change tactics we have described in agency change may also be applied to community change. In the next section of this chapter, some of these tactics are discussed again in regard to community change, and other tactics will be introduced as well. We will be selecting those tactics that we believe are appropriate to interpersonal practitioners and will not be covering those tactics that students would study in their community practice and social policy courses.

● COMMUNITY CHANGE

As the reader has seen throughout this book, our approach to practice requires that the social worker be ecologically oriented and focused on the transactions between individuals and social systems. When these systems are the clients' communities, workers may help the clients to work toward changes in their communities, they may seek changes in community conditions on behalf of clients, or they may encourage others to work toward community changes. In the chapter on organizational and community assessment (Chapter 16), we presented a conceptual framework for understanding communities, and we will use this five-sector framework to talk about how social workers help clients to engage in community change.

The reader justifiably may ask whether community change is the proper role for those interpersonal practitioners whose clients are individuals, families, or groups. Our answer is a resounding yes. Other human service professionals, such as psychologists, rehabilitation counselors, activity therapists, and nurses, may define their roles differently, but we see this concept as central to our definition of what social work is. In addition, we see this as at the heart of any approach that seeks to help clients become empowered.

In practice, social workers frequently are involved in the client's community issues, even when their models of practice are narrowly perceived as "clinical." Social workers may encourage clients to affiliate with neighborhood organizations, self-help groups, or community services when these are related to the client's needs being better met. They may talk with clients about difficulties they have fulfilling their roles in community organizations such as church programs, neighborhood watches, etc. They may help clients seek changes in community institutions by joining advocacy watchdog groups that are designed to improve various neighborhood services such as day care institutions, nursing homes, and recreational programs. They may approach influential figures in community institutions on behalf of clients such as city council members, precinct captains, and representatives in state and federal legislatures. And they may contact other social workers who are full-time community organizers, community planners, and social policy analysts about the needs of their clients. These colleagues should be mindful of what interpersonal practitioners are seeing daily in their work with individuals, families, and groups.

A few examples will make these points clearer.

Improving Child Care Resources in a Community

A school social worker was meeting with a group of parents whose children were experiencing school difficulties. The parents complained that the local community center did not plan children's activities with any attention to the school calendar. This caused these parents—most of whom were employed—severe child care problems. Additional child care problems relating to their younger children were created because of the inadequacy of local day care centers. The worker helped these parents convene a community conference on improving child care resources.

Working With a Community Council to Meet the Needs of Youth

In another community, a worker was told by a young adolescent with whom she was working that she and many of her friends were harassed by the police, park officials, and older adolescents when they hung out in a local park. The worker discussed this with a staff member of the neighborhood's community council. With the permission of the young woman, the worker gave her name to the staff member, who called her and arranged to meet with her and several of her friends. This led to a subsequent meeting that involved the police, park officials, community recreation workers, and both older and younger teens on the ways the community could meet the needs of teenagers.

Strategies, Tactics, and Interventions

In this section of the chapter, we focus on how interpersonal practitioners and client systems can engage in community change. In the chapter on organizational and community assessment (Chapter 16), we presented a framework for understanding communities. This five-sector framework was borrowed from Dimension II in the person-in-environment (PIE) system: (1) economic/basic needs system; (2) education/training system; (3) judicial/legal system; (4) health, safety, and social services system; and (5) voluntary association system. We will also assume—as the PIE system does—that a fundamental dynamic in community systems is discrimination that clients experience when they attempt to connect to resources and opportunities in their community systems (Karls & Wandrei, 1994a).

In community change, we want clients to connect with existing watchdog and advocacy groups that are working to create and/or change community resources. We do not expect clients to organize their own grassroots organizing groups but to locate existing groups that they may join. We view the efforts to locate these advocacy groups to be both the client's and the worker's responsibility. The client may approach neighbors, relatives, and friends in the community and ask about advocacy groups. The worker will also try to locate advocacy groups by professional networking with colleagues, searching through databases, and looking in local papers for schedules of community meetings and activities. Once one or several groups have been discovered that engage in advocacy in the area of the client's issues, then worker and client will find out more about the group and when and where it meets.

For example, an interpersonal practitioner may help a family get access to a community swimming pool that has been denied to them because they live just outside the geographical catchment area of the pool. Their own community does not have a public swimming pool. After talking with the pool manager, the family and social worker are able to arrange a special exception to this rule, which allows the family to use the pool. This would be an example of successful case advocacy. This example does not, however, address the issue that many other families in their community do not have access to the community pool in the other community. This resolution for the one family does not address an underlying social justice issue that is embedded in this case situation. For example, the community surrounding the pool is middle-class and white, whereas the community with no pool is mostly poor and black. Racism and classism may underlie the enforcement of the boundary issue. This would be obvious if the family who is allowed in as the exception happens to be white and will not be a flag that the white community is being "invaded" by a family from "the other side of the tracks."

Community change in this issue would involve resource development and working to modify long-held racist beliefs in each of the communities. However, these goals are way beyond the capacity of an interpersonal practitioner and would be met with giant resistance. Resource development is a long and costly enterprise, and tackling racism can be extremely contentious in communities as reflected in the history of school busing to promote integration and the backlash against affirmative action to open up opportunities for women and minorities.

There are things the interpersonal practitioner can do to plant seeds for change, in spite of the huge resistance forces that exist in this example. An interpersonal practitioner can suggest to clients that they locate existing community groups that are lobbying for recreational resources. Clients may also be encouraged to talk with their neighbors about community issues and discover whether there are informal neighborhood groups that they might join. Joining such groups will be empowering to clients while simultaneously creating a sense of community through shared action.

The interpersonal practitioner may also contact her fellow social workers who are community practitioners and policy analysts in the client's community to get them involved. There may be many initiatives in the community that the interpersonal practitioner and client do not know about. For example, there may be white and black churches in the community that are trying to bridge the racial divide by holding joint religious services and activities to expand understanding between the two groups of parishioners. Clients may already know about many of these groups, and it may only require a gentle nudge to get them more involved in their neighborhood and community.

In the next section of this chapter, we give some examples of advocacy and watchdog groups that exist in the various sectors of a community. This list is suggestive because there may be many small grassroots groups that only exist in a particular neighborhood. These can only be discovered when the client and interpersonal practitioner do networking in the client's neighborhood and surrounding community. For example, in Detroit, there is a group called Save Our Sons and Daughters (SOSAD), which was started by a mother who lost a child to gun violence. Many teens were being killed on the streets, and she wanted to do something to stop this carnage. This would be an example of a grassroots advocacy group in the Health, Safety and Social Services sector of her community.

For example, in the economic/basic needs system of the community, there may exist grassroots client groups and nonprofit agencies that are working to change procedures and policies of public welfare, public housing, and programs for the homeless. Examples of such organizations include the National Welfare Rights Union (NWRU), the Kensington Welfare Rights Union (KWRU), and the National Coalition for the Homeless (NCH; www.nationalhomeless.org).

In the education/training system of the community, there may be nonprofit organizations such as the Student Advocacy Center (SAC) of Michigan (www.studentadvocacycenter.org).

The SAC was established in 1975 to focus on the educational experience of students and to identify successful practices and policies as well as the barriers to effective service. Using a strengths-based approach, the SAC works in partnership with families and schools to promote educational practices that result in success for students, as well as to challenge those exclusionary policies that may have a harmful impact on students and families.

In the judicial/legal system of the community, there may be many kinds of advocacy groups: National Center for Victims of Crime (www.ncvc.org), which represents 10,000 grassroots agencies that are working to help crime victims rebuild their lives; Legal Experts Network (www.legal-experts.net), which was designed to connect consumers to expert, low-cost legal aid; the National Senior Center Law Center (www.nsclc.org), which was designed to empower elders to remain independent in their own homes and promote community-based long-term care for elders and their families; and the National Center on Domestic and Sexual Violence (www.ncdsv.org).

In the health, safety, and social services system, the National Alliance on Mental Illness (www.nami.org) sponsors educational and support groups for the mentally ill and promotes legislative action to protect the rights and services of the mentally ill.

Citizens for Better Care of Michigan (www.cbcmi.org) is a watchdog group that monitors nursing homes, adult foster care, and assisted living institutions.

There are many advocacy groups that cut across community sectors and focus on particular populations or age groups: Federation for Children with Special Needs (http://fcsn.org); The Gray Panthers (www.graypanthers.org); Disabled American Veterans (www.dav.org); and the National Council of La Raza (www.nclr.org), which is the largest national Latino civil rights and advocacy group in the United States.

The point of this discussion of these many advocacy groups is to inform the interpersonal practitioner that there are many opportunities in the client's community that the client may be encouraged to contact and join. These groups already exist and may be actively involved in working to change various aspects of the client's community.

There may be some serendipitous situations in which the interpersonal practitioner and the client may want to engage in their own advocacy efforts to change aspects of the community. We give several examples of this kind of work, but it involves more time and effort than encouraging the client to locate and join an already established advocacy group.

Encouraging Youth to Influence City Council

The first example involved a school social worker who was working with a group of students in a high school. This support group of high school students complained about a lack of recreational facilities in their public housing project. The worker agreed to help them assess the location of recreational facilities—none of which were easily accessible. He then helped them list

(Continued)

(Continued)

the reasons why such facilities are desirable. The group then agreed to attend (with their parents' permission) an open meeting of the city council in which group members asked questions about whether there were any plans for the development of recreational resources. On the basis of this preliminary information, the worker helped the group members appear on the agenda of the city council at a later meeting. The worker helped the students present a well-prepared statement on their recreational needs, which also included suggestions for how the community should proceed to meet them. This was an educational, empowering, and participatory experience for this group of high school students.

Support Group of Elders Advocating for Their Needs

Another example involved a social worker who was assigned to a group of clients in a center serving senior citizens. The worker learned that a city department was working on a comprehensive plan for services to the elderly in the community. The worker encouraged group members, who were ambulatory, to attend a series of hearings on the plan and report back to the support group. Subsequently, the worker acquired a preliminary draft of the plan and made it available to group members. When hearings on this plan were held, several group members testified and presented powerful examples of issues facing seniors, which was based on group discussions from the senior citizen group. This is an example of how an existing support group can be encouraged to become an advocate for changes in their community.

SUMMARY •

This chapter described the ways that interpersonal practitioners work with and on behalf of clients to change organizations and communities. We began our chapter with a discussion of the ethical issues that arise when social workers are trying to make changes in agencies and the client's community. We pointed out that ethical issues that apply to client systems do not necessarily apply to target systems. The rest of the chapter was devoted to a discussion of change procedures. Although there are some similarities between the ways social workers work for organizational and community change, there are also differences, and for this reason, we discuss these sets of change procedures separately.

We began our discussion of organizational change with a presentation of theories of organizational change. We found that the ideas of Patti and Resnick

(1972) were particularly compatible with our approach to practice, and we fully discussed their ideas on "changing organizations from within." We elaborated on such principles as low visibility, starting small, least contest, and client participation. We also described the problem solving steps to be taken by the practitioner who seeks organizational change.

Organizational change approaches used by interpersonal practitioners are often directed at influencing a "DM," so we focused our attention on this kind of influence. This discussion also incorporated an analysis of sources of resistance from the DM and how to deal with such resistance.

In our discussion of community change, we differentiated between the role of the interpersonal practitioners when working for community change from the more extensive roles of community organizer and social policy analyst.

The role of the interpersonal practitioner in community change involves two roles of broker and advocate. The practitioner helps clients to locate and link with established advocacy groups in their community. When the interpersonal practitioner is working with groups, it is possible that the group can be helped to engage in advocacy efforts.

CHAPTER 18

TERMINATION

Great is the art of beginning, but greater is the art of ending.

—Henry Wadsworth Longfellow (1902, p. 464)

Interpersonal practitioners must approach the end of the relationship with clients with as much understanding and skill as they did the beginning and the middle stages of service. Each stage has its own impact and tasks. As we stated in the relationship and clienthood chapters (Chapters 6 and 7), applicants approach the beginning of service with mixed feelings. Some responses are positive when applicants anticipate relief from the pain, deprivation, or conflict of their situations. Some responses are negative when clients are mandated to have service or are pushed in by significant others. Some responses are ambivalent when clients fear that they will not be helped or may even be harmed, and they will invest money, time, and other scarce resources for services that may not produce results.

Clients approach the middle phases with analogous concerns. They have tentatively, at least, committed themselves to the service; identified problems and goals; and understood in general terms what the service will be. The hard work is to make these dreams come true. Even under optimal circumstances, changes will occur in the client's interaction with systems that will be both beneficial as well as troublesome. Rarely is any change an unmitigated blessing.

The end also brings with it a number of other issues that are portrayed in this chapter along with the interpersonal practitioners' tasks in resolving these issues. Our contention is that in any phase of work, if the issues are well handled, the client will be able to proceed into the next phase. For termination, the next phase for the client is to invest herself in living without the supportive and ameliorative inputs of the social work service. If service has been successful, the client should be able to bring to her life the strengths and skills obtained through the service and to retain these. On the other hand, no social work service guarantees that the client will not have additional problems. The client, therefore, should feel free to return to the previous service agency for further help, if that becomes necessary.

In some case situations, the service may not have been successful. Clients may terminate before they accomplish their goals, or the interpersonal practitioner may leave or be replaced. In group situations, some members may leave while others continue. In family work, some family members may also drop out of service or only subsystems of the family may continue. In this chapter, we therefore consider problems that arise through these and other events in the termination process.

The way social work services are offered is highly affected by agency policies and the manner in which service is reimbursed. In the current situation, many social work services are financed under managed care arrangements, which limit the number of sessions that will be covered under the client's managed care or employee assistance plan. Clients may be allocated as few as 1 or 2 or as many as 20 sessions. If the client wishes to use more sessions, she has to pay for these herself.

These types of arrangements require the interpersonal practitioner to establish quickly with the client the goals that are attainable within the time limit. The practitioner also must help the client deal with her feelings about time-limited service. This has many implications for how interpersonal practitioners and clients deal with termination issues, and we note some of these as we discuss termination throughout this chapter.

We now turn to a consideration of the skills required of the interpersonal practitioner during this stage. In this part of the chapter, we discuss "nonproblematic" endings—that is, situations in which the termination occurs through the mutual agreement of the worker and client system when at least some of the client's goals have been attained. Later in the chapter, we discuss endings that are less satisfying.

We discuss these skills in relationship to a series of tasks that confront the client and practitioner during the termination phase. These tasks are:

1. to warn the client about termination and initiate the process,

2. to evaluate the effectiveness of the service experience,

3. to understand and cope with feelings about termination,

4. to plan ways to maintain the beneficial changes that have occurred,

5. to utilize these beneficial changes in a variety of situations, and

6. to seek out and engage the client in new services when this is indicated.

The order in which we have listed these tasks is an arbitrary one. The actual order in which they are accomplished will depend on the unique nature of each case situation and the way in which the client wishes to proceed. For example, when one client became aware that his goals were only partly achieved, he expressed feelings of discouragement. These feelings were dealt with by the interpersonal practitioner by supporting his plan to return for more service in the new community to which he was moving.

THE TASKS OF TERMINATION •

Warning and Initiation

It is the interpersonal practitioner's responsibility to be aware of the time limits of service and to warn the client when termination is approaching. In time-limited models of practice, this warning is often given in the first session when the client and interpersonal practitioner establish a date for their last session and again as that date approaches. For example, in a school situation, the interpersonal practitioner and the members of a student support group agreed to meet until the end of the semester, which was three months away. When the semester was 2 weeks from ending, the interpersonal practitioner reminded the members that they had two more sessions in the semester, and they should begin to talk about the impact the group has made in their lives.

In another situation in which the client's stay in the agency was long term, such as a youth detention facility or a nursing home for elders, the social work intern would have to take responsibility to remind these clients about the length of the internship. For example, if the internship was 9 months, then the interpersonal intern would warn her clients about her departure as she nears the end of the internship. The practitioner would then begin to prepare her clients for the transition to another worker.

The case situation determines when the warning should be given and how much time should be allocated to termination issues. In some time-limited sessions with adults, it may only be necessary to reserve one session for termination issues, whereas with longer term service with young children it may be wise to reserve several sessions as the deadline approaches. With young children and needy clients, it may take a number of sessions to deal with the feelings of loss and abandonment that are expressed in the termination process. Warning is an important part of the termination process and involves a professional decision by the interpersonal practitioner about when it should be given and how many sessions termination should take up in the service process.

Evaluation

In the chapter on monitoring and evaluation (Chapter 9), we presented many of the ways that changes in individuals, families, and groups can be monitored and evaluated. We now consider how these tools are used by the interpersonal practitioner as part of the termination process. One important decision that should be made during termination is to select from among the measurement approaches implemented earlier in the service process. The measurement approach chosen should be one that will demonstrate most clearly to the client what degree goals have or have not been achieved. From a research point of view, this may not be the most valid and reliable form of measurement, but it should be the most graphic one from the client's standpoint. See for example the graph in Figure 18.1 that was prepared at termination for a client whose goal was to improve her self-confidence. The visual analog scale (VAS) was applied on every other session as she worked on becoming more assertive, joined a women's consciousness-raising (CR) group, and decided to look for another job that did not involve the sexual harassment of her manager.

Figure 18.1 Visual Analog Scales Graphed at 1st, 3rd, 5th, 7th Sessions

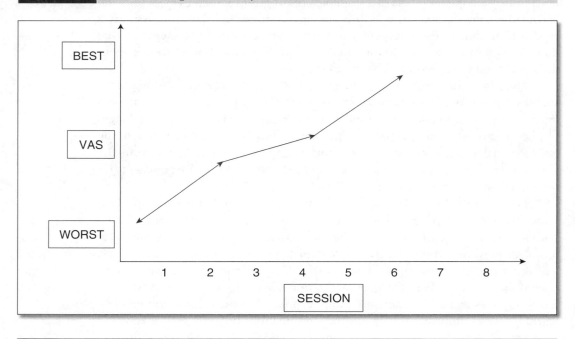

Note: VAS = visual analog scale.

In addition, clients at termination should select the types of information they want most to review, and this choice will also govern what data are reviewed.

New information relevant to the evaluation of the interpersonal practice experience is likely to emerge at this time. Part of the evaluation process at termination may also involve an evaluation in the client's own words, independent of any formal evaluative procedure that has been employed. Formal measurement procedures are likely to present isolated bits of information such as the grades the child has received, the amount of satisfaction in a marriage, or that a decision was reached on an important issue. The client's more qualitative response to an open-ended question, such as "In your own words, how do you think things are different now from the way they were when you began?" will suggest how a number of aspects link together and how the client may have benefited or been hurt by the service experience.

During the evaluation, the interpersonal practitioner may also inquire into the client's perceptions of the "causes" of change. Although these may or may not be more "true" than the worker's ideas of cause, they can suggest hypotheses of what is effective and ineffective in social work techniques that can then be tested in more systematic ways. For example, one client told her practitioner that she attributed her improvement to an explanation she received of the reasons why her husband treated her as he did. This led her to stop blaming herself for all her problems. The practitioner had attributed her progress to specific instructions she had given the client on how to be more assertive. There was no certainty in the practitioner's mind as to which factor was the most important, but she did rethink the strategies she will employ in similar situations.

Another important function fulfilled by evaluation is the reinforcement of changes that have taken place in the client. When the client recognizes and receives recognition for change, this may more firmly establish new behaviors. The client's perception that change has taken place also may reinforce client efforts to seek changes in other parts of her life situation.

Another aspect of evaluation during termination should be the client's evaluation of the interpersonal practitioner. This does not mean that practitioners must wait until termination to seek feedback on their behaviors, as ongoing feedback can be helpful throughout the process. We believe that professional growth requires this kind of personal information. When practitioners ask for personal information, they are providing the client with a positive model of how to ask for and receive evaluative information about oneself.

The evaluation of the worker by clients can be written or oral. If it is written, the worker will usually discuss the clients' reactions so that additional information can be secured. In group situations, the worker has to reach the additional decision with the group members whether the evaluation should be anonymous. Generally, we favor evaluations in which the evaluator takes responsibility for what is shared. This transparency may be difficult in groups conducted in social control settings, such as prisons, where clients may fear the consequences of offering a negative evaluation. This is a reasonable stance under those circumstances. The following are some questions that may be used in asking clients to evaluate the interpersonal practitioner:

1. What actions did you find most (least) helpful?

2. What actions would you have liked me to take that I did not take?

3. Were there personal qualities of mine you found helpful or not helpful (e.g., ways of speaking, timing of comments, sense of humor, ways of expressing myself)?

4. How well did you think I understood what you were thinking and feeling?

5. How honest and open did you experience me as your worker?

6. In what ways did you (or did you not) experience me as supportive and caring?

It is not easy for clients to provide this kind of information because they may not wish to hurt the feelings of the interpersonal practitioner. Many people have a sense that this kind of feedback is impolite, although it is hoped the practitioner and client have a relationship based on honesty and openness. Our experience, however, is that when the interpersonal practitioner unequivocally asks for such information, clients respect the practitioner's wishes.

There is a lot of information to collect in a face-to-face discussion between the practitioner and the client during termination. In agencies that routinely mail out client satisfaction questionnaires (CSQs), many of the items just suggested may be inserted in that type of questionnaire. It may also be helpful for the interpersonal practitioner to develop her own written questionnaire that briefly covers those points that seem most salient to the service process. For example, a practitioner might develop a written feedback form for literate clients about items 1, 5, and 6:

1. What were some of my actions that you found most helpful?

2. What were some of my actions that you found least helpful?

3. Did you experience me as honest and open mostly, sometimes, or rarely?

4. Did you experience me as supportive and caring mostly, sometimes, or rarely?

Coping With Feelings

During termination, a variety of feelings will emerge in clients and interpersonal practitioners that should be expressed, explored, and understood. Earlier in this book, we discussed transference as a dynamic that may emerge in the relationship between the client and their practitioner. Termination activates a number of feelings that may appear when the reality begins to set in that the relationship between the client and the interpersonal practitioner is coming to an end.

Some clients may feel relief and joy that the service is finally winding down—especially when positive changes have been achieved. Clients may be grateful for the efforts made by the interpersonal practitioner in helping them achieve their goals. The practitioner may also feel good about the relationship that was established and should acknowledge these positive feelings. The interpersonal practitioner must be careful to recognize that there will be feelings of loss for the client with whom they now have a strong relationship. The practitioner may wish to continue service, instead of facing a new client in which relationship building will have to take place all over again. Clients may also feel this loss and wonder whether service should not continue. The danger here is that both practitioner and client should work through termination feelings and not talk themselves into continuing when service goals have been achieved.

We want to raise a controversial issue at this point that may make for an interesting class discussion. Review the quote by Franz DeWaal at the beginning of the relationship chapter (Chapter 6). From his studies of primates, he believes that women are hardwired for relationships and men are hardwired for achieving tasks. In the developing literature of behavioral interventions and time-limited models of practice during the 1960s and 1970s in social work, almost all of the authors were men (e.g., Charles Garvin, William Reid, Sheldon Rose, and Edwin Thomas). The traditional, open-ended models of practice, however, were all women (e.g., Florence Hollis, Carol Meyer, Helen Harris Perlman, and Ruth Smalley). The coauthor of Task Centered Casework *was Laura Epstein (Reid & Epstein, 1972), and in a workshop in the mid-1970s, she expressed great doubts about the task-centered model when she first encountered this brief model of practice but later embraced it when practice research demonstrated its efficacy. Do women interpersonal practitioners need to be much more aware of their propensity to value relationships that may make termination and accompanying feelings more problematic?*

In other situations, clients—in response to termination—may become angry and upset that the service is ending. They may accuse the practitioner of abandoning them even though they may have made many changes in their life. This reaction is often difficult for the interpersonal practitioner to take because the client had never expressed such negative feelings in the service process, and they had achieved many of their goals in service. The practitioner must recognize that this strong reaction is probably a transference reaction to endings. The interpersonal practitioner should be empathetic and respond to the underlying anxiety and feelings of abandonment. She may point out that these kinds of feelings are common in terminations and will be part of the work that client and practitioner must do together to put them into perspective—that is, the strong, negative feelings are about ending the relationship and not about the service received.

For some clients, these negative transference feelings may be so strong that they cannot express them to the practitioner but instead will deal with them by acting out and dropping out of service at this point. The difficulty for the practitioner is that it is almost impossible to get these clients to return to work on these termination feelings. For these clients, termination is experienced as a rejection by the worker, and it is easier for them to reject the worker than to come back and work through these feelings.

Another fairly common reaction of clients who are struggling with termination feelings is the sudden return of the issue or symptom that brought them into service. Because so many of the gains that can be achieved in practice are easily reversed (e.g., families can stop communicating, youth may stop attending class, elders may become withdrawn and stop going to activities, or individuals may start drinking again), it is easy for clients to bring up this backsliding during the termination process. Clients may suggest that obviously they are not ready to make it on their own. This kind of unconscious bargaining must be resisted by the interpersonal practitioner, who must try to get the client to express, discuss, and understand their underlying feelings about ending the relationship with the practitioner. It can be empathetically stated that symptoms sometimes return during termination but that client and worker can develop plans to help gains be stabilized and continue after service is over.

A most dramatic display of this issue occurred when I (Brett A. Seabury, or BAS) terminated with a marital couple who had achieved several significant gains in their marriage. In the final session, they displayed a marital argument that was more intense than any I had seen in the previous four sessions. I was able to get them to calm down, listen to each other, and communicate more effectively. At the very end of the session, they queried whether they were really ready to end and whether they shouldn't continue for a few more marital sessions. I explained that I believed they had achieved some major changes and that it was time to end our sessions together as planned. I also stated that if in the future they felt a need for more sessions that they could always return to the agency for more marital counseling. When they got up and left the office, I followed them out the door. Their tense demeanor in the session had completely vanished, and the husband turned to his wife and asked her where she wanted to go for lunch. The performance in my office was about termination and not what they had achieved in the marital counseling, and they never returned for more marital sessions in the future.

The interpersonal practitioner may have various feelings stirred up by the termination process. Sometimes we feel that we were the best thing that ever happened to the client and that we are irreplaceable. When clients are transferred to other workers, we may feel that the next worker will never be as good as we were with the client. Sometimes practitioners are unable to recognize and deal with their own feelings that accompany termination, so they put off giving the client the warning about termination and do not complete the work of termination. The most negative and unethical example can be seen in the worker who waits until the last session with a client and then announces near the end, "This will be our last session and I hope all will be well with you!" The struggles in termination can also be seen in the behavior of some students who continue to "volunteer" at their field placement after their term has expired.

In support groups that are formed to help members cope with loss, the feelings associated with termination can be intense. In grief groups for survivors who have lost a loved one, terminations may involve a great amount of catharsis, grieving, crying, and demands that the group continue. The interpersonal practitioner may be caught up in all of the intense feelings of loss and must create many structured activities and rituals to help members cope with the feelings of ending the group.

One of the most common structured activities is a group party and celebration to recognize the end of the group. In this ending celebration, members of the group may bring food and drink to share and may agree to participate in a variety of symbolic rituals in order to mollify the feelings of loss (Laird, 1988). Some groups plan elaborate ceremonies in which candles are lit and extinguished or the group plans a "fantasy reunion," which will not actually take place. Another termination ritual that is effective with very cohesive groups is the practitioner creates some kind of generic card that each member will take from the group. Each member's card is passed around to all of the other members of the group who will then write short notes to express their feelings about the other member and some memorable event that may have happened earlier in the group process. This exercise can be seen repeatedly at the end of school years when fellow students write memories in each other's yearbook.

Another creative, structured activity involves three colored strands of yarn. The group decides what each of the three colors represent in the work they have done together such as *strength* to continue working on personal issues, *hope* that things will continue to change, and *relationships* that will support continued growth. The leader has the group members stand in a circle facing inward and has each of the members hold on to the long colored strands of yarn. The members tie a single knot in the strands—a tight slipknot will work. The leader then moves around the group and "snips" the strands of yarn consistently on one side of the knot. Before ceremonially cutting the yarn, the leader may ask each member to reflect on the group process. When the leader has cut all members strands, the members of the group are told they can take their strands home as reminders of what they have accomplished in the group. The snipping of the strands of yarn can be a powerful metaphor for terminating the group.

In group sessions, members may accept some feelings regarding termination and deny others. A member may speak about missing the other members of the group but disclaim any feelings about the worker. Sometimes members may share feelings about the worker but deny they have feelings about the other group members. The worker may have to employ a more direct approach to enable members to share feelings. The worker may acknowledge with members that endings are difficult and that talking about feelings is stressful. A worker may then suggest that each member will rotate around the group giving each other an opportunity to say farewell to everyone else in the group. This activity often elicits many feelings. Members observe other members who are more expressive of their feelings, and this kind of vicarious learning helps the more reluctant members to express their feelings about termination.

The emotion of anger—at termination or any other phase—is a difficult one for members and workers to handle. In the chapter on group change (Chapter 15), we discussed in detail some of the interventions that leaders can employ to help groups deal with interpersonal conflict. During the termination process, workers may feel guilty because of things they had done or not done to help their clients. The clients, in turn, may fear that positive components of the experience will be lost if they express anger. They may also believe that anger during termination shows a lack of gratitude for what the worker has done or may cause the worker to experience feelings that are too painful to handle.

Interpersonal practitioners, therefore, should indicate to clients that experiencing some anger is appropriate during endings. Practitioners can also reiterate that the principle that has governed all the work together has been an open and honest expression of feelings and that this is as important a component of the final stage as of all other stages. A feeling of anger has a legitimate basis, as all helping experiences are in some ways imperfect.

The question regarding anger, in addition to expressing it in a constructive manner, is what to "do" with it. The anger must be channeled so that the clients consider how to make future situations more responsive to their needs and themselves more effective in those situations. For example, clients may be encouraged to think of an experience in their past in which they expressed anger toward a significant other and in the present think about other ways they might have expressed their anger.

This discussion of feelings associated with termination is not meant to suggest that all feelings during this period are painful and must be defended against. Quite to the contrary, most clients have pleasurable feelings that the experience is coming to an end—particularly if the outcome has been satisfactory. These positive feelings can be increased when the worker reminds clients that they have continued in the service relationship and have invested their energy in it, even when the "going was rough." This fact can enhance the clients' conception of themselves as empowered individuals who have the strength to seek help when it is necessary and to commit themselves to the process.

Maintaining Change

For a variety of reasons, workers cannot assume that beneficial changes the clients have attained will continue. One reason, for example, is that the environment may not be supportive of changes. Parents, spouses, employers, teachers, or others may be unwilling to make changes in their own reactions that complement changes occurring in the client. This may cause them to criticize or in other ways undermine the client's new ways of coping. Labels placed on the client such as "delinquent" or "nutcase" or "neglectful mother" may continue to be attached to the client orally, as well as in recorded materials. The client may also have received recognition and other forms of reinforcement from the interpersonal practitioner and from other individuals in their family and from other members in the support group that are not forthcoming from other people outside the action system developed by the practitioner. For change to be maintained, therefore, one or more of the following factors must be present:

1. The client system, whether individual, family, or group, must have changed in ways that are directly related to the life situation that brought them into service. The client system must have acquired the knowledge, skills, and attitudes required to function better in that situation. For example, in the case that follows, a student who wished to do better in school decided to meet with a school social worker. These sessions with the school social worker resulted in better study habits, an understanding of how to establish an effective study environment, and the value that studying was important to his future.

2. The client system must continue to receive reinforcement rather than punishment for the behaviors associated with changes. In the example cited in the first factor, the student contracted with his parents to allow him to meet with his friends after he had spent a designated amount of time studying. He also decided to associate with friends who would praise him for studying rather than those who would criticize him for being a "nerd."

3. The client system must have access to the resources they will need to continue the changes. The student in our example was allowed to use his father's

home office for several hours in the evening, which would allow for privacy with adequate lighting and space for studying.

4. The client system must have a means of "self-control" for resolving problems that arise in the future that prevent a continuation of the new pattern of behavior. The youth in our example was confronted with conflicts between his desire to study and a desire to see his girlfriend. He was able to assess the circumstances in which he most felt this conflict, using a framework taught him by his worker. As a result of this assessment, he contracted with himself and with his girlfriend to make seeing her contingent upon a specified amount of completed homework.

As termination approaches, the interpersonal practitioner must develop a plan with the client how change will be maintained. This plan will include some of the following procedures, each related to the principles cited for maintaining change: (1) *overlearning*, (2) *problem solving with regard to the environment*, (3) *performing network interventions*, (4) *creating support groups*, (5) *securing reinforcement*, and (6) *enacting self-control*.

Overlearning is used to help clients practice the new ways of coping after they learn them initially. The clients are helped to plan ways to use their understanding and skills in a number of situations—often situations that are quite different from one another. For example, one client had worked to develop assertive behaviors. He was helped before termination to act more assertively with his fellow workers as well as with his family. Another client worked to form new relationships. Before termination was considered, she was helped to initiate new relationships with several neighbors as well as with coworkers. In group situations, overlearning can occur when group members role-play their skills with one another.

Problem solving with reference to the environment begins with helping the clients to predict possible environmental opposition to their changed ways of coping. The practitioner may help the client consider ways of responding to this opposition. These include negotiations with people in the environment who are unsympathetic to changes, recommendations that such persons also seek professional intervention, and protective actions to insulate oneself from responses that undermine the changes.

The idea that others in the environment may also require professional help recognizes the frequent finding of interpersonal practitioners that, as the client improves, others, such as family members, may develop dysfunctional behaviors. This is one of the strongest reasons for involving family members and others in the process from its beginning. Unfortunately, this is not always possible as the client, as well as the relevant others, may oppose this approach. Some family-oriented practitioners refuse to work with individuals on a one-to-one basis when problems are seen as family problems. We do not take such an unequivocal stance because it ignores the empowerment value that client's perspective should be honored.

The third way of maintaining change is network interventions. We do not mean by this term the type of network therapy (Attneave, 1969) that enlists the participation in the process of all the people with whom the client interacts. During the termination process, the interpersonal practitioner interacts or helps the client to interact with specific people who will help the client to maintain changes. A school social worker, for example, worked with a boy to help him improve his classroom behavior as well as to complete assignments on time. The practitioner, with the knowledge of the boy, had contact with his teacher during this period and also held conferences with the teacher and parents at the time of termination to discuss a plan for maintaining the child's excellent progress.

Another way of helping the client to maintain change is through the creation of support groups. When the form of helping has been the group, some or *all* of the members may decide to maintain contact with each other. In other situations—whether the client system is an individual or group—a new group may be formed for this purpose or an existing group in the community may also be located. These formats are necessary for clients who do not belong to other networks with the potential to provide necessary support. Isolated individuals who are discharged from VA hospitals, psychiatric facilities, or penal institutions may need to locate support groups in the community. Such support also may be required for people who seek to maintain a lifestyle that is regarded as deviant by many groups in the society—for example, a gay lifestyle, single-parent status, or living alone as an emancipated adolescent. We should not assume that people who need such support will become chronically dependent if they receive it. All of us are able to function in life because of the existence of supporting networks. For some people, such networks have not emerged "naturally" and must be created.

The principle associated with all these measures is that of ensuring the kinds of reinforcement the client will need to maintain change. Sometimes this issue must be confronted directly. For specified periods of time, individuals in the client's environment may be asked to guarantee support for the change. In addition, the client can be taught to understand the kind of reinforcement he or she wants and to request it from teachers, family members, employers, and others. It is unfortunate that in our society many folks are unable to offer praise or encouragement spontaneously for desired behavior, such as "warm fuzzies" but instead focus on criticism of undesired actions such as "cold pricklies" (Steiner, 1983). Clients can be helped through role playing and other simulated experiences to ask for recognition of their accomplishments. The anxiety that such requests cause clients and the assumption that such a request is immodest can be overcome. This is in some small measure a step toward the creation of a community in which norms favoring positive responses properly outnumber those favoring aversive ones.

A number of these processes are included in what is called self-control. This procedure is based on the client's understanding of the process of change—usually from a behavior modification perspective. We previously discussed in the individual change chapter (Chapter 11), the problem solving process that may be taught to individual clients. A close corollary is a behavior modification process that may also be taught to individual clients. In the behavioral model, the client learns how to state a problem in behaviorally specific terms, develop a baseline of the behavior to be changed, determine a goal, make a contract with herself to secure and utilize reinforcements for steps toward the goal, and monitor change. The client may alternatively choose to modify some antecedent (prior condition) rather than consequence (following condition) or to self-modify some disabling emotion, such as anxiety, through a relaxation procedure previously taught by the practitioner. Many of these stress reduction procedures were discussed in the individual change chapter.

An example of a use of a self-control procedure taught during the termination process is the following.

Self-Control After Termination

At the time of termination, Susan had attained her goal of making new friends. She had accomplished this through learning a number of techniques for initiating relationships, and she had also been helped to lessen her anxiety in social situations. Subsequently, she found she was in danger of losing a new friend because she did not know how to roller-skate, and this was a favorite activity of the friend. She contracted with herself to learn to roller-skate and was able to set up a series of appropriate learning steps with the help of an attendant at the local rink. She engaged her friend to reinforce her for accomplishing these steps by having the friend agree to join in an activity of the client's choosing. One antecedent she changed was that she did not like the music or decor of one rink, and she felt uncomfortable learning to skate there. She was able to locate another rink that did not have this effect on her.

Utilizing Changes in a Variety of Circumstances

Another task of the termination process—one closely associated with that of maintaining changes—is to use such changes in a variety of circumstances. Clients, at the beginning of the helping process, are helped to state their problems in terms of specific situations. Examples are discomfort in a marriage, anxiety while at work, nonperformance in school, or inability to act in desired ways in the community. When clients do not base their problems on specific situations, the practitioner helps the client to select and focus on a specific situation so that problem solving, goal formulation, and evaluation of changes may have an unambiguous foundation.

Nevertheless, the solutions achieved and learned by clients are likely to have relevance in more circumstances than the ones focused on during the helping process. The worker can aid the client in selecting other circumstances and generalizing learned skills to these other circumstances. For example, in a group, the worker may take trips with the members to several different environments that require the members to adapt their skills to a variety of circumstances. Groups also offer the opportunity to simulate different situations in which the members can practice new behaviors. For this reason, even when the form of helping is on a one-to-one basis, the worker may help the client join a group that has this potential.

In family treatment, the worker, as part of the termination process, may raise issues that have not previously been emphasized so that family members can practice new patterns of adapting. This procedure can also be accomplished with families during termination phases through a series of "homework assignments." Thus, one family had worked on learning better means of problem solving. The content of the discussions in which they acquired problem solving skills was the use of money. The worker, during the termination phase, asked the family to select a problem around child behavior and subsequently a problem around responding to a troublesome relative to see if this approach to problem solving would "work" with those issues.

An important skill that helps clients to apply what they have learned to a broad variety of circumstances is the ability to analyze the relevant aspects of those situations. This ability enables the members to know how to employ the right skill in the right place. In the chapter on individual change (Chapter 11), we discussed the role of teacher as a part of interpersonal practice. Educating and enhancing the client's understanding of their situation is an important procedure in interpersonal practice. The process of interpersonal practice should add to the client's understanding of human behavior.

An example of this kind of generalized learning can be seen in the following case.

Generalizing Skills to Other Situations

In the beginning of the helping process, the client tended to blame himself exclusively for any problem that developed in his interpersonal relationships. When he argued with his girlfriend, he felt very guilty and looked solely at his own present and past actions for the source of the difficulty. In the course of his experience with the interpersonal practice process, he learned to discuss with his girlfriend and to work out with her what she or he contributed to the problem and what each was willing to do to solve it. In the termination phase, the worker reviewed with this client the ways in which he could examine his actual behaviors in other conflict situations as well as those of the other person, the goals of each, and the motivation of each to seek to change the interaction.

The way in which the worker helps the client acquire cognitive skills for the assessment of situations will be heavily influenced by the theoretical bias of the worker. Behaviorists among social workers will teach clients to analyze antecedents and consequences, and ego psychologists will introduce notions of the importance of feeling states, levels of awareness, and ways of coping. In addition to the issue of the truth or falsity of any of these ideas, clients are often strengthened by their sense that they have a "handle" on understanding the behavior of themselves and others.

Engaging in New Services

One interpersonal helping experience can be a preparation for another one. A client who used one service to determine whether or not she wished to place her baby for adoption decided to use another one to help her seek a career after she placed the child. Another client used one group experience to prepare for leaving the mental hospital and a subsequent one to secure support when she returned to the community. A family that used family therapy at one time decided to seek a "preparation for retirement" program later.

Although subsequent services are not always selected as part of termination, when they are, preparation for them should be part of the termination process. This should be more than a brief presentation of information. Clients should be helped to identify their subsequent needs, and the relationship of these needs to available services should be made clear. The worker should help clients discuss their expectations of the new service as well as any barriers they see to its use. When barriers are anticipated, the worker should help the clients plan ways of overcoming them.

An example of this process occurred with a student in a school for adolescents with developmental disabilities.

Helping a Youth Plan for Future Services

The social worker helped this student plan for his future vocational training. The social work service was focused on the choices the student had to make. As part of the termination phase, the worker reviewed the kinds of services the client needed, such as obtaining a counselor to provide support and help in problem solving. The worker helped him to consider what his expectations were for this type of counseling. The client and the worker knew that the counselors in the program were overworked and might spend their scarce time with less motivated students. The worker, therefore, helped this client think of clear and direct ways for expressing his desires for services to the counseling staff.

TERMINATION ISSUES IN GROUP WORK •

Prior issues and discussions in this chapter have generally been applied to individuals, families, and groups. Work with groups, however, involves specific, additional issues. In the group assessment chapter (Chapter 14), we have already described in open groups that members are joining and leaving constantly throughout the group sessions. In closed groups, where members are expected to continue until some designated time limit, sometimes a member may terminate and the other members may continue.

In a closed group, a termination process should occur with the member who leaves. In the beginning of closed groups, often a contract is established between members that if a member desires to leave the group, he or she will attend at least one meeting to deal with termination issues after the decision is reached. This meeting should be used to accomplish the same termination tasks, although in a briefer form, as when the entire group ends. Thus, the member is encouraged to evaluate what he or she has attained through the group experience and how the group has or has not been helpful. The leader and other members help the member express his or her feelings about leaving. The other members, in addition, are invited to talk about their feelings about the departure of the person terminating. These feelings, which can include both hope and anger, can impair the continued development of the group if they are not expressed at this time. The terminating member also uses knowledge of these feelings to deal with the reality of the group's response as well as to avoid the perception that the group members do not care for him or her.

All the tasks of termination noted for individual clients are also undertaken with group members who terminate. They are encouraged to reinforce what they have learned and to apply their skills as broadly as possible. They also should be helped to consider new resources, particularly if their termination is a result of dissatisfaction with this group experience. Another by-product of this process is that other members will learn about the termination process and will also be convinced that their presence matters to the group, and their leaving will be appropriately responded to when they leave the group.

Sometimes a group begins to disintegrate and attendance falls off. When this occurs, the worker should ask the members to attend a formal ending to the group. At this time, a decision on termination can be clearly made, feelings about this can be dealt with, and an evaluation that includes a consideration of the reasons for the group's failure can be conducted. Occasionally, the reasons for the group's failure are responded to in ways that allow for changes in the group to be made, and the group proceeds in a more vigorous and successful way.

When the group members all terminate at the same time because the group itself is ending, members can help each other with each of the termination tasks described earlier. Members will evaluate the progress made by each individual, the effectiveness of the group as an entity, and the effectiveness of the worker. Although the content of the first and last of these evaluations is similar to that in one-to-one terminations, the evaluation of the group is a new issue. This can include an evaluation of the tasks and programs the group undertook, the nature of interpersonal relationships in the group, the kinds of norms the group adopted, and the group's overall emotional atmosphere.

Members will also help each other to express feelings about termination. These feelings will be not only those regarding the loss of associations with other individuals, including the worker, but also the loss of the group as an entity. Members should be helped to recognize this and deal with the empty space created by the disbanding of the group.

Regarding the remaining three issues of maintaining change, generalizing change, and planning future activities, members can also help each other. Because members often have similar problems or come from similar backgrounds or both, they may be more adept than the practitioner at spotting future problems as well as support systems. If this does not violate a goal of termination, members may be encouraged to contact each other on a one-to-one basis after the group ends to help with problem solving or to reinforce the use of a self-control procedure.

● TERMINATION ISSUES WITH FAMILIES

The unique aspect of family treatment compared to group work is that the family remains together after it discontinues services from the worker. The exception is when family treatment ends with divorce or child placement. Some family work also ends when one member of the family continues to receive service from the same or a different worker while others do not. This ending occurred in the Romano family case in the chapter on family change (Chapter 13). Each of these circumstances raises different termination issues.

When the family continues intact, the sense of loss of the interpersonal practitioner may be less than in one-to-one treatment or even group work, as in the latter, termination is associated with the concurrent loss of other members. In some approaches to family therapy, also, the worker withdraws when the family structure is more functional than it was before the family entered service. The worker assumes that the family has become equipped to resolve its own problems and is more likely to do so "on its own" than when it is dependent on the worker. Termination is associated, therefore, with greater problem solving capacity rather than problem solution as such, and the job of the worker is de-emphasized. We hypothesize that this type of termination may be easier for the family than for other client systems, although this proposition should be examined through research on family terminations.

If family work ends in divorce or placement of a family member outside the household, the worker should continue to offer service to the separated parties or ensure that they have access to services they need. Under these circumstances, the feelings of loss from both the worker *and* other family members can be devastating. These clients will require the supportive presence of the worker (or other workers) as they embark on their new roles. The emotions associated with other types of termination will appear among the family members, and they will require help to cope with this separation process.

WORKER TERMINATION ●

In individual, family, and group work, it is possible for the interpersonal practitioner to terminate the services, although the client system desires to continue with them. The practitioner's termination may occur when the practitioner leaves for a new job, becomes ill or pregnant, is laid off or fired, or reaches the end of a student field placement. Because the National Association of Social Workers (NASW) *Code of Ethics* prohibits practitioners from precipitous terminations with clients, the interpersonal practitioner must inform the client, if possible, several sessions in advance of the practitioner's departure.

The client should be helped to express and cope with transference feelings associated with the pending loss of the practitioner. These feelings can include sadness as well as anger that the worker is leaving when the client needs him or her. Practitioners should not minimize the likelihood that the client will have these feelings. The loss of the practitioner can recall other circumstances to the clients when important persons deserted them when they were in need. Clients who have experienced rejection from parents or other crucial people in their lives will be particularly vulnerable to the loss of the worker. Children are also highly susceptible to worker loss because of their dependence on parental figures for security. Sometimes these transference feelings may also occur when the practitioner takes a short vacation.

Clients will require reassurance that the practitioner's termination is not due to their own behavior. Some clients may assume that if they had been "better" clients the practitioner would have remained. This reassurance will be therapeutic to those clients who have believed that earlier losses of other persons in their life was a consequence of their "bad" behavior. Workers should be aware of their own feelings about terminating from the agency, as these feelings can inhibit them from being sensitive to the feelings of their clients.

Worker's Feelings at Termination

For example, a student social worker believed that he had not responded to some of the client's problems as skillfully as he should have. His guilt over this blocked him from accepting that he also had been helpful to the client and had expressed a great deal of caring to him. He was unresponsive at first to the client's sense of loss and was unable to approach this until he had discussed his feelings with his supervisor.

At times it is wise to have the client's termination coincide with that of the practitioner, especially if the client's termination would have occurred soon after that of the worker. The amount of readjustment to a new interpersonal practitioner in these cases may not be worth the additional steps toward goal attainment. On the other hand, the practitioner may leave when the client is nowhere near her appropriate termination time. Ideally, a new practitioner will be chosen before the departure of the previous one and can be introduced to the client. In this situation, both practitioners should be present for at least one session to create continuity. Unfortunately in practice when students finish their internship, there may be a hiatus of several months before the next student arrives. Clients may drop out during this hiatus or may be angry when the new practitioner finally arrives. Because there is no continuity, the start for the new student and the client may be very stormy.

Even under the best of circumstances, the client is likely to spend several sessions discussing feelings about the departure of the previous worker. This discussion of feelings helps the client determine the degree to which the new worker can be empathetic but also may be a test whether the new worker has plans to terminate soon. The client may extol the virtues of the previous worker or condemn his or her shortcomings. The client may hint at either the assumed superiority or inferiority of the new worker. This is often a repetition of how the client coped with previous separation issues, and exploration at this time may help the client gain new insights into his or her previous relationship patterns.

In all cases, the departure of one practitioner and the appointment of another can provide useful learning. Our lives are inevitably composed of shifts in our relationships in which loyalties must be transferred from one individual to another. The new practitioner may be able to help the client recognize functional as well as dysfunctional ways of coping with transitions. This recognition may be generalized to other occasions when the client must cope with such transitions.

PROBLEMATIC TERMINATIONS ●

A common issue that arises in termination is gift giving. This is a dilemma for the interpersonal practitioner because one section of the NASW *Code of Ethics* is in conflict with another. The code prescribes that workers should comply with agency policies and also prescribes that workers should be culturally sensitive and competent. What should an interpersonal practitioner do when a client brings a gift for the practitioner in the last session and the agency has a policy against accepting gifts from clients? This event happens regularly when the practitioner and the client have established a good relationship and service has been successful.

In my (BAS) interpersonal practice classes on termination, I raise this issue of giving and receiving gifts. Many students are aware of agency policies that proscribe receiving gifts from clients. Some agencies strictly prohibit practitioners from receiving any gifts from clients. Other agencies allow some slippage to this policy. If the gift is of low monetary value or made by the client (such as a food item), the practitioner can accept the gift. If the client offers a gift of large monetary value, the gift can only be accepted as a gift for the agency, and it will be added to agency resources. For example, if the client brings money then this should be turned over to the agency, or if the client purchases an expensive item, such as a large floral arrangement, then this will be placed in the waiting areas for all clients to enjoy. Curiously these agency policies do not state the monetary value of a gift that is too large for the practitioner to accept.

The other side of the dilemma is whether it is desirable to reject a gift from a client when it is offered as a symbol of appreciation. We teach students that it is important to be ethnically sensitive, and with some ethnic groups, rejecting a gift is a major insult. Rejecting a gift of appreciation is like a slap across the face and would be experienced as a rejection of the gift giver. With all of the ambivalent feelings that clients are experiencing during termination, why would we add to this turmoil by rejecting a gift? Some students believe that if you explain the agency policy that you cannot accept the gift, this explanation will satisfy the client. Other students do not find such an explanation satisfactory, and these students accept gifts from clients because of the importance that receiving the gift has for the practice relationship.

I point out to students that if they decide to violate their agency policy and engage in "banditry" (Seabury, 2001) then they need to carefully explore the meaning behind the gift and think out their rationale for accepting it. Besides their rationale that accepting the gift is an example of culturally competent practice as presented in the NASW *Code of Ethics*, one principle for resolving competing values in the code of ethics is the "primacy of client interests." This principle suggests that any ethical code that involves the treatment of client interests should take precedence over any other section of the NASW *Code of Ethics*, such as responsibilities to agencies. I point out to students that this issue will surely arise in their practice and they will have to decide what to do. Most students figure out that I will side with client interests. I end this class discussion with two case examples during termination in which a marital couple wanted to give me a used car and another couple, who bred border collies, wanted to give me a runt from one of their litters. These examples produce all kinds of turmoil in class trying to figure out what I did and what they would do in the same situation.

Terminations can be more difficult when the worker, the clients, or both view the service process as having been unsuccessful in attaining the client's objectives. An absence, however, of efforts to fulfill termination tasks in these situations can increase their negative impact. This can be in the form of exaggerating the client's sense of failure, thus making it difficult for the client to seek out a new helping experience that can be more effective than the existing one.

Each of the termination tasks outlined earlier in the chapter can be appropriately adapted to times when the service has been a partial or complete failure. An evaluation of the experience can help to show that there may have been success as well as failure. It can also determine aspects of the process responsible for the failure so that these may be avoided in the future. It is possible that the evaluation will produce material that is critical of the worker. This is always difficult for the worker, but the worker should seek to overcome feelings of guilt and regret. This is a valuable opportunity for the worker to identify ways of improving his or her practice skills. In addition, the way in which the worker copes with failure can provide an important model to clients how they can cope with occasions when they are not successful. Thus, the ways that workers help clients deal with feelings when termination follows an unsuccessful service can, in itself, be one of the most valuable aspects of the service. After all, the client has usually sought service because of unsuccessful coping and can learn from the worker how the latter responds to an analogous situation.

The worker may wish to help the client reach out to a new service that will be more helpful to the client. Because the client may fear a repetition of the present unsuccessful experience, the worker will have to handle this termination in such a way as to avoid this. As we have sought to demonstrate, the worker must use all the skills at his or her disposal to free the client from the emotional bonds of an unsuccessful helping experience so that the client's energies can go into locating and investing in a new one.

Another problematic situation related to the one that we have just discussed is the client's desire to terminate in opposition to the worker's recommendation for continuance. The client may wish to do this because of his or her resistance to change. The client's investment in "things as they are" or fear of new patterns may overwhelm the client's hope that a better life will be attained. The client may also meet with pressures on the part of "significant others" who cannot adapt to changes in the client, although workers should try to identify and ameliorate this type of response, often through a redefinition of the client system, when it occurs.

If the client contracts to meet with the worker for a session after he or she has decided to terminate, such a "premature" termination can sometimes be avoided. On other occasions, no matter how skillful the worker is, a termination cannot be prevented. The client should still be helped to participate in the termination tasks we have outlined because this process will make it more likely that the client will reapply for some service when he or she has coped with internal or external sources of resistance or when the pain associated with dysfunctional life patterns grows more intense. The worker's understanding of and ability to work with the client's feelings in these type of terminations will be a vital factor in the likelihood the client will seek help again.

SUMMARY ●

The interpersonal practitioner helps the client through the termination process fulfilling a series of tasks that include initiating the termination process, evaluating the experience (including the worker's performance), coping with feelings about termination, planning ways to maintain beneficial changes, generalizing changes to a variety of circumstances, and engaging in new services when they are required.

These basic tasks of termination were presented as general issues that occur whether the client system is an individual, a family, or a group. There are, however, special issues around termination in multiperson client systems, and the chapter presents special issues that emerge in termination with families and formed groups. Presented in the chapter were various kinds of endings that take place in practice, such as members dropping out of closed groups and situations in which the worker leaves service before the client is ready to stop. Problematic endings were presented, such as service that does not achieve its goals, clients who are dissatisfied with service, and the relationship between practitioner and client is so intense that termination is overwhelming for the client. Also discussed in this chapter were the ethical conflicts in the issue of gift giving, which often arises in termination.

BIBLIOGRAPHY

About.com: Alcoholism. (2010). *Online diagnostic tools.* Retrieved from http://alcoholism.about.com/od/tests/Online_Diagnostic_Tools.htm

Ad Hoc Committee on Advocacy. (1969). The social worker as advocate: Champion of social victims. *Social Work, 14*(4), 16–22.

Adams, R., Figley, C., & Boscarino, J. (2008). The compassion fatigue scale: Its use with social workers following urban disaster research on social work practice. *Research on Social Work Practice, 18,* 238–250.

Addams, J. (1935). *Forty years at Hull House.* New York: Macmillan.

Adelman, L. (2007). Unnatural causes: Is inequality making us sick? [Editorial]. *Prevention of Chronic Disease, 4*(4). Retrieved from www.unnaturalcauses.org

Aguilera, D. (1990). *Crisis intervention: Theory and methodology* (6th ed.). St. Louis, MO: C. V. Mosby.

Aguilera, D., & Messick, J. (1984). *Crisis intervention: Theory and methodology* (5th ed.). St. Louis, MO: C. V. Mosby.

Alberti, R., & Emmons, M. (1990). *A manual for assertiveness trainers.* San Luis Obispo, CA: Impact Publishers.

Alexander, J. F., Holtzworth-Munroe, A., & Jameson, P. B. (1994). The process and outcome of marital and family therapy: Research review and evaluation. In A. E. Bergin & S. L. Garfield (Eds.), *Handbook of psychotherapy and behavior change* (4th ed., pp. 595–630). New York: John Wiley.

Alexander, L. (1983). Professionalization and unionization: Compatible after all? *Social Work, 28*(4), 476–482.

Alexander, L. (1987). Unions: Social work. *Encyclopedia of Social Work XX* (20th ed., pp. 793–800). Washington, DC: National Association of Social Workers.

Allen, W. F. (1978). The search for applicable theories of black family life. *Journal of Marriage and the Family, 40,* 117–129.

American Psychiatric Association. (2000). *Diagnostic and statistical manual of mental disorders (DSM-IV-TR)* (4th ed.). Washington, DC: Author.

Anderson, M., & Collins, P. H. (Eds.). (1995). *Race, class, and gender: An anthology* (2nd ed.). New York: Wadsworth.

Anthony, W. A., Cohen, M., Farkas, M., & Cohen, B. F. (1988). The chronically mentally ill case management: More than a response to a dysfunctional system. *Community Mental Health Journal, 24,* 219–228.

Arluke, A. (1979). Reexamining the sick role concept: An empirical assessment. *Journal of Health and Social Behavior, 20,* 30–36.

Aronson, H., & Overall, B. (1966). Treatment expectations of patients in two social classes. *Social Work, II,* 35–41.

Atherton, C., Mitchell, S., & Schein, E. (1971). Locating points for intervention. *Social Casework, 52,* 131–141.

Attneave, C. (1969). Therapy in tribal settings and urban network intervention. *Family Process, 8,* 192–210.

Attneave, C. (1976). Social networks as the unit of intervention. In P. J. Guerin (Ed.), *Family therapy: Theory and practice* (pp. 192–210). New York: Gardner.

Bales, R. F. (1958). Task roles and social roles in problem-solving groups. In E. F. Maccoby, T. M. Newcomb, & E. L. Hartley (Eds.), *Readings in social psychology* (3rd ed., pp. 437–446). New York: Holt, Rinehart & Winston.

Bales, R. F., & Cohen, S. P. (with Williamson, S. A.). (1979). *SYMLOG: A system for the multiple level observation of groups.* New York: Free Press.

Bandler, R., & Grinder, J. (1982). *Reframing, neuro-linguistic programming and the transformation of meaning.* Moab, UT: Real People Press.

Barker, P. (1985). *Using metaphors in psychotherapy.* New York: Brunner/Mazel.

Barker, P. (1996). *Psychotherapeutic metaphors: A guide to theory and practice.* New York: Brunner/Mazel.

Barker, R. L. (1995). *The social work dictionary* (3rd ed.). Washington, DC: National Association of Social Workers.

Barlow, C., Blythe, J., & Edmonds, M. (1999). *A handbook of interactive exercises for groups*. Boston: Allyn & Bacon.

Beagle, C. R. (1974). Social service supports cardiac patients. *Hospitals, 48*, 135–136, 140–141.

Beal, L. (1972). Corrupt contract: Problems in conjoint therapy with parents and children. *American Journal of Orthopsychiatry, 42*, 77–81.

Beck, A. T., Steer, R. A., & Garbin, G. M. (1988). Psychometric properties of the Beck Depression Inventory: Twenty-five years of evaluation. *Clinical Psychology Review, 8*, 77–100. Retrieved from http://www.fpnotebook.com/psych/exam/bckdprsninvntry.pdf

Becker, H. (Ed.). (1967). *The other side: Perspectives on deviance*. New York: Free Press.

Beinecke, R. H. (1984). PORK, SOAP, STRAP, and SAP. *Social Work, 9*, 554–558.

Belle, D. (1982). The stress of caring: Women as providers of social support. In L. Goldberger & S. Breznitz (Eds.), *Handbook of stress* (pp. 496–505). New York: Free Press.

Bem, D., & Bem, S. (1970). The power of non-conscious ideology. In D. Bem (Ed.), *Beliefs, attitudes and human affairs*. Belmont, CA: Brooks/Cole.

Bennis, W., Benne, K., & Chin, R. (1969). *The planning of change*. New York: Holt, Rinehart & Winston.

Benson, H. (1975). *The relaxation response*. New York: William Morrow Co.

Benson, H., & Klipper, M. (2000). *The relaxation response*. New York: HarperTorch.

Benson, H., & Stark, M. (1997). *Timeless healing: The power and biology of belief*. New York: Fireside.

Berger, J., & Zelditch, M. J. (1977). *Status, rewards, and influence: How expectations organize behavior*. San Francisco: Jossey-Bass.

Berman, S. (1962). *Why do we jump to conclusions?* San Diego, CA: International Communications Institute.

Bertcher, H., & Maple, F. (1996). *Creating groups* (2nd ed.). Thousand Oaks, CA: Sage.

Bertsche, A., & Horejsi, C. (1980). Coordination of client services. *Social Work, 25*, 94–98.

Beutler, L., Machado, P., & Neufeldt, S. (1994). Therapist variables. In A.E. Bergin & S. L. Garfield (Eds.), *Handbook of psychotherapy and behavior change* (4th ed., pp. 229–269). New York: John Wiley.

Biddle, B., & Thomas, E. (Eds.). (1966). *Role theory: Concepts and research*. New York: John Wiley.

Biestek, F. (1957). *The casework relationship*. Chicago: Loyola University Press.

Billings, A., & Moos, R. (1995). Psychosocial stressors, coping, and depression. In E. E. Beckham & W. R. Leber (Eds.), *Handbook of depression*. New York: Guilford Press.

Billingsley, A. (1964). Bureaucratic and professional orientation patterns in social casework. *Social Service Review, 38*, 400–407.

Bixby, A. R. (1995). Public social welfare expenditures. In R. L. Edwards (Ed.), *Encyclopedia of social work* (pp. 1992–1997). Washington, DC: NASW Press.

Black, M. (1962). *Models and metaphors: Studies in language and philosophy*. Ithaca, NY: Cornell University Press.

Blatner, A. (1996). *Acting in: Practical applications of psychodramatic methods*. New York: Springer Publishing Company.

Blatner, A. (2004). *Foundations of psychodrama: History, theory and practice* (4th ed.). New York: Springer.

Blatner, A., & Blatner, A. (1988). *The art of play: An adult guide to reclaiming imagination and spontaneity*. New York: Human Science Press.

Blenkner, M. (1964). *Serving the aged: An experiment in social work and public health nursing*. New York: Community Service Society of New York.

Bloom, B. (1981). Focused single-session therapy: Initial development and evaluation. In S. Budman (Ed.), *Forms of brief therapy*. New York: Guilford Press.

Bloom, B. (1988). Focused single session therapy: Initial development and evaluation. In S. Budman & A. Gurman (Eds.), *Theory and practice of brief therapy*. New York: Guilford Press.

Bloom, B. (1992). *Planned short-term psychotherapy: A clinical handbook*. Boston: Allyn & Bacon.

Bongar, B., Berman, A. L., Maris, R. W., Silverman, M. M., Harris, E. A., & Packman, W. L. (1998). *Risk management with suicidal patients*. New York: Guilford Press.

Boscarino, J., Charles, R., Figley, C. R., & Adams, R. E. (2004). Compassion fatigue following the September 11 terrorist attacks: A study of secondary trauma among New York City social workers. *International Journal of Emergency Mental Health, 6*(2), 57–66.

Boulding, K. (1956). *The image: Knowledge in life and society*. Ann Arbor: University of Michigan Press.

Boyd-Franklin, N. (1989). *Black families in therapy*. New York: Guilford Press.

Brager, G., & Purcell, F. (Eds.). (1964). *Community action against poverty*. New Haven, CT: College and University Press.

Braham, R., Furniss, K., Holtz, H., & Stevens, M. E. (1986). *Hospital protocol on domestic violence*. Morristown, NJ: Jersey Battered Women's Services, Inc.

Brattberg, G. (2008). Self-administered EFT (emotional freedom techniques) in individuals with fibromyalgia: A randomized trial. *Integrative Medicine: A Clinician's Journal*, 7(August/September).

Briere, J., & Zaida, L. (1989). Sexual abuse histories and sequelae in female psychiatric emergency room patients. *American Journal of Psychiatry*, 146, 1602–1606.

Brim, O., & Wheeler, S. (1966). *Socialization after childhood*. New York: John Wiley.

Brody, C. M. (1987). *Women's therapy group: Paradigms of feminist treatment*. New York: Springer.

Brown, G., & Harris, T. (1989). *Life events and illness*. New York: Guilford Press.

Buchanan, D., & Badham, R. (2008). *Power, politics, and organizational change: Winning the turf game* (2nd ed.). Thousand Oaks, CA: Sage.

Budman, S., & Gurman, A. (1988). *Theory and practice of brief therapy*. New York: Guilford Press.

Burns, G. (2007). *Healing with stories: Your casework collection for using therapeutic metaphors*. Hoboken, NJ: John Wiley.

Bush, S. (1977). A family self-help program that really works. *Psychology Today*, 10, 48–50, 84–88.

Byers, P., & Byers, H. (1972). Nonverbal communication and the education of children. In C. Cazden (Ed.), *Functions of language in the classroom*. New York: Teachers College Press.

Cade, B., & O'Hanlon, W. (1993). *A brief guide to brief therapy*. New York: W. W. Norton.

Call, D. (1990). School based groups: A valuable support for children of cancer patients. *Journal of Psychosocial Oncology*, 8, 97–118.

Campbell, D., Draper, R., & Crutchley, E. (1991). The Milan systemic approach to family therapy. In A. S. Gurman & D. P. Kniskern (Eds.), *Handbook of family therapy* (Vol. 2, pp. 325–362). New York: Brunner/Mazel.

Campbell, M. (1962). Extensional and intentional levels of abstraction. In M. S. Morain (Ed.), *Teaching general semantics*. San Francisco: International Society for General Semantics.

Canda, E. R. (1988). Spirituality, diversity, and social work practice. *Social Casework*, 69(4), 238–247.

Caplan, G. (1964). *Principles of preventive psychiatry*. New York: Basic Books.

Caplovitz, D. (1963). *The poor pay more: Consumer practices of low income families*. New York: Free Press.

Carrell, S. (2000). *Group exercises for adolescents: A manual for therapists*. Thousand Oaks, CA: Sage.

Carrol, M. (1988). Social work's conceptualization of spirituality. *Social Thought*, 18(2), 1–13.

Carroll, L. (2008). *Alice in Wonderland*. Rancho Cucamonga, CA: Brandywine Press

Carter, B., & McGoldrick, M. (Eds.). (1988). *The changing family life cycle*. New York: Gardiner.

Carter, J. B. (1993). *Racketeering in medicine: The suppression of alternatives*. Norfolk, VA: Hampton Roads.

Cartwright, D. (1968). *Group dynamics: Research and theory*. New York: Harper & Row.

Chaiklin, H. (1973). Honesty in casework treatment. *Social Welfare Forum, 1973*. New York: Columbia University Press.

Chau, K. L. (1991). *Ethnicity and biculturalism: Emerging perspectives of social group work*. New York: Haworth.

Child Welfare Information Gateway. (2008). *Child abuse and neglect fatalities: Statistics and interventions*. Retrieved from www.childwelfare.gov/systemwide/pubs/factsheets/fatality.cfm

Child Welfare Information Gateway. (2010a). *Child abuse and neglect statistics*. Retrieved from www.childwelfare.gov/systemwide/statistics/can.cfm

Child Welfare Information Gateway. (2010b). *Program evaluations & studies*. Retrieved from www.childwelfare.gov/famcentered/evaluating/preserve_eval.cfm

The ChildTrauma Academy. (2010). Retrieved from http://www.childtrauma.org/

Cloward, R., & Ohlin, L. (1960). *Delinquency and opportunity*. Glencoe, IL: Free Press.

Cohen, M., & Mullender, A. (2003). *Gender and group work*. New York: Routledge.

Coll, B. D. (1969). *Perspectives in public welfare: A history*. Washington, DC: U.S. Government Printing Office.

Collins, A., & Pancoast, D. (1976). *Natural helping networks*. Washington, DC: National Association of Social Workers.

Collins, J. (1977). The contractual approach to social work intervention. *Social Work Today*, 8(February).

Comas-Diaz, L., & Greene, R. (1995). *Mental health and women of color*. New York: Guilford Press.

Comas-Diaz, L., & Griffiths, E. W. (Eds.). (1988). *Clinical guidelines in cross-cultural mental health*. New York: John Wiley.

Compton, B., & Galaway, B. (1979). *Social work processes* (Rev. ed.). Homewood, IL: Dorsey.

Compton, B., & Galaway, B. (1994). *Social work processes* (5th ed.). Pacific Grove, CA: Wadsworth.

Cooper, J. F. (1995). *A primer of brief psychotherapy*. New York: W. W. Norton.

Corcoran, K., & Fisher, J. (2000). *Measures for clinical practice: A sourcebook* (3rd ed.). New York: Free Press.

Corey, M., & Corey, G. (2006). *Groups: Process and practice* (6th ed.). Pacific Grove, CA: Brooks/Cole.

Corey, M., Corey, G., & Corey, C. (2010). *Groups: Process and practice* (8th ed.). Pacific Grove, CA: Brooks/Cole.

Coser, L. (1956). *The functions of social conflict.* New York: Free Press.

Coulton, C., Rosenberg, M. L., & Yankey, J. A. (1981). Scarcity and the rationing of services. *Public Welfare, 39*(Summer), 15–21.

Cowan, B. et al. (1969). Holding unwilling clients in treatment. *Social Casework, 50*(3), 146–151.

Craig, G. (2008). *The EFT manual.* Santa Rosa, CA: Energy Psychology Press.

Crazy Wisdom. (2009). *The Ann Arbor holistic resource guide.* Ann Arbor, MI: Author.

Croxton, T. (1974). The therapeutic contract in social treatment. In P. Glasser, R. Sarri, & R. Vinter (Eds.), *Individual change through small groups.* New York: Macmillan.

Cummings, E. (1968). *Systems of social regulation.* New York: Atherton Press.

Dalton, D. (Ed.). (1996). *Mahatma Gandhi: Selected political writings.* Indianapolis: Hackett Publishing. Retrieved from www.madd.org

Davies, L. (2006). 25 years of saving lives. *Driven: A MADD Publication,* (Fall), 8–17.

Davis, L. (1984). Essential components of group work with Black Americans. *Social Work With Groups, VII,* 97–110.

Davis, L., & Proctor, E. (1989). *Race, gender, and class.* Englewood Cliffs, NJ: Prentice Hall.

Davis, M., Eshelman, E., & McKay, M. (2000). *The relaxation and stress reduction workbook* (5th ed.). Oakland, CA: New Harbinger Publications.

de Saint-Exupery, A. (1986). *Wartime writings, 1939–1944.* Orlando, FL: Harcourt.

DeJong, P., & Berg, I. K. (2002). *Interviewing for solutions* (2nd ed.). Pacific Grove, CA: Wadsworth.

Delgado, M., & Humm-Delgado, D. (1982). Natural support systems. *Social Work, 17*(1), 83–90.

Demaria, R., Weeks, G., & Hof, L. (1999). *Focused genograms.* New York: Routledge.

DeWaal, F. (2009). *The age of empathy: Nature's lesson for a kinder society.* New York: Harmony Books.

Dohrenwend, B., Krasnoff, L., Askenasy, A., & Dohrenwend, B. (1982). The psychiatric epidemiology research interview life events scale. In L. Goldberger & S. Breznits (Eds.) *Handbook of stress: Theoretical and clinical aspects.* New York: Free Press.

Dolan, M., & Doyle, M. (2000). Violence risk prediction: Clinical and actuarial measures and the role of the psychopathy checklist. *British Journal of Psychiatry, 177,* 303–311.

Domestic Violence Resource Center. (2010). *Domestic violence statistics.* Retrieved from http://bjs.ojp.usgov/content/intimate/circumstances.cfm#type

Dossick, J., & Shea, E. (1988, 1990, 1995). *Creative therapy I, II, III: 52 more exercises for groups.* Sarasota, FL: Professional Resource Exchange.

Dover, M. A., Hunter, B., Joseph, R., Paris, R., DeVoe, E. R., Schwaber Kerson, T., et al. (2008). Human needs. In T. Mizrahi & L. E. Davis (Eds.), Encyclopedia of social work. New York: Oxford University Press.

Dowie, M. (1977). Pinto madness. *Mother Jones,* (September/October), 18–32.

Duhl, F., Kantor, D. & Duhl, B. (1973). Learning, space, and action in family therapy: A primer of sculpture. In D. Bloch (Ed.), *Techniques of family psychotherapy.* New York: Grune & Stratton.

The Earth Charter Initiative. (2010). *Mission.* Retrieved from http://www.earthcharterinaction.org/content/pages/Who-we-Are.html

Edwards, B. D., Edwards, M. E., Francis, E. A., Montalvo, F. F., & Murase, K. (1992). Ethnic minority social work mental health training programs: An assessment of the experience. *Journal of Multicultural Social Work, 1*(4), 31–45.

Eisenberg, D., Davis, R., Ettner, S., Appel, S., Wilkey, S., Van Rompay, M., et al. (1998). Trends in alternative medicine use in the United States, 1990–1997. *JAMA: The Journal of the American Medical Association, 280,* 1569–1575.

Eisenberg, S., & Delaney, D. J. (1977). *The counseling process* (2nd ed.). Chicago: Rand McNally.

Eitzen, D. S., & Zinn, M. B. (2005). *Social problems* (10th ed.). Boston: Allyn & Bacon.

Eitzen, D. S., Zinn, M. B., & Smith, K. E. (2009). *Social problems* (11th ed.). Boston: Allyn & Bacon.

Ekman, P. (2001). *Telling lies: Clues to deceit in the marketplace, politics, and marriage.* New York: W. W. Norton.

Epstein, I. (1969). *Professionalization and social work activism.* Unpublished doctoral dissertation, Columbia University, New York.

Everstine, D. S., & Everstine, L. (1993). *The trauma response: Treatment for emotional injury.* New York: W. W. Norton.

Fanshel, D. (1971). The exit of children from foster care: An interim report. *Child Welfare, 50*(February), 65–81.

Faust, J. (2008). Clinical social worker as patient advocate in a community mental health center. *Clinical Social Work Journal, 36,* 293–300.

Feagin, J. R., & Feagin, C. (1986). *Discrimination American style: Institutional racism and sexism* (2nd ed.). Malabar, FL: Robert Krieger.

Feinstein, D., & Krippner, S. (1988). *Personal mythology: The psychology of your evolving self.* Los Angeles: Jeremy P. Tarcher.

Feld, S., & Radin, N. (1982). *Social psychology for social work and the mental health professions.* New York: Columbia University Press.

Figley, C. (1989). *Helping traumatized families.* San Francisco: Jossey-Bass.

Finn, J., (1999). An exploration of helping processes in an online self-help group focusing on issues of disability. *Health & Social Work, 24,* 320–331.

Fisher, P. A., & Chamberlain, P. (2000). Multidimensional treatment foster care: A program for intensive parenting, family support, and skill building. *Journal of Emotional and Behavioral Disorders, 8*(3), 155–164.

Forsyth, D. R. (1990). *Group dynamics* (2nd ed.). Pacific Grove, CA: Brooks/Cole.

Foster, D. F., Phillips R. S., Hamel, M. B., Eisenberg, D. M., & Renouf, D. (2000). The use of complementary and alternative medicine in older adults. *Journal of the American Geriatrics Society, 48,* 1560–1565.

Fox, J. (Ed.). (1987). *The essential Moreno: Writings on psychodrama, group method, and spontaneity.* New York: Springer.

Frame, M. W. (2001). The spiritual genogram in training and supervision. *The Family Journal: Counseling and Therapy for Couples and Families, 9,* 109–115.

Frank, R. (2007). *Richistan: A journey through the American wealth boom and the lives of the new rich.* New York: Three Rivers Press.

Frankl, V. (1984). *Man's search for meaning.* New York: Washington Square Books.

Freire, P. (1973). *Education for critical consciousness.* New York: The Seabury Press.

Fremouw, W., De Perczel, M., & Ellis, T. (1990). *Suicide risk, assessment, and response guidelines.* New York: Pergamon Press.

Fusco, L. J. (1977, November). *Power, authority, and influence in social work treatment and the two-contract model of practice.* Paper presented at the National Association of Social Workers Fifth Biennial Professional Symposium, San Diego, CA.

Gallagher, R. C. (n.d.). *BrainyQuote.com.* Retrieved from http://www.brainyquote.com/quotes/quotes/r/rober tcga104504.html

Gallant, C. (1982). *Mediation in special education disputes.* New York: National Association of Social Workers.

Gallo, F., & Robbins, A. (2007). *Energy tapping for trauma: Rapid relief from post traumatic stress using energy psychology.* Oakland, CA: New Harbinger.

Galloway, J. (2002). Personal safety when visiting patients in the community. *Advances in Psychiatric Treatment, 8,* 214–222.

Galper, J. (1980). *Social work practice: A radical perspective.* Englewood Cliffs, NJ: Prentice Hall.

Garfield, S. L. (1980). *Psychotherapy: An eclectic approach.* New York: John Wiley.

Garfield, S. L. (1994). Research on client variables in psychotherapy. In A. E. Bergin & S. L. Garfield (Eds.), *Handbook of psychotherapy and behavior change* (4th ed., pp. 190–228). New York: John Wiley.

Garland, J., Jones, H., & Kolodny, R. (1965). A model for stages of development in social work with groups. In S. Bernstein (Ed.), *Explorations in group work* (pp. 12–53). Boston: Boston University School of Social Work.

Gartner, A., & Reisman, F. (1984). *The self-help revolution.* New York: Human Sciences.

Garvin, C. (1974). Task-centered group work. *The Social Service Review, 48*(4), 494–507.

Garvin, C. (1996). *Contemporary group work* (3rd ed.). Boston: Allyn & Bacon.

Garvin, C., & Glasser, P. (1974). The bases of social treatment. In P. Glasser, R. Sarri, & R. Vinter (Eds.), *Individual change through small groups* (pp. 483–507). New York: Free Press.

Garvin, C., & Reed, B. G. (1994). Small group theory and social work practice: Promoting diversity and social justice or recreating inequities. In R. Greene (Ed.), *Human behavior theory: A diversity framework* (pp. 173–202). New York: Aldine de Gruyter.

Garvin, C., & Reed, B. G. (1995). Sources and visions for feminist group work: Reflective processes, social justice, diversity, and connection. In N. V. Bergh (Ed.), *Feminist social work practice in the 21st century* (pp. 41–69). Washington, DC: National Association of Social Workers.

Germain, C. (1968). Social study: Past and future. *Social Casework, 49,* 406–409.

Germain, C. (1970). Casework and science: An historical encounter. In R. Roberts & R. Nee (Eds.), *Theories of social casework.* Chicago: University of Chicago Press.

Germain, C., & Gitterman, A. (1980). *The life model of social work practice.* New York: Columbia University Press.

Gift, A. (1989). The visual analogue scale's measurement of subjective phenomena. *Nursing Research, 38,* 286–287.

Gilbert, N., & Specht, H. (1976). Advocacy and professional ethics. *Social Work, 21,* 288–293.

Giller, E. (1999). *What is psychological trauma? Sidran Institute: Traumatic stress education and advocacy.* Retrieved from http://www.sidran.org/sub.cfm?contentID=88&sectionid=4

Ginsberg, L. (Ed.). (1993). *Social work in rural communities* (2nd ed.). Alexandria, VA: Council on Social Work Education.

Gitterman, A. (1983). Uses of resistance: A transactional view. *Social Work, 28,* 127–131.

Glasser, P., & Navarre, E. (1967). Structural problems of the one-parent family. In E. J. Thomas (Ed.), *Behavioral sciences for social workers* (pp. 145–155). New York: Free Press.

Glasser, P., Sarri, R., & Vinter, R. (1974). Group work intervention in the social environments. In P. Glasser, R. Sarri, & R. Vinter (Eds.), *Individual change through small groups* (pp. 292–306). New York: Free Press.

Glenn, E. (1944). Education behind barbed wire. *Survey Midmonthly, 80,* 347–349.

Goffman, E. (1967). *Interaction ritual: Essays in face-to-face behavior.* New York: Doubleday.

Golan, N. (1978). *Treatment in crisis situations.* New York: Free Press.

Golan, N. (1980). Intervention in times of transition: Sources and forms of help. *Social Casework, 61,* 259–266.

Goldberg, N. (1986). *Writing down the bones.* Boston: Shambala Publ.

Goldberger, L., & Breznitz, S. (Eds.). (1982, 1993). *Handbook of stress: Theoretical and clinical aspects.* New York: Free Press.

Goodwin, P., Leszcz, M., Ennis, M., Koopmans, J., Vincent, L., & Guther, H. (2001). The effects of group psychosocial support on survival of metastic breast cancer. *The New England Journal of Medicine, 345,* 1719–1726.

Googins, B., & Davidson, B. (1993). The organization as client. *Social Work, 38,* 477–484.

Gordon, J. (2008). *Unstuck: Your guide to the seven stage journey out of depression.* New York: Penguin.

Gould, M., & Kramer, R. (2001). Youth suicide prevention. *Suicide and Life Threatening Behavior, 31,* 6–31.

Green, J. (1982). *Cultural awareness in the human services.* Englewood Cliffs, NJ: Prentice Hall.

Green, J. (1995). *Cultural awareness in the human services* (2nd ed.). Englewood Cliffs, NJ: Prentice Hall.

Greene, R. (1994). *Human behavior theory and social work practice: A diversity framework.* New York: Aldine de Gruyter.

Grinnell, R. (1973). Environmental modification: Casework's concern or casework's neglect? *Social Service Review, 47,* 208–220.

Gross, E. (1979, December). *Curanderismo, espiritismo, shamanism, and social work.* Unpublished paper, University of Michigan, Ann Arbor.

Gutierrez, L., & Lewis E. (1994). Community organizing with women of color: A feminist approach. *Journal of Community Practice, 1,* 23–44.

Gutierrez, L., & Lewis, E. (1999). *Empowering women of color.* New York: Columbia University Press.

Gutierrez, L., Lewis, E., Nagda, B., Wernick, L., & Shore, N. (2005). Multicultural community practice strategies and intergroup empowerment. In L. Weil (Ed.), *Handbook of community practice.* Thousand Oaks, CA: Sage.

Haley, J. (1973). *Uncommon therapy: The psychiatric techniques of Milton Erickson.* New York: W. W. Norton.

Haley, J. (1987). *Problem solving therapy: New strategies for effective family therapy* (2nd ed.). San Francisco: Jossey-Bass.

Halleck, S. (1963). The impact of professional dishonesty on behavior of disturbed adolescents. *Social Work, 8*(2), 48–55.

Hamilton, G. (1951). *Theory and practice of social casework* (2nd ed.). New York: Columbia University Press.

Haney, H., & Leibsohn, J. (2001). *Basic counseling responses in groups: A multimedia learning system for the helping professions.* Belmont, CA: Wadsworth.

Haney, W. V. (1969). The inference-observation confusion: The uncritical inference test. In M. S. Morian (Ed.), *Teaching general semantics.* San Francisco: International Society for General Semantics.

Hardman, D. (1975). Not with my daughter you don't! *Social Work, 20*(3), 278–285.

Hardy, K., & Laszloffy, T. (1995). The cultural genogram: Key to training culturally competent family therapists. *Journal of Marital and Family Therapy, 21,* 227–237.

Harmon, M. (1991). The use of group psychotherapy with cancer patients: A review of recent literature. *Journal of Specialists in Group Work, 16,* 56–61.

Harris, A., & Lurigio, A. (2007). Mental illness and violence: A brief review of research and assessment strategies. *Aggression and Violent Behavior, 12,* 542–551.

Hartman, A. (1978). Diagrammatic assessment of family relationships. *Social Casework, 59*(8), 465–476.

Hartman, A., & Laird, J. (1983). *Family-centered social work practice*. New York: Free Press.

Hartmann, T. (2006). *Screwed: The undeclared war against the middle class*. San Francisco: Berrett-Koehler Publishers.

Haus, A. (1988). *Working with homeless people: A guide for staff and volunteers*. New York: Columbia University Community Services.

Hawton, K., Appleby, L., Platt, S., Foster, T., Cooper, J., Malmberg, A., et al. (1998). The psychological autopsy approach to studying suicide: A review of methodological issues. *Journal of Affective Disorders, 50*, 269–276.

Hearn, G. (1993). General systems theory and social work. In F. Turner (Ed.), *Social work theory and skills* (4th ed.). Pacific Grove, CA: Brooks/Cole.

Herman, J. (1992). *Trauma and recovery*. New York: Basic Books.

Hill, R. (1972). *The strengths of African American families*. New York: Emerson Hall Publishers.

Hill, W. G. (1960). The family as a treatment unit: Differential techniques and procedures. *Social Work, 11*(2), 62–68.

Ho, M. K. (1987). *Family therapy with ethnic minorities*. Newbury Park, CA: Sage.

Hoefer, R. (2008). "Social welfare expenditures." In T. Mizrahi & L. E. Davis (Eds.), *Encyclopedia of social work*. Washington, DC, and New York: National Association of Social Workers and Oxford University Press, Inc. (e-reference edition).

Hoehn-Saric, R., Frank, J., Imber, S., Nash, E., Stone, A., & Battle, C. (1964). Systematic preparation for patients for psychotherapy. *Journal of Psychiatric Research, 2*, 267–281.

Hoff, L. A. (1989). *People in crisis* (3rd ed.). Redwood City, CA: Addison-Wesley.

Hoff, L. A. (2001). *People in crisis: Clinical and public health perspectives* (5th ed.). San Francisco: Jossey-Bass.

Hoffman, D., & Remmel, M. (1975). Uncovering the precipitant in crisis intervention. *Social Casework, 56*, 259–267.

Hoffman, L., & Long, L. (1969). A systems dilemma. *Family Process, 8*, 211–234.

Hollis, F. (1964). *Casework: A psychosocial therapy*. New York: Random House.

Hollis, F. (1968). *A typology of casework treatment*. New York: Family Service Association of America.

Hollis, F., & Woods, M. (1981). *Casework: A psychosocial therapy* (3rd ed.). New York: McGraw-Hill.

hooks, b. (1984). *Feminist theory: From margin to center*. Boston: South End Press.

Hopman, E., & Werk, A. (1994). A comparative study of family bereavement groups. *Death Studies, 18*, 243–256.

Howe, I. (1976). *World of our fathers*. New York: Simon & Schuster.

Hsu, C. (2010, February 18). Trauma focus added to MSW curriculum. *UB Reporter*. University of Buffalo, The State University of New York. Retrieved from http://www.buffalo.edu/ubreporter/2010_02_17/soci al_work_curriculum

Hudson, W. W. (1987). *The clinical assessment system*. Talahassee, FL: WALMYR.

Hulko, W. (2009). The time and context-contingent nature of intersectionality and interlocking oppressions. *Affilia, 24*(1), 44–55.

Iannelli, V. (2010). Child abuse statistics. *About.com guide*. Retrieved from http://pediatrics.about.com/od/childabuse/a/05_abuse_stats.htm

Imber-Black, E. (1988). *Families and larger systems: A family therapist's guide through the labyrinth*. New York: Guilford Press.

International Federation of Social Workers & International Association of Schools of Social Work (2004). *Ethics in social work, statement of principles*. Retrieved from http://www.ifsw.org/p38000324.html

Jackson, B., & Hardiman, R. (1994). Multicultural organizational development. In E. Cross, J. Katz, F. Miller, & E. Seashore (Eds.), *The promise of diversity*. New York: Irwin Press and NTL.

Jacobs, J. (1966). *The fables of Aesop*. New York: Shocken Books.

Janzen, C., & Harris, O. (1986). *Family treatment in social work practice* (2nd ed.). Itasca, IL: F. E. Peacock.

Janzen, C., Harris, O., Jordan, C., & Franklin, C. (2005). *Family treatment in social work: Evidence based practice with populations at risk* (4th ed.). Pacific Grove, CA: Brooks/Cole.

Jayaratne, S., Davis-Sacks, M. L., & Chess, W. (1991). Private practice may be good for your health and well-being. *Social Work, 36*(3), 224–229.

Jayaratne, S., & Levy, R. (1979). *Empirical clinical practice*. New York: Columbia University Press.

Jones, E. (1972). *Attribution: Perceiving the causes of behavior*. Morristown, NJ: General Learning Press.

Jones, R. (1977). *Self-fulfilling prophecies: Social, psychological, & physiological effects of expectances*. Hillsdale, NJ: Lawrence Erlbaum.

Jongsma, A., Peterson, M., & Jongsma, K. (1996). *TheraScribe for windows*. New York: John Wiley.

Jourard, S. (1971). *Self disclosure: An experimental analysis of the transparent self*. New York: John Wiley.

Kabat-Zinn, J. (1990). *Full catastrophe living: Using the wisdom of your body and mind to face stress, pain, and illness*. New York: Dell Publishing.

Kadushin, A. (1983). *The social work interview* (2nd ed.). New York: Columbia University Press.

Kantor, D., & Lehr, W. (1975). *Inside the family.* San Francisco: Jossey-Bass.

Kaplan, R. (1987). The current use of live supervision within marriage and family therapy training programs. *The Clinical Supervisor, 5*(3), 43–52.

Karls, J., & Wandrei, K. (1994a). PIE: A system for describing and classifying problems in social functioning. In J. Karls & K. Wandrei (Eds.), *Person-in-environment system.* Washington, DC: National Association of Social Workers.

Karls, J., & Wandrei, K. (1994b). *PIE manual: Person-in-environment system: The PIE classification system for social functioning problems.* Washington, DC: National Association of Social Workers.

Katz, D., & Kahn, R. (1966). *The social psychology of organizations.* New York: John Wiley.

Katz, J. (1988). *Facing the challenge of diversity and multiculturalism: Working paper series.* Ann Arbor, MI: Program in Conflict Management Alternatives.

Keefe, T. (1980). Empathy skills and critical consciousness. *Social Casework, 61,* 387–393.

Keefe, T., & Maypole, J. (1983). *Relationships in social work practice: Context and skills.* Monterey, CA: Brooks/Cole.

Kelley, P. (Ed.). (1990). *The uses of writing in psychotherapy.* New York: Haworth Press.

Kerner Commission. (1968). *Report of the national advisory commission on civil disorders.* Washington, DC: U.S. Government Printing Office.

Kessler, R., Soukup, J., Davis, R., Foster, D., Wilkey, S., Van Rompay, M., et al. (2001). The use of complementary and alternative therapies to treat anxiety and depression in the United States. *American Journal of Psychiatry, 158,* 289–294.

King, M. L., Jr. (1963, August 28). *I Have a Dream* [Speech]. Washington, DC: March on Washington for Jobs and Freedom.

Kiresuk, T., & Garwick, G. (1979). Basic goal attainment procedures. In B. R. Compton & B. Galaway (Eds.), *Social work processes* (2nd ed., pp. 412–421). Homewood, IL: Dorsey.

Kirk, R. S., & Griffith, D. P. (2004). Intensive family preservation services: Demonstrating placement prevention using event history analysis. *Social Work Research, 28*(1), 5–16.

Kirk, S. (1992). *The selling of DSM: The rhetoric of science in psychiatry.* New York: Aldine de Gruyter.

Kirk, S., & Greenley, J. (1974). Denying or delivering services. *Social Work, 19*(3), 439–447.

Klerman, G., Weissman, M., Rounsaville, B., & Chevron, E. (1984). *Interpersonal psychotherapy of depression.* New York: Basic Books.

Knapp, C. (1980). *Service contract use in preventing and reducing foster care: Final evaluation report.* Washington, DC: Administration on Children, Youth and Families, Department of Health, Education and Welfare.

Knowles, L., & Prewitt, K. (1969). *Institutional racism in America.* Englewood Cliffs, NJ: Prentice Hall.

Kopp, S. (1971). *Guru: Metaphors from a psychotherapist.* Palo Alto, CA: Science and Behavior Books.

Kounin, J. (1956). Experimental studies of clients' reactions to initial interviews. *Human Relations, 9,* 265–293.

Koyama, E., & Medve, T. (2003). LARA method of nonviolent response. In E. Koyama & T. Medve (Eds.), *A speaker's handbook for intersex activists & allies.* Portland, OR: Confluere Publications.

Kravetz, D. (1987). Benefits of consciousness-raising groups for women. In C. Brody (Ed.), *Women's therapy groups: Paradigms of feminist treatment.* New York: Springer.

Kravetz, D., & Rose, S. (1973). *Contracts in groups: A behavioral approach.* Dubuque, IA: Kendall Hunt.

Krupnick, J., Rowland, J. H., Goldberg, R. L., & Daniel, U. V. (1993). Professionally led support groups for cancer patients: An intervention in search of a model. *International Journal of Psychiatry in Medicine, 23,* 275–294.

Kuehl, B. P. (1995). The solution-focused genogram: A collaborative approach. *Journal of Marital and Family Therapy, 21,* 239–250.

Kursh, C. (1971). The benefits of poor communication. *The Psychoanalytic Review, 58,* 189–208.

Kurtz, L. F. (1997). *Self-help and support groups: A handbook for practitioners.* Thousand Oaks, CA: Sage.

L'Abate, L. (1992). *Programmed writing: A self administered approach for interventions for individuals, couples, and families.* Pacific Grove, CA: Brooks/Cole.

L'Abate, L. (1994). *Family evaluation: A psychological approach.* Thousand Oaks, CA: Sage.

Laird, J. (1988). Women and ritual in family. In E. Imber-Black, J. Roberts, & R. Whiting (Eds.), *Therapy rituals in families and family therapy.* New York: W. W. Norton.

Laird, J. (1993). *Revisioning social work education.* New York: Haworth.

Laird, J., & Hartman, A. (1987). Women, rituals, and family therapy. *Journal of Psychotherapy and the Family, 3,* 157–173.

Lambert, M. (2004). *Bergen and Garfield's handbook of psychotherapy and behavior change.* New York: John Wiley.

Lambert, M., & Bergen, A. (1994). The effectiveness of psychotherapy. In A. Bergen & S. Garfeld (Eds.),

Handbook of psychotherapy and behavior change (4th ed., pp. 143–189). New York: John Wiley.

Lange, A. I., & Jakubowski, P. K. (1976). *Responsible assertive behavior*. Champaign, IL: Research Press.

Lantz, J., & Lenahan, B. (1976). Referral fatigue therapy. *Social Work, 12*(3), 239–240.

Lazarus, A. (1977). *In the mind's eye: The power of imagery for personal enrichment*. New York: Guilford Press.

Lederer, W., & Burdick, E. (1958). *The ugly American*. Greenwich, CT: Fawcett Publications.

Leiderman, M., Guzetta, C., Struminger, L., & Monnickendam, M. (Eds.). (1993). *Technology in people services*. New York: Haworth.

Lennard, H., & Bernstein, A. (1970). *Patterns in human interaction*. San Francisco: Jossey-Bass.

Lenrow, P. (1982). The work of helping strangers. In H. Rubenstein & M. H. Block (Eds.), *Things that matter influences in helping relationships* (pp. 41–57). New York: Macmillan.

Lens, V. (2004). Principled negotiation: A new tool for case advocacy. *Social Work, 49*, 503–513.

Lens, V. (2005). Advocacy and argumentation in the public arena: A guide for social workers. *Social Work, 50*(3), 231–238.

Leonard, M. (1972). Mutuality as a catalytic power for growth. *Social Casework, 53*, 67–72.

Leveton, E. (1992). *A clinician's guide to psychodrama*. New York: Springer.

Levinger, G. (1960). Continuance in casework and other helping relationships: A review. *Social Work, 5*(3), 40–51.

Levy-Simon, B. (1994). *The empowerment tradition in American social work: A history*. New York: Columbia University Press.

Lewis, E. (1993). Continuing the legacy: On the importance of praxis in the education of social work students and teachers. In D. Schoem, L. Frankel, X. Zuniga, & F. Lewis (Eds.), *Multicultural teaching in the university*. New York: Praeger.

Lewis, E. (1995). Toward a tapestry of impassioned voices: Incorporating praxis into teaching about families. *Family Relations, 44*(2), 149–152.

Lewis, E. (2009). Group versus individual-based intersectionality and praxis in feminist and womanist research foundations. In S. A. Lloyd, A. L. Few, & K. R. Allen (Eds.), *Handbook of feminist family studies* (pp. 304–315). Thousand Oaks, CA: Sage.

Liberman, B., Frank, J., Hoehn-Saric, R., Stone, A., Imber, S., & Pande, S. (1972). Patterns of change in treated psychoneurotic patients: A five year follow-up investigation of the systematic preparation of patients for psychotherapy. *Journal of Consulting and Clinical Psychology, 38*(1), 36–41.

Liberman, R., DeRisi, W., & Mueser, K. (1989). *Social skills training for psychiatric patients*. New York: Pergamon.

Lieberman, R., & Yager, J. (Eds.). (1994). *Stress in psychiatric disorders*. New York: Springer.

Liebmann, M. (1986). *Art therapy for groups: A handbook of themes, games, and exercises*. Cambridge, MA: Brookline Books.

Lindenberg, R. E. (1958). Hard to reach: Client or casework agency. *Social Work, 3*(4), 23–29.

Lippitt, R., Watson, J., & Westley, B. (1958). *The dynamics of planned change: A comparative study of principles and techniques*. New York: Harcourt, Brace and World.

Lipsky, M. (1980). *Street level bureaucracy*. New York: Russell Sage Foundation.

Longfellow, H. W. (1902). *The complete poetical works of Henry Wadsworth Longfellow*. Boston: Houghton Mifflin.

Longres, J. (1990). *Human behavior in the social environment*. Itasca, IL: F. E. Peacock.

Longres, J., & McLeod, E. (1980). Consciousness raising and social work practice. *Social Casework, 61*, 267–276.

Lubove, R. (1969). *The professional altruist*. New York: Atheneum.

Luft, J., & Ingham, H. (1955). The Johari window, a graphic model of interpersonal awareness. *Proceedings of the western training laboratory in group development*. Los Angeles: UCLA.

Lukton, R. (1974). Crisis theory: Review and critique. *Social Service Review, 48*(3), 385–391.

Lum, D. (1992). *Social work practice and people of color: A process stage approach*. Pacific Grove, CA: Brooks/Cole.

Lum, D. (Ed.). (2005). *Cultural competence, practice stages, and client systems*. Belmont, CA: Thompson Brooks Cole.

Lyon, E., Moore, N., & Lexius, C. (1992). Group work with families of homicide victims. *Social Work with Groups, 15*, 19–33.

MacGregor, R., Ritchie, M., Serrano, A., & Schuster, F. (1964). *Multiple impact therapy with families*. New York: McGraw-Hill.

MacKain, S., Soy, R., & Lieberman, R. (1994). Can coping and competence override stress and vulnerability in schizophrenia? In R. Lieberman & J. Yager (Eds.), *Stress in psychiatric disorders* (pp. 53–82). New York: Springer.

Mailich, M., & Ashley, A. (1981). Politics of interprofessional collaboration: Challenge to advocacy. *Social Casework, 62*(3), 131–137.

Maluccio, A. (1975). Action as a tool in casework practice. *Social Casework, 55*(1), 30–35.

Maluccio, A. (1979a). *Learning from clients: Interpersonal helping as viewed by clients and social workers*. New York: Free Press.

Maluccio, A. (1979b). Promoting competence through life experiences. In C. Germain (Ed.), *Social work practice: People and environments* (pp. 282–302). New York: Columbia University Press.

Maluccio, A. (1981). *Promoting competence in clients: A new/old approach to social work practice.* New York: Free Press.

Maluccio, A., & Marlow, W. (1974). The case for contract. *Social Work, 19*(1), 28–35.

Mann, J. (1973). *Time limited psychotherapy.* Cambridge, MA: Harvard University Press.

Maple, F. (1977). *Shared decision making.* Beverly Hills, CA: Sage.

Marger, M. (1994). *Race and ethnic relations: American and global perspectives* (3rd ed.). Belmont, CA: Wadsworth.

Maris, R., Berman, A., Maltsberger, J., & Yufit, R. (1992). *Assessment and prediction of suicide.* New York: Guilford Press.

Marshak, R., & Katz, J. (1992). The symbolic side of OD. *OD Practitioner, 24*(2), 1–5.

Martin, B., & Mohanty, C. (1986). Feminist politics: What's home got to do with it? In T. DeLauretis (Ed.), *Feminist studies/critical studies* (pp. 195–210). Bloomington: University of Indiana Press.

Marziali, E. (1988). The first session: An interpersonal encounter. *Social Casework, 69*(1), 23–27.

Maslow, A. (1954). *Motivation and personality.* New York: Harper and Brothers.

Mayer, J., & Timms, N. (1969). Clash in perspective between worker and client. *Social Casework, 50*(1), 32–40.

McAdams, D. (1993). *Stories we live by: Personal myths and the making of the self.* New York: William Morrow and Co.

McArdle, T. (1995). The (im)migrant community as a context for practice. Unpublished preliminary exam, University of Michigan School of Social Work, Ann Arbor.

McCleary, R. (1978). On becoming a client. *Journal of Social Issues, 34*, 57–75.

McGoldrick, M., Giordano, J., & Garcia-Preto, N. (Eds.). (2005). *Ethnicity and family therapy* (3rd ed). New York: Guilford Press.

McGoldrick, M., Pearce, M., & Giordano, J. (Eds.). (1982). *Ethnicity and family therapy.* New York: Guilford Press.

McIntosh, P. (1995). White privilege and male privilege: A personal account of coming to see correspondences through work in women's studies. In M. L. Anderson & P. H. Collins (Eds.), *Race, class, and gender: An anthology* (2nd ed., pp. 70–82). Belmont, CA: Wadsworth.

McWhirter, E. H. (1994). *Counseling for empowerment.* Alexandria, VA: American Counseling Association.

Medline Plus. (2009, October, 8). *Drug abuse.* Retrieved from www.nlm.nih.gov/medlineplus/drugabuse.html

Mehrabian, A. (1972). *Nonverbal behavior.* Chicago: Aldine.

Meier, A. (2004). Technology-mediated groups. In C. Garvin, L. Gutierrez, & M. Galinsky (Eds.), *Handbook of social work with groups* (pp. 479–503). New York: Guilford Press.

Mencher, S. (1967). *Poor law to poverty program.* Pittsburgh: University of Pittsburgh Press.

Meyer, C. (1976). *Social work practice: The changing landscape* (2nd ed.). New York: Free Press.

Meyer, I. (2007). Prejudice, social stress and mental health in lesbian, gay, and bisexual populations: Conceptual issues and research. *Psychological Bulletin, 129*(5), 674–697.

Meyerson, D. (1989). *The social construction of ambiguity and burnout: A study of hospital social workers.* Unpublished doctoral dissertation, Stanford University Press, Palo Alto, CA.

Michigan Self-Help Clearinghouse. (2010). Retrieved from http://www.mpas.org/mshc1.asp

Middleman, R., & Goldberg G. (1974). *Social service delivery: A structural approach to social work practice.* New York: Columbia University Press.

Miller, T. (1989). *Stressful life events.* Madison, CT: International Universities Press.

Miller, W. L. (1980). Casework and the medical metaphor. *Social Work, 25*(3), 281–285.

Miller, W. R., & Rollnick, S. (2002). *Motivational interviewing: Preparing people for change* (2nd ed.). New York: Guilford Press.

Milnes, J., & Bertcher, H. (1980). *Communicating empathy.* San Diego: University Associates.

Minuchin, S., & Fishman, H. C. (1981). *Family therapy techniques.* Cambridge, MA: Harvard University Press.

Mizio, E. (1972). White worker—minority client. *Social Work, 17*(5), 82–86.

Morgan, G. (1986). *Images of organization.* Beverly Hills, CA: Sage.

Mosley, J. E., Stoesz, D., Cnaan, R. A., Koney, L., & Lopez, K. M. (2008). Contexts/Settings. In T. Mizrahi & L. E. Davis (Eds.), *Encyclopedia of social work.* New York: Oxford University Press.

Mount, S. (2010). *The Constitution explained.* Retrieved from http://www.usconstitution.net/ consttop_mlaw.html

Mowbray, C., Wooley, M., Grogan-Kaylor, A., Gant, L., Glister, M., & Shanks, T. (2007). Neighborhood research from a spatially oriented strengths perspective. *Journal of Community Psychology, 35*, 667–680.

Moxley, D. (1989). *The practice of case management.* Newbury Park, CA: Sage.

Moxley, D., & Freddolino, P. (1994). Client-driven advocacy and psychiatric disability: A model for social work practice. *Journal of Sociology and Social Welfare, 21*, 91–108.

Nagda, B. A. (2006). Breaking barriers, crossing boundaries, building bridges: Communication processes in intergroup dialogues. *Journal of Social Issues, 62*(3), 553–576.

Nagda, B. A., Kim, C. W., & Truelove, Y. (2004). Learning about difference, learning with others, learning to transgress. *Journal of Social Issues, 60*(1), 195–214.

Nathan, P., & Gorman, J. (2002). *A guide to treatments that work*. New York: Oxford Press.

National Association of Black Social Workers. (2010). *Code of ethics*. Retrieved from http://www.nabsw.org/mserver/CodeofEthics.aspx

National Association of Social Workers. (2009). *Social work speaks: NASW policy statements* (8th ed.). Washington, DC: Author.

National Association of Social Workers. (2010). *Social workers and "duty to warn" state laws*. Retrieved from www.socialworkers.org/ldf/legal_issue/2008/200802.asp?back=yes

National Association of Social Workers Delegate Assembly. (2008). *Code of ethics*. Retrieved from http://www.socialworkers.org/pubs/code/code.asp

National Institute on Drug Abuse. (2005). *NIDA InfoFacts: Hospital visits*. Retrieved from www.drugabuse.gov/infofacts/HospitalVisits.html

National Institute on Drug Abuse. (2010). *Diagnosis & treatment of drug abuse in family practice: Drug use questionnaire*. Retrieved from http://archives.drugabuse.gov/diagnosis-treatment/DAST10.html

Nelson, H. W., Netting, F. E., Huber, R., & Borders, K. (2001). The social worker–ombudsman partnership: Using a resident-centered model of situational conflict tactics. *Journal of Gerontological Social Work, 35*, 65–81.

Newman, P., Bogo, M., & Daley, A. (2008). Self-disclosure of sexual orientation in social work field education. *Clinical Supervisor, 27*(2), 215–237.

Nickel, G. (1942a). Evacuation, American style. *Survey Midmonthly, 78*, 99–103.

Nickel, G. (1942b). Evacuation, American style—Part two. *Survey Midmonthly, 78*, 262–265.

Nurius, P., & Hudson, W. (1993). *Human services practice, evaluation, and computers: A practical guide for today and beyond*. Pacific Grove, CA: Brooks/Cole.

Nye, F. I. (1976). *Role structure and analysis of the family*. Beverly Hills, CA: Sage.

O'Hanlon, W., & Weiner-Davis, M. (1989). *In search of solutions*. New York: W. W. Norton.

Orlinsky, D., Grawe, K., & Parks, B. (1994). The relation of process and outcome in psychotherapy. In A. B. Bergen & S. L. Garfield (Eds.), *Handbook of psychotherapy and behavior change* (4th ed., pp. 270–378). New York: Wiley.

Ott, S. J. (1989). *The organization culture perspective*. Pacific Grove, CA: Brooks/Cole.

Overall, B., & Aronson, H. (1963). Expectations of psychotherapy in patients of lower socioeconomic class. *American Journal of Orthopsychiatry, 33*, 421–430.

Overton, A., Tinker, K. H., & Associates. (1958). *Casework notebook: Family centered project*. St. Paul, MN: United Way.

Oyersman, D. (2009). Identity-based motivation: Implications for action-readiness, procedural readiness, and consumer behavior. *Journal of Consumer Psychology, 19*, 250–260.

Oyersman, D., & Benbenishty, R. (1993). The impact of clinical information systems on human service organizations. In M. Leiderman et al. (Eds.), *Technology in people services: Research, theory, & application* (pp. 425–438). New York: Haworth.

Palmer, T. (1973). Matching worker and client in corrections. *Social Work, 18*(2), 95–103.

Paniagua, F. (1998). *Assessing and treating culturally diverse clients: A practical guide* (2nd ed.). Thousand Oaks, CA: Sage.

Papp, P., Silverstein, O., & Carter, E. (1973). Family sculpting in preventive work with "well families." *Family Process, 12*, 197–212.

Parloff, M., Waskow, I., & Wolfe, B. (1978). Research on therapist variables in relation to process and outcome. In A. Bergin & S. Garfield (Eds.), *Handbook of psychotherapy and behavior change* (2nd ed., pp. 233–282). New York: John Wiley.

Patti, R. (1974). Organizational resistance and change: The view from below. *Social Service Review, 48*, 367–383.

Patti, R., & Resnick, H. (1972). Changing the agency from within. *Social Work, 17*(3), 48–57.

Pavenstedt, E., & Malone, C. (1967). *The drifters: Children of disorganized lower-class families*. Boston: Little, Brown.

Pecora, P., Fraser, M., & Haapala, D. (1991). Client outcomes and issues for program design. In K. Wells & D. Biegel (Eds.), *Family preservation services: Research and evaluation*. Newbury Park, CA: Sage.

Pelz, D., & Remley, A. (n.d.). *Principles of respectful dialogue: Suggested guidelines for effective communication on controversial issues*. Retrieved from www.quakerpi.org/QActivism/Compassionate%20listening.pdf

Perlman, H. H. (1957). *Social casework: A problem solving process*. Chicago: University of Chicago Press.

Perlman, H. H. (1960). Intake and some role considerations. *Social Casework, 41*, 171–177.

Perlman, H. H. (1968). *Persona: Social role and personality*. Chicago: University of Chicago Press.

Perlman, H. H. (1979). *Relationship: The heart of helping people*. Chicago: University of Chicago Press.

Perry, B. D. (1999). Memories of fear: How the brain stores and retrieves physiologic states, feelings, behaviors, and thoughts from traumatic events. In J. M. Goodwin & R. Attias (Eds.), *Splintered reflections: Images of the body in trauma*. New York: Basic Books.

Pfeiffer, J. W., & Jones, J. E. (1975). *A handbook of structured experiences for human relations training—Vol. I–V*. LaJolla, CA: University Associates.

Pick, M. (2010). *Emotional well-being and the Emotional Freedom Technique (EFT)*. Women to Women. Retrieved from http://www.womentowomen.com/emotionsandhealth/emotionalfreedomtechnique.aspx

Pincus, A., & Minahan, A. (1973). *Social work practice: Model and methods*. Itasca, IL: F. E. Peacock.

Pines, M. (Ed.). (1985). *Bion and group psychotherapy*. London: Routledge & Keegan Paul.

Plionis, E., & Lewis, H. (1995). Teaching cultural diversity and oppression: Preparation for risk—The Cloverdale model. *Journal of Teaching in Social Work, 12*(1/2), 175–192.

Pondy, L. (1983). The role of metaphors and myths in organization and in the facilitation of change. In L. Pondy, P. Frost, G. Morgan, & T. Dandridge (Eds.), *Organizational symbolism* (pp. 157–166). Greenwich, CT: JAI Press.

Post, E. (1992). *Emily Post's etiquette*. New York: HarperCollins.

Powell, T. (1976). The use of self-help groups as supportive communities. *American Journal of Orthopsychiatry, 45*, 756–764.

Powell, T. (Ed.). (1990). *Working with self help*. Silver Spring, MD: National Association of Social Workers.

Progoff, I. (1975). *At an intensive journal workshop*. New York: Dialogue House Library.

Psych Central. (2006). *Domest violence screening quiz*. Retrieved from http://psychcentral.com/dvquiz.htm

Psych Web. (2008). *Psychology self-help resources on the Internet*. Retrieved from http://www.psychwww.com/resource/selfhelp.htm

Queralt, M. (1996). *The social environment*. Boston: Allyn & Bacon.

Rand, A., & Peikoff, L. (1943). *The fountainhead*. Indianapolis, IN: Bobbs-Merrill.

Rapoport, A. (1974). *Game theory as a theory of conflict resolution*. The Netherlands: D. Reidel Publishers.

Reamer, F. G. (1983). Ethical dilemmas in social work practice. *Social Work, 28*(1), 31–35.

Reamer, F. G. (2006). *Social work values and ethics* (3rd ed.). New York: Columbia University Press.

Reid, K. (1997). *Social work with groups* (2nd ed.). Pacific Grove, CA: Brooks/Cole.

Reid, W. (1975). Test of a task-centered approach. *Social Work, 20*(1), 3–9.

Reid, W. (1978). *The task-centered system*. New York: Columbia University Press.

Reid, W., & Epstein, L. (1972). *Task-centered casework*. New York: Columbia University Press.

Rein, M. (1970). *Social policy: Issues of choice and change*. New York: Random House.

Reissman, F. (1967). The helper-therapy principle. In G. Brager & F. Purcell (Eds.), *Community action against poverty* (pp. 217–226). New Haven, CT: Yale College and University Press.

Rendleman, R. (2009). *2009 in review: People: The legacy of Bonnie Tin*ker. Retrieved from www.justout.com

Resnick, H., & Patti, R. (1972). Changing the organization from within. *Social Work, 17*(3), 48–57.

Resnick, H., & Patti, R. (1980). *Humanizing social welfare organizations*. Philadelphia: Temple University Press.

Reynolds, B. (1951). *Social work and social living*. New York: Citadel.

Richan, W. (1973). Dilemmas of social work advocates. *Child Welfare, 52*, 220–226.

Richmond, M. (1922). *What is social casework*. New York: Russell Sage Foundation.

Ridgeway, C. (1992). *Gender, interaction, and inequality*. New York: Springer-Verlag.

Riley, P. (1971). Family advocacy: From case to cause and back to case. *Child Welfare, 50*, 374–383.

Ripple, L., Alexander, E., & Polemis, B. (1964). *Motivation, capacity, and opportunity: Studies in casework theory and practice*. Chicago: School of Social Service Administration, University of Chicago Press.

Robbins, A. (2010). Newer perspectives on domestic violence. *Psychiatric Times*. Retrieved from www.psychiatrictimes.com/display/article/10168/1546465

Roberto, L. (1991). Symbolic-experiential family therapy. In A. S. Gurman & D. P. Kniskern (Eds.), *Handbook of family therapy* (Vol. 2). New York: Brunner/Mazel.

Roberts, A. (1990). *Crisis intervention handbook*. Belmont, CA: Wadsworth.

Roberts, A. (2005). *Crisis intervention handbook: Assessment, treatment, and research*. New York: Oxford University Press.

Roberts, R., & Nee, R. (Eds.). (1970). *Theories of social casework*. Chicago: University of Chicago Press.

Roberts, R., & Northen, H. (Eds.). (1976). *Theories of social work with groups*. New York: Columbia University Press.

Rogers, C. (1957). The necessary and sufficient conditions of therapeutic personality change. *Journal of Consulting Psychology, 21*, 95–103.

Rooney, R. (Ed.). (2009). *Strategies for work with involuntary clients* (2nd ed.). New York: Columbia University Press.

Roosevelt, T. (1991). *Beyond race and gender: Unleashing the power of your total work force by managing diversity*. New York: AMACOM, American Management Association.

Root-Bernstein, R., & Root-Bernstein, M. (1997). *Honey, mud, maggots, and other medical marvels: The science behind folk remedies and old wives' tales*. Boston: Houghton Mifflin.

Rosano, M., Rotheram-Borus, M. J., & Reid, H. (1998). Gay-related stress and its correlates among gay and bisexual male adolescents of predominately Black and Hispanic backgrounds. *Journal of Community Psychology, 24*(2), 136–159.

Rose, S. (1977). *Group therapy: A behavioral approach*. Englewood Cliffs, NJ: Prentice Hall.

Rosenbloom, D., & Williams, M. B. (1999). *Life after trauma*. New York: Guilford Press.

Rosenfeld, J. (1964). Strangeness between helper and client: A possible explanation on non-use of available professional help. *Social Service Review, 38*, 17–25.

Rossi, E. (1986). *The psychobiology of mind-body healing*. New York: W. W. Norton.

Rothman, J. (1992). *Guidelines for case management: Putting research to professional use*. Itasca, IL: F. E. Peacock.

Rothman, J. (1994). *Practice with highly vulnerable clients: Case management and community based services*. Englewood Cliffs, NJ: Prentice Hall.

Rouse, R. (1991). Mexican immigration and the social space of postmodernism. *Diaspora, 1*(1), 8–24.

Rubenstein, H., & Bloch, M. (Eds.). (1982). *Things that matter: Influences in helping relationships*. New York: Macmillan.

Rueveni, U. (1979). *Networking families in crisis*. New York: Human Sciences Press.

Russel, R. (1998). Spirituality and religion in graduate social work education. In E. R. Canda (Ed.), *Spirituality in social work: New directions* (pp. 15–29). New York: Longman.

Ryan, W. (1976). *Blaming the victim*. New York: Vintage Books.

Sandell, M. (2009). *Justice: What's the right thing to do?* New York: Farrar, Straus, & Giroux.

Satir, V. (1972). *Peoplemaking*. New York: Science and Behavior Books.

Satir, V. (1988). *The new peoplemaking*. Mountain View, CA: Science and Behavior Books.

Scheflen, A. (1974). *How behavior means*. Garden City, NY: Doubleday.

Schein, H. (1971). Organizational socialization. In B. L. Hinton & H. J. Reitz (Eds.), *Groups and organizations* (pp. 210–215). Belmont, CA: Wadsworth.

Schiller, L. (2003). Women's group development from a relational model and a new look at facilitator influence on group development. In M. Cohen & A. Mullender (Eds.), *Gender and group work* (pp. 16–31). New York: Routledge.

Schneider, R. L., & Lester, L. (2001). *Social work advocacy: A new framework for action*. Belmont, CA: Wadsworth.

Schneider, R. L., & Lori, L. (2000). *Social advocacy: A new framework for action*. Pacific Grove, CA: Brooks/Cole.

Schneider, R., & Netting, E. (1999). Influencing social policy in a time of devolution: Upholding social work's great tradition. *Social Work, 44*, 349–357.

Schuerman, J., Rzepnicki, T., & Littell, J. (1994). *Putting families first: An experiment in family preservation*. New York: Aldine De Gruyter.

Schwartz, W. (1969). Private troubles and public issues: One social work job or two. *The social welfare forum, Proceeding of the national conference on social welfare, 1969* (pp. 22–43). New York: Columbia University Press.

Schwartz, W. (1976). Between client and system: The mediating function. In R. W. Roberts & H. Northen (Eds.), *Theories of social work with groups* (pp. 171–197). New York: Columbia University Press.

Schwartz, W. (1994). The social worker in the group. In T. Berman-Rossi (Ed.), *Social work: The collected writings of William Schwartz* (pp. 257–276). Itasca, IL: F. E. Peacock.

Science Daily. (2008, April 22). *Counseling trauma victims causes secondary trauma, study shows*. Retrieved from http://www.sciencedaily.com/releases/2008/04/080421170211.htm

Scott, C., & Resnick, P. (2006).Violence risk assessment in persons with mental illness. *Aggression and Violent Behavior, 11*, 598–611.

Seaburg, J. R. (1965). Case recording by code. *Social Work, 10*(4), 92–98.

Seaburg, J. R. (1970). Systematized recording: A follow up. *Social Work, 15*(4), 32–41.

Seabury, B. (1971). Arrangement of physical space in social work practice. *Social Work, 17*(4), 43–49.

Seabury, B. (1976). The contract: Uses, abuses, and limitations. *Social Work, 21*(1), 16–21.

Seabury, B. (1979). Negotiating sound contracts with clients. *Public Welfare, 37*(Spring), 33–38.

Seabury, B. (1980). Communication problems in social work practice. *Social Work, 25*(1), 40–44.

Seabury, B. (1983, November 3). *Agency change from low power positions: Radical practice for the 80s*. Unpublished paper presented at the Annual Conference of Voluntary Action Scholars and Lincoln Filene Center for Citizenship and Public Affairs, Boston.

Seabury, B. (1995). *Types of groups*. PowerPoint Presentation, Introduction to Interpersonal Practice, University of Michigan, Ann Arbor.

Seabury, B. (2001, June 30). *Banditry: A disobedient role for reactionary times*. PowerPoint Presentation, Social Welfare Action Alliance, National Conference, Philadelphia.

Seabury, B. (2005). An evaluation of online, interactive tutorials designed to teach practice skills. *Journal of Teaching in Social Work*, *25*(1/2), 105–115.

Seabury, B., & Burton, D. (1999). The 'virtual' social work course: Promises and pitfalls. *New Technology in the Human Services*, *12*(3/4), 55–64.

Seabury, B., & Foster, M. (1982, June 11). *Racism and sexism in social work agencies: Casing your agency from within*. Paper presented at the NASW Minority Issues Conference, Los Angeles.

Seabury, B., & Lewis, E. (1994, March 6). *The organizational climate questionnaire: Addressing sexism and racism in social work institutions*. Paper presented at APM '94. CSWE, Atlanta, GA.

Selby, L. (1956). Supportive treatment: The development of a concept and a helping method. *Social Service Review*, *30*, 400–414.

Shapiro, F. (2001). *Eye movement desensitization and reprocessing (EMDR): Basic principles, protocols, and procedures* (2nd ed.). New York: Guilford Press.

Shaw, G. B. (1957). Maxims for revolutionists. *Man and superman*. New York: Penguin Classics.

Sheridan, M., & Amato-von Hemert, K. (1999). The role of religion and spirituality in social work education and practice. *Journal of Social Work Education*, *28*(2), 190–203.

Sherman, W. R., & Wenocur, S. (1983). Empowering public welfare workers through mutual support. *Social Work*, *28*, 375–379.

Shields, S. A. (2008). Gender: An intersectionality perspective. *Sex Roles*, *59*, 301–311.

Shneidman, E. S. (1985). *Definition of suicide*. New York: John Wiley.

Shneidman, E. S., Farberow, N., & Litman, R. (1970). *The psychology of suicide*. New York: Science House.

Shulman, E. (1978). *Intervention in human services* (2nd ed.). St. Louis, MO: C. V. Mosby.

Shulman, L. (1979). *The skills of helping: Individuals and groups*. Itasca, IL: F. E. Peacock.

Shyne, A. (1957). What research tells us about short term cases in family agencies. *Social Casework*, *38*, 223–231.

Siegel, D. H. (1984). Defining empirically based practice. *Social Work*, *29*, 325–331.

Silverman, P. (1970). A re-examination of the intake procedure. *Social Casework*, *51*, 625–634.

Simmons, L. (1972). Agency financing and social change. *Social Work*, *17*(1), 62–67.

Simon, G. E., & Von Korff, M. (1998). Suicide mortality among patients treated for depression in an insured population. *American Journal of Epidemiology*, *147*, 155–160.

Singer, B. (1978). Assessing social errors. *Social Policy*, (Sept./Oct.), 27–34.

Smith, J. (2005). *Relaxation, meditation & mindfulness: A mental health practitioner's guide to new and traditional approaches*. New York: Springer.

Smith, M., Glass, G., & Miller, T. (1980). *The benefits of psychotherapy*. Baltimore: Johns Hopkins University Press.

Sommer, R. (1969). *Personal Space: The Behavioral Basis of Design*, Englewood Cliffs, NJ: Spectrum.

Southern Poverty Law Center. (2010). *Teaching tolerance*. Retrieved from http://www.splcenter.org/what-we-do/teaching-tolerance

Specht, H. (1969). Disruptive tactics. *Social Work*, *14*(2), 5–15.

Spencer, M. S. (2001). Identity and multicultural social work research: A reflective process. *Advances in Social Work*, *2*(1), 1–11.

Spencer, M. S., & Martineau, D. J. (in press). Facilitation training for dialogues on diversity and social justice: Skills for multicultural social work practice. In K. Maxwell, M. Thompson, & B. Nagda (Eds.), *Facilitating intergroup dialogues: Training models, pedagogical practices and research*. Sterling, VA: Stylus Publishing.

Spiegal, D. (1990). Can psychology prolong cancer survival? *Psychosomatics*, *31*, 361–366.

Spiegal, D., Butler, L. D., Giese-Davis, J., Koopman, C., Miller, E., DiMiceli, S., et al. (2007). Effects of supportive-expressive group therapy on survival of patients with metastic breast cancer: A randomized prospective trial. *Cancer*, *110*, 1130–1138.

Speigel, J. (1964). Some cultural aspects of transference and countertransference. In F. Reissman, J. Cohen, & A. Pearl (Eds.), *Mental health of the poor* (pp. 302–320). New York: Free Press.

Spiegel, J. (1974). *Transactions*. New York: Basic Books.

Steadman, H. J., & Cocozza, J. J. (1974). *Careers of the criminally insane: Excessive social control of deviance*. Lexington, MA: Lexington Books.

Stein, T. (1981). *Social work practice in child welfare*. Englewood Cliffs, NJ: Prentice Hall.

Stein, T., & Gambrill, E. (1977). Facilitating decision making in foster care. *Social Service Review*, *51*, 502–513.

Stein, T., Gambrill, E., & Wiltse, K. (1974). Foster care: The use of contracts. *Public Welfare*, *32*(1), 20–25.

Steiner, C. (1983). *The original warm fuzzy tale*. Fawnskin, CA: Jamar Press.

Stotland, E. (1969). *The psychology of hope*. San Francisco: Jossey-Bass.

Straus, M. A. (1979). Measuring family violence: The conflict tactics scale. *Journal of Marriage and the Family*, *41*, 87.

Strean, H. (1985). *Therapeutic principles in practice: A manual for clinicians*. Beverly Hills, CA: Sage.

Stuart, R. (1970). *Trick or treatment: How and when psychotherapy fails.* Champaign, IL: Research Press.

Suarez, Z. F. (1993). Cuban Americans: From golden exiles to social undesirables. In H. P. McAdoo (Ed.), *Family ethnicity: Strength in diversity.* Newbury Park, CA: Sage.

Suarez, Z. F., & Lewis, E. (2005). Spirituality and culturally diverse families: The intersection of culture, religion, and spirituality. In E. P. Congress & M. J. Gonzalez (Eds.), *Multicultural perspectives in working with families* (2nd ed.). New York: Springer.

Suarez, Z., Newman, P., & Reed, B. (2008). Critical consciousness and cross-cultural social work practice: A case analysis. *Families in Society, 89*(3), 1–11.

Sue, D. (1981). *Counseling the culturally different.* New York: John Wiley.

Sue, D., & Sue, D. (2007). *Counseling the culturally diverse: Theory and practice* (5th ed.). New York: John Wiley.

Sundel, M., Glasser, P., Sarri, R., & Vinter, R. (1985). *Individual change through small groups* (2nd ed.). New York: Free Press.

Sunley, R. (1970). Family advocacy: From case to cause. *Social Casework, 51,* 347–357.

Suskie, L. (2009). *Assessing student learning: A common sense guide.* San Francisco: Jossey-Bass.

Swigonski, M. (1994). The logic of feminist standpoint theory for social work. *Social Work, 39*(4), 387–393.

T, B. (2010, May 1). *Short alcohol tests ideal for healthcare screening: Initial diagnosis can be followed up with in-depth testing.* About.com: Alcoholism. Retrieved from http://alcoholism.about.com/od/tests/a/tests.htm

Talmon, M. (1990). *Single-session therapy.* San Francisco: Jossey-Bass.

Temes, R. (2006). *Tapping the cure: A revolutionary system for rapid relief from phobias, anxieties, post traumatic stress disorders and more.* New York: Marlowe.

Thomas, E. (1967). Problems of disability from the perspective of role theory. In E. Thomas (Ed.), *Behavioral science for social workers.* New York: Free Press.

Thomas, E., & Feldman, R. (1967). Concepts of role theory. In E. Thomas (Ed.), *Behavioral science for social workers.* New York: Free Press.

Thorsheim, J. L. (2005). *Guide to using the Kvebæk Sculpture Technique (KST).* Retrieved from www.healthyhumansystems.com

Thurow, L. (1994). To count or not to count by race and gender. In R. Takaki (Ed.), *From different shores: Perspectives on race and ethnicity in America* (2nd ed.). New York: Oxford University Press.

Thursz, D. (1976). Social action as a professional responsibility. *Social Work, 21,* 42–52.

Tolson, E., Reid, W., & Garvin, C. (1994). *Generalist practice in social work: A task-centered approach.* New York: Columbia University Press.

Toren, N. (1973). The structure of social casework and behavior change. *Journal of Social Policy, 3,* 341–352.

Toseland, R., & Rivas, R. (2008). *An introduction to group work practice* (6th ed.). Boston: Allyn & Bacon.

Tracy, E., & Whittaker, J. (1990). The social network map: Assessing social support in clinical practice. *Families in Society, 71*(8), 461–470.

Trice, J., & Beyer, J. (1984). Studying organizational cultures through rites and ceremonials. *Academy of Management Review, 9,* 653–669.

Tropman, J. (1995). *Effective meetings: Improving group decision-making* (2nd ed.). Thousand Oaks, CA: Sage.

Tropman, J., & Morningstar, G. (1989). *Entrepreneurial systems for the 1990s: Their creation, structure, & management.* New York: Quorum Books.

Trotman, F., & Gallagher, A. (1987). Group therapy with black women. In E. Brody (Ed.), *Women's therapy groups: Paradigms of feminist treatment* (pp. 118–131). New York: Springer.

Truax, C., & Carkhuff, R. (1976). *Toward effective counseling and psychotherapy.* Chicago: Aldine de Gruyter.

Tsoukas, H. (1991). The missing link: A transformational view of metaphors in organizational science. *Academy of Management Review, 16,* 566–585.

Tufte, E. (1983). *The visual display of quantitative information.* Chesire, CT: Graphics Press.

Turner, F. (Ed.). (1996). *Social work treatment: Interlocking theoretical approaches* (4th ed.). New York: Free Press.

United Nations. (2010). *The universal declaration of human rights.* Retrieved from www.un.org/en/documents/udhr/

U.S. Department of Health and Human Services, Administration for Children & Families. (2008). *Child maltreatment 2008.* Retrieved from http://www.acf.hhs.gov/programs/cb/pubs/cm08/index.htm

Vaughn, M., Howard, M., & Thyer, B. (2008). *Readings in evidence based social work: Synthesis of the intervention knowledge base.* Thousand Oaks, CA: Sage.

Vinter, R. (1985). The essential components of group work practice. In M. Sundel, P. Glasser, R. Sarri, & R. Vinter *(Eds.), Individual change through small groups* (2nd ed., pp. 11–34). New York: Free Press.

Vugia, H. (1991). Support groups in oncology: Building hope through the human bond. *Journal of Psychosocial Oncology, 9*(3), 89–107.

Waite, W., & Hodder, M. (2003). Assessment of the emotional freedom technique: An alternative treatment for fear. *The Scientific Review of Mental Health Practice, 2*(1), 20–25.

WALMYR Publishing Company. (2002). *Assessment scales.* Retrieved from http://www.walmyr.com/scales.html

Walter, J., & Peller, J. (1992). *Becoming solutions-focused in brief therapy.* New York: Brunner/Mazel Publishers.

Warren, R. (1975). A community model. In K. Kramer & H. Specht (Eds.), *Readings in community organization practice* (2nd ed.). Englewood Cliffs, NJ: Prentice Hall.

Wasserman, H., & Danforth, I. (1988). *The human bond: Support groups and mutual aid.* New York: Springer.

Watzlawick, P. (1966). A structured family interview. *Family Process, 5,* 256–271.

Watzlawick, P. (1978). *The language of change: Elements of therapeutic communication.* New York: Basic Books.

Weiler, K. (1994). Freire and a feminist pedagogy of difference. In P. McLaren (Ed.), *Politics of liberation: Paths from Freire.* New York: Routledge.

Weiner, L., Becker, A., & Friedman, T. (1967). *Home treatment: Spearhead of community psychiatry.* Pittsburgh: Pittsburgh Press.

Weiner, M. (1978). *Therapist disclosure: The use of self in psychotherapy.* Boston: Butterworths.

Weissman, A. (1976). Industrial social sciences: Linkage technology. *Social Casework, 57*(1), 50–54.

Wells, K., & Biegel, D. (Eds.). (1991). *Family preservation services: Research and evaluation.* Newbury Park, CA: Sage.

Wells, S., Polglase, K., Andrews, H. B., Carrington, P., & Baker, H. A. (2003). Evaluation of a meridian-based intervention, emotional freedom techniques (EFT), for reducing specific phobias of small animals. *Journal of Clinical Psychology, 59*(9), 943–966.

Wewers, M., & Lowe, N. (1990). A critical review of visual analogue scales in the measurement of clinical phenomena. *Research in Nursing and Health, 13,* 227–236.

White, B., & Madara, E. (2009). *American Self-Help Group Clearinghouse: Self-Help group sourcebook online.* Retrieved from http://www.mentalhelp.net/selfhelp/

White, R. W. (1956). *The abnormal personality.* New York: The Ronald Press.

Wieman, M., & Stiehler, G. (2005). *Location of the acupoints used in Emotional Freedom Technique.* Retrieved from http:/commons.wikimedia.org/wiki/File:Eft_punkte.jpg.

Will, G. (2007, October 14). Code of coercion. *The Washington Post.*

Wilson, E. (1973). Animal communication. *Scientific American, 227,* 53–54.

Wilson, S. (1978). *Confidentiality in social work: Issues and principles.* New York: Free Press.

Wilson, S. (1980). *Recording: Guidelines for social workers.* New York: Free Press.

Wolpe, J. (1958). *Psychotherapy by reciprocal inhibition.* Stanford, CA: Stanford University Press.

Wylie, M. S. (1995). DSM and the medical model. *The Family Therapy Networker, 19*(May/June), 27–33, 65–69.

Yalom, I. (1995). *The theory and practice of group psychotherapy* (4th ed.). New York: Basic Books.

Zung, W. W. (1965). A self-rating depression scale. *Archives of General Psychiatry, 12,* 63–70. Retrieved from http://healthnet.umassmed.edu/mhealth/ZungSelfRatedDepressionScale.pdf

INDEX

ABAB design, 227–228
ABC design, 227
AB design, 227
Abuse. *See* Child abuse; Substance abuse
Accidental suicide, 112
Acculturation, 74
Actions. *See* Social work
Action system, 35–37, 36 (figure)
Active crisis, 267–273
    dimensions of, 269
    dynamic model of, 272
    stochastic model of, 271–272
    symptoms of, 270–271
    systemic model of, 272–273
    time-limited nature of, 270
    transient nature of disturbed behavior during, 268
Active listening, 146 (exercise)
Acutely suicidal, 112
Adversarial tactics, 524, 525 (figure), 529–530
Advice, receiving and giving, 408–409
Advocacy
    groups, 537–538
    typology of, 324 (figure)
    See also Case, advocacy; Class advocacy
Advocate, 323–326, 514
Aesop, 293
Agency/agencies
    catchment, 497–498, 503 (exercise)
    conditions, 182–183
    functions, 15
    perceptions of, 172–173
    practice and, 14–15
    resistance, and, 75
    sanction and approval, 422–425
    users and, 489–490 (exercise)
Alternating, 314

Alternative healing system, 296–297
Altruism, 409
Angelo family, 350–352
Anger Management, 437
Ann Arbor Holistic Resource Guide (Crazy Wisdom), 296
Anticipatory socialization, 387
Applicability, 18
Applicant, 175
    experience, 164 (exercise)
    process, 179
    worker's tasks with, 175–180
    See also Clients
Assault, screening for, 108–109
Assessments
    crisis, 267–282
    framework, for individuals, 250–262
    group dynamics and, 426–437
    "label," 282–283
    purposes of, 245–246
    sources and, 247–250
    stress, 262–267
    See also Community/communities, assessing;
        Family/families, assessing; Groups,
        assessing; Individuals, assessing;
        Organizations, assessing
Assimilation, 74
Attempted suicide, 112
Authority, 130
Authority structure, 483
Ayurvedic medicine, 306

Bandler, Louise, 380
Bargaining tactics, 525 (figure), 529
Barriers, to individual change, 326–327
Barter, 47

Baseline measure, 226
Beck Depression Inventory, 229
Beck Hopelessness Scale (BHS), 114
Behaviors, interpersonal, 234
"Belling the Cat" (Aesop), 293
"Bent Backs of Chang 'Dong, The," 2–4
Boundaries, family, 346–347, 392–395
Bowen, William, 504
Breath work, 306, 307 (exercise)
Broker, 312–315

CAGE test, 121
Case
    advocacy, 324–326, 536, 572 (bib)
    conference, 318–322
    management, 301
    manager, 381
    See also Social work; Social workers
Catchment area, 294, 417, 495–499, 503, 536
Categorical approach, 71
Catharsis, 410, 466–468
Cause advocacy. *See* Class advocacy
Cementing strategies, 314
Center for Epidemiological Studies-Depression
    Scale (CES-D) (National Institute of Mental
    Health), 234
Centrality, 76
Challenges, as stressful events, 274
Change
    communities, 507–540
    evaluation of, 225–237
    family, 235, 365–400
    group, 236–237, 438–474
    individual, 291–332
    maintaining, 551–554
    measure of, 228–233
    monitoring, 218–225
    organizations, 507–540
    side effects of, 237–243
    utilizing, 554–556
Change agent system, 34
"Change the Organization From Within" (COFW)
    model, 513
Charcot, J. M., 26
Charity Organization Society (COS), 380
Check back, 314
Child abuse
    screening for suspected, 115–117
    signs and symptoms of, 117

Child care resources, improving in a community,
    535 (example)
ChildTrauma Academy (CTA), 100
Child welfare, 12 (table)
Chronically suicidal, 112
Circularity, 336
Class advocacy, 324–325, 327
Clienthood
    entry process, 170–175
    events leading to, 173–175
    feelings about, 171–172
    pathways to, 169–170
    process, overview, 165–169
    See also Clients
Client participation principle, 516
Clients, 162–194
    continuance and discontinuance of, 183–188
    contract, preliminary, 193–194
    definition of, 164–165, 181–183
    involuntary, xxii, 169–170, 575 (bib)
    nonvoluntary, 169–170
    potential. *See* Applicant
    problem solving by, 191–193
    role of, 188–191
    significant others and, 180
    voluntary, 169, 184 (figure)
    See also Clienthood; Client systems; Contracting
Client satisfaction questionnaires (CSQ), 234–235, 546
Client systems, 33
    multiperson, defining the client in, 181–182
    worker's relationship to, 511 (figure)
    See also Clients
Closed groups
    first session of, 450–457
    in-session phases within, 412–413
    stages of development in, 415–416
Cloverdale process, 137
Coded recording forms, 222–223
Code of ethics, for social work, 43–50
Code of Ethics (National Association of Black
    Social Workers), 43
Code of Ethics (National Association of Social
    Workers), 43
Code violations, 49
Coercion, 8, 130
COFW ("Change the Organization From Within"
    model), 513
Cohesiveness, 408, 463–466
Collaborative decision structure, 484

Collaborative tactics, 524, 525 (figure)
Colleagues
    impairment of, 48
    unethical conduct of, 48–49
Colonization, 75
Communication, 427–429
    accurate, 144–149
    full, 149–152
    patterns, family, 346, 391–392
    training, 391–392
Community/communities
    assessing, 499–504
    change, 507–540
    organizers and practitioners, 10
Competence, promoting in chronic psychiatric
        patients, 303
Completed suicide, 112
Conceptions, 127, 127 (exercise)
Conditions, as stressors, 262
Confidentiality, 46
Conflict, interpersonal, 469–473
Conflict of interest, 45–46
Conflicts, value, in practice, 51–53
Conscientization, 82
Consciousness. See Critical consciousness
Consciousness-raising (CR) group, 133,
        404, 516–517
Conscious use of self, 141–142
Continuance, 183–188
Contract
    corrupt, 209–210
    dual, 202
    multiperson client systems and, 214 (table)
    preliminary, 193–194
    sequence, 198 (figure)
    written, 201 (figure)
    See also Contracting; Social work contract
Contracting, 195–215
    families and groups, 211–215
    hidden agenda and, 208–209
    limits of, 207–210
    sabotage and, 210
    values of, 206–207
    See also Social work contract
Co-option, of the change agent, 529
Coordination, in practice situations, 317
Coping, 282, 387
Corrupt contract, 209–210
COS (Charity Organization Society), 380
Council on Social Work Education (CSWE), xv–xix

Countertactics, 524–532
Counter-transference, 126
CR. See Consciousness-raising (CR) group
Crisis
    active, 267–273
    assessment, 267–282
    exhaustion, 269
    intervention, 327–330
Critical consciousness, 60–98, 133, 266–267 (exercise)
    application of, 91–96
    definition of, 65–69
    positionality and standpoint, 81–83
    relationship issues with clients, 136–138 (exercise)
    routes to, 84–91
Critical incident recording, 219
CSQ. See Client satisfaction questionnaires
CSWE (Council on Social Work Education), xv–xix
CTA (ChildTrauma Academy), 100
Cultural competence, 47, 74
Cultural consciousness, 74
Cultural deviance, 91–92
Cultural equivalence, 92
Cultural relevance, 74
Cultural sensitivity, 47, 74
Cultural variance, 92
Culture, transactional approach to understanding,
        71–72
Culture and traditions, family, 345–346, 358–363,
        387–390

Dangerous Behavior Rating Scale (DBRS), 108
DAST (Drug Abuse Screening Test), 120
Data, for family assessment, 338–343
DAWN (Drug Abuse Warning Network), 119
deBecker, Gavin, 123
Decision making structure, 483–487
Descriptive feedback, 406
Diagnostic and Statistical Manual of Mental
        Disorders (4th ed.) (DSM-IV), 26, 120
Differences, 70–74
Discontinuance, 183–188
Discrimination, 47, 75, 87–89
Disease metaphor, 25–27
Dissociation, 104
Distress, 263
Diversity, 18, 20, 70–73
Dix, Dorothea, 25
Documentation, 513–515
Domestic violence, 118–119
Domestic Violence Screening Quiz (Psych Central), 119

Dominance, 74–77
Drug Abuse Screening Test (DAST), 120
Drug Abuse Warning Network (DAWN), 119
DSM-IV. *See Diagnostic and Statistical Manual of Mental Disorders* (4th ed.)

Ecological balance, individual and environment, 301 (figure)
Ecological concepts, use of, 10–11
Ecological transactions, 257 (figure)
Ecomap, 235, 277, 316 (figure), 317, 335, 343, 352, 356–358, 499, 501, 503 (exercise), 506
Efficacy, empirically demonstrable, 18–20
Ego dystonic, 269
Ekman, Paul, 149
Electronic recording, 219–222
Emotional climate, family, 346, 390–391
Emotional Freedom Technique (EFT), 308–312
Emotional injury, symptoms of, 105–107
Empathic response, 147–149
Empathy, 146
Empirically based practice, 217–218
Employee assistance, 12 (table)
Employers, commitment to, 49
Empowerment, 4, 8, 44, 64, 170, 200, 206, 302, 365–366, 389, 400, 402, 489, 510, 516, 552, 569 (bib), 572 (bib), 573 (bib)
Enabler, 16, 291, 302–303, 332, 379
Enactments, 340–341
Engagement, 124–161
Ethical issues, practice cases with, 54–58
Ethics. *See* Organizational change; Social work code of ethics; Unethical conduct
Eustress, 263
Evaluation, 225–237, 544–546
    change, measure of, 228–233
    client satisfaction questionnaires (CSQ), 234–235, 546
    design of, 225–228
    of family change, 235
    of group change, 236–237
    of interpersonal behaviors, 234
    of problem solving skills, 233–234
    session, by workers, 237 (table)
Events, as stressors, 262
Events and conditions
    interplay between, 263 (figure)
    time line of, 276 (figure)
Exhaustion crisis, 269
Expectations, importance of, 127 (exercise)

External advocacy, 325
External factors, 186

Facilitative conditions, 147
Faith-based programs, 13 (table)
Families and Larger Systems (Imber-Black), 381
Family/families
    assessing, 333–364
    behavior, 337, 349–350 (table)
    boundaries, 346–347, 392–395
    circumstances, categorizing, 344–352
    change, 365–400
    change stage, 379–386
    communication patterns, 346, 391–392
    conditions, ways of portraying, 352–363
    contracting with, 211–215
    culture and traditions, 345–346, 358–363, 387–390
    definition of, 334–335
    emotional climate, 346, 390–391
    ending stage, 399–400
    environment transactions, 355 (table), 380–384
    evaluation of, 235
    extended family transactions, 384–386
    interaction with other systems, 348
    interventions, 366–367, 380–384
    life cycle, phases of, 344–345, 386–395
    meetings, pseudo-democracy in, 347
    network therapy, 383
    preservation services, 382
    problem specification in, 192–193
    resources, 347–348, 354–355
    transactions within, 386
    sculpture, 343–344
    sessions, 337, 367–379, 395–399
    situations, relationships in, 158–159
    structure, 337, 347
    termination issues with, 558–559
    treatment, 368
    welfare, 12 (table)
Feedback, 405–406, 462
Fields of service, 11–13
Focus, problem, 13
Focused feedback, 406
Follow-up, 314
Force field analysis, 522, 522 (figure)
Formal rules, 481
Freire, Paolo, 66

Game theory, 469
Garvin, Charles, 547

Gender, complexity of, 61–63 (figure)
Generality, 18, 20
Generalizing skills to other situations, 555 (example)
Genogram, 335, 342, 348, 352, 358–363, 373, 380, 385, 398
Genuineness, 142, 150
Geographic information systems (GIS), 503–504
Geography, 436–437, 495–497
Germain, Carel, 218
Gifts, 47, 561–562
Goal attainment scale (GAS), 228, 231–233
Gordon, James, 240
Groups
    agency sanction and approval, 422–426
    assessing, 401–437
    change, 236–237, 438–474
    composing, 416–420
    development, 411–426
    deviancy, 186–187
    dynamics, 426–437
    evaluation, 236–237
    feelings about, 454–455
    first session, 444–447
    formation stage, 423–424
    individual change, 403
    interpersonal conflict, 469–473
    life span, 402 (figure)
    maturity stage, 425
    membership, 80 (table)
    middle school, 416
    norms and ground rules, 454
    revision stage, 424–425
    second session, 447–450
    self-help, 403
    student reflections, 445–450
    support, 297–301, 403, 439–444, 539 (example)
    systems, problem specification in, 192–193
    task, 402
    termination stage, 426
    types, 402–404
    work, termination issues in, 557–558
"Group Story, The," 464–465

Hamilton, Gordon, 125
Hamilton rating scale for depression (HRSD), 234
"Hard to Reach" (Lindenberg), 171
Harassment, sexual, 48
Haunting, 314, 321
Hazardous conditions and events, 267, 281

Healing system, alternative and indigenous, 296–297
Help-seeking journey, 295 (figure)
Herman, Judith, 100
Hidden agenda, 208–209
Hierarchical decision structure, 483–484, 484 (figure)
Historical Clinical Risk Management Scheme (HRC-20), 108
Historical trauma, 103
Hollis, Florence, 125, 547
Homebuilders model, 382
Hope
    importance of, 143–144
    instilling, 405, 463
Host settings, 478–479
HRC-20 (Historical Clinical Risk Management Scheme), 108
HRSD (Hamilton rating scale for depression), 234
Hudson generalized contentment scale (WALMYR Publishing Co.), 228–231
Human communication, transfer of meaning, 145 (figure)
Humor, 410–411

Iatrogenic illness, 238
Identities, multiple, 80–83
Identity work, 72
Ideology, of the social work profession, 42–43
IFPS (Intensive Family Preservation Services), 382
Imber-Black, Evan, 381
Immediate feedback, 406
Income maintenance, 12 (table)
Indigenous practitioners, examples of, 298 (table)
Individual change, 291–332
    barriers, 326–327
    context of, 292–301
    crisis interventions, 327–330
    interventive roles, 301–326
    role solutions, 330–332
Individualizing, 314–315 (figure)
Individuals, assessing, 245–290
    crisis assessment, 267–282
    individual assessment framework, 250–262
    issues in, 247–250
    labels and, 282–283
    PIE system, 283–290
    purposes of, 245–246
    stress assessment, 262–267
Informal rules, 481
Informational relationship, 130
Information technology, 494–495

Informed consent, 45
Initial contact, 338–339
Institutionalized discrimination, 75
Intensive Family Preservation Services (IFPS), 382
Interactional difficulties, 287 (table)
Internal advocacy, 325, 477
Internalized discrimination, 75. *See also* Oppression
Interpersonal behaviors, rating, 234
Interpersonal change, and individuals, 292–301
    alternative and indigenous healing system, 296–297
    resources, formal and informal, 294–296
    self-help/support groups, 297–301
    treatment plan, 292–294, 332, 494
Interpersonal conflict, in groups, 469–473
Interpersonal learning, 468–469
Interpersonal practice, 9–10
    action system, 35–37
    assumptions and concepts, 17–38
    bases of, 15–16
    client system, 33
    concepts, basic, 32–37
    critical consciousness and, 60–98
    factors in feasibility of change goal, 520–523
    issues, 45–50
    metaphors, 23–32
    principles, 513
    rationale, 17–20
    scope of, 11–15
    target system, 35
    worker system, 33–34
    See also Social work
Interpersonal skills, learning, 409–410
Interpreting, 462–463
Intersectionality, 66–67
Intervention, 15
    crisis, 327–330
Interventive roles, 301–326
    advocate, 323–326
    broker, 312–315
    enabler, 302–303
    mediator, 315–322
    resource developer, 322–323
    trainer, 304–312
Involuntary clients, 170

Janet, Pierre, 26
Job training, 12 (table)
Johari Window, 406–407, 407 (figure), 429, 432, 462, 471

Katz, Judith, 92
Kraepelin, Emil, 26
Kvebæk Sculpture Technique (KST), 344, 345 (figure)

Labels, and assessment, 282–283
LARA (listen, assess, respond, add information) procedure, 392, 472
Law and Order, 41
LDS (Legal Dangerous Scale), 108
Leaders/leadership
    interventions, 457–469
    mismatches and matches in, 420 (exercise)
Learning, vicarious, 5, 410, 466, 468, 550
Least contest principle, 515–516
Legal Dangerous Scale (LDS), 108
Leisure time and youth services, 12 (table)
Leveton, Eva, 466
Lie to Me, 149
Limbaugh, Rush, 51
Linking, 175, 313, 330, 381, 396, 509
Location, privilege of, 89–90
Losses, stressful events as, 274
Lower-class clients, 185–186
Low visibility principle, 515

Maintenance issues, 141
Mandated clients, 177
Marginality, 76
Mary Trueheart, 58 (exercise)
MAST (Michigan Alcohol Screening Test), 122
Measures of Clinical Practice (Corcoran and Fisher), 234
Mediator, 16, 34, 157, 181, 291, 301, 315–322, 321, 332, 386, 431, 470–471
Meditation, 306, 307 (exercise)
Melting pot metaphor, 72
Mental health care, 12 (table)
Mercenary metaphor, 29–32
Metaphors, 23–32
    disease, 25–27
    influence of, 32 (exercise)
    mercenary, 29–32
    moral, 24–25
    nature, 27–29
Meyer, Carol, 547
Michigan Alcohol Screening Test (MAST), 122
Middle school group, 416, 422
Monitoring change, 218–225
    coded recording forms, 222–223
    critical incident recording, 219

electronic recording, 219–222
process recording, 218–219
Moral metaphor, 24–25
MOSAIC threat system, 123 (exercise)
"Mother's Group, The," 5–7
Multicultural competence, routes to, 84–91.
    See also Critical consciousness
Multiculturalism, 69–77. *See also* Critical
    consciousness
Multiple identities, 80–83
Multiple issues, 91

National Association of Black Social Workers
    (NABSW), 43
National Association of Social Workers (NASW), 43
National Child Abuse and Neglect Data System
    (NCANDS), 116
National Institute of Mental Health, 234
Nature metaphor, 27–29, 251
Neuro-Linguistic Programming (NLP), 310
Nicholson, Jack, 437
9 Gamut Procedure, 310–312, 311 (figure)
Noah's Ark principle, 418, 430
Nonclients, tasks with, 180
Nonvoluntary clients, 169–170
Norms, 40, 427, 482–483

Open-ended group, 413–415
Oppression, 75, 87–89
Organizational assessment, 477–499
    climate, 492–494
    decision making structure, 483–487
    geography and, 495–497
    how to, 479–480
    information technology and, 494–495
    norms and operating rules, 480–483
    roles, 488–492
    understanding organizations, 477–479
Organizational change, 507–540
    ethics of, 508–512
    tactics, hierarchy of, 525 (figure)
    theories of, 513–534
Outsiders, 75

Perlman, Helen Harris, 547
Perry, Bruce D., 100
Personal relationships, 129
Person-in-environment (PIE) system, 283–290,
    499–500, 536
Persuasion tactics, 525 (figure), 528–529

Physical health care, 12 (table)
PIE. *See* Person-in-Environment system
Pinel, Phillipe, 25
Pivotal norms, 482
Placebo effect, 143
Policy analysts, 10
Political action, 42, 44, 45, 325, 510
Positionalities, 67, 81–83
Potential clients. *See* Applicants
Power
    definitions related to, 75–77
    dimensions of, in professional relationships,
        129–131
Practice
    agencies and, 14–15
    cases, with ethical issues, 54–58
    critical consciousness, application of, 91–96
    potency, 18–19
    scope of, 11–15
    value conflicts in, 51–53
    See also Interpersonal practice; Social work
Precipitating factors, 267, 280–282
Prejudice, 75
Prescriptive norms, 40, 482
Presuicidal state, 112
Primacy of client interests, 561
Priorities, service, 13–14
Privacy, 46
Private practice, 13 (table)
Privilege, 67, 70, 75, 89–91, 94–96, 98, 128, 131, 133,
        136–137, 256, 265–266, 326–327, 480, 494, 508
Problem
    focus, 13
    family and group systems, 192–193
    specifying, 191–192
Problematic terminations, 561–563
Problems of intimacy, 186–187
Problem solving
    framework, 513–517
    guidelines, 307–308
    initiation to, 191–193
    skills, rating, 233–234
    steps, 517–534
Process recording, 218–219
Professional relationships
    power dimensions in, 129–131
    stages of, 131–135
    transactional nature of, 135–140
    See also Social work relationship
Proscriptive norms, 40, 482

Protocols, risk screening, 107–123
Psychological injury, symptoms of, 105–107
Psychological trauma, 99–100
Psychosocial casework, 125

RAPS4 questions, 122
Recording change, 218–223
Reed, Beth Glover, 60
Referent base, 130
Referral
    fatigue, 312
    for service, 48
Reflective response, 147–149
Reframing, 393–394
Reid, William, 547
Relationships, 124–161
    communication in, 144–149
    complementary roles in, 153–155
    importance of, 141
    in family situations, 158–159
    in group situations, 156–158
    initiation of, 144–156
    personal, 129
    positive and negative, dimensions of, 160–161
        (exercise)
    professional, 129–140
    sexual, 46
    social work, 126–129
    trust in, 155–156
    warmth and caring in, 152–153
Relaxation and Stress Reduction Workbook, The
    (Davis, Eshelman, and McKay), 305
Relevant norms, 482–483
Research-oriented workers, 10
Resistance
    agency and, 75
    value, 523
Resource developer, 322–323
Resources, formal and informal, 294–296
Restructuring, 394
Reward, 130
Reynolds, Bertha, 183
Richmond, Mary, 125
Risk screening protocols, 107–123
Rogers, Carl, 147
Role(s), 431–436
    clarification procedure, 188–190
    clients, 188–191
    complementary, 153–155
    interventive, 301–326

solutions, 330–332
    training, 191
    transitions, 251–256
Romano family, 395–399
Rose, Sheldon, 547
Rules, formal and informal, 481
Rush, Benjamin, 25

Sabotage, 210
SAC (Student Advocacy Center), 537
Safety, in the workplace, 109–111
Salad bowl metaphor, 72
SAMHSA (Substance Abuse and Mental Health
    Services Administration), 119
Sandler, Adam, 437
Sandwiching, 314
Save Our Sons and Daughters (SOSAD), 537
Screening. *See* Risk screening protocols
Sculpting, 343–344, 354, 391
Secondary trauma, 103
Self, conscious use of, 141–142
Self-control, after termination, 554 (example)
Self-disclosure, 142, 150–152, 405, 407, 411, 426, 452
Self-help groups, 297–301, 403
Self-sharing, 221 (table), 236, 300 (exercise), 405–406,
    410, 411, 430, 432, 435, 451, 460–462, 468
Service
    delivery system, 166 (figure), 168 (figure)
    fields of, 13
    priorities, 13–14
    referral for, 48
    termination of, 47
    See also Clients
Settlement movement, 380
Sexual harassment, 48
Sexual orientation, complexity of, 61–63 (figure)
Sexual relationships, 46
SFI (structured family interview), 212
Shapiro, Francine, 224
Shock crisis, 269
"Significant others," of clients, 180
"Singing in the Rain" (Barlow et al.), 463–464
SLAP (specificity, lethality, availability, proximity)
    Scale, 114
Smalley, Ruth, 547
SOAP, 223
Social action, 45, 325, 403, 459
Social disease, 26
Social group categories, 77–80
Socialization, 387, 411

Social justice, xv, xvi, xxi, 10, 42, 44, 59, 60, 62-64, 66, 89, 177, 235, 388, 439, 459, 474, 500, 534, 536
Social network
    map and grid, 280 (exercise)
    support map, 278 (figure)
"Social Network Support Map" (Tracy and Whittaker), 277
Social pathology, 26
Social planners, 10
Social skills training, 304–305, 387
Social supports, 279 (table), 282
Social work
    actions, 15–16
    agencies, 14–15
    assumptions and concepts, 17–38
    code of ethics, 43–50
    code violations consequences, 49
    commitment to employers, 49
    conflict of interest, 45–46
    cultural competence and sensitivity, 47
    definition, 9
    discrimination and, 47
    ethics, 43–50, 54–58
    fields of service, 11–13, 12–13 (table)
    gifts and barter, 47
    ideology of the profession, 42–43
    impairment of colleagues, 48–49
    informed consent, 45
    interpersonal practice in, 1–16
    metaphors, 23–32
    practitioners, competing demands on, 478 (figure)
    problem focus, 13
    privacy and confidentiality, 46
    referral for service, 48
    relationship, 126–129. See also Professional relationships
    service priorities, 13–14
    sexual harassment, 48
    sexual relationships, 46
    social and political action, 45
    termination of service, 47
    unethical conduct of colleagues, 48–49
    values, 51–53
    See also Assessments; Change; Interpersonal practice
Social work contract
    characteristics of, 200–205
    components of, 195–199
    limits of, 207–210
    sequence, 198 (figure)
    terms, 196
    value of, 206–207
    with families and groups, 211–215
    written, 201 (figure)
Social workers
    applicants and, 175–180
    bureaucratic-centered, 491
    client-centered, 490
    nonclients and, 180
    profession centered, 491
    See also Interpersonal practice; Social work
Sociocultural safety, 94
Sociometry, 429–431
Solicited feedback, 406
Solution focused, 13, 195, 293, 302, 307, 459
SOSAD (Save Our Sons and Daughters), 537
Standpoint, 81–83
Status, 70, 74–75, 485 (exercise)
Stereotypes, 70–71
Stress assessment, 262–267
Stressful transition, 274 (exercise)
Stressors, 262, 277 (exercise)
Stress reduction techniques, 305–307
Structured family interview (SFI), 212
Student Advocacy Center (SAC), 537
Subjective Units of Discomfort Scale (SUDS), 224, 243, 307, 311–312
Subordination, 75
Substance abuse, 13 (table), 119–123
Substance Abuse and Mental Health Services Administration (SAMHSA), 119
Suicide, 111–115
Support groups, 297–301, 403, 439–444, 539 (example)
Symptoms, of psychological and emotional injury, 105–107
System variables
    influence of, 476–477 (exercise)
    measurement of, 335

T-ACE test, 121
Tapping sequence, 309–310
Target system, 35, 511 (figure)
Task Centered Casework (Reid and Epstein), 547
Task Implementation Sequence (TIS), 203–205, 330, 395
Task(s), 341–342
    assignment, 394–395
    groups, 402
    issues, 141

Teaching Tolerance (Southern Poverty Law Center), 52
TEC (The Earth Charter), 40, 41 (exercise)
Termination, 541–563
　issues in group work, 557–558
　issues with families, 558–559
　of service, 47
　problematic, 561–563
　tasks of, 543–556
　worker, 559–560
The Earth Charter (TEC), 40, 41 (exercise)
Therapeutic/effectiveness variables, 404–411
　advice, receiving and giving, 408–409
　altruism, 409
　catharsis, 410
　cohesiveness, 408
　feedback, 405–406
　hope, instilling, 405
　humor, 410–411
　interpersonal skills, 409–410
　Johari Window, 406–407
　self-sharing, 405
　socialization, 411
　universality, 407
　vicarious learning, 410
Therapist, 34
Thomas, Edwin, 547
Threats, stressful events as, 274
TIS. *See* Task Implementation Sequence
Tracking, in a family session, 339
Trainer, 304–312
　problem solving and, 307–308
　social skills training and, 304–305
　stress reduction techniques and, 305–307
Transactional approach, 71–72
Transactional nature, of professional relationships, 135–140
Transactions, family, 380–386
Transference elements, 126
Transnational communities, 74
Trauma, 99–123
　assessment of, 103–105
　consequences of, 105–107
　historical, 103
　psychological, 99
　recognition of, 100–102
　secondary, 103
　treatment options, 107
　types of, 102–103
Treatment options, for violence and trauma, 107

Treatment plan, for individual change, 292–294
Trust, 155–156
"T-shirt" (Carrell), 460, 462
Tufte, Edward, 503

Unethical conduct, of colleagues, 48
Unit of attention, 37 (exercise)
Universal Declaration of Human Rights (UDHR) (United Nations), 40, 41 (exercise)
Universality, 407
Unstuck (Gordon), 240
U.S. Constitution, 41 (exercise)

Value conflicts in practice, 51–53
Variables, therapeutic/effectiveness, 404–411
Vicarious learning, 5, 410, 466, 468, 550
Violence, 99–123
　counterthreats of, 531
　domestic, 118–119
　recognition of, 100–102
　risk factors for, 111 (case study)
　screening for, 108–109
Violence Risk Appraisal Guide (VRAG), 108
Violence Risk Scale (VRS), 108
Violent tactics, 525 (figure)
Visual analog scale (VAS), 228–229, 456, 544 (figure)
Visual Display of Quantitative Information, The (Tufte), 503
Voluntary association system, 501
Voluntary clients, 169, 184 (figure)
Vulnerable state, 267, 273–280

Wal-Mart, 510
Warmth and caring, in relationships, 152–153
War on Poverty, 497
"Weeding Your Garden" (Barlow et al.), 460, 461 (figure)
Whistle-blowing, 530
Will, George, 42
Worker(s)
　interventions, 221 (table)
　research-oriented, 10
　system, 33–34, 34 (figure)
　termination, 559–560
Workplace safety, issues in, 109–111

Youth, 535 (example), 538–539 (example)

Zung screening scale, 229

ABOUT THE AUTHORS

Brett A. Seabury (BAS) became interested in social work during his undergraduate education at Wesleyan University in Middletown, Connecticut. He participated in a companion program for chronically mentally ill patients at a nearby state psychiatric hospital. Brett also was a member of Connecticut's First Service Corp, which placed college students in a summer program at Norwich State Hospital and as staff at Connecticut's camping program for psychiatric patients. These progressive programs influenced his decision to pursue a master's degree in social work at Simmons College School of Social Work in Boston. After graduating from Simmons, he enlisted in the U.S. Army Medical Service Corps as a social work officer in lieu of his impending draft. Most of his tour of duty for 3 years was at Fort Jackson, South Carolina, in the Mental Hygiene Consultation Division where he worked with military dependents and also provided psychiatric emergency screening to the ER in the small base hospital. After completing his tour, he attended the doctoral program in social work at Columbia University in New York City. Brett's academic career has involved 4 years at the University of Maryland School of Social Work and 34 years at the University of Michigan School of Social Work. His academic career has included teaching many direct service courses involving individuals, families, and groups; courses in advocacy, metaphors, alternative, and indigenous healing; and contemporary treatment techniques. His publications have focused on pedagogical innovations such as the use of computer conferencing, computer tutorials, and interactive video simulations. Many of these innovations are reflected in the revisions to the third edition of this book. While at Michigan, Brett and his wife, Barbara, have engaged in small scale, natural farming and now have the opportunity to expand their farming operations and to reduce their environmental footprint by raising grass fed beef and sheep for the local community.

Barbara H. Seabury (BHS) began her social work career with an interest in children and their families, which was reflected in her field placements at Simmons College School of Social Work. Upon graduation, her first job in social work was in a child psychiatry clinic and later as a school social worker in Columbia, South Carolina. Later in Maryland, she worked part-time as a social worker in a public health clinic. When she moved to Michigan, she became interested in treating kids who had been physically and sexually abused. Barbara has been in private practice for the past 25 years. As an outgrowth of her earlier work with abused children, she became interested in multiplicity, dissociation, and other consequences of trauma in adults. Her primary interest has been the treatment of adults who have experienced severe trauma. She received additional training in the treatment of dissociative disorders and is a member of the International Society for the Study of Trauma and Dissociation. In addition, Barbara also received training in eye movement desensitization and reprocessing (EMDR). She lives on a farm in Michigan with her husband, Brett. They currently raise grass fed beef, sheep, pigs, and dwarf dairy goats.

Charles D. Garvin, PhD, received his social work master's degree and doctorate from the School of Social Service Administration of the University of Chicago. Before he studied for his doctoral degree, he worked for a dozen years as a social worker at a residential treatment center for children (Chapin Hall), the U.S. Army (into which he was drafted in 1952), a settlement house (Henry Booth House), and the Jewish Community Centers of Chicago. He was a faculty member of the School of Social Work at the University of Michigan from 1965 until 2002 when he became a professor emeritus. During this period, he taught courses in direct practice, group work, community organization, and administration. He also taught research courses and in the 1990s was director of the Joint Doctoral Program in Social Work and Social Science. He was one of the founders of the International Association for the Advancement of Social Work with Groups and its second president. He is the author or coauthor of *Contemporary Group Work*, *Social Work in Contemporary Society*, and *Generalist Practice: A Task Centered Approach*. He was coeditor of *Handbook of Social Work With Groups*. He has written many articles and book chapters on various aspects of social work and social work practice. He is currently a principal investigator of an action research project on training high school students as leaders in intergroup conflict resolution. He is now completing books on group work, group work research, and social justice in social work. He is a consulting editor with SAGE with reference to several social work book series.